ROOTS: AN ASIAN AMERICAN READER

U.S.C. 4⁹⁰

ROOTS: AN ASIAN AMERICAN READER

Design:

Kathy Fukami Glascock   Donna Wong   Mary Uyematsu

Photo Coordination:

Robert A. Nakamura
National Visual Communication Committee-JACL

Distribution:

Sherry Valparaiso   Peter Lin

ROOTS: AN ASIAN AMERICAN READER

Editors:

Amy Tachiki **Eddie Wong** **Franklin Odo** with **Buck Wong**

A project of the UCLA Asian American Studies Center

Copyright © 1971
by The Regents of the University of California

That which is bright rises twice:
The image of FIRE.
Thus the great man, by perpetuating this brightness,
Illumines the four quarters of the world

LI-THE CLINGING, FIRE
The I CHING

Preface

As the title indicates, this volume was written and edited with the intent of going to the "roots" of the issues facing Asians in America. It may, therefore, strike the reader as "radical"--a term which derives from the latin radix, meaning, appropriately enough, roots. Fair enough. The selections were chosen to encourage readers to consider and compare the experiences of Asian Americans, individually and collectively, within the context of the human condition. Our work is designed to meet the particular needs of Asian Americans. At this point in time, the lack of appropriate materials in readily accessible form is one of the greatest immediate problems. Asian Americans who have tried to serve their communities as social workers, organizers, lawyers, businessmen, workers, housewives and students have long expressed the need for a convenient anthology focusing on the lives of our people. Equally important is the increasing number of people who have sought a convenient book with which to begin their reading on this neglected subject.

Several points need to be made about this work. It contains a variety of materials written from a multitude of perspectives. There are scholarly pieces which rely on traditional, academic sources for information and present a mixed sociological and historical picture of Asian Americans. There is, however, equal emphasis on the contemporary expression of the Asian American condition by the people themselves. ROOTS is, therefore, not only a handy repository of secondary writings on the subject but a documentary collection from our time.

These are critical times for Asian Americans and it is imperative that their voices be heard in all their anger, anguish, resolve and inspiration. Many selections have not been edited at all; others only to avoid undue repetition. We have felt it important to preserve something of the person who wrote the piece--thus insisting that the reader make a positive effort to understand the author's intent and examine it critically. The wide variety of styles and viewpoints have helped create a work which, we hope, suggests the riches awaiting those who pursue an interest in the experiences of Asian Americans.

One of the first things to note is the magnitude of interest already exhibited. Asian American studies classes and student groups have formed across the country and a national con-

ference on the subject attracted several hundred participants to Los Angeles in April, 1971. There is a long tradition of interest in the academic uses of Asian Americans--here, limited to Chinese, Japanese, Filipinos, and Koreans--as sociological "case studies" to test (and usually to "prove") the validity of American society as a largely open and democratic one. As the section on identity indicates, however, that type of analysis has done serious disservice to all Asian Americans and has been part of the self-delusion white America has suffered.

Amy Tachiki notes, in her important opening remarks to the section on identity, the range of misconceptions, the mechanisms through which they operate, and the consequences thereof. Identity is a question to which we return time and again. It is never neatly solved and incorporated into the computation of other variables. Identity is crucial to ideology and action--central to the problem of self-determination at any level. The Asian who "identifies" white (or <u>anything</u> other than what he is) faces the insurmountable problem of his physical makeup. Any individual of talent who is "skimmed" from his generally oppressed group faces a lifetime of ambivalence--increasingly regarded as a turncoat by them and as an exception by others.

A few, tortured by their inability to make sense of a crazy world of color, choose to destroy themselves in drugs and/or blind hostility. The rest of us, workers and professionals alike, endure a lifetime of alienation and uncertainty marked by an intuitive sense of powerlessness. Until, that is, some sequence of events forces us to turn to the problem of identity--with whom are we to identify? That turn forces increasing numbers to look to their "roots."

The central section of this volume deals with the history of Asian Americans, from the emigration period to the present. This was another facet of the title's significance--our "roots" go deep into the history of the United States and they can do much to explain who and what we are and how we became this way. Buck Wong's opening section is properly critical of the bland <u>pap</u> that has masqueraded as history--the number of new articles and their various styles should convince all of us that much important work remains to be done in this area.

Interestingly, some of the features of the "generation gap" unique to Japanese Americans seem to disappear when the youth talk to parents and grandparents about the World War II concentration camp experience, or the "picture bride" practice. This should be true for all ethnic groups.

Disregarding or misinterpreting the historical background of the particular group is one of the most important reasons for the failure to make meaningful changes in the ethnic community. All Asians have much in common: the history of their exploitation as migrant farm labor is but one significant theme that continues to this day with the Filipino laborers in Delano. But there are unique qualities to each of the ethnic groups which make united struggles difficult--they need to be understood and discussed rather than shaded or wished away.

Many of those qualities are discussed in the section on Asian American communities. Eddie Wong's introduction sets the articles and interviews in the all-important context--without it they might easily be read as merely interesting reflections on the present state of affairs. The notion of "community" is an elusive one--for decades now social scientists have thought that Asian Americans would be geographically dispersed as they were culturally assimilated. Instead, as the 1970 census will probably show, even those who have achieved middle class economic status are congregating in suburban pockets. Some of the same features from the central city ghetto areas accompany them--an ethnic church, food stores and a few cultural centers offering instruction in the various Asian arts. Why this phenomenon if our assumptions about the gradual assimilation of Asians in the "majority" society are accurate? In fact, the yellow bourgeoisie may be discovering what his black brothers did long ago--racism exists at all levels of American society.

Even Asians who advance to managerial level positions find themselves bound by restrictions on the basis of race. The case of Los Angeles County Coroner Dr. Thomas Noguchi is instructive (see document by J.U.S.T. in the community section). A recent survey of personnel decision-making executives in 50 top corporations in metropolitan California areas (San Francisco, Los

Angeles, San Diego) revealed considerable anti-Asian racism.[1] The fifty companies, each with at least twenty executives, were selcted from 1700 available by means of a chi-square test to ensure a random and representative sample. A surprising number of these executives (39-79%) had served in the Pacific Theater in World War II, Korea or Vietnam. Thirty four (67%) had seen combat against Asians. This preliminary questioning established the strong probability of U.S. foreign policies in Asia serving as a major contributor to anti-Asian racism.

As expected, only two (4%) had ever employed Asians at the executive level while the others rejected the possibility on the basis of one or another function of mistrust. "Sneaky," "conniving," "shifty," are terms they used to express their reservations about hiring or promoting at the executive level. In a tight, competitive situation, the personal prejudices of potential customers are considered important and 35 (70%) of the sample felt they shared personal perspectives with other business associates. The point should be clear--success on any but the basest of material levels will continue to be elusive and even that remains subject to events beyond our control and related to race.

This volume focuses considerable attention, perhaps disproportionately on Asian American youth; their attitudes, their problems, their movements. That focus should be interpreted in two contexts: first, as part of the long and rich heritage of generations of Asian American struggles for equality and justice and, second, in light of contemporary Third World movements. Several writers and interviews allude to problems of conflicts of emphasis and limited vision even among those who see themselves at the forefront of the movement. Two questions of importance have not received adequate attention: one is the relationship of any ethnically based struggle to others such as other ethnic groups or economic class-oriented ones, while a second one is, if anything, even more complex. What should be a "proper" stance toward the inculcation or maintenance of a cultural heritage? How closely, if at all, and in what ways should Asian Americans relate to Asia? Responses vary from "back to Asia" types to a strictly

---

[1] Student paper submitted to course on "Asians in America" (Occidental College, December, 1970).

Americanist, localized, point of view. There are no hard and fast solutions to these problems but the evidence suggests a few guidelines.

Any "answer" which treats symptoms and fails to look to the roots of the condition will be woefully inadequate. Our questioning and thinking must relate directly to the issue of Asian ethnicity in a racist society but they must move from the particular to the universal, from personal identity to the identity of larger groups, to the nature of human experience and the human condition. And in all of this, an essential identification with the people and a redistribution of power must be seen as both possible and necessary; that is, after all, what is meant by the demand for power to the people.

FRANKLIN ODO

TABLE OF CONTENTS

1 IDENTITY

Introduction 1
Amy Tachiki

Success Story of One Minority Group in America 6
U.S. News and World Report

The Emergence of Yellow Power in America 9
Amy Uyematsu

The Intolerance of Success 14
Daniel Okimoto

An Interview with S.I. Hayakawa 19
Editorial Board

The Nature of G.I. Racism 24
Norman Nakamura

G.I.'s and Asian Women 27
Evelyn Yoshimura

That Oriental Feeling 30
Irvin Paik

Selective Acculturation and the Dating Process: the Patterning of Chinese-Caucasian Interracial Dating 37
Melford Weiss

White Male Qualities 44

'I hate my wife for her flat yellow face' 46
Ron Tanaka

Generation and Character: the Case of the Japanese Americans .. 48
Stanford Lyman

Chinese-American Personality and Mental Health 72
Stanley Sue and Derald W. Sue

An Interview with Harry Kitano 83
Editorial Board

Response and Change for the Asian in America: a Survey of Asian American Literature 89
Bruce Iwasaki

Roots 101
Ron Tanaka

A Brief Biographical Sketch of a Newly Found Asian Male .. 105
Ron Low

from a lotus blossom cunt 109
Tomi Tanaka

I Am Curious (Yellow?) 110
Violet Rabaya

Revolution point zero: 1967 (or whenever) 111
Mary Uyematsu

Autobiography of a Sansei Female 112

Rapping with One Million Carabaos in the Dark 114
Al Robles

the trouble with losing face is, you become invisible .. 116
Marie Chung

Stormy Weather 118
Shin'ya Ono

Asian Brother, Asian Sister 121
Lawson Inada

2 HISTORY

Introduction 131
Buck Wong

Causes of Chinese Emigration 134
Pyau Ling

The Issei Generation 138
Roger Daniels

One Hundred Years of Japanese Labor in the U.S.A. 150
Karl Yoneda

xii

Strangers in the City: the Chinese in the Urban Frontier 159
Stanford Lyman

Filipino Immigration: the Creation of a New Social Problem ......,.. 188
Violet Rabaya

Koreans in America, 1903-1945 201
Linda Shin

The Failure of Democracy in a Time of Crisis 207
Isao Fujimoto

The Cherishing of Liberty: the American Nisei 215
Bill Hosokawa

Book Review of NISEI: THE QUIET AMERICANS 221
Yuji Ichioka

The U.S. in Asia and Asians in the U.S. 223
Franklin Odo with Mary Uyematsu, Ken Hanada, Peggy Li, Marie Chung

3 COMMUNITY

Introduction 247
Eddie Wong

AAPA Perspectives 251

Understanding AAPA 252

An Interview with Pat Sumi 253
Editorial Board

Concept of Asian American Studies 264

Need for Awareness: an Essay on Chinatown San Francisco 265
Buck Wong

Asian Community Center 273

An Interview with L. Ling-Chi Wang 275
Editorial Board

New York Chinatown Today: Community in Crisis 282
Rocky Chin

I Wor Kuen: twelve-point program 296

Asian Women as Leaders 297

The Asian American Experience in Sacramento River Delta 298
Ken Suyama

Sour Grapes: Symbol of Oppression 302
Phillip Vera Cruz

An Interview with Phillip Vera Cruz 305
Editorial Board

International Hotel 310

Filipinos: a Fast Growing U.S. Minority - Philipines Revolution ... 312
KALAYAAN Editorial Collective

Save Kalama Valley - Hawaii 316

This Land Is Mine 318

Raising the Fist 319

Tourism: Decline of Aloha 320
Roy Tsumoto

Hawaiian Homestead Struggle 320
Laura Alancastre and Gloria Burbage

Little Tokyo: Searching the Past and Analyzing the Future 322
Jim H. Matsuoka

An Interview with Warren Furutani 335
Editorial Board

J.U.S.T. Platform 341

List of Movement Journals 343

Acknowledgements 344

1
IDENTITY

INTRODUCTION

Asians in America are a strong, vital people who have withstood a century of racist oppression in this country. Their experience might be described as successful, but not according to the dehumanizing criteria that this society has utilized. America has ignored the history and participation of Asians in this country's development; it has distorted the ethnic and cultural identities of Asian people; and still it hails Asian Americans as its most "successful" minority. American society has dictated this seemingly positive identity from its own majority framework - hardly for the benefit of Asians or other nonwhite minorities. To create a truly fulfilling identity, Asian Americans realize they must redefine and articulate Asian American identity on their own terms.

Like all stereotypes, there is some factual support for the success image of Asian Americans, if success is to be defined along economic, materialistic parameters. A sizable number of Chinese and Japanese Americans have attained higher educational, employment, and income levels - that is, compared to other nonwhite groups in the United States. What the mass media selectively overlooks in Asian success are such factors as middle management ranks, de facto segregation, delayed promotion in jobs, and other subtleties of institutional subordination.[1] In addition, the success stereotype does not consider the psychological and cultural costs which have been the price of Asian American success.

The article that opens the identity section, "Success Story of One Minority Group in U.S.," appeared in U.S. NEWS AND WORLD REPORT in 1966, shortly after the release of the McCone Commission's report on the Watts riots. The opening to the article offers a capsule summary of the racist model that America puts forth in the success story:

> At a time when Americans are awash in worry over the plight of racial minorities - One such minority, the nation's 300,000 Chinese-Americans is winning wealth and respect by dint of its own hard work....
> Still being taught in Chinatown is the old idea that people should depend on their own efforts - not a welfare check - in order to reach America's "promised land."

The U.S. NEWS article is representative of a recent surge of writings praising the unparalleled achievement of Asians in this country. Other success stories include the NEW YORK TIMES' "Success Story: Japanese American Style" (1966); Joseph Alsop's "New American Success Story" (on Chinese and Japanese, 1971); and NEWSWEEK's "Success Story: Outwhiting the Whites" (on Japanese Americans, 1971).

Basic to the success story are the means by which Asian Americans have assimilated. They have often adhered to this society's prescribed mode of behavior for minority assimilation: through hard work, education, quietly remaining in the background, inaction in the face of injustice, and blind faith to the American dream of equality and opportunity for all. The danger in upholding this success myth is that it reinforces the underlying value structure that created it. The Asian success story functions to validate the fundamental soundness of this system and to support the "truth" that all deserving people of any color can and should earn a middle-class position and life style within this society. Despite the disadvantaged status of millions in the United States, most Americans cling to the ideal that American democratic capitalism guarantees self-determination for all its people. By accepting the distorted picture of Asian American success, America rationalizes its racist behavior - and fools itself that it is responsive to the people. Furthermore, the Asian model of assimilation frees the white majority from assuming responsibility for its own oppressiveness, since it implies that nonwhite minorities have to earn their rights to American society and it shifts the causes for minority problems away from the society and onto minority communities.

In the late 1960's younger Asian Americans began to question the remarkable success identities that were being publicized about their people. There were basic inconsistencies and ommissions in the one-sided success

1

theory which the emerging Asian movement for awareness and social change criticized. In the excerpted student paper, "The Emergence of Yellow Power in America," Amy Uyematsu disagrees with the success image, which glosses over the continuing realities of such ghetto-related conditions as unemployment, inadequate housing, drug abuse, and juvenile delinquency in Asian American communities. Her paper traces certain origins of the Asian movement to the Black Power movement in America, especially in terms of the psychological effects of American racism on Asians. The Yellow Power article is not a comprehensive treatment either of the success theory or the Asian movement, but it does document many of the feelings, ideas, and problems which were evident at an early stage of the movement's development.

The Asian movement is also discussed in Daniel Okimoto's autobiography, AN AMERICAN IN DISGUISE. In his chapter on "The Intolerance of Success," Okimoto shows many of the negative aspects of Asian assimilation and sees the Yellow Power movement as a welcome and healthy change. Okimoto is alarmed at the "unquestioning, almost mindless acceptance" of white middle-class American values and attitudes in Japanese and other Asian Americans; he feels that quiet conformity has hampered verbal expression and artistic creativity and has encouraged political conservatism and racist behavior toward other minorities.

One concern of the Asian movement is the need for increased personal and social awareness in all segments of the Asian American community. The success image gives a decided white-majority perspective on Asian Americans which many Americans, Asians included, support without question. Those Asian Americans who have 'made it,' in particular, tend to deny the social problems that Asians and other minorities experience by believing the success myth. Perhaps the most publicized spokesman for their position is S.I. Hayakawa, acting president of San Francisco State College, who has suggested that blacks and other minority groups emulate the Nisei in their drive for success. In "An Interview with S.I. Hayakawa," Asian assimilation and success are viewed by Hayakawa in terms of the functional congruity between Japanese and American cultural values. Upon comparing Hayakawa's interview with a later interview with Harry Kitano, one can see that Hayakawa seems to repeat many of white America's misconceptions of Japanese cultural norms. For example, Hayakawa reproduces the narrow Western view of 'quaint' Japanese non-presumptuousness (enryo) as the determinant of proper Japanese-American behavior. White America has appointed S.I. Hayakawa as its spokesman for Asians in America. Yet in his interview, Hayakawa makes clear his past and continuing disassociation with other Asian Americans and their community experience. Emerging as a figurehead for the white power establishment, Hayakawa echoes familiar placebos for those Americans, Asian and white, who prefer fantasy to reality.

Moving from the phenomena or symptoms of the Asian success story, Asian and other Americans should ask why this success stereotype functions in American society. In his studies on Japanese stereotypes in the United States, Dennis Ogawa, acting director of the Ethnic Studies Department at the University of Hawaii, has delineated several specific functions of the success stereotype in relation to changing social, political, and psychological conditions within America.[2] One function previously outlined is the use of the success image as a balancing force between Americans' reputed ideals and actual racist behavior. Another partial explanation lies in the changing international relationship between Japan and the United States. Now that the United States seeks the maintenance of friendly economic ties with Japan as vital to the balance of power in Asia, it would be impractical to continue the "Jap" stereotypes which were so dominant up through World War II. Also, with the growing militancy of larger minority groups, the blacks and the chicanos, many Americans feel both socially and physically threatened; how convenient it becomes to retain the status quo by setting an example from a minority which seems to pose no real threat to the American system: "Every aspect of the stereotype exists to assure America that we are no danger to the White race, the economy, the political system, or anything at all...."[3]

The specific functions of Asian stereotypes become even clearer upon comparing the success stereotype to other Asian stereotypes America exhibits. While American society defines its domestic Asians as commendable people whose success is due partly to their rich Asian cultural heritages, Asians abroad are depicted as inferior human beings, whose lives and cultures are worth sacrificing 'to insure democracy' in their lands. Since the Korean War and increasingly during the Southeast Asian conflict, "Gookism" has played an important role in shaping the behavior of Americans toward Asian people. The "Gook" stereotype portrays Koreans, Vietnamese, Cambodians, Laotians, and other Asians as subhuman beings who do not value individual human life and who all look like the treacherous Chinese Communist enemy. Not only does this grotesque stereotype lend psychological support to America's genocidal, imperialistic role in Asia, but it affects Americans' actions toward Asians in the United States, who are not physically distinguishable from Asians in Asia. Two Asian Americans - Norman Nakamura (an ex-Vietnam veteran) in "The Nature of G.I. Racism" and Evelyn Yoshimura in "G.I.'s and Asian Women" - examine the "Gook" concept and its dangerous implications for all Asians.

One of the most effective ways for conveying Asian stereotypes is through the film media. In a recent article, Tom Engelhardt explains the role of the "Western" film form in preparing a genocidal racist psychology in Americans.[4] Since the early Westerns about cowboys and Indians, American has interpreted history from the racist perspective of the white majority: pioneers are never viewed as invading the homelands of American Indians; rather, the Western depicts the unreasoned Indian attack on a white wagon train or fortress, as if they, the Indians, were the intruders. This type of historical distortion is extended to every American campaign against Third World people, with the recurring message that nonwhites are simply not human beings and that their inferiority makes them expendable. Engelhardt comments on the Western,

> With this form, they...have successfully tied extermination of non-white people to laughable relief and white racial superiority to the natural order of things....It's hardly a wonder that Vietnam did not sear the American consciousness. Why should it have? For years, Americans have been watching the whole scene on their screen: REV DEV WHAM, endless My Lai's, body counts, killing of wounded enemy soldiers, aerial obliterations, etc....[5]

The dehumanization of Asians on films has perhaps in recent years become less blatant but it does continue. Using relevant examples from such television series as HAWAII FIVE-O, THE COURTSHIP OF EDDIE'S FATHER, and the upcoming CHARLIE CHAN, Irvin Paik, an Asian American film-maker and actor, demonstrates the persistent distortion of Asians in his article, "That Oriental Feeling." The media have been increasingly careful in their portrayals of blacks, chicanos, and Indians, largely because of pressure from those groups as well as from major segments in white society. In Paik's analysis of Asian film stereotypes, he suggests that an improved, humanized Asian image on the screen will first require the heightened awareness and active support of the Asian American community for changing the Asian image.

As the subhuman identity of Asians is instilled into the American conscience, the United States' colonialist and neo-colonialist roles with the Third World become justifiable and indeed necessary to the defense and preservation of the white power structure. Colonialist mentality also serves to define sexual relationships between whites and nonwhites in America. Despite the emasculating pressures put on all nonwhites, white Americans still perceive black, chicano, and Indian males as sexually aggressive and threatening to the white woman. In contrast to these stereotypes, Asian American men are characterized as shy, withdrawn, weak, and passive; or in the words of writer Frank Chin, "Ours (referring to the Asian stereotype) is the only one that is utterly without manliness, male sexuality, potency, virility, male strengths."[6] In the past, before Asians had 'made it' and were considered socially inferior to whites, they too were labelled sexually dangerous. Now that the successful Asians are held up as a minority model by white America, their prior image had to be changed. So, the Asian male image became desexed - so emasculated that the boundary between white females and nonwhite males was still maintained.[7] On the other hand, colonialist situations have always encouraged the availability of nonwhite women for the sexual outlets of white males. The image of Asian women is understandably quite the opposite of that of Asian men. Qualities often used to describe Asian females include exotic, feminine, mysterious, charming, and sensuous. Distorted relationships between Asian men and women are frequently the result of these conflicting stereotypes. As Asian Americans try to acculturate according to white social and physical ideals, they can experience great difficulty in accepting their own ethnic identity. Self-hatred and repulsion toward each other is commonly manifested in their trying to escape their full identity by exclusively seeking white friends, white dating and marriage partners. Probably some of the most damaging indictment of Asian males comes from Asian American females, as expressed in two articles, "Inter-Racial Romance: The Chinese-Caucasian Dating Game" by Melford Weiss and "White Male Qualities." Following these articles is a corresponding male response to Asian American women, in a poem by Ron Tanaka entitled 'I hate my wife for her flat yellow face.'

Few academic studies have attempted to search beneath the stereotype image of Asian Americans to understand the actual basic aspects, needs, and problems of Asian American personality. Socio-psychological research usually seems to perpetuate the success myth, having lost its objectivity within a white conceptual framework. Tentative steps are being made to explore Asian American identity development from wider perspectives. In Stanford Lyman's "Generation and Character: The Case of the Japanese Americans," he focuses on the character development of the Nisei generation and how its behavior involves an attempt to merge and balance the values of the American environment with the Japanese culture of its Issei parents. Unfortunately, the implicit tone of the work supports the success stereotype, and although it offers important insights into Nisei character, it suffers from an overriding pro-Nisei rationale: "They have not merely survived the hatred and oppression of America's racism, they have triumphed over it....They have turned almost every adversity into a challenge and met each with courage and cool judgment. In all this their own subcultural character has been an invaluable aid as well as an ever-present source of pride." Pertaining to Chinese identity in America, Stanley and Derald Sue offer a theoretical model for studying Chinese American self-concepts in their article, "Chinese-American Personality and Mental Health." The interplay of Chinese culture, American culture, and racism can be organized into three fundamental personality types that appear to characterize Chinese and other Asians in America: the traditionalist conforms strongly to Chinese or Asian values; the marginal man cannot identify substantially with either culture; and the Asian American is trying to create a stable identity based on both cultures. The authors are careful to mention the limitations of their conceptual scheme, which is not meant to be all-inclusive, but which provides a possible means to gain better insight into Asian American personality.

Identity dynamics of Asian Americans can be related to the fundamental problem of being relatively powerless in American society, due to their small population. One acknowledged authority on Asian Americans is Harry Kitano, sociologist and social psychologist, who has written JAPANESE AMERICANS: EVOLUTION OF A SUBCULTURE and co-authored AMERICAN RACISM with historian Roger Daniels. In "An Interview with Harry Kitano," Kitano contends that Asian Americans are now divided between the Hayakawas and the non-Hayakawas but they have yet to deal with basic questions of a middleman minority, which is caught between two large opposing forces, the whites and the blacks. Should Asians try to join the white majority, unite with other Third World groups, remain aloof from either? Or does their middleman position offer them any choice in deciding their futures? A permanent middleman status for Asian Americans suggests a rather dismal outlook for them. However, Kitano concludes that the middleman analogy stems from existing models of assimilation; and once a person is aware of the realities of his past and present positions, "then a search for newer and perhaps more realistic models will be in order."

The final responsibility for creating alternative models and defining Asian American identity in new terms lies with the people - the community. Bruce Iwasaki, in his paper "Response and Change for the Asian in America: A Survey of Asian American Literature," takes a look into the changing identities of Asian Americans via their literature and indicates that an alternative model for Asians in America is now being created. A recurring theme in Asian American literature for over a century is their search for identity, evolving through experimental forms, withdrawl, return to Asian roots, success stories, and partial community involvement. Iwasaki feels that "in seeking a definition of the 'self,' most of the Asian literature has found expression within limited bounds. The self is always defined in relation to the conceptions of the majority culture, whether it is in opposition to or in agreement with it." He proposes that a valid Asian American literature will combine revolutionary political action and the Asian community experience into one. Iwasaki hopes that this will be the future direction of Asian American writers and their community.

A true Asian American literature along with other art forms will be extensions of an identity which fully recognizes the strengths, the weaknesses, and the total interaction of both Asian and American forces on Asian Americans. The autobiographies and poems which conclude the identity section express the increasing commitment of Asian Americans to redefine and articulate their individual and collective identity. While they reflect a wide range of backgrounds and responses to American society, there can be found a common level of experience with which all Asians in America can identify. The bulk of this section presents Asian American stereotypes and the changing relationships of Asians to them.[8] As Asian Americans define themselves on a human, universal level, they will no longer be restricted to imitations of or arguments against majority dictates. Hopefully, they will regain a sense of ego identity and unity that will allow them to act for changing the oppressed positions of Asians and other Americans.

AMY TACHIKI

[1] Isao Fujimoto, "Don't Mistake the Finger Pointing at the Moon for the Moon," ASIANS IN AMERICA: SELECTED STUDENT PAPERS, Davis: Asian American Research Project, 1970, p. 86.

[2] Dennis Ogawa, FROM JAPS TO JAPANESE, Berkeley: McCutchan Press, 1971, Chapter on the "Functions of the Stereotypes."

[3] Frank Chin, "Letter to Peter," January, 1970.

[4] Tom Engelhardt, "Ambush at Kamikaze Pass," BULLETIN OF CONCERNED ASIAN SCHOLARS, Vol. 3, No. 1 (Winter-Spring, 1971). This paragraph could not do justice to Mr. Engelhardt's excellent article; hopefully, the reader will be encouraged from this brief description to read it.

[5] Ibid., p. 81.

[6] Chin, op. cit., p. 9.

[7] Ogawa, op. cit., p. 58.

[8] Many identity-related articles to which this Reader had access happen to be written by or about Japanese Americans. Issues raised in this section are directed to all Asian groups in America. A major goal of this section is to stimulate further examination and discussion into the identity of all Asian Americans.

SUCCESS STORY OF ONE MINORITY GROUP IN U.S.

U.S. NEWS & WORLD REPORT   *Reprinted from U.S. NEWS AND WORLD REPORT, December 26, 1966.*

At a time when Americans are awash in worry over the plight of racial minorities--

One such minority, the nation's 300,000 Chinese-Americans, is winning wealth and respect by dint of its own hard work.

In any Chinatown from San Francisco to New York, you discover youngsters at grips with their studies. Crime and delinquency are found to be rather minor in scope.

Still being taught in Chinatown is the old idea that people should depend on their own efforts--not a welfare check--in order to reach America's "promised land."

Visit "Chinatown U.S.A." and you find an important racial minority pulling itself up from hardship and discrimination to become a model of self-respect and achievement in today's America.

At a time when it is being proposed that hundreds of billions be spent to uplift Negroes and other minorities, the nation's 300,000 Chinese-Americans are moving ahead on their own--with no help from anyone else.

Low rate of crime. In crime-ridden cities, Chinese districts turn up as islands of peace and stability.

Of 4.7 million arrests reported to the Federal Bureau of Investigation in 1965, only 1,293 involved persons of Chinese ancestry. A Protestant pastor in New York City's Chinatown said:

"This is the safest place in the city."

Few Chinese-Americans are getting welfare handouts--or even want them. Within a tight network of family and clan loyalties, relatives continue to help each other. Mrs. Jean Ma, publisher of a Chinese-language newspaper in Los Angeles, explained:

"We're a big family. If someone has trouble, usually it can be solved within the family. There is no need to bother someone else. And nobody will respect any member of the family who does not work and who just plays around."

Today, Chinese-American parents are worrying somewhat about their young people. Yet, in every city, delinquency in Chinatown is minor compared with what goes on around it.

Strict discipline. Even in the age of television and fast automobiles, Chinese-American children are expected to attend school faithfully, work hard at their studies--and stay out of trouble. Spanking is seldom used, but supervision and verbal discipline are strict.

A study of San Francisco's Chinatown noted that "if school performance is poor and the parents are told, there is an immediate improvement." And, in New York City, schoolteachers reportedly are competing for posts in schools with large numbers of Chinese-American children.

Recently Dr. Richard T. Sollenberger, professor of psychology at Mount Holyoke College, made a study of New York City's Chinatown and concluded:

"There's a strong incentive for young people to behave. As one informant said, 'When you walk around the streets of Chinatown, you have a hundred cousins watching you.'"

What you find, back of this remarkable group of Americans, is a story of adversity and prejudice that would shock those now complaining about the hardships endured by today's Negroes.

It was during California's gold rush that large numbers of Chinese began coming to America.

On the developing frontier, they worked in mines, on railroads and in other hard labor. Moving into cities, where the best occupations were closed to them, large numbers became laundrymen and cooks because of the shortage of women in the West.

Past handicaps. High value was placed on Chinese willingness to work long hours for low pay. Yet Congress, in 1882, passed an Exclusion Act denying naturalization to Chinese immigrants and forbidding further influx of laborers. A similar act in 1924, aimed primarily at the Japanese, pro-

Copyright 1966 U.S. NEWS AND WORLD REPORT, Inc.

hibited laborers from bringing in wives.

In California, the first legislature slapped foreign miners with a tax aimed at getting Chinese out of the gold-mining business. That State's highest court ruled Chinese could not testify against whites in court.

Chinese-Americans could not own land in California, and no corporation or public agency could employ them.

These curbs, in general, applied also to Japanese-Americans, another Oriental minority that has survived discrimination to win a solid place in the nation.

The curbs, themselves, have been discarded in the last quarter century. And, in recent years, immigration quotas have been enlarged, with 8,800 Chinese allowed to enter the country this year.

As a result, the number of persons of Chinese ancestry living in the United States is believed to have almost doubled since 1950.

Today, as in the past, most Chinese are to be found in Hawaii, California and New York. Because of ancient emphasis on family and village, most of those on the U.S. mainland trace their ancestry to communities southwest of Canton.

How Chinese get ahead. Not all Chinese-Americans are rich. Many, especially recent arrivals from Hong Kong, are poor and cannot speak English. But the large majority are moving ahead by applying the traditional virtues of hard work, thrift and morality.

Success stories have been recorded in business, science, architecture, politics and other professions. Dr. Sollenberger said of New York's Chinatown:

"The Chinese people here will work at anything. I know of some who were scholars in China and are now working as waiters in restaurants. That's a stopgap for them, of course, but the point is that they're willing to do something--they don't sit around moaning."

The biggest and most publicized of all Chinatowns is in San Francisco.

Since 1960, the inflow of immigrants has raised the Chinese share of San Francisco's population from 4.9 per cent to 5.7 per cent. Altogether 42,600 residents of Chinese ancestry were reported in San Francisco last year.

Shift to suburbs. As Chinese-Americans gain in affluence, many move to the suburbs. But about 30,000 persons live in the 25 blocks of San Francisco's Chinatown. Sixty-three per cent of these are foreign-born, including many who are being indoctrinated by relatives in the American way of life.

Irvin Lum, an official of the San Francisco Federal Savings and Loan Community House, said:

"We follow the custom of being good to our relatives. There is not a very serious problem with our immigrants. We're a people of ability, adaptable and easy to satisfy in material wants. I know of a man coming here from China who was looked after by his sister's family, worked in Chinatown for two years, then opened a small restaurant of his own."

Problems among newcomers stir worries, however. A minister said: "Many are in debt when they arrive. They have a language problem. They are used to a rural culture, and they have a false kind of expectation."

A youth gang of foreign-born Chinese, known as "the Bugs" or "Tong San Tsai," clashes occasionally with a gang of Chinese-American youngsters. And one group of Chinese-American teen-agers was broken up after stealing as much as $5,800 a week in burglaries this year.

Yet San Francisco has seen no revival of the "tong wars" or opium dens that led to the organizing of a "Chinese squad" of policemen in 1875. The last trouble between Chinese clans or "tongs" was before World War II. The special squad was abolished in 1956.

"Streets are safer." A University of California team making a three-year study of Chinatown in San Francisco reported its impression "that Chinatown streets are safer than most other parts of the city" despite the fact that it is one of the most densely populated neighborhoods in the United States.

In 1965, not one San Francisco Chinese-- young or old--was charged with murder, manslaughter, rape or an offense against wife or children. Chinese accounted for only two adult cases out of 252 of assault with a deadly weapon.

Only one of San Francisco's Chinese youths, who comprise 17 per cent of the city's high-school enrollment, was among 118 juveniles arrested last year for assault with a deadly weapon. Meantime, 25 per cent of the city's semifinalists in the California State scholarship competition were Chinese.

Most Chinese-Americans continue to send their youngsters to Chinese schools for one or two hours a day so they can learn Chinese history, culture and--in some cases --language. A businessman said: "I feel my kids are Americans, which is a tremendous asset. But they're also Chinese, which is another great asset. I want them to have and keep the best of both cultures."

Much the same picture is found in mainland America's other big Chinatowns--Los Angeles and New York.

Riots of 1871. Los Angeles has a memory of riots in 1871 when white mobs raged through the Chinese section. Twenty-three Chinese were hanged, beaten, shot or stabbed to death.

Today, 25,000 persons of Chinese ancestry live in Los Angeles County--20,000 in the city itself. About 5,000 alien Chinese from Hong Kong and Formosa are believed to be in southern California.

In Los Angeles, as elsewhere, Chinese-Americans are worrying about their children. Superior Judge Delbert E. Wong said: "Traditionally, the family patriarch ruled the household, and the other members of the family obeyed and followed without questioning his authority.

"As the Chinese become more Westernized, women leave the home to work and the younger generation finds greater mobility in seeking employment, we see greater problems within the family unit--and a corresponding increase in crime and divorce."

A Chinese-American clergyman complained that "the second and third-generation Chinese feel more at home with Caucasians. They don't know how to act around the older Chinese any more because they don't understand them."

The family unit. On the other hand, Victor Wong, president of the Chinese Consolidated Benevolent Association in Los Angeles said:

"Basically, the Chinese are good citizens. The parents always watch out for the children, train them, send them to school and make them stay home after school to study. When they go visiting, it is as a family group. A young Chinese doesn't have much chance to go out on his own and get into trouble."

A high-ranking police official in Los Angeles found little evidence of growing trouble among Chinese. He reported:

"Our problems with the Chinese are at a minimum. This probably is due to strict parental supervision. There is still a tradition of respect for parents."

New York City, in 1960, had a population of 32,831 persons of Chinese ancestry. Estimates today run considerably higher, with immigrants coming in at the rate of 200 or 300 a month.

Many Chinese have moved to various parts of the city and to the suburbs. But newcomers tend to settle in Chinatown, and families of eight and 10 have been found living in two-room apartments.

"The housing shortage here is worse than in Harlem," one Chinese-American said. Altogether, about 20,000 persons are believed living in the eight-block area of New York's Chinatown at present.

The head of the Chinatown Planning Council said recently that, while most Chinese are still reluctant to accept public welfare, somewhat more are applying for it than in the past. "We are trying to let Chinese know that accepting public welfare is not necessarily the worst thing in the world," he said.

However, a Chinese-American banker in New York took this view:

"There are at least 60 associations here whose main purpose is to help our own people. We believe welfare should be used only as a last resort."

A sizable number of Chinese-Americans who could move out if they wanted to are staying in New York's Chinatown--not because of fears of discrimination on the outside, but because they prefer their own people and culture. And Chinatown, despite its proximity to the Bowery, remains a haven of law and order. Dr. Sollenberger said:

"If I had a daughter, I'd rather have her live in Chinatown than any place else in New York City."

A police lieutenant said:

"You don't find any Chinese locked up for robbery, rape or vagrancy."

There has been some rise in Chinese-American delinquency in recent years. In part, this is attributed to the fact that the ratio of children in Chinatown's total population is going up as more women arrive and more families are started.

Even so, the proportion of Chinese-American youngsters getting into difficulty remains low. School buildings used by large numbers of Chinese are described as the cleanest in New York. Public recreational facilities amount to only one small park, but few complaints are heard.

Efforts at progress. Over all, what observers are finding in America's Chinatowns are a thrifty, law-abiding and industrious people--ambitious to make progress on their own.

In Los Angeles, a social worker said:
"If you had several hundred thousand Chinese-Americans subjected to the same economic and social pressures that confront Negroes in major cities, you would have a good deal of unrest among them.

"At the same time, it must be recognized that the Chinese and other Orientals in California were faced with even more prejudice than faces the Negro today. We haven't stuck Negroes in concentration camps, for instance, as we did the Japanese in World War II.

"The Orientals came back, and today they have established themselves as strong contributors to the health of the whole community."

the emergence of yellow power in america
(an excerpt)

AMY UYEMATSU

Asian Americans can no longer afford to watch the black-and-white struggle from the sidelines. They have their own cause to fight, since they are also victims--with less visible scars--of the white institutionalized racism. A yellow movement has been set into motion by the black power movement. Addressing itself to the unique problems of Asian Americans, this "yellow power" movement is relevant to the black power movement in that both are part of the Third World struggle to liberate all colored people.

Part I: MISTAKEN IDENTITY

The yellow power movement has been motivated largely by the problem of self-identity in Asian Americans. The psychological focus of this movement is vital, for Asian Americans suffer the critical mental crises of having "integrated" into American society--

"No person can be healthy, complete, and mature if he must deny a part of himself; this is what 'integration' has required so far."
--Stokely Carmichael & Charles V. Hamilton[1]

The Asian Americans' current position in America is not viewed as a social problem. Having achieved middle-class incomes while presenting no real threat in numbers to the white majority, the main body of Asian Americans (namely, the Japanese and the Chinese) have received the token acceptance of white America.

Precisely because Asian Americans have become economically secure, do they face serious identity problems. Fully committed to a system that subordinates them on the basis of non-whiteness, Asian Americans still try to gain complete acceptance by denying their yellowness. They have become white in every respect but color.

However, the subtle but prevailing racial prejudice that "yellows" experience restricts them to the margins of the white world. Asian Americans have assumed white identities, that is, the values and attitudes of the majority of Americans. Now they are beginning to realize that this nation is a "White democracy" and that yellow people have a mistaken

Reprinted from GIDRA, October, 1969.

identity.

Within the past two years, the "yellow power" movement has developed as a direct outgrowth of the "black power" movement. The "black power" movement caused many Asian Americans to question themselves. "Yellow power" is just now at the stage of "an articulated mood rather than a program--disillusionment and alienation from white America and independence, race pride, and self-respect."² Yellow consciousness is the immediate goal of concerned Asian Americans.

In the process of Americanization, Asians have tried to transform themselves into white men--both mentally and physically. Mentally, they have adjusted to the white man's culture by giving up their own languages, customs, histories, and cultural values. They have adopted the "American way of life" only to discover that this is not enough.

Next, they have rejected their physical heritages, resulting in extreme self-hatred. Yellow people share with the blacks the desire to look white. Just as blacks wish to be light-complected with thin lips and un-kinky hair, "yellows" want to be tall with long legs and large eyes. The self-hatred is also evident in the yellow male's obsession with unobtainable white women, and in the yellow female's attempt to gain male approval by aping white beauty standards. Yellow females have their own "conking" techniques--they use "peroxide, foam rubber, and scotch tape to give them light hair, large breasts, and double-lidded eyes."³

The "Black is Beautiful" cry among black Americans has instilled a new awareness in Asian Americans to be proud of their physical and cultural heritages. Yellow power advocates self-acceptance as the first step toward strengthening personalities of Asian Americans.

Since the yellow power movement is thus far made up of students and young adults, it is working for Asian-American ethnic studies centers on college campuses such as Cal and U.C.L.A. The re-establishment of ethnic identity through education is being pursued in classes like U.C.L.A.'s "Orientals in America." As one student in the course relates:

"I want to take this course for a 20-20 realization, and not a passive glance in the ill-reflecting mirror; the image I see is W.A.S.P., but the yellow skin is not lily white...I want to find out what my voluntarily or subconsciously suppressed Oriental self is like; also what the thousands of other (suppressed?) Oriental selves are like in a much larger mind and body--America...I want to establish my ethnic identity not merely for the sake of such roots, but for the inherent value that such a background merits."⁴

The problem of self-identity in Asian Americans also requires the removal of stereotypes. The yellow people in America seem to be silent citizens. They are stereotyped as being passive, accomodating, and unemotional. Unfortunately, this description is fairly accurate, for Asian Americans have accepted these stereotypes and are becoming true to them.

The "silent" Asian Americans have rationalized their behavior in terms of cultural values which they have maintained from the old country. For example, the Japanese use the term "enryo" to denote hesitation in action or expression. A young Buddhist minister, Reverend Mas Kodani of the Los Angeles Senshin Buddhist Temple, has illustrated the difference between Japanese "enryo" and Japanese-American "enryo": in Japan, if a teacher or lecturer asks, "Are there any questions?", several members of the class or audience respond; but in the United States, the same question is followed by a deathly silence.

Reverend Kodani has also commented on the freedom of expression between family members that is absent in Asian Americans. As an American-born student in Japan, he was surprised at the display of open affection in Japanese families. This cultural characteristic is not shown in Japanese-American families, who react with embarrassment and guilt toward open feelings of love and hate.

This uneasiness in admitting and expressing natural human feelings has been a factor in the negligible number of Asian Americans in the theater, drama, and literary arts. Not discounting the race prejudice and competition in these fields, yellow Americans cannot express themselves honestly, or in the words of Chinese-American actor James Hong, they cannot feel "from the gut level".

The silent, passive image of Asian Americans is understood not in terms of their cultural backgrounds, but by the fact that they are scared. The earliest Asians in America were Chinese immigrants who began settling in large numbers on the West Coast from 1850 through 1880. They were subjected to extreme white racism, ranging from economic subordination, to the denial of rights of naturalization, to physical violence. During the height of anti-Chinese mob action of the 1880's, whites were "stoning the Chinese in the streets, cutting off their queues, wrecking their shops and laundries."⁵ The worst outbreak took place in Rock Springs, Wyo-

10

ming, in 1885, when twenty-eight Chinese residents were murdered. Perhaps, surviving Asians learned to live in silence, for even if "the victims of such attacks tried to go to court to win protection, they could not hope to get a hearing. The phrase 'not a Chinaman's chance' had a grim and bitter reality."[6]

Racist treatment of "yellows" still existed during World War II, with the unjustifiable internment of 110,000 Japanese into detention camps. When Japanese Americans were ordered to leave their homes and possessions behind within short notice, they co-operated with resignation and not even voiced opposition. According to Frank Chumann, onetime president of the Japanese American Citizens League, they "used the principle of shikataganai--realistic resignation--and evacuated without protest."[7]

Today the Asian Americans are still scared. Their passive behavior serves to keep national attention on the black people. By being as inconspicuous as possible, they keep pressure off of themselves at the expense of the blacks. Asian Americans have formed an uneasy alliance with white Americans to keep the blacks down. They close their eyes to the latent white racism toward them which has never changed.

Frightened "yellows" allow the white public to use the "silent Oriental" stereotype against the black protest. The presence of twenty million blacks in America poses an actual physical threat to the white system. Fearful whites tell militant blacks that the acceptable criterion for behavior is exemplified in the quiet, passive Asian American.

The yellow power movement envisages a new role for Asian Americans:

"It is a rejection of the passive Oriental stereotype and symbolizes the birth of a new Asian--one who will recognize and deal with injustices. The shout of Yellow Power, symbolic of our new direction, is reverberating in the quiet corridors of the Asian community."[8]

As expressed in the black power writings, yellow power also says that "When we begin to define our own image, the stereotypes-- that is, lies--that our oppressor has developed will begin in the white community and end there."

Another obstacle to the creation of yellow consciousness is the well-incorporated white racist attitudes which are present in Asian Americans. They take much false pride in their own economic progress and feel that blacks could succeed similarly if they only followed the Protestant ethic of hard work and education. Many Asians support S.I. Hayakawa, the so-called spokesman of yellow people, when he advises the black man to imitate the Nisei: "Go to school and get high grades, save one dollar out of every ten you earn to capitalize your business."[10] But the fact is that the white power structure allowed Asian Americans to succeed through their own efforts while the same institutions persist in denying these opportunities to black Americans.

Certain basic changes in American society made it possible for many Asian Americans to improve their economic condition after the war. In the first place, black people became the target group of West Coast discrimination. During and after World War II, a huge influx of blacks migrated into the West, taking racist agitation away from the yellows and onto the blacks. From 1940 to 1950, there was a gain of 85.2 percent in the black population of the West and North; from 1950 to 1960, a gain of 71.6 percent; and from 1960 to 1966, a gain of 80.4 percent.[11]

The other basic change in society was the shifting economic picture. In a largely agricultural and rural West, Asian Americans were able to find employment. First- and second-generation Japanese and Filipinos were hired as farm laborers and gardeners, while Chinese were employed in laundries and restaurants. In marked contrast is the highly technological and urban society which today faces unemployed black people. "The Negro migrant, unlike the immigrant, found little opportunity in the city; he had arrived too late, and the unskilled labor he had to offer was no longer needed."[12] Moreover, blacks today are kept out of a shrinking labor market, which is also closing opportunities for white job-seekers.

Asian Americans are perpetuating white racism in the United States as they allow white America to hold up the "successful" Oriental image before other minority groups as the model to emulate. White America justifies the blacks' position by showing that other non-whites--yellow people--have been able to "adapt" to the system. The truth underlying both the yellows' history and that of the blacks has been distorted. In addition, the claim that black citizens must "prove their rights to equality"[13] is fundamentally racist.

Unfortunately, the yellow power movement is fighting a well-developed racism in Asian Americans who project their own frustrated attempts to gain white acceptance onto the black people. They nurse their own feelings of inferiority and insecurity by holding themselves as superior to the blacks.

Since they feel they are in a relatively secure economic and social position, most Asian Americans overlook the subtle but damaging racism that confronts them. They do not want to upset their present ego systems by honest self-appraisal. They would rather fool themselves than admit that they have prostituted themselves to white society.

Part 2: THE RELEVANCE OF POWER FOR ASIANS IN AMERICA

The emerging movement among Asian Americans can be described as "yellow power" because it is seeking freedom from racial oppression through the power of a consolidated yellow people. As derived from the black power ideology, yellow power implies that Asian Americans must control the decision-making processes affecting their lives.

One basic premise of both black power and yellow power is that ethnic political power must be used to improve the economic and social conditions of blacks and yellows. In considering the relevance of power for Asian Americans, two common assumptions will be challenged: first, that the Asian Americans are completely powerless in the United States; and second, the assumption that Asian Americans have already obtained "economic" equality.

While the black power movement can conceivably bargain from a position of strength, yellow power has no such potential to draw from. A united black people would comprise over ten percent of the total American electorate; this is a significant enough proportion of the voting population to make it possible for blacks to be a controlling force in the power structure.[1] In contrast, the political power of yellows would have little effect on state and national contests. The combined populations of Chinese, Japanese and Filipinos in the United States in 1960 was only 887,834 -- not even one-half percent of the total population.[2]

However, Asian Americans are not completely weaponless, in the local political arena. For instance, in California, the combined strength of Chinese, Japanese, and Filipinos in 1960 was two percent of the state population.[3] Their possible political significance lies in the fact that there are heavy concentrations of these groups in San Francisco and Los Angeles. In the San Francisco-Oakland metropolitan area, 55% of the Chinese, 16% of the Japanese, and 33% of the Filipinos live.[4] On an even more local level, Japanese and Chinese in the Crenshaw area of Los Angeles form about one-third of the total residents; and Japanese in the city of Gardena own forty percent of that city's property.[5]

In city and county government, a solid yellow voting bloc could make a difference. As has been demonstrated by the Irish, Italians, Jews, and Poles, the remarkable fact of ethnic political power is it's ability to "control a higher proportion of political control and influence than their actual percentage in the population warrants."[6]

Even under the assumption that yellow political power could be significant, how will it improve the present economic situation of Asian Americans? Most yellow people have attained middle-class incomes and feel that they have no legitimate complaint against the existing capitalist structure.

The middle-class attainment of Asian Americans has also made certain blacks unsympathetic to the yellow power movement. In the words of one B.S.U. member, it looks like Asian Americans "just want more of the money pie." It is difficult for some blacks to relate to the yellow man's problems next to his own total victimization.

Although it is true that some Asian minorities lead all other colored groups in America in terms of economic progress, it is a fallacy that Asian Americans enjoy full economic opportunity. If the Protestant ethic is truly a formula for economic success, then why don't Japanese and Chinese who work harder and have more education than whites earn just as much? Statistics on unemployment, educational attainment, and median annual income reveal an inconsistency in this "success" formula when it applies to non-whites.

In 1960, unemployment rates for Japanese and Chinese males were lower than those for white males in California:

    2.6 percent for Japanese
    4.9 percent for Chinese
    5.5 percent for whites

In the same year, percentage rates for Japanese and Chinese males who had completed high school or college were higher than those for white males:

<u>High School</u>
34.3 percent for Japanese
24.4 percent for Chinese

<u>College (4 years or more)</u>
13.3 percent for Chinese
11.9 percent for Japanese
10.7 percent for whites [8]

Despite these figures, the median annual income of Japanese and Chinese was considerably lower than the median annual income of whites. Chinese men in California earned $3,803; Japanese men earned $4,388; and white men earned $5,109.[9]

The explanation for this discrepancy lies in the continuing racial discrimination toward yellows in upper-wage level and high-status positions. White America praises the success of Japanese and Chinese for being highest among all other colored groups. Japanese and Chinese should feel fortunate that they are accepted more than any other non-white ethnic group, but they should not step out of place and compare themselves with whites. In essence, the American capitalistic dream was never meant to include non-whites.

The myth of Asian American success is most obvious in the economic and social position of Filipino Americans. In 1960, the 65,459 Filipino residents of California earned a median annual income of $2,925, as compared to $3,553 for blacks and $5,109 for whites.[10] Over half of the total Filipino male working force was employed in farm labor and service work; over half of all Filipino males received less than 8.7 years of school education.[11] Indeed, Filipinos are a forgotten minority in America. Like blacks, they have many legitimate complaints against American society.

A further example of the false economic and social picture of Asian Americans exists in the ghetto communities of Little Tokyo in Los Angeles and Chinatown in San Francisco. In the former, elderly Japanese live in run-down hotels in social and cultural isolation. And in the latter, Chinese families suffer the poor living conditions of a community that has the second highest tuberculosis rate in the nation.[12]

Thus, the use of yellow political power is valid, for Asian Americans do have definite economic and social problems which must be improved. By organizing around these needs, Asian Americans can make the yellow power movement a viable political force in their lives.

PART I

[1] Stokely Carmichael and Charles V. Hamilton, BLACK POWER: THE POLITICS OF LIBERATION IN AMERICA (New York: Vintage Books, 1967), p. 55.
[2] REPORT OF THE NATIONAL ADVISORY COMMISSION ON CIVIL DISORDERS (New York: The New York Times Company, 1968), p. 233.
[3] Dinora Gil, "Yellow Prostitution", GIDRA, April, 1969, p. 2.
[4] "UCLA Class on 'Orientals in America,'" GIDRA, May, 1969, p. 6.
[5] Foster Rhea Dulles, CHINA AND AMERICA (Princeton: Princeton University Press, 1946), p. 89.
[6] Ibid.
[7] "Twenty Years After," TIME, LXXVIII (August, 1961), p. 15.
[8] Larry Kubota, "Yellow Power," GIDRA, April, 1969, p. 3.
[9] Carmichael and Hamilton, p. 37.
[10] "Hayakawa Praises Nisei as Sansei Picket Talk," KASHU MAINICHI, April 28, 1969, p. 1.
[11] REPORT OF THE NATIONAL ADVISORY COMMISSION ON CIVIL DISORDERS, p. 241.
[12] Ibid., p. 278.
[13] Kazuo Higa, "What Meaning Does the Japanese-American Experience Have for the Black People of America?", Japanese American Seminar, June 5, 1968.

PART II

[1] Chuck Stone, BLACK POLITICAL POWER IN AMERICA (New York: Bobbs-Merrill Company, 1968), p. 108.
[2] State of California, CALIFORNIANS OF JAPANESE, CHINESE, AND FILIPINO ANCESTRY (San Francisco: Division of Labor Statistics and Research, June, 1965), p. 9.
[3] Ibid., p. 17.
[4] Ibid., pp. 10-11.
[5] Interview with Alan Nishio, May 26, 1969.
[6] Stone, p. 147.
[7] State of California, p. 12.
[8] Ibid., p. 25.
[9] Ibid., p. 14.
[10] Ibid.
[11] Ibid., p. 25.
[12] GIDRA, May, 1969, p. 2.

THE INTOLERANCE OF SUCCESS

DANIEL OKIMOTO

Despite the outpouring of praise from the white community, my own reactions to the celebrated success story of the Japanese minority are not quite so effusive or one-sided. While the many achievements of this minority should be acknowledged, it must also be pointed out that much of the praise that is showered upon us springs from a fountainhead of middle-class assumptions, some of questionable value, and that those neglect to mention the reverse side of success: the sacrifices that had to be made, the shortcomings that are all but overlooked in our pilgrimage into the Land of Milk and Honey. Since to dwell exclusively on our accomplishments is to present an incomplete picture, some of the less attractive aspects of the Japanese-American pattern of acculturation need to be discussed. Of greatest importance, perhaps, are the costs at which our social advancement has been won.

In adapting to American society, we have had to face the persistent and perplexing problem of how to look upon our dual heritage. The difficulty in reconciling these twin aspects of our lives is often revealed in that moment of hesitation many experience when asked, "What are you?" In my own life there have been times when I have been frankly at a loss how to reply. Depending on my mood and the circumstances, my answers have vacillated between "American," "Japanese," and "Japanese American." Whatever the response, it usually felt somehow unnatural. I never considered myself 100-percent American because of obvious physical differences. Nor did I think of myself as Japanese. The social opprobrium associated with being a member of a minority also made me slightly uncomfortable about declaring myself a Japanese American.

Perhaps this question would not pose such problems if an atmosphere of greater tolerance existed in America. Certainly if the United States were a harmonious melting pot in which all races are accepted equally - as myths would have one believe - there would not be any need to feel hesitant about identifying with a minority, particularly one as successful as the Japanese. But in the face of prejudice, it is often hard indeed to resolve the Japanese and American elements.

Like a number of others, I passed through a period when I almost always responded to questions about my nationality with "American." The mere fact of being questioned made me bristle with indignation at the ignorance of those who felt the need to inquire. At the bottom of my eagerness to be recognized as an American, was a deep-seated discomfort about my Asian past. Even at those times when I referred to myself in jest as a "Buddha-head" there was probably some degree of self-derogation.

Unfortunately, as a consequence of this state of mind, we nisei all too frequently attempt to jettison the Asian aspects of our personalities. In our eagerness to scramble to the top of American society, many of us have paid the costly price of abandoning the "baggage" of our cultural heritage, the finest features of which have contributed to the competitive position we now hold. Although Japanese Americans still stick together in closed groups, the substance of our subculture has lost much of its "Japaneseness." Certain old-country stresses, such as that placed on education, survive today, but gradually these have come to be associated less with Japanese-American values than with middle-class American norms.

As any casual conversation will reveal, Japanese Americans are on the whole no better informed about their ancestral homeland than non-Japanese. Few are willing to make an effort to learn anything about it. Although this disinterest may perhaps be inevitable as the struggle to

---

Reprinted from AMERICAN IN DISGUISE by Daniel Okimoto by permission of John Weatherhill, Inc. Mr. Okimoto, a graduate of Princeton, Harvard, and Tokyo Universities, is currently completing his Ph.D. at the University of Michigan.

The term "Nisei" is used in this article to denote all Japanese Americans, and not just the second-generation Japanese Americans.

establish an American identity goes on, it is nevertheless a loss to lament, particularly in view of the richness of Japanese culture. Japanese concepts of aesthetics as expressed in such art forms as ink painting, woodblock prints, folkcrafts, traditional gardens, and architecture stand up well in comparison with the world's greatest artistic achievements. The same can be said of Japanese literature, cinema, martial arts, flower arrangement, tea ceremony, Noh, Kabuki and Bunraku drama, and Zen Buddhism. How unfortunate that so few Japanese Americans consciously seek to keep alive this cultural heritage.

Interestingly, there is a movement taking shape now among the postwar generation to reevaluate the problem of identity and the significance of their ethnicity. No longer apologetic about being members of a minority nor eager to discard their past, many college-age nisei today are rebelling against remnants of racism and old Oriental stereotypes, and are aggressively raising a cry for Yellow Power. Like Afro-American groups, Asian-American organizations are appearing on campuses throughout the country, their members demanding courses that can help them receive a sense of their historical roots. They are redefining their role and place in society and, from a newly delineated perspective, participating in the momentous issues confronting the nation.

The new ethnic consciousness and defiance against racial prejudice owes much to the Black Power movement which, by boldly challenging the status quo, brought vividly to light conditions of injustice that confront all minorities, leading the way for other races to join in the long-delayed fight against discrimination. Borrowing the insights and even some of the rhetoric of the blacks, the Asian-American movement represents a sharp divergence from the old pattern of silence and passivity. While Yellow Power may never become the rallying cry for Orientals in the same way that Black Power has for Negroes, the affirmation of racial ancestry is the kind of major shift in attitude that could have far-reaching implications for Asian subcultures in the United States.

Even though the term "nisei" applies to Japanese in both North and South America, the two groups are quite different in their identification with their Japanese past. Nisei in Latin America appear on the whole to have come under less compulsion to shed their Asian identity than those in North America. Not only do they tend to speak better Japanese, retain more Oriental customs, and maintain closer ties with relatives in Japan, but they also hold their ancestral culture in higher esteem than their counterparts in the States. This may be the result of timing; large scale immigration to South America took place more recently than that to the United States. But it is probably more directly related to differences in the area into which Japanese culture was carried. Location helps explain why Japanese Americans on the mainland and in Hawaii are not the same. In the presence of more Japanese and perhaps less anti-Japanese prejudice, Hawaiian nisei seem to retain more of their racial identity, maintain a larger and more cohesive ethnic community, and in general appear less frantic about Americanizing than those on the continent.*

The successes of the Japanese in mainland America have been predicated on a thoroughgoing accomodation to white-class norms. The high degree of conformity is evident in the general behavioral patterns of nisei students: in the classroom they are extremely well-behaved, seldom make noise, never talk back to teachers, faithfully finish their school assignments on time. Neatly dressed, cleanly scrubbed, polite and deferential, nisei on the whole would be among the last to join hippie communes or participate in avant garde movements. Although some postwar youths are beginning to defy traditional modes, the majority of Japanese are still the epitome of the clean-cut all-American prototype in all but physical appearance.

Quiet conformity has no doubt helped to minimize social deviation and outbreaks of crime; in this sense it has functioned positively in gaining Japanese American admission into American society. However, from quite another perspective, the unquestioning, almost mindless acceptance of middle-class standards has given rise to an insensate conservatism that has all but deadened impulses toward individualism and creativity. It is rare to find among the Japanese community individualists who not only think heretically but dare to court strong social disapproval by disregarding convention. Accolades from the Caucasian community, inadvertently perhaps, have reinforced this timidity by convincing Japanese Americans that it is better to be safe than conspicous. As a result, nisei are proud of their upstanding reputation and are reluctant to risk damaging it with unorthodox activity. Told what exemplary citizens we are, we have responded gratefully by continuing to embrace the order and norms of the white mainstream. How dull the United States would be, I have thought at times, if it were populated only by those of Japanese ancestry.

Given this social orientation it is hardly surprising that artistic creativity, except perhaps in certain fields of the visual arts, is not an attribute for which Japanese Americans are noted. Strict conformity to established norms will probably insure continued prominence in traditional middle-class occupations. Successful nisei dentists, pharmacists, engineers, and businessmen there will always be in great abundance. But the odds are stacked against writers of originality or poets of genius. So long as nisei swallow set standards of social propriety so unquestioningly, so long as they are intent on following the well-known paths to middle-class success, they will probably lack the raw material of experience, the social relevance, individual perception, and artistic vision, to say nothing of the personal daring needed to assume the high risk of failure, that are basic ingredients for genuine creative expression. Though of course the possibility cannot be ruled out, it appears unlikely that literary figures of comparable stature to those of minorities like the Jews and blacks will emerge to articulate the nisei soul. Japanese Americans will be forced to borrow the voices of James Michener, Jerome Charyn, and other sympathetic novelists to distill their own experience. Even if a nisei of Bernard Malamud's or James Baldwin's talents did appear, he would no doubt have little to say that John O'Hara has not already said.

The drive to adapt to white standards of success has recently prompted some postwar nisei to make the charge that behind our conformity and ambition lies a strong desire to become white. Once securely esconced in high social positions, some Japanese Americans have become yellow Uncle Toms, or in the lively jargon of the militant young, "bananas"--yellow on the outside, white inside. Currently ranking as Top Banana is S. I. Hayakawa, who was appointed president of San Francisco State College during its bitter strike. Although Dr. Hayakawa became the darling of the silent majority in California by ripping out wires from student microphones and by following a get-tough policy against recalcitrant blacks, he hardly endeared himself to many postwar nisei who felt he had sold out completely to the white Establishment. To them it was unforgivable that he had callously misused his ethnicity to thwart the aspirations of another minority. They pronounced him guilty of willingly becoming the flunky of reactionary white politicians in need of a Japanese lackey to lead the "holy alliance" against the "lawless" insurrection of the blacks.

Nor is Hayakawa the only banana. Combined with their apolitical bent, the conformity of the Japanese Americans has prevented many from involving themselves in the great social issues facing the nation today. The nisei in southern California seem at times as allergic to liberal causes, such as fair housing and civil rights, as other residents in the area whose reactionary political views are notorious throughout the country. The aversion to participate in just causes is puzzling in light of the historical suffering of the community; but it is yet another aspect of our adaptation that has been largely overlooked.

There are happily some signs of change, at least insofar as self-interests are at stake. The dismissal of Dr. Thomas Noguchi as Los Angeles County Coroner is a case in point. When complaints against the alleged sadism and morbid personality of Dr. Noguchi were made public, many of the good citizens of L. A. screamed for the "Jap's" removal from office. Whether such a hue would have been raised against a white or whether such charges would have been so readily believed is doubtful. Operating on the assumption that a minority suspect is guilty unless proven innocent, the County Board of Supervisors acceded to pressures by dismissing the doctor without investigating carefully the facts of the matter or granting him the right of a public hearing. Although some influential Japanese typically recommended that he accept the dismissal without a fight, thousands of others grouped together in an ad hoc organization called JUST--Japanese United in Search of Truth--which collected over 10,000 signatures of protest, raised large sums of money, took the case to court, proved Noguchi's innocence, and won his reinstatement as County Coroner.

However, the nisei community is in little danger of winning medals for social crusading on the behalf of those outside its own circle. Socio-political apathy continues to be one of our most debilitating defects. Lack of concern for fellow humans is graphically captured in the statement I have heard expressed much too often: "We've made it. We've overcome the barriers of racial prejudice without help from anyone else. Why can't the others?" S. I. Hayakawa embodied this hardhearted outlook in its extreme when he simplistically suggested that Negroes emulate nisei in their struggle to find a place in society.

Such attitudes raise the question of whether an ethnic minority such as ours can really be considered successful. True, Japanese Americans have succeeded in securing a comfortable bourgeois life, an accomplishment for which we have earned the rousing commendation of the white majority. But this praise, it must be realized, has been based on value judgments that ultimately serve the purposes of the established social order. Professor Harry Kitano, in his informative book, correctly points out that "the judgment of Japanese Americans as the 'model American minority' is made from a strictly majority point of view. Japanese Americans are good because they conform--they don't make waves--they work hard and are quiet and docile."* When this lauded minority sits back indifferently and says, "We've made it, why can't they?" I doubt whether we have succeeded in any but the narrowest materialistic definition of the word. For in a broader spiritual and humanistic sense we have failed abysmally, not only as a minority group but as compassionate human beings.

The spiritual dimension of the nisei success story is obviously as important as the material, yet this aspect is often overlooked by those whose eyes catch only the glitter of our position and possessions. Failure of the human spirit does not register in sociological studies--intangibles of the heart are not amenable to points on a graph or lines on a chart. Ours is not a failure of wrong action; rather it is one of omission, which is no less reprehensible because it involves doing nothing at all. Indeed, passivity in the face of injustice is particularly insidious because it often goes unnoticed or is subject to deceptive rationalization.

Perhaps my reaction to the conservatism and political lethargy of the ethnic community may strike some delicate Japanese Americans, particularly those incorrigible optimists who insist America is indeed the Promised Land, as excessively harsh. But "don't rock the boat," "let them work for it" attitudes strike me as basically immoral. Perhaps this is because my family, having lived in the ghetto after the war, takes the civil rights movement very personally and has become involved in it in one way or another. My brother, Joe, has in effect dedicated his life to working with the poor and oppressed.

After graduating from Harvard Medical School, Joe was moving safely along the established tracks toward the security of a job as a surgeon, a most prestigious and lucrative profession. During his residency, however, he began to feel deeply uneasy about the disconnection between the wonders of modern medicine and the world of human misery inhabited by blacks and other minority groups. Health care seemed to be largely a middle-class luxury, out of the reach of those poverty-stricken people who most needed it. Unhappy with the elitist orientation of the career he was headed for, Joe quit surgery to devote himself to that area of medicine--public health and social medicine-- where he believed he could best help the minority races and the poor.

Joe's decision to throw away assured wealth and status was perplexing for many of his colleagues and friends, who could only conclude that he was hopelessly confused. Within their hierarchy of values, he indeed will never reach the pinnacle of success epitomized by a surgical career; nor will he boost statistics about the nisei success story. For Joe, who lived in the slums of San Diego, it is back to the "ghettoes, Indian reservations, and other areas of poverty," as he put it in his letter of resignation. This move may be both foolish and foreign to some nisei, particularly those whose prime ambition is to set up practice on East First Street of Little Tokyo, an area about as remote in spirit from the ghettoes, Indian reservations, and other areas of poverty as the Japanese Americans are from the struggles of those minorities. But regardless of what others think of him or his decision, he will have the satisfaction of knowing he acted as his heart and conscience dictated.

It is unfortunate that so many nisei, climbing up the social ladder, have given primacy to material over humanistic values. Gradually, many have assumed some of the less desirable features of their newly acquired status. Preoccupied with materialism as are the majority of Americans, many are deeply committed to the stylish life. Comfortable houses, sleek cars, and fashionable clothes are the accouterments of the middle-class success they have pursued so single-mindedly. Conversations with some nisei friends have left me wondering at times whether our values supersede material accumulation in their view.

With the passage of time the Japanese in America have also begun to display more of the patterns of delinquency and crime found in other American groups. Acculturation has resulted in the erosion of some of the principle qualities that set Japanese apart as a particularly law-abiding minority. While crime statistics still fall substantially below other groups', violence and other forms of destructive behavior have become increasingly prevalent. Unthinkable in the past, crime rates and juvenile delinquency have risen to such a point that it is no longer rare to witness gangs of Japanese youngsters marauding through the streets of Los Angeles, fighting with knives and guns and aimlessly destroying property.

In taking an overview of the Japanese American road to success it might seem that the pattern of adaptation through passive conformity to the structure and norms of society points beyond the simple abandonment of ethnic legacy and the assumption of certain middle-class values ultimately toward total assimilation. Although there may be a long-term trend in this direction, powerful currents are moving counter to the drift toward assimilation, as shown by the resistance of the subculture to diffusion within the larger framework of society. It is true that the postwar generation of Japanese Americans, unlike the prewar breed, no longer need to band together defensively in the face of such blatant discrimination as existed before the war, yet social barriers continue to exist, and today's generation seems to prefer the company of its kind. Quite apart from the question of whether this is desirable or not, the presently visible evidence indicates that it is premature to forecast dissolution of the Japanese subculture.

The matter of marriage, the key to final assimilation, is a complicated question for which no clear tendencies are discernible. There appears to be a growing open-mindedness about marrying into other racial groups, which is nevertheless offset to a certain extent by definite preferences, even among many of the postwar set, to find spouses within the ethnic community. The whole marriage issue has been, and still is, overladen with all sorts of volatile emotions and stubborn prejudices. Even when young Japanese Americans choose marital partners from the subculture, as many prefer to do, difficult problems can still arise. The issei did not come to America wholly unfettered by social biases; even today issei grandparents occasionally object to marriages involving partners whose ancestry can be traced back to "undesirable" social origins: those from Okinawa or worse, *eta* (outcast class in Japan), are anathema to many issei, who might try to prohibit marriages despite the freedom of the youngsters from such biases.

The situation becomes even more complex when hakujin (whites) or kokujin (blacks), enter the picture. This is partly because some Japanese Americans continue to harbor a distrustful attitude toward non-Japanese. This defensive suspicion is unlikely to disappear so long as the remnants of anti-Japanese hostility are not erased. The arsenal of arguments against interracial marriage from the standpoint of Japanese Americans is frequently well stocked with racial and social myths, some of which are quite farfetched, concerning the physical incompatibility of races, the alleged ease with which whites divorce, unresolvable differences of background, and social difficulties for mixed children. It is my impression that many nisei parents will try just as hard as, if not more so than, non-Japanese families, to dissuade their children from marrying out of their race. My parents as ministers have frequently been called upon by desperate parents to discourage nisei-white, nisei-Mexican, nisei-Chinese, and sometimes nisei-Negro couples from intermarrying. The tranquility of a number of households has been shattered by the eruption of emotions over prospective non-Japanese in-laws. If persuasion fails, some parents as a last resort will threaten to disown the children. But the passage of time, particularly if a grandchild has been born, generally restores harmony within the family.

The issues of intermarriage and ultimate assimilation, like a host of other complex questions, await answers from future generations of Japanese Americans, beginning with the postwar group now reaching adulthood. The nisei community has come to a new, and in some ways decisive, turning point in its comparatively short history in the United States. The questions that face my generation will undoubtedly require new answers in determining our future role in American society from those that have brought us to our present position.

The imminent danger that confronts us now is not so much the obstacle of social oppression or the threat of another bitter internment experience or the looming specter of potential failure. Unlike our prewar predecessors we face comfort not hardship, security not uncertainty, and general tolerance not discrimination. Our challenge stems, paradoxically, from an excess of success. The question that will concern us is not whether we can make it in American society, but whether the price of achieving social success is too high. Concretely, this means: Can we adjust to middle-class living without necessarily accepting wholesale the inbuilt prejudices and undesirable characteristics? Can we relish our newly won social status and material affluence without forgetting the misfortunes of those who are still seeking them? Can we enjoy our freedom without forgetting the oppression other minorities suffer?

These challenges demand no less determination or courage, because they arise from the very successes that have been passed on to us, than did the imposing barriers that pushed the issei and older-generation nisei to the limits of their abilities. Indeed they are perhaps in the long run even more demanding and difficult, because they represent internal challenges, not external obstructions, involving the human spirit and heart. Whether we possess that extra measure of inner strength and spiritual greatness to rise up to these subtle but stern tests is a matter only the future will tell. Our present response to them, however, will determine whether the much publicized Japanese American experience is really a success story.

AN INTERVIEW WITH
S. I. HAYAKAWA
PRESIDENT OF SAN FRANCISCO STATE COLLEGE

EDITORIAL BOARD
JUNE, 1971

HAYAKAWA: I was born in Vancouver. At that time my father was a worker on a Japanese-American newspaper. He also was a labor contractor. He was just a kid, you know, about 22 or so and he was the only English-speaking Japanese around so he acted as a semi-lawyer for Japanese who got in trouble with the laws. And he was a community leader in that small Japanese colony in Vancouver in 1904, 1905, 1906.

QUESTION: How did this role as a leader in the community show itself in your family?

HAYAKAWA: In no way at all, because we left that community. And I was brought up in Cranbrook, B. C., only Japanese family there; Calgary, only Japanese family there, Winnipeg, only Japanese family there. And I stayed in Winnipeg through the end of grade school, through high school, through college, so I was never a member of the Japanese-Canadian community. And one important thing about being a one-man minority, is that there is no such thing. You're just part of the gang. There are no generalizations about what Japs are like or what Chinese are like you see in a community like Winnipeg, they just accept you or they don't. Hell, you can go to school with the kids and you're part of the community. I was brought up according to Cub Scouts, Boy Scouts, National Guard, everything, loyal Canadian, taking great pride in being a Canadian, that's all.

QUESTION: Did your family speak Japanese in the house?

HAYAKAWA: We spoke Japanese at home but not to Father, because Father was a student of English history before I was born. He used to translate Ruskin and Carlyle into Japanese, and publish essays in Japanese-language papers.

QUESTION: What about your mother? Did she speak English?

HAYAKAWA: Not very well, she never did learn.

QUESTION: So you communicated in Japanese?

HAYAKAWA: Yes. I communicated with her in young baby Japanese with English words tacked on.

QUESTION: There's a recent article in Newsweek and many other journals labelling Japanese-Americans as a model minority, or as whiter than white. Do you agree with this analysis?

HAYAKAWA: I haven't read the article in Newsweek. But there is a sense in which they are a model minority in that the cultural values of Japanese, not Japanese-Americans, but Japanese, are congruent with the values of middle-class America.

QUESTION: What values for example?

HAYAKAWA: Well, postponement of gratification is the most important one. That's what education is about; you study now in order to enjoy the fruits of education later, so the high value placed upon education which is congruent to Japanese, Chinese, Jews and Americans...that's a very important congruence of middle-class values in America with Japanese cultural values. Then, one very important Japanese value is propriety in public behavior. Don't make yourself ridiculous, don't make yourself conspicuous, don't get yourself laughed at...this is congruence with middle-class American behavior...don't make a nuisance of yourself. So there are many ways in which the restraint of emotion, of public expression of emotion, of the Japanese is congruent with that of middle-class Americans.

QUESTION: Dr. Kitano, in his book, Japanese Americans, Evolution of a Subculture, writes about many of these norminative values --the enryo syndrome...

HAYAKAWA: I hate that expression "enryo syndrome". I think its an absolute distortion of reality. Some smart son-of-a-bitch thought that up and they have been using it ever since --and I think it's nonsense.

I can give you a very simple explanation of it. You know what the Jews mean by the term "chutzpah." Now "chutzpah" is the very opposite of the Japanese characteristic I am talking about. When they say "enryo syndrome," notice that the word syndrome makes it sound like some kind of illness instead of a real cultural characteristic. Now, the characteristic is non-presumptuousness, and chutzpah is being presumptuous as all hell. You are just assistant manager but you act as if you own the whole damn store. And if you can get away with it, that's chutzpah and you are admired for it. In Japanese culture, you don't do this. If you are a manager, you behave like a manager and acknowledge the authority of the manager and the owner, etc., and acknowledge the line of authority. This is congruent with American culture too, although American culture has more chutzpah than Japanese. But for an immigrant group, not to have chutzpah, to be non-presumptuous, is tactfully a very smart thing. And the Chinese have had this characteristic too of non-presumptuousness, of not barging in and making demands and making noise about it--just simply being quiet about it.

Now you asked the question, "In what respect are Japanese Americans ideal immigrants?" From the point of view of immigration, a small minority trying to get themselves integrated into a larger culture... that's the most tactful thing that you can do is not to be presumptuous.

QUESTION: But what happens in an adverse situation like the relocations experience?

HAYAKAWA: This is where the non-presumptuousness paid off fantastically. Because a number of Sansei behave today as if they should have shot if off with the authorities, and they feel ashamed that the Issei and Nisei didn't fight, and quietly and meekly went off to concentration camps--well, there were only 110,000 of them including small children to start with against a population of 150 million--so what the hell is the use of fighting? The second thing--my aunt represents this so well. She says "There is a war on--what do you expect?" So they went into the concentration camps and behaved themselves extraordinarily well. You put a bunch of Irish, or Italians, or Portuguese or anyone else in there and they wouldn't have behaved that well, but Chinese and Japanese would have behaved that well.

QUESTION: Do you yourself feel that relocation is a necessary measure for the United States government to put forth?

HAYAKAWA: It was not necessary for the defense of America, but there was no way of telling in January, 1942. The United States had suffered serious serious naval defeats at Terawa or at the Battle of Midway --American people would have felt this terrible sense of frustration about having been defeated by the Japanese in the mid-Pacific and they would have lynched the local Japanese if they had been around.

QUESTION: So you feel that it was more or less for their protection then?

HAYAKAWA: I think that ultimately it turned out for their own protection. I still think that it was a hell of a terrible thing to have to do, but as my aunt said,--"You know, there's a war on."

QUESTION: Do you see any negative effects on the psychology of the Japanese after camp?

HAYAKAWA: No. All the people I know have a very positive attitude towards it. The ones I know in Chicago say, "We would have never gone to Chicago, if it hadn't been for the wartime relocation. We would have all been hung along a little strip of the Pacific coast and would have never discovered San Francisco, or New York, or Chicago, Omaha, or Minneapolis, where the Japanese are scattered all over the place. So this really gave us a chance to really become Americans instead of residents of Little Tokyo in Los Angeles.

QUESTION: Then you think that, given the exigencies of a national war going on, there was no way to avoid the violence of Hiroshima and Nagasaki, that was dictated by military necessity?

HAYAKAWA: My father said that if Hiroshima and Nagasaki had not happened, then the die-to-the-death type of samurai mentality would have taken over and we would have fought until every last woman and child in Japan would have been killed, because that is what the samurai code requires. There are enough romanticists in the military of Japan in that it might very well have happened.

QUESTION: Then you think that despite the destruction that ultimately resulted, it was probably a good thing for the cause--the end of the war and ultimately peace.

HAYAKAWA: My father said, "I think, in a way, that those atomic bombs saved Japan. Without that, everyone in Japan would have fought until everyone was slaughtered. That was the saying in Japan--until every female fought to the death in the streets. With the atomic bomb, everything was shattered, although after the war Japanese were very very bad off, they gradually regained prosperity." I am just repeating what my father said. I have never quite known what to think. . .the trouble right now is all minorities, including yourselves, are undergoing fashions established by the Panthers and black militants,--a fashion of paranoia; "We are all being picked upon, we are all discriminated against, we are all not given an equal chance --they bombed yellow people with the atomic bomb. They never did that to anyone else. . .they are picking on us." I say it is an emotional fad, because after the Black Panthers took it up, then everyone else started taking it up. The Mexican American Political Alliance takes it up, the Asian American Political Alliance takes it up --they all use the same kind of language --and the Women's Lib uses the same kind of language and the American Indians are taking it up now. It's a fad.

QUESTION: Do you think the same thing can be true of Sansei millitants or Japanese-American militants?

HAYAKAWA: Sansei-American and Chinese-American militants, as far as I'm concerned, are taking up somebody else's ball game. They are the children of prosperous men,-- advertising executives--they go to USC and UCLA, San Francisco State --they've got nothing to complain about. They have the same kind of sentimental identification with the lower classes as Russian children of archdukes who became communist and helped the revolution along--the privileged classes. The Sansei who become militants are usually the privileged classes.

(To one of the interviewers)--You go to Yale, for example. You are of the privileged class.

QUESTION: Do you see any problems, such as drug abuse among the Sansei, that would require Sansei movements?

HAYAKAWA: If there are problems of drug abuse among Sansei, that means that they are so goddamned completely white that they have become lost to Asia. They are just like whites. . .they have already lost their cultural identity.

QUESTION: You mentioned before that you felt the Sanseis were taking over someone else's cause. How does that apply to minorities supporting general progressive movements?

HAYAKAWA: The one advantage that the Oriental has is that we are not a big problem at all. There is not that many of us. The Negro-White problem is the biggest problem this country has. One advantage that you and I have is that we are not white and we are not negro; therefore, we can take an objective view of both. We really can--and when people want to line you up with the whites who oppress the negro, you can pull back and say, "Look what you are doing", and when the blacks want to line you up with the Third World and create r verse racism against white people, you can pull out of that too--you can say "Look, that's racism too." My criticism of Sansei and the radical Orientals --third generation, University students, usually the children of prosperous families --is that. . they play Black Panther--in other words, they play Yellow Panther. . .they have not developed their own critical style which says "We are not white, we are not black. When blacks make a mistake, we can pick it out. When whites do something very just, we can pick it out. When they do something very unjust we can pick it out." Of course, that damn newspaper <u>Gidra,</u> --silliest damn thing I ever saw.

(Talk about the tam-o-shanter.)

QUESTION: How did you come by that?

HAYAKAWA: My Scotch background, my childhood.

QUESTION: Your tam-o-shanter is kind of a symbol. Is that in keeping with the Japanese-American attitude of being retiring, keeping back. . .?

HAYAKAWA: I don't have this non-presumptuousness. First of all, because I was brought up in Canada, and so many of my friends were Jews. Secondly, because I was very much spoiled, indulged as eldest son --and mother being sort of aristocratic, and we living in a lower class neighborhood, she kept separating me from my playmates, saying "We are the representatives of another class of people". I didn't have this non-presumptuousness.

QUESTION: Do you feel that this had anything to do with rather large success in academic circles?

HAYAKAWA: It had to do with the fact that, seeing a terribly big emergency situation at this college, in which the college was already closed down, someone had to step in. Most people say "Well, its not my job", but I had the conviction that I could do something about it.

QUESTION: Looking back at the San Francisco State strike three years ago, would you have handled it any differently?

HAYAKAWA: Yes, I would have been tougher. My Christian friends said "Don't be mean, don't be nasty, don't be disagreeable, --and everytime you yield to Christian impulse you have reason to regret it.

QUESTION: What future direction do you see for the Asian American community in terms of relations with the larger society, and also for all the minority community?

HAYAKAWA: I don't know where its going from here. One terrible thing that has happened in the last few years since the rise of the civil rights movement--your parents ceased to be Japanese pretty much. They got themselves assimilated, they got themselves elected to the West Rotary Club, to the Kiwanis; they just became members of the community in the largest sense. Then the Sansei, or a certain element among the Sansei, started whooping it up all over again about being Japanese at a time where their parents have damned near forgotten about it. This is sort of a revival of a racial consciousness that your parents' generation spent a lot of time trying to overcome. Because if you are the first Japanese to get to the University of Cincinnati Medical School, you don't sit around worrying about the fact that you are Japanese--you worry about the fact if you are going to do well in medical school. So the Nisei generation kept their minds off the fact that they were Japanese, in order to become good nurserymen, good physicians, bankers, good photographers --whatever they became. It is an era of the relative prosperity that the Nisei created that the Sansei can ask themselves the question "What is my identity?" They didn't have a problem of identity in the Nisei generation because they were too ambitious, they had a goal for themselves; they didn't have a problem. They had too much work to do. It's the college-educated, affluent Sansei who have an identity problem. I think its funny as hell.

QUESTION: Do you feel it is a real problem or it's sort of an artificial thing?

HAYAKAWA: I think it's sort of a fictitious problem, but I think it's terribly real.

QUESTION: Do you believe that the Vietnam War has any impact on the image of the Asian American community now?

HAYAKAWA: No, but here is something that bothers me. . .Why should Asian Americans say the same things about the Vietnam War that white people do? Because if you talk to a Korean from Korea or a Filipino from the Philippines, they are damn grateful for the American intervention in Vietnam. South Koreans like the South Vietnamese, are deeply, deeply grateful for the American intervention in South Vietnam and so are all the Filipinos I know. Now, you guys are Asian Americans. You say the same things as the S.D.S. and the white radicals. That makes me so damn sick. Why don't you have your own eyes? You are not white, you are not Jewish intellectuals from New York. But you are aping the same things that Jewish intellectuals are saying.

QUESTION: Recently there have been some Asian American veterans from Vietnam who are organizing demonstrations to protest the war on two grounds: one, that the American Army treats them in a racist manner, and two, that the Army presents a racist stereotype of the enemy on the battlefield. There have been very close situations where they have been shot at by their own troops. Would you consider that an Asian American perspective on the war?

HAYAKAWA: No. That may be one of them but there is another perspective on the war that involves racism. Notice that white people, generally W.A.S.P., especially New York Jews--are ready to fight for freedom of white people all over Europe and the Middle East. They are not ready to fight for the freedom of yellow men. There is a hell of a lot of racism in this. What does it matter if the South Vietnamese become conquered by communists? They are just a bunch of yellow people. Who cares? But if Israel is threatened, Jesus, you hear the warlike noises coming out of New York City.

QUESTION: There have been some new groups of Asian Americans for Peace in Los Angeles and other anti-war groups that come from Asian backgrounds. What sort of position should they or can they take?

HAYAKAWA: One position that can be reasonably taken now is --and it can be consistent with being opposed to the indefinite continuation of the war --to back President Nixon and the orderly withdrawal as quickly as possible. The bug-out-tomorrow-morning kind of people seem to me to be terribly irresponsible. They are leaving the South Vietnamese a terrible, terrible future to confront. Also, they are not taking into consideration the fact that if the United States pulls out of South Vietnam in a precipitated way without a stable South Vietnamese government in operation, then Japan will have to rearm. You don't want the Japanese to rearm again. But they will have to have it because note twice or three times in Japan's history when a hostile power occupied the southern end of the Korean Peninsula, Japan went to war.

If North Vietnam was triumphant in Southeast Asia, North Korea will feel their oats. They will wipe out the South Koreans and Americans will have to pull out. Japan will have to arm to the teeth all over again. And Japan is technologically capable now of developing its own atomic weapons without any help from anybody.

QUESTION: Your analysis of Korean and Vietnam seems to indicate that they are capable of invading other countries. In light of the New York Times articles, do you still feel that. . .

HAYAKAWA: I am not going to take out a position on this. I don't have one. I am just raising some questions.

QUESTION: Where would an Asian American who was interested in becoming more Asian --where would he go to learn that? You said that he might go back to his grandparents. What if they speak Japanese and he doesn't speak Japanese?

HAYAKAWA: There are a lot of things he can do. He might cultivate non-college Filipino or South Vietnamese friends. He might start right out by going to the consulate general of South Vietnam, getting himself invited to some parties--the other point-of-view. He might go to the Korean Consulate.

QUESTION: How does it relate to Japanese radicals in Japan who are far more militant than radical Japanese-Americans?

HAYAKAWA: The Japanese radicals have their own big problem too. They too are upper class. That radicalism is...do you know Louis Sawyer's book, THE CONFLICT OF GENERATION. It's a really profound book on the radicalism of the children of the upper classes right through the Russian revolution to the German revolution of 1848, and so on. It's a fascinating book. There's an awful lot of that in Japan.

QUESTION: You mean like it's an anti-father image?

HAYAKAWA: Yeah.

QUESTION: What kinds of associations do you have with the Bay Area Japanese community?

HAYAKAWA: Very little. They're parents of guys like you.

THE NATURE OF G.I. Racism

NORMAN NAKAMURA

One finds it hard not to sarcastically laugh when he hears that the United States is fighting in Vietnam to save and maintain the Vietnamese people, while many American G.I.'s do not treat the Vietnamese as people but as animals. How can we be fighting and supporting a war when the very people who we are supposed to be helping by this costly action begin hating us because of the racist antagonisms of the U.S. soldier?

For some G.I.'s in Vietnam, there are no Vietnamese people. To them the land is not populated by people but by "Gooks", considered inferior, unhuman animals by the racist-educated G.I. Relieved in his mind of human responsibility by this grotesque stereotype, numerous barbarities have been committed against these Asian peoples, since "they're only 'Gooks.'"

Out on the roads of Vietnam the G.I. more overtly exhibits antagonisms against the Vietnamese civilians, for there he is more or less free from the direct restraints of military control that exist in the main base camps. He also has the security in the knowledge that other G.I.'s consider these people as "Gooks" and will not deal with him too severely if he should be caught antagonizing "Gooks." Furthermore, the G.I. does not seem to be subject to Vietnamese law, so any civilian's complaint would have to be executed through the U.S. military if he could identify his antagonizer and if he felt that justice would be done.

Throwing empty cans at children along the roadside is so common that G.I.'s are told not to do this over the radio. Although they have been told otherwise, I have seen this more and more. Driving alongside Vietnamese on motorcycles to either hit them on the head or steal their hats is a daily practice of a courier on Q.L.13. Having acquired tear gas cannisters for his grenade launcher, one officer shot tear gas into a group of Vietnamese as he drove through their village during a non-military action. He also shot tear gas into a Lambretta mini-bus filled with civilians. Obscene gestures and phrases are also hurled at the Vietnamese along the roads, especially at any Vietnamese girl, for many G.I.'s believe that all Vietnamese women are whores. Meaningless petty thefts by G.I.'s also occur on the roads. One G.I. in his dump truck asked a roadside seller to hand her tray of miscellaneous goods up to him for close examination. When she did this, he took off with everything without paying her a cent. In a group effort, some G.I.'s surrounded a roadside seller and kept her busy by examining various products. While she was looking at one G.I., the others would slip some of her goods into their pockets. In both of these cases, the thefts were not done out of need but were done to play a clever trick on a "Gook".

Unfortunately, some G.I.'s get malevolent on the roads. One G.I. threw a piece of lumber into the windshield of a moving Vietnamese bus from his vehicle for no apparent reason. Some G.I. drivers recklessly drive at high speeds, running motor scooters and ox carts off the road. Furthermore, they drive this way through villages, which have no signals so that the civilians in these villages must be cautious. The regard for these people is so low that in Lai Khe Base Camp you may hear a driver say to a new driver that it is better to run over a "Gook" than a chicken, because when you kill a chicken, you have to also pay for the number of eggs that this chicken would have layed in a year. I saw a Vietnamese mother in the road through her village squatting in front of a small object covered with a gunny sack in a pool of blood; she had her face covered with her hands and was rocking back and forth crying. Upon seeing the driver of the murder vehicle with an expression of guilt and horror on his face, I am sure that he would have rather killed a chicken.

For no apparent reason, a child was shot to death and another wounded by a drunken American G.I. in Lai Khe Base Camp on day tower guard duty. In no way could one interpret the actions of these Vietnamese children as hostile. This soldier, who had spent at least 11 months in Vietnam as an engineer in a construction

Reprinted from GIDRA, June/July, 1970.

engineer unit, was not a combat-fatigued soldier. Had there not been a stereotype that pictured Vietnamese to be inferior, unhuman animals, this and other atrocities in Vietnam would not have happened. I do not believe that this drunken soldier actually felt that he was shooting at human beings; he was "only shooting at 'Gooks.'"

The antagonisms against the Vietnamese by some G.I.'s have been severe at times since they are acting in accordance with a severely negative stereotype. Since most G.I.'s have not been prepared to associate with the other peoples of the world in terms of fraternity, the G.I. has reacted to his situation in Vietnam as he would have in the United States. He has taken this physically, culturally and linguistically distinct group and created an ethnocentrically negative stereotype of these people with racist overtones, which colors his behavior and attitude towards these people.

"You can't trust a 'Gook'" is a common expression among G.I.'s. During the G.I.'s Vietnam orientation training, he is told by the Army not to trust any Vietnamese, because any one of them may be a Viet Cong terrorist or sympathizer. When out of the confines of military installations, the G.I. is told to carry a weapon and to avoid contact with Vietnamese, for there may be terrorists lurking about. In addition, the G.I. is told that many V.C. are civilians during the day doing their regular work and guerillas at night planting mines and booby-traps or firing rockets into military targets. Since one cannot physically tell who is a civilian or V.C. due to guerilla warfare and since one's life is at stake, the G.I. is suspicious of all Vietnamese.

Secondly, the G.I. is told during his mandatory Vietnam orientation that the A.R.V.N.'s, soldiers of the South Vietnamese Army, are not dependable soldiers and may run away upon hostile contact, whereas the North Vietnamese soldiers troops will not run and are good soldiers. The G.I. is told to respect the enemy as soldiers but not to trust the South Vietnamese soldiers. Since the G.I. feels that he has been sent to Vietnam to possibly die for civilians who may be his enemy and for soldiers who are too cowardly to fight for their own country, the G.I.'s feeling towards the Vietnamese is initially hostile and negative, and it is through these eyes that the G.I. examines and judges the South Vietnamese people.

"Why do they cheat and steal from us; they should be grateful that we're here to help them" is another familiar exclamation by G.I.'s in reference to both Vietnamese civilians and soldiers. Having seen too many war hero movies, the G.I. seems to expect the Vietnamese to show appreciation for the U.S. presence in Vietnam by being the humble and honest Oriental. The Vietnamese seem to treat the G.I. as another entity and not as a super-hero, which embitters the G.I. ego. As in Hong Kong, the saying, "Let the buyers beware," is very appropriate in describing the Vietnamese system of buying and selling. In Vietnam it is the buyer's fault for being stupid, if he buys an item that will not work after a few days or buys an item without bargaining down the price. Unfortunately, the G.I. does not look upon this as custom but as cheating, which reinforces his feelings of mistrust towards the Vietnamese. When there is an act of theft by a Vietnamese from a G.I., the G.I. does not treat it as an act by an individual but as an act by the whole Vietnamese population. Rather than curse at one's own stupidity in buying or in allowing someone to steal from you, the G.I. curses the Vietnamese and their ingratitude.

"How can these people live like this; why do they want to live like animals'." is a common ethnocentric statement by G.I.'s when viewing the different customs and relative poverty of the Vietnamese. Since many G.I.'s have had exposure only to American culture and mores, they use U.S. mores as a measure of what is right or wrong in the world and judge the Vietnamese accordingly. To such G.I.'s the Vietnamese live in poverty and in low standards of personal hygiene to a degree that is shocking to them. Ethnocentrically and naively feeling that human beings cannot live in such low standards, the G.I. feels that these people must want to live like animals when he sees the whole nation living in what he thinks to be animal-like standards. He makes this judgment assuming that the Vietnamese have the same education, goals, and opportunities that he has. Rather than having compassion for the Vietnamese, many G.I.'s are disgusted by them.

Since there is tendency in the United States to equate poverty with intellectual or moral weakness on the part of the impoverished people, many G.I.'s feel superior to the Vietnamese and feel that they are inherently stupid and immoral. The fact that many Americans measure cultural level by the quality and quantity of material goods and technology also reinforces this viewpoint. Rather than see a non-technological culture, many G.I.'s see the Vietnamese as people who are too dumb to ever be technological.

The sum total of this ethnocentric and racist negative stereotype is summarized in the term "Gook". The ugly sound of this word indicates the feeling of many G.I.'s that the people and culture of Vietnam are ugly. The word is impersonal and does not connote human beings, which goes along with the fact that many G.I.'s do not consider the Vietnamese to be human beings but animals. Furthermore, it makes the people seem so impersonal that one could commit barbarous acts upon them from malice or military expediency without feeling guilty of commiting crimes against human beings. The word "Gook", which is used by most G.I.'s instead of the word "Vietnamese", is definitely a racist term in Vietnam.

The G.I. in Vietnam is a frustrated individual and takes out his frustrations upon the Vietnamese either in derogatory words or in malicious acts. Many G.I.'s have used this physically, culturally, and linguistically distinct group to take out their frustrations upon since the Vietnamese have been negatively stereotyped in an impersonal manner by the G.I.

The G.I. feels culturally and physically superior to the Vietnamese, yet they are being killed or wounded by some of these people. Since the enemy does not fight out in the open but plants mines and booby-traps, fires rockets or mortar rounds into the base camps, and usually does most of his fighting under the cover of darkness, the G.I. is frustrated at not being able to see or distinguish his enemy. Since the enemy is all around him and not isolated to a certain area of the country with marked lines of battle, the G.I. is always in danger of his life, which is quite a frustrating thing to have on one's mind. Since he cannot easily strike out at the enemy to rid himself of this frustration, the G.I. strikes out at the Vietnamese civilians, which are the closest thing to the enemy that is readily available.

Just being under military discipline with all its restrictions and silliness is frustrating enough, but to be in the military far away from home in Vietnam creates further frustrations. Marriages and love relationships can suffer while one is far away from home. In the company that I was in, which numbered around 150, one G.I.'s wife stopped writing. Two G.I.'s had their wives move to an unknown location, and two other G.I.'s were sued for divorce by their wives. Some of the guys in my company received "Dear John" letters or letters of illness in the family. Some were even notified of deaths in their family. Those who were so adversely affected were frustrated over their inability to do anything about it since they were in Vietnam and not at home, and those who were not so affected worried about these things possibly happening to them.

The G.I. in Vietnam is also sexually frustrated due to a lack of meaningful female companionship and sex. For those who needed prostitutes, many G.I.'s found the Vietnamese to be frustrating prostitutes, for many of them would only spread their legs and lie limp. Since there is a great barrier in language, the G.I. has a frustrating time trying to develop a meaningful relationship with any Vietnamese girl even if he has an opportunity to meet some Vietnamese girls. Furthermore, there is a cultural and a racial barrier to overcome.

Many G.I.'s try to escape from their frustration by drinking heavily or taking drugs, marijuana or even narcotics. However, this is usually done at night after work, which leaves the daytime free for antagonisms against the Vietnamese.

Frustration and racism have made racist bullies out of many G.I.'s in Vietnam, but will it end in Vietnam or will it color a negative stereotype toward all Asians? For some G.I.'s this is the first contact with Asian peoples, so it is highly unlikely that this experience would not affect them. Some G.I.'s would only go to Australia on their rest and recuperation leave from Vietnam, excluding various Asian nations and Hawaii, because they wanted to get away from people with "slanted eyes".

Since guerilla warfare depends upon the support of the people and since many G.I.'s are antagonizing the people, it seems that the presence of such G.I.'s in Vietnam is perpetuating the war. It seems ridiculous and hypocritical to be antagonizing the very people who you are supposed to be aiding if such is the case. There can only be a military victory in Vietnam, for rather than bringing civilization to Vietnam, the American G.I. has brought syphilization and racism to the Vietnamese people.

G.I.'s and Asian Women

EVELYN YOSHIMURA

The Vietnam War has touched the lives of the American people in many ways, and the Asian American community has not been immune. Our brothers have been drafted into the military to face fighting and possibly dying in a war that even the legislators of our country cannot wholly support; and for Asian American brothers, there is the added contradiction of killing other Asian people in the name of a country that itself is divided in its support of the war. The drafting of our brothers into the military, and the taxes that we must pay for this war are two very concrete ways in which we are touched. There are other ways in which we feel that ugliness of that war.

GIs are sent to Vietnam by the U.S. government and its Military armed with martial training, sophisticated weapons and a view of Asian people as sub-human beings. A vast number of Asian American GIs have unpleasant memories of being called gook, charlie, Jap, Chink, Ho Chi Minh by superior officers and fellow GIs in their basic training. And the phrase Asians have no value for human life has been used too often to detract from the horror of rumored and proven atrocities against Vietnamese civilians.

Because of the lack of self-motivation and justification on the part of the GIs to fight against the Vietnamese people, it is necessary for the U.S. Military to psychologically break down GIs so they can instill the values and mentality that is necessary to become effective killers. One method employed by the Military towards this end is the use of women, or more correctly, the sexual symbol of women, which proves very effective because of the long and complete separation from women that GIs experience, especially in basic training. This use of women to oppress GIs many times manifests itself in the way GIs relate to women they come in contact with after boot-camp. Because of World War II, the Korean War and now, the Vietnam War, many times these women are Asian women. An Asian American brother recalls his experiences in boot-camp:

"In Marine Corps boot-camp, the military goes through a psychological and physical breakdown trip of the men so they (the Military) can instill their values. And a heavy part of that trip is the mentioning of women in certain sexual contexts.

Some guys really believed this shit too. Like when you get overseas afterwards, you kind of trip on the jokes you heard and look for things you remember from the jokes."

We had these classes we had to go to taught by the drill instructors, and every instructor would tell a joke before he began class. It would always be a dirty joke usually having to do with prostitutes they had seen in Japan or in other parts of Asia while they were stationed overseas. The attitude of the Asian woman being a doll, a useful toy or something to play with usually came out in these jokes, and how they were not quite as human as white women. For instance, a real common example was how the instructor would talk about how Asian women's vaginas weren't like a white woman's, but rather they were slanted, like their eyes.

By using Asian women in this manner, the Military gains in two ways. First, they use Asian women as a symbolic sexual object. The Military knows that the GIs aren't able to seek sexual satisfaction during basic training and a large part of their combat time, so they use this knowledge to keep the men down. They continually remind them of their desire by talking about women all the time, yet they keep the gratification of this desire from their reach. Again, the psychological breakdown.

According to Wilhelm Reich, noted psychologist (from his book MASS PSYCHOLOGY OF FASCISM, p. 25-26), "The goal of sexual suppression is that of producing an individual who is adjusted to the authoritarian order and who will submit to it in spite of all misery and degradation."

Reprinted from GIDRA, January, 1971.

He goes on to say, "...the suppression of the gratification of primitive material needs (food, shelter, clothing) has a result different from that of the suppression of the gratification of the sexual needs. The former incites rebellion. The latter, however--by repressing the sexual needs and by becoming anchored as a moralistic defense--paralyzes the rebellion against either kind of suppression."

The second way the Military gains from using the symbol of Asian women is by the racism against Asians that it encourages and perpetrates. The image of a people with slanted eyes and slanted vaginas enhances the feeling that Asians are other than human, and therefore much easier to kill. More than a few Vietnam veterans tell of incidents of GIs who spend time in combat; then during their Rest and Recuperation periods, suddenly and with no apparent provocation, will kill a Vietnamese civilian out of a paranoid concept of gooks. And according to many vets, civilian massacres like My Lai are not exceptional happenings. Reich has something to say about this too.

"The suppression of natural sexual gratification leads to various kinds of substitute gratifications. Natural aggression becomes brutal sadism which then is an essential mass-psychological factor in imperialistic wars."

And there is another dimension in the use of Asian women as sexual objects. The view that Asian women are less than human helps perpetrate another myth--that of the White woman "back home" being placed on a pedestal. (This is not to say that the White woman's position is to be envied. Her position on that pedestal is also an oppressive situation). A good illustration of this attitude is the attitude towards the Red Cross nurses on some bases in Vietnam and throughout Asia. Another Vietnam veteran recalls those Red Cross workers:

"I remember these Red Cross broads-- they were called Do-nut Dollies because they'd sell donuts and coffee. Anyway, on the side they would hustle the guys on the base. The average price for a Vietnamese prostitute was about $10.00, but these Red Cross broads, because they were White, could get $65. Most of them didn't even look that good, and some of them were kind of old, but the men were really hungry for round-eyed chicks. Oh yeah, and $65 was how much you got a month for combat pay. So you risk getting killed for a month to get that $65, and a lot of guys blew it in one shot just to lay a round-eyed chick."

Another example of the "White woman on a pedestal" can be seen in the words of another Asian American brother's experiences with the Military when he tried to marry a Vietnamese girl:

"I wanted to get married when I was in Vietnam, but they (the Military) wouldn't let me. I didn't push it because of the static and all the feedback I got from the beginning. You see, you have to go through the chain-of-command to get married, even in Vietnam because I was in the rear at the time. That's when I met this Vietnamese girl. First, I went to my Section Chief, and he said, 'Man, you don't want to marry one of these "gooks" over here. They're not civilized, and if you take her back home with you, people won't be able to handle her cause she's not civilized.' And so I said, 'Well, that's my problem.' So then I went to the Gunnery Sergeant, and he lectured me for like all day, and he told me to come back. And I came back, and he lectured me and told me to come back again. Then I got to the First Sergeant and he did the same thing. Finally, I got to the CO (Commanding Officer) and he ran down all the bureaucratic stuff that I'd have to go through before I could even get the consent to get married. You see, you have to go through this waiting period, and they make you wait until after your rotation time, like if you have five months before you're moved out, then they'll give you a waiting period of six months so they can get you out of there."

"Man, they'd say stuff like, 'She's not an American so she wouldn't be able to handle it in the States; and you wouldn't be able to trust her once you got back to the States.' They said, 'Okay. You think you want to marry her now, but that's because there are no round-eyed chicks around. They said that to me, you know, I'm an Asian too, but they said that to me. They'd always talk about 'round-eyed' chicks--you know, Caucasian chicks. They'd say, 'And once you get back, you'll see all those blondes and stuff, and you'll look at your wife and she'll be this old farmer chick--this gook--and you'll want to get rid of her. You'll be embarrassed when you get back because she's Vietnamese.'"

To most non-Asians in the U.S., there is little if any difference between Asian Americans and Asians in America. We Asian Americans are either lumped with Asians, and therefore considered "foreigners", or we are invisible. The brother who wanted to marry the Vietnamese girl experienced both. On one hand, the Military, completely insensitive of the fact that he too was an Asian, talked about the 'round-eyed' chicks waiting back home. This same brother, upon entering basic training was called a gook and was made to stand in front of his platoon as an example of "what the enemy (the Vietnamese) looked like." Asian Americans are also victims of the stereotypes put on Asian people. Therefore, Asian American women are susceptible to the stereotypes that GIs have of women in Asia. An example of this is shown in the following story of still another Asian American brother in basic training.

"Before everybody crashes, the drill instructor comes through and checks to see that all foot-lockers are locked, and that you have your wallet. So you stand up on top of your locker at attention in your drawers and teeshirt and he comes around and he yells at everybody and he'll punch a few people; and he always picks somebody and he'll take their wallet and he'll look at their pictures. I had some pictures of these Asian girls I went to high school with. He made some derogatory comments like, 'This looks like this whore I knew back over there (Japan).' Then he took three or four pictures out of my wallet and he kept them. I couldn't do nothing about it. I don't know what he did with them. I think he believed they were the best looking out of all of them. And I didn't see them after that. That's when he saw the picture of my sister.

After lights were out and everyone was supposed to be sleeping, he would come into our barracks, and he would bring a chair next to my bunk and act like he was my friend. Then he started rapping about when he was overseas in Japan, and how he had this prostitute for quite a while. He said her last name was the same as mine. Then he said, 'What was your sister's name?' He knew I had an older sister, and he had seen the picture of her, and I guess he flashed back on his experiences. Then he started harassing me by saying my sister looked like his prostitute. He said, 'What'd you say her name was?' And I'd tell him and he asked, did she have a Japanese name, so I'd tell him her Japanese name, and he'd say, 'Yeah, that's her. That's the prostitute I had.'"

As long as there are U.S. troops in Asia, as long as the U.S. government and the Military wage wars of aggression against Asian people, racism against Asians will serve the interest of this country. And that racism will be perpetrated. We, as Asian Americans cannot divorce ourselves from this reality, and we as Asian American women cannot separate ourselves from our Asian counterparts. Racism against them is too often racism against us. The stereotypes fit us much too easily. The mentality that keeps Suzy Wong, Madam Butterfly and gookism alive; the mentality that turns human beings into racist, murdering soldiers, also keeps Asian Americans from being able to live and feel like human beings. We must destroy the stereotypes of Asian women, and Asian people, as a whole, so we can define ourselves, and be free to realize our full and total potential. Just as the U.S. government, through forced control, denies the Vietnamese people of their right to self-determination and self-definition, the racism needed to maintain that control cripples us as Asians in America.

Suzy Wong, Madame Butterfly and gookism must die, along with the Monster who created them--whose tentacles hungrily suck riches out of Asia, and pride and dignity out of Asian Americans.

drawing by Donna Wong

THAT ORIENTAL FEELING

A LOOK AT THE CARICATURES OF THE ASIANS AS SKETCHED BY AMERICAN MOVIES

IRVIN PAIK

It often comes as a shock to Asians to realize that they are not human beings. At least, not human beings as represented by movies and tv. The greatest educational and propaganda devices ever devised by mankind, still depict Asians as stereotypes created in the early 1900's. With rare exceptions, Asians are always portrayed as waiters, laundrymen, cooks, villians, warmongers, Geishas, house servants, gardeners, karate experts, and prostitutes. Movies and tv have failed to reflect the achievements of Asian Americans in education, medicine, finance, art, music, or any other equivalent field.

When a script calls for an Asian, it is to provide a backdrop or "an Oriental feeling" to the main story. TV's HAWAII FIVE-O is a consistent offender. In the state with the largest percentage of Asian-Americans, two blue-eyed yankee devils had to be imported from the mainland to solve the Asians' crimes. Jack Lord (white) is head of the police department, James MacArthur (white) is his assistant. Over both of them is the governor (white). After the three whites come the Asians, one is a fat Chinaman stereotype, and the other a fat Hawaiian stereotype. On a typical program their lines are simply statements of fact: "Steve, take a look. Finished." "The governor wants you." "So far no trace anywhere." "There it is, Steve." "This the one?" The producers and writers allow them no character development or participation in the plot other than to draw guns and kick down doors. Other Asians are shown as technicians who feed facts to the whites. So much for the good guys.

The bad guys get a bigger part of the pie indicating that the writers of the show find it easier to depict Asians as villians than as heroes. One of the running villians is a bald-headed mustached Chinese Communist master spy, who acts like a cross between Genghis Khan and Jack the Ripper. Rarely has tv produced a more cruel and vicious stereotype. His motivation on the show is to cause physical and mental suffering in as many persons as possible using the latest technical and psychological devices. No reason is ever given for his behavior. The audience can only assume that no explanation is necessary as it is common knowledge that "All communist-Asians are born that way." He is a direct steal from the Asian villian featured in the Fu Manchu films.

Fu Manchu was a kindly man with a scientific aptitude created by Sax Rohmer and featured in THE MYSTERIOUS DR. FU MANCHU (1929) starring Warner Oland (a Swede) as Fu Manchu. The film introduces Fu Manchu as an ordinary man with no diabolical intentions. Then, during a revolutionary riot in China, a British officer, Petrie, kills his wife and child. Fu Manchu follows Petrie to London and begins taking revenge on all his family using drugs, black magic, scientific invention, and Oriental slyness. An excerpt from an advertisement read "...terror in each split second of his slanted eyes."[1] A 1965 reviewer said, "Lovers of unabashed melodrama will respond to the machinations of the slant-eyed villain with delight."[2] A secondary theme of Asiatic world dominance played upon the "yellow peril" theme popularized by pulp magazines, cheap novels, and the Hearst press. This treatment of Asians was widely accepted and very popular as judged by the sequels, DAUGHTER OF THE DRAGON (1931), THE MASK OF FU MANCHU (1932), DRUMS OF FU MANCHU (serial, 1940), re-released (1943), THE FACE OF FU MANCHU (1965), and BRIDES OF FU MANCHU (1967). Fu Manchu was a radio show in the thirties and the fourteen Sax Rohmer novels which first appeared in 1911 were serialized in COLLIER'S MAGAZINE in 1957. A popular joke in the thirties was "Many man swallow

---

Copyright 1971 Irvin Paik. The author, of Korean-American background, obtained his B.A. and M.A. degrees in theater arts from U.C.L.A. and is currently a film-maker and member of East-West Players, Inc..

but Fu Manchu."[3]

This hideous characterization justified Asian immigration exclusion, encouraged Japanese relocation and paved the way for W.W. II anti-Japanese propaganda films. Today, China is stereotyped as a world conquerer. With a law on the books that appears to legalize the imprisonment of 110,000 Japanese in America, how safe can the Chinese in America feel with the perpetuation of the Asian villain stereotype? A writer in HOLIDAY MAGAZINE in 1965 praises the Asian villain as follows: "...he (Fu Manchu) fulfills a need for a 'safe' villain who won't hurt anybody's feelings...The Chinese must have seemed a happy answer, with the fictional Fu Manchu all ready and waiting, and Red China looming ominously in real life as the latest thing in world menaces. Who, other than the Chinese--and nothing could make them madder than they already are--would protest the image of a Chinese villain out to dominate the white world? Albania?"[4] Will all Asians in America please check your mirror as you have just disappeared. A reporter from the WALL STREET JOURNAL notes as follows: "On television and in the movies, more and more of the guys in the black hats have a definite Oriental look...It's probably all part of the changing tone in foreign relations and the cold war...Mr. (Khigh) Dhiegh in fact, doesn't like the trend toward the Oriental heavy. 'We're getting back to the era of the Yellow Menace,' he says, 'and I don't think this contributes anything to prospects for world peace." Although Khigh Dhiegh (who is not Asian) claims he doesn't want to play the villain he has done so in the style of Fu Manchu in THE MANCHURIAN CANDIDATE (1962), THE HAWAIIANS (1970), HAWAII FIVE-O (tv) and MISSION IMPOSSIBLE (tv).

On another segment of HAWAII FIVE-O in the 1969-70 season, Jimmy Hong plays a slimier version of the Oriental villain, this time with a blond "secretary." The director and actors were trying to establish a sexual relationship between the Asian and the blond without violating the American taboo that Asian men must not touch white women. When the phone rang, the secretary was discovered sitting not on his lap, but on his desk. The camera was placed so that her thighs and breasts seemed to be thrust into his easy reach, yet allowing enough distance to observe the taboo. Though each line was delivered with passionate looks and sensual tones, they never touched each other. However, the phone, the desk, the chairs, pencils and pens received enough caresses to practically bring them to life. How silly and immature, but typical of tv. "Naughty, naughty, the slimy Asian must not put his hands on the pretty white lady."

This unwritten taboo stems from the Don't and be Carefuls of the Motion Picture Producers and Distributors of America (The Hays Office) censorship guide in 1927 as follows: "Miscegenation (sex relations between the white and black races) is forbidden." The casting of Asian roles and the films with Asian themes show that this rule applied to Asians as well as blacks. A proud announcement of the application of this rule appeared in a national magazine as favorable publicity for the film, THE GOOD EARTH (1937). Irving Thalberg, producer, was determined to maintain the authenticity of Pearl Buck's novel at almost any cost. He sent a camera crew to China for a year to photograph backgrounds. The Nanking Censorship Board approved all the footage to insure that a good image of China would be shown. Authentic props were bought and shipped to Hollywood. Whole farms were sometimes obtained. A vast talent search was initiated for an all Chinese cast which lasted many months. Incredibly, no Asian male could be found that suited M.G.M.'s idea of a Chinese peasant, so Paul Muni was given the role. The talent search did, however, find a female Asian that fit M.G.M.'s idea of a Chinese peasant. Then the Hays office stepped in. The Asian girl was dropped and replaced by Luise Rainer as the following quote explains: "The introduction of a few white principles into a predominatingly yellow cast brought up new problems. Mr. Will Hays is very sensitive on the subject of miscegenation in films. Not only is he thumbs down on a white character being married to a yellow one, but he won't permit a white actor playing a yellow role, or vice versa. Muni and Luise Rainer were O.K. They were both Caucasians, albeit of different breeds."[3]

The Hays Office did not create new morals, but reflected prevailing and long standing attitudes of white Americans. BROKEN BLOSSOMS (1919), D.W. Griffith's well-known classic, featured a kindly Chinese played by Richard Barthelmess, who adopts and cares for a mistreated white girl (Lillian Gish) and kills himself because he cannot tolerate society's condemnation of his love for her. Killing one of the main characters is a favorite trick of writers who wish to bring up controversial issues but never reach any conclusions and never offend whites in the audience. Another solution is as follows. In EAST IS WEST (1930), a Chinese girl played by Lupe Valdez falls in love with a white man. Society condemns the romance until it is discovered that she is really a missionary's daughter and not Chinese after all. The situation is reversed in a film of that same year, SON OF THE GODS, in which a wealthy Chinese (Richard Barthelmess) falls in love with a white girl and they are condemned until it is discovered that he is the son of a missionary and not really Chinese.

Though the Hays Office lost its influence in the late forties, the "miscegenation is forbidden" taboo remained for many years and is still in effect for Asian men. William Holden makes love to a Eurasian girl in LOVE IS A MANY SPLENDORED THING (1955), but it's "all right" because she is really Jeniffer Jones in a Chinese high collar dress. In TEAHOUSE OF THE AUGUST MOON (1956), Machiko Kyo is told by Glenn Ford that he would be happy to marry her but American society would make her unhappy, so he deserts her. SAYONARA (1957) finally broke the taboo by allowing Red Buttons to make love to Miyoshi Umeki and Marlon Brando to make love to Miiko Taka. While there is no love making in BRIDGE ON THE RIVER KWAI (1957), William Holden is the object of the affection of four Thailand actresses. William Holden makes passionate screen love to Nancy Kwan in THE WORLD OF SUZIE WONG (1961). Nancy Kwan plays the prostitute with a heart of gold. The other Asian girls treat prostitution in Hong Kong as if it were ping pong and all the Asian males are pimps, servants and rickshaw pullers. DIAMOND HEAD (1962) concerned itself with bigotry in Hawaii. Charleton Heston opposed the marriage of his sister, Yvette Mimieux, to a full-blooded Hawaiian played by James Darren (he wore dark makeup) while he maintained France Nuyen as his mistress. In the end, George Chakiris, playing a half-breed, runs off with Miss Mimieux. What might have been a significant film ended up as a travelogue for the island paradise that got lousy reviews. Replacing France Nuyen is Miko Miyama, who plays the willing mistress of Charleton Heston in THE HAWAIIANS (1970), simply because he gets into the bath tub with her.

While the Hays office recognized the film as an art form and as an influence on morals and sexual behavior among whites, it ignored the devastating effects upon all minority races. While white men have broken the miscegenation taboo with Asian women, Asian men are still where they were in 1900. Leading Asian roles are almost always played by white men in yellow face. The most notorious examples are Richard Barthelmess in BROKEN BLOSSOMS (1919), Warner Oland in FU MANCHU (1929) and CHARLIE CHAN (1931-1937) SIDNEY TOLER and Roland Winters CHARLIE CHAN (1937-1949) Paul Muni, THE GOOD EARTH (1937), Alec Guiness in A MAJORITY OF ONE (1961), James Darren in DIAMOND HEAD (1961), Marlon Brando in TEAHOUSE OF THE AUGUST MOON (1956), J. Carroll Naish in CHARLIE CHAN tv (1957) and Ross Martin, CHARLIE CHAN tv (1971).

Producers claim that Asian women lend a special Oriental charm, feeling, and atmosphere to an Oriental production, but Asian men are never talented enough. White men have access to Asian women, but Asian men are forbidden to touch white women. The news that the white man is publishing is obvious, Asian men are inferior to white men. The white male maintains his sexual superiority over all races.

It is ironic that Jack Lord had to be imported to Hawaii to solve crimes when one of the most popular detectives in movie history was originally with the Honolulu police. Charlie Chan, a Chinese master detective was featured in twenty-two movies in the thirties and twenty-four in the forties. In a star role, Charlie Chan was never played by an Asian. The ugly visual fakery of a white man in "Oriental" makeup trained audiences to accept the idea that white men should play Asians, if the role was big and the character sympathetic. So Warner Oland, Sidney Toler, and Roland Winters, deprived Asians of an opportunity to portray themselves, for eighteen years. J. Carroll Naish continued the insult in 39 tv films in 1957.

It was these films which popularized the phrase "Confucius say" and caused Asian Americans to be the butt of many jokes concerning prophet-like phrases. An excerpt from the review of the first Charlie Chan indicates the importance of these sayings. "Another of his lines is that 'man should never hurry except to catch a flea.' 'A good wife, opines Chan, 'is the best household furniture.' He also asserts that 'he who feeds the chicken deserves the egg,' and that 'only a very sly man can shoot off a cannon quietly.' Needless to say these lines told upon the audience yesterday afternoon so well that one could have listened to Charlie Chan for an hour longer."[8]

For eighteen years, Charlie Chan was for most people in America, the only contact with Asians. He was intelligent, wise, cool-headed and always outwitted the white police. How could America accept an Asian outwitting whites in forty-six feature films? Easy. Charlie Chan was not Asian, he was a white actor pretending to be Asian. So, anything good that Charlie Chan did, the audience could attribute to the white actor. Any disparaging aspects of his character (eyes, accent, syntax) would be attributed to the Asian character he was playing. To further reinforce white supremacy, Charlie Chan had several sons, a few of which would appear in each film. The sons were played by Asians, such as Keye Luke,

Victor Sen-Young and Benson Fong. They provided the "Oriental atmosphere" and the comic relief. "Comedy romance between Chan's son (Keye Luke) and a Chinese performer (Shia Jung) is developed for laughs."[9] "His 25 year-old son (Keye Luke) supplies rather lightweight humor by his bumbling when trying to independently track down the villain."[10] The implication in this type of casting is that a white man can depict an Asian as a normal or exceptional person, but Asians can only depict themselves as fools.

Twenty-two years after the last Charlie Chan film was made, and fourteen years after it flopped on tv, NBC brings him back to life in the fall of 1971. What has America learned about Asians since then? The answer is apparently almost nothing. A white actor will again put on the "Oriental eyes" and with it blind himself to all of his experience and training as an actor as he proceeds to become not a person, Charlie Chan, but a white man trying to convince people he's Chinese. Back again is the inscrutable attitude, the faked accent, the folded hands, the slight bow, the pigeon toed stance. Ross Martin is a fine actor of long experience. Yet he has fallen into the trap of trying to act a stereotype rather than being a real person. The most disgusting aspect of this episode is that the producers have ignored any new Asian subject matter in preference to spending close to a million dollars for grave robbing to parade the corpse of a 1930 stereotype. Rest well America, your stereotype of the Asian will not be disturbed by tv's ploy to get you to buy more deodorant, soap, or whatever.

The burden to be borne by Asian Americans for this exhumation is another round of derisive gibes as illustrated in this quote from the LOS ANGELES TIMES, 16 May 1971: "My first day in boot camp, we were supposed to be equal" (Nick) Nagatani said, "I was the only Asian. The drill instructor could not pronounce my name so when he got to it he called me 'Charlie Chan.' I didn't acknowledge because I had no idea he was talking to me" he said. "I thought there was actually a Charlie Chan in the platoon. Finally he said 'Yeah Jap, I'm talking to you.' After that, people in the platoon themselves, started calling me Charlie Chan," said Nagatani. "In my own way, I had to straighten them out."[11] A Doral cigarette ad on the back of the FAMILY CIRCLE MAGAZINE, July 1971 shows an Asian waiter saying of the product "Confucius say: Don't knock it till you've tried it!"[12] That's as offensive as saying "Jesus Christ say: Don't knock it till you've tried it!"

"The Quiet American" award, if there were such a thing, would probably be given to Miyoshi Umeki. She was discovered for SAYONARA (1957) in which she married Red Buttons and chose to die silently in double suicide rather than part with him. In FLOWER DRUM SONG (1961) she plays a shy "wetback" from China who finds happiness with a shy Asian American. Today, as Mrs. Livingston, on THE COURTSHIP OF EDDIE'S FATHER tv, she plays a soft-spoken understanding housekeeper. She represents the American Dream as in one episode she prefers to stay in America as a housekeeper, to marrying a fabulously wealthy Japanese businessman and returning to Japan. The producers, by using her in this way, contribute to the idea that all Orientals can take care of themselves and they have no social or economic problems.

Other roles which dehumanize the Asian are the karate expert, the polynesian beauty, the gardner or farmer, and the Chinese Communist. Harold Sakata played the deadly karate expert Odd Job in GOLDFINGER (1964). His character was similar to that of Fu Manchu. The karate expert is used more for comic effect as in A SHOT IN THE DARK, (1964) Vicks tv commercial, milk billboards, and tv sketches. The polynesian beauty was most recently exemplified by Irene Tsu in the tv Chevron Island commercials of 1967. Travel agencies and airlines continue this exotic stereotype to lure choked city dwellers away to the islands. Sugar commercials continue the idea that the islands are covered with sugar cane and all the Hawaiians are farmers. The Chinese Communist is pictured as a fat politician who is astounded by Fruit of the Loom (with difficulty in saying "L"). Another group of Chinese Communists are astounded by a Volkswagon bus.

These stereotypes are not obviously evil characterizations but are insidious in their innocence. They cause Asians to be thought of as certain types or caricatures, rather than as human beings. Asians become inanimate robots who are only made in definite predictible styles, and as such they can be ignored when convenienet, used when convenient or destroyed when convenient as in Vietnam, Korea, or Hiroshima.

One attempt to break stereotypes resulted in more reinforcement than reversal. FLOWER DRUM SONG (1961) used Asian stereotypes as the punch lines of jokes and the themes for songs creating a happy contented image of the Asian living in Chinatown San Francisco. It perpetuated as many stereotypes as it exposed. The father and aunt are not wise ancestors, but practical stubborn activists. The younger son is interested, not in karate, but baseball. The older son is not the quiet studious hardworking number one son, but a young man in love. The leading Asian girl is a loud, hip, shapely, swinging night club dancer. The friend of the family is a hustler and nightclub entrepreneur. Still, family loyalty is an accepted fact of Oriental life. Miyoshi Umeki again plays the shy, soft-spoken Oriental girl. The older characters wear expensive Chinese costumes all the time. The whole practice of arranged marriages and picture brides smuggled into the country is taken as a cute everyday reality. The effect of the film is to put Asians into a white man's doll house that he can "coo" over but never let into his real household.

There have been some films that portray the Asian outside of the stereotype character and situation but their success has been minimal. GO FOR BROKE (1951) told of the heroic action of the famed all Nisei 442nd Regimental Combat Team. One line hinted at relocation camps. The film was advertised as "another BATTLEGROUND" starring Van Johnson and made little mention of the Japanese subject matter. HELL TO ETERNITY (1960) is based upon the true story of Guy Gabaldon, an orphaned Chicano who is raised by a Japanese family in California and then joins the Marines and captures 2,000 Japanese soldiers on Saipan through his fluency in their language and his compassion for them as human beings. The film points out the irony of Japanese American relocation and in the great American tradition the "Chicano" is played by Jeffrey Hunter. There were Japanese Americans who performed similar feats as United States soldiers, but their stories have yet to be told. James Shigeta plays a Japanese diplomat who marries Carroll Baker (playing a white) in BRIDGE TO THE SUN (1961). The film examines her difficulty in living in wartime Japan. WALK LIKE A DRAGON (1960), featured James Shigeta as a Chinese gunslinger in America. It is one of the few times when an Asian defeats a white man in a fair fight on a one to one basis. Six years later, Mako defeats a white man in a boxing match in THE SAND PEBBLES. Burt Kwouk forces Anthony Quinn and the Catholic church to capitulate in THE SHOES OF THE FISHERMAN (1968). Toshiro Mifune (from Japan) and Lee Marvin fight to a draw in HELL IN THE PACIFIC (1968). In a similar situation, Mako and Darren McGavin fight to the death on the tv 69-70 season show THE CHALLENGE. The Japanese as a nation score a resounding triump over the U.S. in TORA! TORA! TORA! (1970), but a disclaimer at the end makes it an empty victory. Mako and Tina Chen are allowed to develop the secondary theme of THE HAWAIIANS (1970) as a family unit. This is unique in that minorities rarely have real family relationships. They seem to be plopped onto earth full blown. George Takei played Dr. Sulu on Star Trek, now on syndicated tv. He had no special characteristics due to being Asian. He plays a college student in a soon to be released film. Aaron Spelling Productions will release a movie made for tv dealing with a love affair between a young Japanese American boy and a white girl in a midwestern town during W.W. II. It will be aired in the '71-'72 season. It's the first time a tv show will allow an Asian male to marry a white girl. It will be the first mention of the Japanese relocation. Although the script divided the problems of this marriage equally between the two families, the shooting and editing emphasize what a terrible problem the white family has.

I do not mean to imply by this puny listing of reverse stereotypes that tv and movies have reached maturity in dealing with minorities. HAWAII FIVE-O grinds on as does the COURTSHIP OF EDDIE'S FATHER. These stereotypes will continue to live on syndicated tv again and again. As recently as the '70-'71 season a vicious and offensive caricature of Asians appears on the cartoon show for children, WILL THE REAL JERRY LEWIS PLEASE SIT DOWN? This travesty named Hong Kong Flewis has huge buck teeth, a shoddy "Oriental" accent, slanted eyes, and is full of wise sayings. His son, One Ton Son, is a fat dumb Oriental who spouts hip sayings. Like Charlie Chan's son, he provides a comic relief. They make fun of an Asian's physical appearance and cause Asians to be thought of as clowns and idiots.

Where does the child see the Asian as a human being? Nowhere as often as he sees him as a fool. The white child learns that Asians are subjects for laughter, but what does the Asian child learn? Does he learn that he is a fool and so rejects his Asian identity to "join" his white friends? Does he learn that he is a fool and so hides from his white friends? But why must he be pushed into these corners?

Producers of films and tv that blatantly parade stereotypes have defended their creations by saying that white people are depicted in degrading situations also. That's true, but for every bad white image there are ten good ones to shift the balance. Whereas a single caricature of a white person is accepted as an exaggerated truth, a stereotype is often accepted as the whole and complete truth about all Asians. When is the last time you saw an Asian American on tv? When is the last time you were asked, "How long have you been in this country?"

White people claim that there is nothing wrong with the stereotype as they believe stereotypes truthfully depict the Asian. The extreme example of a person in this condition is John Wayne. He was asked by a reporter if he thought the Indians had any right to protest their stereotype as blood-thirsty savages. He replied that they did not and instructed the reporter to look at Indian history to prove him right. John Wayne's history book must be the American western movie, of which he has made many. Not only does he perpetuate the stereotype, but he has that stereotype reinforced as he sits watching his own films. How easily then, does the unsophisticated viewer accept the stereotypes on the screen as he knows that "the camera never lies." One such viewer states her reaction to Fu Manchu: "I hate to admit it, but I grew up with a fear of the Chinese that emanated solely from movies I saw as a child--and I still can't walk through Chinatown in New York or San Francisco without an uneasy feeling even though I know it is stupid and ridiculous. Those old pigtailed villains of my childhood made a lasting impression, slinking around (in that kind of film, the Chinese never walk, they slink) in their opium dens, thinking up unspeakable tortures for kidnapped white girls."[13] THOROUGHLY MODERN MILLIE (1967) spoofs white slavery while CONFESSIONS OF AN OPIUM EATER (1967) treats it seriously. TRUE GRIT (1969) shows where John Wayne thinks the Chinese belong and the GREEN BERETS (1968) gives his position on the Viet Cong.

For a moment, let's turn the tables. If the only white actors who ever got parts were Red Skelton, Jackie Gleason, Shelly Winters and Raquel Welch, would anyone consider casting white people in Shakespeare? That's where Asian performers are today. No one considers them outside of their stereotyped roles. Whites have played Asians in leading roles so often that producers look for the stereotype mannerism when they cast. When they audition a real Asian, he's a human being and not a stereotype. Therefore, since he doesn't fit into their idea of an Asian, they say he lacks personality, charisma, or talent.

Writers follow the same pattern. White writers do not write for Asians. They write for the stereotype. Is it any wonder that producers think white people fit better in roles that were written for white people in yellow face? If real Asians were cast, the writers could see how shallow and hollow their Asian characterizations are. If a white man can play an Asian better than an Asian, then there's something wrong with the part, not the actor.

It may seem as if I'm saying that only Asian writers should write Asian stories, and only Asian actors should play Asian roles. It seems that I'm putting race before talent. Well, I am. But just for now until a balanced image of the Asian is evidenced. Then it will be perfectly acceptable for any actor of any race to play any part. And this period of adjustment is not really unfair. After all, only white people have been playing white parts as well as Asians, Indians, Chicanos and Blacks. And only white writers have been writing about white people as well as Asians, Indians, Chicanos and Blacks. Is it so much to ask to let Asian writers and Asian actors express themselves? Apparently it is. N.B.C. executives claim that Charlie Chan is a positive image of the Asian. They say he corrects and guides his sometimes foolish sons. It may look that way in the script, but on the screen we see Ross Martin (in yellow face) telling real Asians how to behave. They believe that the stereotype is the true picture of the Asian.

While actors can talk to directors and producers about stereotypes, they are jeopardizing their futures as they depend upon these directors and producers for their livelihood. Minority theatrical endeavors like the Inner City Cultural Center and the East West Players, Inc., in Los Angeles offer opportunities for Asians to play human beings, but they often use more of the actors' money than he receives. Actors' objections can easily result in their replacement by some insensitive person anxious to make that $120/day. Producers have always managed to find somebody to fit their stereotyped ideas, or they will put some white person in makeup to do it. A producer is really only sensitive to one person, the man with the money. In the case of tv, the sponsor. Actors can inform they community of the stereotypes, but the community must act and say, we will not buy your product and we will discourage our friends from buying it if you continue to portray us in menial roles; if you continue to make fun of our physical appearance by slapping "Oriental" makeup on white actors.

There are a few people in the industry who are sincerely concerned about Asian stereotypes. These people can do very little by themselves. However, a few thousand letters from you, the community, can give them the leverage to effect change. Your silence maintains the status quo. You must tell the producers and writers that their stereotype is no longer acceptable, that your life is richer and fuller than a few wise sayings and a bowed head. The Japanese American Citizens League made A.B.C.-T.V. swallow the loss of the first F.B.I. tv segment because it dealt with a Japanese spy and sabotage ring in the United States. The producers of that show are now aware of Asian-Americans. However, they seem to have retaliated by hiring almost no minorities at all. If N.B.C. loses close to a million dollars on Charlie Chan, they will also become aware of Asian-Americans and may also retaliate in a manner similar to A.B.C. The picket of the Civic Light Opera made Edwin Lester aware of Asian-Americans and inspired the formation of The Brotherhood of Artists, a multi-racial organization addressing itself to stereotypes in film and tv.

Everyday I meet people who are dumbfounded to learn that Asians are stereotyped. From that initial shock it takes about six months to a year and several more conversations to clear their minds of the stereotype and reveal to them the dehumanization of Asians in film and tv. Asians too must go through this metamorphosis. I am a recent example. Asians must educate themselves, along with everyone else. We must unlearn the old stereotype and rebuild our image as human beings.

---

[1] Dorothy B. Jones, THE PORTRAYAL OF CHINA AND INDIA ON THE AMERICAN SCREEN, 1896-1955, (Cambridge: Massachusetts Institute of Technology, 1955).

[2] "The Face of Fu Manchu" (film review), THE FILM DAILY, October 20, 1965.

[3] Helen Lawrenson, "The Critical Eye--Fu Manchu Strikes Again," HOLIDAY, (February, 1965).

[4] Loc. cit.

[5] Norman Sklarewitz, "The New Bad Guys: Orientals Take Over As TV, Film Villains," WALL STREET JOURNAL (New York), October 12, 1966.

[6] Frederick L. Collins, "Paul Muni Becomes a Heathen Chinese," LIBERTY, (August 22, 1936).

[7] Ibid.

[8] Mordaunt Hall, "Charlie Chan Carries On," WEEKLY VARIETY (New York).

[8] Mordaunt Hall, "Charlie Chan Carries On," (film review), NEW YORK TIMES, March 21, 1931.

[9] Land, "Charlie Chan at the Circus," (film review), WEEKLY VARIETY, (New York), March 25, 1936, p. 15.

[10] Bert., "Charlie Chan at Monte Carlo," (film review) WEEKLY VARIETY, (New York), December 22, 1937, p. 17.

[11] "Asian Americans Tell of Bigotry in Vietnam," LOS ANGELES TIMES, May 16, 1971.

[12] "Doral Meets a Smart Cookie!" (advertisement) FAMILY CIRCLE, vol. 79 (July, 1971), back cover.

[13] Lawrenson, op. cit.

selective acculturation and the dating process: the patterning of chinese-caucasian interracial dating

MELFORD S. WEISS

● Abstract

The recent increase in Chinese-Caucasian dating may reflect a growing Chinese-American female preference for Caucasian courtship behavior. Chinese-American girls have internalized the dominant dating values of the Caucasian teenager to a greater extent than Chinese-American boys.* Because many boys have not successfully deciphered these social values they often cannot meet the girls' expectations and may seek romance, companionship and adventure in Caucasian arms.

Divergent dating behavior of Chinese-American boys and girls may be related to: 1) the pervasive influence of American racial stereotyping; 2) Chinese-American inter-personal relationships in American society; 3) sex-linked socialization practices; and 4) the closed nature and efficient information exchange system in the Chinese community.

● Perspective

This study suggests that the relative success of the acculturation and assimilation of ethnic and racial minorities into the processes of American life can be related to the sex of the assimilating member. This paper is an initial attempt to explore social and psychological factors responsible for divergent inter-racial successes and failures of Chinese-American boys and girls.

● Methodology

This paper is based upon anthropological fieldwork in a Chinese-American community (1967-1968). Fieldwork methodology included individual and group in-depth interviews in both synchronic and diachronic perspective with Chinese-American boys and girls and their families, attendance and participation at Oriental and mixed dances, parties, organizational meetings, and other social events as well as visiting Chinese-American homes and attending numerous Chinese community celebrations and dinners.

Supplementing traditional techniques of participant-observation, questionnaires were administered to eighty (80) of the 400 Chinese students at a local junior college. Twenty-five (25) Chinese-American students (13 females, 12 males) completing the questionnaire were subsequently interviewed about their dating attitudes and behavior.

Conclusions substantiated and/or suggested by this study are applicable to the teenagers and young adults (14-21) presently living in the Chinese-American community in which this research was conducted. It may however, have general applicability to other Chinese-American communities as well.

● Background: The Chinese experience in America

The early Chinese communities in America (1850-1900) have previously been characterized by the dominance of traditional family and district associations in Chinese economic and political life, the acknowledged unchallenged superiority of the male elders, the subservient position of women in the family, and the acceptance by the younger generation of parental controls in matters of courtship and mate selection (Kung:1962, Lee:1960).

By contrast, Chinese-American communities of the 1960's are intensely involved in the processes of urban socio-cultural change-processes of acculturation and assimilation often responsible for divergence from traditional practices. With the decentralization of the community and the dispersion of its members, the Family Associations are declining in importance as they can no longer meet all the needs of

---

Reprinted from JOURNAL OF MARRIAGE AND THE FAMILY, Volume 32, Number 2 (May, 1970), by permission of the National Council on Family Relations. The author is on the faculty of the Department of Anthropology at Sacramento State College.

contemporary community life (Willmott: 1964, Lee:1949). Male elders are rapidly losing the ability to control inappropriate behavior of the younger generation--a generation more responsive to the nuances of American life than bonds of family and community (Lee: 1956). As women gain a more equal footing in the financial, recreational and socialization practices of the family, the dominant position of the father is weakened (Barnett: 1958).

One of the more dramatic departures from traditional Chinese-American life is evidenced in Chinese-Caucasian dating patterns--patterns which emphasize Chinese youth's new-found independence from familial restrictions and increasing adherence to western romantic demands; resulting in an eager attempt on the part of the Chinese-American female to embrace Caucasian courtship rituals and the concomitant social dictums that accompany them.

● The pattern of inter-racial dating

Chinese-American females have internalized the dominant dating values of the Caucasian teenager, have better adjusted to American social custom, and are better accepted by the Caucasian community as dating partners and potential mates than the young Chinese-American male. Consequently Chinese-American boys cannot meet these expectations and as a result, the girls may seek romance, companionship and adventure in Caucasian arms.

Chinese-American males have experienced many successes in American society. They have proven themselves as scholars in our educational system and as enterprising entrepreneurs in business ventures and as professionals (Kwoh 1947:113). Yet in the area of inter-racial social relationships, dating and marriage, many Chinese-American males fail to exhibit the successes achieved by the female-- and it is specifically in these interpersonal arenas that the future of assimilation of ethnic and racial minorities into American life will be determined (Gordon:1964).

The divergent dating habits of young Chinese-American males and females and their differential treatment by white American society are both a consequence and a result of continuous exposure to, and partial Chinese acceptance of, American racial stereotyping; and are directly related to Chinese-American inter-personal relationships in American society, sex-linked psychological profiles of Chinese-Americans, and the closed nature and efficient information-exchange system (grapevine) of the Chinese community.

● The nature of Chinese stereotypes

American society has historically been given to negative stereotypes of the Chinese male. In early years male Chinese arrivals to America have been characterized as "bestial celestials," "atheistic heathens," "opium smokers," "gamblers," and "gangsters" (Barth, 1964:129-156; Farwell, 1885:97-114). More recent Chinese character profiles include the evil and cunning Dr. Fu Manchu, the inscrutable Charlie Chan, and the agreeable but puzzled and simple proprietor of a hand-laundry shop (Sung, 1967). Although the Chinese male has also been popularly characterized as "clever, honest, industrious, and studious," "a paragon of family virtue," "respectfully obedient to his elders" (traits acceptable in business and family success), he is still identified as "shy," "introverted," "with-drawing" and "tongue-tied" (traits unacceptable to current ideas of romanticism) (Sung, 1967). Furthermore, the Occidental stage, screen and television image of the "hero" and the "he-man," emphasizing virility and sexual attraction--a prime factor in the courtship game--includes too few physical or cultural features of Oriental men. Chinese males are rarely mentioned as "herioc" and "adventuresome" and have never been popularized in American fiction as "dashing impulsive lovers."

The Chinese female image, on the other hand, has been better accepted by the American public. "Suzie Wong" is portrayed as slim, sexy and loveable in tight cheong-sam. The "Oriental dishes" of Flower Drum Song and the well-publicized Miss Chinatown beauty pageants have particularly emphasized Chinese feminine beauty and charm. Chinese women have a appeared in Playboy's centerfold and lend support to the exaggerated tales of servicemen returning from Far Eastern duty ports. As a result, Chinese girls with Caucasian escorts receive few disparaging public stares, while Chinese men walking hand-in-hand with white women are often the subject of malicious gossip.

American stereotypes of "Chinese"-- although based upon much fictitious characterization--accept the Chinese female as a satisfactory sexual and dating companion but reject the Chinese male in a similar category. Caucasian "social indices" reflecting an unfavorable Chinese male image discourage the Chinese-American male from seeking dates with Caucasian girls. With little confidence as a romantic competitor, he is often unsuccessful with Chinese-American females as well. Perhaps the most illustrative example of the Chinese-American females' acceptance of American sex-linked discrimination is the Chinese-American girl dining with her Caucasian date who just can't help staring at the Chinese boy and his white girlfriend and wondering what in the world she sees in him.

- Image and identity: the Chinese-American male

Perhaps the most damaging indictment of Chinese-American male "dating ineptness" comes from the dating age Chinese-American female. Girls who regularly date Caucasians can be quite vehement in their denunciation and disapproval of Chinese-American males as dating partners. But even the foreign-born Chinese girls--who do not usually inter-date--also willingly support a demeaning courtship image of the Chinese-American male. Moreover, "Chinese inadequacies" and "failures" are contrasted with Caucasian "confidence" and "success" in similar situations. Chinese-American girls report that getting-to-know-you chatter with most Chinese-American boys is basically shallow and tends to revolve around common experiences as Chinese. Males are often considered to be egocentric and to rarely consider the girls as an equal partner in a common dating activity. Conversation is less likely to contain introspective elements. Questions relating to personal identity ("who am I") and social meaning ("what is it all about") are usually excluded from Chinese-American male repertoire. The boys tend to joke about such matters ("you must be kidding") or to further ridicule the girl ("you're sick in the head").

Chinese-American dating activities are often limited to evening hours and to private or predominately Chinese settings with the drive-in movie a favorite--leading one Chinese-American girl to sarcastically remark: "One more Chinese date this month and I'll have seen every drive-in in town." Chinese-American boys are often accused of behaving "childishly" at dances and parties and embarrassing their dates by not displaying "mature" and "sophisticated" mannerisms. Hurried, clumsy love-making attempts in parked cars do not meet the girls' romantic expectations leading them to characterize Chinese-American boys as sexually inept. More often they complain about his "lack of advance," but one Chinese-American girl reports: "It's easy to get pregnant with a Chinese boy; he never knows how to take precautions."

The aforementioned comments on Chinese-American male dating behavior are less the observations of this researcher than the reporting of Chinese-American girls. Furthermore, current American dating ideology makes it fashionable to belittle and demean "traditional" behavior of Chinese-American males. When presented with these "stories" Chinese-American males deny the more derogatory accusations yet basically agree that they are more inhibited and less aggressive than Caucasian males, and admit to feeling uncomfortable if not insecure in racially mixed company and in predominantly Caucasian settings. Caucasian males on the other hand, express more confidence in inter-racial dating, seem more familiar with dating procedures and in the absence of a shared "identity" with girls of Chinese descent, give the appearance of broadening their conversational horizons. When comparing Caucasian to Chinese-American males, the former are easily accorded more social and sexual maturity, and are often referred to as "suave," "cool," "sophisticated," "swinging," and "sexy" --adjectives rarely associated with Chinese-American males.

In order to elicit more definitive information about attitudes toward Caucasian and Chinese-American dating partners, Chinese-American females were asked to specifically describe their reasons for dating the above-mentioned boys. Those who preferred to date Chinese-Americans constantly indicated "parental coercion," "Chinese and Caucasian community pressures," "respect for tradition," "the sharing of a common heritage with other Chinese," race consciousness," and "the many problems associated with inter-racial marital unions " Responses for

Caucasian dating preferences are of an entirely different nature: "Caucasians know better dating places," "more fun on dates," "more considerate," "sexy and good-looking," "easy going personality," and "they are the fun part of American culture."

These differing preference typologies for Chinese-American and for Caucasian dates suggest that the girls prefer the adventure, romance and easy familiarity associated with Caucasian life, and by accepting these "wants" have accepted many of the mores of "Americans." Although they prefer the Caucasian dates as best representative of the individuality and free-expression of this society the realities of family life and a future within this community channel their marital choice to a Chinese mate.

Thus, Chinese-American boys who demonstrate proficiency in the "Caucasian-style" dating game are in much demand as friends, dates and eventually husbands. One Chinese-American girl neatly summarized her dating desires by posting on her dormitory door: WANTED...A NON-CHINESE AMERICAN--OF CHINESE DESCENT."

●Social interaction and dating expectations

The results of the questionnaire indicated that Chinese-American college males usually carry a full-time course load (fifteen or more credits), demonstrate an intense commitment to their academic study program (predominantly science, math, and engineering) and spend many after-class hours at the school library. Many of these students hold part-time jobs in Chinese-owned restaurants and grocery markets as clerks, checkers, busboys, and waiters. Their on-the-job relationships with both Chinese and Caucasian clientele are subordinate and superficial.

Chinese-American female students, however, take fewer courses (twelve hours or less) in more non-academic subjects (cosmetology, home economics, typing) and spend less time in library confines than Chinese-American boys. Most females are not employed after school, and those with part-time jobs are more likely to work for Caucasian employers. Chinese-American females spend many "leisure" hours in snack bars and on campus grounds in the company of the Chinese-American and Caucasian peers. The girls "tune in" to social conventions concerning heterosexual activities and quickly learn the expectations and frustrations of American teen-age dating styles. Although Chinese-American extra-curricular organizational life is largely spent with other Chinese-Americans; females are more likely to be escorted to Caucasian dances, invited to Caucasian parties and attend predominantly Caucasian churches than are males.

As Chinese-American females continue to participate in inter-racial activities they learn the current fads and fashions associated with Caucasian courtship ritual and come to expect similar consideration. Chinese American males, whose participation in the non-Chinese world is limited, are either unaware, or more commonly uncertain of these "social graces." Since the males must take the initiative for arranging dates, Chinese-American males find themselves at a distinct dating disadvantage when compared with their Caucasian peers.

Chinese-American males do participate in "Caucasian" school organizations, but these activities do not demand the same social sophistication as parties and dances. Chinese-American boys rarely join the predominantly Caucasian fraternities while Chinese-American females are better represented in women's social associations. Females declare they are usually "at ease" in the company of Caucasian peers. Males often indicate insecurity and anxiety in competitive inter-racial situations. The females consider themselves "more Americanized" than the males.

Our data suggests that the nature and degree of inter-racial social participation adjust to contemporary American life. Male feelings of "inadequacy" are not complemented by female "adjustments" to acculturation. Because Abel and Hsu's analysis is applicable to this community study, it takes but little imagination to project these suggested sex-role discrepancies directly into the dating situation.

●Community grapevine and closed system

Most Chinese parents (native and foreign born) disapprove of inter-racial dating, yet certain features of social life in this Chinese-American community not only encourage Chinese-American females to date non-Chinese men, but even discourage casual and/or consistent dating within the Chinese-American group.

Although dispersed throughout the city, the Chinese "sense of community" is nevertheless consciously maintained by an efficient yet informal information exchange system which unites the community by cutting across age, sex, and generational barriers. This Chinese "grapevine," strengthened by long-standing friendships and cross-cutting organizational and social activities, functions through the spreading of news and rumor to maintain a running commentary upon the activities of its younger members. "Grapevine" gossip exposes dating activities to "Chinese public view" by rapidly relaying dating stories to parents, relatives, dating partners and potential mates.

While foreign-born Chinese parents consider "dating" a direct prelude toward serious intentions, and see consecutive and/or consistent dates with one individual as swiftly leading to a future marital commitment, Chinese-American youth (particularly females) consider "dating as a pleasant end in itself." Thus, non-serious dating styles mean unwanted gossip. Caucasian society more readily approves of casual courtship practices (particularly those of an inter-racial nature) and are unable to directly contribute to Chinese gossip sessions. Therefore a "Caucasian date" may spare the girl from a "double-pronged" feedback into the Chinese community, and much of the dating "activity" can remain unexposed; allowing the girl multiple and varied dating experiences without necessarily endangering her reputation. The grapevine functions most successfully with spicy and risque episodes. Rebuffed and jealous Chinese-American males have been known to tell "tall tales" to enhance their social reputation--tales which add little to the girl's reputation, as scandal is appreciated neither by parents nor potential mates. In any event, Chinese-Chinese "heavy dates" rarely remain secret, and girls may keep their dates a private affair by dating non-Chinese. Although Caucasian males are also prone to ego building "stories"--because they are not plugged into the Chinese network--their fictional and factual adventures are unlikely to reach Chinese ears.

Chinese parents opposed to inter-racial marriages may not seriously view a Caucasian escort as a possible choice, and are sometimes less concerned with multiple Caucasian outings than would be the case with a Chinese suitor. Two important structural features in this Chinese community are a stable population for persons under twenty-five and the tendency for the Chinese to split into "foreign-born" and "native-born" social groupings. Because the total community population is under 9,000; scattered throughout the city; and further split into separate groups, eligible dates can be a considerable problem, particularly for American-born Chinese females, who rarely date foreign-born Chinese boys. Moreover, close childhood and school ties continue with age-mates within groups and friendship does not easily become romance. Thus Chinese-Americans frequently go outside the Chinese community in search of dating companions. Caucasians, whose life style already appeals to the Chinese-American female are able to furnish an immediate identity and find it easy to meet "date searching" Chinese-American girls. The Chinese-American male finding it difficult to date Caucasian girls, remains frustrated.

● Summary

The social and cultural orientations and sentiments of the Chinese in America are gradually shifting from the ethnic subculture to the larger American society. As Caucasian society continues to become a positive reference group, its norms and values begin to guide as well as modify the behavior and perspectives of the Chinese (Fong 1965:271).

Yet, cultural and structural assimilations of the Chinese-American into white America have always resulted in a similar acceptance of both Chinese-American males and females. Sex-linked American discriminatory practices have contributed to a male-negative/female-positive dichotomy. The effects of this "stereotyping" are further validated and reinforced by the Chinese-American female successes in inter-racial social activities and personality adjustment to American life. The sex-linked demands upon its youngsters also share in the responsibility for the continuance of the female's success and many males' failures in inter-racial dating activities.

● Suggestions

Although the focus of this study is dating with an obvious emphasis upon the cross-sex relationship, Chinese-American males still remain ill at ease with Caucasians of BOTH sexes. The lack of successful inter-racial personal relationships in social activities carry over into adult lives where the inability of the Chinese-American male to relate positively to Chinese-Caucasian social/sexual situations continues.

Chinese-American females have a less rigid role to maintain than their male counterparts. They are not responsible for carrying on family "tradition" and are less subjected to parental pressures to conform. They therefore find it less challenging to significantly affects dating expectations, and that Chinese-American females spend more time in "mixed" activities than Chinese American males; thus hastening the females' incorporation into American social life.

● Psychological profiles and sex-related differences

Abel and Hsu (1949:286) support differential sex-linked attitudes when reporting the responses for American born Chinese males and females. Rorschach protocals suggest that Chinese-American females approach the American response pattern to a greater degree than do Chinese-American males. The males seem insecure about their sex roles, their acceptance in relation to Americans as people, and their relationship to girls in general. Although the females expressed adjustment difficulties, they marshalled their resources, faced their conflicts squarely, and handled sexual preoccupations more directly. Hsu further suggests that because Chinese-American males are more responsible for carrying on the family name and following in their "ancestors' footsteps," that their exposure to Chinese and western ideals often involves conflicting emotions. They are less sure of the roles they should or could lead. In attempting to break away from tradition and better fit into the American patterns, they encounter many difficulties within both the Chinese and American community. Their protocols suggest that many may be emotionally disturbed since they show frequent anxiety signs, repressed feelings of rebellion, a dilemma in the sexual sphere, and the inability to work out sexual difficulties.

American sex-linked discriminatory practices and "poor" social interaction experiences combine to isolate the Chinese-American male from active participation in community-wide organizational activity. When Chinese-American males do join in extra-Chinese city events, they do so as members of all-Chinese groups rather than as assimilated individuals. Moreover, these activities are usually limited to business or "Chinese community" functions and rarely specifically "social events."

....

REFERENCES CITED

ABEL, THEODORA M. and HSU, FRANCIS L.K.
   1949   *Some aspects of personality of Chinese as revealed by the Rorschach tests. Research exchange and Journal of Projective Techniques XIII:385-401.*

BARTH, GUNTHER
   1964   *Bitter strength: a history of the Chinese in the United States, 1850-1870. Harvard University Press, Cambridge, Mass.*

BARNETT, MILTON L.
   1958   *Some Cantonese-American problems of status adjustment. Phylon XVIII:420-427.*

FARWELL, WILLARD B.
   1885   *The Chinese at home and abroad. A.L. Bancroft and Company, San Francisco.*

FONG, STANLEY
   1965   *Assimilation of Chinese in America: changes in orientation and social perception. American Journal of Sociology IXIII 3:265-273.*

GORDON, MILTON M.
    1964   Assimilation in American life. Oxford University Press, New York.

KUNG, S.W.
    1962   Chinese in American life: some aspects of their history, status, problems a and contributions. University of Washington Press, Seattle.

KWOH, BEULAH ONG
    1947   Occupational status of the American-born Chinese college graduate. (unpublished doctoral dissertation, University of Chicago).

LEE, ROSE HUM
    1960   The Chinese in the United States of America, Oxford University Press.
    1956   The recent immigrant Chinese families of the San Francisco-Oakland area. Marriage and Family Living 18:14-24.
    1949   The decline of Chinatown in the United States. American Journal of Sociology LIV 5:422-432.

SUNG, BETTY LEE
    1967   Mountain of Gold: the story of the Chinese in America. The Macmillan Company, New York.

WEISS, MELFORD S.
    1968   Selective acculturation and dating process: the patterning of Chinese Caucasian inter-racial dating, Paper presented at the 67th annual meeting of the American Anthropological Association, Seattle, Washington.

WILLMOTT, W.L.
    1964   Chinese clan associations in Vancouver. Man 49:33-36.

I intend to marry a White man. But what were my attitudes leading up to our decision to marry?

My parents have tried to encourage me to marry an Oriental, but they also wanted me to marry a man of my own choosing. I have met many Oriental men, and they seem to lack many qualities that I would need in any man I would marry. My fiancee possesses all these qualities and many more. It seems that they are all the White stereotype qualities that are important to White middle and upper class mothers. His qualities: 1) tall, 2) handsome, 3) manly, 4) self-confident, 5) well-poised, 6) protective, 7) domineering, 8) affectionate, and 9) imaginative. These are all Prince Charming characteristics that all White women instill in their daughters for the ideal mate.

My future-husband seems to possess all of them, and he's also White.

It seems that Oriental girls who marry White men are looking for this stereotype and will not settle for the short, ugly, unconfident, clumsy, arrogant Oriental man that we are all plagued with.

Oriental women also have stereotypes --small, long black hair, gentle, obedient, loving, soft, very womanly, quiet, and beautiful.

None of these are derogatory, but all complimentary. Women like to be thought of in this way.

In the pre-marital relationship between an Oriental couple, the boy will first woo the girl by taking her out on expensive dates; once he knows she will be his girl friend, he takes her for granted, causing many heartaches for her; but necessary for him, to show his masculinity.

The Oriental man seems to have a very distorted picture of masculinity. More and more Asian American girls are seeing that there is a better life--dating the White male. He treats her as the woman she really is, and doesn't have a hangup about proving his masculinity.

The Oriental girl is unique to a White male, because of her Oriental face, her Oriental body; but the Oriental boy seems to like those girls who evoke little of their Orientalness.

White Male Qualities

Name Withheld

One of my old boyfriends was a Japanese American and he seemed to dislike all and any interest exhibited about Yellow identity. He wanted to continue to pretend he was White.

My fiancee wants me to retain all my cultural ties. Perhaps he sees me as a little Japanese doll in kimono, but at least I know what I am. We want to have children, and he wants them all to have black hair. He would also like me to learn to make all Japanese dishes and specialties from my grandmother.

I am much more Oriental now, marrying him.

One of my girl friends mentioned that although she doesn't like the idea of stereotypes, she doesn't really mind it with White men. They seem to appreciate one much more. She feels much better adjusted not dating Orientals.

It seems to me that Sanseis marrying Sanseis will grow up to be exactly like their parents, not better, not worse. I have much higher aspirations for myself and family. I want my children to be free of all hangups. My fiancee and I don't dwell upon my being Japanese and he being white--we think much more about being a man and woman.

Another aspect that may be brought into this project could be the attitudes concerning sex. I think most Orientals have hangups about sex. More than our White counterparts. The cultural ties to duty and honor may have a lot to do with this.

After an Oriental boy has seduced his girl friend, she will expect to marry him, and he begins to take her for granted. He has proved his masculinity, and for once, she feels truly loved.

If an Oriental girl were seduced by a White boy friend, she would probably enjoy the relationship much more and not dwell upon marriage.

Oriental girls have two forms of behavior, one for Oriental boys, and one for White boys. When they find the one that is typically them, as I did--they make their decision.

I have been lucky in my decision--my parents want me to marry for love and happiness, and not for preservation of the blood.

They will let me go ahead and marry him. They trust my judgment completely, and realize that I am just as they raised me--with White ideals.

I feel that if I make any contributions to the community, they will be better for having married him.

Reprinted from GIDRA, January, 1970.

憎

'I hate my wife for her flat yellow face'

*I hate my wife for her flat yellow face
and her fat cucumber legs, but mostly
for her lack of elegance and lack of
intelligence compared to judith gluck.*

*I married my wife, daughter of a rich
east los angeles banker, for money.
of course, I thought I deserved better, but
suffering is something else altogether.*

*She married me for love but she can't love
me, since no one who went to Fresno State
knows anything about Warhol or Ginsberg or
Viet Nam. She has no jewish friends.*

*She's like a stupid water buffalo from
the old country, slowly plodding between
muddy furrows, and that's all she knows of
love beneath my curses and sometimes blows.*

*I thought I could love her at first, that she
could teach me to be myself again, free
from years of bopping round LA ghettos,
western civilization and the playmate of the month*

*since she was raised a buddhist with all
the arts of dancing, arranging and the
serving of tea, and I thought I saw in my
arrogance some long forgotten warrior prince.*

*But I wanted to be an anglican
too much and listened too long to dylan
or maybe it was the playmate of the
month or poetry and judith gluck.*

*So I hate my gentle wife for her flat
yellow face and her soft cucumber legs
bearing the burden of the love she has
borne for centuries, centuries before*
                *anglicans and dylans
          playmates and rock
          before
          me or judith gluck*

                        RON TANAKA

Reprinted from GIDRA, September, 1969.

GENERATION AND CHARACTER:
the case of the Japanese Americans

STANFORD LYMAN

INTRODUCTION

When the first Japanese Embassy arrived in the United States in 1860, the DAILY ALTA CALIFORNIAN, a San Francisco newspaper, reported with mingled approval and astonishment:

"Every beholder was struck with the self-possessed demeanor of the Japanese. Though the scenes which now met their gaze must have been of the most intense interest for novelty, they seemed to consider this display as due the august position they held under their Emperor, and not one of them, by sign or word, evinced either surprise or admiration."[1]

Thus, with their first major debarkation in the New World,[2] the Japanese appeared to Americans to lack emotional expression. Indeed, San Francisco's perceptive journalist went on to observe: "This stoicism, however, is a distinguishing feature with the Japanese. It is part of their creed never to appear astonished at anything, and it must be a rare sight indeed which betrays in them any expression of wonder."[3]

In the eighty-five years which passed between Japan's first embassy and the end of the second World War, this "distinguishing feature" of the Japanese became the cardinal element of the anti-Japanese stereotype. Characterized by journalists, politicians, novelists and film-makers as a dangerous, enemy people, the Japanese were also pictured as mysterious and inscrutable.[4] Supposedly loyal to Japan, cunning and conspiratorial, most of the Japanese Americans were evacuated and incarcerated throughout the second World War. This unusual violation of their fundamental civil rights was justified in the minds of a great many ordinary Americans by the perfidious character they imputed to Japanese.[5]

The anti-Japanese stereotype was so widespread that it affected the judgments of sociologists about the possibilities of Japanese assimilation. Thus, in 1913 Robert E. Park had been sufficiently depressed by the orgy of anti-Japanese legislation and popular prejudice to predict their permanent consignment to minority status: "The Japanese ... is condemned to remain among us an abstraction, a symbol, and a symbol not merely of his own race, but of the Orient and of that vague ill-defined menace we sometimes refer to as the 'yellow peril'."[6] Although Park later reversed his doleful prediction, his observations on Japanese emphasized their uncommunicative features, stolid faces and apparently blank characters. The Japanese face was a racial mask behind which the individual personality was always hidden. "Orientals live more completely behind the mask than the rest of us," he wrote. "Naturally enough we misinterpret them and attribute to disingenuousness and craft what is actually conformity to an ingrained convention. The American who is flattered at first by the politeness of his Japanese servant will later on, perhaps, cite as a reproach against the race the fact that 'we can never tell what a Japanese is thinking about.' 'We never know what is going on in their heads'."[7]

Since the end of World War II recognition of the evils of racism has reduced the negative and pejorative effects of racial stereotypes, but it has not brought about an end to their popular usage or academic study. Recent scholarship, while eschewing antipathetic and hostile stereotypes, has begun to lay great emphasis on the role of character and character formation for achievement and assimilation. Thus, in one study, the success of Jews in America is attributed in part to their belief "that the world is orderly and amenable to rational mastery;" to their willingness "to leave home to make their way in life;" and to their "preference for individualistic rather than collective credit for work done."[8] Another study points out that the child rearing practices of Jews, Greeks and white Protestants lay the emphasis on independence and achievement, while those of Italians, French-Canadians and Negroes emphasize cooperation and fatalistic resignation.[9]

Reprinted from THE ASIAN IN THE WEST by Stanford M. Lyman by permission of the Western Studies Center, Desert Research Institute, University of Nevada System. Mr. Lyman is currently on the faculty of the Department of Sociology at the University of California, San Diego.

The remarkable record of achievement by Japanese Americans has been noted frequently in reports of both journalists and sociologists. As early as 1909, Chester Rowell pointed to their refusal to accept unprofitable contracts, their commercial advancement beyond the confines of the ghetto and to their geniality and politeness.[10] Seventeen years later Winifred Raushenbush, Park's assistant in his race relations survey of the Pacific Coast, admonished the Japanese of Florin, California, for their impatience with racial restrictions and praised the Japanese community of Livingston, California, for its propriety.[11] More recently, Rose Hum Lee vividly contrasted the Chinese Americans with their Japanese counterparts, noting that the Nisei "exhibit greater degrees of integration into American society, than has been the case with the Chinese, whose settlement is twice as long."[12] Broom and Kitsuse have summed up the impressive record of the Japanese in America by declaring it to be "an achievement perhaps rarely equalled in the history of human migration."[13] The careful statistical measures of Schmid and Nobbe indicate that present-day Japanese in America have outstripped all other "colored" groups in America in occupational achievement and education.[14]

Analyses of Japanese American achievement have laid stress on the same character traits which once made up the notorious stereotype. Thus, Caudill and deVos have pointed out that the Nisei appear to be more acculturated than they are in fact because of "a significant compatibility (but by no means identity) between the value systems found in the culture of Japan and the value systems found in American middle class culture."[15] "What appears to have occurred in the case of Japanese-Americans is that the Nisei while utilizing to a considerable extent a Japanese set of values and adaptive mechanisms, were able in their prewar life on the Pacific Coast to act in ways that drew favorable comment and recognition from their white middle class peers and made them admirable pupils in the eyes of their middle class teachers."[16]

The experiences of prewar California were repeated in Chicago during the second World War. Personnel managers and fellow workers admired the Nisei. "What has happened here," wrote Caudill and deVos, "is that the peers, teachers, employers and fellow workers of the Nisei have projected their own values onto the neat, well-dressed and efficient Nisei in whom they saw mirrored many of their own ideals."[17] What were these ideals? They included patience, cleanliness, courtesy and "minding their own business,"[18] the same ideals capable of distortion into negative characteristics. Thus, Japanese patience has been taken to be silent contempt; cleanliness and courtesy, as matters for comic ridicule or dark suspicion; minding their own business as unwarranted aloofness and "clannishness."[19] What was once caricature is now recognized as character.

The fact that the same, or very nearly identical, traits can be used to denigrate the Japanese, as well as account for their unprecedented success, suggests the possibility that behind these traits there exists a unique character structure. Indeed, the Japanese Americans themselves believe this and, as we shall presently show, they regard each generation of Japanese Americans as possessed of a unique character. That there should exist a correspondence between a racist stereotype and culturally-created character should not cause too great a concern. The haters of a people have often correctly picked out elements of their enemies' character and spun webs of viciousness out of them. Indeed, one reason for the survival of a stereotype through time and other changes is its origin in a kernel of fundamental truth which it distorts for evil purposes.

Recently a great advance in the understanding of the nature of slavery and Negro personality was made by a recognition of the truth value of personality elements in the "Sambo" stereotype and an attempt to discover just how such a personality could arise.[20] Progress in the social analysis of culture and personality might be enhanced by sociologists and social psychologists undertaking the unpalatable task of assuming for the sake of research that the worst statements made about a people have their origins in some fundamental truth which needs first to be abstracted from its pejorative context and then subjected to behavorial and cultural analysis.

This paper presents an analysis of Japanese American character. Fortunately, no anti-Japanese mood is currently widespread in America, and the analysis may proceed without fear of being distorted for pernicious purposes. A conceptual framework first developed by Alfred Schutz and effectively employed by Clifford Geertz to study the Balinese[22] is here used to analyze Japanese American character. A somewhat similar formulation of concepts by Clyde Kluckhohn has been applied to Japanese character by Caudill and Scarr.[23] Although this paper relies heavily on Schutz, the conceptual schema of Kluckhohn and the findings of Caudill and Scarr will be noted when appropriate. In addition, the findings of numerous researchers on Japan and the

Japanese Americans have been employed and interpreted throughout.

TIME PERSON PERSPECTIVES

In every culture and in many sub-cultures there is a predominant time-person perspective. This perspective organizes the relevant temporal and personal categories in order to structure priorities with respect to past, present and future, and to structure orientations with respect to intimacy or impersonality. Any culture may be viewed then with respect to its priorities of predecessors, contemporaries, consociates and successors.[24] Predecessors are all those who have lived in some past time, in history, and with whom no contemporary can have direct subjective knowledge. Successors are all those who shall live in some future time and with whom no contemporary can share a mutual inter-subjective identity because they have not yet lived. Contemporaries are all those fellow men who share the same spatio-temporal environment. Among contemporaries are those about whom one has only categorical but no intersubjective knowledge, and those whom one knows intimately and in regular association. The latter are consociates. Now, for any culture or subculture, we may ask how these distinctions appear--not merely as analytic features, but rather as members' understandings of their own world. Note that it is possible for any one of these time-person perspectives to be experienced subjectively by members as prior to, having precedence over, or exclusive from any one or group of the others. The relative subjective weight placed on any one or more of these perspectives over and against the others has profound consequences for the organization of behavior and is, in turn, reciprocally related to other elements of culture and the institutional order.

In the case of the Japanese in America, time and person are perceived in terms of geographic and generational distance from Japan. The Japanese are the only immigrant group in America who specify by a linguistic term and characterize with a unique personality each generation of descendants from the original immigrant group.[25] In contrast, for example, to the United States Census[26] and the Chinese,[27] the Japanese do not merely distinguish native-born from foreign-born but rather count geo-generationally forward or backward with each new generational grouping. Moreover, from the standpoint of any single living generational group, the others are imputed to have peculiar and distinctive personalities and attendant behavior patterns which are evaluated in positive and negative terms. Each generation removed from Japan is assumed to have its own characterological qualities, qualities which are derived at the outset from its spatio-temporal position, and are thus not subject to voluntaristic adoption or obviation. Thus, each generation is living out a unique, temporally governed lifetime which shall not be seen again after it is gone.

Immigrants from Japan are called Issei, literally "first generation," a term referring to all those who were born and nurtured in Japan and who later migrated to the United States. The children of at least one Issei parent are called Nisei, literally "second generation," and this term encompasses all those born in the United States of immigrant parentage. The grandchildren of Issei are called Sansei, literally "third generation," and include all those born of Nisei or Kibei parentage. The great-grandchildren of Issei are called Yonsei, literally "fourth generation" and include all those born of Sansei parentage. The great-great grandchildren of Issei are called Gosei and include all those born of Yonsei parentage. In addition, there is both terminological and characterological distinction imputed to all those persons who were born in the United States of Issei parentage, educated in Japan and then returned to the United States. These are called Kibei,[28] literally "returned to America," and their children, as mentioned, are considred Sansei.

Age and situation may modify the strictness of membership in these generational groups, but while persons might be informally reassigned to a group to which they do not belong by virtue of geographical or generational criteria, the idea of the groups remains intact as a working conception of social reality. Thus, a young Japanese American friend of the author's who enjoys the social status of a Nisei jokingly refers to himself as an Issei since he was born of Nisei parents during their temporary residence in Japan. Older Nisei whose social and personal characteristics are similar to those of Issei are somtimes treated as if they were the latter.[29] Sansei age peers of Nisei are treated as the latter if they behave accordingly. But Nisei who appear to their fellow Nisei age peers as "too Japanesy" are sometimes associated in the minds of their more Americanized friends with Kibei, while those who are "too American" are associated with Sansei. Finally, the offspring of geogenerationally mized parentage--e.g., Issei-Nisei, Nisei-Sansei, Nisei-Yonsei, etc.--and of racially mixed parentage are not easily classifiable. In practice they tend to demonstrate the sociological rule that status is as status does; that is, they enjoy the classification which social relations and personal behavior assign to them and which they assign to themselves.[30]

In terms of the temporal categories with which we began this discussion, the Japanese in America lay great emphasis on contemporaries. This does not mean that they have no sense whatsoever of predecessors, successors and consociates. Rather, their ideas about these categories--in practical terms about the past and history and the future of other generations, as well as about intimates--are vague and diffuse, or in the case of consociates, deemphasized and deprecated. From the point of view of the Nisei--and especially those Nisei who grew up on the West Coast and received cultural and group reinforcement from the Japanese American communities--Issei, other Nisei and Sansei, white Americans, Negroes, Chinese Americans and other persons whom they encounter are contemporaries in the formal sense since they are capable of being known to one another and of sharing similar, but not especially identical, situations. Moreover, while individuals live through an age-demarcated life cycle with rites de passage to mark off birth, marriage, death and certain ceremonies, for the Nisei it is the common lifetime of the whole generational group that circumscribes social and personal orientations. The generational group has a life cycle of its own internally indicated by its appropriate behavior patterns and externally bounded by the temporal duration of the whole group.

To the Nisei--and for the balance of this paper it is this group's perspective we shall be examining--the world of their predecessors is known through whatever their parents have told them about old Japan and what they have learned in afternoon "language" schools, college history courses and Japanese movies. Nisei parents are concerned about their own children in particular and the Sansei and Yonsei successor generations in general, partly in terms of achievement and advancement--which Nisei efforts have facilitated--but more significantly they are worried about the future generations' character. Sansei and Yonsei do not exhibit Nisei character, and Nisei regard this fact as both inevitable and unfortunate.

It is as and with contemporaries that Nisei feel both pride and apprehension. The basic conception of the Nisei phenomenon ultimately depends on the objective existence of their own generational group. The Nisei geogenerational group inhabits time and space between that of the Issei and the Sansei. The Japanese community in general and the Nisei group in particular provides a Nisei with emotional security and a haven from the turbulence and unpredictable elements of the outer world.[31] But the Nisei group is threatened by both centripetal and centrifugal forces, by individual withdrawal and acculturative transcendence.[32] Should collective identity be dissolved by the overarching precedence of atomized individuals, dyadic relationships or small cliques, then Nisei would lose both its objective existence and its subjective meaning. Should individuals transcend the generational group by moving out into the world of their non-Japanese contemporaries, by "validating their acculturation,"[33] then too would both the objective and subjective senses of Nisei identity lose their compelling force. Thus, Nisei must worry on two fronts about the risks of intimate association. On the one hand, the very close contacts inherent in the segregated yet secure Japanese community allow for intimate association "below" the level of the generational group; on the other hand, the breakdown of prejudice and discrimination threatens to seduce the Nisei individual away from the confines of his racial group.[34] Hence, it follows that for Nisei social and interpersonal relations are governed by a permanent interest in maintaining an appropriate social distance, so that individuals do not "escape" into integration or withdraw themselves from group solidarity. Either of these would jeopardize if not destroy the Nisei as a group and an idea.

Nisei, do not speak of their social and personal life in this fashion; rather, they exhibit in numerous ways a quiet but deep and pervasive pride in their Nisei identity. This pride is not rooted in their material success, as it might be among other ethnic groups in America, but instead in their character. Nisei believe that they combine in themselves a perfect balance of Japanese and American traits. They are not "too Japanesy" as are the Issei by definition and the Kibei by virtue of imposed culture and education; they are not "too American" as are their white American contemporaries and the Sansei. Nisei character at its best is exhibited in cathectic management and by control over and suppression of spontaneity, emotionalism and inappropriate expressiveness. It is this character itself, in which the Nisei take so much pride, that reacts back on the Nisei group to maintain its objective existence. It is this character which operates to orient behavior in such a manner that contemporaries are not converted to consociates, that fellow men are not brought too close into the intimate circle.

MANNERS, MORES AND MEANINGS

For the Nisei to preserve the objective identity of its own generational group, to deemphasize the biological aging of its members in favor of preserving the single moment-to-moment simultaneity of the generational group, it is necessary to remove interpersonal relations from the intimate or consociate level and push them back toward the formal or contemporary plane. In behalf of this objective, the Nisei have a built-in aid, Japanese culture, especially as it had developed by the late Meiji-early Taisho eras, the periods in which the bulk of Issei came to America. Although this culture had its origins in an environment far different from that which the Nisei experienced, it served the goal of anonymization of persons and immobilization of individual time through its emphasis on etiquette, ceremony and rigid status deference.

The emphasis on etiquette in Japanese culture has been such a frequently mentioned feature that it hardly needs demonstration here.[35] The Japanese language itself is one of social forms, indicative politeness and status identifiers.[36] Moreover, Japanese language is one of indirection, removing the subject (speaker) in a sentence from direct relation to the predicate, and utilizing stylistic circumlocutions so that the intended object of the particular speech is reached by a circular rather than linear route.[37] The net result of these forms is that individuals are held at arm's length, so to speak, so that potential consociates remain contemporaries--quasi-stranger, quasi-friends.

The Issei were able to transmit the basic ideas of this culture to their offspring, but its manifestation took place in an American idiom interpenetrating the only society with which Nisei were familiar. Thus, Japanese etiquette appeared in the form of a sometimes seemingly Victorian politeness. Although the bow, whose rigid rules the Japanese imposed upon themselves while exempting all foreigners,[38] did not survive the generational passage, except in a limited vestigial form,[39] other forms especially verbal ones, could be translated into English. Thus, Japanese Americans are likely to pay careful attention to titles, to employ the terms of genteel propriety, to avoid obscenity and to use the passive voice.[40] In all this the Nisei succeed simultaneously in keeping associations under management and emotions under control.

The primary concern of a Nisei male is the management and control of his emotional economy. He truly cannot countenance an emotional economy governed, or should we say ungoverned, according to principles of behavioristic laissez-faire; he desires ultimately a "socializing of that economy," and in the absence of complete "socialization, he introduces a constant "Keynesian" watchfulness over it. The human state that is idealized is that of inward quiescence--that is lauded, is an outward appearance of emotional equanimity. An outward appearance that is boisterous, excessively emotional, visibly passionate, obviously fearful, unabashedly vain or blushingly embarrassed, is distasteful and itself shameful, fit perhaps only for children and foreigners.

"Etiquette," as Clifford Geertz has pointed out in his study of Java, provides its user "with a set of rigidly formal ways of doing things which conceals his real feelings from others. In addition it so regularizes behavior, his own and that of others, as to make it unlikely to provide unpleasant surprises."[41] The manner in which Nisei attempt to tonal control, euphemisms and circumlocutive forms in speaking English illustrates the role of etiquette in language. Although English-speaking Europeans and most native-born Americans employ tonal change for emphasis and object indication, the Nisei strive after a flatness of tone and an equality of metre in their speech. For those who are unfamiliar with this style--as are a great many white Americans--it becomes difficult to distinguish the important from the insignificant items in any speech encounter. For the Nisei, it provides a continuous demonstration of the proper state of emotional equanimity; for the uninitiated "foreigner," it presents the Nisei as a blank slate. Since no one believes that a fellow human is in fact a blank slate, it causes wonder about what "really" is being said and in some instances arouses suspicion of ulterior motives.[42]

Nisei employ euphemisms whenever the simpler and more direct form might indicate a state of emotional involvement or evoke an undesirable emotional response from others. Euphemisms and round-about expressions are especially employed when the direct and precise term would or could be insulting or otherwise emotionally provocative. Where no English euphemism is available, or where one is so awkward as to introduce an embarrassment by its very usage, a Japanese term may be employed. This is especially the case in using nouns to designate racial or ethnic groups. Nisei rarely say "whiteman," "Negro," "Chinese" or "Jew" in their everyday speech. Nisei understand that race is a touchy subject in America with ambiguous meanings and ambivalent feelings deeply embedded in the subterranean value structure.

To avoid possible emotional entanglements, they employ substitute and usually neutral terms derived from Japanese. This is the case despite the fact that Nisei tend not to speak Japanese to their peers. For "white man," the term "Caucasian" is sometimes used, but one is more likely to hear

Hakujin, literally "white man," and occasionally one might overhear the pejorative Keto, literally a "hairy person," but freely translated as "barbarian." For "Negro," the Nisei who combine a culturally derived, mild antipathy to blackness[43] with an unevenly experienced and ambivalent form of the American Negrophobic virus, almost never employ such vulgar terms as "nigger," "coon," "Jigaboo" or "black boy." Rather, they use the denotatively pejorative Kuron-bo, literally "black boy," usually in a neutral and unpejorative sense, at least on the conscious level. For "Chinese," another people toward whom Nisei are ambivalent, the mildly pejorative Hawaiian term, Pakē, is quite commonly employed.

For "Jew" the terminology is especially interesting and provides an unusual example of trans-Pacific linguistic transmogrification. Anti-Semitism was almost unknown in Japan at the time the Issei came to America, and neither they nor their offspring readily adapted to this essentially European prejudice.[44] While growing up, however, Nisei learned of the special attitude held by Americans toward Jews, and in their own inimitable way invented a term whereby they could express one central idea of the anti-Jewish stereotype without using the emotion-laden English term, "kike." Nisei employ the "Japanese" neologism ku-ichi to express this idea. Now, ku-ichi in its everyday use among Nisei does not refer so much to the Jews as such but rather to the idea of stinginess and miserliness and the representation of "cheapskate." The etymology of ku-ichi is the combination of the Japanese numbers "ku," meaning "nine" and "ichi" meaning one. Nine plus one is ten, and the Japanese term for ten is "Ju," the hononym for the English word "Jew." This Nisei linguistic innovation is not used or or even widely known in Japan. The denotative word for Jew in Japan is yudaya-jin.[45] Nisei do not apply ku-ichi exclusively to Jews, but rather to fellow Nisei or to anyone who openly displays an attitude of cheapness or stinginess.

Circumlocutions and indirect speech are regular features of Nisei conversations serving to mute one's own feelings and prevent the eruption of another's. In the Chicago researches employing the Rorschach test, Nisei males resorted to a significant amount of "confabulatory" responses when faced with a perplexing or emotionally troubling perception.[46] Indirect speech is a regular feature of conversations in Japan and is matched there by the circular placing of household furniture and the use of open space in streets and homes.[47] It also affects the quality of translations from Japanese to another language.[48] Among the Nisei English usage is preferred, except when propriety dictates otherwise,[49] and circumlocutions and indirections are not too difficult to develop. Abstract nouns, non-committal statements and inferential hints at the essential meaning are regular features.

Indirection is also effected by the use of go-betweens to mediate in delicate situations. Anthropologists have emphasized the role of the marriage-arranger (nakyo-do or baishakunin) in traditional Japan, and some Nisei are prevailed upon to employ a baishakunin to ceremonialize an engagement after it has been effected in the American pattern.[50] On a more personal level, intermediaries may be employed to inform one friend that another wishes to borrow money from him and to sound out the former on his willingness to loan it. In this manner the would-be borrower is prevented from having to go through a direct face-losing refusal should the hoped-for creditor decide not to loan the money, and the borrowee is saved from the mutually embarrassing situation that would arise if he had to refuse his friend the money. An intermediary is also employed, occasionally, to warn someone that he will receive an invitation to a social affair or to inform someone quietly that a "surprise party" is going to be given for him. In the former case, the affective linkage hinted at by the extension of an invitation is blunted, the embarrassment of a refusal to attend is reduced, and the invitee is given the opportunity to mobilize himself for the receipt of the formal invitation. In the latter case, the "surprise" is rendered unprovocative of an undesirable, excessive, emotional display.

Bluntness of speech is not a virtue among Nisei. Here again the trait is also found in Japan where it is accompanied by a high tolerance for lengthy monologues and a polite indifference to complete comprehension.[51] Among the Nisei as among their forbears in Japan, the main point of a conversational episode is not approached immediately. Moreover, as mentioned earlier, the monotonal flatness of affect prevents it from being readily identifiable to those who, like Europeans and white Americans, are accustomed to a tonal cue which indicates that what is being said now is more important than what has preceded or will follow it. Indeed, conversations among Nisei almost always partake of the elements of an information game between persons maintaining decorum by seemingly mystifying one another.[52] It is the duty of the listener to ascertain the context of the speech he hears and to glean from his knowledge of the speaker and the context just what is the important point.

Violations of this tacit ritual speech relationship occur fairly often, sometimes among Nisei themselves, but more often in encounters between Nisei and Hakujin, Nisei and Sansei, and Nisei and other Gaijin. Exasperation with the apparent pointlessness of talk, frustration with vain attempts to gauge the meaning of sequential utterances, and the desire to reach a conclusion often lead these non-Nisei to ask a pointed question directed at the heart of the matter. Nisei are troubled by this; they may refuse to answer, change the subject or, more subtly, redirect the conversation back to its concentric form. The idealized aim in a conversation is to maintain the appropriate ritual and calm state of speaker and audience. To do this, important items (i.e., those charged with potential affect and those likely to disturb speaker-audience homeostasis) are buried beneath a verbal avalanche of trivia and, in the most perfected of conversations, are never brought to the surface at all--they are silently apprehended by the listener.

This emphasis on calmness and composure lends itself to unstated but widely held norms of conversational propriety appropriate to different social occasions. Since it is at informal social occasions -- parties, dinners, tete-a-tetes--that one's speech partners and oneself are vulnerable to conversion from contemporaries to consociates, it is precisely such occasions, seemingly just the ones for intimacy and spontaneity, that require careful monitoring for excessive affect.[53] Nisei "rules" for social gatherings, therefore, include (1) an emphasis on "democratic participation" in speech; i.e., no one should speak too long or too much and everyone should have an opportunity to speak; (2) circulation; i.e., small clusters of conversationalists are permissible but these should be governed by fusion and fission, regularly decomposing and reforming with new elements; lengthy dyadic conversations at a gathering of ten or twenty people are discouraged; (3) unimportance; i.e., the content of conversations should be restricted to trivial matters, things that can always be kept "external," items that do not reflect directly on either the speaker's or listener's inner life. The most fruitful items for conversation are sports, stocks and bonds and technical subjects, for all of these can be kept "outside" the inner domain of individual personhood and every speaker can be fairly confident that he is not likely to be importuned or embarrassed.[54]

Further exemplification of Nisei emotional management is seen in their handling of the erotic and their emphasis on form over function. The erotic is everywhere emotionally exciting and thus is a source of potential emotional discomfiture to Nisei. Two examples--that of wedding receptions and pornographic movies--illustrate modes of mitigation and neutralization of the erotic.

One "survival" of the rural customs of Japan among current Nisei is the employment of a "master of ceremonies" at wedding receptions. Originally, this role was usually enacted by the baishakunin,[55] but among Nisei a good friend of the groom is often requested to assume this post. At the banquet or reception following the wedding, the master of ceremonies formally introduces the bride and groom and their families to the assembled company, presents one or several toasts to the newly-wed couple, calls people out of the audience to perform as comedians, storytellers, or singers, and tells jokes, droll anecdotes and humorous incidents about the groom. Now, in the rural prefectures of traditional Japan, this part of the reception was often accompanied by ribald jokes and risque stories.[56] When Issei participate in such a reception, they sometimes introduce humorous obscenities into them. However, Nisei usually instruct their appointed masters of ceremonies to "keep it clean" and to refrain from any drolleries which would "embarrass" bride, groom, or company.

Watching pornographic films constitutes one instance of "watching the unwatchable" since they depict activities usually carried out in private with no audience except the participants. Viewing them is not governed by well-known ubiquitous norms.[57] Pornographic films are typical fare at an American stag party for a groom-to-be and his male friends. When Nisei are watching such films two kinds of response are prevalent. On the one hand, jibes and catcalls will tease one or another of the assembled company about his excessive interest in the films, alleged similarities or dissimilarities in his behavior and that depicted on the screen, or his remarkable quietness in the presence of an obviously stimulating event. On the other hand, it sometimes happens that a Nisei will verbally transform the meaning of the activities on the screen, emphasizing their form irrespective of content. Thus, the nude bodies copulating on the movie screen can be treated in terms of their physical anatomy, aesthetic quality or gymnastic innovation.

Emphasis on form over and against content is not only a protective device against possible emotional disturbance in the presence of the erotic, but also a generally utilized mechanism in the presence of anticipated or actual performance failure. Thus, Nisei golfers and bowlers who are performing poorly, or who believe they will do so, may justify their bad scores by pointing out that they are working on their stance, body form, follow-through, etc. Since it is widely accepted that form and content are analytically separable but related aspects of a variety of activities, the claim to be emphasizing the former irrespective of the latter is an acceptable account.[58] Moreover, it prevents any effective referral of the poor scores to the inner or actual state of the performer. Thus, inner equanimity may be maintained and outer calmness may be exhibited even in the presence of apparently contradictory evidence.

SOCIAL AND PERSONAL CONTROLS

The ideal Nisei is one who has mastered the art of personal control. This requires management of body, mind and feelings.[59] If these are properly under control the outward appearance is that of a calm, collected, blasé sophisticate.[60] This state is rarely reached in fact, but Nisei have mechanisms of impression management and mutual monitoring that keep any appearance approximating the ideal from being damaged too much by emotional breakdowns. Among these mechanisms are face controls, dissimulation and avoidance.

The face, as Simmel observed long ago,[61] is the most significant communicator of the inner man. This is especially true of the eyes, nostrils and mouth and the color exhibited by the face.[62] For Nisei the face is a most vulnerable object in any interpersonal encounter, for its uncontrolled expression, if met by the searching gaze of another, may lock them into a consociative relationship from which extrication would be both difficult and embarrassing. Nisei faces tend to be "set" at the expressionless level or at least to strive after that effect. This is achieved more easily in America perhaps because of the stereotypical interpretation of Japanese faces by Caucasians and Negroes, and because of the epicanthic eye fold and smooth skin face make face "readings" difficult. However, some Nisei are disturbed over their vulnerability to facial disclosure; they avoid facing others for any length of time or erect barriers and involvement shields against another's gaze.[63] Newspapers and magazines provide objects for scanning during a conversation, and, although too close attention to these might be considered rude, a deft employment of them will serve to reduce eye contact. Finally, the fact that Nisei share a common concern over face management facilitates a mutual avoidance of staring or fixed gaze, and a tendency to avert one's eyes.

Dissimulation is a regular feature of everyday life among Nisei. Its most elementary form is the self-imposed limitation on disclosure. Nisei tend not to volunteer any more information about themselves than they have to. Thus, to a listener, a Nisei's autobiographical statements appear as a series of incompletely presented episodes, separated by voids which are not filled in with events or information unless it is unavoidable.

Beyond silence about much of personal life is the half-truth or "little white lie" which bridges the gap between information requested and personhood protected. Thus, Nisei will sometimes not tell about an important event, or will casually dismiss it with a denial or only a partial admission, suggesting by style and tone that it was not important at all. Direct questions are usually answered with vague or mildly meretricious replies.[64] Still another element of dissimulation is concealment of feelings, opinions or activities, especially in the presence of employers, colleagues and guests. As Nisei have been promoted into middle-management and other decision-making posts, their colleagues and superiors have sometimes been astonished at their silence during conferences or executive meetings. And, as with the Javanese practice of etok-etok (pretense),[65] the Nisei do not feel the need to justify these omissions, "white lies" or evasions; rather, the burden would appear to be on the listener to demonstrate why such tact and tactics should not be employed.[66]

Nisei attempt to avoid those persons and situations that are likely to evoke embarrassment, personal disorganization and loss of self-control. When a new line of endeavor is undertaken, especially if it requires learning a new skill or taking a risk, it is usually entered into in secret or with those persons whom the Nisei does not know well or wish to know. After it has been mastered, or after the risk has been evaluated as worthwhile, or sometimes after the endeavor has already begun, the Nisei will inform his close associates in a casual manner that he thinks he might be about to undertake the line of action in question. To fellow Nisei this will be understood not as a probablistic statement, but as an absolute one, and they will further understand that all preparations, rehearsals and calculations have already been made. Later, if his associates see a performance of the new skill, they remain silently aware that it is in fact an exhibition of an already perfected ability.

Persons who are importunate, who demand too much display of interpersonal commitment, or who violate norms of emotional propriety are an ever-present threat to the cathectic equanimity of a Nisei. A concept usually employed with respect to Japanese child-rearing practices is relevant here.[67] Japanese speak of amaeru, an intransitive verb by which they mean "to depend and presume upon another's benevolence." Not only children but adults suffer from too much amae, and their behavior toward those whom they wish to express affection toward them is regarded as overly demanding and excessive. A person suffering from too much amae feels himself to be kodawaru; i.e., he feels inwardly distrubed over his personal relationships. A recognition of one's own feeling of kodawari leads to sumunai, guilt over one's failure to do as one should. Behind many Japanese people's feeling of sumunai, as Professor Doi has pointed out, lies "much hidden aggression engendered by frustration of their wish to amaeru."[68] Nisei do not employ this terminology generally, but several studies have pointed to a complex of dependency needs and consequent personal difficulties in Nisei individuals, needs which have their roots in the wish to be loved, and the guilt over this wish or the shame over its expression.[69]

For Nisei, the entire complex of amae-kodawari-sumunai is rarely admitted to be a personal problem; rather it is most frequently perceived to be a problem in another's interpersonal relations. When a Nisei recognizes a close associate's excessive amae toward him, he may become upset by this fact, retreat even further behind a formal facade of etiquette and attempt to establish greater social distance. Or he might hope, or even clandestinely request, that a third party, recognizing the difficulty between the two friends, tactfully explain the problem to the defalcating party and urge upon him an approach to his friend which is less demanding and less obviously a display of excessive amaeru. Still another alternative is to gently but firmly tease the offending party until he realizes that he has overstepped the bounds of propriety. Finally, another tactic is to make sure that all contacts with the offending party will take place with other friends present, so that his excessive affection will be "diffused" among the whole body of friends rather than centered on just one person.[70]

BUILDING NISEI CHARACTER

There can be little doubt that the fundamental source of Nisei character is to be found in the samurai ethic which developed from the Tokugawa through the Meiji Eras (c. 1601-1912). Nisei find representative expression of this ethic in the brilliant epic films made in Japan to celebrate the feats and character of warriors of that period.[71] At one time shown in basements and church social halls in Nihonmachi (the Japanese quarter of the city), these movies are now known to many non-Japanese Americans because of their general popularity when exhibited at public theaters. Chambara (samurai) stories always emphasize the stoic character of the solitary and often tragic warrior who, though beaten about on every side by personal or clan enemies, political misfortunes and natural disasters, nevertheless retains an outward appearance suggesting inner psychic strength and emotional equanimity.[72] Such characters--poignantly portrayed on the screen in recent years by such actors as Toshiro Mifune and Tatsuya Nakadai--serve as ideal character models and reminders of the appropriate presentation of self.

The patterns of hierarchical society, rigid formalism, etiquette and shame were routinized features of the early life of the Issei, who grew up in a time of great technological and political--but little ethical or interpersonal--change in Japan.[73] The modernization of Japan, actually begun in the Tokugawa Period, was achieved not by overturning the old cultural order but rather by adapting western industrial, educational and military forms to the framework of that order. "Within this general context," writes Reinhard Bendix, "the samurai were transformed from an estate of independent landed, and self-equipped warriors into one of urbanized, aristocratic retainers, whose privileged social and economic position was universally acknowledged. They remained attached to their tradition of ceremonious conduct, intense pride of rank and the cultivation of physical prowess."[74] The educational system fostered not only study of classics and, later, the more technical subjects, but also, and more importantly, directed its major attention to the development of virtue, humble modesty before superiors, self-control and etiquette.[75] Thus, the Issei bore the cultural marks which had been part of the Japanese tradition for at least two centuries.

Few of the Issei were of samurai rank,[76] but in the two hundred years before emigration began, a complex melding process had helped to "nationalize" the samurai ethic and remove it from encapsulation within a single status group. First, after 1601 many samurai became displaced ronin (masterless warriors) obliged to sell their services to other lords, to cities as policemen or magistrates, even to commoners on occasion or, as a last resort short of suicide, they felt compelled to give up official samurai status entirely and become merchants.[77] All of these acts caused a certain filtering of the samurai ethic through the social order. Second, the educational system founded in the Tokugawa period, and universalized in 1873, though undecided about whether heredity or merit was more conducive to learning, admitted increasing numbers of commoners to the schools, thus affording them direct access to samurai indoctrination.[78] Third, samurai status itself was muddied by the practice, begun after 1700, of selling the right to wear a sword and bear a surname (i.e., the status symbols of samurai) to commoners.[79] Finally, it would appear that a significant portion of America's Issei came from prefectures in southeastern, central and western Japan, prefectures in which the "democratization" of "ethical" education had been well advanced at the time of emigration.[80]

In addition to the samurai ethic, elements of the rural farmer's outlook also helped forge the orientation with which the Issei reared their children. The ie system, by which Japanese farmers represented both the contemporary physical house and the permanent family household, operated through this notion of preservation and continuity to forestall the development of individualism.[81] In Japan's rural villages the honke-bunke (stem-branch family system) allowed nuclear families to split off from one another in a partial sense, so that nothing like the extended Chinese clan system developed,[82] but atomization below the ie, or household, level was strongly discouraged. Village people spoke of the iegara, or kakaku; i.e., the "reputation" or "standing" of a family, rather than the hitogara or jinkaku, the "personality" or social "standing" of individuals. The ie "was also far more important than the individuals who at any one time composed it, and hence if 'for the sake of the ie' the personal wishes and desires of those individuals had to be ignored or sacrificed, this was looked on as only natural."[83] The ie "required its members each to keep their proper place under the authoritarian direction of the househead, resigning themselves to the suppression of personal desires unbecoming to their position. Thus, was order within the ie preserved and its harmony guaranteed-- a harmony not of liberated cheerfulness, but of smouldering reserve and the frustration of still incompletely repressed desires."[84]

In America the Issei men, often married by proxy to women whom they had only seen in pictures (shashin kekkon) and who were sometimes quite a bit younger than they,[85] applied the principles of late Tokugawa-early Meiji child rearing to their Nisei offspring. In certain respects--notably for the Issei, the lack of Japan's bath houses and geisha for outlet; for the Nisei, in the inhibitions on physical expression and open sensuality, and because of the absence of an indulgent grandmother to assuage the harshness of parental authority--child rearing was more harsh than in Japan.[86] Physical punishments were rarely used, although the moxa treatment was sometimes practiced by Issei parents not only for punishment and and moral training, but also as a curative.[87] In one instance known to the author, an Okinawan Nisei reported that his father purposely cut his ears when giving him a haircut. When the boy screamed in pain, his father would slap him across the face with stern admonition: "You don't scream. Japanese boys do not scream." However, resort to physical punishment is rare among Issei-Nisei families. Much more likely is the use of ridicule and teasing.

Several reports on Japanese child rearing have emphasized the role of ridicule.[88] Among these is the common theme of teasing a recalcitrant, noisy, emotionally upset or otherwise obstreporous boy about behaving like a little girl. That a young man should be ashamed of his emotional expressions because they remind him of behavior associated with women is a frequent theme in Japanese biographies.[89] Nisei boys were also reprimanded by their parents for acting like little girls.[90] In addition, they were reminded that they were Japanese and therefore obligated to avoid arai (crudeness); to speak "good" Japanese and not zuzu (the dialect characteristic of northern Japan);[91] and to avoid any association with or even mention of Eta (Japan's pariah caste, some of whose members had unobtrusively settled in Florin, California, and a few other places).[92]

Moreover, emphasis was placed on individual superiority, achievement and education as a criteria for both individual and group maturity.[93] Thus, Nisei children were not invited to discuss family matters at the dinner table, but rather were instructed to withdraw from participation until age and achievement had demonstrated their worth. Nisei children and adolescents were admonished with the statement, Nisei wa mada tsumaranai; that is, they were told that the Nisei generation was still worthless. Until manhood had been achieved, a manhood indicated not merely by coming of age but, far more importantly, demonstrated by independent status achieved through steadfastness, determination and single-minded purposefulness, the Nisei were treated as immature but developing children.

Central to the demonstration of maturity among growing Nisei was self-control. Although independence and real achievement could not be actually demonstrated until adulthood, emotional management was always worthy of exhibition and often tested for its own sake. Issei tended to be oriented toward their children in terms of the latter's position in the birth order and their sex.[94] A line of direct authority extended down from the father through the mother to the first-born, second-born, third-born and so on. A line of obligation extended upward from the youngest to the eldest. The authority system was not infrequently tested by an elder brother harshly rebuking his younger brother, sometimes for no apparent reason. Younger brothers learned that if they could "take" these rebukes with an outwardly calm detachment, they would ultimately be rewarded with a recognition of the "maturity." Firstborn sons received similar treatment from their fathers, and daughters sometimes found that they had to live up to both the precepts of manhood maturity and womanliness.[95] Brothers who threw tantrums or gave way to violent emotional expression were regarded as "immature" and were teased or otherwise maneuvered into conformative cathectic quiescence.

In the case of the Nisei, teasing and ridicule are characteristic not only of parent-child discipline but also of intra-group relations. They function to monitor behavior. Among Nisei, peer groups begin to share authority over the individual with parents with the onset of adolescence, and they begin to supersede parental authority, though not parental respect, in late adolescence and early manhood. No one who has not been intimately associated with adolescent second generation Japanese groups can testify adequately to the remarkable, pervasive atmosphere and social effect of ridicule among Nisei teenagers. A veritable barrage of "cuts," "digs," "put-downs" and embarrassing stories are the stuff of verbal life. Moreover, as if a survival of the cultural collective unconscious,[96] Nisei youth, like their Japanese forebears across the sea, have a facility and interest in the organization of clubs, cliques and gangs.[97] These associations are the units through which Nisei character is manifested, sustained and reinforced.

Nisei teasing is not randomly directed. Targets for the verbal "cuts" are those fellow Nisei and other close friends who exhibit outward signs of tension, embarrassment, excessive emotional display or boisterousness. Persons who blush, tremble, give way to tears or raise their voices too often in anger or too much for emphasis are the "victims" and recipients of jibes and cajolery designed to bring them back into line. Many Nisei are self-consciously aware of the didactic purpose of this teasing, and regular "victims" have on occasion reported to me their heartfelt gratefulness for it.

In addition to its teaching and control functions, two other "rules" appear to govern Nisei teasing. First, the status position of any particular Nisei vis-a-vis his fellow Nisei may render him ineligible or preferable for teasing. For instance, in the joking relationship there is a tendency for Nisei whose parents hail from peasant and poor prefectures not to tease those whose parents are from urban and socio-economically better-off areas; for Nisei from rural parts of California to be somewhat awed by those from San Francisco or Los Angeles; and for clique leaders to be less eligible for "cuts" than ordinary members. The "inferior" statuses are themselves the butt of jokes which earmark offensive behavior and gauche ways as stemming from poor, peasant and rural origins. Thus, Nisei whose parents came from Shiga, Kagoshima and a few other prefectures, and those whose parents are from Okinawa and Hokkaido, are often teased mercilessly about their culturally acquired agrestic characters, or are perceived as persons incapable of realizing the Nisei characterological ideal. More mild in form, but no less felt, are the ridicule and humor directed at Nisei from rural America by their urban compatriots. An informal avoidance and segregation sometimes set boundaries between Nisei of different status groups and prevents confrontations that would be mutually embarrassing.[98]

The second so-called "rule" governing teasing centers on that Nisei ridicule and joking which must steer a careful course between the Scylla of ineffectiveness and the Charybdis of associative break-up. If jokes and "cuts" are too mild, too obscure, usually misunderstood or always mitigated by apologies and explanations, then the intended objective is frustrated and the defalcating party is not brought to heel. If, on the other hand, the jokes are too damning, too pointed, if they cut to the very heart of a person and leave him no room to maneuver or retreat, then the defalcating party may withdraw from the group in unredeeming shame or anger and be lost, perhaps forever, to its benefits and protections. To indicate that a person has gone too far in his teasing, a Nisei "target" may warn him of his offense by directing a telling remark at a third party in earshot of the two. Thus, watching two youthful Nisei friends of mine escalate their reciprocal "cuts," I became the third party in such a situation. The offended party turned to me and said, "Man, he's a chilly dude, isn't he?" The warned person recognized the rebuke for what it was and proceeded to deescalate his humorous assaults on the other. And so the appropriate relationship--not too close, not too distant--was maintained.

The characterological ideal of any Nisei is best realized when others do not know his emotional state. To achieve this, he must, as one Nisei put it to me, build a wall around his emotions so that others cannot see what they are. Their "authoritarian" upbringing on the one hand, and the "samurai" code of stoicism and endurance on the other, helped them to construct this social and psychic edifice. The functions of this wall have been described by Beertz in his study of Java where he found an identical ideal: "If one can calm one's most inward feelings...one can build a wall around them; one will be able both to conceal them from others and to protect them from outside disturbance. The refinement of inner feeling has thus two aspects: the direct internal attempt to control one's emotions...; and secondly, an external attempt to build a (wall) around them that will protect them. On the one hand, one engages in inward discipline, and on the other in an outward defense."[99] However, while this impregnable "wall" is the ultimately desired objective, most <u>Nisei</u> point out that few can fully attain it.

The character displayed or aimed at by <u>Nisei</u> in everyday life is not unfamiliar to other Americans. Indeed, while at one time it was thought to be the unique trait of aristocrats, Orientals and urbanites, mature industrial societies seem to require it of everyone today.[100] Ordinary men describe it by such adjectives as "blasé," "sophisticated" and, in more recent time, "cool." Other related terms describing aspects of this character are "self-possessed," "detached," "aloof," "sang-froid" and "savoir-faire." What is referred to is the "capacity to execute physical acts, including conversation, in a concerted, smooth, self-controlled fashion in risky situations, or (the capacity) to maintain affective detachment during the course of encounters involving considerable emotion."[101] Ideally for the <u>Nisei</u>, this means combining courage, a willingness to proceed on a course of action anticipated to be dangerous without any manifestations of fear; gameness, sticking to a line of action despite set-backs, injury, fatigue and even impending failure (<u>Yamato damashii</u>);[102] and integrity, the resistance of temptations which would reduce the actor's moral stance. Finally, <u>Nisei</u> character places its greatest emphasis on composure, including all its ramifications of physical and mental poise during any act, calmness in the face of disruptions and embarrassing situations, presence of mind and the avoidance of "blocking" under pressure, emotional control during sudden changes of situation, and stage confidence during performances before audiences.[103]

As has been intimated, <u>Nisei</u> find it difficult to live up to this ideal. However, there are strategies and tactics whereby its appearance can be generated and its failures avoided or hidden. Thus, courage is balanced by a realistic appraisal of risks and opportunities. Studies of <u>Nisei</u> estimates of first salaries, for example, show that they almost almost always guessed the salary to the nearest dollar,[104] suggesting perhaps a procedure whereby face could be protected from the loss it would suffer by a rejection of an incorrect estimate of self-worth. Gameness is partially mitigated by choosing lines of action--such as jobs, sports, games, etc.--in which one has secretly tested oneself for potentiality and ability. Violations of absolute integrity are neutralized by the practice of situation ethics and the invocation of a layman's version of the international legal principle <u>rebus sic stantibus</u>. Composure, as has been mentioned, is guarded by self-discipline, protected by barriers and involvement shields, and tested and supported by teasing and ridicule. Finally, disasters and misfortunes, either personal or collective, may be accepted with equanimity by assigning them to fate (or as the Japanese would say, shikata-ganai[105]).

CONSEQUENCES OF NISEI CHARACTER

The everyday practice of the <u>Nisei</u> way of life has certain consequences which both reflect its essential nature and react back upon <u>Nisei</u> as sources of pride or problems. These consequences may be discussed under the headings of perception and projection, communication confusion, stage fright and real and imagined illnesses.

In everyday discussions with <u>Nisei</u> any non-<u>Nisei</u> listener would be impressed by their pointed perceptions and shrewd observations of others. These perceptions and observations are made about absent third parties and are never uttered in the presence of the party under discussion. Many people would be surprised at how keenly quite ordinary <u>Nisei</u> have paid attention to the minute details of interpersonal situations, placed brackets around particular sets of events, and interpreted words and gestures in light of the general "theory" of <u>Nisei</u> character. Most <u>Nisei</u> analyses of fellow <u>Nisei</u> concentrate on the degree to which the latter fail to carry off the appropriate presentation of self and attribute any failings to some inner-lying maladaptation or maladjustment. Parlor "Freudianism" is quite common in these analyses, and one <u>Nisei</u> may speak of another in terms of the latter's essential inability to mask his "inferiority complex," "fear of failure" or "feelings of inadequacy."

It is my impression that these "perceptions" are in fact "projections." <u>Nisei</u> tend to function as one another's mirror images, showing up the defects in each other's character. This is possible because the "wall" which <u>Nisei</u> have built to prevent others from seeing their own emotions is actually only a set of personal blinders keeping the individual from introspection. To put it another way, the <u>Nisei</u> have attempted to separate personal feeling from particular action and in doing so have "alienated" their emotional from their behaving selves.[106] This "alienation" gives

Nisei the peculiar advantage of self-detachment and an angular vision of their fellow men not shared by those not so detached from self. But the angle of perceptive advantage, reinforced by the similarity of life styles among Nisei results, as I see it, in the imputation to others of the perceiver's own partly recognized failings. Thus, their common life and general self-alienation permit projections and perceptions to coincide without the latter necessarily being seen as having derived from the former.

Nisei character is an ideal which few Nisei in fact ever feel they have achieved. In trying to live up to the ideal, many Nisei find they are confused or are confusing to others. These confusions occur over mutual misreadings of intentions or meanings, misunderstandings of jokes and ridicule and problems arising out of the episodic nature of Nisei life. Because tonal cues are not used as indicators of significance, Nisei sometimes fail to grasp the relevant item in a conversation; more often their non-Nisei colleagues or friends miss the important point and fail to act appropriately. Since Nisei often take it for granted that those with whom they converse will automatically understand them and will be able to separate the chaff from the wheat of their speech, they are frustrated and exasperated when this fails to happen.[107]

Mention has already been made of the role of jokes and ridicule in Nisei social control. Despite their importance, or perhaps because of it, these "cuts" and "digs" create problems. Discussing the problem of what a humorous jibe at another Nisei really means, a Nisei friend and I distinguished analytically three kinds of barbs: (1) those that are given just in fun; i.e, "pure" humor having neither intent nor consequences beyond the ensuing laughter; (2) those that are didactic, i.e., having as their objective the redirection of another's behavior so that it is no longer embarrassing or inept; and (3) those that are intentionally destructive having as their object another's degradation.

Nisei tend to disbelieve that many jokes can have no object at all, preferring instead to believe that some intent must lie behind the ostensibly humorous utterance. However, they experience difficulty in ascertaining whether a jibe is didactic or destructive, because, in fact, the line between them is difficult to draw. Witty repartee is a well-developed and highly prized art among Nisei, but precisely because skill at it is differentially distributed, no Nisei can feel entirely comfortable in an encounter.

Beyond adolescence, Nisei occasionally confess discomfiture about being permanently locked into a system of competitive relations with fellow Nisei. Social visits are occasions for the reciprocal giving and receiving of humorous remarks calling attention to invidious distinctions. Birth, sex and growth of children, richness and style of furniture, occupational advancement, skill at leisure time activities and many other everyday things may become grist for the wit's mill. Indeed, a young Nisei told the author that one reason Nisei oppose the continuation of the Japanese residential ghetto is that they "just know" that they would be constantly "looking in each other's windows."

Nisei encounters with friends and colleagues tend to be episodic rather than developmental. Non-Nisei, however, usually assume a developmental sequence to be the operative norm in continued interactions. Thus, among non-Nisei Americans a sequence of social encounters usually proceeds upon the assumption that each new encounter will begin at the emotional level or feeling-state reached at the end of the last meeting. Among Nisei, however, there is a limit to expressed feeling-states that is quickly reached and may not be deepened without loss of inner equanimity or outer poise. Hence, Nisei tend to treat each encounter almost as if the participants were meeting for the first time. This permits the limited range of feeling-states to be reached again each time but not transcended. For those content with a permanently established line beyond which interpersonal relations may not go, this pattern may go unnoticed. However, those who expect that each new encounter will bring increased "depth," or those who expect to open any "second" encounter with a Nisei with a reciprocated expression of the warmth typical of Occidental friendships, may be startled or exasperated by an apparent coldness of response. Episodic encounters function to keep potentially consociative relationships at the contemporaneous level, and thus, to protect the integrity of the Nisei group.

Unlike many middle-class Occidentals in America, Nisei are more conscious on display, so to speak, before a hyper-critical audience. "A simile is useful in pointing up the similarities and differences between Japanese America and white middle-class achievement orientations: the ultimate destinations or goals of individuals in the two groups tend to be very similar; but Japanese Americans go toward these destinations along straight, narrow streets lined with crowds of people who observe their every step, while middle class persons go toward the same destinations along wider streets having more room for maneuvering, and line only with small groups of people who, while watching them, do not observe their every movement."[108]

People who believe that their every move is under scrutiny are liable to suffer from "stage fright."[109] In the case of Nisei this would appear to be an inevitable consequence of their need to exhibit an appearance of poise and equanimity in the face of a constantly intrusive and challenging world. Moreover, the exhibition of "stage fright" is itself a flaw in Nisei character management and must be avoided if the illusion of composure is to be maintained. Among Nisei one finds a fear-- usually mild, occasionally quite intense-- that an encounter will be spoiled by a collapse of formality and a revelation of the actual personality hidden behind the facade of etiquette. Nevertheless, Nisei lend support to the belief system that generates this fear by observing in quite ordinary conversations, and insisting in their reprimands given to fellow Nisei, that the entire community is watching them, and that they must, therefore, behave with circumspection.[110]

It sometimes occurs that ceremony and etiquette collapse and Nisei find themselves locked in the mutually embarrassing relationship of consociates. More often this happens to one party who during an encounter is, for some reason, unable to sustain appropriate emotional equipoise. When this does occur, the other parties present will try to repair the psychic bridge which has kept them at the proper social distance from one another by studied non-observation of the other's embarrassment, by aversion of the eyes from the other's discomfiture in order to allow the latter time to repair his social front, or by a warm but unmistakably triumphant grin which simultaneously signals a "victory" in the ever-played "game" of social testing and also the social reinstatement of the "losing" player. Social life for Nisei is a contest something like tennis: a single faux pas is a "game" victory; an evening full of them may be a "set," but it takes an entire lifetime to play out the "match."

Many observers have pointed to the noticeable hypochondria in the Japanese character,[111] and at least one has stated that it indicates a remarkably compulsive personality.[112] It is questionable whether, or to what extent, hypochondria is a feature of Nisei life; for a sociologist the very question raises problems for which an unambiguous answer is difficult if not impossible.[113] Disease, or the outward signs of disease, threatens the equanimity so cherished by Nisei. On the other hand, admission that one has a disease is also potentially damaging. In traditional Japan a history of disease in a family was sufficient reason to cancel a marriage, and it was the task of the nakyo-do to discover if such a history existed.[114] Shame over illness is found to some degree among doctors to have their symptoms analyzed. Instead, they rely on Nisei pharmacist friends and colleagues, of whom in California there are a great many, to diagnose their symptoms and prescribe a remedy or a relief. Seeing a Nisei pharmacist friend is not too threatening apparently since it keeps the information localized and requires far less elaborate explanation by either "patient" or pharmacist than would or might be required by a physician. The suffering Nisei need only hint at his ailment, and the pharmacist, who may suffer from the same problem, will know what not to say and what medecine to prescribe. By eliminating the "middle man"--in this case, the physician--the Nisei sufferer preserves his poise while at the same time protecting his health. Moreover, he avoids that source of potentially embarrassing or frustrating information, the doctor or psychiatrist, who might show him that his pain and discomfort arise directly out of the unresolved problems created by his subcultural outlook. That ultimate revelation might be too much to bear; one logical conclusion to be drawn from it is that abandonnment of the Nisei way of life is the price for permanent relief rom pain.

THE CRISIS OF THE FUTURE

The geogenerational conception of time and person which predominates in Nisei life evokes the recognition that any generation with Nisei and extends also, with numerous individual variations, of course, to cover any involuntary loss of control over body stasis such as occurs when vomiting or in a state of intoxication. A Nisei is vulnerable to "attacks" from his body, which enjoys for him something of the sociological status of the stranger as conceived by Simmel:[115] It is ever with him but is mysterious and not quite subject to perfect control.

It is my impression that the Nisei suffer from an unusual amount of that kind of psychosomatic disease--ulcers, colitis, psoriasis, falling hair, etc.--which results from permanent unresolved tensions.[116] That the tensions are real should be clear not only from what I have written thus far, but also from the findings of clinical studies.[117] Proof of the actual existence of these diseases is more difficult to obtain, not only because of the desire on the part of Nisei to conceal and deemphasize the sickness in themselves, but also because of the structural arrangements in current America which aid them in their efforts. Many of my Nisei friends have informed me of the abdominal pains from which they silently suffer. Others are startled and ashamed of their seemingly incurable mottled finger nails or falling hair. Few Nisei, however, visit

its attendant character structure will eventually decline and pass away. Although the Issei generatiom has by no means passed out of existence, its influence began to decline after 1942 when the enforced incarceration of all persons of Japanese ancestry propelled the Nisei into positions of prison camp and community leadership.[118] At the present time, as the Sansei generation comes to maturity and establishes its independent existence and special group identity in America, the Nisei group is beginning to sense its own decline and eventual disappearance.

The Nisei can clearly see the end of their generational existence in the not too distant future. The census of 1960 reported that 82% of all Japanese in thirteen western states were born in the United States, its territories or possessions; in other words, a little more than eight-tenths of the persons of Japanese descent in that area are Nisei, Kibei, Sansei, Yonsei and Gosei. The manner of taking the census prohibits any further breakdown of these figures into respective geogenerational groupings. However, by looking at age distribution, we can arrive at a crude approximation. In California, where 159,545 persons of Japanese descent live, the 1960 census recorded 68,015 of these between the ages of zero and twenty-four. Most of these are the children, grandchildren or occasionally great-grandchildren of Nisei, and thus will soon equal and then outstrip the latter in number.

The inevitable end of the Nisei group has provoked a mild crisis in the Lebenswelt ("life-world") of the Nisei.[119] Nisei are coming to realize with a mixture of anxiety, discomfort and disillusion--but primarily with a sense of fatalistic resignation--that the way of life to which they are used, the presentation of self which they have always taken for granted, the arts of self-preservation and impression management which they have so assiduously cultivated and so highly prized, will soon no longer be regular features of everyday existence among the Japanese in America. Thus, Nisei perceive that what has been a valid way of living for so many years will not continue to be so, and that what they have accomplished by living this way will no longer be accomplished this way or perhaps at all. The Sansei and, for that matter, the other successor generations will be different from the Nisei in certain fundamental respects. Moreover, some of these respects are viewed with considerable misgivings by contemporary Nisei.

Nisei have always seemed to recognize the socio-cultural and psychic differences between themselves and the Sansei. Some of these differences are based on clearly distinguishable generational experiences.

Few of the Sansei are old enough to remember or have experienced the terrible effects of imprisonment during World War II; most Sansei have not grown up in homes marked by a noticeable cultural division between America and Japan; most Sansei have benefitted from the relative material success of their parents and have received parental support for their educational pursuits without difficulty; finally, few Sansei have borne the oppressive burden of racial discrimination or felt the demoralizing agony of anti-Japanese prejudice. In all these respects Nisei recognize that the Sansei are the beneficiaries of Issei and Nisei struggles and perseverance, and they acknowledge that if, because of these things, the Sansei do behave differently than an immigrant or oppressed people, then it is only right and proper for them to do so.

There is one aspect of Sansei behavior, however, that worries and disappoints Nisei: It is their lack of appropriate (that is, Nisei) character. Some Nisei see this characterological loss as a product of increased urbanization and Americanization; others emphasize the loss of Japanese "culture" among the third generation. Whatever the explanation, many Nisei perceive a definite and irremediable loss of character in their successor generation. To illustrate this point, note that Nisei often use the term Sansei to indicate at one and the same time the existence and cause of social impropriety. Thus, in the face of an individual's continued social errors in my presence, a Nisei explained to me, "What can you expect? He's a Sansei."

Ironically, Nisei child-rearing and parental practices contribute to the creation of the very Sansei character that disappoints them, just as their own Issei parents helped to lay the groundwork for Nisei character.[120] Despite the great general respect and personal deference which the Nisei pay to their parents, they tend to see them as negative role models when it comes to rearing their own children. The isolation, loneliness, harshness and language and communication difficulties of their own childhoods are vividly recalled, and a great many Nisei have vowed that their children will not experience any of that. As a result, the ethics of samurai stoicism and endurance and the discipline associated with them are rarely emphasized by Nisei parents. Rather, they choose to order their child-rearing by following the white middle-class ethos of love, equality, and companionship. The principles of Bushido gave way to those of Dr. Spock; the idea of age-graded obligation is supplanted by the age-cohort theory of Gesell; the social distance that separated parent and child is replaced by the idea that parents and children should "grow up together."

The resultant product of this upbringing is, of course, quite different from that of its parents. Worse, from the point of view of most Nisei, it is a disappointing one. Nisei complain that Sansei seem to lack the drive and initiative which was once a hallmark of the Japanese; that they have no interest in Japanese culture, especially its characterological elements; that they are prone to more delinquency and less respect for authority than were the Nisei; and that they are "provincial" and bound to the "provincialisms" of Los Angeles, perhaps the city that encloses the single largest aggregate of Sansei.[121] Nisei often complain of the lack of psychological self-sufficiency and independent capacity for decision-making among Sansei. Thus, a Nisei scoutmaster pointed out to me how his scout troop, mostly Sansei, became emotionally upset and homesick when away for but a week's camping trip, and how their projected weiner roast would have been ruined if he had not stepped in and directed the planning for food purchases. He attributes these "failings" to their Sansei background, and he admitted that his own intervention in assisting the scouts in their plans was a distinct departure for what his own parents would have done in a similar situation during his childhood. Issei parents, say many Nisei, would probably have "let" their children "fail" in such an endeavor in order to help them cultivate responsibility and initiative. But such a seemingly cold and unfeeling response to their own children is anathema.

Sansei indicate an ambivalence and a mild anxiety over their own situation. They do exhibit a certain "Hansen effect"—that is, a desire to recover selected and specific elements of the culture of old Japan[122]—but in this endeavor itself they discover that their own Americanization has limited the possibility of very effective recovery. If juvenile delinquency among them is on the rise—and the evidence is as yet inconclusive[123]—they attribute it in small part to parental misunderstandings and in greater part to the effects of the great social changes taking place in America. Their parents often appear "old-fashioned" to them, unprepared to understand their "hang-ups" and unwilling to offer sufficient love and understanding to them.[124] Finally, they seem at times to be about to claim the right to dissolve their own geogenerational identity and that of their successor generations in favor of both deeper intimate associations below the level of the generational group and inter-racial intimacies transcending them.[125] Yet, they also wonder how and in what manner they can or should retain their "Japanese" identity.[126]

Unlike many groups, the Nisei do not stand at a crossroads. Their fate is sure and their doom is sealed by the moving hands of the generational clock. They have not merely survived the hatred and oppression of America's racism, they have triumphed over it. In nearly every "objective" measure they outstrip their minority "competitors," and in education they have surpassed the white majority.[127] They have turned almost every adversity into a challenge and met each with courage and cool judgment. In all this their own subcultural character has been an invaluable aid as well as an ever-present source of pride. Now they see the coming of the end of their own generation and of this character, and they can only wonder what psychic supports will provide mental sustenance for future generations. In one sense the Nisei are the last of the Japanese Americans; the Sansei are American Japanese. As Jitsuichi Masuoka observed over two decades ago, "It is the members of the Sansei who, having been fully acculturated but having been excluded by the dominant group because of their racial difference, really succeed in presenting a united front against exclusion by the dominant group. A genuine race problem arises at this point in the history of race relations."[128]

---

[1] Quoted in Lewis Bush, 77 SAMURAI: JAPAN'S FIRST EMBASSY TO AMERICA, Tokyo and Palo Alto, California: Kodansha International, 1968, p. 132. (Based on the original manuscript in Japanese by Itsuro Hattori.) Bush does not give the date of this newspaper article. It would appear to be April 2, 1860 or thereabouts.

[2] The Embassy was not the first visit of Japanese to America. It is probable that a Japanese ship was wrecked off the coast of South America in 3,000 B.C. Betty J. Meggers, Clifford Evans and Emilio Estrada, EARLY FORMATIVE PERIOD OF COASTAL ECUADOR: THE VALDIVIA AND MACHALILLA PHASES, Washington, D.C.: Smithsonian Institution, 1965, pp. 167-178. The Hashikura Embassy arrived in New Spain in 1614 and some of its members remained until 1615, not returning to Japan until 1620. William Lytle Schurtz, THE MANILA GALLEON, New York: E.P. Dutton, 1959, pp. 99-128. Moreover, twenty-four Japanese ships were wrecked off western North America in the period between 1613 and 1850 and some of the survivors resided temporarily among Occidentals. Charles Wolcott Brook, JAPANESE WRECKS STRANDED AND PICKED UP ADRIFT IN THE NORTH PACIFIC OCEAN, Fairfield, Washington. Ye Galleon Press, 1964 (originally published in 1876); Shunzo Sakamaki, "Japan and the

United States, 1790-1853," THE TRANSACTIONS OF THE ASIATIC SOCIETY OF JAPAN, XVIII (1939), Second Series, pp. 3-204. See also J. Feenstra Kuiper, Ph.D., "Some notes on the Foreign Relations of Japan in the Early Napoleonic Period (1798-1805)," Ibid., I (1923-1924) Second Series, pp. 55-82.

[3] Bush, op. cit., p. 132.

[4] See Jacobus ten Broek, Edward N. Barnhart and Floyd Matson, PREJUDICE, WAR AND THE CONSTITUTION, (Japanese American Evacuation and Resettlement, Vol. III), Berkeley: University of California Press, 1954, pp. 11-98.

[5] See Anne Reeploeg Fisher, EXILE OF A RACE, Sidney, British Columbia: Peninsula Printing Co., 1965; Morton Grodzins, AMERICANS BETRAYED: POLITICS AND THE JAPANESE EVACUATION, Chicago: University of Chicago Press, 1949, pp. 1-230, 400-422. For a typical example of the rhetoric of that period see Alan Hynd, BETRAYAL FROM THE EAST: THE INSIDE STORY OF JAPANESE SPIES IN AMERICA, New York: Robert M. McBride & Co., 1943.

[6] Robert E. Park, "Racial Assimilation in Secondary Groups with Special Reference to the Negro," in RACE AND CULTURE, Glencoe: The Free Press, 1950, p. 209. (The Collected Papers of Robert E. Park, Vol. I, edited by Everett C. Hughes, et al.).

[7] Robert E. Park, "Behind Our Masks," SURVEY GRAPHIC LVI (May 1, 1926), p. 137. This essay emphasized its point with photographs of NOH masks on each page.

[8] Fred L. Strodtbeck, "Family Interaction, Values, and Achievement," in Marshall Sklare, (Editor), THE JEWS: SOCIAL PATTERNS OF AN ETHNIC GROUP, New York: The Free Press, 1958, pp. 162-163.

[9] Bernard C. Rosen, "Race, Ethnicity, and the Achievement Syndrome," AMERICAN SOCIOLOGICAL REVIEW, 24 (February, 1959), pp. 47-60.

[10] Chester Rowell, "Chinese and Japanese Immigrants--A Comparison," ANNALS OF THE AMERICAN ACADEMY OF POLITICAL AND SOCIAL SCIENCE, XXIV (September, 1909), pp. 223-230.

[11] Winifred Raushenbush, "Their Place in the Sun," SURVEY GRAPHIC, LVI (May 1, 1926), pp. 141-145.

[12] Rose Hum Lee, THE CHINESE IN THE UNITED STATES OF AMERICA, Hong Kong: Hong Kong University Press, 1960, p. 425.

[13] Leonard Broom and John I. Kitsuse, "The Validation of Acculturation: A Condition of Ethnic Assimilation," AMERICAN ANTHROPOLOGIST LVII (February, 1955), p. 45.

[14] Calvin F. Schmid and Charles E. Nobbe, "Socioeconomic Differentials Among Nonwhite Races," AMERICAN SOCIOLOGICAL REVIEW, 30 (December, 1965), pp. 909-922.

[15] William Caudill and George de Vos, "Achievement, Culture, and Personality: The Case of the Japanese Americans," AMERICAN ANTHROPOLOGIST, 58 (December, 1956), p. 1107.

[16] Ibid, p. 1116.

[17] loc. cit.

[18] Alan Jacobson and Lee Rainwater, "A Study of Management Representative Evaluations of Nisei Workers," SOCIAL FORCES, 32 (March, 1953), pp. 35-41.

[19] See, e.g., Wallace Irwin, LETTERS OF A JAPANESE SCHOOL BOY, New York: Doubleday, Page. 1909, pp. 172-173 et passim.

So powerful was Irwin's caricature of the Japanese that the distinguished Negro novelist and statesman, James Weldon Johnson, felt he could not be sure whether a letter he received from a Japanese student offering to assist in the Negroes' struggle for equality was genuine or a product of Wallace Irwin's mischievous hand. After a conference attended by Chinese and Japanese diplomats, Johnson noted: "I myself reacted differently to these two peoples; the Japanese left me rather cold. Not during the time I was at the Conference did I form cordial relations with warm friendships." James Weldon Johnson, ALONG THIS WAY, New York: Viking, 1968, pp. 399-401.

[20] Stanley M. Elkins, SLAVERY: A PROBLEM IN AMERICAN INSTITUTIONAL AND INTELLECTUAL LIFE, Chicago: University of Chicago Press, 1959, pp. 81-139.

[21] Alfred Schutz, THE PHENOMENOLOGY OF THE SOCIAL WORLD, Evanston: Northwestern University Press, 1967, pp. 139-214 (translated by George Walsh and Frederick Lehnert).

[22] Clifford Geertz, PERSON, TIME AND CONDUCT IN BALI: AN ESSAY IN CULTURAL ANALYSIS, New Haven: Yale University Southeast Asia Studies, Cultural Report Series No. 14, 1966.

[23] William Caudill and Henry A. Scarr, "Japanese Value Orientations and Culture Change," ETHNOLOGY, I (January, 1962), pp. 53-91.

[24] Schutz, op. cit., pp. 142-143, 194-214.

[25] Cf. Edward Norbeck, PINEAPPLE TOWN, HAWAII, Berkeley: University of California Press, 1959, pp. 5, 86-104.

[26] See the interesting discussion in Clyde V. Kiser, "Cultural Pluralism," THE ANNALS OF THE AMERICAN ACADEMY OF POLITICAL AND SOCIAL SCIENCE, 262 (March, 1949), pp. 118-129.

[27] Chinese prefer to distinguish by a common "middle name" all persons born in the same generational cohort of a single lineage, but they do not continue a genealogical measurement of geo-generational distance from China. See Maurice Freedman, CHINESE LINEAGE AND

SOCIETY: FUKIEN AND KWANGTUNG, New York: Humanities Press, 1966, pp. 44-45, 179-180.

[28] The *Kibei* have been the most frequently discussed group among the Japanese Americans because of their socio-cultural marginality and because of their alleged disloyalty to the United States during the Pacific War. See E.K. Strong, Jr., THE SECOND-GENERATION JAPANESE PROBLEM, Stanford: Stanford University Press, 1934; Andrew W. Lind, HAWAII's JAPANESE: AN EXPERIMENT IN DEMOCRACY, Princeton: Princeton University Press, 1946, pp. 33-34, 183-188, 212-213, 245; Carey McWilliams, PREJUDICE: JAPANESE AMERICANS: SYMBOL OF RACIAL INTOLERANCE, Boston: Little, Brown, 1944, pp. 321-322; An Intelligence Officer, "The Japanese in America: The Problem and the Solution," HARPER'S MAGAZINE, 185 (October, 1942), pp. 489-497; "Issei, Nisei, Kibei," FORTUNE, XXIX (April, 1944), pp. 8, 21. 32, 74, 78-79, 94, 106, 118; Bradford Smith, AMERICANS FROM JAPAN, Philadelphia: J.P. Lippincott, 1948, pp. 253-255, 275, 315-321; Dorothy Swaine Thomas and Richard Nishimoto, THE SPOILAGE, (Japanese American Evacuation and Resettlement, Vol. I), Berkeley: University of California Press, 1946, pp. 3, 69, 78-81; Dorothy Swaine Thomas, with the assistance of Charles Kikuchi and James Sakoda, THE SALVAGE, (Japanese American Evacuation and Resettlement, Vol. II), Berkeley: University of California Press, 1952, *passim*; ten Broek, Barnhart, and Matson, *op. cit.*, pp. 142, 177, 275-285; Alan Bosworth, AMERICA'S CONCENTRATION CAMPS, New York: W.W. Norton, 1967, *passim*.

[29] Norbeck, *op. cit.*, p. 94.

[30] For a poignant account of the social and personal adjustment of the daughter of an Irish-American mother and an *Issei* father, see Kathleen Tamagawa, HOLY PRAYERS IN A HORSE'S EAR, New York: Ray Long and Richard R. Smith, 1932.

[31] See Daisuke Kitagawa, ISSEI AND NISEI: THE INTERNMENT YEARS, New York: Seabury Press, pp. 26-31.

[32] The phenomena discussed here are analogous to the issues involved in romantic love and incest on the one hand and group dissolution through loss of function on the other. For perceptive theoretical insights, see Philip Slater, "Social Limitations on Libidinal Withdrawal," AMERICAN JOURNAL OF SOCIOLOGY LXVII (November, 1961), pp. 296-311 and Talcott Parsons, "The Incest Taboo in Relation to Social Structure," BRITISH JOURNAL OF SOCIOLOGY, V (June, 1954), pp. 101-117; Parsons, "The Superego and the Theory of Social Systems," PSYCHIATRY, 15 (February, 1952), pp. 15-25.

[33] Broom and Kitsuse, *op. cit*.

[34] Discussions of this group breakdown through withdrawal or transcendence usually focus on juvenile delinquency, although the issues clearly go beyond this element of behavior. See, e.g. Harry H.L. Kitano, "Japanese-American Crime and Delinquency." JOURNAL OF PSYCHOLOGY 66 (1967), pp. 253-263.

[35] See, e.g. Ruth Benedict, THE CHRYSANTHEMUM AND THE SWORD: PATTERNS OF JAPANESE CULTURE, Boston: Houghton Mifflin, 1946; Nyozekan Hasegawa, THE JAPANESE CHARACTER: A CULTURAL PROFILE, Tokyo: Kodansha International, 1966; Fosco Maraini, MEETING WITH JAPAN, New York: Viking Press, 1960, pp. 22-23, 217-218 (translated by Eric Mosbacher).

[36] Joseph K. Yamagiwa. "Language as an Expression of Japanese Culture," in John W. Hall and Richard K. Beardsley, (Editors), TWELVE DOORS TO JAPAN, New York: McGraw-Hill, 1965, pp. 186-223.

[37] Hajime Nakamura, WAYS OF THINKING OF EASTERN PEOPLES: INDIA-CHINA-TIBET-JAPAN, Honolulu: East-West Center Press, 1964, pp. 409-410 (Edited by Philip P. Wiener).

[38] See Benedict, *op. cit.* pp. 48-49. Professor Shuichi Kato informs me that *gaijin* (i.e. foreigners) will be automatically exempted from the rigid requirements of the Japanese bow. *Nisei* in Japan, however, may suffer loss of face for their lack of knowledge in this area of etiquette, especially if they are not recognized as American-born.

[39] Among *Nisei* I have observed a quick jerk of the head in genuflection before elders, *Issei* and visitors from Japan, but this vestigial bow is far from the careful employment of body idiom required of traditional Japanese.

[40] Among my *Nisei* associates it is widely professed that the Japanese language contains no obscenities, and many *Nisei* utter English scatological phrases softly and under their breath. In contrast, Chinese Americans of the same generation, especially those who speak *Sz Yup* dialect, employ a rich variety of epithets, curses and obscenities.

[41] Clifford Geertz, THE RELIGION OF JAVA, London: Collier-Macmillan, The Free Press of Glencoe, 1960, pp. 241-242.

[42] As a general phenomenon of human behavior, this suspiciousness has been described by Erving Goffman. See THE PRESENTATION OF SELF IN EVERYDAY LIFE, Edinburgh: University of Edinburgh Social Science Research Centre, Monograph No. 2, 1958, pp.1-46.

[43] See Hiroshi Wagatsuma, "The Social Preception of Skin Color in Japan," DAEDALUS 96 (Spring, 1967), pp. 407-443.

[44] Jews had reached China as early as the twelfth century, and the synogogue at K'ai-feng was still standing in 1851. See William Charles White, CHINESE JEWS: A

COMPILATION OF MATTERS RELATING TO THE HEWS OF K'AI-FENG FU, New York: Paragon Book Reprint Corp., 1966 (Second Edition), pp. 9-204. A few Jews came to Japan in the ninth century, and another group in the sixteenth, but it was not until the nineteenth century that the Jewish religion had even a small establishment there. In the early twentieth century Kobe became a center for European Jewish merchants, and this colony was enlarged by refugees from Nazi Germany. See Abraham Kotsuji, FROM TOKYO TO JERUSALEM: THE AUTOBIOGRAPHY OF A JAPANESE CONVERT TO JUDAISM, New York: Bernard Geis, Random House, 1964, pp. 58-59, 159-161. The Nazis had a difficult time converting their Japanese allies to anti-Semitism. Kotsuji, (op. cit., pp. 131-200) provides a personal report of his own activities in behalf of Jews in Manchuria and Japan. See also Norman Cohn, WARRANT FOR GENOCIDE: THE MYTH OF THE JEWISH WORLD CONSPIRACY AND THE PROTOCOLS OF THE ELDERS OF ZION, New York: Harper and Row, 1966, pp. 242-243.

[45] I am indebted to the Rev. Taro Goto and Mr. Nobusuke Fukuda for explaining this term and its origins to me.

[46] George de Vos, "A Quantitative Rorschach Assessment of Maladjustment and Rigidity in Acculturating Japanese American," GENETIC PSYCHOLOGY MONOGRAPHS, 52 (1955) p. 66.

[47] Edward T. Hall, THE HIDDEN DIMENSION, Garden City, Doubleday, 1966, pp. 139-144.

[48] Bernard Rudofsky, THE KIMONO MIND, Garden City: Doubleday, 1965, pp. 159-161.

[49] Japanese, like English, is a language that betrays the speaker's social and regional origins. Japanese Americans, highly conscious of the poor quality of their spoken Japanese and wary lest it betray peasant origins, tend to rely on English whenever possible.

[50] See Ezra Vogel, "The Go-Between in a Developing Society, the Case of the Japanese Marriage Arranger," HUMAN ORGANIZATION, 20 (Fall, 1961), pp. 112-120. For the go-between among Japanese in America, see Shotaro Frank Miyamoto, SOCIAL SOLIDARITY AMONG THE JAPANESE IN SEATTLE, Seattle: University of Washington Publications in the Social Sciences, Vol. II (December, 1939), pp. 87-88; Robert H. Ross and Emory S. Bogardus, "Four Types of Nisei Marriage Patterns," SOCIOLOGY AND SOCIAL RESEARCH, 25 (September, 1940), pp. 63-66; John F. Embree. "Acculturation Among the Japanese of Kona, Hawaii," Memoirs of the American Anthropological Association. Supplement to AMERICAN ANTHROPOLOGIST 43 (1941), pp. 74-77; Toshio Yatsushiro, "The Japanese Americans," in Milton Barron (Editor), AMERICAN MINORITIES, New York: Alfred A. Knopf, 1962, p. 324.

[51] Rudofsky, op. cit., pp. 161-163.

[52] For a discussion of information games, see Stanford M. Lyman and Marvin B. Scott, "Game Frameworks," in SOCIOLOGY OF THE ABSURD, New York: Appleton-Century-Crofts, forthcoming.

[53] For the most perceptive theoretical analysis of social occasions, and one that is applicable to the Japanese American scene, see Georg Simmel, "The Sociology of Sociability," AMERICAN JOURNAL OF SOCIOLOGY, LV (November, 1949), pp. 254-261 (translated by Everett C. Hughes).

[54] Cf. David Riesman, et al. "The Vanishing Host," HUMAN ORGANIZATION, XIX (Spring, 1960), pp. 17-27.

[55] John Embree, THE JAPANESE, Smithsonian Institution War Background Studies Number Seven. Washington, D.C.: Smithsonian Institution, 1943, p. 25.

[56] John Embree, A JAPANESE VILLAGE: SUYE MURA, London: Kegan Paul, Trench, Trubner, 1946, pp. 155-156.

[57] See Lyman and Scott, "Stage Fright and the Problem of Identity," in SOCIOLOGY OF THE ABSURD, op. cit.

[58] See Marvin B. Scott and Stanford M. Lyman, "Accounts," AMERICAN SOCIOLOGICAL REVIEW, 33 (February, 1968), pp. 46-62.

[59] Cf. Edward Gross and Gregory P. Stone, "Embarrassment and the Analysis of Role Requirements," AMERICAN JOURNAL OF SOCIOLOGY, LXX (July, 1964), pp. 6-10; Erving Goffman, "Embarrassment and Social Organization," AMERICAN JOURNAL OF SOCIOLOGY LXII (November, 1956) pp. 264-271; Stanford M. Lyman and Marvin B. Scott, "Coolness in Everyday Life," in Marcello Truzzi (Editor), SOCIOLOGY AND EVERYDAY LIFE, Englewood Cliffs; Prentice-Hall, 1968, pp. 92-101.

[60] Cf. Georg Simmel, "The Metropolis and Mental Life," in THE SOCIOLOGY OF GEORG SIMMEL, Glencoe: The Free Press, 1950, pp. 409-426 (Edited and translated by Kurt Wolff).

[61] George Simmel, "The Aesthetic Significance of the Face," in GEORG SIMMEL, 1858-1918, Columbus: Ohio State University Press, 1959, pp. 276-281)Edited by Kurt H. Wolff).

[62] Georg Simmel, "Sociology of the Senses: Visual Interaction," in Robert E. Park and Ernest W. Burgess, INTRODUCTION TO THE SCIENCE OF SOCIOLOGY, Chicago: University of Chicago Press, 1921, pp. 356-361.

[63] Cf. Erving Goffman, BEHAVIOR IN PUBLIC PLACES: NOTES ON THE SOCIAL ORGANIZATION OF GATHERINGS, London: Collier-Macmillan, the Free Press of Glencoe, 1963, pp. 38, 42.

[64] Cf. Maraini, op. cit., p. 23.

[65] See Jerry Enomoto, "Perspectives: Enryo-Syndrome?" PACIFIC CITIZEN, 64 (June 16, 1967), p. 1; "Perspectives: Enryo," Ibid., 65 (July 7, 1967), p. 1. In 1953 John H. Burma wrote:

> There is evidence that Nisei leaders are not so aggressive and consistent in their leadership roles as are Caucasian leaders. In their thinking Nisei leaders seem very often to be liberal, progressive, or radical, but these attitudes are often not carried over into aggressive action because such behavior will call down censure from the by-no-means impotent Issei, and because of the tradition that no Japanese leader should assert himself too strongly or too often or place himself in the limelight too frequently. Nevertheless, the leader is expected to be able to speak on his own initiative in keeping things running smoothly, and to speak out when Nisei rights are being infringed upon. The problem involved here is that Nisei are likely to be much concerned with "doing the proper thing," meeting requirements placed upon them, and being careful not to do anything which would too much disturb the Japanese community or disrupt the status quo. This tends to penalize initiative and aggressiveness and to slow down the dynamics of leadership as the Caucasian knows it.

"Current Leadership Problems Among Japanese Americans," SOCIOLOGY AND SOCIAL RESEARCH, 37 (January, 1953), p. 162.

[66] Geertz, RELIGION OF JAVA, op. cit., pp. 245-247.

[67] See three essays by L. Takeo Doi, "Japanese Language as an Expression of Japanese Psychology," WESTERN SPEECH, 20 (Spring, 1956), pp. 90-96; "'Amae': A Key Concept for Understanding Japanese Personality Structure," in Robert J. Smith and Richard K. Beardsley (Editors), JAPANESE CULTURE: ITS DEVELOPMENT AND CHARACTERISTICS, Chicago: Aldine, 1962, pp. 132-139; "Giri-Ninjo: An Interpretation," in R. P. Dore (Editor), ASPECTS OF SOCIAL CHANGE IN MODERN JAPAN, Princeton: Princeton University Press, 1967, pp. 327-336.

[68] Doi, "'Amae'. . . " op. cit., p. 133.

[69] See Charlotte E. Babcock and William Caudill, "Personal and Cultural Factors in Treating a Nisei Man," in Georgene Seward (Editor), CLINICAL STUDIES IN CULTURE CONFLICT, New York: Ronald Press, 1958, pp. 409-448; Charlotte E. Babcock, "Reflections on Dependency Phenomena as Seen in Nisei in the United States," in Smith and Beardsley, op. cit., pp. 172-188. See also Katharine Newkirk Handley, "Social Casework and Intercultural Problems," JOURNAL OF SOCIAL CASEWORK, 28 (February, 1947), pp. 43-50; Mamoru Iga, "The Japanese Social Structure and the Source of Mental Strains of Immigrants in the United States," SOCIAL FORCES, 35 (March, 1957), pp. 271-278.

[70] For this last point I am indebted to Hideo Bernard Hata.

[71] See Joseph L. Anderson and Donald Richie, THE JAPANESE FILM, New York: Grove Press, 1960, pp. 63-71, 223-228, 315-331.

[72] Cf. Robert Frager, "The Psychology of the Samurai," PSYCHOLOGY TODAY, 2 (January, 1969), pp. 48-53.

[73] Douglas G. Haring, "Japanese National Character: Cultural Anthropology, Psychoanalysis, and History," in PERSONAL CHARACTER AND CULTURAL MILIEU, Syracuse: Syracuse University Press, 1956 (Third Edition, compiled and edited by Douglas G. Haring), pp. 424-437; George A. De Vos, "Achievement Orientation, Social Self-Identity, and Japanese Economic Growth," ASIAN SURVEY, 5 (December, 1965), pp. 575-589.

[74] Reinhard Bendix, "A Case Study in Cultural and Educational Mobility: Japan and the Protestant Ethic," in Neil J. Smelser and Seymour Martin Lipset (Editors), SOCIAL STRUCTURE AND MOBILITY IN ECONOMIC DEVELOPMENT, Chicago: Aldine, 1966, pp. 266-267.

[75] Herbert Passin, SOCIETY AND EDUCATION IN JAPAN, New York: Bureau of Publications, Teachers College, East Asian Institute, Columbia University, 1965, pp. 149-160; R. P. Dore, EDUCATION IN TOKUGAWA JAPAN, London: Routledge and Kegan Paul, 1965, pp. 124-251.

[76] The early student migration to America was of samurai rank, a fact attested to by their each having two swords. See Charles Lanman, THE JAPANESE IN AMERICA, London: Longmans, Green, Readers, and Dyer, 1872, pp. 67-79. See also Charles F. Thwing, "Japanese and Chinese Students in America," SCRIBNER'S MONTHLY, XX (July, 1880), pp. 450-453; John W. Bennet, Herbert Passin, and Robert K. McKnight, IN SEARCH OF

IDENTITY: THE JAPANESE OVERSEAS SCHOLAR IN AMERICA AND JAPAN, Minneapolis: University of Minnesota Press, 1958, pp. 18-46. Although students, some of whom were of samurai rank, continued to migrate to the United States thereafter, the settler and sojourner immigrants who came after 1880 were largely of peasant, handicraft, and merchant origin. Some of these undoubtedly descended from noble lineage or ronin (masterless warrior) backgrounds. See Hirokichi Mutsu, "A Japanese View of Certain Japanese-American Relations," OVERLAND MONTHLY, 32 (November, 1898), pp. 406-414; Yosaburo Yoshida, "Sources and Causes of Japanese Emigration," ANNALS OF THE AMERICAN ACADEMY OF POLITICAL AND SOCIAL SCIENCE, XXIV (September, 1909), pp. 157-167. The Japanese American History Project now carrying on research at UCLA may produce more data on the social origins of Issei.

[77] George Sansom, A HISTORY OF JAPAN, 1334-1615, Stanford: Stanford University Press, 1961, pp. 333, 398; A HISTORY OF JAPAN, 1615-1867, Stanford: Stanford University Press, 1963, pp. 32-34, 54-58, 79, 92-93, 133-138; JAPAN: A SHORT CULTURAL HISTORY, New York: Appleton-Century-Crofts, 1943 (Revised Edition), pp. 356, 496-498.

[78] Passin, op. cit., pp. 117-121, 177-179, 190, 191, 226-228; Dore, op. cit., pp. 214-251.

[79] George B. Sansom, JAPAN: A SHORT CULTURAL HISTORY, op. cit., pp. 520-521.

[80] Paul T. Takagi, "The Japanese Family in the United States: A Hypothesis on the Social Mobility of the Nisei," Revised version of a paper presented at the annual meeting of the Kroeber Anthropological Society, Berkeley, April 30, 1966.

[81] Tadashi Fukutake, JAPANESE RURAL SOCIETY, Tokyo: Oxford University Press, 1967, pp. 39-59, 212-217 (Translated by R. P. Dore).

[82] Chie Nakanee, KINSHIP AND ECONOMIC ORGANIZATION IN RURAL JAPAN, New York: Humanities Press, 1967, shows a distinct difference between Japanese rural social structure and that of China described in Maurice Freedman, LINEAGE ORGANIZATION IN SOUTH-EASTERN CHINA, London: Athlone Press, 1958, and CHINESE LINEAGE AND SOCIETY: FUKIEN AND KWANGTUNG, op. cit. See also Stanford M. Lyman, "Contrasts in the Community Organization of Chinese and Japanese in North America," CANADIAN REVIEW OF SOCIOLOGY AND ANTHROPOLOGY, 5 (May, 1968), pp. 51-67.

[83] Fukutake, op. cit., p. 40.

[84] Ibid., p. 212. See also Robert J. Smith, "The Japanese Rural Community: Norms, Sanctions, and Ostracism," AMERICAN ANTHROPOLOGUST 63 (June, 1961). Reprinted in Jack M. Potter, et al. (Editors), PEASANT SOCIETY: A READER, Boston: Little, Brown, 1967, pp. 246-255.

[85] Sidney L. Gulick, THE AMERICAN JAPANESE PROBLEM, New York: Charles Scribner's Sons, 1914, pp. 90-96; T. Iyenega and Kenoske Sato, JAPAN AND THE CALIFORNIA PROBLEM, New York: G. P. Putnam's Sons, 1921, pp. 109-119; Thomas, et al., THE SALVAGE, op.cit., pp. 7-8, 10-12. For a poignant account of the meetings between young brides and their older husbands, see Sessue Hayakawa, ZEN SHOWED ME THE WAY. Indianapolis: Bobbs-Merrill, 1960, pp. 84-88. Accounts of the adjustments to proxy marriages may be found in OUR CHRISTIAN TESTIMONY, Loomis, California: First Methodist Church, 1967 (Compiled and translated by Rev. Taro Goto).

[86] See William Caudill, "Japanese American Personality and Acculturation," GENETIC PSYCHOLOGY MONOGRAPHS, 45 (1952), p. 32. In rural areas and in some of the ghetto residences of urban Nihon-machi, the hot bath was transplanted from Japan. I have taken a "Japanese bath" in a traditionally operated boarding house in the Japanese community of Walnut Grove, California. Saké, Japanese rice wine, was also manufactured or purchased by the Issei. Drunkenness was a common complaint among the wives of Issei settlers. OUR CHRISTIAN TESTIMONY, op. cit.

[87] Benedict, op. cit., pp. 266-267. Personal interviews with Nisei indicate that moxa was used or threatened against naughty, overly-excited, tantrum-throwing children. See also Monica Sone, NISEI DAUGHTER, Boston: Little Brown, 1953, p. 28.

[88] Douglas G. Haring, "Aspects of Personal Character in Japan," PERSONAL CHARACTER AND CULTURAL MILIEU, op. cit., pp. 417-419; Betty B. Lanham, "Aspects of Child Care in Japan: Preliminary Report," Ibid., pp. 565-583; Edward and Margaret Norbeck, "Child Training in a Japanese Fishing Community," Ibid., pp. 651-673; Benedict, op. cit., pp. 261-264.

[89] See, e.g., THE AUTOBIOGRAPHY OF YUKICHI FUKUZAWA, New York: Columbia University Press, 1966, pp. 113-114, (Revised Translation by Eiichi Kiyooka).

[90] Caudill, op. cit., p. 30.

[91] Takagi, op. cit.

[92] For the Eta in Florin see Winifred Raushenbush, "Their Place in the Sun," SURVEY GRAPHIC, LVI (May 1, 1926), pp. 154-158; Hiroshi Ito (Pseudonym), "Japan's Outcastes in the United States," in George de Vos and Hiroshi Wagatsuma (Editors), JAPAN'S INVISIBLE RACE: CASTE IN CULTURE AND PERSONALITY, Berkeley:

University of California Press, 1966, pp. 200-221.

[93]Takagi, op. cit.

[94]Cf. Edward Norbeck, "Age-Grading in Japan," AMERICAN ANTHRPOLOGIST, 55 (June, 1953), pp. 373-384.

[95]Caudill, op. cit., p. 30. On the other hand, in Meiji Japan girls were expected to observe certain proprieties--including a proper body position when sleeping--from which boys were exempted. See Etsu Inagaki Sugimoto, A DAUGHTER OF THE SAMURAI, Rutland, Vt.,: Charles E. Tuttle, 1966, p. 24; Baroness Shidzue Ishimoto, FACING TWO WAYS: THE STORY OF MY LIFE, New York: Farrar and Rinehart, 1935, pp. 13-76.

[96]See Edward Sapir, "The Unconscious Patterning of Behavior in Society," in David G. Mandelbaum (editor), SELECTED WRITINGS OF EDWARD SAPIR IN LANGUAGE, CULTURE, AND PERSONALITY (Berkeley: University of California Press, 1963), pp. 544-559.

[97]George A. De Vos and Keiichi Mizushima, "Organization and Social Function of Japanese Gangs: Historical Development and Modern Parallels," in R. P. Dore, (Editor), ASPECTS OF SOCIAL CHANGE IN MODERN JAPAN, op. cit., pp. 289-326.

[98]Takagi, op. cit.; Stanford M. Lyman, "The Nisei Personality," PACIFIC CITIZEN, 62 (January 7, 1966), p. 3.

[99]Geertz, THE RELIGION OF JAVA, op. cit., p. 241.

[100]Lyman and Scott, "Coolness in Everyday Life," op. cit.

[101]Ibid., p. 93.

[102]Caudill, op. cit., pp. 66-68.

[103]For an excellent discussion of these phenomena in general, see Erving Goffman, INTERACTION RITUAL: ESSAYS ON FACE-TO-FACE BEHAVIOR, Chicago: Aldine, 1967, pp. 218-226.

[104]William Petersen, "Success Story, Japanese-American Style," THE NEW YORK TIMES MAGA-ZINE, January 9, 1966, p. 40.

[105]Professor Harry H. L. Kitano has suggested that most Japanese Americans did not resist incarceration in detention camps during World War II because of their engrained sense of fateful resignation. Joe Grant Masaoka, "Japanese tailor-made for Army order, says Kitano," PACIFIC CITIZEN, 64 (June 9, 1967), pp. 1-2.

[106]There is cultural support for this phenomenon, summed up in the Buddhist ideal of muga, carrying on activities effortlessly; that is, having eliminated the observing self in one's acts. The observing self is seen as a hindrance to smooth performance. See Benedict, op. cit., pp. 247-251.

[107]Cf. the remark by Sapir: "We do not really know what a man's speech is until we have evaluated his social background. If a Japanese talks in a monotonous voice, we have not the right to assume that he is illustrating the same type of personality that one of us would be if we talked with his sentence melody." "Speech as a Personality Trait," SELECTED WRITINGS. . . op. cit., p. 539.

[108]Caudill and de Vos, op. cit., p. 1117.

[109]Geertz, PERSON, TIME, AND CONDUCT IN BALI. . . , op. cit., pp. 53-61; Goffman, INTERACTION RITUAL. . . , op. cit., pp. 226-233; Lyman and Scott, "Stage Fright and Social Identity," SOCIOLOGY OF THE ABSURD, op. cit.

[110]The Japanese term jicho sums up this sense. Literally "a self that is weighty," it refers to circumspection in social relations. A person loses jicho when he commits an impropriety. See Benedict, op. cit., pp. 219-222.

A nice example is found in the autobiography of a daring, youthful Japanese sailor. Writing of an older sailor whom he admired very much, he tells of his surprise when his "idol" actually spoke to him:

Takeuchi was a man with a superb record as a yachtsman at Kansai University. He was always one of my idols. . . He seemed like a big shot to me, so much that I never even used to say "hello" to him because he might not recognize me or return my greeting. But on this day there was something different about him, because he spoke to me first. I was sure that I hadn't done anything wrong, but I still wondered why Takeuchi would want to talk to me.

Kenichi Horie, KODOKU: SAILING ALONE ACROSS THE PACIFIC, Rutland, Vermont: Charles E. Tuttle, 1964, pp. 26-27. (Translated by Takuichi Ito and Kaoru Ogimi.)

[111]George de Vos and Hiroshi Wagatsuma, "Psycho-Cultural Significance of Concern over Death and Illness Among Rural Japanese," INTERNATIONAL JOURNAL OF SOCIAL PSYCHIATRY, V (Summer, 1959), pp. 5-19; George de Vos, "Social Values and Personal Attitudes in Primary Human Relations in Niike," OCCASIONAL PAPERS, Center for Japanese Studies, University of Michigan, 1965; Babcock and Caudill, op. cit., pp. 436-437; Marvin K. Opler, "Cultural Dilemma of a Kibei Youth," CULTURE AND SOCIAL PSYCHIATRY, New York: Atherton Press, 1967, pp. 360-380.

[112]Weston LaBarre, "Some Observations on Character Structure in the Orient: The Japanese," in Bernard S. Silberman (Editor), JAPANESE CHARACTER AND CULTURE, Tucson:

The University of Arizona Press, 1962, pp. 325-359, esp. pp. 349-351.

[113] See Thomas S. Szasz, THE MYTH OF MENTAL ILLNESS: FOUNDATIONS OF A THEORY OF PERSONAL CONDUCT, New York: Dell-Delta, 1967, pp. 100, 110, 129-130, 139-143, 248-258.

[114] Ezra Vogel, "The Go-Between. . .," op. cit.

[115] Georg Simmel, "The Stranger," in THE SOCIOLOGY OF GEORG SIMMEL, op. cit., pp. 402-408.

[116] See Franz Alexander, "The Psychosomatic Approach in Medical Therapy," THE SCOPE OF PSYCHOANALYSIS: SELECTED PAPERS OF FRANZ ALEXANDER, 1921-1961, New York: Basic Books, 1961, pp. 345-358.

[117] George de Vos, "A Comparison of the Personality Differences in Two Generations of Japanese Americans By Means of the Rorschach Test," THE NAGOYA JOURNAL OF MEDICAL SCIENCE, 17 (August, 1954), pp. 153-261. Recent medical evidence lends support to my observations. British psychiatrist Dr. H.H. Wolff reports that psychosomatic illness may be a substitute for "healthy" discharge of aggressive impulses, impulses that arise from fear of loving or being rejected. SAN FRANCISCO CHRONICLE, November 25, 1968, p. 7.

[118] See five articles by Emory S. Bogardus: "Current Problems of Japanese Americans," SOCIOLOGY AND SOCIAL RESEARCH, 25 (July, 1941), pp. 562-571; "Culture Conflicts in Relocation Centers," Ibid., 27 (May, 1943), pp. 381-390; "Relocation Centers as Planned Communities," Ibid., 28 (January, 1944), pp. 218-234; "Resettlement Problems of Japanese Americans," Ibid., 29 (June, 1945), pp. 218-226; "The Japanese Return to the West Coast," Ibid., 31 (January, 1947), pp. 226-233. See also Leonard Bloom, "Familial Adjustments of Japanese-Americans to Relocation: First Phase," AMERICAN SOCIOLOGICAL REVIEW 8 (October, 1943), pp. 551-560; Bloom, "Transitional Adjustments of Japanese-American Families to Relocation," AMERICAN SOCIOLOGICAL REVIEW, 12 (April, 1947), pp. 201-209; Robert W. O'Brien, "Selective Dispersion as a Factor in the Solution of the Nisei Problem," SOCIAL FORCES, 23 (December, 1944), pp. 140-147; Richard A. Niver, "Americanizing the Issei," FREE WORLD, 11 (March, 1946), pp. 31-34; John H. Provinse and Solon T. Kimball, "Building New Communities During War Time," AMERICAN SOCIOLOGICAL REVIEW, 11 (August, 1946), pp. 396-410; Bernard L. Hormann, "Postwar Problems of Issei in Hawaii," FAR EASTERN SURVEY, 15 (September 11, 1946), pp. 277-280; John H. Burma, op. cit., pp. 157-163.

[119] For this concept, see Alfred Schutz, "Some Structures of the Life-World," COLLECTED PAPERS III: STUDIES IN PHENOMENOLOGICAL PHILOSOPHY, The Hague: Marinus Nijhoff, 1966, pp. 116-132 (Edited by I. Schutz).

[120] Studies of Issei with teen-age children in the 1950's suggest that these Issei were relaxing their standards and grudgingly accepting the fact of their children's "Americanization." See Dennie L. Brigges, "Social Adaptations Among Japanese American Youth: A Comparative Study," SOCIOLOGY AND SOCIAL RESEARCH, 38 (May-June, 1954), pp. 293-300; Melvin S. Brooks and Ken Kunihiro, "Education in Assimilation of Japanese: A Study in the Houston Area of Texas," SOCIOLOGY AND SOCIAL RESEARCH, 37 (September, 1952), pp. 16-22; Mamoru Iga, "The Japanese Social Structure...," op. cit., p. 278.

[121] See T. Scott Miyakawa, "The Los Angeles Sansei," KASHU MAINICHI, Holiday Supplement, Christmas Edition, December 20, 1962, Part 2, pp. 1,4.

[122] For the "Hansen Effect," see Marcus Lee Hansen, "The Third Generation in America," COMMENTARY, 14 (November, 1952), pp. 492-500; Eugene I. Bender and George Kagiwada, "Hansen's Law of 'Third-Generation Return' and the Study of American Religio-Ethnic Groups," Paper presented at the annual meeting of the Pacific Sociological Association, Vancouver, B.C., Canada, April, 1966. For its application to Japanese Americans, see George Kagiwada, "The Third Generation Hypothesis: Structural Assimilation Among Japanese-Americans," Paper presented at the annual meeting of the Pacific Sociological Association, San Francisco, March, 1968.

[123] See Harry H.L. Kitano, "Is there Sansei Delinquency?" KASHU MAINICHI, op. cit., p. 1.

[124] See "A Sansei's Opinion," KASHU MAINICHI, op. cit., p. 2; Ken Yoshida, "Contra Costa Youth Trade Views with Nisei Parents," PACIFIC CITIZEN, 64 (March 3, 1967), p. 4; Donald Kazama, "On Focus: The Sansei and Nisei," PACIFIC CITIZEN, 64 (May 26, 1967), p. 4.

[125] Recently World War II Nisei air ace Ben Kuroki observed that "We're losing our Japanese heritage through intermarriage." His public "blast" at intermarriage [PACIFIC CITIZEN, 64 (February 17, 1967), p. 1] was criticized in letters to the editor [Ibid., 64 (April 14, 1967), p. 6] and by a young columnist: Ken Kuroiwa, "Mampitsu: Interracial Dating," [Ibid., 64 (March 24, 1967, p. 5.]

[126] "Sansei in California divided on Integration, FEPC Told," PACIFIC CITIZEN, 64 (May 19, 1967), p. 1; Jeffrey Matsui, "Sounding Board: Anonymously Integrated," Ibid., p. 4; Bill Strobel, "Japanese Heritage in the United States," OAKLAND TRIBUNE, March, 1966. Reprinted in PACIFIC CITIZEN, 62 (April 1, 1966), pp. 1, 3, 4. See also Daisuke Kitagawa, "Assimilation or Pluralism?" in Arnold M. Rose and Caroline B. Rose (Editors), MINORITY PROBLEMS, New York: 1965, pp. 285-287.

[127] Isao Horinouchi, EDUCATIONAL VALUES AND PREADAPTATION IN THE ACCULTURATION OF JAPANESE AMERICANS, Sacramento Anthropological Society Paper Number 7, Fall, 1967.

[128] Jitsuichi Masouka, "Race Relations and Nisei Problems," SOCIOLOGY AND SOCIAL RESEARCH, 30 (July, 1946), p. 459.

CHINESE AMERICAN PERSONALITY & MENTAL HEALTH

STANLEY SUE AND DERALD W. SUE

In writing this article, we have tried to integrate personal observations, clinical impressions, and available research findings. Where clinical cases have been described of individuals in therapy, care has been taken to insure anonymity. Since there is a lack of research on Chinese-American personality and mental health, much of our discussion should be regarded as tentative rather than as the "final" word. Hopefully, this article will stimulate further thinking and raise issues.

THE DEVELOPMENT OF PERSONALITY

Sometimes it seems as though a Chinese-American must possess great ego strength in order to survive the conflicts surrounding him. He must develop within the interplay of forces such as parental upbringing, the clash between Chinese and Western values, and racism. As a basis for developing a conceptual scheme of personality, let us briefly examine them.

The Traditional Chinese Family

Although generalizations of the "traditional" Chinese family do injustice to differences among families, we have decided to define the traditional family as having certain values and behavioral characteristics. A more extensive analysis can be found in studies by DeVos and Abbott[1] and Cattell.[2]

In the traditional family, ancestors and elders are viewed with great reverence. The primary family unit is strong and typically exerts great control over its members. Emphasis is placed on obtaining a good education, on being obedient to parents, and in giving the family a good name. "Bad" behavior on the part of a member (exhibiting antisocial or criminal behavior, disobedience, low achievement, or even psychopathology), brings shame on the entire family. In order to control members, parents use guilt-arousing techniques such as threatening to disown the person, verbally censuring the individual, or having the individual engage in activities that accentuate his feelings of guilt and shame. Many times disappointed Chinese parents may say, "How could you do this to us," or "after all we have sacrificed for you, you are still like this." An interesting example of the accentuation of shame is provided by Lowell Chun-Hoon[3] in his analysis of Jade Snow Wong. After Jade Snow Wong had stolen a piece of cloth from a visiting peddler, her father made her sit outside the house for a day with the item she stole. Thus, her wrongdoing was publicly displayed.

In addition, the Chinese learns strong patterns of self control which have an effect on his personality. Fenz and Arkoff state that investigators have...

> stressed the strong family ties of Chinese families, as well as the traditional adherence of Chinese youths to parental mores. Chinese children are said to be taught by their parents to live up to a role of detachment and self control. This is said to be responsible for a lack of spontaneity and self-expression and for a strong control over affective impulses which is said to have become characteristic of the Chinese personality.[4]

In their study utilizing the Edwards Personal Preference Schedule, Fenz and Arkoff found that Chinese were generally more deferent and less autonomous, exhibitionistic, and heterosexual in interest than Caucasians. In a preliminary study of the Chinese community of San Francisco, DeVos and Abbott[5] attempted to conceptualize family life through interviews, a questionnaire, and a problem situation test. These investigators found that (a) educational achievement was consistently valued above other types of achievement, (b) Chinese-Americans usually react passively to authority, (c) respect for elders was equated with respect for authority, (d) there is a strong sense of responsibility for relatives, (e) when a younger person failed to live up to the elders' expectations, self-blame was the result, and (f) proper methods of socializing the child was seen to exclude physical violence and punishment.

Western Influences

Against this family background, the Chinese-American also develops within the host culture. Peer group influences may begin to erode parental authority. He is con-

---

Reprinted from AMERASIA JOURNAL, Volume 1, Number 2, by permission of AMERASIA and the authors. At the time of the article's writing, Stanley Sue was on staff at Student Health Psychiatry, University of California, Los Angeles, and Derald Sue was on staff at the Counseling Center, University of California, Berkeley.

stantly bombarded with Western values in the schools and in the mass media. These values reflect the attitudes, norms, emotional expressions, and other behaviors characteristic of the dominant society. It is inevitable that some changes will occur. For example, Fong[6] studied 336 Chinese college students by using three different instruments. He administered a personal data form to obtain background factors such as generational level, area of residence, citizenship status, etc. An assimilation-orientation inventory assessing social, cultural, and political attitudes was also employed. Finally, a stick figures test was administered to demonstrate an individual's ability to perceive culturally-determined modes of expression. Results indicated that as the Chinese-American becomes increasingly exposed to the values and standards of the larger host culture, there is progressive inculcation of those norms. In fact, Chinese-Americans whose families had been in the United States for two or more generations were largely assimilated.

Racism

Finally, the Chinese-American also experiences direct and subtle forms of discrimination in his exposure to the host society. While it is beyond the scope of this paper to analyze racism, we note that racism can be individual and institutional. Individual racism involves a _person's_ attitudes and behaviors toward the Chinese. He may believe that Chinese are "sneaky" or may try to prevent them from moving into his neighborhood. Interestingly, prejudice can also work in favor of the Chinese-American in specific situations. Teachers may believe that Chinese are intelligent and hard working and thus give them better grades. In the long run, side effects often develop. The individual may strive to maintain his hardworking image by being obedient and conforming. A Chinese who rebels against this stereotype faces the wrath of his teachers for violating _their_ notions of a "good" Chinese.

Institutional racism refers to systematic discrimination in various institutions. For example, in the past, laws in some states prevented Chinese from marrying Caucasians; and current business practices may prevent Chinese from attaining high executive positions in large corporations. Blacks have often been systematically denied admission to institutions of higher education because of failure to attain certain admission requirements. Although these requirements may be applied equally, they are insensitive to the factors behind the Blacks' inability to meet the standards. These forms of racism leave their mark on the personality of many ethnic minorities.

PERSONALITY: A CONCEPTUAL SCHEME

Personality development can proceed in many ways. At this time, we are not prepared to present the possible factors determining which direction the individual ultimately takes. In order to examine some of the underlying dynamics and conflicts which many Chinese-Americans have, we will concentrate on only three typological characters. Figure 1 illustrates a conceptualization of the Traditionalist, the Marginal Man, and the Asian-American.

Traditionalist

The Traditionalist has strongly internalized Chinese values. There is an attempt to be a "good" son or daughter. Primary allegiance is to the family into which he was born. In fact, eventual obligations as father and husband may be secondary to his duty to

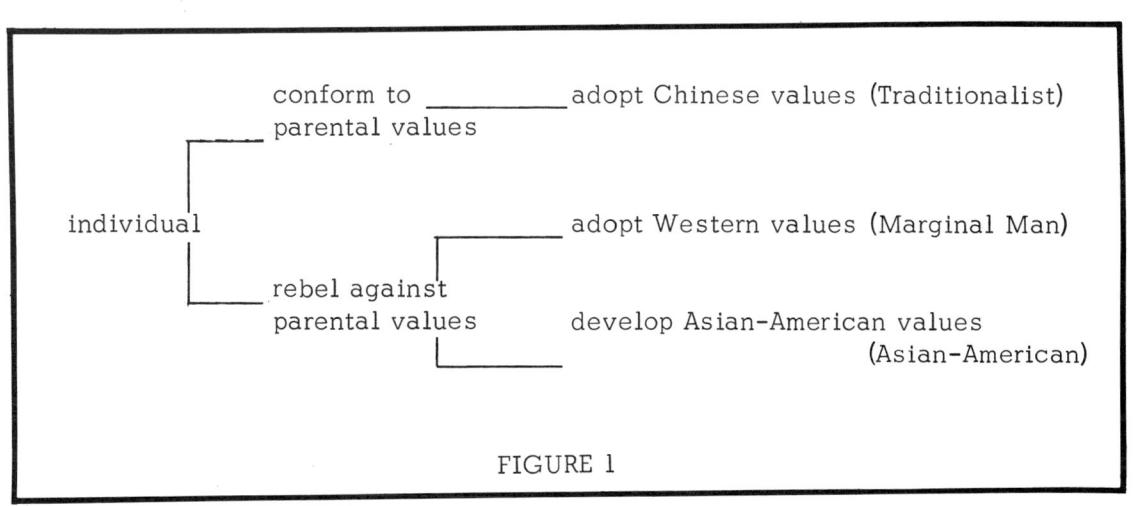

```
                    conform to _____ adopt Chinese values (Traditionalist)
                    parental values
                                        
        individual                       adopt Western values (Marginal Man)
                    
                    rebel against
                    parental values     develop Asian-American values
                                                (Asian-American)
```

FIGURE 1

parents. Self worth and esteem are defined by his ability to succeed in terms of high educational achievement, occupational status, etc. With success he feels respectable in American society; he has brought honor to the family name and has accomplished this all as a minority member. Gordon Allport, a social psychologist, notes that

> People admire the cripple who has persevered and overcome his handicap... Accordingly, some members of minority groups view their handicap as an obstacle to be surmounted by an extra spurt of effort.[7]

Thus feelings of pride are felt because he has achieved despite adverse conditions. Allport also states that...

> they may evoke abuse for being *too* industrious or clever.[8]

This statement points to the limitations on achievement by the host society. The Chinese must work hard to achieve; but if he works too hard and is too manipulating, he runs the risk of being stereotyped a "Chinese Jew."

We believe that the personal conflicts that the Traditionalist suffers come primarily from two sources. The first involves his attempts to be a good son. He must give his parents unquestioning obedience and must achieve well in order to maintain a good family name and to feel self worth. However, if he feels that his parents are wrong or demanding too much from him, what will he do? In these situations his personal feelings are in conflict with parental expectations. His acquiescence to them means he must suppress or repress his indignation; his defiance of them brings on intense feelings of guilt and shame. Guilt feelings often emerge because his identity is defined within the family.

The Traditionalist feels responsible for his failure to obey parents or to achieve well. Since he has internalized values of respect for parents, he finds it difficult to blame them. On the other hand, he cannot blame the host society, since he has been taught by his parents that success is possible with hard work. He alone bears the responsibility for failure. The following is a description of a Chinese student seen by one of the authors for therapy.

The Case of John C.

John C. is a 20 year-old junior student, majoring in electrical engineering. He is the oldest of 5 children, born and raised in San Francisco. The father is 58 years old and has been a grocer for the past 20 years; and the mother is a housewife. The parents have always had high expectations for their eldest son and constantly transmitted these feelings to him. Ever since he could remember, John's parents had decided that he would go to college and become an engineer--a job they held in high esteem.

Throughout his early school years, John was an outstanding student and was constantly praised by his teachers. He was hard-working, obedient and never gave his teachers any trouble. However, his parents seemed to take John's school successes for granted. In fact, they would always make statements such as "you can do better still."

John first came to the counseling center during the latter part of his junior year because of severe headaches and a vague assortment of bodily complaints. A medical check-up failed to reveal any organic malfunctioning, which led the psychologist to suspect a psychophysiological reaction.

Throughout the interviews, John appeared excessively concerned with failing his parents' expectations. Further exploration revealed significant sources of conflict. First, his grades were beginning to decline and he felt that he was letting his parents down. Second, he had always harbored wishes about becoming an architect, but felt this to be an unacceptable profession to his parents. Third, increasing familial demands were being placed on him to quickly graduate and obtain a job in order to help the family's financial situation. The parents frequently made statements such as "Once you are out of school and making good money, it would be nice if you could help your brothers and sisters through college." John's resentment to these imposed responsibilities was originally denied and repressed. When he was able to see clearly his anger and hostility towards his parents, much of his physical complaints vanished. However, with the recognition of his true feelings, he became extremely depressed and guilty. John could not see why he should be angry at his parents after all they had done for him.

John exhibited a great deal of anxiety throughout the interviews. He seemed suspicious of the psychologist and found it difficult to talk about himself in a personal way. As the sessions progressed, it became evident that John felt a great deal of shame about having come to a therapist. John was concerned that his family not be told since they would be disgraced.

The second source of conflict occurs because the Traditionalist must interact with the dominant society. Despite his attempt to confine his social life to the Chinese subculture, he is unable to fully isolate himself from members of the host society. Learned patterns of obedience and conformity are transferred to his interactions with them. Since role expectations in the Chinese family are well defined and structured, he may find it difficult to interact with Caucasians who are often behaving under different expectations. Frequently, these expectations are diametrically opposed to one another. For example, Caucasian patterns of relating tend to stress assertive and spontaneous behaviors. The Chinese patterns of deference and reserve are at odds with these values. This causes the Traditionalist great discomfort in his interpersonal relations with Caucasians who may view his behaviors negatively. In addition, individual forms of racism increase his level of anxiety and discomfort. He has not been taught how to aggressively respond to racism. He seeks to make the best of the circumstances without challenging the host society. Allport notes that the individual...

> escapes being conspicuous, has no cause for fear, and quietly leads his life in two compartments: one (more active) among his own kind, one (more passive) in the outer world.[9]

As for institutional racism, the Traditionalist is often less aware or concerned since he believes he can overcome obstacles if he works hard enough. This belief is similar to the Protestant ethic.

Marginal Man

Both the Marginal Man and the Asian-American cannot give unquestioning obedience to traditional parental values. The Marginal Man attempts to assimilate and acculturate into the majority society. Existing between the margin of two cultures, he suffers from an identity crisis. In attempts to resolve this conflict, the person may reject traditional Chinese ways by becoming over-Westernized. We believe that the Marginal Man finds his self worth defined in terms of acceptance by Caucasians. For the Chinese male, the number of Caucasian friends he has and such things as his ability to speak without an accent are sources of pride. He may feel contemptuous of Chinese girls who are "short legged" and "flat chested" when compared to Caucasian girls.

Likewise, an anthropological field study in a Chinese-American community by Weiss revealed that many Chinese-American females view their male counterparts as inhibited, passive, lacking in sexual attractiveness. Data was obtained through attendance at social functions and by the administration of questionnaires. The investigator states that

> Perhaps the most damaging indictment of Chinese-American male "dating ineptness" comes from the dating age Chinese-American female. Girls who regularly date Caucasians can be quite vehement in their denunciation and disapproval of Chinese-American males as dating partners. But even the foreign born Chinese girls--who do not usually inter-date--also support a demeaning courtship image of the Chinese-American male. Moreover, "Chinese inadequacies", and "failures" are contrasted with Caucasian "confidence" and "success" in similar situations.[10]

Weiss feels that Chinese-American females are better accepted by American society than the Chinese-American male. Stereotyping of the Chinese-American male has been generally unfavorable as compared to the female. As a result, the highly Westernized female begins to expect her boyfriends to behave boldly and aggressively. Because the Chinese male is perceived to lack these "desirable traits", many of the Chinese females begin to date outside their own race.

The Marginal Man is not without a great deal of conflict. Hostility and denial of his minority culture may cause him to turn his hostility inward and to develop a form of "racial self hatred". An extreme form of self hatred is demonstrated in the observations of Bruno Bettlheim as described by Gordon Allport:

> Studies of Nazi concentration camps show that identification with one's oppressor was a form of adjustment... At first prisoners tried to keep their self respect intact, to feel inward contempt for their persecutors, to try by stealth and cunning to preserve their lives and their health. But after two or three years of extreme suffering many of them found that their efforts to please their guards led to a mental surrender. They imitated the guards, wore bits of their clothing (symbolic power), turned against new prisoners, became anti-Semites, and in general took over the dark mentality of the oppressor.[11]

Self hatred can result in violence as well as in derogatory attitudes towards one's own group. It is our belief, however, that the Marginal Man has not resorted to widespread physical violence toward his own group because of subcultural values emphasizing restraint of disruptive feelings and because of underlying guilt feelings regarding violence to one's own group.

The Marginal Man's over-Westernized behavior is frequently in opposition to parental values and to Chinese culture, and may arouse intense feelings of guilt. Again, Allport describes a similar process in the Jew:

> ...the member who denies his allegiance suffers considerable conflict. He may feel like a traitor to his kind. A Jewish student confessed with remorse that in order not to be known as Jewish he would sometimes "insert in my conversation delicate witticisms pertaining to Jewishness which, while not actually vicious, conveyed a total impression of gentile malice."[12]

Although the Marginal Man cannot disguise his appearance, he too may experience conflict and anxiety for telling jokes about Chinese or for contemptuously stating that other Chinese are old fashioned.

Since he cannot escape his own group, he thus in a real sense hates himself ... To make matters worse he may hate himself for feeling this way. He is badly torn. His divided mind may make for furtive and self-conscious behavior, for "nervousness" and a lasting sense of insecurity.[13]

Allport's observations point to the double conflict involved in self hatred. First, the Marginal Man may hate himself for possessing "Chinese" characteristics. For example, he is frequently disgusted by his own physical characteristics such as shortness of height, round-flat nose, narrow eyes, and lack of a "manly" physique. Second, he may hate himself for hating himself! In the course of our work, we have observed many of these conflicts in Chinese-Americans. The following is the case of a student exhibiting problems typical of a Marginal Man.

The Case of Janet T.

Janet T. is a 21 year-old senior, majoring in sociology. She was born and raised in Portland, Oregon, where she had limited contact with members of her own race. Her father, a second generation Chinese-American, is a 53 year-old doctor. Her mother, age 44, is a housewife. Janet is the second oldest of three children and has an older brother (currently in medical school) and a younger brother, age 17.

Janet came for therapy suffering from a severe depressive reaction manifested by feelings of worthlessness by suicidal ideation, and by an inability to concentrate. She was unable to recognize the cause of her depression throughout the initial interviews. However, much light was shed on the problem when the therapist noticed an inordinate amount of hostility directed towards him. When inquiries were made about the hostility, it became apparent that Janet greatly resented being seen by a <u>Chinese</u> psychologist. Janet suspected that she had been assigned a Chinese therapist because of her own race. When confronted with this fact, Janet openly expressed scorn for "anything which reminds me of Chinese". Apparently, she felt very hostile towards Chinese customs and especially the Chinese male, whom she described as introverted, passive, and sexually unattractive.

Further exploration revealed a long-standing history of attempts to deny her Chinese ancestry by associating only with Caucasians. When in high school, Janet would frequently bring home white boyfriends which greatly upset her parents. It was as though she blamed her parents for being born a Chinese, and she used this method to hurt them.

During her college career, Janet became involved in two love affairs with Caucasians, both ending unsatisfactorily and abruptly. The last break-up occurred 4 months ago when the boy's parents threatened to cut off financial support for their son unless he ended the relationship. Apparently, objections arose because of Janet's race.

Although not completely conscious, Janet was having increasing difficulty with denying her racial heritage. The break-up of her last torrid love affair made her realize that she <u>was</u> Chinese and not fully accepted by all segments of society. At first she vehemently and bitterly denounced the Chinese for her present dilemma. Later, much of her hostility was turned inward against herself. Feeling alienated from her own subculture and not fully accepted by American society, she experienced an identity crisis. This resulted in feelings of worthlessness and depression. It was at this point that Janet came for therapy.

Finally, the Marginal Man must somehow handle instances of individual and institutional racism. For example, if he dates Caucasian girl and is rejected by her parents, he faces conflict. He is not being accepted by individuals of the very group into which he aspires. In an attempt to resolve the conflict, the Marginal Man may overcompensate. He believes that rejection by the girl's parents is an isolated situation rather than a reflection of pervasive individual racism. Although he feels that it can happen again, the situation does not change his desire to assimilate. He may even double his efforts to date Caucasians since they are now more symbolic of acceptance by the host society, i.e., the Caucasian girls are "forbidden fruits". The Marginal Man finds it difficult to admit widespread racism since to do so would be to say that he aspires to join a racist society.

As in individual racism, the Marginal Man also minimizes or denies the impact of institutional racism. For example, he may believe that if Chinese do not attain high executive positions, it is because they are too unassertive and reserved. His inability to be fully accepted by the host society is not so much a matter of personal failure or pervasive racial discrimination. He attributes blame to his own group for perpetuating Chinese values, which are maladaptive and which make the Chinese appear even more foreign and unacceptable to the host society.

Asian-American

Since he is in the process of self definition, the Asian-American is much harder to define. Thus we would like to pose some general impressions. Unlike the Traditionalist and the Marginal Man who have found existing models, the Asian-American tries to formulate a new identity by integrating his past experiences with his present conditions. Unquestioning obedience to parents is too painful; racism is too pervasive to ignore; and pride in self is too underdeveloped. He also shares common patterns with the other two. For example, he associates with other Chinese without embarrassment as does the Traditionalist. And like the Marginal Man, he experiences some guilt for his unwillingness to fully accept the dictates of his parents. However, the Asian-American's defiance is less a rejection of Chinese ways than an attempt to preserve certain Chinese values in the formation of a new identity. He feels that complete obedience to traditional values limits his self growth. Self pride cannot be attained if his behaviors are completely determined by his parents or by society. Parental emphasis on high achievement is too materialistic for the Asian-American who is trying to find meaning and self identity. In addition, his political and social awareness is more fully developed He is more sensitive to the forces in society which have shaped his identity and have too often been left unchallenged. Problems such as poverty, unemployment, individual and institutional racism, and juvenile delinquency are of primary concern to him. More than anything, society is to blame for his present dilemma and must be changed. Emphasis is placed on raising group esteem and pride, for it is only through collective action that society's perception of the Asian-American can be efficiently altered.

The Asian-American's orientation also includes other Asian groups as a basis for identity. Allport believes that group cohesiveness is often due to a common-enemy hypothesis. For example, he states that

> Threats drive them to seek protective unity within their common membership. The prevailing belief on the west coast during World War II that "a Jap is a Jap" created a strong tie among Issei (foreign born) and Nisei (American born), although before the persecution set in, these groups were frequently at odds with each other.[14]

The united of Chinese-Americans with other groups (Japanese, Korean, Filipino, etc.), however, seems to be more than just a common reaction to racism or stereotypes. There appears to be a positive effort by the Asian-American to develop and form an identity which will enable him to reconcile viable aspects of his heritage with his present situation. The notions of "viable aspects" and of "present situations" are hard to define. The former probably includes pride in one's heritage, knowledge of one's culture, and united with his group. The latter is the consideration of Chinese-Americans as a minority group and as Americans. The Asian-American must be assertive, questioning, and active in order to develop in his present environment.

The Asian American also faces conflicts. Since he is attempting to find an identity with other Asian-Americans, the group is extremely important to him. Anyone who is perceived to threaten the Asian-American group is, in a real sense, threatening his identity. Thus he may feel quite intolerant of the Traditionalist and particularly of the Marginal Man who wants to assimilate. Since he feels that much of the problems of minority groups are due to the host society, he must somehow reconcile this belief with the observations that there are "uncle toms" in his own racial group. That is, while he is contemptuous of the Marginal Man, he also believes that the Marginal Man is a product of the society.

In addition, the Asian-American may become extremely militant in his reaction to racism. While militancy may have valuable contributions in gaining civil rights, feelings of self pride, and power, it may also make the Asian-American obsessively concerned with racism. He may become extremely sensitive and suspicious. Allport notes that this is not uncommon among Jews:

> One day in the late 30's a recently arrived refugee couple went shopping in a village grocery store in New England. The husband ordered some oranges. "For juice?" inquired the clerk. "Did you hear that," the woman whispered to her husband, "for Jews? You see, it's beginning here, too."[15]

Finally, the Asian-American may experience a great deal of guilt and frustration in his relationship with his parents. His parents tend to view his disobedience, assertiveness, tendency towards long hair, and deemphasis on academic achievemement as signs that he is disrespectful to them and to traditional values. He finds it difficult to communicate that he is attempting to gain self respect; that his parents have not failed in raising him; that he is, indeed, growing and achieving in his *own* way. Thus the Asian-American may feel a real sense of loss. He is trying to help his people, many of whom do not understand his efforts. The following is a description of an Asian-American student seen for therapy.

The Case of Gale K.

Gale K. is a 22 year old, first year graduate student in biochemistry. His father, once employed in an engineering firm, died recently from cancer. His 52 year old mother is currently employed at the San Francisco airport as a receptionist. Gale was born and raised in Oakland, California. He has three sisters, all of whom are married.

Much of Gale's early life was filled with conflict and antagonism between him and his parents. Like Janet T., Gale did not confine his social life exclusively to other Chinese-Americans. Being the only son, his parents were fearful that they would lose their son should he marry a Causian. Five years earlier, their eldest daughter had married a Caucasian which caused great turmoil in the family and the subsequent disowning of the daughter.

Throughout much of his life, Gale attempted to deny his racial identity because he felt shameful about being Chinese. However, within the last four years, a phenomenal change occurred in Gale. He actively participated in the Third World Strike at the University and became involved in a number of community change committees. Gale recalls with great fondness the "esprit de corps" and the contagion he experienced with other concerned Asians. His parents had been delighted about his reorientation towards certain Chinese values. They were especially happy to see him dating other Asian girls and volunteering his time to help tutor educationally deprived children in Chinatown. However, they did not understand his activist thinking and outspoken behavior towards authority figures.

Throughout our sessions, Gale exhibited an understanding and awareness of economic, political, and social forces beyond that of the average student. He attributed the plight of Asian-Americans to the shortcomings of society. He was openly suspicious of therapy and confronted the therapist on two different issues. The first objection dealt with the use of tests in therapy. Gale felt them to be culturally biased and somewhat inapplicable to ethnic minorities. The second issue concerned the relationship of therapy to the status quo. Since therapy has traditionally been concerned with the adjustment of individuals to society, Gale questioned the validity of this concept. "Do you adjust people to a sick society?" Only after dealing with these issues, was it possible for Gale and the therapist to focus on his feelings regarding the death of his father.

Gale came for therapy because he had not fully resolved guilt feelings concerning the recent death of his father. Several weeks prior to his father's death, Gale had a violent argument with him over his recent participation in a demonstration. When his father passed away, Gale felt a great deal of remorse. He had often wished that his father would have understood the Asian-American movement.

A final word should be said before we move on with our discussion. It has been our feeling that the Marginal Man comes in for therapy at a much higher rate than either the Traditionalist or the Asian-American. Our clinical impressions seem to indicate that since psychotherapy is a white middle-class activity, the three types are affected differentially. The Traditionalist does not understand therapy and feels great shame about admitting psychological problems; the Asian-American equates psychotherapy with the status quo and is openly suspicious of this type of activity; and the Marginal Man, in his attempts to assimilate, may view therapy more favorably than the other two. As a result, the Marginal Man would be more prone to utilize mental health facilities when he encounters problems.

LIMITATIONS AND IMPLICATIONS

At this point, we would like to note some limitations of our analysis. First, this conceptual scheme does not deal with important factors such as foreign versus American-born Chinese, residence in - versus outside of Chinatowns, and length of residence in the US. In doing so, problems involving juvenile delinquency, poverty, educational and language difficulties, and peer group factors have been largely ignored. Second, individual differences and variations are submerged in this kind of analysis. For example, we know Traditionalists who are quite aware of the social and political forces surrounding them; we know of Marginal Men who function without much internal conflict and without "racial self hatred"; and we have seen parents of Asian-Americans who are as "Third World" as their sons and daughters. Third, sex differences within and between each character types have not been adequately handled. Finally, we have used many examples from Allport's analysis of Jews. Our purpose in presenting these examples is to illustrate some of the underlying processes and conflicts rather than to argue for the personality similarity between Chinese and Jews.

These typological characters have been carried to their logical extremes in an attempt to gain insight into some of the underlying dynamics and conflicts. Any typological analysis tends to limit the number of relevant variables it can handle. A tabular summary of the three types is given in Figure 2.

It is our impression that these polar types have been used in reality. Note the following terms: "F.O.B." or "typical Chinese" for the Traditionalist; "Banana" or "Uncle Tom" for the Marginal Man; and "radical" or "militant" for the Asian-American. These terms are often derogatory and demonstrate within-group divisions. Our position is that all three types can attain self pride. This possibility has not been recognized since each type has defined pride and self esteem from different reference points. The Traditionalist's failure to see how one can attain self respect by not obeying parents is a result of defining pride and esteem within the family unit. The evaluation from his family is the critical factor. Evaluations

	Traditionalist	Marginal Man	Asian American
Self worth defined by...	Obedience to parents... Behaviors which bring honor to the family...	Ability to acculturate into White society...	Ability to attain self pride through defining a new identity...
Behavior which arouses guilt	Failure to live up to parental values...	Defiance of parental values...	Defiance of parental values...
Attribution of blame for one's lack of success	Self... White society...	Chinese values... Minimal blame on White society...	White society...
Handling or prejudice and discrimination	Deferring and minimizing effects...	Denying and minimizing effects...	Anger and militancy...

FIGURE 2

from the host society, while being important, are secondary.

The Marginal Man's self pride is determined by his relationship to the host society. He cannot see how one can attain pride by not assimilating. He views the traditionalist as perpetuating outdated values. On the other hand, the Asian-American is seen to be "rocking the boat" by his militancy. The Marginal Man feels that both groups have difficulty in maintaining "real" pride since the host society fails to accept them as well as it has accepted him.

Finally, the Asian-American's pride is in the reconciliation of past and present values. He may believe that the Traditionalist cannot have "real" pride since the Traditionalist ignores racism and is unassertive. Between the Traditionalist and the Marginal Man, however, most of his wrath is directed to the Marginal Man who is perceived to be completely denying his cultural heritage.

We feel that in all cases, there is a confusion between "self" and "pride". Self pride, by definition, must involve the individual's own conception of pride. Although self pride is often determined by one's environment, we do not feel that any of the typological characters have the "exclusive" definition of self pride. It must be defined by the individual in his circumstance.

The real name is the attainment of pride at what cost to one another. In this regard, the Traditionalist is the least threatening. With each succeeding generation, Chinese in America are becoming less "traditional". The possibility that immigrants can maintain traditional values is highly unlikely since their number is relatively small. According to our conceptual scheme, the only viable alternatives for Chinese (Asians) in the U.S. are between the Marginal Man and the Asian-American.

To the extent that the Marginal Man feels "racial self hatred" and contempt for Chinese, then he demonstrates his willingness to gain self pride at the expense of other Chinese. On the other hand, the Asian-American seeks pride by raising group esteem. As long as he rejects dogma and intolerance in his approach, he can do much to raise the esteem of Chinese-Americans and to give himself some choice in preserving aspects of his subculture. In terms of pride, each type can reconcile some of their differences, although social and political differences may always exist. We do not believe that assimilation necessarily involves hatred for self. The Marginal Man can try to assimilate without derogating the Chinese once he feels secure in saying that he is a <u>Chinese</u>-American. Like the Marginal Man, the Asian-American is assimilating in many ways. Once the Asian-American's identity is firmly rooted, the "banana" will be less threatening and less an object of scorn. Again, the issue is not assimilation versus separatism; it involves the striving for personal respect at the expense of disrespect for others.

MENTAL HEALTH PROBLEMS

Thus far, our discussion has focused on the problems and conflicts of Chinese-Americans. Aspects of culture-conflict and racism place Chinese-Americans under greater emotional distress than members of the host society. When these sources of stress become too great, mental health problems are frequently the result. Although no direct statistics exist concerning the rate of mental illness, Tom[16] suggests that the rate is quite high in San Francisco Chinatown. He notes that there is an extremely low utilization rate of mental health facilities among the Chinese. Tom believes that cultural factors such as (1) the manner of symptom formation (low acting out such as inhibiting expression of strong impulses), (2) the traditional handling of difficulties within the family, and (3) fear of social stigma contribute to the low visibility of mental illness. However, the suicide rate in San Francisco has historically been the highest in the nation. Chinatown has an even higher rate than the city. Since suicide indicates severe personal disorganization, Tom believes mental illness to be quite high among the Chinese.

In a comprehensive investigation performed by Sue and Kirk[17] at the University of California, Berkeley, the entire entering Freshman class was surveyed and given various tests. Approximately 90% of the students completed at least one of the tests which included the Omnibus Personality Inventory, the Strong Vocational Interest Blank, and the School and College Ability Test. Chinese-American students (128 males and 108 females) were then identified and compared to all other students. Results indicated that Chinese-American students appeared more inhibited, conventional, and socially withdrawn. While they had higher quantitative ability scores, they demonstrated less verbal facility on the College Ability Test. A bilingual background could partially account for the latter result.

Our conclusion is not that Chinese-Americans have an extremely high rate of than other females. These results show intra-consistency. If Chinese are inhibited, socially withdrawn, and lower in verbal skills (but higher in quantitative abilities), then they understandably have interests in fields minimizing interpersonal interactions.

Recently, we[18] conducted a study on the students seen at the Student Health Psychiatric Clinic, University of California, Los Angeles. Preliminary results based on the Minnesota Multiphasic Personality Inventory (MMPI) and on clinical impressions indicate that Chinese (and Japanese) males exhibit more severe problems than non-Asians. Although test profiles for Asian and for non-Asian students were similarly patterned, the severity was clearly greater for Asian males. The combined test profiles for Chinese males also indicated problems involving blunted affect, dependency, inferiority feelings, ruminations, somatic complaints, and lack of social skills. The most common diagnosis for these problems is pseudoneurotic schizophrenic. Interestingly, Chinese females exhibited less disturbance than males, perhaps because 20% of the females applied for theraputic abortions rather than for "purely" psychological problems.

Finally, Chinese males and females exhibited more somatic complaints and more familial discord on the MMPI. Somatic complaints are often the result of emotional conflicts. Perhaps the Chinese is reluctant to admit psychological problems since there is much shame associated with these problems. Physical conditions are better recognized and more acceptable. As for family discord, it is apparent that most Chinese-Americans face not only a generation gap but also a wide cultural gap from their parents.

Obviously, these findings can be quite disquieting. Not only do they point to the ills of Chinese mental health, but they can easily be used to maintain negative stereotypes of the Chinese. Furthermore, the findings have social and political implications far beyond the scope of this paper. For example, if Chinese as a group exhibit maladaptive characteristics, then what will this mean in terms of their struggle to attain self identity and pride through Chinese culture?

When viewed in its proper perspective, however, Chinese need not be ashamed nor embarrassed by seeing themselves as being reserved, emotionally inhibited, etc. These characteristics are highly valued and are a great part of traditional Chinese culture. Instead, concern should be addressed to the functional value of Chinese traits under the present circumstances. If the traits are no longer adaptive for attaining proclaimed goals, then they must be changed.

Furthermore, Chinese-Americans preferred concrete and practical approaches to life. This may reflect a dislike for uncertainty, ambiguity, and unpredictability. The Chinese males tended to avoid the social sciences, business contact occupations, and verbal-linguistic fields; they showed predominant interests in the physical and biological sciences. Chinese-American females were much more domestically oriented mental illness as Tom suggests in his Chinatown sample. We do feel, however, that the mental health needs of Chinese are sufficient to warrant great concern, especially since few individuals have addressed themselves to these needs. Attempts to rationalize the results on the grounds that the research instruments are culturally biased are no longer adequate. They tend to deny the urgency of the problem and to undermine effective search for solutions.

THE INADEQUACY OF MENTAL HEALTH CARE

If one accepts the notion that the mental health needs of Chinese-Americans are of great concern, then the problem is especially urgent since mental health care seems to be inadequate. Klein states that

...the individual facing any hazard is dependent on the resources that a particular community has to offer and is affected by the means of coping that the community either makes available to him or denies him.[19]

In this regard, the Chinese-Americans have not found appropriate facilities to handle their problems. They do not turn to professional mental-health facilities. Furthermore the results of our study[20] indicate that Chinese (and other Asian) students tend to underutilize the Psychiatric services at UCLA. While Asians represent 8.1% of the student body, they comprise only 3.9% of the clinic population. This underutilization is also evidenced in the mean number of therapy sessions. Chinese students are seen for an average of approximately three sessions while non-Asians attend an average of over five sessions. Thus, Chinese (and other Asians) are underrepresented; and those who apply to the clinic terminate therapy earlier.

Of course, one might argue that Chinese do not seek the clinic services because they have a low rate of behavioral problems. Furthermore, early termination may be due to quick recovery from personal problems. Neither of these possibilities appear to have much support. First, Chinese and Japanese males seem to exhibit more severe problems than non-Asians. This finding points to the possibility that the most disturbed males come for therapy. Chinese experiencing milder problems merely avoid using clinic services. (An additional possibility--that Chinese have a low rate of mental illness but greater severity of problems among those affected--seems unlikely. We believe that mental health problems in groups follow a normal distribution). Second, the early termination of sessions by Chinese seems to be due to a negative response to therapy rather than to a quick recovery.

These ideas seem consistent with our belief that psychotherapy is essentially a white middle-class activity. Therapy is not well understood by Chinese, and they frequently enter with much apprehension and suspicion. In addition, their lower verbal facility, greater inhibition, and low tolerance for ambiguity may make Chinese extremely uncomfortable in therapy. Psychotherapy is often geared for individuals who have high verbal functioning, high emotional expressiveness, and great tolerance for ambiguity.

Another barrier to the seeking of professional help is the Chinese-American's value judgement of psychological problems. He frequently equates such problems with shameful and disgraceful behavior. To enlist the aid of mental health professionals would be to publicize the disgrace of the individual and his family. It is unfortunate that unless a family member becomes overtly psychotic, he may not receive professional help.

Furthermore, professional help itself may be unresponsive to the needs of certain groups of Chinese-Americans. There is a critical shortage of bilingual therapists. More importantly, few attempts have been made to nodify traditional theraputic approaches to the cultural experiences of Chinese. Since Chinese may feel ashamed and suspicious in seeking help for emotional problems, the therapist may be able to establish more rapport by not making early demands for him to be open and expressive. Such demands can easily be interpreted by the Chinese as disrespect for his behavior. In addition, the Chinese may feel uncomfortable with a therapist who initially provides too little structure and too much ambiguity. The therapist may be more effective if he gives guidelines and takes an active part in the interaction.

Perhaps the most fruitful direction is in the area of community mental health. This involves the use of community resources in programs of primary prevention and of community intervention. Although we are not prepared to present an analysis of the problems involved in community organization, we would like to offer a few suggestions for programs. First, mental health professionals who work with ethnic minorities must be more aware of the fears, concerns, and aspirations of the people they work with. They should have an understanding and appreciation of minority group experiences. Second, the mental health needs of Chinese must be assessed through research. Community leaders, special organizations (social agencies and schools), and the community members must be made aware of these needs. Third, proposals for special programs can be offered. Such programs may involve the use of community personnel briefly trained in counseling to offer their services to Chinese.

Other projects can focus on early detection and prevention of emotional problems such as in school children. Finally, continuing assessment of the effectiveness of these programs is necessary.

References

[1] DeVos and Abbott, K. THE CHINESE FAMILY IN SAN FRANCISCO. MSW Dissertation, University of California, Berkeley, 1966.

[2] Cattell, S. HEALTH, WELFARE, AND SOCIAL ORGANIZATION IN CHINATOWN, NEW YORK CITY. Report prepared for the Department of Public Affairs, 1962.

[3] Chun-Hoon, L. Jade Snow Wong and the Fate of Chinese-American Identity. AMERASIA JOURNAL, 1971, 1, 52-63.

[4] Fenz, W. and Arkoff, A. Comparative Need Patterns of Five Ancestry Groups in Hawaii. JOURNAL OF SOCIAL PSYCHOLOGY, 1962, 58, p. 82.

[5] DeVos and Abbott, op. cit.

[6] Fong, S.L.M. Assimilation of Chinese in America: Changes in Orientation and Social Perception. AMERICAN JOURNAL OF SOCIOLOGY, 1965, 71, pp. 265-273.

[7] Allport, G.W. THE NATURE OF PREJUDICE. Garden City, New York: Doubleday & Co., 1958, p. 152.

[8] Ibid., p. 153.

[9] Ibid., p. 143.

[10] Weiss, M.S. INTER-RACIAL ROMANCE: THE CHINESE-CAUCASIAN DATING GAME. Paper presented at the Southwestern Anthropological Association. Las Vegas, Nevada. April, 1969, p. 3.

[11] Allport, op. cit., p. 147-148.

[12] Ibid., p. 142.

[13] Ibid., p. 147.

[14] Ibid., p. 145.

[15] Ibid., p. 141.

[16] Tom, S. MENTAL HEALTH IN THE CHINESE COMMUNITY OF SAN FRANCISCO. Paper found in Asian American Studies Center, UCLA, 1968.

[17] Sue, D.W. & Kirk, B.A. PSYCHOLOGICAL CHARACTERISTICS OF CHINESE-AMERICAN STUDENTS. Paper submitted for publication, 1971.

[18] Sue, S. & Sue, D.W. THE REFLECTION OF CULTURE CONFLICT IN THE PSYCHOLOGICAL PROBLEMS OF CHINESE AMERICANS. Parts of this paper presented at the First National Conference on Asian American Studies, Los Angeles, California, April, 1971.

[19] Klein, D.C. COMMUNITY DYNAMICS AND MENTAL HEALTH. New York: John Wiley & Sons, 1968, p. 13.

[20] Sue & Sue, op. cit.

AN INTERVIEW WITH
HARRY KITANO

Acting Director of the Asian American Studies Center, Professor of Social Welfare at the University of California, Los Angeles

EDITORIAL BOARD
JUNE, 1971

QUESTION: How valid a description do you think the success image of the Japanese-Americans and other Asian Americans is?

KITANO: When you define success, you have to define it along different parameters. If you use education as one criterion, they come out (the Asians) reasonably well. For occupations and income and jobs, there is some evidence that they don't get paid as much for the same amount of work as the average white person, so on that level, they are less successful. If you come to behavior such as crime, delinquency, mental illness--in those the Japanese and Chinese come out relatively good, at least in terms of official hospitalized rates. But if you analyze areas like creativity or personality development, I think that you can start seeing how racism can affect a "very successful" minority group. It means that, generally for the Asians, they don't have the full range of possibilities offered to the white person, given a similar status and background or whatever else. The greatest disservice is to take just one or two of those dimensions like occupation and income and then indicate that this is an overall successful group, because success is made up not only of different criteria, but also what you value as successful. For some people being comforming and quiet and being accepted gets to be a very high value; if you equate that with success, you come out differently than if you value something else.

The fundamental problem of a small, powerless minority group (and I think we can use the Asians in this whole context) really does raise a whole series of questions that very few of us are even aware of. One of the problems of a small group such as ours, especially if there are two other dominant groups, the whites and the blacks, is that probably the most difficult position, sociologically anyway, would be that of a permanent middleman minority. Just by that description, I think you can get a pretty clear implication that if you are in the middle between two opposing forces, in one way you can first never achieve what you want because you are being determined by two other large groups, or the middleman obviously sometimes becomes the scapegoat of all the ills of that kind of social system and that kind of society. I think we have some evidence that the whites use us and the blacks may use us; the question that people in the middle should think about is "Where does the middleman minority go? Does it try to become a majority; does it try to join the subordinated minorities; does it try to remain somewhat aloof?" It might be very wise to stop and think because even in terms of color, we are in the middle, and that until we first come to some sort of agreement among ourselves of "What is the best way?", then we end up in a sense fighting each other, which we do. Right now we are fighting between the Hayakawas and the non-Hayakawas, but I don't think that we have really addressed ourselves to the major questions yet. As far as I know, historically no middleman minority has ever handled this position quite well, because the final power may lie outside the group, but still, if we think that we have some choice, we may be able to decide some of the consequences of the ways that we might be going.

QUESTION: Do you see any division between the class aspect or caste aspect of being yellow? Would that be a factor in deciding which way the Asians might go?

KITANO: One of the solutions for the middleman minority is to try to emphasize other modes of stratification such as class, which means that instead of color being the most dominant criterion--occupation, income, and position are, and that's certainly been the answer of many Asians. Historically, many have tried to deny and hide the fact that yellow was an important variable and it was hard work and achievement that lead to economic success. At least that's the way that a large number of the middleman group have tried to answer the question-- maybe not consciously but this is the way they have behaved. Now the problem with that approach is that it will serve those who have, if you want to call it, the mobility and drive, but it certainly doesn't answer the question of what happens to those yellow people of less motivation or capabilities. Again, I think this is why we are seeing certain problems within our own ethnic community. Those who have become successful on the social class level almost deny the importance of color and yet when you see large proportions of our group now not making it (at least in the traditional sense) then it raises another spectra of an unresolved issue. I think that's essentially where the problem lies.

QUESTION: Is there a tendency among Japanese-Americans to believe in the success story about themselves too much? Is there a danger in that?

KITANO: The danger with the Japanese-Americans is that there is enough empirical evidence to indicate that they have become relatively successful in this narrow fashion; and they forget that they may have paid an extremely high price for it. I think that we have some evidence that the most successful Japanese, at least according to the stereotype, are those who really paid for it psychologically; if you look at things like stomach cancer, ulcers, and other internalized modes of adaptation, that is one price. But I think the other price that comes out so clearly is that we have developed either a servant or a second-class mentality. Our drive for acceptance has really been to follow the cues of the dominant white society, and they have told us that to be successful you have to be quiet and humble and those other characteristics. If we really believe that that's the way we can become successful, then one can become rather pessimistic about the future of our group because that means that we have been "conned" or that we have "conned" ourselves almost completely into taking a second-class role.

QUESTION: It's always been an interesting point in your book that it's not so much that Japanese cultural values are the same as American middle-class cultural values, but that Japanese have one value of adapting or accommodating to a situation. There is a functional compatibility when American cultural values dictate that minorities should be quiet and work hard, even though for Americans, being quiet is not highly emphasized. How does that carry out with the younger generation when that cultural value is no longer followed to the same degree?

KITANO: The validity of one set of prescriptions for one generation may not hold for another because of the changes in not only time and place but situation. I still think the adaptation syndrome that was a part of not only the first but also the second generation has been instilled to a large degree in the third, current generation. And like all role prescriptions that are put forth, it does have validity if it works--it's like any other kind of tool; if you do certain things and it works out for you, then you continue in this fashion. Part of it may be simple generational reaction. So even if it does work, a lot of the Sansei may very well take an opposite tact, which is not too unusual in all groups and is labelled adolescent rebellion. At this stage one would almost predict two levels: they will try newer ways of adapting and they will hold and maintain that kind of adaptation that they feel gets them closer to what they want.

QUESTION: You have done a lot of research on mental illness of Japanese-Americans. Why is there relatively low incidence of mental illness among Japanese-Americans?

KITANO: It's both intriguing and very tricky to interpret this question because in all of these areas there is what we call official rate: in crime and delinquency--that's what appears on the police records and the FBI records; in mental illness --the number in mental hospitals, and things like that. But I think the true incidence is generally hidden, and a lot depends on how the culture defines it. If Japanese-Americans thought that exposing mental illness to the larger culture was the source of either embarrassment or shame or at least a negative characteristic, then I think that in many ways they would try to hide this; I think there is some evidence that this is what they do. The shame on the family and the shame on the ethnic group would mean that even if you had a "mentally ill" person, and that again is a debatable term, the average Japanese might deny that he has a mentally ill person and not send the person in for treatment. He would most likely try to handle the mentally ill person within his own ethnic group, community or family. Therefore, this person never shows up in a mental hospital. There are other factors that go with that too. Economic independence often leads to taking care of one's own. Japanese sometimes have a pride in that. Another one which is a sheer functional kind of thing is that if the average Japanese, especially of another generation, went into a mental hospital and all he spoke was Japanese, the chances are very good that he will never get well, because who is going to know that he is getting better? You can probably come out with a reasonable generalization that the Japanese are not superior or inferior, if you want to use those terms, to other groups in terms of mental illness; the rates are probably very similar. But the second part of that generalization is that they don't show up in mental hospitals or those facilities at the same rate as most of the other groups.

QUESTION: Can we pursue alienation as a source of the identity crisis? Let's take the family as a contributor to the Asian identity crisis. How does the Japanese-American family contribute to that problem?

KITANO: From my point of view, you have to answer it from a relative sense. If you compare it with different families, then I see the alienation of the Japanese much less than the average white families, the average black families, and perhaps most similar to the Jewish families. Although it is changing, the Japanese family still retains sort of a unit and a function that is still qualitatively different from the average American family. You can even use simple statistics such as separation and divorce as one example. Another one might be mobility. Chances are good for many white families that they might have moved five or six times within a lifetime, and the moves may have been from New York to Miami. So when you follow that kind of pattern and think that the family can contribute to alienation by not providing either a consistent background or in some degree of stability through an intact family and all the amenities that go with that, then I think the Japanese and Chinese families are much more cohesive. For all of us who live in Asian families, that cohesion as told to us by the white man is really a myth--the white man really thinks that the families think together, do things together, and everyone obeys, etc. But I think there is still enough truth in a relative sense in that compared to the average white family, we do come up as a less alienated group. Now the other question which is interesting is alienation in the Jewish family. In some ways it may almost be a reaction to the over-closeness and over-dependency that sometimes appears to be a stereotype of a Jewish family; you look for ways of breaking away from that kind of interdependency.

QUESTION: The Portnoy syndrome.

KITANO: Look at the Asian family--there are enough parallels. I think that some of the chuckles and insights when we discuss Portnoy point up the similarities.

QUESTION: Do you feel that if the family stays together as a unit, it leads to conservatism among its members?

KITANO: That may very well be. Family units generally are much more conservative, especially if you get input from different generations. The grandmothers and grandfathers have lived or experienced a more conservative era, so the risk that you pay obviously is much more conservatism.

QUESTION: Has the family prompted the "quiet American" stereotype?

KITANO: I think the average Japanese-American family usually has his own home, has a late model car, is given all the material things, and thinks that the one way he achieved this is through his quiet demeanor. Many feel the maintenance of this kind of posture may be very important in getting even a greater proportion of the goods of the society.

QUESTION: A lot of parents will encourage quiet behavior and say it's because they brought it over from Japan. Isn't it more of a response to succeeding in this society?

KITANO: I would say that generally, if you are from lower classes or less powerful groups of any immigrant population, the chances are high that you had to adapt to the system in Asia, and that if you didn't adapt, then you paid some kind of price. It's this kind of psychological orientation that many Asians might have brought over here. It was a translation of one group in power to another; it was not that difficult. That's what I mean by the congruence. But to mistake that as part of the Japanese culture. . .I think this is the error that many Americans make. White Americans start saying, "That's the culture." But they forget that depending upon your class and your position in Japan, you will behave appropriately; if you came from the upper class or the upper middle class, then you can be arrogant or loud, depending on the time, place, and situation. The mistranslation of the characteristics of a small social class group over here and saying that it's part of Japanese culture is a misperception.

QUESTION: How does the relocation experience fit into this model of quiet Americans?

KITANO: I think that the evacuation has now become the Japanese-American Rorschach test, which I think is quite appropriate. It means that now we can go back to a concrete event, but interpret it in a way that we think appropriate. The facts themselves are not really as important as the interpretation and its symbolic meaning. Again, as in any event like this, you can line up the positive and the negative and then remake your analysis from there. I think that if I had to interpret the event, it becomes the symbol of a racist, oppressive society that does this thing to one ethnic group. The problem with getting too hung up with that approach is that one may forget what it did to an essentially conservative community. I am for family interaction, but not for that oppressive kind of family interaction that was characteristic of many Japanese families right up and through that World War II era. Your father almost determined your occupation, who you were going to marry, where you were going to live, and because most Japanese were poor and dependent, you had to follow through on what your parents told you to do because there were no alternatives. A cohesive family really is good if it's somewhat voluntarily entered into. But if a cohesive family was forced upon you because there was no there was no other choice, then I suspect that it could become very restrictive. It would deny opportunities. I can give you a rigid way of looking at the world. But you still can't over-react to the racism and that's the one thing. The other thing about the evacuation was that it forced young Japanese, especially, to go to live in Chicago and New York and other places where they experienced different kinds of input--we saw how white families lived, we saw upper classes, middle classes, lower classes--and that kind of exposure is quite necessary so that you can get some newer perspectives. Now whether it should be forced on one through something like the evacuation obviously is unfair.

QUESTION: Looking back at recent history, how do you re-evaluate the assimilation process in America?

KITANO: I think inevitably, in the long run, when you have different racial groups, especially so visible as in our culture, there are two main choices: One is to go completely pluralistic so that each visible ethnic group develops its own culture, language, styles, institutions, and organizations. So you have within that one system a whole series of different cultures living side by side with almost minimal interaction with each other. The ultimate would be perhaps several states set aside. I don't think that that will ever come about, because I guess it's so impractical. The other way would be complete integration, some sort of assimilation so that out of this melange comes a new kind of American--maybe some part Asian blood, some part black blood, and Indian, and whatever else. That too, I suspect would be an almost impossible reality at the recurrent time. I think where we're at now--is where the white man is still on top and all the other groups are fighting for the scraps and trying to become something. The direction towards pluralism may be one feasible direction for the ethnic groups. As ethnic groups develop their own identities and skills, they will develop a social class system within their own ethnic group. The minute you develop a social class or other kind of stratification within your own ethnic group, the probabilities are very, very high that if you are say, upper-class, middle-class, or lower-class Japanese, that you will be much more similar to the white and the black and the Chicano across that line rather than within your own ethnic group. As they develop their own stratification systems, then that stratification would no doubt lead to cross-ethnic kinds of interaction. I think the obvious example (it's almost becoming a cliche) is that one may then ask "Is he a doctor?" rather than "Is he Japanese?" And if your beloved daughter brings home a Jewish doctor or a black doctor, eventually that may be more salient in terms of what you want than, "Is he Japanese?" I see the stage of ethnic puralism as almost a pre-stage for some kind of integration on a different level.

QUESTION: In your position as a researcher, what do you feel should be your relationship to the Asian American Community?

KITANO: I don't know. That's a question most researchers never face. I think there is a dimension of ethnic responsibility and that you try very hard to do research on several levels, and what comes out is a value choice. Anything that I think will be extremely damaging to the Asian Community, I would probably not research; and if I did find something at a period that in my judgment might be misused grossly, I would probably not publish. One tries to report back to the ethnic community in those areas where one thinks, at least from my point of view, they could stand some sort of improvement. But with sound empirical data. If I think that there's a high degree of discrimination going on by Asian groups, then at least among Asian groups I try to point this out as gently as I can. But if I had to make a blatant remark saying, "The Asians are as racist as anybody else," I probably would not say that because obviously that could not only be used, but misused. And the empirical evidence will be mixed on that score.

This is why if it comes out that Japanese are less criminal, less delinquent or whatever, I find that it's something I will publish without any difficulty, at least in the scholarly journals. But always in the interpretations, I try to indicate that there are other features of the culture that should also be assessed; and the second thing is not to compare the Japanese with any other groups with the implication that we're good and the others are bad.

QUESTION: Hayakawa said during the San Francisco State Strike that there is no such thing as an innocent bystander. You're either there or not. His warning was to go watch the demonstrations on T. V. So that's what really concerns me about being a middleman minority, it's not your choice to be a middleman minority. It's decided for you. How is that going to work when Sanseis say that they have a Third World perspective because they see the future not with white people and that their values lie with the struggles of Third World peoples?

KITANO: Except that the Third World concept is a nebulous one too. And so I don't know what any of these systems has to offer to people in the middle. Previous generations tried to join the White World and, depending on your definition, were successful in certain areas and not successful in others. I think a lot of the younger generation feel that joining the Third World is a possible solution. And I don't doubt at all that many Asians have joined the White World, others the Third World, and if they've achieved a degree of identity and comfort, I say, "Good, join those." But that still leaves a large group of people in the middle who aren't too sure which to join, and I think that's why the middleman thing is of such a personal interest to me. I don't want to join the White World wholeheartedly; I don't think the Third World makes more than a certain degree of sense. If the Blacks took complete power of the United States and the Whites were at the bottom, we would still be in the middle. The middleman by definition will fare no better or worse at the top or the bottom--you're the middle of that sandwich whether the wheat bread goes on top or the white bread goes on top. So in some ways a permanent middleman position is maybe what the Asian in the United States has to look forward to. Then you start thinking, "What does that mean?"

QUESTION: I don't see much optimism in your conclusion that we're going to be a middleman minority no matter who's on top in America. Do you feel you have a responsibility to find alternate models?

KITANO: Yes and no. I think for me, the best solution is to achieve a sense of reality. Whether what I see is a good world or a bad world, that's the next question; but as long as I know what the realities are, then I think I can make my own choices. But if I don't know what the realities are, if people give me myths and dreams and illusions and lies and falsehoods, then I would be in bad shape. So I don't use the term pessimism or optimism although eventually I'll have to, but the first stage is that once any human being knows the realities of the world and the realities of his choices, then hopefully he can make whatever choices he thinks are appropriate. This is why I think I'm wiser now knowing that I live in a racist state as a member of a middleman minority group than when I was younger, when I felt that I lived in an open demoncracy and I could do exactly what I wanted; I was really living in a dream world.

It's really a cliche, "Know yourself"--know yourself, your world, your enemy, and your friends.

I think that once you are reasonably clear as to where the problem lies, then a search for newer and perhaps more creative models will be in order. But if you are not clear and have an illusory grasp of the world, then there may never be a creative next step.

Response and Change for the Asian in America:
A Survey of Asian American Literature

BRUCE IWASAKI

The experience of Asians in America has been such a neglected area of study, there is no wonder that the literary output of Asian Americans is virtually unknown. True, there have been no Japanese-American Saul Bellows; no Chinese-American Ralph Ellisons; no Filipino-American N. Scott Momadays. But there have been--and are--noteworthy authors of Asian descent in the United States. The literature of Asian Americans has themes running through it which in turn reflect how this literature has been received. That is, just as the historical study of Asians (indeed, all minority groups) in the United States is actually a critical study of the majority culture, so an examination of Asian American literature sheds light upon the exclusionary literary tradition of white America. There is then, a self-reflexivity in this writing; the social experience of Asians is closely tied to the subject, and, as we shall see, the form of the literature.

The problems of Asians in America--the dynamics of change and the response to this change--are unique. By studying how a wide variety of Asian American writers have responded to this country, we hope to discern some pattern to the literature. Then we may examine some of the contemporary writing of Asian Americans and analyze its limitations and speculate on its possibilities.

American literature in the last century has dealt at length with the spiritual nature of man and the changing values of his society and institutions. Henry Adams, Twain, Faulkner and Fitzgerald, for example, have written of man's sense of displacement and fragmentation, and the society's decline. In a more compact, but more intense form, this sense of individual "self-lessness" has been a major influence upon the Asian American experience.

The first Asian immigrants encountered fierce racism in the legal system, physical violence, and economic exploitation. Beyond the struggle for physical survival, differences in culture and language were additional sources of alienation. More recently, an ambivalent, even ambiguous, ethnic and social identity has been manifested. Conflicts caused by a culturally reinforced stratification of generations have further added to the peculiar situation of Asians in America.

The response to this situation by Asian writers has been so diverse it may be fallacious to speak of an Asian American literature at all. But the variety is what is so interesting. Asian American literature cannot be easily categorized as, for example, simply non-existent; or linked with the Old Country; or a quaint blending of East and West. Majority culture critics will have to disabuse themselves of their stereotypes toward Asian people, and the type of literature produced by them. Perhaps some Asian Americans will too.

Yone Noguchi exemplifies the search for new forms of artistic expression. He was the first Japanese-American poet to publish in the United States. Born in Japan in 1875, he came to America at eighteen and became a protege of California poet Joaquin Miller. His collection, FROM THE EASTERN SHORE (1905) reflects the traditional forms and images of Japanese verse:

Lines

When I am lost in the deep body of the mist
   on a hill,
The universe seems built with me as its pillar
Am I the god upon the face of the deep, nay
   deepless deepness in the beginning?[1]

Reprinted with permission of the author. Mr. Iwasaki is presently a senior at UCLA, majoring in English and psychology.

The daring tone and metaphors of a later poem show quite another influence:

To Robert Browning

You are a smoking-room story-teller of the pageant of life seen by senses,
Your gusto in speech turns your art into obscurity,
Again from the obscurity into a valedictory:
You are a provincialism endorsed by eccentric pride.
You are sometimes riotous to escape from anarchism,
Your great thirst for expression makes you a soul-wounding romancer,
You often play the mystagogue, and appear cruel.
You are a glutton by colorful adventures,
You are a troubadour serenading between the stars and Life,
Your love song on a guitar torments us even physically;
You are a realist who under the darkness purifies himself into the light
    of optimism;
You are a griffin wildly dancing on human laughter.[2]

A friend of Noguchi's, Jun Fujita, also wrote in English, and also published in noteworthy magazines like POETRY. In his book TANKA: POEMS IN EXILE (1923), more traditional Oriental forms express the loneliness of living in Chicago.

To Elizabeth

Against the door dead leaves are falling;
On your window the cobwebs are black.
Today, I linger alone.

The foot-step?
A passer-by.[3]

The most radical artist/writer of new forms--in any literature--is Sadakichi Hartmann. Kenneth Rexroth has called this Bohemian the "court magician to two generations of American intellectuals."[4] Carl Sadakichi Hartmann was born in Japan in 1867, the son of a German trader and a Japanese mother. Because of rebellion from his father's strict discipline, he was sent off to America at the age of thirteen. There he studied art and literature, and was soon championing American art and pioneering the recognition of Oriental art. Sadakichi gained great notoriety by his off-beat behavior, but his undisciplined eccentricities also put him far ahead of his time.

> After all, he was writing haiku and tanka as early as 1898, long before
> the Imagists. In 1895, he drafted the script for the first psychedelic
> light show, noting that its presentation would have to await the inven-
> tion...means of projection. In 1902, he held the first perfume concert
> in New York City.[5]

He fought against the rigidly conforming mass consciousness; "the average mind accepts wisdom, beauty, or any gift of the Muses as sluggishly as magnesium absorbs moisture,"[6] he wrote. His was certainly an atypical Asian response to America. Sadakichi was an atypical man. But our wonder may partly reflect our expectancies of sedately acceptable Oriental writing.

Another writer who sometimes experimented with new forms was José Garcia Villa. Born in the Philippines, he came to the United States in 1930. He wrote short stories, but is most noted for his poetry; Dame Edith Sitwell, Mark Van Doren, David Daiches, Richard Eberhart and others have lauded his work. Villa's poems do not dwell on his Filipino heritage, rather his mystical Blakean quality transcends all experience.

> Inviting a tiger for a weekend.
> The gesture is not heroics but discipline.
> The memoirs will be splendid.
>
> Proceed to dazzlement, Augustine.
> Banish little birds, graduate to tiger.   [5]
> Proceed to dazzlement, Augustine.

> Any tiger of whatever colour
> The same as jewels any stone
> Flames always essential morn.
>
> The guest is luminous, peer of Blake. 10
> The host is gallant, eye of Death.
> If you will do this you will break
>
> The little religions for my sake.
> Invite a tiger for a weekend.
> Proceed to dazzlement, Augustine.[7]

Villa made two innovations in verse form: the peculiar use of the comma to regulate the lines' "verbal density and time movement,"[8] and the exploratory use of "reverse consonance." Reverse consonance is a new method of rhyming,

> The last sounded consonants of the last syllable, or the last principal consonants of a word, are reversed for the corresponding rhyme. Thus a rhyme for <u>near</u> would be run, rain, green, reign.[9]

An exerpt:

> It's a hurricane of spirit--
> That's genius! Not God can tear
> It from itself, though He is the rose
> In this skull that's seer.[10]

All of these diverse writers share a collective individuality--they all seek innovative forms to express their experiences in a new culture. They were among the earliest Asians to publish in America. Their search for new patterns of communication surely reflect--however unconsciously--the search for a new self definition, amidst numerous hardships, of the Asian pioneers to this country.

The search for an Asian American identity is a central problem in much of the literature. One response to this dilemma is to look back to Asia. Several authors have done this, in different ways, for different reasons. Lin Yutang, born in China in 1895, was educated there, and then earned an M.A. at Harvard and a Ph.D. at Leipzig. He has written over thirty books in English over a wide spectrum of subjects: history, philosophy, art, and novels. CONFUCIUS SAW NANCY AND OTHER ESSAYS ABOUT NOTHING (1936) contains a witty tragicomic play, as well as essays on topics ranging from Chinese calligraphy, to feminist thought in ancient China. Most of his novels are set in Asia; THE FLIGHT OF THE INNOCENTS (1964) for example, about refugees fleeing to Hong Kong, is a tendentious criticism of the People's Republic of China. In CHINATOWN FAMILY (1948), Tom, a young man brought to America and trained in its scientific attitudes, comes to accept the traditional Eastern philosophies of his ancestors.

Lee Yu-Hwa was also born and educated in China. She moved to America in 1947, took an M.A. at Pennsylvania, and has published short stories in several American literary magazines. Her narratives, though set in China, parallel the cultural conflicts between generations in Asian American families. In "The Last Rite," originally published in THE LITERARY REVIEW and included in the 1965 collection of THE BEST AMERICAN SHORT STORIES, the progressive thinking Chou Nan-An acquiesces to the matrimonial demands of his staunchly traditional family. But the ending is not so much a triumph of old ways over new as one of spontaneous emotion over both traditional and modern mechanization.

A third writer who sets his fiction in Asia is the Korean-born Richard Kim. His three novels, THE MARTYRED (1964), THE INNOCENT (1968), and LOST NAMES (1970), explore human identity and belief against the background of the Korean War. His stark style imitates--some critics feel unsuccessfully--Albert Camus, by whom he is deeply influenced.

These three authors, who have experienced America after growing up in Asia respond to cultural and generational conflict by setting their fiction in the Orient. Perhaps this more familiar scene frees them from otherwise artificial modes, and permits a wider expression of human experience.

Still another group of writers has chosen to relate the simple daily occurances of the Asian communities. Otherwise sharing little in common, these writers usually dwell on the private and public isolation of this experience.

Bienvenido Santos, born in the Philippines in 1911, came to this country as a lecturer before World War II. Later he returned to the islands where he was the president of Legazpi College. Since coming back to study writing at the State University of Iowa in 1957, Santos has written several books of poetry and fiction as well as publishing widely in literary journals. His stories are set both in the Philippines and the States, but their common theme is loneliness, pathos, and quiet desperation His characters self-consciously search for love or friendship or sometimes just ordinary human contact. In "Footnote to a Laundry List," he describes a college professor in the Philippines.

> At forty, he didn't feel too old; still, there were the bleak years ahead he kept seeing before him. Dr. Carlos was not unattractive, but he was shy. In class, his voice barely reached the back row.... After a while, they stopped trying to understand whatever it was he was saying. He didn't make sense.[11]

Dr. Carlos remembers his trip back from America,

> It was a lonesome, miserable trip back home. He was sick every day of the first week, but he mailed her a letter. Each letter was a passionate avowal of love, no mention of seasickness. And he meant every word he wrote her then and since. Paula was quick to answer in the beginning. She owed him a couple of letters now.[12]

One of Santo's achievements is that though his content invites a merely sentimental rendering, his consciously simple style undercuts any response in excess of the situation. One very brief tale, "My Most Memorable Christmas in America," deals with self-pity, is a story about a sentimental experience. But the story itself is remarkably free of maudlin bathos.

Toshio Mori is not always in control of this feeling. But the short stories in his only book, YOKOHAMA, CALIFORNIA (1949), though often stylistically crude, are just as often charming and poignant portraits of the Japanese community just prior to World War II. Each story is an eagerly hacked off slice of life--what Mori's ear misses, his curious, penetrating eye picks up. Each tale seems to end with an optimistic look to tomorrow; it is ironic that the book's publication was postponed eight years partly spent by Mori in the wartime concentration camps. Sadly, he never published again.

One of the more talented Japanese-American authors is Hisaye Yamamoto, who was born in Redondo Beach in 1921. Immediately after the war, when jobs for Japanese were not forthcoming, she was hired by a black newspaper in Los Angeles. Since then, she has published in the ethnic press, as well as such prestigious journals as the PARTISAN REVIEW, KENYON REVIEW, and FURIOSO. In "Yoneko's Earthquake" she conveys with great subtlty the close interpersonal dynamics of a Japanese family in rural California. This tale was chosen for the 1952 collection of Martha Foley's BEST AMERICAN SHORT STORIES. All of her stories are about Japanese-Americans, but she skillfully generalizes this experience by a fascinating preoccupation with social deviance--sexual, psychological, and artistic. Treating such atypical themes with cool understatement, she exposes tensions of a socially oppressed, and emotionally repressed, minority group.

The last of these writers who focus specifically upon the Asian experience in America is not a fiction writer. In ISSEI AND NISEI: THE INTERNMENT YEARS (1967), Daisuke Kitagawa describes the tense conflict between generations in the Japanese community,

> The division was remarkably clear-cut: Issei--Japanese in culture and nationality, Buddhist in religion; Nisei--American and Christian. The Issei were already past middle age, and the Nisei were barely past adolescence. The former were separated from Japan by the Pacific Ocean and the ever-increasing distance of time, and the latter were segregated from American society by barriers of social discrimination and race prejudice.[13]

Kitagawa is overly biased toward Christianity, somewhat irritatingly accomodationist, and rather simplistically glib. He feels that,

> ... the war, with the wholesale evacuation, changed the entire situation so completely that it can almost be said to have served as shock therapy for the collective neurosis of the Nisei community.[14]

If racist stereotypes have always plagued the Asian American community, today there is a stereotype promoted in part by that community. That is the success story. Asians have no problems; Asians have made it. Ingratiatingly cheerful autobiographies such as Monica Sone's NISEI DAUGHTER (1953) and Pardee Lowe's FATHER AND THE GLORIOUS DESCENDANT (1943) are examples. But this position, as shown in the following narratives by "successful" Japanese and Chinese may tell us something about the current situation of Asian Americans they did not intend to convey.

Daniel Inouye's JOURNEY TO WASHINGTON (1967) and Jade Snow Wong's FIFTH CHINESE DAUGHTER (1945) read like Horatio Alger novels. In both, the Protestant virtue of hard work--*very* hard work, is stressed. One must not detract from the achievement: Inouye, through heavy self-sacrifice became a war hero and finally a United States senator; Miss Wong, by scrupulous saving and fierce ambition, overcame finances and tradition to graduate with honors from Mills College, and eventually established her own ceramics shop. Both stories are true, yet both are myths. They are myths when they are taken as lessons: few people have the spartan self-discipline of an Inouye, few the thorough intelligence of a Wong. They are also myths when taken as a realistic response to a racist society. No mistake: both writers are fully conscious of the discrimination they've encountered. However, the implicit message in both books is that by succeeding in terms of the majority culture's norms, a sort of victory over racism can be won. Neither person perceives how accepting those standards actually reinforces this racist society. Neither one, however well intentioned, quite get to the root of things; they react more to white middle class values of success than to the problems common to the entire Asian community. Inouye and Wong are individuals of good will, but their books quite miss the mark. Unintentionally they tell us how America likes its minorities to behave; and deeper, how America behaves. Change without any.

A more realistic autobiography is Daniel Okimoto's AMERICAN IN DISGUISE (1971). Born in a relocation center, Okimoto at least has no illusions about the depth of American racism. Also, despite both his parents being ministers, he does not heave Christianity at us the way Inouye and Wong do, nor does he preach about the "success" of Asians compared to other minority groups in the U.S. Still, we're unsure about Okimoto. For example, he puts forward a potentially dangerous half-truth about the Japanese community being an interdependent extended family. But this leads to the stereotype that Asians can take care of their own problems, and finally, that Asians have no problems. In addition, this generally enlightened book has left unexplored the paradox of Nisei social clannishness and the drive to assimilate white middle class values that wrenches the identity of so many post-war Japanese Americans.

Finally, there is a contradiction--no fault of Okimoto's--not *in* the book, but *of* the book. AMERICAN IN DISGUISE is not written as a success story; nevertheless its author has moved from the San Diego ghetto to an education at Princeton, Harvard, and the even more prestigious Tokyo University. What publisher would have it otherwise?

But step back: Once again the central concerns of Asian American literature--conflicts of adjustment, isolation, alienation due to racism, i.e., Asian identity--encapsulate, and even determine the form (sometimes even the presence) of the work itself. That is, the different responses to the Asian experience are not only reflected in the subject of this literature, but also in the manner this literary response is undertaken and explored. So far, in seeking a definition of the "self," most of the Asian literature has found expression within limited bounds. The self is always defined in relation to the conceptions of the majority culture, whether it is in opposition to, or in agreement with it. Perhaps this initial overview of past Asian American writing indicates that acceptable, graduate-school American literature is not exclusionary--but like the one-dimensional society, is all inclusionary. Asian American literature, whose theme is "identity" has as yet no identity by itself; Asian American literature, a response to racism, has its form greatly dictated by the racism in the society. No exit.

Is this ironic situation also true in the modern writing of younger Asians? It's hard to show, since in contemporary literature perspective is difficult to attain. And especially in poetry, where the range of expression is wider, the form is as important as the content, and where crude didacticism will both sink a poem and obstruct subtle criticism.

Diana Chang published in POETRY magazine when she was twenty-two (1946), and is an accomplished poet by any standard. Born in New York, her family moved to China before she was a year old. She returned to the United States after the war. Though her first novel, THE FRONTIERS OF LOVE (1956) examines ethnic identity in the romantic encounters of Eurasians in wartime Shanghai, her poetry is more concerned with mortality and the inner consciousness.

        Mood

I watch one by one
Strands from my cigaret
Float to the ceiling
Water-marked with sun.

One by one
Late fall's leoparded leaves   5
Float down like stray
Discarded thoughts.

The clock nudges noon up on me
With each of twelve fingers
While I float among the little things--   10
    Warm window-sill
      Three cornered cactus

That make a mood,
And pin me there
The way a moth is held
Between glass-panes.[15]

It is probably straining to assert that "Filiae" deals with a response to traditional Chinese filial piety. The element is certainly there, but the poem is far richer and more subtle than that line of criticism allows:

Daughters may have sons at twenty.
Innocence nursing nature.
We cease to be young
Quite early, sweet with sobriety,

Harmonious as wives. But mothers   5
Of daughters do not know,
Gargoyles at our backs
Spew in all weathers

Affection, rivalry,
Hurt feelings, delusioned,   10
Debts and fire

These familial persuasions
Rain down old sluices
Kept open by birthdays,
Christmas, duty,   15
Snapshots and baby spoons[16]
. . . .

Wing Tek Lum, winner of the 1969 Poetry Center award, says of being Chinese-American, "The hyphen is like the tightrope I walk... I draw from both cultures, and yet I am part of neither."[17] "Scar" is his prize winning poem:

> Living together
> usually you cooked
> and I washed.
> Once though
> Helping you slice onions 5
> I was blurred by my own tears
> knicking my wrist.
>
> Scrambling an egg
> this morning 10
> I found the whitish scar
> remembering
> when we had to call
> the doctor, explaining then
> that I was no suicide.[18]

    Certainly the work of both Miss Chang and Wing Tek Lum is very well crafted indeed, but one does not explode from the study upon reading it. This is fine. Our purpose is not to classify any writers by their level of gusto. However, these particular talents have chosen a different response to the Asian experience. It is _not_ "no" response. But it does not confront change--either in new verse forms or in new definitions of the self--and to that extent it is "safe." It is within bounds. Beautiful art, but if we seek a more vigorous confrontation between Asian American writers and their oppressive social-literary experience, we must move on.

    Here we are on rather slippery ground. Several reasons: first, we will move away from historical analysis, through criticism, to literary speculation. And on the topic of Asian American literature--in primary material a past of barely eighty years, in commentary no past at all--future projection seems quite rash. Also with the two writers we will discuss, a level of objectivity is lost; both writers are known to this critic though not personally beyond their published record. So.

    Lawson Fusao Inada is a third generation Japanese-American poet from Fresno, California. In his early thirties, he has been writing for about ten years. His first collection, BEFORE THE WAR was published in early 1971. He has also appeared in THE CARLTON MISCELLANY, CHICAGO REVIEW, KAYAK, NORTHWEST REVIEW and others. In addition, his poems have been anthologized in 3 NORTHWEST POETS (1970), DOWN AT THE SANTA FE DEPOT (1970), and NEW DIRECTIONS 23 (1971).

    Frank Chin is a thirty-one year old Chinese-American from San Francisco. His short story "Food For All His Dead" was published in CONTACT magazine in 1962; it has since been included in the anthology THE YOUNG AMERICAN WRITERS edited by Richard Kostelanetz. An exerpt from this yet unpublished novel, A CHINESE LADY DIES appeared in Ishmael Reed's collection 19 NECROMANCERS FROM NOW. He is also the editor of a forthcoming anthology entitled ASIAN AMERICAN LITERATURE.

    Both writers attended U.C. Berkeley and the Creative Writing Program at the State University of Iowa. They also know each other (Chin wrote a highly laudatory review of Inada's book). Both are concerned with the Asian experience--Inada primarily from his life in the concentration camps, Chin from growing up in Chinatown. Both are very talented writers--of considerable accomplishment and greater potential. But for both, it is their literary criticism; specifically their outlook on Asian writing as Asian writers that we will analyze.

Exerpts; Lawson's poems:

from "From Our Album"

. . . .

> When the threat lessened,
> when we became tame,
> my father and friends
> took a train to Chicago

>   for factory work,   5
>   for packaging bolts.
>   One grew a mustache
>   and called himself Carlos.
>
>   And they all made a home
>   with those of their own--
>
>   rats, bed bugs, blacks.[19]

from "The Great Bassist":

>   And when I walk the streets
>   wind
>   flattens my beard
>   and I look tired, tattered.
>
>   That doesn't matter.   5
>
>   But I need your love.
>   We need
>   each other.
>
>   So when I come down your street
>   with my Great Bass--   10
>
>   toss us your love--
>
>   we'll play you
>   love petals.
>
>   Love us back
>
>   If you don't, we'll kill you.   15
>
>   All of you.
>
>   We will.[20]

No Bashō, he. Inada's poetry has a forcefully insistent--but very deft--sense of rhythm. Crafted but powerful. But when Inada read at UCLA May 28, 1971, I (no scholarly detachment here), though enjoying the poetry, was peculiarly uncomfortable with his opening remarks. He said that as a writer he was little concerned with his Oriental heritage since his experience was solely an American one. Of the few Asian American writers he knew those he had read he considered inferior for trying to sound acceptably "Oriental." Lawson commented that some of his relatives might have expected him to write haiku. In a letter to the PACIFIC CITIZEN after they had published an idiotic review of his book, Lawson suggested, "No doubt a quaint collection of cricket haikus would have been cause to praise my Oriental sensitivity."[21] Lawson is correct: moving away from an affected stereotyped style is progress. But his critical outlook holds implications I suspect he is unaware of. Let us turn to Frank Chin.

In "Food For All His Dead," Johnny, an educated young Chinese-American maintains a strained relationship with his tradition-minded parents and with Chinatown in general. The story, by its intelligent manipulation of dialogue and accents, is secondarily about language and the limits of language. It opens with an announcement in Chinatown dialect:

>   "Jus' forty-fie year 'go, Doctah Sun Yat-sen free China from da
>   Manchus. Dat's why all us Chinee, alla ovah da woil are celebrate
>   Octob' tan or da Doubloo Tan...!"
>
>   The shouted voice came through the open bathroom window. The
>   shouting and music was till loud after rising through the night's dry
>   air; white moths jumped on the air, danced through the window over
>   the voice, and lighted quickly on the wet sink, newly reddened from

> his father's attack. Johnny's arms were around his father's belly, holding the man upright against the edge of the sink to keep the man's mouth high enough to spit lung blood into the drain.[22]

Later Johnny accompanies his father to the square where the man will give a speech. Here Johnny most hurts his father, and in his mother's opinion, kills him, when he points out the problem of language as it relates to his Chinese identity.

> "Maybe I'm not Chinese, pa! Maybe I'm just a Chinese accident. You're the only one that seems to care that I'm Chinese." The man glared at the boy and did not listen. "Pa, most of the people I don't like are Chinese. They even _laugh_ with accents, Christ!" He turned his head from the man, sorry for what he said. It was too late to apologise.
>
> "You dare talk to your father like that?" the man shouted in Chinese. He stood back from the boy, raised himself and slapped him, whinning through his teeth as his arm swung heavily toward the boy's cheek. "You're no son of mine! No son! I'm ashamed of you!".[23]

Frank Chin's preoccupation with diction is central to his critical theory as well. "America has taught us to lie about ourselves, to avoid facing our American history and experience. Maintaining Oriental culture translated reads, 'keep your place.'"[24]

> Blacks, Chicanos, Jews all write what could be called bad English. Their particular badmouth is recognized as being their own legitimate mother tongue. Only Asian-Americans are driven out of their tongue and expected to be home in a language they never use and a culture they encounter only in books written in English.[25]

In a letter to Peter ___ dated January 14, 1970, Chin criticizes a Chinese-American journalist,

> Generally speaking, Ben Fong-Torres' attempts at colloquial English come off as effeminate. He writes a mutant language that sometimes is great. If it were Chinese-American, it would be great. By the standards of English, it's awful.
> . . . .
> If the language of Chinese-America has to be called English, it is the English of Ralph Williams and Chick Lamber . . . .[26]

The problem of language that so bothers Inada and Chin is the key to understand both the value and limits of their art. Inada rejects the cute safe diction expected of an Oriental poet by writing in earthy, jazzy rhythms and muscular metaphors. In his fiction, Chin brings it even closer; he uses shifts in language to examine the implications of language and speech. It is easy to see why they reject such stereotypes about the degree centuries of Eastern culture influence third generation Asian Americans. But they seem to reject the culture too. Furthermore, it is understandable to expect recognition as a _writer_ without condescending labels of being a fine Asian American writer. Chin is right, Pearl Buck-talk never was part of the Asian American vocabulary. But the problem is not analagous to say, the blacks. Whites considered the blacks' tonuge unacceptably bad; the Asian stereotype--equally pernicious for being a stereotype--was quaint, and ultimately acceptable. The problem isn't diction--or tone, style, accents, speech, or even language. They're off the mark and, finally, (again) trapped if they assert that the problem of Asian Americans is that they mimic--either the classic Orient, black rhetoric, or white colloquialisms. Here Inada and Chin are responding to the majority culture's stereotypes instead of confronting the actual root problems of the Asian American community.

Again, we have the limitation, the absorbtion, of both content and form. No matter how "universal" the language and style, a piece of literature will not convey a universal human experience as long as the community is used merely as source material. Employed in this way, the community becomes little more than "local color"--in writing, not at all less deplorable than an affected style. We are at the point where art touches society, for here artistic decisions are tied with moral, and finally, political decisions. And by ignoring this crucial interrelationship, Chin and Inada remain within the bounds that makes so much literature "safe."

What's the escape? Well, to choose not to confront the problems of change in the Asian community (at least not on its terms), like Diana Chang and Wing Tek Lum. Or to extend the first (and really praiseworthy) efforts of Chin and Inada. One must escape the closed system where Asian literature is written and judged in terms of Anglo literary conceptions. A closer involvement with the very roots of the Asian experience (both subject and mode of the literature) is required. Thus, the final extension of this rather extravagant literary theory is the merging of political action and literature.

We have dealt with the various literary responses to the Asian experience: experimental forms, return to Asia, focusing on the everyday events of people in the community, success story, withdrawal, and (partial) involvement. Upon inspection, each of these can easily be translated into political responses. Perhaps then, the means for breaking the closed circle that structures much of the literary imagination are the same means necessary for removing the bonds of political oppression. Literature and literary criticism then, instead of numbing the reader of his capacity to struggle realistically with social problems, can unleash the creative force and human potential that make qualitative social change possible. Thus, revolutionary political action and the expression of universal experience in, say, poetry, become as one. Literature and change no longer <u>describe</u> each other--they become the <u>same thing</u>.

Well, we said we'd be on slick ground. Of course there are no examples of the ultimate product yet. But perhaps we can point toward this final merging.

Joann Miyamoto is a radical activist in New York, working in the Latin and Asian communities. With Chris Iijima, they write and sing original revolutionary songs. The following is an example. We do not think it is merely a "political poem." It represents an entire community's experience. This may not be the poetry of the burning brush, but is a worthy piece of Asian American writing. Hopefully, the direction of Asian American writing too.

(meant to be read aloud)

when I was young
kids used to ask me
what are you?
I'd tell them what my mom told me
I'm an American
chin chin Chinaman
you're a Jap!
flashing hot inside
I'd go home
my mom would say
don't worry
he who walks alone
walks faster

people kept asking me
what are you?
and I would always answer
I'm an American
they'd say
no, what nationality?
I'm an American
that's where I was born
flashing hot inside
and when I'd tell them what they wanted to know
Japanese . . . .
Oh I've been to Japan

I'd get it over with
so they could catalogue and file me
pigeon-hole me
so they'd know just how

to think of me
priding themselves
they could guess the difference
between Japanese and Chinese
they had me wishing I was what I'd
been seeing in movies and on T.V.
on billboards and in magazines

and I tried
while they were making laws in California
   against us owning land
we were trying to be American
and laws against us intermarrying with white people
we were trying to be American
when they put us in concentration camps
we were trying to be American
our people volunteered to fight against their own country
trying to be American
when they dropped the atom bomb on Hiroshima and Nagasaki
we were still trying.

finally we made it
most of our parents
fiercely dedicated to give us
a good education
to give us everything they never had
we made it
now they use us as an example
to the blacks and browns
how we made it
how we overcame.

but there was always
someone asking me
what are you?

now I answer
I'm an Asian
and they say
why do you want to separate yourselves
now I say
I'm Japanese
and they say
don't you know this is the greatest country in the world
now I say in America
I'm part of the third world people
and they say
if you don't like it here
why don't you go back.

            12-70 JM

    finis.

Notes

[1] Yone Noguchi, FROM THE EASTERN SEA, fourth ed., (Tokyo: Fuzabo & Co., 1905), p. 16.
[2] Yone Noguchi, DOUBLE DEALER, November, 1923, v. 5, no. 30., p. 200.
[3] Jun Fujita, TANKA: POEMS IN EXILE, (Chicago: Covici-McGee Co., 1923), p. 52.
[4] Sadakichi Hartmann, WHITE CHRYSANTHEMUMS, George Knowland and Harry W. Lawton, eds., (New York: Herder and Herder, 1970), p. xi.

[5] Hartmann, p. xxv.
[6] Hartmann, p. 41.
[7] Jose Garcia Villa, POEMS 55, (Manila: Alberto S. Florentino, 1962), p. 16.
[8] Villa, p. 59.
[9] Villa, p. 58.
[10] Villa, p. 9.
[11] Bienvenido Santos, THE DAY THE DANCERS CAME, (Manila: Bookmark, 1967), p. 24.
[12] Santos, p. 29.
[13] Daisuke Kitagawa, ISSEI AND NISEI: THE INTERNMENT YEARS, (New York: Seabury, 1967), p. 39.
[14] Kitagawa, p. 31.
[15] Diana Chang, POETRY: A MAGAZINE OF VERSE, November, 1946, p. 74.
[16] Diana Chang, NEW YORK QUARTERLY, Fall 1970, p. 111.
[17] Lucille Medwick, "The Chinese Poet in New York," NEW YORK QUARTERLY, Fall 1970, p. 108.
[18] Wing Tek Lum, NYQ, p. 110.
[19] Lawson Fusao Inada, BEFORE THE WAR, (New York: Morrow, 1971), p. 20.
[20] Inada, p. 124.
[21] Lawson Fusao Inada, "Letter to PACIFIC CITIZEN," 31 March 1971.
[22] Frank Chin, "Food For All His Dead," CONTACT, vol. 3., no. 3., August 1962, p. 82.
[23] Chin, p. 84.
[24] Frank Chin, rev., LOS ANGELES FREE PRESS, vol. 8, no. 15, April 9-15, 1971, p. 31.
[25] Ibid.
[26] Frank Chin, "Letter to Peter," A READER OF ASIANS IN AMERICA, vol. 1, (Los Angeles: U.C.L.A. Asian American Studies Center, 1970), p. 66.

ROOTS

I

it was my last
           weekend in the states and
I didn't know
           whether I'd ever be able to come back so
there was no doubt where I had to go, man
  south
      from San Francisco to
                  LA
back to the ghetto
           and maybe even back to Poston -
Poston, Arizona
        where I was born, man
                    June 2nd, 1944
    Camp 2, shit
              but it
was too fucking hot, being August
                to drive all the way to
Poston, Arizona since
           my new Alfa Romero 1750 GTV
           didn't have
           air-conditioning or
           sleeping accomodations for two, so
I just went to LA (besides
           Poston?
where's that?
           just another ride in the
           coney island of my mind)

II

the final remarks of the preceding section (in fact the
whole fucking section) were the presentation of
           my credentials, designed
to let you know
           I'm literarily inclined and
           have an Alfa and
           the need for sleeping accomodations for two
           (which should have filled your dirty little
           minds with wild visions of sexy naked girls
           with flowing blond hair and mouseybrown cunts)
to let you know
           I'm therefore better than
           the average Japanese
           which means therefore
           I'm very typical
               very average
                  Japanese
hence the
      presentation of my credentials

Reprinted from GIDRA, December, 1969.

III

I was

              going back to East LA, to
              Brooklyn Avenue and Soto Street
              and the Evergreen cemetery,
              going back to the roots
              going back to the ghetto
(only we didn't call it a ghetto then, ten years ago
shit we didn't even know what a ghetto was, just like
we didn't know camp was a place for concentration
instead of relocation, ten years ago)
                                but it felt good

going back
down home
and, baby
        everything I was gonna do was gonna be so funky
                                (right on)

IV

of course, I had to see Jii-chan and Baa-chan
              I knew I'd never see Jii-chan again
                              alive
I cried for him but had a fight with Baa-chan
about the war in Vietnam which was stupid so
              I split
                    knowing I'd miss her too
                    even though she talks too much
                    feeling bad
                              but then
my cousin Johnny in
              Monterey Park
                            (where all the good people
                            seem to be moving)
told me there was a gang somewhere with
              "two thousand dudes"
and Barry (who's coaching B football and playing in a rock band)
        said
            he hates Japanese girls too
            but really digs on
            Mexican chicks
and I said
        I wished I could
        dig on Mexican chicks
              too

V

    saturday night
                driving, cruising around
                checking out the broads
                none of them digging my new
                silver fuel-injected Alfa at
                all (shit)
                          but
there were places I had to go
                      Tommy's (for a burger and a pepsi)
then to Acapulco
                (for the hottest burritos in LA)
and, round midnight, past
                the old drugstore
on the corner of Soto and St Louis (is it
    still there? I was too drunk to notice.)
a long time ago
when I had friends
we would go to that drugstore and
        have a suicide for 5¢
                    Ronnie Minami
                    Richard Kami
                    Sam Iwaoa
                    and
                    Ron Tanaka
                    from Madera

VI

                      but
I had to leave that place
                      it
wasn't really my place
                Tommy's
                Monterey Park
                or even
    the hottest burritos in LA, I
had to get on that freeway and drive
    out of there
    and out of California
    and away from ghettos and
    suburban housing developments
    and shit like that
                    to the place
                    where I would find
                    that ideal woman and
have her
without guilt or fear
                where
                    I could find myself at peace with myself
                and
                    I could look at that face in the mirror
again
    I
didn't really want those roots
those shitty little streets in East LA
but I needed them and wanted them to
                    speak to me
                          like a child
              this is how far you've come
              this is how far you'll have to go
              this is what you're leaving and
              this is the happiness you'll find
              two-thousand miles
                    from Tommy's

VII

    Vancouver, B.C.

I went to an opening last night
                      having received an
                      engraved invitation
                      from the director
of the gallery where
                    I had just purchased something
                (very pricey).
I stepped out of my silver Alfa,
flicked that imaginary speck of dust off
my new H. Freeman, and,
                  holding a cigarette (in one hand)
                  sipping champagne (with the other)
                  I was placed just to be there
                  looking at her
                  wondering if
she was part of the exhibit
                  and whether
she fucks
                  and (supposing that
her very elegant boy friend had
taken her away
because she
might have been looking too
                  interestingly) I
                wondered whether I ought to
                feel flattered, until
       (after two hours)
       the director
              stumbled
                    to that corner
                    where I had been
                              and
            asked
                (in his elevated danish accent)
if, though not remembering for not ever having known my name,
I
                  might not be so kind as to
                  step outside
                  and show
                  him and (what I understood to be)
                  his new mistress
                  a few
                  judo chops

(well!)

                                          RON TANAKA

A BRIEF BIOGRAPHICAL SKETCH OF A NEWLY-FOUND ASIAN MALE

RON LOW

I am a typical freshman, looking for a self and attempting to find a place for myself in the American society. This quarter I have, for the first time, begun to really participate actively towards my development as an Asian-American. Throughout my life I have experienced confusion, rejection and self-hostility because I lacked an awareness of who "Ron Low is, was and wants to

This article was written for an Asian American studies course at Cal State, Hayward, with instructor Magoroh Maruyama, in 1970.

be." Through a historical sketch of my life I will attempt to make these points more clear.

My parents ran a small grocery store in West Oakland. Because there were eight mouths to feed at that time, my parents had to send me away to attend nursery school. This way they were able to work in the store full-time and not worry or care for the baby, which was me. My first experience with people other than my immediate family was in nursery school. Nursery school was cool--no conflicts. Everyone got along fine with each other. There were no color differences or race differences whatsoever. All the other little kids were just looking for someone to play with. We were all friends, we played together, ate together, slept together, etc. It was really cool, I thought the whole world was like this. I could see no difference in them as they could not see any difference in me. Then came time for a new experience, elementary school.

Elementary school was the shits, I mean it really blew my mind, man was it a far out trip. With what I had experienced in nursery school, I thought it would be the same in elementary school, but it wasn't. Because we lived in a predominantly black area, the school which I attended was also predominantly black. At Prescott there were only 3 or 4 non-blacks in the whole school. I was the only Asian attending the school at that time. My experience at this elementary school was pure hell. All the other kids referred to me as being white or non-black. The classic phrase of "Ching Chong Chinaman sitting on a fence, trying to make a dollar out of fifteen cents" was tossed at me constantly. Because I was physically smaller than most of the other kids, I was getting the shit kicked out of me just about every day, even by the girls. It wasn't a normal school day if I didn't get picked on or beat up. Some of the older kids who knew my parents owned a store, threatened to beat me up if I didn't steal them some candy or something from my parents. By the end of my first year in elementary school, I was hurt, confused and didn't know what to do or who to turn to. Fortunately by this time my parents had earned enough money for us to move out of this area and settle down elsewhere. We still continued to operate the store, we just lived in a newly bought house. With the idea that I would be attending a new school this fall, I thought things would be different and even better than before. The new school I was to attend was Franklin. Franklin was an integrated school. My parents who had, by this time, sensed what I had encountered at Prescott, felt I would be better off attending this school. They also were white-conscious and wanted me to assimilate into the white society. They also felt that this was as good a place to start as any. But they were wrong and so was I. I still suffered the same rejections and hurts as I had experienced at Prescott, but this time it was twice as bad. Not only did the Blacks not accept me and considered me white, the whites wouldn't accept me either and labeled me non-white or even black on various occasions. I was in the middle as many other Asians were. Because I was a sensitive kid at the time, it sort of hurt me a little more than the others to be in the middle and to take all the shit and garbage that was thrown our way. Classic cut-down phrases seem to become more plentiful now. I can even recall one of my teachers reciting one in front of the whole class, which didn't help the situation any. It goes something like this: "You know how Chinese kids get their Chinese names? Well, they take a silver platter and toss it up into the air, then when it lands the sounds it makes is the name given to him or her. "kng! Ding! Chong! Etc." It took me a month to live that one down.

By the time I reached the third grade I was desperate. I had to do something, I couldn't stand it anymore. I was even at the point where I would cry sometimes when the other kids made fun of me. Then I discovered a way to get the kids off my back and to make allies. I noticed that if you cry or get mad when they're shooting on you, you just prolong it by crying and getting mad. But if you laugh and start to come down on yourself they let up real soon. I quickly became the school clown by cutting myself and my race down. The other kids started to become my friends because of this. One of the things I did as the school clown was sneak into the girls' bathroom. Man! Was that a trip. It blew my mind when I didn't see any of those wall-troughs or things on the walls like they had in the boys' bathroom. They had mirrors, doors on the stalls, it even smelled better than the boys'! I think that was the first time I realized that there was a difference between the girls and the boys. Oh! You think that was bad--you should have been there when we raided the lady teachers' bathroom. <u>Far Out</u>!! It was built much the same way as the girls' but in bigger dimensions. We also noticed a few new items like the Kotex containers. At first we couldn't figure out what they were. When I saw that there was blood on it, I thought it was for bloody noses. Teachers have bloody noses just like anyone else, young or old. But the thing I couldn't figure out is how it fits on the face. Not until I found out what they were for years later, it was one of my most puzzling mysteries of my life.

Cutting down on myself and race didn't bother me too much. I sort of enjoyed it. I hated what I was, being Chinese that is; my parents had the most to do with that. They expected too much from me. They wanted me to be this, do that, go here, read this, etc. What I couldn't understand was that when I received S's, which stand for Satisfactory, on my report card, I would catch hell. All the other Black kids and some of the Whites would receive praise and even money for each one they got. Why was I so different? If my parents were Black would I get the same treatment? I loved sports, but my parents were against it. They never let me participate in any athletic events. That really pissed me off. The thing that annoyed me most about being Chinese was having to go to Chinese school. Boy! Did I hate that. I just couldn't dig it. I couldn't figure out why I should spend two extra hours each day after school attending this crummy institution. I was practically forced to go by my parents. Although I hated to attend Chinese school, there was one important thing that took place there that influenced my transition in the later years. This was the only place where I no longer was being pushed around. Instead I was doing the most pushing. I was Mr. Big, the bully of the whole school. I didn't care if I learned anything or not; if anything I learned how to speak most of the bad words in Chinese, cuss, swear, etc. I could do what I wanted, didn't have to listen to the teacher, cheat on tests, etc. I was also ashamed of my family because of our different culture, customs and language.

By the sixth grade I had developed a philosophy. "There are only two groups of people in the world, Blacks and Whites, and if you're gonna make it in this world you'd better be part of one or the other." Because I grew up in a Black neighborhood and that most of my buddies or friends were Black, I chose to become a member of the Black group.

When I entered Junior High School I soon found out that fitting into the group is to feel and act Black. I found out that being a tough bastard with the vulgar and profane mouth and ideas, I was more accepted because I was not the classic Chinaman anymore. I associated less and less with the whites and Asians, and more and more with the Blacks. I started getting in good with the fellows by telling some pretty good jokes and stories. They may not seem too cool now, but back in them days you were rated by the jokes and stories you told. I had some pretty good ones alright. I heard some real rockers too. My grades started to drop to C's and D's. I started to groove with the guys after school and nights as well as in school. I continued to drop by once in a while with the Asians to check their scene out. Because I was a cool cat I started to attract some of the Asian chicks who thought I was hot stuff. I was also a few years ahead of my peers at hustling the women. I began hustling all the bitchin' looking chicks around, Black, Brown, Yellow, White. I didn't give a damn as long as they were <u>fine.</u> At that stage they determined also how cool you were by how many chicks you had scored on. To put it mildly, guys came to me for advice and pointers. I had become very proficient in sports such as football and basketball. Instead of being last choice and told what to do and where to play, I was now first or second, even fought over at times and giving orders out now. When I graduated from junior high, I not only graduated from the education institution but from tennis shoes to pointed shoes, jeans to tight black slacks, crew cut to long hair well-styled, no glasses to shades, flyaways to highboys and crew socks to pimp socks. My whole junior high career could be summed up in one phrase: "Happiness was being cool and Black." I was caught up in the wrong crowd according to Chinese standards and values, but I was comfortable and proud. The Blacks were saying, "Man! Ron is cool, he talks like a Black Brother, dresses like one, dances like one and even makes love like one!"

In high school I was still messing around. College was the farthest thing from my mind. I know that I was able to get into a college after I graduated even if it was Lancy or Merritt. I was accepted by both the Asians and the Blacks and was able to drift back and forth, but I primarily stuck with the Blacks. Being a member of the football team I became even more close to the Black group. By the eleventh grade the beginnings of the Black Identity and Black Power came to the high school campuses. Now I was faced with the problem I had managed to avoid for four years. "What would happen to me now?" I gradually began to drop off from the group and was spending more and more time with the Asians. I started to feel uncomfortable among them as I sensed they felt uncomfortable around me. Everyone began wearing naturals, their identities changed from being tough guys to together power people. What I realized then was that I wasn't together with myself or my people. Later on in the year the Chicanos and Asians were beginning to get together. An Asian Caucus formed at Oakland High and called itself Asian Bloc. I quickly jumped on the bandwagon. Actually I really didn't care, but I wanted and needed a group to relate with. Everyone else was doing it, so why couldn't I.

Asian Bloc continued to operate my senior year at Oakland High. I was still a bandwagonist and apathetic towards the Asian Crisis. Then I had a date with one of the very heavy chicks on the Asian Caucus. Not only was she very heavy but a very fine chick. On the date we started talking. I started showing her my usual jive that the other chicks really dug. I felt uncomfortable, then she really laid it on me. "What's wrong with you? You're not Black, you're yellow, quit talking and acting like one! Start thinking about your brothers and sisters. About how you can help them and yourself." She saw right through me. I didn't get over that experience for almost half a year. When I saw her at school or came across her, I felt very down and shitty. Although I felt this way I respected her for what she had done.

No one up to that point had ever put me down for being or acting like I was. She proved to me that you can act and play all the parts of something or someone else, but you'll never truly be that something or someone else. You are what you are, so be proud of it.

My feelings started changing. I stopped trying to play it cool. I was myself at last. At the same time, my sister got married to a White. I had naturally expected her to turn White and abandon the Chinese ways. What happened instead was that her husband took on the Chinese ways. I thought to myself, "If a White can be proud of being Chinese, why can't I?"

During the latter part of my senior year I was selected to go to Washington, D.C. to attend a Presidential Scholars program. At the conference I was the only Asian, there were also only four Blacks. One night we were allowed to rap all night. During our rap session I sat and listened. There were many southern whites at the conference. One of them started coming down on the Black movement. He said that the Blacks wanted too much too soon. I just sat there at first because I couldn't relate. Then the whitey pointed at me and said, "Look at him, he's not complaining and demanding, look how well off the Orientals are!" This blew my mind completely. I got up quickly and started rapping on his ass real good. This was the first time I had ever got up and defended my race instead of cutting it down. I will never forget that incident for as long as I live. I believe that was the catalyst for my search and involvement in Asian awareness and identity.

To me the movement of today's minority youth toward THIRD WORLD identities is a vital part of growing up. I have gone through my identity changes and at my age I know that I as a human being will go through many more changes. But my awareness of my lack of an Asian's Spirit will always have an effect on my development as Ron Low, that will influence me for the rest of my life. As I see my Asian peers now, too many are robbing themselves of their Asianess and I cannot do anything but talk and discuss how I feel about Asian awareness. With those who feel the same way as I do, we must participate and work together to develop an Asian awareness through community projects and gatherings.

from a lotus blossom cunt

so you come to me for a spiritual piece
my eyes have the ol' epicanthic fold
my skin is the ideologically correct color
a legit lay for the revolutionary
well, let me tell you, brother
revolution must be total
and you're in its way
yeah, yeah, I'm all sympathy
your soul and your sexuality has
been fucked over by Amerika
well, so has mine
so has ours
we chronic smilers
asian women
we of the downcast almond eyes
are seeing each other
sisters now, people now
asian women
I'm still with you, brothers
Always
But I'm so damned tired
of being body first, head last
wanting to love you when all
you want is a solution to glandular discomfort
that I thought I'd better say my say
Think about it, brothers
We are women, we are Asian
We are freeing ourselves
Join us
Try to use us,
and you'll lose us
Join us.

                    Tomi Tanaka

Reprinted from GIDRA, July, 1971.

I AM CURIOUS (YELLOW?)

VIOLET RABAYA

It is very difficult to describe my plight. Being raised in a white society and having acquired white "habits" is difficult enough to cope with when attempting to find pride in one's ancestry, but even more difficult is the alienation I find among my own people (if I may be so liberal as to include myself in the oriental race).

I have found that the Filipino oriental has three basic differences when comparing him with other "typical orientals," that is, the Japanese and Chinese. First of all, as the term oriental has been interpreted by most to mean peoples of yellow skin, the Filipino is not yellow, but brown. Secondly, the heritage of the Filipino has definite and pronounced Spanish colonial influences, which have nearly obliterated most Asian customs associated with orientals. And thirdly, the sense of unity among Filipinos, where it is most needed, precisely within the people themselves, is not strong.

Filipinos, also, like most other orientals, have basic racist tendencies. This phenomena is admittedly not uncommon among other races, but there exists a looming discrepancy in the racial attitude of the Filipino. Unlike most other groups of people where racism stems from the belief in one's superiority, or at least, in one's equality, the Filipino has accepted, though reluctantly, his place on the "white social ladder." Caucasians are number one, orientals are number two, Mexicans number three, then Negroes. Asking my parents or any other Filipinos I have known from the old country[1] to evaluate their status on this ladder, I was, at first, naturally greeted with the "We are the greatest orientals" line, mostly because no one took me seriously. But, upon pressing the point, I was shocked (not really, because I expected as much) to find that Filipinos, even though their hatred for the Japanese is still great because of the war and their dislike of the Chinese apparent, believe that they are inferior to whites and other orientals (Japanese and Chinese), but superior to Mexicans and blacks. Of course, this opinion is not true for all Filipinos, but it generally serves to illustrate the fact that the Filipino, himself, does not "see" his place among other orientals.

Possibly, because of the rift culturally, religiously and politically between the Japanese, Chinese, and Filipino, the Filipino like the Japanese and Chinese did not care to be assimilated in earlier times. But the Filipino in America today has realized that, because of the racial climate of the times, it is more beneficial to be considered oriental than any other minority group. The white middle class has, at least, verbally "accepted" the oriental. Thus, it becomes mandatory for the Filipino to assert his oriental origin.

Japanese and Chinese are at once categorized as oriental, but no so the Filipino. Whenever anyone in this society thinks "what is an oriental?" the answer immediately comes back Chinese or Japanese, maybe Korean, that is, unless one is a Filipino. This failure of inclusion of the Filipino is, of course, unconscious to the non-oriental and probably at least partially understandable, since most non-orientals care little to make distinctions when referring to orientals, or have a profound stupidity and general lack of knowledge concerning the oriental. "They all look the same to me!" is the cry. The fact is that they don't all look the same. But, alas, for the observant non-oriental, the problem of identifying the Filipino as different is not so great. The real problem lies in the classification of the Filipino. I have always been met with this dilemma. I have been called Vietnamese, Hawaiian, Indian, Chinese, Japanese, Korean, and even Polynesian just to be safe. Only once or twice in my memory can I recall being said to be Filipino, and one of these times was an absolute absurdity. To illustrate the height of obscurity in Filipino identification, I was once told that I didn't look Mexican and I couldn't be oriental, so I must be Filipino. To put it lightly, I, like other Filipinos, have become "disoriented."

All of this is not to say that I believe my cultural identity has the ultimate importance in my life, or that I wish to be classified. Certainly, I find that a classification as an individual is to be more greatly desired, but the question of recognition as both a Filipino and an oriental is of great significance to me. And, because this is not the case, I find myself, and I daresay, many other American born Filipino orientals, torn not only between my white-Filipino identity, but my oriental-Filipino identity as well. It seems illogical that a Filipino, being an oriental, should be faced with such a crisis. But, it is only too real.

"One of the peculiar situations in which the Filipino has found himself is that relating to his racial status. Laws prohibiting the marriage of Caucasians and Orientals do not specifically mention Filipinos. There was nothing Oriental in the Filipino's tradition, and his language was Spanish. He felt no bonds with Orientals in the United States--nor they with him. For a time the legality of Filipino-Caucasian intermarriage became the province of each county clerk in California. Whether it was permitted or not depended on their individual viewpoints and the extent of their knowledge of racial groups."[2]

To be an outcast in a white society and an outcast among other orientals leaves the Filipino in that never-never land of social obscurity. It is almost no wonder that the Filipino might not mind being stereotyped as a "typical oriental."

---

[1] *My father operated a labor camp in Delano for 15 years under the Di Giorgio Fruit Corporation where most of the laborers were Filipino and Mexican. The Japanese-Chinese labor camp was adjacent to ours. My observations were partly due to my relationships with them.*
[2] *Ritter, Dr. Ed; Ritter, Helen; and Spector, Dr. Stanley: OUR ORIENTAL AMERICANS, p. 96.*

Revolution point-zero: 1967 (or whenever).
Hey, who's that groovy guy
Who-sits-in-the-corner-near-the-clock-
of-West-Wing-Powell-Sunday-nights--
(I could sure dig on his ass)...

Revolution 1: 1968 (or whenever)...
The coop's full of laughter--Asian laughter.
How come it stops,
When I come in with my white boyfriend?

Revolution 2: 1969 (or whenever)--
"Hey sister...I want to turn you on to Revolution.
Let me rap with you awhile."
The sister looked at me
Then shifted her gaze back
To her loving peace freak (or whatever).
Her eyes told me to go to Hell.
(--I did!)

Revolution 3: 1970 (or whenever).
Another year, another face...
"Hey, don't I know you?"
--well, if i don't it really doesn't matter;
we'll-be-recognizing-each-other-just-the-same--
The familiar Asian eyes say yes.
And my smile creeps up from my stomach.
"Right on brother...right on!"

MARY UYEMATSU

Reprinted from Gidra, January, 1971.

AUTOBIOGRAPHY OF A SANSEI FEMALE

Never before have I seriously attempted to dissect my feelings and attitudes about myself as a Japanese-American. Aborted attempts were made but never brought to final fruition. I suspect because certain truths about oneself are unbearably painful, I preferred to postpone my confrontation with reality until I was able to cope with the consequences of such a confrontation.

I am Japanese and there is no denying this. On the other hand, I am also American, not a White American, but a diluted, yellow-White one. I say yellow-White American because no matter how hard I try to reject the values of the dominant White society, these very values remain ingrained in me. So much so that I am unconscious of their presence. This truth I have had to face in spite of my newly-found pride in ethnic origin. To accept myself as a total person, I also have to accept the dual existence of Asian and American values in my life. For the modern Asian raised in the Asian-American style, the struggle for a clear-cut identity is a very real dilemma, in spite of the similarities between the two culture's value systems. My parents urged me, unconsciously I am certain, to perpetuate the stereotype of the quiet, polite, unassuming Asian. But survival in American society requires one to speak up vociferously to defend one's rights and gain recognition. Slowly, I am rejecting the Asian stereotypes in order that by doing so, I am contributing to the elimination of the Asian stereotypes held by White America. A change in attitudes of Caucasians toward Asians will not occur until we alter the attitudes we have toward ourselves.

Discrimination toward Asian Americans today is usually so subtle that one of Asian ancestry may not be able to recognize prejudices at work. I am very sensitive to verbal and non-verbal reactions of Whites to me. I have to be able to distinguish between discriminatory remarks and "non-color" remarks or actions. Asian Americans, much like the Blacks, are on the defensive. Only after carefully examining each situation can we attribute an action or remark to prejudice. For example, if I fail to get a desired job, can I blame my failure on racial prejudice or on my own lack of ability? The circumstances of the situation must be considered before any conclusions are drawn. I feel I have experienced subtle discrimination ... the kind of discrimination which is more difficult to detect, define and to cope with. While shopping at so-called "better stores," I have come into contact with rather aloof saleswomen who have treated me with cold indifference. I could almost sense their thinking, "What could she possibly want or afford in this store?" At first, I felt their superior, haughty behavior was a reaction to the way I was dressed on those occasions. But no, even when I was properly attired, I was treated in like manner.

I have had similar experiences in restaurants where I have been treated differently and made to wait a bit longer. Once, a friend and I had lunch at San Francisco's Fisherman's Wharf. I had chosen the wharf because this particular friend was a first-time visitor to the city. We were seated and our orders were taken before those of the older White women who had come in after us. Well, those two White women were served before us. We noticed this but preferred to believe the waiter had had a slight mix-up of orders. I knew the oversight was not because our dishes took longer to prepare as the women were having the same lobster dish I had ordered. When our meals arrived, they were overdone. I know I should have refused to accept the dishes but I remained silent as the waiter suspected I would. (Stereotype: Asians never complain; for that matter, most people don't.) My friend, when asked by the waiter upon completion of the meal if she had enjoyed it replied, "Not really, it was overcooked."

I had a very painful experience while in Europe with my mother. People are always saying how tolerant the Europeans are of race, creed and color. A Black friend told me about his wonderful experiences in Europe where he never encountered discrimination. I did in Vienna, Austria. I was particularly aware of being constantly stared at--the staring was not always friendly. My unpleasant experience with the hotel concierge is still fresh in my memory. One morning before going out on a tour, I went to the hotel desk to use a pen to sign a traveller's cheque. I used the concierge's pen, then placed the pen on the desk. Mom and I left for the tour and returned several hours later. When I arrived at the desk, the concierge asked me brusquely, "May I have my pen back please?" I told him I did not have it as I distinctly remember

---

Reprinted from "Diversities in the Development of Ethnic Identifications among the Sanseis" by Magoroh Maruyama with his permission. This study was based on autobiographic materials written by third-generation Asian students from the East Bay Area in California.

returning it. But he was certain I had it on my person. He then asked me to check my handbag which I did reluctantly...still, no pen. I explained to him that I was not in the habit of stealing pens. He then said, "I had that pen for five years." Obviously, he did not believe me. I was never so insulted in my life. I am certain this man would never have approached any other hotel guest as he did me. He was either terribly rude and unworldly or he was just prejudiced. I believe he was the latter.

I think most Asian Americans have experienced discrimination, overt or subtle, directed against them. I asked a number of my friends if they had ever been discriminated against. To my surprise, they said no. This made me wonder if I was subtlely harassed because of my personality and not because of my color. I also wondered if I was being too sensitive and a bit paranoid. But knowing my friends led me to one conclusion...if they had encountered prejudice, they did not recognize it or they refused to recognize it. By recognizing prejudice directed at you, you are forced to look at yourself and what you are. You are compelled to see yourself as different, as a member of a minority group. Facing the truth can be a painful experience. You are not quite as White as the White society you wish to identify yourself with.

I have finally faced this reality. I am yellow--I cannot change what I am. I can say honestly now that I am proud of being Japanese. This pride is based upon our illustrious history as a people, our culture, and our undying spirit. Even as imprisoned peoples during World War II, the Japanese displayed courage and ethnic pride. My mother told me a great deal about her camp experiences. She fondly recalls the unity and high morale of the group during internment. As an act of defiance and also as an exercise in keeping the morale high, the Japanese in the Rivers, Arizona camp celebrated all of the traditional festivals and holidays of their native land by donning native costumes (kimonos, yukatas), dancing native dances, and eating traditional foods. Once, during the big New Year's celebration, a few daring, young Japanese boys stealthily climbed a small hill within the compound and hoisted up the flag of Japan emblazened with the symbolic rising sun. The Army officials quickly removed it and demanded to know who put the flag up. They never found the culprits. The Japanese enjoyed the stunt immensely. This was just one incident my mother recounted. To my memory, my father on the other hand, has never discussed his camp experiences. For a man, such involuntary imprisonment was an emasculating experience. The role of "breadwinner" and protector of the family was taken away from him. My dad will never again reside on the U.S. mainland...he prefers to remain in Hawaii which boasts large Asian population.

In spite of their internment during the war, my parents feel a sense of gratitude toward the U.S. For them, the "American Dream" has been realized...they have enjoyed a modest success in their business, they have earned and saved enough for their dream home, they have purchased that second new car and now look forward to a life filled with more leisure and less struggle. I am happy for them but for me, such attainment is not enough. I feel where real equality is concerned, we still have a long way to go. Unlike my parents, I don't feel a sense of gratitude toward the U.S. What we have, we earned. We made our opportunities when there were none and capitalized on them.

I feel a common bond with my Asian brethren, whereas at one time I did not. As a Japanese raised in Hawaii, I looked upon the Asians on the U.S. mainland as a different breed. I felt they were too American because they thought, acted and spoke like the Caucasian. I now realize this was an Island stereotype of the West Coast Asian. Also, if there is truth in the belief that the West Coast Japanese are stand-offish and less open and friendly, then it is probably due to their greater exposure to racial prejudice. The Japanese here have always been aware of their minority group status. Now that I reside in California and have Asian friends here, I find the Asians friendly, informed and involved. I have changed... I am aware of our group's social problems as well as the problems of other minority groups. I identify with these minorities and feel we need the strength of unity to attain our goals in this society...our goals being 1) recognition as individuals and not as stereotyped peoples; 2) equality; and 3) eradication of racial prejudice, etc.

I am already looking forward to the day when I start my family. My husband, who is White, and I want our children to be proud of their Japanese-American heritage. Presently, we are tracing my family lines back to my early Japanese ancestors who lived in the old country hundreds of years ago. Then we will be able to pass on this valuable knowledge to our children. We want them to be familiar with the Japanese language and customs. Sadly, I, a third-generation Japanese in the U.S., have lost a great deal of the Japanese traditions. I wish I had paid closer attention to the traditional Japanese ways of my parents and grandparents. My mother told me years ago when I turned my back on things Japanese, that one day, I would regret not learning more about Japanese culture. She was right.

So, as inadequate a teacher as I may be, I will attempt to transmit to my children one day, what little I have retained of my Japanese heritage. I hope our half-White, half-Yellow children will be proud of being Japanese-American.

RAPPING WITH ONE MILLION

All night session--ocean of words
Legazpi - Frank - Bob - Bill Sorro - Marty and myself
and someone else.

Put down your white mind
    with your dark eyes
    behind brown skin

Brown
    like fallen coconuts
        on a cold
            cold winter day

Brown
    like fish drying
    in the hot summer sun.

Bill Sorro: "You know when I go into the poolhalls
and see my Filipino brothers--you know--
I want to say to them--you know--
I know how they feel and think--you know
I want to say to them, "manong, manong,
monong, don't you know? you are being fucked."

Come down from those white flaky hills
    the smell of the carabao shit stills the mind
    keeps the pampino
    swimming in your belly.

Throw away those knives and forks
    and eat rice and raw fish
    with brown winter-soiled hands

Jump and wallow
    in the grass heap shit
    of the carabao

Don't you know
you smell like the deep brown earth
if you only knew
if your eyes were only opened
you would see the sun come down
if you only knew
you would bring the sun down
underneath brown children's feet.
You can't hide these

CARABAOS IN THE DARK

You can't hide these
               fish heads
                    in your pockets
  the smell is too strong.

If you only know how brown you are
you would slide down
from the highest mountain top
you would whip out your lava tongue
and scoop up all that white shit
that's keeping your people down.

I'll whip out a sharp bamboo leaf
        and push it down your throat
but I'll be gentle
I'll push it down
with my bolo
and you will cry out
        maybe see into the dawn
hear the water buffaloes
        gallopping along the river

        On the sand
        By the water
        In the mountains

You will have your sharp bolo
        and sing and dance
        and eat   and fight

All day into
        the hot blazing sun

through the cool night
onto the next morning

Behind the early morning fog
A million brown Filipino faces
chanting: makibaka, makibaka, makabaka.

                        AL ROBLES

Reprinted from KALAYAAN, July, 1971.

the trouble with losing face

is,

you

become

invisible

i never looked at my skin,
i knew it was yellow. . .
i played in the sun
all the time. . .
maybe i was indian.
i wore pigtails--
indians did too.
they didn't have
slanted eyes
though.
no one did but me
all the other kids
had
red hair
green eyes
long noses
funny spots on their
faces
tiny hairs growing
out of their eyes. . .
i didn't complain

i thought i was special
that's what my mother said
(you're better,
than them)
not in those exact words. . .
she didn't know those words
neither did my father--
but he tried to say them

i thought it was pretty funny,
like the other kids. . .
say something--
nay-hao-ma-ha-ha-ha
i had a nice friend
she came to visit
me
one day.
she asked me
what those funny
machines
were
in my house.
i couldn't make up
anything to say.

116

*she wanted to make
her eyes
go up
like mine--
she combed her hair
into a tight
pony tail
to pull
her eyes--back.
i went to school
the house was too
crowded
i brought home
goody-goody marks
to my parents
so they could smile
because they worked all day
rinsing out the
bok guoi's
underwear
and forgot how to
smile
or laugh.
this limbo of
motionless flight--
my world hangs
faded
dingy
i love my brothers
and sisters
but i don't know
what they look like.
we used to play
house
together.
you look familiar
you are me
they are we
and i just became
an anti
anti-them
anti-us
anti-words
here's my
anti-parenthesis)*

*one day
i wanted to have
a fit.
my father said
(no) (you can't)
angry. . .
i wanted to
break everything
in sight.
but impulse made me
glance
at the portrait
of grandfather
suspended over
the fireplace.
i vomited words
confucius is
alive. . .
crush confusionism
exterminate the seeds
of this
bao-bab.
i smeared a can
of red paint
over his eyes,
then i draped it
carefully
over the
honorable wrinkles
of his visage--
so. . .
this is losing face.
now i can
take off my
skin
without being watched
no, you can't. . .you can
"you're invisible now
you got no secrets
to conceal"
just open your
eyes--
but keep them
covered. . .
so no one
can
see you.*

MARIE CHUNG

This poem was written for an Asian American studies course at UCLA, in 1970. Miss Chung is a recent graduate in political science at the University of California, Los Angeles.

Stormy Weather

I am an Ono,
who once was
a good Japanese
obeying Mother (OKĀSAMA)
Did well at AZABU Academy
Forest Hills High School,
Columbia College (Class of '64)
and all that.

When I was little
OKĀSAMA said: whatever you do
don't be satisfied unless you become
the top person in it.
Maids and neighbors used to say:
what a brilliant child! He could even be
a foreign minister
someday.

I'm in jail now
one of the two black sheep
in the ONO FAMILY (military officers, educators,
bankers, ambassadors, and me)
YOKO and SHIN'YA.

What would mother's peasant father, KUBO TSUNEZO,
think of me now? Living with robbers, pimps, thieves,
and hustlers like I do? What would he think?
He, a proud Japanese who led ISSEI farm-workers
against hakujin vultures in L. A. of 1910's?
He, an angry ISSEI who left for home in 1921,
saying "fuck America!" He wasn't one to knuckle under.

I am ONO SHIN'YA
who once was a Japanese patriot
proud of his father
(missing in action; presumed dead
Manila, Philippines
April, 1945).

When I was little,
I rooted for Tokyo Giants
valiantly defending the honor of our race
against the players from N.Y.
who smelled of butter.

I'm in Chicago now, #70086474
serving five months
for bringing two hakujin poliko
down to the ground (allegedly).

What would the tutors of my boyhood
(Habo niichan and Yoichi niichan)
think of me now?
They who barely survived their training as young Kamikaze?
They who taught me the difference between
being a Japanese and being a mish-mush.

I am a 29 year old Asian
who once was a radical teacher in NY Chinatown,
for four years, I went through a thousand routines
making kids feel small, hating myself every minute of it.

When I was little,
I used to be good, taking all the shit in school,
keeping anger inside,
and regarded with contempt
any kid who couldn't be as good as me.

I like with bad people now
people who said: Fuck you! to the same teacher who praised
me to the skies. The bad ones who were marked in
the teacher's black book,
the ones who defiantly left the room, to be sent to the
Dean's office
Mad people. CRAZY MOTHERFUCKERS! every one of them!

What would my friends of AZABU days think of me?
Where are they now? MITSUI? MITSUBISHI?

BANK OF TOKYO? FOREIGN MINISTRY, perhaps
Still good Japanese, most of them, recreating the glorious Japan
that once murdered 20,000,000 Asians. . .
only 25 years ago.

I am Shin'ya
and Asian,
who in the film Vietnam
cannot help
seeing
his own face
in the faces of the Vietnamese.

When I was 4
mother had to huddle us
daily
to protect us from the strafings and bombings
of p51's
which always disposed their unused ordinance
on our village. As a safety precaution.

When I was 5,
GI's used to laugh
in that Amerikan way
watching us scramble for chewing gums
thrown from their jeep.

Elders used to say:
"Have a pride. You're a Japanese."

By the time I was 6 or 7
mother, Tad, and me had subsisted
for 2 whole years
on diet of pumpkins and sweet potatoes,
in the occupied Japan.

When I was 8, Tad and me hurt mom's feeling
refusing to wear Amerikan style mittens.
which she spent night after night making.
We didn't like being called pum-pum-no-fu
just because we wore Amerikan style clothes
sent to us by our nisei relatives in L. A.

When I was 9
I went to Tokyo
to attend my father's funeral,
five years late.
I remember
a white box with only a piece of paper in it.
It said "The Honorable Spirit"
or something like that.

When I was 10
AMERIKA WAS
murdering
Asians
again.
The principal of my school said:
"Our neighbors in Korea are
suffering a disastrous fire"

I'm happy now,
having faced the deadness and
bankruptcy of my previous life,
accepting, fully
what it means to be
a bad Japanese in the
white
imperial
Amerika.
Living the way I want to,
living and fighting for myself,
daring to be me.

What would my father think of me?
He, whose death weighed so heavily on all of us.
He, who tried to fight for tragic Japan?
(Japan, whose only way to save herself from
the greedy, presumptuous, brutal, devilish,
smelly hakujin was to become
devilish and imperialistic herself)
what would he think of me,
like this?

I don't know.
It doesn't matter, really.
As long as I am me.
As long as I keep on feeling the Japanese
and the Vietnamese inside me.

Inside us. With all my brothers and sisters
out there.
Our history.
Our biography
Keep on
feeling
the sadness of that.
the power of that.

SHIN'YA ONO

Reprinted from GIDRA, November, 1970.

Asian Brother, Asian Sister

For Yoshiko Saito

I.

*Not yet dawn,
but the neighbors have been here,
bringing condolences, assurances
that my pupils will be seen to:*

*though I am new to their village
they include me, are grateful
for what I do.*

*The teacups are rinsed.
The bedding is stacked.
While my wife wraps our basket
the children kneel on the tatami,
fingering the beads of the rosary like an abacus.
In their way, they are hushed,
and seem to sense the solemnity.*

"Sa. Iki-ma-sho."

*A cold wind greets us.
There will be snow soon
in this prefecture.*

*Burnt wood, sweet fields.
Not yet dawn.
In one of these houses,
my grandmother is rising to go to school.*

II.

*By sixteen,
she was in this country--*

*making a living, children
on the way.*

*I don't know what it cost
in passage, in the San Joaquin.*

*I'm beginning
to understand the conditions.*

III.

To get back to the source,
through doors

of dialects and restrictions...

Brazil to the south, this blue
shore on the horizon...

To get back to the source,
the need to leave

and bring it with you:

in 1912, they opened
the Fresno Fish Store.

IV.

Ika, the squid,
to slither down your throat.

Saba, the mackerel,
to roast.

Maguro, the tuna--
slice it thin and raw.

Kani, the crab.
Aobi, the abalone.

All these
shipped in slick and shiney.

All these
to keep our seasons.

All these.

V.

Grandmother never learned the language--
just a few
choice phrases to take care of business.
Grandfather ordered the fish.

But when the nice white man
bent down to her level and said
"How long you been here, Mama?"
she told him
"Come today fresh."

VI.

Before the war, after
the old scrape of stench and scale,
she'd come to see what her new grandson could do.

Nine o'clock, but you've got to wake him,
so I can flip him in his crib.

Bring him down to the store tomorrow
so I can get him some manju,
let him chew on an ebi.

Part his hair in the middle,
slick it down,
so I can wheel him around to the people.

Listen, big baby--Mexican tunes
moving around the jukeboxes.
Listen, big fat round-headed baby in white shoes.

What chu mean
he's got small eyes?
What chu mean?
That's how he
supposed to be.
What chu mean?
Big fat baby in a hood.

In depths of bed,
to roll to where the shore was, undulating
coves and folds...

Drunks dancing wounded
under a wounded streetlight...

Then the Danish Creamery
screaming about its business
and we couldn't sleep.

Sing me. Sing me. Sing me
please about the pigeons
cooing home to the temple to roost.

Sing me. Please.

For our sweet tooth,
she kept a store
of canned fruit buried in the dirt
beside her barracks in Arkansas.

Water flopping over the furo's edges
as we entered, feet
sliding on slats,
a soft iceberg in the heat and steam...

So you've got a son in New Guinea,
another at some fort.
What do you do?
What have you been doing?--

try to keep busy and eat.

And as the children leave
to dicker with the enemy,
try to keep busy and eat.

*Float around him,
bump and nudge him,
and try to keep busy and eat.*

*Shuffle off to the store
ten feet behind him
and try to keep busy and eat.*

*And when the sons take over,
try to keep busy and eat.*

*Go in and scream about the business.
Grandchildren stumbling
over their own skin in the suburbs,
hubcaps and money
cluttering the driveways...*

*One day they found her
flipping in a driveway like a fish.*

*If your hip is broken,
you can't ever go home--
roaming through Wakayama
for what the War didn't own.*

*If your hip is broken,
you can't ever go to Oregon.
You've got to wheel to your drawer
for your Issei medallion--*

that steamer riding a starry-striped sea.

*If your hip is broken,
you've got to give that medallion
with a moan--*

as though you could know.

VII.

*My grandmother is in the beauty
of release.
As the heart subsides,
as the blood runs its course,
she is gowned and attended,
chanting incantations to Buddha.*

*I am touched by the beauty,
by the peace
that is the end of her life--*

*fluttering eyelids,
the murmuring barely audible.*

It is goodbye.

It is beautiful.

I do not need to cry.

*As the sheet flows over in its purity,
I note the smoothness
of skin, the grey-blue hair
echoed faintly over the lips.*

*Then the sheet becomes a paper bag,
and she slips out of that sack
off the kitchen table*

*and lands on her back
on the linoleum,*

*naked, moaning, the impact
having stunned her into fright.*

*And she grabs both legs of mine
and bends the knees
and brings me down upon her*

*blue mouth without teeth,
food beginning to swell
in her belly*

where I am

crying, and not yet born.

VIII.

*This house. This house.
The paths become trenches to the telephone, the bathroom...
This house. The scent of Orient
and seven existences.
This house. The bedrooms
tacked-on then sealed-off
as each moved to the colonies.*

*This house. Fifty years in this house.
Lie in front of the heater and dream,
flames eating the snowflake
mica that shudder with color
like fish-scales--blue, red--dream...*

*Lie in front of this heater
and knead the pus
where fish-fins stuck,
your dreams a fish
wilting over this heater...*

*This house. Creamery and cleavers
going at each other down the wintery street.*

*Bitches in alleys,
bottles in dreams...*

*Who knew the black whore in the alley
of this house--
dead a week, wrapped in leaves...*

Tread lightly in this house.
Appliances try the edge of trenches.
Grandchildren balance on the shelves--
tassled
offspring of another culture...

This house. The basement
crammed with ballast--
dolls, kimonoes, swords...

This house. That survived the War
and got stoned.
This house. Exhausted fumes

gnawing the garden on the shore.

In the mist of that shore,
the chrysanthemum
droops and nods.

This house.

It drops into the freeway
and I drown.

IX.

Then the doors burst open
and the people come flooding in--

from all over the San Joaquin
come to form the procession.

There is a trench to the temple.

When you are in that trench,
there is no room
for much movement:

all that you move from
comes in on you;
all that you do
is judged upon.

Trapped in the trench,
I am smothered in my people,
chanting in procession to the   temple.

And when we emerge in the temple
I am five feet two,
flat-faced, bent-legged, epicanthic
as I will ever be...

Do my eyes lie?

My people see I am beautiful.

Yes. I am rocked in the lap of Buddha.
Yes. Incense owns my clothes.
Yes. I am wrapped in beads.

Yes. My people.
Grandmother, take me in your arms.

What you say, I will do.

X.

The procession continues...
My grandfather migrates
to my mother's house, in the suburbs.
Even the chrysanthemum
finds new root, in the suburbs.

I have the medallion
forever sailing on my breast--
a family and the seven gods of luck
in the hold.

Brothers, Sisters,
understand this:

you are in passage--
wherever you go
you are slanted
down to the bone.

Do your eyes lie?

Brothers, Sisters,
understand this:

you are beautiful.

And your beautiful grandmother
is dancing in your eyes,

cooing and cooing you
home to roost.

LAWSON INADA

Reprinted by permission of the author. Mr. Inada is a third-generation Japanese American who is now on the faculty of Southern Oregon College at Ashland.

2
HISTORY

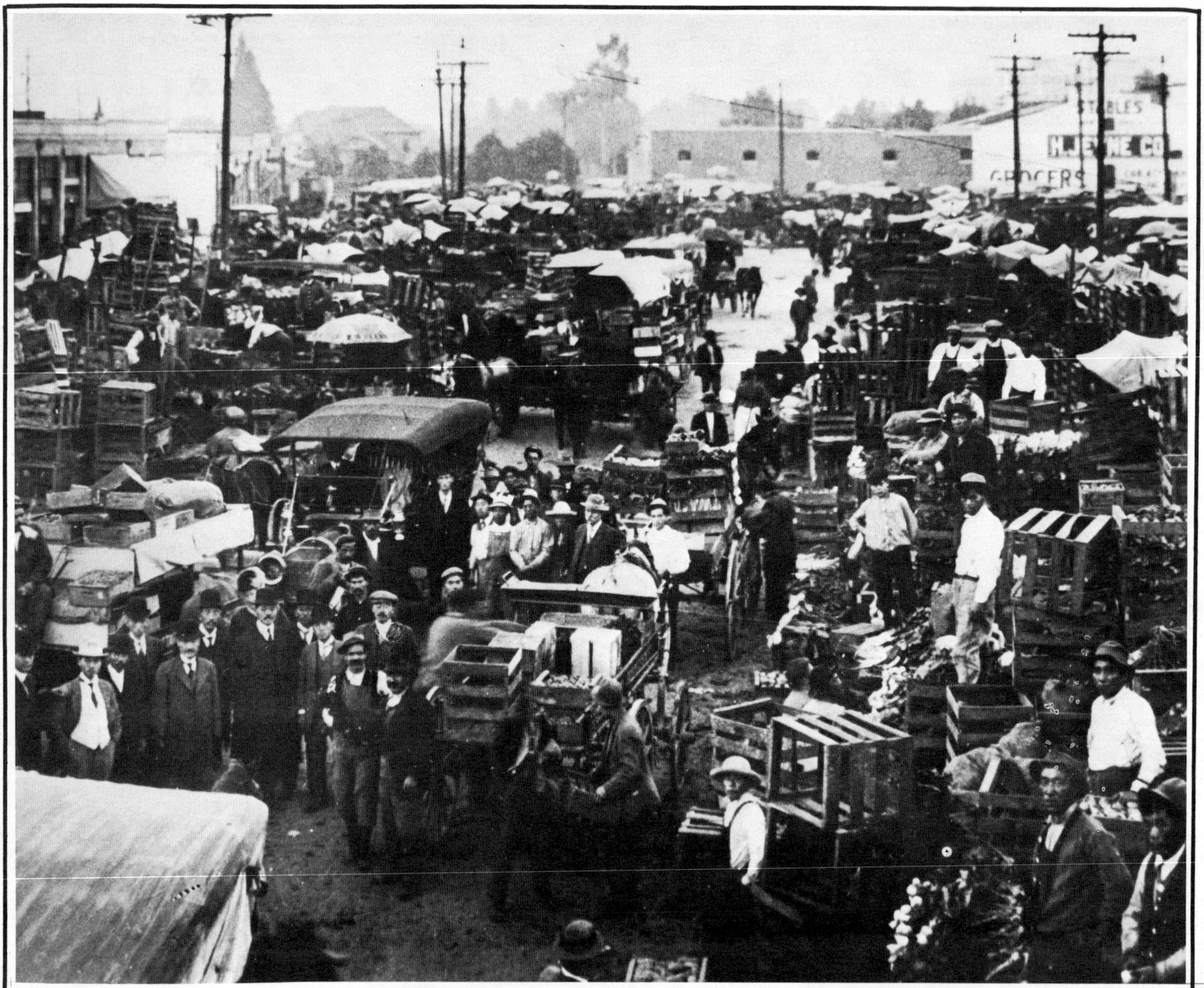
STABLES
GROCERS

INTRODUCTION

Asian Americans and the Apotheosis of American Democracy

Let's face reality! Despite governmental assurances to the contrary, the American democratic society is one more concerned with order and stability than with minority rights. As a result, the typical American approach is to leave crucial social problems unattended until they can no longer be ignored. Then attempts are made to deal with the dilemma without changing any of the basic institutions which may be responsible for creating them. In effect, the system itself becomes sacred, and the flaws within the democratic framework are perpetuated and institutionalized.

The prevailing concern of the government to project the system as responsive to all people leads to the apotheosis of American democracy. The idea is that as long as people believe in the popularized concept of democracy, they will not question any of the mechanisms of the governing process. If people are dominated by the belief that there is a never-failing democratic tradition, they will tolerate and even acquiesce in the inequalities that exist in society. Government "for the people" becomes an unquestioned fact, and faith in democracy reigns absolute.

The apotheosis of American democracy has had tremendously damaging consequences for Asian Americans. There is a popular concept of the democratic system as supposedly functioning as a panacea for all social ills and this breeds the misguided philosophy into the area of race relations, the greater society points to the Asian Americans as the successful minorities. Unfortunately, such a policy effectively covers up the general inadequacies of this country in satisfactorily resolving racial conflict and inequities. It only hides reality. The social gains made by Asians are important for what they portend rather than for indicating any basic changes within society. The barriers are lowered for some individuals, but the mass of the Asian Americans have yet to break through these openings.

One of the major tragedies in the attempt to deal with racial issues in America is that there is a propensity to develop a concept of history which reinforces the American democratic ideal. The general theme as it relates to Asian Americans states that they have faced and overcome much prejudice in society and, thus, serve as an example of the responsiveness of the democratic system. The tragedy lies not in using history to show that positive changes have occurred, but in utilizing the past in a manner that disguises the persistent racism (overt, covert, and institutionalized) that still plagues the Asian American. Through such a manipulation of the Asian identity, the desired result is to have the Asian riding in the back of the bus and digging it.

A scheme of viewing the history of the Asian American must be used which is _essentially_ devoted to analyzing historical events in terms of their significance for Asian Americans rather than a concept that is _primarily_ concerned with lavishing praise upon the mechanisms of American democracy. It is hoped that the wide-ranging selections offered in this history section will help provide such an analytical framework for understanding the status of the Asian American in society today. Through an understanding of the circumstances which produced the contemporary situation, human awareness will hopefully be enriched; thereby enhancing the capacity to cope with the existing dilemmas.

The early experience of all the Asians is that of an immigrant group. In every case there existed strong social and economic pressures in the homeland which created the impetus for the Asian emigration. The similarities of those factors, however, were only of a generic sense. For example, the Taiping Rebellion in China (1850-1864) played a major role in encouraging Chinese emigration while the social forces of overpopulation and economic changes leading to Japanese emigration were much less traumatic. Good indication of the various forces which initiated the emigration process appear in the article by Pyau Ling, "Causes of Chinese Emigration."

From the beginning, the Asian immigrant encountered tremendous difficulties. He not only had to cope with the problem of leaving a familiar environment and adjusting to life in a strange land but had to face the factor of cultural and racial prejudice. Roger Daniels in "The Issei Generation" reveals many of the complexities involved when the Japanese settled in America. For instance, the early experience entailed the struggle to earn money as a seasonal farm laborer in order to buy farm land; the lack of Japanese women in America before 1907 which handicapped the functioning of a family structure; and living in socially visible ethnic communities. Karl Yoneda's "One Hundred Years of Japanese Labor in the USA" illustrates how racial prejudice hindered the Japanese in their quest for equitable working conditions and fair wages.

The Chinese, who had arrived in America earlier, went through similar difficulties in adjustment. Stanford Lyman gives an excellent overview of the early period in "Strangers in the City." He depicts the movement of Chinese into the cities as a result of white racism plus congregative sentiments and investigates two important factors--the vital role of Chinese social organizations and the shortage of Chinese women. He feels that anti-Chinese agitation left the new immigrants demoralized, isolated, and neglected by 1900.

The other Asian groups, such as the Filipinos, Koreans, and Hindus, also faced difficulties in their adjustment to the American environment. More needs to be written on these groups, but many of their experiences are mentioned in Violet Rabaya's article, "Filipino Immigration," and Linda Shin's article, "Koreans in America, 1903-1945." The Filipinos found that they could only find three basic types of work: in domestic service, the fishing industry, and agricultural labor. They faced constant discrimination which led to anti-Filipino riots in the early 1930's and to Filipino exclusion after the Philippines Independence Act of 1934. While there were very few Koreans in America until recently, those who came after the turn of the century served primarily as laborers and have developed their communities on the edge of other Oriental enclaves. Also few in number, the Hindus in America have faced strong discrimination and are severely isolated. They came into America by way of Canada in the early 1900's and quickly became an object of the Asiatic Exclusion League. The Alien Land Laws affected them as well as the Japanese, and in 1917, they were also excluded.

For those who already have or will read beyond the selections in this book, it will become clearer that the Asiatic people's adjustment to American society has been complicated and, at times, stymied by cultural and racial prejudice. Another means of examining this trend is in viewing the history of the Oriental in Hawaii. This island region is constantly presented as the melting pot of the Pacific, but as Carey McWilliams stated, Hawaii actually provides a history of racial prejudice in its purest form. Since the whites controlled the economic system, the Hawaiians, Chinese, Japanese, and Filipinos were completely subordinated to them. The Hawaiian economy revolved around the plantation crops of sugar cane and pineapples so a clear dichotomy developed between the rich white plantation owners and the Asian laborers. Despite the overwhelming majority of Asians in Hawaii, it has only been in recent years, through unionization, that the labor situation has improved. The Hawaiian experience is replete with examples of racial conflict; and with a deeper analysis of it and the Asian experience on the mainland, an understanding will be reached of the forces that subjected Asians to a second class status in America.

California agriculture has been marked by specialization, seasonality, and reliance on migratory labor. Specialization in California meant large quantities of perishable commodities requiring extremely large numbers of farm laborers for short periods, particularly the harvesting season from May through October. Unorganized, migratory, skilled and docile--these were the qualities demanded of the laborers by the farmers. For the workers the system meant a wretched existence with back-breaking labor in the hot summer months, underemployment pay much of the year and unemployment during the winter season. Arbitrary treatment by farmers and labor contractors meant no security for the laborers, while the lack of social services such as health and educational facilities doomed most of their children to lives of continuous struggle. Both in the past and present, many Asians have worked as agricultural labor and have continually been the object of exploitation. The large agriculturists in California have very successfully resisted efforts to unionize farm labor and attain fair wages and working conditions. While farm labor unions got nowhere in the 1930's, the Associated Farmers, a union of employers, appeared. The large growers have often used the "divide and rule" policy in which one ethnic group is used to compete against another ethnic group. In such a situation strikes are diffcult to sustain. It was only after much hard work and sacrifice that the Filipinos united with the Mexicans to successfully carry out the Delano grape boycott.

One variable that seems to be ignored during times of social calm is the ingrained character of racial prejudice. For example, after Japanese exclusion in 1924, racial antipathy entered a submerged state but in no way did it disappear. As a result, war in 1941 against Japan led to the internment of almost all of the Japanese on the mainland. Much work has been written on the forces leading to and the mechanisms of the relocation experience, but Isao Fujimoto's article, "The Failure of Democracy in a Time of Crisis," relates the feelings of one who has undergone the relocation years. His article raises the crucial question of how to combat racism when it is submerged and camouflaged by rhetoric.

The different criteria for viewing Asian American history are reflected in Bill Hosokawa's article, "The Cherishing of Liberty: The American Nisei," and the book review of Hosokawa's book, NISEI: THE QUIET AMERICANS, by Yuji Ichioka. Hosokawa states that it is a credit to America that it has gradually repealed discriminatory laws and abolished discriminatory practices until the Japanese and other Asians have relatively little to complain about today. On the other hand, Ichioka criticizes Hosokawa's book for indulging in filiopietistic banalities and being out of touch with the hard realities of society. He sees the book as projecting an ethnic Horatio Alger story without questioning an Americanism that still practices racism and super-patriotism.

The last article, "The U.S. in Asia and Asians in the U.S.," by a UCLA seminar on "Asian Americans and U.S. Policy in Asia" explores the relationship between U.S. policy in Asia and the position of Asian Americans. It deals with the question of whether or not a colonialist paternalism directed at the Third World nations will manifest a dangerous superiority complex toward Asian Americans whose heritage lies in these countries. The article discusses the various mechanisms of U.S. foreign policy such as economic exploitation, use of foreign aid, cultural exchanges, and manipulation of underdeveloped countries for an American global power struggle. Just as international events affected the Japanese in World War II, the U.S. policy today in Asia has consequences for Asian Americans.

Hopefully, these articles will prompt a person into viewing the Asian identity in American society in terms of the forces that have shaped its history rather than in terms of glorifying the status quo and simply reaffirming faith in American democracy. Human attitudes are strongly resistant to change, and the deep and fierce strain of racism directed toward Asian Americans in the past is still imbedded in society and will not be easily erased. The American democratic system must be made to rectify the inequities that still exist for Asian Americans. So, while Asian Americans should treat <u>all</u> men as their brothers, it is vital that they be cognizant of the existing realities and act accordingly.

BUCK WONG

Causes of Chinese Emigration

PYAU LING

Chinese emigration is a movement of the most singular character. It is one which differs in purpose from emigration from European countries. Europeans come to America because of surplus of population which depresses wages and drives the ambitious to better their economic conditions or to secure a greater degree of personal freedom. Apparently the same conditions lie back of Chinese emigration. In China the land is truly thickly peopled and the economic condition wretched. Still we cannot safely say that the Chinese emigrate entirely for these two purposes. Europeans may leave their abodes for political freedom or for religious tolerance. The Chinese do not. The Chinese government is indeed despotic at the top, but it is democratic at the bottom. Religious persecutions, such as Catholics against Protestants and churchmen against dissenters which have been so prevalent in Europe, are entirely unknown in China. There are other factors which make Chinese emigration peculiar. Europeans come from all parts of the country; the Chinese come from certain parts only. Europeans go everywhere; the Chinese go somewhere only. Europeans come to teach, to trade, to work and to till the soil; the Chinese primarily come to labor, although trading is a later result. With Europeans, no matter male or female, old or young, they all come, with the Chinese only the young men emigrate. Europeans intend to settle permanently; the Chinese intend to go back. Europeans become citizens and are assimilated into American citizenship; the Chinese do not care for naturalization, nor for the native customs, manners and dress. Europeans emigrate to countries where they are most favored; the Chinese persist in landing where they are opposed by legislation and public opinion. With Europeans only the most favored class come; with the Chinese only the least favored classes come.

Chinese emigration has peculiar territorial limits not only in its destination but in its source. It is chiefly composed of young peasants coming from only six perfectures of the two southeastern provinces, Fookien and Kwantung, lying between Foochow and Canton. These adventurous emigrants have for centuries penetrated through the Indian archipelago, have pushed through the Indian Ocean to Ceylon and Arabia, have reclaimed Formosa and Hainan, have established a remarkable trade with Cochin China, Cambodia and Siam and have introduced useful arts into Java, the Philippines and the Malay Peninsula. To-day they venture southward to Australia and far westward to Peru, Mexico, Canada, Cuba, and America in spite of the stringent laws those uncourteous countries have adopted to exclude them.

Still while we are pointing out the reasons why the other provincials would not emigrate and why only the Cantonese and Fookienese emigrate, we cannot deny that the density of population in these provinces has an important influence. It is a world-known fact that China is overpopulated. Comparing the area and population of the Chinese empire and America, we find that in territory China is just about as large as the United States. But her population is five times as great. In China every square mile supports a hundred people, but in America

Reprinted from the ANNALS OF THE AMERICAN ACADEMY OF POLITICAL AND SOCIAL SCIENCES, Volume 39 (January, 1912), pages 74-82, by permission of the American Academy of Political and Social Sciences.

twenty only, one-fifth as many. The mild climate of Southern China also encourages the increase of population. So Canton, one of the treaty ports, has an enormous population which, by the census of 1899, was 2,500,000--compared with that of the northern cities, we find that this is more than thrice that of Hankow (709,000) or four times that of Shanghai (615,000), the great commercial center at the mouth of the Yangtse River. Much has been written by travelers about people living in boats on the Pearl River and about growing potatoes in the kitchens. Both these facts, though more or less exaggerated, show that the southeastern provinces are densely inhabited.

When we think of the peculiarities surrounding this emigration, we cannot help believing that there are certain local characteristics which make Kwangtung and Fookien differ from the other provinces of the empire. The inborn independent idea, the seafaring spirit, the early contact with western nations, the stress of war, the "Golden Romance," the traveling facilities, the social prejudice at home and the attachment to kindred--all these are factors that are laboring to make the Cantonese and Fookienese a migratory people.

Aside from rapid multiplication, another influence impelling the people to emigrate is the peculiar family tradition which entitles the eldest son of the family to occupy the ancestral house. Suppose a man has five sons, which is not uncommon in Canton; his eldest son will have the house. The other four sons have each to build themselves a house. Again supposing these five sons each has a family of five children, how can these children, the land of Canton being so dear and labor so cheap, manage to house themselves? Generally they cannot, and emigration is the result.

If China is overpopulated, why do not the people of the provinces emigrate? Because China is not a migratory nation. The Chinese are home loving; the Middle Kingdom is to them the center of civilization and all the surrounding countries are savage nations, nations where there is little to gain but much to lose. Until the present time the outside world has been a chaos of mystery, unknown and forbidding to the Chinese. Not only would the respectable people not voluntarily go outside the limits of the Celestial Empire, but even the desperate convicts and exiles dreaded banishment to these distant lands. It is in democratic Canton that every man is considered the equal of every other man and all countries worthy of consideration. Even there the well-to-do do not emigrate. Students and merchants who can afford to stay, consequently stay. Conventional ideas, of course, keep the women at home. It is the wretched economic condition that has driven the young peasant out.

What is this economic condition then? The emigrants are almost exclusively peasants. At home they till their own soil and support their own families. Their income is little, but their families are enormous. When the harvest is good, they get barely sufficient to satisfy their hunger. In time of droughts which often occur in winter and in the southeastern provinces they suffer from the failure of crops. We have also to remember that it is the well-to-do peasants that have their own land to till. Those that have no land, labor for those that have. The misery of these laboring peasants in times when food is scarce we need not picutre. When they are out of work, they seek to cut wood in the hills. By this new occupation they can obtain only enough to meet the demand of their homes and an extra meal, the reward of the whole day's labor being twenty or thirty cents. But hills are soon deforested and their families are constantly threatened with starvation. Naturally these able-bodied, young peasants aspire for something greater, something by which they can better their own economic conditions and secure the ease and comfort of life. At home such excellent opportunities are lacking. They have to seek them abroad.

But the economic condition like overpopulation, though having a good deal to do with emigration, cannot be said to be the sole cause. This is shown by the fact that in the north the provinces along the Yellow River are often not less disturbed by floods than are Kwangtung and Fookien by droughts. The great plague that ravaged the North last spring is one of the calamities that often befall those provinces and drive many to starvation and untimely graves. Yet the Northerners do not come out, not entirely because they are less ambitious, but because China is primarily not a migratory country. The emigration of the Cantonese and Fookienese can be accounted for only by the peculiar local characteristics of those two provinces.

A marked characteristic of the people of Kwangtung and Fookien is their independent, adventurous and unbending spirit. The independent spirit of the Cantonese for instance, has long been fostered by the independence of their province which despised submission to the Son of Heaven and which did not join the Celestial Empire till the Ming Dynasty about three hundred years ago. This unruly spirit their northern neighbors designate as "savageness," and they call the Cantonese tauntingly "the southern savages." Whether savage or not, Kwangtung preferred independence to servile submission to the despotic rule of the central government and homage which their northern neighbors take pride in as a sign of civilization. The tribute, however, they did not fail to send to the throne even during the turbulent time of anarchism at the latter part of the Tong Dynasty (907 to 959 A.D.), when the other provinces revolted against the government. So Kwangtung always preserves its individuality. What the northern provinces did, it would not do; what the northern provinces would not do, it did. This deep-rooted independent spirit no emperor could extirpate. Even the powerful Chen Chi Wong, who had in 249 B.C., brought the Six Feudal Kingdoms to subjugation, did not know what to do with Kwangtung. The expedition he sent there met with firm resistance. Half was starved and half slain. The emperors of the Sung Dynasty (960 to 1279 A.D.), instead of requiring the servile homage from the Cantonese, sought to curry their favor. They built a wall for them against the depredations of Cochin China. This independent spirit is what the Northerners lack, is what the Northerners envy. It is, therefore, no wonder that, while their northern countrymen were bound by the idea of absolute seclusion, the people of Kwangtung and Fookien, on the other hand, traversed the South China Sea and crossed the Pacific Ocean to Hawaii and America.

Their adventurous spirit has been fostered by their distant commercial enterprises. Their early commercial history showed considerable trade with the Romans. During the period of luxury Rome stood in want of silk, and silk came only from China. We can trace this as far back as the time of Virgil and Pliny. Virgil spoke of the soft wool obtained from the trees of the Seres or Chinese. Pliny, on the other hand, condemned the useless voyages made merely for that luxurious stuff. Smarkand and Bokhara were in these days the emporiums between the West and the East. Caravans traveled through the desert of Gobi till they reached the northwestern province of Shensi. This route would have led the northwestern provincials to trade with the Westerners, if it was not cut short by the Tartar robbers who constantly pillaged the loaded caravans. A more expeditious way was pursued, which was destined to confine the commerce entirely to Canton. The merchants took their ships from that port to Ceylon, where they sold their goods to the Persian merchants who crowded thither.

During the Mohammedan ascendancy the Arabs penetrated the dreary deserts into China and established considerable trade in Canton, at that time known as Kanfu, literally the Cantonese Prefecture. From the "Voyages of the Two Arabian Travelers," we learn that Chinese junks loaded in Siraf for Maskat, thence for India and Kau-cammali. Having watered at Kau-cammali, they entered the Sea of Harkand and touched at Lajabalus whence they sailed for Kalaba. Thence they steered for Betuma and Senef. Having gotten through the gates of China, they waited for the flood tide to go to the fresh water gulf where they dropped their final anchor at Canton. This trade like the Roman trade was entirely confined to the southern port of Canton. So was the trade with the Indies.

The Indian archipelago has always offered a field to the Chinese trade. Even in the Han Dynasty (202 B.C. to 220 A.D.), many Chinese junks laden with emigrants sailed southward in quest of fortune. They went as far as Arabia, traded with Ceylon and Malacca and penetrated Borneo. As they had touched Archeen, they might have ventured to West Africa, if their junks had been adapted to such voyages.

The Manchu inroads also forced many a Cantonese to leave his abode for the Straits Settlements. The Fookienese likewise preferred shipwreck and death to an ignominious subjection to the Manchus. Able-bodied, young men from the eastern parts of Canton (Chaouchoofoo) and the southern districts of Fookien, Tunggau, Tseueuchoo and Changchoo sailed in large numbers for the islands of the Indian archipelago.

This adventurous spirit was rendered unbending by the many struggles and difficulties they encountered, when they came into contact with the Western explorers. These haughty explorers, after their success in maritime discoveries in the sixteenth century, had rude ideas about the civilization of the colossal empire. Because China was peaceful, they thought they had found an easy prey--all their early acts being marked by blooshed and violence. In 1520 the marauding Portuguese violated the family sanctuary of the Ningpo people. In 1543 the Spaniards occupied the Philippines and massacred the Cantonese in Formosa. In 1635 the British fleet attacked the Bogue Fort of Canton. All these events led the Manchu government to stringent measures, resulting in the closing of all ports against the Westerners, confining the trade to Canton only. This gave the Cantonese the opportunity of dealing with these aggressive Westerners who were to them less mysterious than to their northern neighbors. Gradually it came to their knowledge that there was still land beyond the Four Seas and that there were countries rich in opportunities and fortune besides the Indies; when the great demand for labor in America arose, they flocked over the Pacific into the promised land.

Other occurrences were destined to make the emigration inevitable. First, the stress of war. At the end of the Ming Dynasty (1368 to 1644 A.D.), China was thrown into a chaos. The whole empire was at the mercy of dynastic aspirants and marauding soldiers. Other disasters naturally resulted from the war. The Manchus came in. Their ruthless spirit was such as, to quote the phrase of a celebrated Chinese historian, "to make a patriot's hair stand on end." Thousands and thousands were put to the sword. Cities were sacked and looted. The Manchurian invaders spread terror everywhere they went. The most unfortunate province was Kwangtung, where the survivors of the Ming Dynasty took refuge. Every means was employed to extirpate the royal family so every means was employed to destroy the place of regue. A traveler who visits Southern China can still see the great wastes which were formerly sites of flourishing towns and villages. Not only this, adventurous Canton could not enjoy a quiet day. The aggressive Westerners, who were disgusted with the haughty manner of the Manchu officials, not infrequently sent their cannon balls against the Bogue Fort and marched upon Canton. Twice did Canton enormously suffer from the Opium Wars. The British soldiers marched to the Viceroy's Yamen, causing consternation among the people. The Taiping Rebellion, which had its origin in Kwangsi, did not spare the cities of its neighboring province, the houses of which were as much robbed and destroyed as those of the northern provinces.

At the time of these disasters, there were also certain attractions to quicken the emigrating movement. The sugar plantation in Cuba, the demand of labor in Mexico, Canada, and Peru for other economic purposes, and especially the discovery of gold in California had stirred the whole world with hopes of unexpected fortune. The call of the Gold Mountains, the name given by the Chinese laborers to the Californian ranges, was ringing in the air of the distressed regions of Canton. To go over there and dig the gold up was the thirsty desire of the poor sufferers. "To be starved and to be buried in the sea are the same," said some young adventurers. "Why not plunge right into death rather than wait for death!" With this spirit they even embarked in their crude, old junks and combatted with the dangerous element of the sea without any fear or the least idea of receding. They sailed in these days directly for California before reaching Hawaii. Those who had made their fortune returned and spread the news of the "Golden Romance." The public spirit was stirred. Thousands and thousands forsook their homes.

We must also not forget the traveling facilities which the foreign agents in Hongkong and Macao afforded to the Chinese laborers. Placards were posted on every street wall narrating the charming news of getting fortune quick and the attractive facilities of going to these wonderful lands. Every able-bodied man, no matter whether he could afford the passage money or not, was induced to emigrate, if he could borrow the money to go. Those who could not pay for the passage readily received the most cordial assistance from the agents. A certain amount of money was advanced to the family. A certain amount was paid for clothing and other traveling equipment. What the employers needed was labor, labor of any sort. Nothing would interfere with the Chinese custom, dress and manners. Emigrants need not necessarily know the foreign languages. They need only to work and get good pay. So farmers laid down their spades, carpenters put aside their chisels, and woodcutters said good-bye to their old companions, the axe and the pipe.

Among the classes of peasantry who emigrate, there are in some parts of Canton another class, the class of semi-slaves, who run errands for the villagers and receive pay for their services. In form they are entirely independent. But, nevertheless, they cannot enjoy certain social privileges which the common people can. In spite of the social prejudice, this class has grown to be very intelligent and prominent. This also aroused the prejudices of the ignorant against them the more. Naturally in accord with the independent spirit of the Cantonese, they prefer to die abroad where they can enjoy freedom than to endure the social prejudice at home. Liberty, above all, is the star that guides these people to America.

Having taken a comprehensive view of the causes of emigration--the stress of war, the gold attraction, the traveling facilities and social prejudice at home--which render an unmigratory nation migratory, it is easy to see why the Chinese laborers come to America. But aside from all these there is still another cause that accounts for the non-emigration to Europe. That is the Chinese sense of family attachment. To make clear what I mean, I may say that the Chinese stick to their friends and relatives. Where their friends and relatives do not go, there they do not go. Formerly they flocked to the Straits Settlements only, and not a single one came to America, nay, not even by the gold attraction or any means of inducement. But as soon as a beginning was made, the adventurous emigrant was soon followed by his friends and relatives. That is why, notwithstanding, only three Chinese emigrants appeared in San Francisco in 1830, by 1857, only forty-five years later, we find quite a large settlement in that city. From three, the immigration had changed to eighteen thousand, twenty-one, an increase wonderfully rapid when compared with that long period between American independence and 1830, when not a single Chinese stepped on American soil. Since the passage of the exclusion laws, of course, the number of Chinese entering the United States has been curtailed, but the inducement to come has not stopped. In fact as the unfavorable conditions in China have not changed, the attractiveness of America to the Chinese emigrant still increases. High wages, higher by far than were obtainable in the old mining camps days continue to beckon him eastward. When such attractions are present, it is hardly to be expected that the Chinese laborers will look with respect upon an exclusion law which contradicts with their interests and seems to them an affront to their race. So I dare to predict, no matter how stringent the exclusion law is, it cannot keep them off. I may also say that no matter how much less promising the economic opportunity of Europe may be, if these laborers have once set foot on that continent and become accustomed to living there as they have in America, there is sure to be a constant emigration thence as remarkable as is the present neglect of that field by the Chinese emigrants.

THE ISSEI GENERATION

ROGER DANIELS

"Of sea and the first plantings and the men,
 And how they came in the ships, and to what end."
                    --S.V. Benet, WESTERN STAR

This study will tell the story of California's anti-Japanese movement through its first major triumph, the Japanese exclusion provisions of the Immigration Act of 1924. The emphasis will thus be on the excluders rather than the excluded. But before our narrative can begin we must take an all too brief look at the real focus of the movement: the Issei in California and how they came there.[1]

Originally published by the University of California Press; reprinted by permission of the Regents of the University of California. Professor Daniels is presently with the University of Wyoming.

In comparison with the vast stream of more than thirty million immigrants who came from Europe in the years between the end of the Civil War and 1924, the modest flow from Japan seems an insignificant trickle. Immigration from Japan may be conveniently divided into five periods:[2]

1.	1861-1890 Unrestricted and scattered..........................	3,000
2.	1891-1900 Unrestricted and growing...........................	27,000
3.	1901-1908 Peak, unrestricted immigration......................	127,000
4.	1909-1924 Gentlemen's Agreement in effect....................	118,000
5.	1925-1952 Exclusion; no immigration..........................	....
	Grand total (about)...............................	275,000

Less than 300,000 souls, then are what all the agitation was about. But even this is a misleading figure. Many of the immigrants were birds of passage who returned to Japan or went elsewhere; some made more than one trip, while of course others died. The census figures for Japanese immigrants and native-born give a much more accurate picture:

	United States	California
1880	148	86
1890	2,039	1,147
1900	24,326	10,151
1910	72,157	41,356
1920	111,010	71,952
1930	138,834	97,456

When compared with the total populations of California and the United States, the figures show that at the time of their highest incidence in the population, Japanese immigrants and native-born comprised two and one-tenth per cent (.021) of the population of California and one tenth of one per cent (.001) of the population of the continental United States. The reader will do well to keep these figures in mind, for he will encounter some strange statistical manipulations thereof.

As the tables show, large numbers of Japanese did not begin to migrate to the United States until late in the nineteenth century. Their failure to do so earlier was not owing to their ignorance, for Japanese had been in the New World exactly a decade before the Pilgrim Fathers; in 1610 and 1613 Japanese diplomatic missions visited Mexico.[3] Their passage had been made relatively simple by nature. The Japanese Current will, almost automatically, bring eastbound ships from northern Japan to the Puget Sound area and on down the coast. This was the route of the fabled Manila Galleon.[4] A hypothetical geographic determinist in the early seventeenth century could have concluded that while Europeans were destined to settle the eastern half of the North American continent, Japanese and other Orientals might well colonize its western slopes. This, of course, was not to be. After almost a century of intercourse with the Occident, the human beings who controlled the destinies of Japan decided, in 1638, that their country would be better off without such exotic influences. In that year Japan embarked on a policy of isolation which lasted for more than two centuries until its forcible rupture by Perry in 1853. Emigration did not become legal until 1886.

This does not mean that all contact was broken; curtains, whether of iron or bamboo, have never been a hundred per cent effective. Stranded and castaway Japanese seamen were frequently brought into contact with Americans. In the period from 1782 to 1856 at least thirteen Japanese vessels were shipwrecked on the Pacific Coast and a number of Japanese seamen were picked up at sea, with more than a few of the latter being brought to the United States.[5] These contacts were largely ephemeral and have little significance for our story, although at least two such sailors received an American education and, upon their return to Japan, exerted some influence.[6] After Perry and his black ships reopened Japan to the West, this hitherto accidental intercourse became regularized. Direct shipping between San Francisco and Japan was begun in 1855, and reciprocal diplomatic relations date from 1860.[7]

It is impossible to pinpoint the date of the earliest immigration from Japan to the United States, but it seems to have begun in the 1860's. Starting with a lone traveler in 1861, the statistics record that 185 Japanese entered the country in that decade, but it is not certain that all of them were immigrants.[8] As we have seen, the census could find only 55 in 1870. The earliest group of Japanese settlers that I have been able to discover settled in Alameda County sometime in 1868. According to a local newspaper report they were educated men--there is no mention of any women--who spoke "English and French" and were "gentlemen of refinement and culture in their own country." They seem to have been political refugees.[9] The following year saw the founding of the celebrated but short-lived agricultural colony at Gold Hill, Eldorado County, which has been regarded as the first Japanese colony in the state. The settlers were led by J.H. Schnell, a German who had a Japanese wife and who claimed that he had been the consular representative of "Germany" in Japan. Encouraged by reports of the success of the earlier group, he tried to establish a large-scale agricultural colony which would produce commodities exotic to California--tea and silk. Schnell had a flair for publicity, but lacked talent for or experience in farming. He acquired 600 acres and probably invested at least $10,000 in his experiment, but the dry California summers proved too much for the tender tea bushes and mulberry trees; the colony failed and dispersed after two or three years.[10]

Despite the fact that California was, by the end of the 1860's, already violently anti-Chinese, it is interesting to note that these early colonists from Japan were received with great favor. A typical newspaper editorial pointed out that "the objections raised against the Chinese...cannot be alleged against the Japanese...They have brought their wives, children and...new industries among us."[11] If there was a single word of protest raised against these early immigrants, I have failed to find record of it. This, then, was the early pattern of Japanese immigration--isolated colonies and educated individuals who were accepted and even absorbed with very little ado.[12] This early immigration was minuscular; the total Japanese population of the United States was only 148 persons according to the census of 1880, and in all probability the majority of these were students rather than immigrants.

In the next decade the whole pattern of Japanese immigration was to change. The reasons for that change were several: the socioeconomic dislocations brought about within Japan by the Westernization embarked upon during the Meiji restoration, the need of Hawaiian sugar planters for cheap labor, and the passage of the Chinese Exclusion Act by the United States Congress.

Almost everyone is aware of the rapid transformation which industrialization on the Occidental model wrought in nineteenth-century Japan. In 1850 she was isolated, her warriors crudely armed; by the turn of the century she was, militarily, a first-class power, although this did not become evident until 1905, when she defeated Russia. The measures necessary to bring about so striking a change naturally caused serious dislocations on all levels of Japanese life, and, as is usually the case, the heaviest burdens fell upon those least able to bear them--in this instance, the small farmers. By 1884 the leading English-language Japanese weekly could say:

> The depression...has increased month by month and year by year...Most of the farmers have been unable to pay their taxes...In more than one case self-destruction has been resorted to... If any other territory can (support them) then we should say that it would be a judicious step to get them there as fast as possible.[13]

There was such a territory--the kingdom of Hawaii--and it had been trying to get Japanese laborers for its booming sugar plantations for several years, but the Japanese government had been unwilling to have its citizens emigrate as contract laborers because it rightly concluded that this would, in the long run, lower the prestige of Japan as a nation. The Chinese coolie trade had long been a stench in the nostrils of most of enlightened mankind, and Japan's one previous experience with the Hawaiian plantations had not been good. In 1868 (the year 1 of the Meiji era) one shipload of Japanese-- 141 men, 6 women, and 1 child--had been brought to Hawaii as contract laborers by the Hawaiian Board of Immigration. The terms of their contract called for the Japanese to perform thirty-six months of actual labor in Hawaii at the rate of $4 per man per month, half of which was to be withheld until the contract had been completed. Labor contracts were enforceable in Hawaii under the provisions of the Masters' and Servants'

Act of 1850, which was modeled after the current laws governing merchant seamen. In Hawaii a worker could be sent to jail for breach of contract, i.e., quitting his job. To those who suggested, after the American Civil War, that such contracts smacked of slavery, the planters insisted that the law merely required that "a man do what he has contracted to do," and like to argue that "the right to break a voluntarily made contract with impunity (did not constitute) any part of the system of free labor."[14]

Evidently the Japanese newspapers were aware of the conditions in Hawaii, for a loud roar of protest arose. A Yokohama newspaper compared the recruiting methods in Japan to "stealing Negroes" and pointed out that because of the revolution then in progress "even the government does not have time to deal with things of this sort," but it assured its readers that as soon as peaceful conditions were restored the government would put a stop to such practices. Actually, labor emigration was illegal under Japanese law (and remained so until 1886), but the government did issue the passports. These Gannen Mono ("First Year People"), as they are known in Japanese, were not a great success as plantation workers, probably because, having been recruited on the streets of Yokohama during a period of civil war, "very few, if any, were farmers."[15] Nevertheless, the Hawaiian planters wanted more.

The planters could not afford to be particular. They were faced with the converse of most modern population problems, in that the native Hawaiians were dying faster than they were being born. When, in 1778, Captain Cook chanced upon what he named the Sandwich Islands, the Hawaiian population was perhaps 200,000 thriving pagans. By 1853, thanks to the progress of the white man's civilization and concomitant diseases, there were about 70,000, and their number continued to decline.[16] With a booming sugar industry--Hawaii produced 4,286 pounds of sugar in 1837 and 17,127,161 pounds in 1868-- the American planters who dominated Hawaii knew that they would have to import labor. They would have preferred white labor, but, as a committee ruefully reported, such labor could only be had under "onerous conditions which would result in the complete demoralization of labor in these islands."[17] Forced to make a choice between maintaining a low wage scale and their desire to make Hawaii a white man's country, the planters chose the former. In 1851 they began to import Chinese laborers under five-year contracts.[18] By 1884 there were almost 18,000 Chinese in the islands, comprising more than 22 per cent of the population.[19] Many of these had worked out their contracts and, instead of continuing to work on the plantations or returning to China, had chosen to remain in Hawaii and set up their own businesses. Exhibiting that genius for commerce which has characterized Chinese communities throughout Asia, they became what Professor Conroy has aptly called "troublesome elements in a class society." To counterbalance the economic power of the Chinese, the planters continued to search for other sources of labor. After 1868 Japan had refused all further requests for laborers. But in April, 1884, the economic realities noted above caused the Japanese government to compromise its principles. The Hawaiian envoy in Japan was informed that the government was "not inclined to interpose any obstacle" to large-scale contract labor immigration.[20] Once the green light had been given, the immigration--the first large-scale migration from Japan in history--poured forth in an ever-broadening stream. In the nine years that the contract immigration continued, 1885-94, more than 30,000 Japanese were brought to the Hawaiian Islands.[21] Since the patterns of this immigration were to influence, in more ways than one, the immigration to the United States, it will be worthwhile to examine it in some detail. Fortunately, very complete statistics are available for this period.

It has been noted by almost every student of Japanese immigration, both to Hawaii and to the United States, that a surprisingly high percentage of the immigrants came from four prefectures in one small area of southwestern Japan. The territory around the then obscure city of Hiroshima sent forth more than any other.[22] One of the earliest studies of Japanese immigration pointed out that all four of the prefectures were among the poorest in Japan, although there were other poor districts which did not contribute many immigrants.[23] There the matter rested until Professor Conroy's researches into the Hawaiian archives revealed a hitherto unknown human factor. The agent in Japan for the Hawaiian Board of Immigration, Robert W. Irwin, was determined to avoid the error of his predecessor. He deliberately selected his laborers from a rural backwater "about 1000 miles from Tokyo."[24] Thus all the contract immigration came from one general area. This influenced the later immigration to the United States in two ways. First, a very large percentage of California's Issei came by way of Hawaii. Second, since these areas were the only part of Japan whose people had had experience with transpacific migration, it naturally followed when the period of heavy free immigration ensued that this area furnished a disproportionate share of the migrants. In the five years from 1899 to 1903 more than 60 per cent of the non-Asian passports issued by the Japanese government went to residents of the four prefectures, and in 1908 a survey conducted by the semiofficial Japanese Association of America showed that the same group controlled almost half of the acreage tilled by Issei in California.[25]

The origins of the Hawaii-California transmigration, like that of the Japan-California migration, are shrouded in obscurity. When the first group of contract laborers arrived in Hawaii in 1868, they "found three Japanese in Honolulu, two of whom left immediately for the United States!."[26] These two unknown travelers may well have been the first Japanese to make the Hawaii-California trip, but we cannot even be sure they arrived safely. By the end of the contract labor period (1894), at which time, unfortunately, the keeping of accurate statistics lapsed, 771 laborers whose contracts had expired were listed as having "left for America."[27]

Wages on the highly unionized Pacific Coast of the United States, where employers chronically complained of a "labor shortage" (usually they meant a shortage of labor willing to work at close-to-subsistence levels), were substantially higher than in Hawaii, where unions were almost unknown until after American annexation annulled the contract labor laws. From that time (June, 1900, was the effective date) until the Gentlemen's Agreement went into effect (1908), more than 40,000 Issei made their way to the Pacific Coast, most of them to California.[28] The passage of the Chinese Exclusion Act of 1882 had barred Chinese from the United States, and, after their numbers began to diminish, the so-called shortage of cheap and reliable agricultural labor in California acted as an inducement to prospective Japanese immigrants. Had Chinese immigration continued, the total number of Japanese immigrants would certainly have been smaller.

If must have taken a good deal of courage to make the trip from Hawaii. Although the immigrants from Japan to California or Hawaii did not travel under conditions that could be called luxurious by any stretch of the imagination, the Japanese government, always solicitous for the welfare of its subjects, insisted upon at least a minimum standard of decency. On the Hawaii-California trip, before 1900, these standards sometimes completely disappeared. A San Francisco newspaper described one such immigrant ship as loaded with a cargo of 24,494 sacks of sugar and an unspecified number of Japanese, who were packed aboard the Potter "much in the fashion cattle are imported, only with less regard to the health and comfort of the Japs," and added that "A sheep or a cow costs money (but) a Jap more or less does not count." The master of the Potter, a vessel of 1,803 tons, merely stowed the "passengers" in on top of the sacks without even the pretense of bunks. For several days, during a storm, they had been enclosed under battened-down hatches in "Cimmerian darkness," without water, since "water in a cargo of sugar is like fire in a cargo of gunpowder." Somehow, according to the amazed shipping reporter of the Call, all the immigrants survived conditions that "would have killed a waterfront tough outright."[29]

Having survived such a voyage, or a more pleasant one, what did the newly arrived immigrant do? If he had come from Hawaii, he would know at least a little of Western ways, but in the course of a short term on a sugar plantation, surrounded by fellow Japanese, he might acquire only a very limited English vocabulary. Immigrants from Japan often could not boast even that. How did they get their bearings in an alien world? They did so exactly as non-English-speaking Europeans were doing in New York and other Eastern centers. They were assisted, and exploited, by fellow immigrants who were often themselves "just off the boat." There rapidly developed, along the Pacific slope, clusters of boardinghouses run by Issei who doubled as small-scale labor contractors. Although most of the officials who commented on this system regarded it as a unique product of "Asiatic cunning," similar institutions had developed spontaneously in the East. There, supplying unskilled industrial employment, it became known as the padrone system. In the West an agricultural proletariat was needed. Both systems had a common basis: a need for varying amounts of unskilled labor, a mass of newly arrived immigrants unfamiliar with the language and customs of the country, and a group of small-scale entrepreneurs--"padrones" in the East, "boardinghouse keepers" in the West--who served as convenient and perhaps necessary middlemen. It was the constant complaint of officials in the West, state and federal, that they could never prove that these Issei entrepreneurs were violating the contract labor laws. Since these officials, who, as a body, were zealously anti-Japanese, could never prove a single violation against resident Issei, the historian must assume their innocence.[30]

We can get a glimpse into the far-flung activities of these contractors from advertisements that frequently appeared in the Japanese-language press of Hawaii. A typical example, from the HAWAIIAN-JAPANESE CHRONICLE of March 22, 1905, proclaimed:

GREAT RECRUITING TO AMERICA
Through an arrangement made with Yasuwaza, of San Francisco we are able to recruit laborers to the mainland and offer them work. The laborers will be subjected to no delay upon arriving in San Francisco, but can get work immediately through Yasuwaza. Employment offered in picking strawberries and tomatoes, planting beets, mining and domestic service. Now is the time to go! Wages $1.50 a day. Tokujiro-Inaya-Niigata Kejin--care of the Nishimura Hotel. Apply to the Honolulu agencies for further particulars, giving the name of your plantation.[31]

The contractors thus served as an adjunct to California agriculture, which, in contrast with the usual American pattern of family-sized farms, has always been dependent upon large numbers of seasonal workers. As a recent authority put it: "Many localities (in California) are dependent for their farm operations on a mobile labor supply which has neither stability in employment nor in domicile."[32] In the decades after the Civil War this transient labor supply was, in the main, Chinese. After the passage of the Chinese Exclusion Act of 1882, it is often asserted, a vacuum was created by the ensuing shortage of cheap agricultural labor, and this vacuum attracted the Japanese to America.[33] This is an oversimplification. California, like the rest of the nation in the curiously named "gay nineties," was in the throes of the most prolonged panic of the century. The earliest Japanese labor gangs were in direct competition with the remaining Chinese, and had to resort to wage cutting to get employment. In 1894, in Santa Clara County, Japanese were working for 50 cents a day and boarding themselves. The normal scale for Chinese had long been established at a dollar a day. Similarly, in 1896, Japanese reduced the sugar beet harvest price from $1.20 to 70 cents per ton.[34]

Naturally, employers welcomed these early Issei recruits to the ranks of American agriculture, particularly since the Chinese, abetted by their rapidly diminishing number, were trying to raise wages. Within a few years the growers were singing a different tune. Around the turn of the century business conditions improved, both in California and the nation, and the decline in number of the Chinese laborers became even more noticeable. At the same time, as a group, Japanese labor began to serve notice that it would not be long content with the lowest rung of the economic ladder. Although the earliest recorded strike of Japanese agricultural laborers occurred in 1891, strikes do not seem to have become a frequent tactic until 1903. A standard device was to wait until the fruit was ripe on the trees and then insist upon renegotiating the contract. The growers protested that this was unethical, since a contract was a contract, and remembered that the Chinese, to their credit, had never done such things. But, as there were no longer enough Chinese to go around, in many instances the Japanese demands had to be met. From about this date, 1903, we begin to hear invidious comparisons of the two races from agriculturalists, almost always to the detriment of the Japanese. One grower even complained about the "saucy, debonair cuffs and white collar accompaniments." That is, of course, hyperbole, but it can be taken as a symptom of something quite tangible; the intense desire of many Issei to move up the social and economic ladder.[35] From 1910 on, despite the prewar slump, the earnings of Japanese in agriculture were generally equal to, and sometimes above, those of other groups. This latter condition was particularly true when piecework rates were in force.[36]

But a seasonal farm laborer, no matter how well paid, could never climb very high. Many, perhaps most, Issei had their eyes fixed on the same goal; they wanted to work their own land. Because of lack of capital, it often took many years of toil before this goal could be realized. In many instances the individual would first sharecrop, then rent or lease, and finally, if possible, buy land. The statistics of Japanese land tenure in California dramatically illustrate the upward climb of thousands of Issei. In 1900 the holdings of thirty-nine Issei farmers, unspecified as to tenure, aggregated 4,698 acres. From 1904 on, the statistics are more detailed:[37]

28,800 acres actually in production and, by means of marketing agreements, handled the produce of thousands more. His working force numbered over five hundred, from engineers and boat captains (the islands were then accessible only by water) to common laborers, and included Japanese, East Indians, and Caucasians, both native and foreign born. At his death, in 1926, a newspaper estimated his estate at $15 million; his pallbearers included David Starr Jordan,

	Owned (in acres)	Leased (in acres)	Shared Crop (in acres)
1904	2,422	35,258 1/2	19,572 1/2
1909	16,449 1/2	80,232	59,001 1/2
1919	74,769	383,287[a]	....

[a]*Lease figure includes cropping contracts.*

In 1919 the market value of crops produced by the Issei was over $67 million, a bit more than 10 per cent of the total value of California crops.[38] At this time agriculture occupied about half of the 70,000 Japanese in California. One of them, George Shima, an emigrant from Fukuoka Prefecture, was undoubtedly the best-known Issei. Although his career is certainly not typical, it is surely worth considering, since he probably symbolized the aspirations of many of the first generation.

Shima, who was born in 1863 in pre-Meiji Japan, came to this country in 1889 with less than a thousand dollars in capital.[39] After working first as a common laborer and then as a labor contractor, he formed a partnership with several other Issei and leased 15 acres of reclaimed land. By use of the latest techniques, both agricultural and managerial, Shima and his associates created an agricultural empire on the virgin "drowned islands" of the San Joaquin delta and were among the first to raise potatoes successfully for the market in California. As early as 1909 Shima was referred to as the "Potato King," and each year the press speculated as to his net income. By 1920 it was alleged that he controlled 85 per cent of the crop, whose total value was over $18 million. Thanks to a graduate student at the University of California, who visited the Shima holdings in 1913 as part of his research, we can get an accurate picture of his operations at that time. In that year Shima controlled

the chancellor of Stanford University, and James Rolph, Jr., the mayor of San Francisco. Shima's was surely a Horatio Alger story without any trace of kind benefactor or boss's daughter; but when the real-life hero was a California Issei there was bound to be a bitter twist not found in dime novels. Shima, despite his millions, was still an "alien ineligible to citizenship"; and when, in 1909, he bought a house in one of the better residential neighborhoods of Berkeley, a cry of protest went up from the citizens of that quiet university town. Although obviously embarrassed, Shima stayed. He informed the protestants, who included a University of California professor, that they need not worry, since he was putting up "a high... fence to keep the other children from playing with his."[40] If even a millionaire had problems finding a home, what must it have been like for his less prosperous compatriots?

Those in the cities, when they became numerous enough, were crowded into a ghetto which soon became a "Little Tokyo" or "Little Osaka" to its residents and "Japtown" to most outsiders. Although they practiced many occupations (a group of shoemakers had been among the first to come), the vast majority fell into two groups: domestics--house servants and gardeners--and small businessmen. Most of the latter catered to the growing Japanese community; a few, but ever increasing in number, dealt primarily with Caucasians.

The servant problem--for the well to do,

at least--seemed quite important in an earlier America. In California, first Chinese and then Japanese immigrants offered temporarily successful solutions. After the 1882 exclusion act, Chinese servants, a traditional leisure-class symbol in San Francisco (as even television has discovered), became increasingly scarce. As in the case of agricultural laborers, the Japanese substitutes were only a stopgap, for their ambition would not permit many Issei to remain domestics. Thus arose the phenomenon of the "Japanese schoolboy", usually a very recent immigrant and often not at all involved in higher education, although many students from Japan did work their way through college in domestic service. The "schoolboy", however, wanted to learn English and the "ropes," then move on to greener pastures. To get a foothold, he accepted what seemed almost token wages--in 1900 $1.50 per week, plus board (by 1907 this had gone up to $2, while a trained servant earned from $15 to $40 per month, plus board). The classified sections of the San Francisco newspapers during the height of immigration (1904-1907) give striking evidence of the situation. Ads such as "Good Japanese boy wants situation as schoolboy," or "Japanese nice boy wants position as school boy in small family," dominated the "situations wanted" column. By 1909 their number had decreased. In that year there were an estimated 2,000 Japanese domestics in San Francisco; a few years earlier there had been more than twice as many.[41] Another, but more permanent, upper-class symbol was the Issei gardener, whose green thumb made California lawns and shrubs bloom as never before. Since anything connected with the soil had status in the Japanese culture, the gardeners are a continuing feature of California life; the indoor domestics have almost completely disappeared.

What did the "schoolboy" do when he left domestic service? Because of the high degree of unionization in northern California and the anti-Oriental agitation which had been prevalent since the 1860's, no significant number of Issei were ever hired by white firms for factory or office work. The "schoolboy," if he stayed in town, had to go into business for himself, or, more probably, go to work for an already established Issei.[42] Commenting on the relatively large number of businesses owned by Orientals in America ("In 1929 they owned one-and-a-half times as many (businesses) per 1,000 population as other residents of the United States") and contrasting this with the proportionately fewer establishments owned by Negroes, Gunnar Myrdal seemed not to realize that he was comparing two different kinds of phenomena. Most Oriental businesses (restaurants, laundries, and curio shops were, to a degree, exceptions) catered primarily to Orientals.[43] This practice was not just the result of clannishness; unlike the Negroes, whose wants and needs were purely American, the Issei, bringing their own language and culture with them, had special requirements. Patronizing Mr. Watanabe's grocery store was not only a convenience (the store was closer and he spoke the language even if his prices were a little higher than those of the A & P) --if one wanted Aji-no-moto Sauce, or some other Japanese delicacy, it was a necessity. The basic function of most Issei businesses can be summed up in a phrase--"they took in each other's washing."[44]

The United States Immigration Commission's 1909 survey located and categorized 1,380 Japanese businesses in California; thirteen years later Matsui found the total had grown to 2,176. Both agreed that these were essentially family businesses, having small capital and serving primarily their own community. Both studies found that when Issei businessmen competed with Caucasians price cutting was apt to be used as an entering wedge, but that after a time price agreements would be made with Caucasian trade associations, which Issei were rarely able to join. Within the Japanese community, however, wages were generally lower and hours longer than in other businesses. All these generalizations would apply almost equally well to most first-generation immigrant businesses in the United States irrespective of the origin of the proprietors.[45]

Whether they lived on farms or in cities (for the period under consideration the rural-urban division was roughly equal) the Issei and their descendants tended to cluster in certain areas, thereby heightening what the sociologists like to call their "high social visibility." Although the distribution pattern within the state was to change, the tendency to congregate became, if anything, more pronounced. Even without the extra-legal segregation which existed everywhere, such concentrations would be understandable from both social and economic points of view. Up to about 1907, the San Francisco Bay area, the area around Sacramento, and the upper San Joaquin Valley were the major foci of immigrant population. After that date the population grew more rapidly in the south. This was owing both to the fact that the anti-

Japanese agitation started in San Francisco and had not yet become serious in southern California, and that the latter region, particularly Los Angeles County, was, for all newcomers, much more a land of economic opportunity than the more heavily populated middle part of the state. By 1910 Los Angeles, which at the previous census had contained less than one per cent of the state's Japanese population, had more Japanese than any other county. By 1920 almost 20,000 (18 per cent) lived there. The other centers of Japanese population were Sacramento, Fresno, San Francisco, Alameda, and San Joaquin counties; the remaining 10 per cent were scattered in thirty-four counties, and in eight counties the enumerators failed to find a single Japanese.[46]

Demographically, the outstanding feature of the immigration before 1907 was its imbalance. There was an overwhelming preponderance of young adult males, the majority of whom came from "the agricultural class." The Immigration Commission, whose agents personally interviewed 12,905 Issei, reported that more than 75 per cent had been less than thirty years old when they arrived in the United States. Since many of them had come by way of Hawaii, the median age at the time of original emigration had been less than twenty-four years.[47] The next year the census reported that there were almost eight Japanese males of more than fifteen years of age for each Japanese female in the same age group. Only 28 per cent of these men were married (more than half of their wives were still in Japan), while almost half of the comparable group of native white males were no longer single. For Issei girls and women, catching a husband was no problem; more than 86 per cent of the women over fifteen years of age were married, compared to only 57 per cent of their native white sisters. The predominantly female immigration of the next decade helped equalize the sex ratio, but there were still several thousand more men than women by the next census, at which time the "picture bride" immigration was stopped.[48] Some of these Issei bachelors were able to go to Japan and bring back brides before the exclusion provisions went into effect (the Japanese steamship lines did a thriving "peace excursion" business in those years); others later married Nisei women much younger than themselves (these marriages were often arranged in the old-country manner); but the majority of these unmarried men was doomed to be the last of their line, a particularly cruel fate for the strongly family-oriented Japanese.

Those Issei males able to marry generally did so rather late in life, and took wives much younger than themselves. Statistical verification can be found in the data compiled when the West Coast Japanese were incarcerated during the Second World War. At that time most of the Issei males were between fifty and sixty-four years of age, and most of the Issei females were between forty and fifty-four. The major group of the Nisei were between twenty and twenty-four years of age.[49] When these and other data are plotted on a chart, it becomes apparent that there was a "missing" generation of Japanese, i.e., the generation which, under conditions of a normal population-sex ratio, would have been born in the years 1905-1915. The figures also indicate that in a typical Issei family, children were born in the years 1918-1922 to a thirty-five-year-old father and a twenty-five-year-old mother. In the years to come, the absence of this generation would exacerbate the tension between Issei father and Nisei son, although it should be noted that "rejection" of the immigrant parents by the second-generation children is one of the classic motifs of the history of immigrants in America.[50]

The Nisei were born into homes which they made bilingual; most Issei continued to use Japanese among themselves, and some had no alternative. Their homes partook of both cultures. One Nisei remembered that he

> sat down to American breakfasts and Japanese lunches. My palate developed a fondness for rice along with corned beef and cabbage. I became equally adept with knife and fork and with chopsticks. I said grace at meal times in Japanese, and recited the Lord's Prayer at night in English. I hung my stocking over the fireplace at Christmas and toasted "mochi" at Japanese New Year. The stories of "Tongue-cut Sparrow" and "Momo-taro" were as well known to me as those of Red Riding Hood and Cinderella...On some nights I was told bedtime stories of how Admiral Togo sent a great Russian fleet down to destruction. Other nights I heard of King Arthur or from GULLIVER'S TRAVELS and TOM SAWYER. I was spoken to by both parents in Japanese and English. I answered in

whatever was convenient or in a curious mixture of both.[51]

The homes were generally modest, especially in the earlier years, but most Issei were not economically disadvantaged. Matsui concluded, in 1922, that "in general...the standard of living of the Japanese is still a little lower than the well established American, although it is not inferior to that of (other) recent immigrants."[52] In general, by the 1920's, the Issei were what in modern parlance might be called "lower-middle class," although it cannot be overemphasized that, for the Issei, associations were ethnically rather than economically determined. They lived in a world modeled on what they had known in Japan, but a world strangely and eccentrically transmuted by the omnipotent American environment. Some Issei were or became Christians, but even Buddhism, the religion of the majority, became Americanized. It was not uncommon, for example, for Protestant hymns to be swallowed almost whole; one of the most popular thus evolved into "Buddha loves me, this I know." Other, more malleable, aspects of life changed even more. Culturally, then, the Issei generation was transitional, neither Japanese nor American; the Nisei, their children, became, in law and fact, Americans.

But the role of the Issei was not unique, except for their peculiar status. Along with other Asians, they were "aliens ineligible to citizenship." The selfsame transitional role has been played out by millions of immigrants from Europe, particularly those of the new immigration whose exodus from southern and eastern Europe occurred at about the same time. Operating in the freer and more expansive California economy, the Issei, as a group, undoubtedly were economically better off than the new immigrants in the East.[53] Their acceptance into American society, however, was greatly retarded by ever-growing fires of social antagonism. The flames were deliberately fanned by the assorted individuals and groups who collectively comprised the anti-Japanese movement.

---

[1] *The Japanese terms "Issei" ("first generation," for immigrants from Japan) and "Nisei" ("second generation," for their children born in the United States or Hawaii) will be used frequently for precision. The terms "Japanese-Americans" and "Americans of Japanese ancestry" are not appropriate for the period under discussion because the vast majority of the adult population (except for a handful of Issei "illegally" naturalized) were "aliens ineligible to citizenship" and remained, in law, Japanese nationals. Therefore I will often use the term "Japanese" to cover both immigrants and their citizen offspring, although it is to be understood that many of both generations had more of the spirit of America in them than some whose forefathers were the first to settle the land. For linguistic and historical convenience, the terms "Caucasian" and "white" are used as if they were altogether meaningful, which of course they are not. The semantic problems involved in doing otherwise a work of this nature are dreadful to contemplate.*

[2] *For statistics of Japanese immigration see Appendix A.*

[3] *Z. Nuttall, "Earliest Historical Relations Between Mexico and Japan," UNIVERSITY OF CALIFORNIA PUBLICATIONS IN AMERICAN ARCHAEOLOGY AND ETHNOLOGY, 4 (1906), 1-47.*

[4] *William Lytle Schurz, THE MANILA GALLEON (New York, 1959), p. 15.*

[5] *Sacramento UNION, Dec. 14, 1876; San Francisco ALTA CALIFORNIA, March 5, 6, 17-20, 22, and 23, and April 5, 1871; the ALTA for Feb. 21 and March 2, 1852, gives a running account of one group of castaway Japanese.*

[6] *For the stories of two wandering Japanese of this period see Joseph Heco, THE NARRATIVE OF A JAPANESE; WHAT HE HAS SEEN AND THE PEOPLE HE HAS MET IN THE COURSE OF THE LAST FORTY YEARS (Tokyo, 1895) and Hizakazu Kneko, MANJIRO, THE MAN WHO DISCOVERED AMERICA (Boston, 1956).*

[7] *San Francisco ALTA CALIFORNIA, Sept. 19, 1855; C. Yanaga, "The First Japanese Embassy to the United States," PACIFIC HISTORICAL REVIEW, 9 (March, 1940), 113-138.*

[8] *REPORTS OF THE IMMIGRATION COMMISSION (Washington, 1911), Vol. 23, p. 5.*

[9] *San Francisco CHRONICLE, June 17, 1869.*

[10] *Paolo Sioli, HISTORICAL SOUVENIR OF EL DORADO COUNTY, CALIFORNIA (Oakland, 1888), p. 112. ALTA CALIFORNIA, June 16 and Oct. 24, 1869, Sacramento UNION, June 5, 7, 18, 19, and 21, and Oct. 24, 1869; March 2, April 5, June 11, Sept. 1 and 3, and Dec. 31, 1870; April 7, 1871.*

[11] *San Francisco CHRONICLE, June 17, 1869. One suspects that the expectation of a thriving tea and silk industry weighed heavily with the editor. The West's lack of manufactures was a chronic complaint in California newspapers. For an even later favorable comment see the Sacramento UNION, Jan. 19, 1888.*

[12] *That is, absorbed literally. California then could take interracial marriage in its stride. On Jan. 12, 1877, the Sacramento UNION published in its exchanges a report from the Truckee REPUBLICAN telling of a marriage between "a large good looking white man" and "a delicate fragile looking Japanese woman." There was no derogatory comment. Twenty-eight years later, California would be in an uproar because Japanese boys sat in the same classrooms with Caucasian girls.*

[13] JAPAN WEEKLY MAIL, Dec. 20, 1884, quoted in Hilary Conroy, THE JAPANESE FRONTIER IN HAWAII, 1869-1898 (Berkeley and Los Angeles, 1953), pp. 61-62. As the notes will show, this chapter relies heavily on Professor Conroy's excellent monograph.

[14] *Ibid.*, pp. 11-12, quoting from the HAWAIIAN GAZETTE, Jan. 19, 1870. See also Ralph Kuykendall, THE EARLIEST JAPANESE LABOR IMMIGRATION TO HAWAII (Honolulu, 1935). For a good account of the Chinese coolie trade see Persia Campbell Crawford, CHINESE COOLIE EMIGRATION TO COUNTRIES WITHIN THE BRITISH EMPIRE (London, 1923). Strictly speaking, there was never any "coolie" emigration to the United States.

[15] Conroy, *op. cit.*, pp. 15, 21.

[16] REPORT OF THE COMMISSIONER OF LABOR ON HAWAII, 1901 (Washington, 1902), p. 26.

[17] Quoted by Conroy, *op. cit.*, p. 133.

[18] Donald Rowland, "The United States and the Contract Labor Question in Hawaii, 1862-1900," PACIFIC HISTORICAL REVIEW, 2 (Sept., 1933), 249-269.

[19] REPORT OF THE COMMISSIONER OF LABOR ON HAWAII, 1901, pp. 26, 34.

[20] Quoted by Conroy, *op. cit.*, p. 58.

[21] *Ibid.*, p. 154.

[22] See the map in Yosaburo Yoshida, "Sources and Causes of Japanese Immigration," ANNALS OF THE AMERICAN ACADEMY OF POLITICAL AND SOCIAL SCIENCE (hereinafter cited as ANNALS), 34 (Sept., 1909), 161.

[23] *Ibid.*

[24] Conroy, *op. cit.*, pp. 82-83. Irwin had doctors inspect the laborers as part of the selection process and naturally chose as good physical specimens as he could, since the work on the plantations was grueling. As Conroy notes, this means that the later physical comparisons of Nisei children with those in Japan (Nisei were larger) do not prove as much as once was thought, the original migrants having been selected for their superior physical qualities (see pp. 80-89).

[25] Yoshida, *op. cit.*, pp. 160-162.

[26] Conroy, *op. cit.*, p. 28.

[27] *Ibid.*, Appendix E, p. 154. Romanzo Adams, THE JAPANESE IN HAWAII (New York, 1924), Table C, p. 12 gives the numbers as 712. For an excellent fictional treatment of the Japanese in Hawaii from about 1900 on see James A. Michener, HAWAII (New York, 1959), particularly the section entitled "From the Inland Sea."

[28] Contract labor was abolished by sec. 10 of the Act of April 30, 1900, 31 Statutes at Large 141, chap. 339 (2 Supp., Revised Statutes 1141); REPORT OF THE COMMISSIONER OF LABOR ON HAWAII, 1901, p. 19; REPORTS OF THE IMMIGRATION COMMISSION, Vol. 23, p. 6.

[29] San Francisco CALL, June 25, 1892.

[30] See, for example, the affidavit of Cleveland L. Dam, former deputy labor commissioner of the State of California, Feb. 16, 1900 in REPORTS OF THE INDUSTRIAL COMMISSION (Washington, 1901), Vol. 15, pp. 767-768. For a federal official's reminiscences, see Hart H. North, "Chinese and Japanese Immigration to the Pacific Coast," CALIFORNIA HISTORICAL SOCIETY QUARTERLY, 28 (Dec., 1949), 343-350. For an adverse appraisal of North's treatment of Chinese immigrants see letter, Theodore Roosevelt to Victor H. Metcalf, June 16, 1905, in E.E. Morison (ed.), THE LETTERS OF THEODORE ROOSEVELT (Cambridge, Mass., 1951), IV, 1235-1236; hereinafter cited as Roosevelt Letters.

[31] Quoted in REPORTS OF THE IMMIGRATION COMMISSION, Vol. 23, p. 14.

[32] Varden Fuller, "The Supply of Agricultural Labor as a Factor in the Evolution of Farm Organization in California," in HEARINGS BEFORE A SUBCOMMITTEE OF THE COMMITTEE ON EDUCATION AND LABOR, UNITED STATES SENATE, SEVENTY-SIXTH CONGRESS, THIRD SESSION PURSUANT TO S. RES. 266 (74TH CONGRESS), (Washington, 1940), Part 54, p. 19778. Another authority comments that California's specialized farming "was made possible by a long continued supply of cheap migrant labor.... In the years preceding the First World War [the Japanese] constituted the primary supply.... By the 1920's [many] had migrated to cities or had set themselves up as farmers." Clarke A. Chambers, CALIFORNIA FARM ORGANIZATIONS (Berkeley and Los Angeles, 1952), pp. 1-2.

[33] See the testimony of John Powell Irish, a large-scale California agriculturist and long-time advocate and defender of Orientals, in U.S. Congress, House of Representatives, Committee on Immigration and Naturalization, HEARINGS ON JAPANESE IMMIGRATION (Washington, 1921), pp. 43-49.

34Fuller, "The Supply of Agricultural Labor...," op. cit., pp. 19827-19833.

35Ibid., pp. 19834-19835. The employer's complaint is in the CALIFORNIA FRUIT GROWER, 28 (Aug. 15, 1903), 2. The Immigration Commission shrewdly comments, on this stated preference, that it must be remembered that "these opinions are expressed... after the [Chinese] had largely disappeared from the industry.... There is at least a question whether the Chinese have not risen in the appreciation of the growers with their scarcity and at the expense of the reputations of the races at present employed." REPORTS OF THE IMMIGRATION COMMISSION, Vol. 24, p. 108.

36Shichiro Matsui, "Economic Aspects of the Japanese Situation in California" (Unpublished M.A. thesis, University of California, Berkeley, 1922), p. 93; REPORTS OF THE IMMIGRATION COMMISSION, Vol. 23, pp. 33-45.

37Data for 1900, 1904, 1909 are in REPORTS OF THE IMMIGRATION COMMISSION, Vol. 23, p. 79; for 1919 in California State Board of Control, CALIFORNIA AND THE ORIENTAL (Sacramento, 1922), p. 48.

38CALIFORNIA AND THE ORIENTAL, p. 49.

39The date of arrival is variously given as 1888, 1889, and 1890; but see letter, Shima to Hiram Johnson, Feb. 11, 1911 (Johnson MSS, Bancroft Library, Berkeley).

40The sketch of Shima is drawn from: Kaizo Naka, "Social and Economic Conditions among Japanese Farmers in California" (Unpublished M.A. thesis, University of California, 1913), pp. 55-60. K.K. Kawakami, THE REAL JAPANESE QUESTION (New York, 1921), pp. 44-47. San Francisco CHRONICLE March 8, 1909; Jan. 6, April 7, and Dec. 15, 1910; Jan. 21, Sept. 1 and 16, 1911; June 25, 1912; Jan. 19 and 26, 1917; Nov. 20, 1919; March 27, 28, 29, and 30, and April 18, 1926; July 19, 1927; April 26, 1952. San Francisco EXAMINER Feb. 23, 1917. Dorothy Swaine Thomas, THE SALVAGE (Berkeley and Los Angeles, 1942), pp. 181 ff. The home incident is from the CHRONICLE of March 13, 1909.

41Statistics from REPORTS OF THE IMMIGRATION COMMISSION, Vol. 23, pp. 183-184. Viewers of television may recall that the "western" serial show "Have Gun, Will Travel" has repeatedly used a stereotyped Chinese servant as a late-nineteenth-century status symbol; see also the Californian novels of Gertrude Atherton.

42REPORTS OF THE IMMIGRATION COMMISSION, Vol. 23, pp. 97-99.

43Gunnar Myrdal, AN AMERICAN DILEMMA (New York, 1944), I, 310.

44A student of the Japanese in the State of Washington finds that "cultural differences have tended to isolate the Japanese and make of them a discrete unit...[They have developed] a complementary economic organization." John A. Rademaker, "The Japanese in the Social Organization of the Puget Sound Region," AMERICAN JOURNAL OF SOCIOLOGY, 40 (Nov., 1934), 338-343.

45REPORTS OF THE IMMIGRATION COMMISSION, Vol. 23, pp. 99-103; Matsui, op. cit., pp. 53-57.

46FOURTEENTH CENSUS OF THE UNITED STATES, 1920 (Washington, 1920), Vol. 3, pp. 109-110. The term "southern California" traditionally refers to the area south of the Tehachapi Mountains which are north of Los Angeles.

47REPORTS OF THE IMMIGRATION COMMISSION, Vol. 23, pp. 3-4, 7-8.

48THIRTEENTH CENSUS OF THE UNITED STATES, 1910 (Washington, 1910), II, 159. FOURTEENTH CENSUS OF THE UNITED STATES, 1920 (Washington, 1920), II, passim. Among all immigrants to the United States from 1865 to 1924 the ratio was about 6.5 males to 3 females according to Harry Jerome, MIGRATIONS AND BUSINESS CYCLES (New York, 1926), p. 38. For the best treatment of the problems immigration laws caused Oriental familes see R.D. McKenzie, ORIENTAL EXCLUSION (Chicago, 1928), pp. 79-97.

49For an excellent chart see Dorothy S. Thomas and Richard Nishimoto, THE SPOILAGE (Berkeley and Los Angeles, 1946), p. 31. The same work states that the "average modal age of Issei was 56, of Nisei 21" (p. 68). It is obvious that the Issei figure refers to males only, but not clear whether those figures have relevance outside the particular camp under discussion (Gila River). See also, ibid., p. 4.

50One of the best treatments of the problems of the Nisei is in Carey McWilliams, PREJUDICE (Boston, 1944), pp. 96-105. For generalizations about American immigration see Marcus L. Hansen, "The History of American Immigration as a Field for Research," AMERICAN HISTORICAL REVIEW, 32 (April, 1927), 500-518.

51Aiji Tashio in NEW OUTLOOK, Sept., 1934, quoted in McWilliams, op. cit., p. 99. Tashio's parents were undoubtedly much better educated than the average Issei, since they read to him in English; but all Nisei would, by their attendance in public schools, have comparable experience.

52Matsui, op. cit., p. 98.

53Without being able to cite any data, I would also suggest that "new immigrants" in California--Italians, Armenians and Greeks in particular--were economically better off than their contemporary compatriots in the East.

100 Years of Japanese Labor History in the USA

KARL YONEDA

The history of Japanese migration to this country cannot be separated from that of the Chinese because they are interwoven. When gold was discovered in California, Chinese began to migrate to Hawaii and the West Coast seeking "a tree that bears money." The first contract-labor group of 180 Chinese was brought to Hawaiian sugar plantations in 1852 under a 5-year contract with pay of $3.00 per month. More came, toiling under the hot sun and watchful eyes of lunas (overseers) who constantly beat the workers with whips for not working "fast enough." However, the owners were not happy with the Chinese, saying "they are clannish, secretive, as well as dirty and full of sex diseases," etc. Then, in 1868, the first group of 148 Japanese arrived and were sent to 6 plantations under 3-year contracts at $4.00 per month pay. The conditions were so unbearable that three committed suicide; some were fined $4.00 --a month's pay--for talking back to the luna; and one was jailed for one year. In spite of some "rebellious" Japanese, the owners preferred them, in order to maintain and increase their profits through the "divide and rule" policy against other immigrants. (The first Koreans were brought to Hawaii in 1903, followed by Filipinos in 1906).

The employers' and their lackeys' treatment was so inhuman and vicious that even "docile and obedient" Chinese and Japanese, as well as others including native Hawaiian workers, resorted to sabotage, work stoppages and strikes. From 1868 to 1920, Japanese alone participated in more than 60 such incidents. A total of some 72,000 Japanese workers were involved: 600 jailed, 350 fined, and one, Katsu Goto, an ex-sugar worker, store keeper and interpreter, was lynched on the Island of Hawaii in 1889 for refusing to testify falsely in the courts on behalf of plantation owners.

Two of the big strikes on Oahu Island were in 1909 when 8,000 Japanese sugar workers struck--this was crushed after a 3-month heroic struggle; and in 1920 when 6,000 Japanese and 2,700 Filipino workers jointly struck--this was also lost after 6 months. Today, the working people in Hawaii enjoy the fruits of their labor, after many years of untold suffering and sacrifices. By no means do the workers there live in "paradise." Their fight to maintain better conditions is still the order of the day. Local 142 of the International Longshoremen's & Warehousemen's Union (ILWU) is one of the most influential in the Islands; a great number of its 24,000 members are of Asian ancestry. The Local's secretary, Newton Miyagi, a Japanese. Hawaiian labor history is full of rich experiences of solidarity and the dignity of man.

These remarks have just scratched the surface, as we must move on to the mainland. Some 26 Japanese known as the "Wakamatsu Colonists" are good examples of exploitation and adventurism. A German named Henry Schnell brought the first contract laborers to establish a tea and silk farm near Coloma, California, in 1869, without first investigating that area's fitness for such farming. Two years later Schnell abandoned the colonists including the now famous nursemaid Okei. Perhaps he had gold in back of his mind, since he was a young ambitious adventurer who had made a fortune in gun-dealing with feudal lords in Japan.

Japanese migration to the United States began at a snail's pace not because of the Wakamatsu Colony failure, but due to the more than 200-year isolation policy of Japan. On the other hand, Chinese came to the shores of San Francisco by the thousands and went to work mainly in the mines, railroads, farms, sawmills and fish canneries; some became cigar makers, shoemakers, laundrymen and domestic workers. As their numbers increased, so did the anti-Chinese campaign, mostly from organized

---

The following is excerpted from lectures given by Karl G. Yoneda at various campuses based on his book JAPANESE LABOR HISTORY IN THE USA, written in Japanese and published in 1967. Yoneda was born in 1906 in Glendale, California. At age 7, he was taken by his father to Japan for his education. He bacame a drop-out during Hiroshima high school days and joined the then student and labor movements in Japan. At age 20, he was drafted by the Japanese Imperial Army and escaped to America. Some of his activities, from 1926 are covered in the body of the article.

labor. In 1870, the Anti-Chinese Convention of the State of California was organized in San Francisco. The following year in Los Angeles, a white mob raided the Chinese quarters and lynched 19 Chinese. In 1877, unemployed whites and hoodlums attacked the Chinese and demolished 25 warehouses in San Francisco. In that same year, a petty San Francisco politician named Dennis Kearney formed the mis-named "Workingmen's Party of California" based on the slogan "Chinese Must Go." In 1882, the United States Congress passed the Chinese Exclusion Law with the help of organized labor, including Samuel Gompers--who later became president of the American Federation of Labor (AFL)--but the operators of the mines, railroads and farms soon found "satisfactory substitutes" in the Japanese.

In 1886, two Englishmen named Amore and Goldman brought 9 Japanese farmers to Soquel near Santa Cruz to plant tangerines. This failed. They then moved on to Woodland to operate a farm; however, the Englishmen abandoned the men because of financial difficulties. Some 80 Japanese started to work on farms in the Vacaville-Winters area in 1888, alongside the Chinese. The young, determined Japanese were no match for the aging Chinese who had toiled on the farms for many years. The growers welcomed them because the Japanese had fallen into the "divide and rule" trap and showed that they could produce more. This was true in the mines and on the railroads along the Pacific Coast and midwestern states.

We must not ignore the fact that the Japanese producing more than others, stemmed not only from their strong desire to get rich-quick and return to their homeland, but from their deep-rooted nationalism-- "Yamato damashii"--which increased its tempo after Japan's military victories over China and Russia in the 1895 and 1905 wars. In 1890, not withstanding the anti-Oriental policy of the AFL, Fusataro Takano, Tsunetaro Jo, Hannosuke Sawada, and others formed the Friends of Labor in San Francisco and studied the program of the AFL for the purpose of establishing a similar union in Japan. The three named returned to Japan and in 1897, together, with Sen Katayama, whose activities in the USA I will deal with later, organized the first trade union in Japan.

Japanese immigrants faced untold discrimination and oppression, not only from employers, politicians and labor misleaders, but also from their own countrymen--contractors--just as their Chinese predecessors had experienced at the hands of the Chinese Six Companies. Let us take the railroad industry as an example: Japanese contractors collected 10¢ per day from the $1.00 per day's pay from each man they secured. Hajime Nishiyama of Rock Springs, Wyoming, once had 500 under him and his rake-off was $50.00 per day, which was an enormous sum at the beginning of this century. Kyutaro Abiko, who is known as one of the successful pioneers, set up the Japanese American Industrial Corporation in 1903 in San Francisco, supplying Japanese workers to the farm, mine and railroad industries. At one time, the company had as high as 3,000 men under contract, charging them $1.00 each per month for "handling mail and other services."

The First Farm Workers Union

Early in 1903, some 2,000 Japanese and Mexican sugar beet workers in Oxnard, where Chinese formerly toiled, went on strike against low pay and mistreatment. During the strike, they formed the Sugar Beet and Farm Laborers Union of Oxnard and elected Kosaburo Baba, president; Heizo Otomo, vice president; and J. M. Larraras, secretary. The company brought in scabs, including Japanese from San Francisco. A shooting took place in which a Mexican union member was killed and four were injured. Police arrested all union officials. The California State Federation of AFL dispatched a Mr. Wheeler to aid in the defense of all those arrested. Finally, the men were released and the strike was won. This was the first instance of the AFL aiding any Japanese.

When Larraras applied for an AFL charter, its president, Samuel Gompers replied in writing: "Your union must guarantee that it will under no circumstance accept memberwhip of any Chinese or Japanese." Larraras wrote a strongly worded protest letter telling Gompers "to go to hell" in so many words. This is a historically beautiful document of solidarity and brotherhood; therefore I quote it:

> "Your letter...in which you say the admission with us of the Japanese members into the AFL cannot be considered is received. I beg to say in reply that our Japanese here were the first to recognize the importance of cooperating and uniting in demanding a fair wage scale. They were not only with us, but they were generous when one of our men was murdered by hired assassins of the oppressors of labor. They gave expression of their sympathy in a very substantial form.
> In the past we have counsels, fought and lived on very short rations with our Japanese brothers, and toiled with them in the fields and they have been uniformly kind and considerate. We would be false to them and to ourselves and to the cause of unionism if we now accepted privileges for ourselves which are not accorded to them. We are going to stand by men who stood by us in the long, hard fight ended in a victory over the enemy.
> We therefore respectfully petition the AFL to grant us a charter under which we can invite all the sugar beet and field laborers of Oxnard without regard to their color or race. We will refuse any other kind of a charter except one which will wipe out race prejudice and recognize our fellow workers as being as good as ourselves."

Gompers, however, continued his vicious attack on Japanese, stating at the 1904 AFL National Convention, "the American God was not the God of the Japanese." The convention then passed an anti-Japanese resolution in which is stated, "Japanese were as difficult to assimilate into the American culture as were the Chinese." The San Francisco Chronicle fired its first shot against Japanese on February 23rd, 1905, in an editorial titled "The Menace to the Country from Japanese Immigration." When in 1907, the United Mine Workers of America, AFL/UMWA, in Rock Springs, Wyoming, took in more than 500 Japanese miners, Gompers instructed John Mitchell, president of UMWA, to exclude them stating "it was unthinkable that Orientals sat in the same lodge room with whites and that the union demands the same wages for the yellow men as for whites."

Sen Katayama - Pioneer Socialist

The tirades of Gompers were also heaped upon a Japanese socialist, Sen Katayama, who first came to this country in 1884 to study theology. He returned to Japan and helped organize the first trade union there. Katayama came back to this country in 1904 and spoke against the Russo-Japanese War. He attended the Congress of the Second International in Amsterdam, where he shook hands with the Russian delegation pledging to fight against the war. Katayama went on to organize labor as well as socialist groups among the Japanese in this country and later became one of the founders of the Communist Party, USA, in 1919. He then went to Moscow, becoming a world renowned leader of the communist movement. He died in Moscow and is buried in the Kremlin.

Industrial Workers of the World

I would be remiss if I did not relate some of the history of the Industrial Workers of the World (IWW) in its relation to immigrants. It was born in 1905, because of the do-nothing policies of the AFL bureaucrats and issued a special appeal to foreign born workers, including Orientals, to join them. Unknown numbers of Japanese cannery and farm workers joined the IWW throughout the years. In 1906, Shisui Kotoku, a well known Japanese anarchist, came to the Bay Area where he met with the leaders of the IWW, Socialist Party, and other radicals in the Japanese communities. This resulted in the forming of the Social Revolutionary Party (SRP) on June 1, 1906, with 50 Japanese members. During the 1906 strike of Pacific Coast seamen, the SRP members held street meetings in Oakland and asked Japanese not to scab! Tetsugoro Takeuchi and several Japanese socialist followers of Kotoku formed the Labor League of Fresno in 1908; the IWW actively aided the League in organizing 4,000 Japanese grape pickers. As an aside, you may be interested to know that Kotoku returned to Japan in 1906 and subsequently was executed, in 1911, along with 11 others for allegedly "plotting to assassinate Emperor Meiji." This case aroused protest throughout the world including the US, where Jack London and others aided in the defense of the Kotoku group.

The IWW established local 283 in an Alaska Ketchikan cannery in 1913. Among its members were 100 Japanese. That same year, the IWW called a strike of 2,800 hop pickers, including Japanese at the Durst Brothers Ranch in Wheatland (Northern California). During the dispute, four, including the District Attorney and Deputy Sheriff, were killed in a shoot-out. Shorty Ford and H.D. Suhr, IWW leaders, were arrested and charged with murder. The following year, the IWW called another strike against the Durst Ranch. This time, AFL Central Labor Councils of Sacramento, Fresno and San Diego endorsed the strike. Although Japanese were among those who walked out from the beginning of the strike, they withdrew from the area because of their fear that non-Japanese strikers might lose the support of the traditionally anti-Oriental AFL. These Japanese inserted ads in the Japanese language press asking their countrymen to stay away from the Durst Ranch until Ford and Suhr were released and other strike demands granted. This was a meaningful gesture of working class solidarity and should be remembered by all of us.

In 1917, 106 employees of a refinery in Tooele, Utah, struck against their contractor, Mitsugoro Watanuki, for firing Saburo Tanaka who had been outspoken against the rake-off system and mistreatment by the contractor. The strike lasted 3 months; meanwhile strikers had been replaced by Japanese scabs.

Another early Japanese labor leader was Ryosho Yamane, who helped to organize Local 1736, Brotherhood of Maintenance-of-Way Employees, AFL, in Roosevelt, Washington, on May 5, 1919. The Local had 120 Japanese railroad workers. Yamane became its secretary. The union successfully eliminated the 10¢ per day rake-off to the contractor and the company agreed to deliver the men's needs free of charge. During World War II, Yamane moved to Denver, where he became president of Local 6511, UMWA. Incidently, the Local sent Franklin Sugiyama as a delegate to the UMWA convention in Atlantic City in 1946.

Japanese Mine Workers in Colorado

Speaking of the UMWA, their members, which included some of Japanese ancestry, had to go through more bloody strikes to improve conditions than the rest of the American labor movement in the early part of this century. An irony was that Japanese were originally used as strikebreakers in the mines, but later were taken into the union. Take for example, the Japanese in the Colorado mines, which were owned by old man John D. Rockefeller, were scabs during the big 1910 strike. The strike was lost. In 1913, the union, 12,000 strong, struck and this time most of the Japanese miners were on the side of the union. Again, the Colorado Fuel and Iron Company--owned by John D.,--sent in scabs including Japanese. During the height of the fight, on April 20, 1914, company thugs and militia raided the strikers' tent colony, in Ludlow-- which is in the southern part of Colorado-- setting fire to 200 tents. Thirteen women and children were burned to death. Angered, striking miners retaliated by marching to the scab camp, called upon them to come out or suffer the same fate as had befallen the strikers. A number of Japanese scabs, along with some of the guards who refused to come out, perished in the resulting fire. When the battle ended, the strikers marched out of the burning camp singing:

"The Union Forever, Hurrah! Boys,
 Hurrah!
Down With The Militia, To Hell With
 The Law,
For We Are Coming Colorado, We Are
 Coming All The Way,
Shouting The Battle Cry Of Union!"

Many Japanese miners were among the victims of mine explosions. In 1923, a Frontier Wyoming mine exploded, killing 99 miners--17 were Japanese. The following year, another mine nearby exploded, 39 killed--6 were Japanese. All were members of the UMWA. Mrs. Tanimura, widow of the only married Japanese miner killed in that area, received $2,000 compensation from the employers and $1,000 from the union--a considerable amount in those days and was the result of the union contracts.

However, agitation and "yellow peril" attacks upon the Japanese were continuing, especially on the West Coast and brought about the passage of the 1924 Japanese Exclusion Act.

Now about some of the activities in which I participated. Upon returning to Los Angeles in 1926, I found an "open shop" city where hundred of Japanese, Filipino, Chinese and Mexican restaurant workers were getting only $1.00 per day for a 10 to 12 hour shift; the same poor conditions were also true for several hundred Japanese fruit-stand employees. Elsewhere--thousands upon thousands of unorganized farm workers getting 15-20¢ per hour for a 10 hour day. Mooney and Billings, militant San Francisco labor organizers imprisoned in San Quentin and Folsom on framed charges; Sacco and Vanzetti, Italian anarchists, facing the electric chair in Boston--both cases brought world-wide protest against U.S. injustice. And where millions of Negro people were toiling and living under slave conditions. Therefore, I joined other activists as an organizer for the Agricultural Workers Organizing Committee of Southern California.

17 Million Unemployed in 1929

During the great economic crisis of 1929, 17 million unemployed were looking for jobs and food. The Socialist Party had collapsed ideologically many years before. The IWW was no longer an active force, the AFL leaders were collaborating with the employers and betraying those who dared to strike. The Communist Party was the only organization which helped in establishing the National Unemployed Council Branches. From 1930 on, hundreds of thousands demonstrated throughout this country, demanding "food and jobs", "immediate public works programs", "unemployment relief and insurance", etc.. Several Japanese were among those arrested in the Los Angeles March 6, 1930 hunger march. The following year, I was arrested under the name of Karl Hama (assumed name to protect family members and mother in Hiroshima from harassment) in the Los Angeles February 10, 1931 hunger march and served 90 days for "disturbing the peace"--this I did, by holding up a sign "OUR CHILDREN NEED FOOD!" We need thousands of similar signs today because the thirties are here again.

Militant trade unions outside the AFL were making great strides in organizing the unorganized. One was the Agricultural Workers Industrial Union of Trade Union Unity League (AWIU-TUUL), which sent 10 organizers, including Tetsuji Horiuchi and Danny Roxas, a Filipino, into Imperial Valley, Southern California, to organize 7,000 Mexicans, 1,000 Japanese and several hundred Filipinos in 1930. Horiuchi and others were arrested and sent to prison on Criminal Syndicalism Act charges. After serving 2 and 1/2 years in Folsom Prison, Horiuchi was ordered deported. The International Labor Defense (ILD) including its Japanese language branches, which had over 100 men and women members, tried to have deportation charges dropped against Horiuchi and 20 other Issei activists, who had been arrested on various political charges, and then ordered deported as "undesirable aliens --communists". Failing in having the charges dropped, the ILD then campaigned for "voluntary departure" to a country of their own choice, as they faced torture, jail and even death if returned to Japan on those charges. They finally secured the right to go to the Soviet Union.

In 1931 about 50 employees of the SAN FRANCISCO NICHIBEI, one of the oldest Japanese language papers in the USA, owned by Kyutaro Abiko, went on strike for reinstatement of a union leader, dismissal of 4 senior editors and back pay. Abiko promised to grant these demands after a two-month bloody strike; however, he reneged and the workers were forced to strike again within a month.

California Farm Strikes In 1933

1933 was one of the most historical years in California farm labor because the Japanese Section of the AWIU conducted more strikes than in any other year. My records show that more than 20 strikes took place on farms where strawberry, raspberry, pea, peach, asparagus, grape, lettuce and other crops were raised, covering the areas from Chico, Lodi, Walnut Grove, Fresno, Visalia, Bakersfield down to Stanton, San Gabriel Valley, etc.. These actions involved more than 5,000 Japanese and tens of thousands of Mexicans, Filipinos and whites, as well as small numbers of Negroes.

Strikes of agricultural and cannery workers continued into the following year 1934. Imperial Valley Japanese Association secretary Miura, writing in the NICHIBEI (2/11/34), advocated that "all strike leaders be lynched because they were communists."

During the 1934 Pacific Coast maritime strike, which later developed into the world famous San Francisco general strike, the Japanese Section of the AWIU collected truck loads of vegetables and fruit for the strikers. Also the RODO SHIMBUN, a Communist Party language newspaper published in San Francisco, issued an appeal to Japanese not to scab! Incidently, I was editor of the RODO SHIMBUN.

In 1934, I, Karl Hama, ran on the Communist Party ticket for the then San Francisco 22nd Assembly seat in the white, black and Japanese section--the Fillmore District, receiving 1,017 votes. That same year, the late Clarence Arai, an attorney for Japanese contractors in Alaska canneries, was the Republican candidate for the Seattle 37th Assembly sea--he got only 320 votes. We were the first Asian Americans to run for political office on the mainland.

In spite of my communist affiliation, Alaska Cannery Workers Union, Local 20195, AFL, appointed me as one of its organizers in 1935; I was elected to serve as one of the Local's delegates to the San Francisco Central Labor Council, which had been traditionally anti-Oriental (first Asian delegate). In 1936, I became a longshoreman, and still pack a hook; in other words, I am a working member of Local 10, ILWU.

The California Japanese Agricultural Workers Union should not be overlooked. It was organized in 1935 with 800 enthusiastic members in Los Angeles. Its program called for living wages, aid to old timers, work with small farmers, collective bargaining, social security and unemployment insurance, work with AFL, etc.. The union was well received among Japanese farm workers and achieved numerous gains for them. One of its successful strikes was conducted in 1936 jointly with Mexican and Filipino celery workers in the Venice area; it spread to other farms in Southern California. This resulted in wage increase and union recognition.

The AFL helped 3,000 Filipinos as well as its own white shed workers in the 1936 Salinas lettuce strike. Shamefully, I still feel 15 Nisei, mostly growers, were among those deputized to brutally break that strike. The AFL in Los Angeles organized thousands of Issei and Nisei into Local 20284 of the Produce Market Employees Union, Local 630 of the Teamsters and Local 770 of the Retail Clerks Union. All had Nisei officials. The emergence of the Congress of Industrial Organizations (CIO) in 1936 saw many Japanese and other minorities join the ranks of organized labor. In Seattle 500 Japanese cannery workers were among those who formed the CIO Farm and Cannery Workers Union. Its vice president --George Taki. The Alaska Cannery Workers Union switched its affiliation to the CIO in 1937 and elected Karl Yoneda, 1st vice president; Fen Fee, second vice president; C. Caballero, a Filipino, 3rd vice president; Frank Fukuda, recording secretary. This Local was the most integrated union in the Bay Area with 2,000 members--all meetings were conducted in English, Spanish, Chinese and Filipino languages.

In 1938, the CIO successfully established cannery workers locals in Monterey, Stockton, Terminal Island, etc.. Some 1,000 Japanese men and women were among the members--Mary Imada and Karl Yoneda among the CIO organizers.

In spite of the vigorous organizing drive during the thirties, we succeeded only in organizing about one-fourth of the Japanese agricultural workers in California. On the other hand, more than twice as many Issei and Nisei worked as scabs. In 1935, there were 18,000 Japanese farm workers in California according to Tamezo Takomoto, general secretary of the Japanese Association of America. Of the 18,000, 3,000 were over 60 years old, 10,000 were between ages of 50 to 60, and significantly 90% were single. Some of them responded to our drive with open arms. However, although we conducted many strikes, most failed.

The question then arises "why were Japanese less willing to join unions than Mexican, Filipino and other workers?" Perhaps, the following will explain some of the reasons: (1) strong desire to go back to Japan because of the racial prejudice they had encountered; (2) language barrier--dependency on labor contractor to arrange employment, housing, etc.,; (3) mistrust of labor in general, because of their historical racist stand; (4) swallowed propaganda that unions were communistic and feared deportation if they joined; (5) strong nationalism--<u>Yamato demashii</u>--which gave them a false sense of superiority over Mexican, Filipino and other minority workers; (6) lack of understanding democratic principle, and the need for workers solidarity; and (7) hope of becoming independent growers and having families.

Jack Shirai Killed In Spain

Looking around at the world in those years, one could see rising fascism in Germany: a civil war going on in Spain-- Jack Shirai, a New York restaurant worker, the only Japanese in the Abraham Lincoln Battalion, fighting on the side of the Loyalists against Franco and the rest of the fascists, was killed July 11, 1937 near Madrid; and the Japanese militarists waging an unjust war upon the Chinese people. In the US, notably in San Francisco, many Japanese and other trade unionists joined hands with thousands of Chinese on picket lines against shipping scrap iron to Japan. Placards in Chinese, Japanese and English were carried in San Francisco and New York: "Don't Buy Japanese Goods", "Silk Stockings Kill Chinese", and "Scrap Iron Becomes Bullets".

Did any of the Japanese American Citizens League (JACL), Buddhist and Christian leaders in the Japanese communities join the picket lines or speak out against Japan's invasion of China? The answer is NO! As a matter of fact most Buddhist and Japanese Christian church members, Japanese Overseas Ex-Servicemen's Association, Japanese comapny unions, Japanese language newspapers, Japanese language schools, Japanese Associations and others strongly campaigned to raise war relief, war chest funds, collected scrap iron and tin foil, and wrote so-called comfort letters to the Japanese Imperial Army soldiers in North China.

Then Pearl Harbor! It was a great hey-day for the "yellow peril" jingoists and super-patriots, spearheaded by the Hearst press, Native Sons and Daughters, American Legion, Veterans of Foreign Wars, Grower Associations, labor misleaders and politicians, who for years had beaten the drums of racism, kept out Issei parents from becoming citizens and shunted most of us into "little Tokyo." And saw the vocal rebirth of anti-Japanese hysteria, which led to the destruction of the trade union structure among the Japanese on the Pacific Coast and to the evacuation into 10 concentration camps of more than 110,000-- citizen and non-citizen--persons of Japanese ancestry.

But first a pause, to remember this was not the first time that racist America drove out a racial minority. In 1830, the Indian Removal Act passage resulted in the US Army removing tens of thousands of unwilling Indians from their ancestral land west across the Mississippi--the full story of this crime against the native Americans as well as against Japanese-Americans, blacks, Chicanos and others must be studied, told and retold. A long time anti-Japanese organization, mis-called The California Joint Immigration Committee, headed by H.J. McClatchy, submitted a statement to the Tolan Committee investigating problems of evacuation in February, 1942, in which it was declared "the determination of the Caucasians to keep their country and their blood white, and involves no claim on superiority...only to free white persons...grave mistake was the granting of citizenship to the Negroes after Civil War."

Only a handful--some church members and leaders of the then California CIO like Lou Goldblatt (now Secretary-Treasurer of the ILWU)--spoke out in defense of the Japanese before the evacuation order was issued in the spring of 1942--99 percent of the American people kept quiet, just as did the Germans under Hitler.

Racism Behind Evacuation

Yes, the racists succeeded in sending us behind barbed wire and tried to dehumanize us. The question arises "Why did not the Japanese Americans fight the evacuation order?" We must remember that the Japanese Americans were not strong politically on the mainland in 1942, the average age of the Nisei was only 19, our alien parents were not allowed to become US citizens; therefore we did not have a strong political-oriented organization nor political connections in Washington, D.C. as did those of German and Italian descent. Secondly, we were not an economic or social factor--as were those of Japanese ancestry in Hawaii where they made up one third of the population, had become a political force, held elective offices; where workers were organized and rooted especially in the sugar, pineapple and shipping-longshore industries and where the ILWU and other unions were on the road to becoming powerful integrated unions. And most important of all, we were at war with the facistaxis (Germany, Italy, and Japan). We had not choice but "to accept" America as it was at that time over Hitler's ovens and the Japanese military rapists of Nangking.

Some Nisei and Sansei have recently been glorifying those who took part in relocation camp riots. But let me tell you like it was in Manzanar, which I know first hand. A group, mostly Kibei, calling themselves Black Dragons, headed by Joseph Kurihara and Ben Kishi, openly predicted victory for Japan; physically attacked those working on the camouflage net project; threatened the lives of those they considered to be pro-democratic Americans including my family and myself; intimidated those who had relatives in Japan saying that they would inform the Japanese government about opposition to emperor-militarist cliques; constantly creating turmoil and not once raising a finger to try to improve camp conditions for the benefit of all residents. The camp administration took a "no-see" attitude toward these misguided "protesters" and fascist elements.

But, we who wanted to see the fascist-militarist-axis destroyed and democracy triumphant, campaigned through the Manzanar Citizens Federation (MCF) to save the crops--thousands of us went to Idaho and Utah to top sugar beets. The MCF circulated petitions in August, 1942, to the US government urging utilization of Japanese Americans confined in the camps for war duties. In November, 1942, 14 of us were the first to enlist from behind barbed wire, into the Military Intelligence Service to fight in the Pacific. On December 6th, a riot instigated by the pro-Japan group resulted in two killed, many wounded. 60 pro-democratic Americans, including my wife and 4 year old son, were taken into "protective custody" and moved to an abandoned CCC camp in Death Valley.

Despite the hanky-panky of American imperialists who had aspirations even then of control over Asia, I do not regret my part in World War II, including active service with the China-Burma-India Psychological Warfare Team. Significantly, 33,300-- Isei, Nisei, men and women, mainly from War Relocation Centers--volunteered their services in the US Armed Forces and helped in the defeat of the Berlin-Rome-Tokyo axis. However, the war crimes committed by the US such as dropping of A-bombs over Hiroshima and Nagasaki should not be forgotten nor should the atrocities and senseless killing committed today in Indochina be taken lightly.

There were a few courageous Nisei who defied the evacuation order, such as Gordon Hirabayashi and Fred Korematsu (who resisted the order on different grounds)-- one a Conscientious Objector, the other, for love of a Caucasian girl--and were imprisoned. Their cases went to the U.S. Supreme Court which upheld the guilty verdicts under the myth of "military necessity" thus evading the crux of the question-- CIVIL RIGHTS!

Under the infamous McCarran Act passed in 1950, 3 Japanese ex-communists were deported and 5 other Issei faced deportation. They were all trade union activists. The charges against the latter were dropped. All of them had been fingered by Japanese, including paid informers.

Forced Scab Activities

Now to touch on the forced strike-breaking activities of some Japanese nationals who were brought to work on California farms after World War II. In 1956, the Japanese government, with the help of Nisei growers and Mike Masaoka of the JACL, formed a Council to Dispatch Short Term Farm Laborers to the USA. It was to send 1,000 nationals every year. None of the growers lived up to the agreement in toto, which provided such things as sightseeing trips, English study, NO STRIKEBREAKING, decent living conditions, etc.. In fact, the first group that landed in the Kawasaki camp in Delano ran away because there was not enough work, the poor living quarters (in railroad cars) and the outhouse setup. In 1960, they were used as scabs on the Katsuta farm in Oxnard and Inouye farm in Yuba City. Opposition to the program became widespread, especially throughout organized labor ranks, and had to be discontinued by the Japanese government. However, the Ag Trainee Program goes on, with 200-300 trainees from Japan coming under one year contract with pay of $50.00 per month.

In 1965, the internationally known Delano grape pickers strike of the United Farm Workers Organizing Committee, under the leadership of Cesar Chavez started. Japanese were among those scabbing. The union successfully concluded agreements with many growers after 5 years of striking. Thousands of farm workers, including several hundred Japanese, are still outside the ranks of organized labor, working for low pay, no job guarantee, no unemployment insurance or health coverage, etc.. They are at the mercy of big agri-business, among those whose number are Nisei growers.

Experiences and lessons from Japanese Labor History in the US and the evacuation are varied and complex, and certainly could not be adequately covered here, but I hope we can all agree that no one should be downgraded because of his occupation, color, political or religious beliefs, and that there shall be NO CONCENTRATION CAMPS in this country for any one ever again.

As to the question being raised by some: "Is our ethnic history and studies thereof relevant in today's fast changing world?" I would say, "Yes." There is much to learn; there are many heroes whose records are unsung and unknown. We can enrich ourselves from the past in order to help create the kind of society all of us are hoping and striving for. Asian immigrants contributed greatly in enriching the US mine, railroad, farm, sawmill, fishing, cannery, sugar and pineapple industries. We, their descendants, have every right to have a say in its destiny. Let us not prostitute our heritage by becoming lackeys or spokesmen for the reactionary dominant racist power structure as has Samuel Ichiei Hayakawa.

It is heartening to see more and more Nisei, Sansei and Yonsei and those of other Asian descent beoming active in their professional, trade union, anti-war and student organizations, as well as communicating and learning the needs of others in order to achieve justice and dignity for all.

It is important to recognize and remember that our history is beautiful as is that of the blacks, browns, redmen and others.

Cross, Ira B. A HISTORY OF THE LABOR MOVEMENT IN CALIFORNIA. Berkeley: 1935.

DOHO. Los Angeles, 1937-1942.

Foner, Philip S. HISTORY OF LABOR MOVEMENTS IN THE UNITED STATES. Vols. 3,4,5. New York, 1964-1968.

Fuchs, Lawrence H. HAWAII PONO. New York, 1961.

HOKUBEI MAINICHI. San Francisco, 1955-65.

HONOLULU RECORD. December 2, 1948.

Johannesson, Edward. THE HAWAIIAN LABOR MOVEMENT. Boston, 1956.

KAIKYUSEN. San Francisco, 1928-1929.

Katayama Sen Kinenkai, ed. KATAYAMA SEN CHOSAKUSHU. Tokyo, 1960.

Kimura, Ryukichi. HAWAII NIHONJIN SHI. Honolulu, 1921.

LOS ANGELES TIMES. February 11, 1931.

McWilliams, Carey. FACTORIES IN THE FIELD. New York: 1939.

NICHIBEI. San Francisco, 1934, 1937-38.

RODO SHIMBUN. San Francisco, 1930-36.

SAN FRANCISCO CHRONICLE. February 23, 1905.

Shakai Bunko, ed. ZAIBEI SHAKAISHUGISHA-MUSEIFUSHUGISHA ENKAKU. Tokyo, 1964.

SHINSEKAI. San Francisco, 1905, 1906, 1911, 1915, 1936-41.

Tani, Motohiro. HAWAII NIHONJIN IMIN SHI. Honolulu, 1964.

Tatsumi, Takashi. 1920 NENDO HAWAII SATOKICHI RODOUNDO SHI. Honolulu, 1921.

THE DAILY PACIFIC COMMERCIAL ADVERTISER. Honolulu, October 31, and December 21, 1889.

WYOMING LABOR JOURNAL. September 19, 1923.

Yoneda, Karl G. MANZANAR DIARY (to be published). December 7, 1941-December 7, 1942.

Yoneda, Karl G. ZAIBEI NIHONJIN NO REKISHI. Tokyo, 1967.

ZAIBEI RODO SHIMBUN. San Francisco, 1929-30.

Strangers in the City: the Chinese in the Urban Frontier

STANFORD LYMAN

To speak of the Chinese in San Francisco--and, for that matter, in Seattle, Vancouver, New York City and other large cities as strangers, is to describe them in terms first projected by the great sociologist George Simmel. "The stranger," he wrote in his essay of that title, "is...not ...the wanderer who comes today and goes tomorrow, but rather is the person who comes today and stays tomorrow."[1] Chinese immigrants who journeyed to America and other foreign shores in the last century were wanderers to be sure, but they were not without fixed places to go. Their course took them where opportunity beckoned, but never without the hope of one day returning to the homeland which would call them back from their diaspora and invite them once more to the warmth of hearth and domesticity.[2]

While abroad they were in the host society, but never were they of it. The culture, ideas, and ideals they brought were foreign to native Americans and would never have seen birth among the host society's people had it not been for the influx of these strangers.

As strangers, the Chinese aroused much interest and curiosity, but not without hostility. Ideas about the newcomers were not based on actual knowledge; they were, rather, stereotypes, categorical images built upon flimsy shreds of information about China and supplemented by cursory observations devoid of any profound cultural, social or historical intelligence.[3] As time passed, the original pejorative impressions were reinforced by reiteration and legitimized by the proclamations of social and political elites. At last the stereotypes became the basis for both legislative restrictions and popular uprisings against the Chinese. Only after the newcomers had declined somewhat in numbers and accommodated themselves to a ghetto existence within the urban structure--only when it appeared that other racial and ethnic groups posed a greater threat-- did hostilities toward the Chinese begin to subside. The stereotypes did not vanish, but they took on more benign forms. These, unfortunately, were couched in patronizing and indulgent terms. As both symbol and artifice they facilitate the social distance that persists even to today.

Chinese Immigration To America

American interest in China antedates immigration from that nation by more than a half century. The Chinoiserie movement[4] which swept over Europe from the sixteenth century had by the end of the eighteenth left its mark on America where Chinese bric-a-brac was to be found in colonial homes and by the nineteenth century in frontier cabins as well.[5] Chinese art collections were the early prized possessions of both private individuals and museums.[6] Several magnificent houses were built in the "Chinese style" in Colonial America, and Chinese tapestries adorned many a wall of American gentlemen and traders.[7] Indeed, one of the compelling economic reasons for the American Revolution was the desire of American merchants and traders to wrest control of the China trade from British domination. China's importance to the new republic was symbolized by the early appointment of Major Samuel Shaw as Consul at Canton in 1786, the first American Consulate beyond the Cape of Good Hope.[8]

Interest in China's art, architecture and government was not however accompanied by much knowledge of or deep compassion for the Chinese people. To be sure, the Jesuits in sixteenth century Peking had exaggerated an image of efficient public administration and lack of military aggression

---

Reprinted from ETHNIC CONFLICT IN CALIFORNIA HISTORY edited by Charles Wollenberg by permission of Tinnon-Brown, Inc.. The author is currently on the faculty of the Department of Sociology, University of California, San Diego.

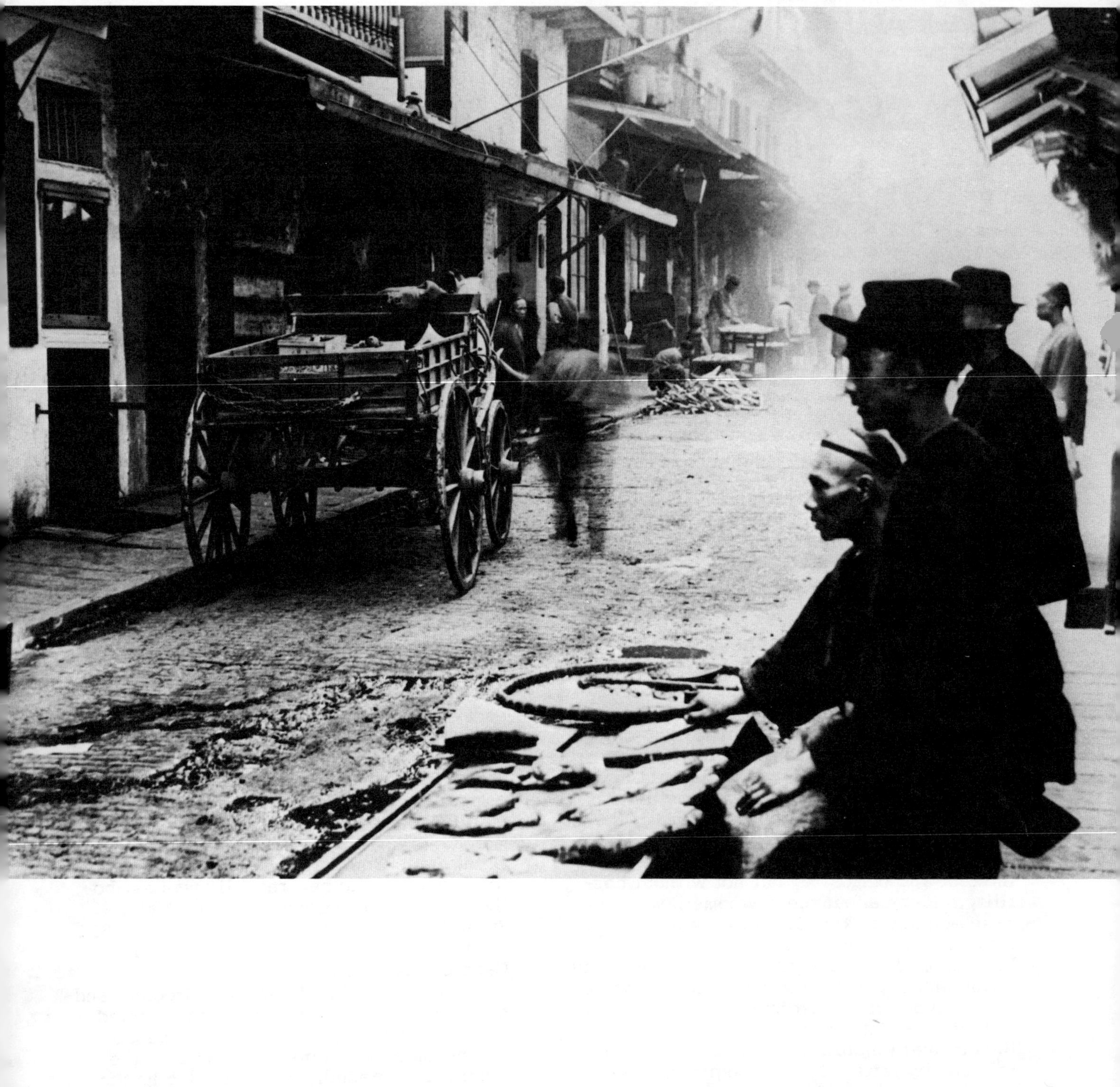

in China which had impressed Europeans and some Americans.[9] But these ideas were not spread far and wide in America; rather, there was a general indifference about Chinese people and only occasional approval of China's policy of isolation from foreign influence.[10]

From 1787 until 1848 few Chinese visited the United States. A Chinese colony, settled in Nootka Sound in 1788 only lasted until 1789, and other Chinese brought to the Northwest coast of America travelled on ships along the Pacific coast until around 1791, a few deserting in Mexico.[11] An earlier Chinese settlement in Mexico City in 1635 had also come to naught.[12] A few Chinese seamen had been temporarily abandoned in Pennsylvania in 1785-1786, while others worked occasionally as sailors on the New England ships that engaged in the China trade, even though an American law of 1817 limited foreign sailors on American ships to no more than one-third of the crew. One Chinese cook shipped as "George Harrison of Charlestown, Mass."[13] By representing one of his Chinese crew members as an important mandarin who had to be returned to his native land, in 1809, John Jacob Astor persuaded President Jefferson to exempt his ship from the embargo on China then in force.[14] Four years later the American ship Sally docked in Plymouth with a Chinese passenger who attended the Sabbath meeting the following Sunday in full mandarin regalia.[15] In 1830 John P. Cushing, one of the most influential merchants in China trade, retired with a retinue of Chinese servants.[16]

The education of Chinese in America had interested some Americans, such as James Magee who brought a Chinese over to learn English in 1800.[17] In 1818 the first of five Chinese youths was admitted to the school for foreign students at Cornwall, Connecticut. This institution was begun for the "education in our own country of Heathen youth, in such manner, as with subsequent professional instruction, will qualify them to become useful Missionaries, Physicians, Surgeons, School Masters, or interpreters, and to communicate to the Heathen Nations such knowledge in agriculture and the arts as may prove the means of promoting Christianity and civilization."[18] The students' history at the school, as well as the denouement of the school itself, has been reported by a descendant of the school's founders:

> Wong Arce came in 1818 from Canton. He was brought by a New York merchant who had employed him in Canton and was soon dismissed for disobedience and immorality. In 1823 Ah Lan and Ah Lum came from Philadelphia, stayed two years and were also dismissed for misconduct.
> In 1825 Chop Ah See was in the school for a while. From 1822-25 Lieaou Ah See, known also as William Botelho, came from Boston and is regarded as the first Protestant convert. Lieaou who was reported as faithful but far from brilliant, is supposed to have died a Christian in China. The boys were supported partly by charity but mainly by manual labor. The school was closed in 1827 because two Cherokee Indians married two prominent white girls in Cornwall. There was no correspondence recorded with the Chinese after their departure from the school and the experiment seems, as far as the Chinese were concerned, to have been a failure.

Forty-five years were to pass before the Chinese Government, urged by Yung Wing, who had become America's first Chinese college graduate when he matriculated from Yale University in 1854,[20] would send over one hundred Chinese young men to study in America as part of the ill-fated Chinese Educational Mission. In 1881, concerned over the growing Americanization of these Chinese youth--their popularity with white girls, their neglect and even deprecation of Chinese studies, ethics, and practices (including the wearing of the queue which they had petitioned their tutor for permission to sever[21])--the Chinese government recalled the entire mission and required that the students return to China.[22]

That Americans regarded Chinese persons with a mixture of curiosity and amazement is indicated in the reactions to some of the early visitors. In 1808 a Chinese equestrian was employed as a stage performer in New York City. A Chinese juggler performed in the same city in 1842.[23] Chinese sailors and their dog, aboard the junk Ke Ying docked at Providence in 1847, were nearly as great a curiosity to the Rhode Island visitors as was the ship itself.[24] One year after the junk left, P. T. Barnum opened his Chinese museum in New York City.

Two traits of the Chinese continued to puzzle and astonish Americans throughout the nineteenth century. One was the plaited queue worn by Chinese men, a mark of subjection imposed on them by the Manchu conquerors in 1645. The queue was a constant source of amusement and derision to Californians who plagued Chinese immigrants by cutting off or pulling on their "pigtails,"[25] and who in the 1870's attempted to punish Chinese by prohibiting the wearing of this badge of citizenship.[26] The other was the practice among Chinese of binding the feet of women, a custom so remarkable to Occidentals that as late as 1834 a Chinese women in traditional dress and with bound feet was exhibited as a freak attraction on Broadway.[27] Although "pigtails" and footbinding were the most commented upon features of Chinese life--not only by American but other peoples, such as the Japanese, who tried to extirpate the practices when they assumed rule in Taiwan[28]--other traits and customs aroused curiosity, astonishment or indignation. The fact that they had "yellow" complexions and "slanted" eyes, that Chinese men all wore the same style of clothing,--a loose blue blouse, with matching trousers and a broad brimmed hat,--that they regularly remitted money and the corpses of their dead to China, that they spoke an "unintelligible" cacophanous language, that they seemed to adopt only a crude "pidgin" English, that they appeared to gamble incessantly and be addicted to opium smoking, that they carried peculiar diseases, and that they came without their wives or sweethearts--each and everyone of these real and imagined, alleged and exaggerated traits contributed to the belief that the Chinese were a strange, exotic and even a dangerous people.

Chinese immigration to America effectively began in 1847. A coincidence of catastrophe in China and opportunity in California supplied the expulsive and attractive elements that linked the Middle Kingdom to the United States. Political unrest had been a constant feature of life in Kwangtung and Fukien Provinces since the Manchu conquest of 1644.[29] Overpopulation, once considered no problem at all, presented ever-increasing pressure on agricultural production and distribution after 1800.[30] In addition, foreign intrigues by several of the European nations and the United States had seriously encroached upon Chinese sovereignty, arousing an incipient nationalism directed against both the foreigners and the Manchu regime.[31] Then, in 1849, a terrible flood wreaked havoc on the already wretched lives of southeastern China's peasants. "The rains have been falling for forty days," said a memorial to the emperor, "until the rivers, and the sea, and the lakes, and the streams, have joined in one sheet over the land for several hundred li (three li are equal to one English mile) and there is no outlet by which the waters may retire."[32] The observer who wrote for Blackwood's Magazine noted that on the basis of missionary reports,

> ten thousand people were destroyed, and domestic animals drowned in untold numbers; crowds even of first families were begging bread, and (horror of horrors to the pious Celestials!) coffins were floating about everywhere on the face of the waters...Such an inundation is too stupendous for the European mind adequately to comprehend its extent, and is said to have exceeded any similar disaster within the memory of the present generation.[33]

Natural disaster was followed by rebellion and revolution. In 1851 the Taiping revolutionaries raised their standard against the empire in a civil insurrection that lasted fourteen years and resulted in casualties estimated to be greater than 30,000,000.[34] In the same period the Cantonese unsuccessfully fought against invasions from British, French and American mercenary forces and also against Hakkas invading from the northwest.[35] The stage was set for continuous anti-Manchu rebellions and anti-foreign uprisings.[36] As a result of all these catastrophic and dislocating events, hundreds of thousands of Chinese were uprooted from their villages. Many fled to the coastal seaports of Canton, Hong Kong and Macao where they hoped to find work, to secure aid from kinsmen, or to go abroad temporarily until they could recoup their losses and return to loved ones as wealthy men.

Then gold was discovered in California.[37] A few Chinese merchants had already arrived in California, and they sent word back to kinsmen and friends of the remarkable discovery.[38] Meanwhile shipping lines and independent sea captains, realizing the profits to be made in adding passenger traffic to the brisk commercial trade with China, sailed into southeastern Chinese ports with circulars advertising the gold discovery and offering cheap passage to California.[39] The excitement created by the news, coupled with the fabulous accounts brought back by the first Chinese returnees, started a brisk passenger trade which, while its vicissitudes were many during the period of "free" immigration, did not subside markedly until American law placed restrictive limits on it in 1882.[40]

The method by which most Chinese came to California was a variant of the indenture system which two centuries earlier had brought Englishmen to the colonies[41] and which a few decades hence would bring southern and eastern Europeans to work in the burgeoning industries of the Northeast.[42] The "credit-ticket" system, as it has been called,[43] enabled an impoverished Chinese to come across the ocean without putting up any cash, find food and lodging in San Francisco, and assistance in going to work in the mines, on the railroads, or in the midwest or east as a strikebreaker...Money for his passage was obtained from kinsmen or fellow-villagers who assigned the collection of the debt to kinsmen or Landsmanner in San Francisco. The latter, organized into caravansaries, met the immigrant at the point of debarkation, accompanied him to the hostel in which his compatriots dwelt, provided him with food, a place to sleep, and a certain amount of protection from anti-Chinese elements. Most important, the merchant leaders of the hui kuan (Landsmannschaften) acted as contracters or subcontractors and sent gangs of men out to work. The debts incurred by the Chinese immigrants were deducted from their wages by Chinese headmen, and defalcating debtors were prevented from escaping back to China by special arrangements between the Chinese creditor associations and the merchant fleet. The entire system was fraught with corruption and undoubtedly not a few Chinese found themselves poorer off in the end than they had been when they began their American adventure, and many were forced to stay overseas much longer than they had anticipated.[44]

Although an American law of 1862 forbade the immigration of involuntary contract labor, the ignorance and corruptibility of American consuls at Canton and the nefarious methods of Chinese "crimps" combined to effect the illegal traffic in human flesh.[45] One incident is of particular importance because it introduced Chinese laborers into the South and indicates the limited interest held by Americans in the Chinese. Following the Civil War there was a severe labor shortage on plantations in Louisiana, Arkansas and other states of the defunct Confederacy. This vexing situation resulted in a bizarre scheme to import Chinese. Originated at the Memphis convention of 1869, subsidized by two major railroads, supported by newspapers in the North as well as the South, and effected by the "crimping" activities of the notorious contractor Tye Kim Orr and the mysterious shipmaster Cornelius Koopmanschap, the "Chinese experiment" resulted in the inveiglement of 200 Chinese aboard the ship Ville de St. Lo in 1870. Some jumped overboard when they learned their fate; others bided their time and ran away when the ship deposited its human cargo in New Orleans.[46] Some of them may have made up the early Chinese settlement in the south; others probably migrated into the midwest, journeyed to California, or moved into the industrial northeast.[47]

The appearance of Chinese in the midwest and south took place after the anti-Chinese movement had begun in California. Riots against the Chinese seem not to have occurred in the former Confederate states, largely because the Chinese there were not perceived as a competitive but rather as an exploitable element in the labor force, often to be used as a club against recalcitrant Negro laborers. In Colorado, however, where Chinese began to settle in 1870, one of the worst riots ever against the immigrants from the Middle Kingdom took place in Denver on October 31, 1880.[49] It was one of the signals that the Sinophobic virus, once but a localized malady, had become nearly a national epidemic.

The Beginnings of the Anti-Chinese Movement

At first there were but a few Chinese in America. Most of them were located in San Francisco where they acted as purveyors of art goods, foods and prefabricated houses which they floated across the Pacific and reassembled in the city crowded with gold-seekers.[50] During the first few months of their stay in California, Chinese merchants were regarded as a curious but welcome addition to the already heterogeneous population composed of Mexicans, Indians, Americans, Chileans, Australians and various Europeans. They participated in civic festivals, thrived in their mercantile establishments and were expected, as one San Francisco newspaper prophesied, soon to serve in the legislature.[51] "We shall undoubtedly have a very large addition to our population;" wrote an editor of the Daily Alta Californian on May 12, 1851, "and it may not be many years before the halls of Congress are graced by the presence of a long queued Mandarin sitting, voting, and speaking beside a don from Santa Fe and a Kanaker from Hawaii... The 'China boys' will yet vote at the same polls, study at the same schools, and bow at the same altar as our own countrymen."

However, this period of welcome, this sense of social toleration and sympathetic response, this recognition of California as a culturally plural society, disappeared quickly when Chinese began to appear in the gold mines.[52] The gold mines of California and other states where the precious ore was discovered were never dominated by the Chinese. Indeed, it would appear that they often worked mines already abandoned by white men.[53] Nevertheless, they were attacked vigorously and viciously by both public laws and popular uprisings. California's infamous Foreign Miner's Tax, first enacted in 1850, and then repealed, reenacted and reset irregularly until it was declared void in 1870, was from the beginning enforced almost exclusively against the Chinese who paid 50 percent of the total revenues obtained from it during its first four years and 98 percent during its final sixteen years of enforcement.[54] Moreover, beginning in 1852, the California legislature began what would be more than a quarter of a century of vain experimentation with laws designed to restrict or exclude altogether the coming of Chinese to the state.[55]

In addition to harassing and restrictive legislation, the Chinese were subjected to popular tribunals and mob violence in the mines. In the town of Chinese Camp as early as 1849 an uprising took place against 60 Chinese miners. At Marysville white miners drew up a resolution in 1852 asserting that "no Chinaman was to be thenceforth allowed to hold any mining claim in the neighborhood."[56] There followed a general uprising in the area against the Chinese and, accompanied by a marching band, white miners expelled the Chinese from North Forks, Horseshoe Bar and other neighboring mining camps.[57] By 1856 the following laws were in operation in California's Columbia mining district: "Neither Asiatics nor South-Sea Islanders shall be allowed to mine in this district, either for themselves or for others." Any person who shall sell a claim to an Asiatic or a South-Sea Islander shall not be allowed to hold another claim in this district for the space of six months."[58] In New Kanaka Camp, Tuolomne Colony, the Chinese were excluded entirely, "not allowed to own either by purchase or pre-emption."[59] As late as 1882 the laws of Churn Creek District forbade any miner to sell a claim to the Chinese,[60] and Chinese were rarely to be seen in that county. In 1858 and 1859 there were again attempts to expel the Chinese from the placers, and Chinese were routed out of Vallecito, Douglas Flat, Sacramento Bar, Coyote Flat, Sand Flat, Rock Creek, Spring Creek and Buckeye.[61]

By the end of the decade gold mining was coming to an end for Chinese and other pioneers alike. Gold strikes in British Columbia in 1858, and gold, silver and copper mining in the Rocky Mountain area attracted some Chinese for the next thirty years, extending the miners' anti-Chinese movement eastward and northward into Canada. However, by the mid-1860's many Chinese were beginning to move into other occupations: railroad building and food, laundry, manufacturing, mercantile and domestic services, occupations which located them in cities. As the 1850's closed, the Chinese accounted for twenty-five percent of California's miners, yet this fact alone, as Rodman W. Paul has pointed out, suggests the decline of the mines.[62] Descriptions of the Chinese miners in the 1860's indicate the reduced state of the industry. Writing in the 1860's an anonymous erstwhile miner described the area around Sonora: "Whole acres of land have been upturned and the earth and sand passed through a second and third washing, and apparently every particle of gold extracted; yet the less ambitious Chinese and Mexicans find enough in these deserted places to reward them for their tedious labors."[63] In Tuolomne County Chinese worked mines so far below the streams that the ore had to be "packed" up to the water: "Here we see troops of sturdy Chinamen groaning along under the weight of huge sacks of earth brought to the surface from a depth of eighteen feet and deposited in heaps after a weary tramp along the banks of a muddy pool."[64] William H. Brewer who traveled throughout California between 1860 and 1864 described the town of Weaver as "a purely mining town... so it is like California in bygone times." There he found a church "sluiced around until only enough land remains for it to stand upon... and multitudes of Chinese--the men miners, the women 'frail,' very frail, industrious in their calling." At Eureka: "Ten white men and two Chinamen slept in the little garret of the 'hotel'. Our horses fared but little better, and our bill was the modest little sum of fifteen dollars." Along the Klamath River: "Here and there a poor Chinaman plies his rocker, gleaning gold from sand, once worked over with more profit, but there are a few white inhabitants left until we reach Happy Camp."[65]

Despite the decline of the mining industry, or perhaps because of it, Chinese were still expelled from areas in which they had settled to work or were forcibly driven out of their jobs. A few Chinese were employed in and around some quicksilver mines near Calistoga until 1900; they were indulged as servants so long as they appeared docile and obsequious, but they were often suspected of thievery and kept under surveillance.[66] The Chinese who had been employed in quartz mining, often "for certain inferior purposes, such as dumping cars, surface excavations, etc.,"[67] were driven out of that occupation in Sutter Creek as a concession to striking white miners in 1871.[68] In 1885, the leading citizens of Eureka ordered the entire Chinese population to leave Humboldt County on one day's notice or suffer the injuries of an outraged mob. When a few Chinese were brought to the area in 1906 the town again forcibly reviewed them. As late as 1937 Humboldt County boasted of its riddance of the hated Chinese.[69] The 1880's witnessed the beginning of over two decades of public threats, popular agitation and prejudicial reporting about the Chinese in Napa County which ended with their decline or departure around the turn of the century.[70] By the end of the nineteenth century the California Chinese had, for the most part, died off, returned to China, moved eastward or settled into those ghettos of American cities referred to as "Chinatowns." There they would remain to the present day.

The mining frontier of the west moved eastward and with it went some of the Chinese--and after them came nativist movements to remove their tiny colonies or restrict their meager opportunities.[71] Oregon, Idaho, Montana, Nevada and Wyoming felt a Chinese presence in the last three decades of the nineteenth century. British Columbia and Alaska also employed Chinese at first and then attempted to exclude them during this period. Chinese entered Oregon in the late 1860's, apparently following after the whites who worked in the newly discovered gold fields in the eastern part of that state. By 1870 mining had declined considerably in Oregon as was evidenced by the fact that of the 3,965 miners there the Chinese numbered 2,428.[72] A similar decline in Idaho mining caused many whites to sell out to Chinese so that by 1870 more than one-half the state's miners were Chinese; by 1880 the ratio of Chinese to whites in Idaho was higher than in any state or territory in the Union.[73] Chinese settlement in Montana began at least as early as 1869 and continued to increase irregularly until 1910, after which it declined until in 1940 only 258 were left in Butte, a city which had once complained of over 2,500 Chinese.[74] Nevada had a small Chinese population by the mid-1850's, a fact testified by the renaming of the settlement first known as Hall's Station to Chinatown;[75] by the 1870's a thriving Chinese community had been established at Virginia City as a result of the Comstock mining boom, and it was soon the object of curiosity and suspicion.[76] The Chinese community at Rock Springs, Wyoming was the scene in 1885 of one of the worst riots ever spawned by the anti-Oriental feeling in America.[77] Chinese settlement in British Columbia began with the Fraser River gold strike in 1858 which brought several thousand Chinese from California's sluiced out fields,[78] and it was increased by the importation of Chinese to build the Canadian Pacific Railroad.[79] In Alaska the Chinese stay was as brutish as it was short. Imported to work the picked-over gold mines of John Treadwell in 1885, they were confronted by the angry, demoralized, unemployed white and Indian mine laborers and attacked with dynamite. One year later they were incarcerated and expelled from the Territory; after 1886 no more Chinese were employed in Alaskan mines.[80]

The Sinophobia which gripped California spread to the Rocky Mountain area in the wake of the Chinese miners. An editorial in an Arizona newspaper is typical of its genre and reveals both the nature and depth of the hatred against the Chinese:

The Chinese are the least desired immigrants who have ever sought the United States. . . the Almond-eyed Mongolian with his pig-tail, his heathenism, his filthy habits, his thrift and careful accumulation of savings to be sent back to the flowery kingdom.

The most we can do is to insist that he is a heathen, a devourer of soup made from the fragrant juice of the rat, filthy, disagreeable, and undesirable generally, an incumbrance that we do not know how to get rid of, but whose tribe we have determined shall not increase in this part of the world.[81]

Similar views inflamed the people of other states in the Rockies, occasionally modified by a recognition of the benefits obtained from the Chinese. Thus, in Silver City, Idaho, the *Owyhee Avalanche* asserted, "They are in many respects a disgusting element of the population but not wholly unprofitable."[82] However, more people seemed to agree with the Montana journalist who wrote, "We don't mind hearing of a Chinaman being killed now and then, but it has been coming too thick of late. . . soon there will be a scarcity of Chinese cheap labor in the country. . . Don't kill them unless they deserve it, but when they do--why kill 'em lots."[83] Opposition to the Chinese was not merely a pastime of journalists; Montana Governor James M. Ashley expressed the views of much of the citizenry and many of his fellowship governors in the west when he said that his state needed "Norwegian, Swedes, and Germans," not Chinese:

It will be conceded by all practical men who have given this subject any thought, that Montana is better adopted (sic) to the hardy races of men and women from Great Britain and Northern Europe. . . I am. . . opposed to the importation of laborers from any of the barbarous or semi-civilized races of men, and do not propose to co-operate in any scheme organized to bring such laborers into Montana, or into any part of the country.[84]

By 1880 the drive to exclude Chinese, which started in California and moved eastward to the Rockies, had spread throughout the nation and laid the basis for America's first bill to restrict immigration on the basis of race. In 1870 Chinese laborers had been shipped from California to North Adams, Massachusetts, to break a strike of shoemakers. Hailed at first by those opposed to the striking union, the Knights of St. Crispin, the Chinese were subsequently the objects of anti-coolie meetings held in Boston to protest the reduction of American labor to the standards of "rice and rats."[85] In 1877 another gang of Chinese coolies were imported from California to break a cutlery manufacturing strike in Beaver Falls, Pennsylvania.[86] The *Cincinnati Enquirer* and other Ohio papers protested against the use of Chinese labor in the cigar-making industry,[87] the industry whose union leader, Samuel Gompers, was to become a lifelong foe of the Chinese and one of the most potent forces in denying them equal opportunity in craft work.[88] America's labor unions fulminated against the Chinese and demanded their exclusion from the nation and their expulsion from the labor force. "The political issue after 1877 was racial, not financial, and the weapon was not merely the ballot, but also 'direct action'--violence. The anti-Chinese agitation in California, culminating as it did in the Exclusion Law passed by Congress in 1882, was doubtless the most important single factor in the history of American labor, for without it the entire country might have been overrun by Mongolian labor and the labor movement might have become a conflict of races instead of one of classes."[89] That a historian of labor, writing in the twentieth century, could make this statement is indicative of the depth to which Sinophobia had worked itself into at least one sector of the American population.

Settlement in Cities

One of the outstanding characteristics of the Chinese in America is their settlement in cities. Unlike the Japanese, for example, the Chinese have not had a long habitation on agricultural hinterlands followed by the migration of second and third generation offspring to urban areas.[90] A few Chinese agricultural settlements existed briefly in the California interior,[91] and some Chinese farmers are to be found in the rural environs of Vancouver, British Columbia, but the bulk of Chinese have always dwelt in cities or small towns.[92] Even when Chinese were employed on railroads--such as the Central Pacific in the late 1860's--or in digging the tunnels of California's vineyards,[93] their places of work were but temporary abodes; when the work was done they returned to the city. "San Francisco," testified Frank M. Pixley, politician, publisher and opponent of Chinese immigration, "is the heart and hive and home of all the Chinese upon this coast. Our Chinese quarter, as it is called, is their place really of residence. If they go to a wash house in the vicinity, to a surburban manufactory, to gardening near the town, or if to build railroads in San Bernadino or on the Colorado, or to reclaim tule lands in the interior, their departure here is temporary, and their return here is certain; therefore the number in San Francisco depends upon seasons and the contract labor market."[94]

The Chinese population of San Francisco grew both in an absolute and a proportional sense in the decades after 1860. In 1860 the Chinese in San Francisco numbered 2,719 persons and were only 7.8% of the state's total Asian population. By 1870 it had jumped to 12,030 and 24.4%; ten years later it had risen to 21,745 and 28.9%; in 1890 the Chinese in San Francisco had grown to 25,833 and 35.7%. Only in 1900 did the Chinese in San Francisco show a decline. The enforcement of the exclusion laws, the return of numerous successful or discouraged Chinese to China, and the departure of others for the midwest and beyond left the number at 13,954, still 30.5% of the state's Chinese population.[95]

The city always meant the Chinese quarter, a ghetto called "Chinatown." It was in Chinatown that the lonely Chinese laborer could find fellowship, companions, social familiarity and solace. Chinatown acted as a partial buffer against the prejudices, hatreds and depredations of hostile whites. Chinatown included the offices and hostelries of the various Chinese benevolent and protective associations, places where one could get a bunk for the night, some food, a stake, and a knowledge of the number, kinds, and conditions of available jobs. Chinatown also housed the Chinese elite, the merchants of the ghetto who acted as spokesmen for and protectors of the laborers and who held the latter in a state of political dependence and debt bondage. The Chinatowns of America and elsewhere[96] cannot be said to be either products of white racism on the one hand or congregative sentiments among the Chinese on the other. Rather, they must be seen as complex emergents produced by these two elements acting simultaneously. A powerful sense of group feelings and social needs found institutionalized expression in Chinatown at the same time that white aversion and hostility gave added reasons for those Chinese institutions to continue to flourish.

Chinese Social Organization

The Chinese quarter of San Francisco and other cities where Chinatowns have been established are characterized by a high degree and complex mesh of organization. To the present day most Americans are unaware of the actual nature and functions of Chinese associations and tend to regard them in unilluminating stereotypy. There are three basic types of association established in Chinatown as well as subsidiary and ancillary groupings. At the apex of the organizational pyramid is a confederation of association which tends to govern the community. First there are clans. Clans have their origin in the Chinese lineage communities so prevalent in southeastern China, communities which united their male inhabitants with bonds of blood loyalty based on descent from a common ancestor.[97] In the New World the lineage unit was replaced by a net sprung wider than the original geographically compact village of origin to include all those bearing the same surname. The clan provided the boundaries of the incest taboo by prohibiting marriage within the same surname group.[98] Clan officials established hostelries for their kinsmen, and the clan association became a kind of immigrant aid society providing food, shelter, employment, protection and advice. The clans further served to remind the sojourner of his ties to village and family in China, and in the absence of the original lineal authorities, assumed a role in loco parentis.[99] In some instances clans obtained a monopoly over some trades or professions in Chinatown and effectively resisted encroachments on these monopolies by ambitious Chinese from other clans.[100] More recently clan authority has been undermined by the acculturation of Chinese born in America and by a resentment against both its traditional despotism and the clans' failure to ameliorate social conditions.[101]

In addition to clans, however, there developed among immigrant Chinese a functionally similar but structurally different type of association. The hui kuan united all those who spoke a common dialect, hailed from the same district of origin in China or belonged to the same tribal or ethnic group. The hui kuan, like the clan, originated in China, and by the mid-nineteenth century there were associations of this type throughout the Celestial Empire. In many ways these Chinese associations were similar to those immigrant aid and benevolent societies formed by Europeans in America, and the German term which has been applied to the latter, Landsmannschaften, is applicable to the Chinese hui kuan as well.[102]

The several Landsmannschaften established in San Francisco and other cities where Chinese dwelt served as caravansaries, hostelries, credit associations and employment agencies for their members. They also represented their constituency in dealings with other Landsmannschaften and with white officials. Finally, they conducted arbitration and mediation hearings between individuals and groups and adjudicated disputes. In San Francisco, Vancouver and New York City the several hui kuan confederated together with other associations, often including clans and secret societies, to form a supra-community association. The Chinese Benevolent Association, as it is usually called, provides Chinatown-wide governance on the one hand and a united front in relations with white America on the other.[103] During the first half century of Chinese settlement in America the consolidated association of hui kuan commanded at the least the grudging allegiance and obedience of the toiling Chinese laborers and the respect of many well-meaning whites; however, in more recent times the association's alleged involvement in illegal immigration, its failure to meet the needs of San Francisco's new Chinese immigrant youth, its conservative and traditional orientation toward welfare, and its anachronistic appearance to acculturated American-born Chinese have led to a certain decline it its community power and a slight dampening of its popularity with white America.[104] Nevertheless, it retains considerable authority and can still exert sanctions against recalcitrant and defalcating Chinese in the ghetto.[105]

The third major type of organization in Chinatown is the secret society. Like the clan and the hui kuan, the secret society originated in China where for centuries it served as the principal agency for protest, rebellion and banditry. It also provided a haven for those who blamed officialdom for their agricultural or professional failures, for those who had been expelled from their village, expunged from their lineage or who had run afoul of the law.[106] After 1644 in Kwangtung and Fukien secret societies where the most notorious opponents of Manchu rule, and for more than 250 years they pursued sporadic guerilla warfare against Ch'ing officials, seaport towns and wealthy merchants. The overseas branches contributed to Sun Yat-sen's revolution in 1911, but in China secret societies continued to plague both revolutionary forces and republican power holders--both of which tried to crush or co-opt them--well into the middle of the twentieth century. After the advent of the Communist regime, attempts were again made to "coordinate" them or stamp them out, although it is by no means clear how successful these efforts have been.[107]

Nineteenth century migrants from Kwantung and Fukien included not a few of the members of the Triad Society, the most famous of China's clandestine associations. In nearly every overseas Chinese community of size secret societies sprang up as chapters of or models based on that order. In Malaya, an area in which much information on these societies has been gathered, the several secret fraternal brotherhoods not only organized much of the social, economic, political, criminal and recreational life of the Chinese community, but also played a significant role in the industrial and political development and the foreign relations of the British colony.[108]

In the United States and Canada early immigrants established Chinese secret societies in the cities and in the outlying areas where Chinese miners gathered to organize their meager elements of livelihood and daily life. In the mining country of British Columbia, for example, a Chinese secret society provided a carefully run hostelry, adjudicated disputes and regulated the boundaries of the claims.[109] In the cities the secret societies soon took over control of gambling and prostitution in the American Chinatowns, and it is with these activities rather than with their political or eleemosynary work that they are most often associated in the minds of non-Chinese in America.

The different associations often fell out with one another; their so-called "tong

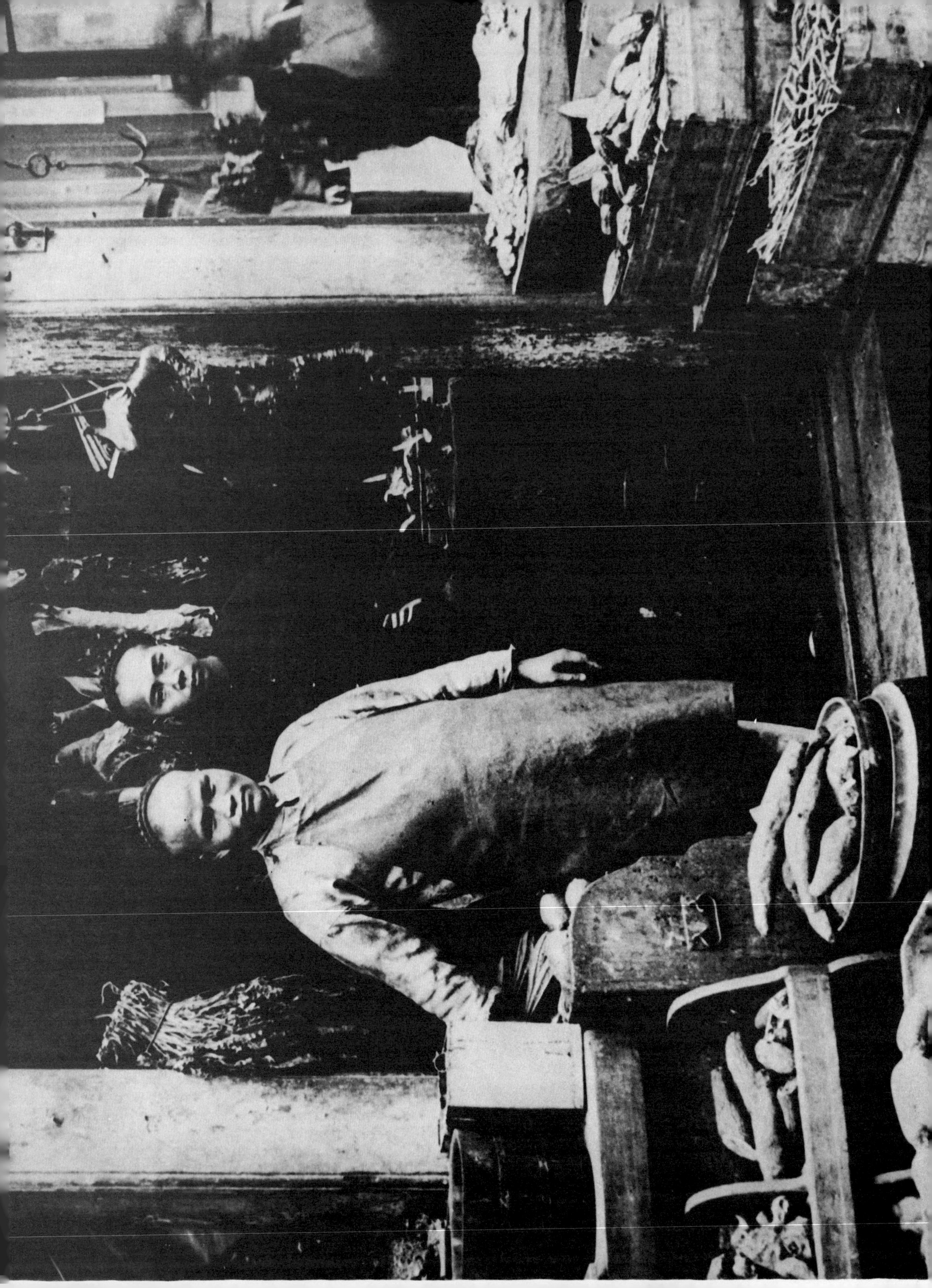

wars"--in actual fact, violent altercations that involved clans, hui kuan and secret societies--are a frequent source of apocryphal history and stereotypy of the Chinese in America. The charitable works of secret societies were confined for the most part to mutual aid to their constituents, the establishment of buildings and club-houses where fraternity might be found, and, in recent years, some care and solicitation for their aged and infirm members. Political activities of the secret societies in North America were limited to occasional interest in the fortunes of China's regimes, and they did not interfere with or participate in the national politics of the United States or Canada.

At the turn of the century and in the decade thereafter Sun Yat-sen obtained considerable financial support from chapters of the Chih-kung T'ang in North America.[110] In San Francisco over 2,000,000 dollars in revolutionary currency were printed, while in rural California a few hundred inspired Chinese young men drilled in preparation to join the fighting foces of Sun's revolution.[111] When Dr. Sun was stranded without funds in New York City at a critical moment in the revolution, Seto May-tong, a Triad Society official who was to continue to exercise influence on the international relations of China and secret societies for more than thirty years, raised the necessary funds to finance his fateful return to China. In 1912 Seto mortgaged the society's buildings in Victoria, Vancouver and Toronto, raising $150,000 for the revolution.[112]

In more recent years Chinese secret societies may have lost some of their erstwhile functions and declined in influence and power. Their unity in support of Sun Yat-sen collapsed with the failire of the Republic to establish consensus and legitimacy. Although the Triad Society reorganized as a political party in 1947, it was ineffectual in arranging a peace between the Communist and Kuomintang forces, and since has been devoid of political influence.[113] Meanwhile, in the Chinatowns of America prostitution and gambling--the traditional sources of secret society revenue--have declined with the infirmity and death of the bachelor immigrants, the establishment of families in America, and the acculturation of the American-born Chinese.[114] Finally, the general rejection of traditional Chinese societies by the present generation of immigrants and Chinese-Americans has added to secret society desuetude.[115] At the present time it would appear that, barring some unforseen source for their rejuvenation, Chinese secret societies will soon disappear from the American scene.

The Shortage of Women

The principal social problem affecting the Chinese in America was the shortage of women. So few Chinese women came to America that it was not until the middle of the twentieth century that there occurred even a proximity in balancing the sex ratio. During the entire period of unrestricted immigration (1850-1882) a total of only 8,848 Chinese women journeyed to American shores. In that same period over 100,000 men arrived in the United States. Many of the women could not stand the rigors of life in America and died or returned to China. By 1890 only 3,868 Chinese women were reported to be in the country. The number of Chinese males continued to grow during the latter three decades of the nineteenth century. In 1860 the census reported 33,149 male Chinese; in 1870, 58,633; in 1880, 100,686; and in 1890 there were 102,620 Chinese men in America. Only in 1900 did the census of Chinese males reveal a halt in the growth of this portion of the Chinese population in America. In that year 85,341 Chinese males were reported. Between 1860 and 1890 the ratio of Chinese males per 100 Chinese females was alarmingly high: 1,858 in 1860; 1,284 in 1870; 2,106 in 1880; 2,678 in 1890; and 1,887 in 1900.[116]

The imbalance in the sex ratio was slowly reduced during the first half of the twentieth century. By 1920, despite the birth of a few females among the Chinese in America, the males still far outnumbered the females; for every 100 women there were more than 695 men. By 1960 the situation had been only partially mitigated. The number of males had grown to 135,430, but the number of females was only 100,654.[117] The low number of females among the Chinese in America and elsewhere[118] has been one of the most salient features shaping their personal, social and community life.[119]

Ideally, Chinese custom held that a wife should remain in the household of her husband's parents, even in the event that her husband went abroad. Should his parents die during his absence, the wife was expected to perform the burial and mourning rites.[120] Village headmen often secured a prospective emigrant's loyalty to his village by requiring that he marry before departing and that he promise to remit money for the support of his wife and family and the village community.[121] Overseas the clan or hui kuan often assumed the obligation of collecting the remittances from the laboring immigrants and sending them to the appropriate village in China.[122] The lonely laborer toiled in the hope that one day he would return to his wife and family as a wealthy and respected man. In fact, however, this rarely occurred; instead, the sojourner was usually forced to put off his remigration to China year after year. The promise of America's gold turned to dross, but still he labored. For some there was a temporary respite in a visit to China, siring of a son there, and the hope, sometimes realized, that the son would join the father in the American adventure when he came of age.[123]

If Chinese custom, often misunderstood in America,[124] prevented Chinese women from joining their husbands overseas in the first three decades of unrestricted immigration, American law continued the bar against them after 1882. According to the Chinese Exclusion Act of that year, as interpreted by the courts two years later,[125] a Chinese woman acquired the legal status of her husband upon marriage. Thus, the wives of Chinese laborers were excluded by the same law which excluded Chinese laborers from coming to the United States. In the many changes made in the immigration laws before they were all repealed and a quota system imposed in 1943, the few liberalizations that were granted were applied almost exclusively to the Chinese wives and offspring of Chinese merchants and other classes exempted in the original exclusion act.[126]

The consequences of the barring of Chinese women were many and tragic. In the rural mining areas the few Chinese women who had come abroad often became unwilling prostitutes servicing the sexual needs of homeless, lonely Chinese laborers.[127] "The Chinese are hardly used here," wrote Horace Greeley from a California mining camp in 1859. He went on to say that "he has no family here (the few Chinese women brought to this country being utterly shameless and abandoned), so that he forms no domestic ties, and enjoys no social standing."[128] "Very few bring wives with them," wrote Henryk Sienkiwicz in 1880 in one of his letters from America, "and for that reason it so happens that where among ten Chinese occupying a dwelling place there is but one woman, they all live together with her. I encountered such examples of polyandry quite frequently, particularly in the country."[129]

In the cities in which the Chinese congregated, prostitution was organized under the direct or tributary control of the secret societies. Young girls were brought to America from China after being kidnapped, sold into indentured servitude by their parents, captured by pirates or raiding bands, or lured abroad by a meretricious promise of proxy marriage. Once having arrived in America they were placed under contract to individual Chinese, or more often, to brothels in the Chinese quarter. They might be sold and resold again and again. The brothel keepers guarded their interest in "slave girls" by bribing court interpreters and offering perjured testimony in numerous litigations, and by invoking the assistance of secret society thugs to put off Chinese men who wished to marry a girl under contract.[130]

Organized prostitution and secret society vice domination continued well into the twentieth century.[131] A close observer of Chicago's Chinatown wrote in 1934: "Women are another temptation. Be it remembered that out of a total of some 5,000 Chinese in Chicago there are only about 40 women, and one can imagine the social problem involved. The Chinese Exclusion Act has prevented the Chinese from importing their women. Taking advantage of this situation, the tong men smuggle young girls from China for this purpose. The owner of the prostitution house owns the victims and pays tax to the tong which delivered the girls, and gives to the owner protection. Prostitution houses in the town are in the guise of hotels, and gambling houses, as stores."[132] Rather than recognize that the source of the problem was America's restrictive immigration laws, most journalists and politicians were content to rail against the Chinese on the grounds of immorality. Only Jacob A. Riis, himself an immigrant, having toured New York's Chinatown in 1890, seemed to grasp the enormity of the problem. He offered a solution: "This is a time for plain speaking on this subject. Rather than banish the Chinaman, I would have the door opened wider--for his wife; make it a condition of his coming or staying that he bring his wife with him. Then, at least, he might not be what he now is and remains, a homeless stranger among us. Upon this hinges the real Chinese question, in our city at all events, as I see it."[133]

The Anti-Chinese Movement in the Cities

The presence of Chinese in large numbers in San Francisco should not have seemed so strange in view of the polyglot population already in that city. The heterogeneous denizens of San Francisco were described in an observant report in 1852:

The population of both the State and city was largely increased in 1852. The departures by sea from San Francisco were only 23,196 while there were 66,988 arrivals. This immigration was about double the amount that had taken place in 1851. The immigrants from the Atlantic States generally crossed the Isthmus, while the greater number of European foreigners came round Cape Horn. The Germans, a most valuable and industrious class of men, and the French, perhaps by nature not quite so steady and hard-working a race, though still a useful body of citizens, were year by year arriving in large numbers, and were readily remarked among the motley population. The most untutored eye could distinguish and contrast the natural phlegm and common-sense philosophy of the fat Teutor, and the "lean and hungry look" and restless gestures of the Celt. . . The English, Scotch, and Irish immigrants, were also numerous, but their characteristics, although something different, were less distinguishable from those of native Americans than were the manners and customs of other foreigners. Besides there were always arriving numerous specimens of most other European nations,--Spaniards, Portuguese, Italians, Swiss, Greeks, Hungarians, Poles, Russians, Prussians, Dutch, Swedes, Danes, Turks, too--all visited California. Many of them went to the mines, although a considerable proportion never left San Francisco. The country and city were wide enough to hold them all, and rich enough to give them all a moderate independence in the course of a few years...

Upwards of twenty thousand Chinese are included in the general number of arrivals above given. Such people were becoming very numerous in San Francisco... at one period of 1852 there were supposed to be about 27,000 Chinese in the state. A considerable number of people of "color" (par excellence) also arrived. These were probably afraid to proceed to the mines to labor beside the domineering white races, and therefore they remained to drudge, and to make much money and spend it in San Francisco, like almost everybody else. Mexicans from Sonora and other provinces of Mexico, and many Chileans, and a few Peruvians from South America, were likewise continually coming and going between San Francisco and the ports of their own countries. The Chinese immigrants had their mandarins, their merchants, rich educated, and respectable men, in San Francisco; but all the Mexicans and Chileans, like the people of negro descent, were only of the commonest description. The women of all these various races were nearly all of the vilest character, and openly practiced the most shameful commerce. The lewdness of fallen white females is shocking enough to witness, but it is far exceeded by the disgusting practices of these tawny visaged creatures.[134]

As late as 1875, San Francisco still attracted comment because of its many peoples, cosmopolitan atmosphere and colorful character. Samuel Wells Williams, the noted missionary to China, wrote of it in tones of genuine rapture:

San Francisco is probably the most cosmopolitan city of its size in the world. Nowhere else are witnessed the fusing of so many races, the juxtaposition of so many nationalities, the Babel of so many tongues. Every country on the globe, every state and principality, almost every island of the sea, finds here its representative. Your next door neighbor may be a native of Central Asia; your vis-a-vis at the restaurant table may have been born under the shadow of the great wall of China; the man who waits on you at table may be a lascar from the East Indies. If you go to the theater, you may find sitting next to you a lady from the Sandwich Islands; if you go to the Opera, you may hear, in the pauses of the music, French, German, Italian, Spanish, Russian Swedish, Modern Greek, spoken by people dressed in the most scrupulous evening costume. If you take a ride in the horse-cars, you may find yourself wedged in between a parson from Massachusetts and a parsee from Hindostan; if you go to the bank, you may be jostled by a gentleman from Damascus, or a prince of the Society Islands. In three minutes' walk from your place of business, you enter an Oriental city--surrounded by the symbols of a civilization older than that of the Pharaohs."[135]

Yet, the strange customs, peculiar habits and frugal life of the Chinese seemed to astonish, alarm, or disgust the San Franciscans within a short time after the arrival of Chinese laborers. Chinese merchants, with their indispensable supply of hot cooked foods, objects d'art and household necessities, were a small but favored group. Chinese laborers on the other hand, were "unfair" competition in the mines and elsewhere, and morally degenerate, socially undesirable and politically irrelevant. The derision of the Chinese, the hatred directed against them, and the vicious half-truths and distortions that were to make up the anti-Chinese stereotype were already visible in 1852. Although, according to San Francisco's annalists of that year, the Chinese were described as "generally quiet and industrious members of society, charitable among themselves, not given to intemperance and the rude vices which drink induces, and. . . reputed to be remarkably attached to their parents," they were despised in California:

The manners and habits of the Chinese are very repugnant to Americans in California. Of different language, blood, religion, and character, inferior in most mental and bodily qualities, the Chinaman in looked upon by some as only a little superior to the Negro, and by others as somewhat inferior. It is needless to reason upon such a matter. Those who have mingled with "celestials" have commonly felt before long an uncontrollable sort of loathing against them. John's "person does not smell very sweetly; his color and the features of his face are unusual; his penuriousness; his lying, knavery, and natural cowardice are proverbial; he dwells apart from white persons, herding only with countrymen, unable to communicate his ideas to such as are not of his nation, or to show the better part of his nature. He is poor and mean, somewhat slavish and crouching, and is despised by the whites, who would only laugh in derision if even a divine were to pretend to place the two races on an equality. In short there is a strong feeling,--prejudice it may be,--existing in California against all Chinamen, and they are nicknamed, cuffed about and treated very unceremoniously by every other class.[136]

That the racial hostility toward the Chinese stemmed in great measure from their alleged competition with urban white labor was indicated in 1852 when the California State Senate turned down Senator Tingley's infamous Bill number 63, "An Act to Enforce Contracts and Obligations to Perform Work and Labor," commonly known as the "Coolie Bill."[137] In the committee's minority report, eventually adopted by the Senate, Senator Philip Roach, who was to be a leader in the fight for Chinese exclusion for the next thirty years, wrote that he did not oppose the importation of Oriental contract labor for agriculture: "There is ample room for its employment in draining the swamplands, in cultivating rice, raising silk, or planting tea. Our State is supposed to have great natural advantages for those objects; but if these present not field enough for their labor, then sugar, cotton, and tobacco invite their attention. For these special objects I have no objection to the introduction of contract laborers, provided they are excluded from citizenship; for those staples cannot be cultivated without 'cheap labor'; but from all other branches I would recommend its exclusion." Roach's conclusion about Chinese in the skilled labor occupations was quite emphatic. "I do not want to see Chinese or Kanaka carpenters, masons, or blacksmiths, brought here in swarms under contracts, to compete with our own mechanics, whose labor is an honorable and as well entitled to social and political rights as the pursuits designated 'learned professions.'"[138] By the 1870's California labor's "social and political rights" took the form of an organized movement dedicated to the restriction of Chinese immigration and the exclusion of Chinese workers from the labor market.

After two decades of mining and railroad building, work which had kept large number of Chinese away from the cities, the Chinese began to settle down in the urban Chinatowns of the west and to become a principal part of the labor force in newly developing urban industries. During the 1870's and 1880's Chinese in San Francisco were employed in the woolen, textile, clothing, shoe, cigar, gunpowder and a few other industrial factories which at that time played a vital part in the city's economy.[139] When the depression of the 1870's put large numbers of white laborers out of work, Chinese workers became the objects of labor union hostility. Popular demagogues--of whom Denis Kearney was the most famous[140]--railed against their presence in industries which, they held, belonged to white labor exclusively. Mob actions against the Chinese were organized, harassing laws were passed, and eventually the Chinese were driven out of the industries and in many cases out of the cities as well.

The polemics against the Chinese were inflammatory and exaggerated allegations against their character and culture, and they served as incitements to riot and abuse. Mark Twain, one of the most acute observers of the western scene, bitterly satirized the mistreatment of Chinese, calling attention to the unequal protection of the laws, popular prejudices and injurious practices from which they suffered daily. He had hoped that the Burlingame Treaty of 1868 would put an end to these abuses, but when its protective provisions were winked at, he fulminated against the street boys and politicians, workers and legislators who perpetrated torture and terror on the inoffensive Chinese. As he so carefully observed, the popular attacks on Chinese were not simply the outrages of sick or savage individuals, but rather the product of the campaign of Sinophobic vilification which had been created by the political, labor and media leaders.[141] Similarly, Thomas Nast, the political cartoonist, turned his sharp pen to satirizing the inconsistent laws and hate-ridden ideologies that barred Chinese from citizenship and the franchise and condemned them to be the mudsills of America. Later, however, Nast appears to have withdrawn the bite from his criticism and to have accepted the permanent place of Chinese in this country as an abused minority.[142]

Negro leaders such as Frederick Douglass carefully distinguished their opposition to the coolie trade and to the exploitation of Chinese laborers from any opposition to Chinese as laborers or citizens,[143] but occasionally a California Negro journalist would take up the anti-Chinese cry contrasting the latter's alleged inability to assimilate with the rapidly Americanizing Negro.[144] As the racist movement spread throughout the United States, the anti-Chinese diatribes became confused with those levelled against the Negro. Comparisons, sometimes favoring one, sometimes the other were made, but in the end both Negroes and Chinese were declared inimical and inferior to white society in general and to white labor in particular.[145]

The demagogic voice of Denis Kearney of California was a major factor in elevating the anti-Chinese movement to National importance. In a letter to Lord Bryce, Kearney defended himself against Bryce's criticism, stating, "My only crime seems to have been that I opposed the Mongolization of my State in the interest of our own people and their civilization."[146] The Workingmen's Party of California, led by Kearney, adopted the slogan "The Chinese Must Go," and as its numbers and influence increased, affected California politics and legislation in a remarkable manner. In 1879 it sent a large and vociferous delegation to the state constitutional convention and played an important part in bringing about the infamous Article XIX of the California Constitution. In its vitriolic volley against the Chinese the Workingmen's Party rose to new heights of rhetorical invective:

The Chinese coolie represents the most debased order of humanity known to the civilized world. No touch of refinement can ever reach him. He comes to this country in a condition of voluntary servitude, from which by insidious precautions of the Chinese Six Companies, under whose auspices this immigration is carried on, he is scarcely ever able to escape--brings with him all the loathsome and vicious habits of his native country.

No amount of association or example can change in the least iota his repulsive filthiness, or wean him in the slightest degree from the ways of his race. His personal habits are of the most loathsome. He knows nothing of the family relation, nothing of the sanctity of an oath, regards no right of property except as controlled through absolute fear, and utterly refuses to assimilate in any measure with the people to whom his presence is a curse. As a race, the thirty years of their presence in California has not been able to influence them to a solitary change of habit. They maintain their separate dress, retain their language and religion, institute their own secret courts, levying fines and enforcing decrees, even to the applying of the death sentence, in utter defiance of the laws of the State.

They establish and carry on the most thorough and complete system of gambling, protect and encourage debauchery in its worst form, and under the cover of their laws, openly provide the most polluted system of prostitution ever known. Wherever they locate as a class in a city or town, it is as if the horrid touch of leprosy had grasped it. Straightway all Caucasian civilization is driven away from the quarter they settle upon; property values are destroyed, and as is the case in San Francisco a proscribed quarter known as "Chinatown" is made, with as exactly defined limits and as complete an isolation from the civilized portion of the community as the line by the Great Wall which divided their own country from Tartary.

Disgusting and nauseating as is the contemplation of the personal habits of the race, it is, however, to the influence which their competition with the intelligent and civilized labor of the State in all our industries will have upon the future, that the people are looking with most concern, and from which unwholesome and unnatural competition the people are anxiously seeking for relief. . . .[147]

The vicious anti-Chinese stereotype was perhaps never so well combined with a fanatical religious anthropology and the racist interests of white labor organizations as in the testimony presented by Frank M. Pixley before the Senate committee investigating Chinese immigration in 1877:

The Chinese are inferior to any race God ever made. . . I think there are none so low. . . Their people have got the perfection of crimes of 4,000 years. . . The Divine Wisdom has said that He would divide this country and the world as a heritage of five great families; that to the Blacks He would give Africa; and Asia he would give to the Yellow races. He inspired us with the determination, not only to have prepared our own inheritance, but to have stolen from the Red Man, America; and it is now settled that the Saxon, American or European groups of families, the White Race, is to have the inheritance of Europe and America and that the Yellow races are to be confined to what the Almighty originally gave them; and as they are not a favored people, they are not to be permitted to steal from us what we have robbed the American savage of. . . I believe the Chinese have no souls to save, and if they have, they are not worth the saving. . .

The burden of our accusations against them is that they come in conflict with our labor interests; that they can never assimilate with us; that they are a perpetual unchanging and unchangeable alien element that can never become homogeneous; that their civilization is demoralizing and degrading to our people; that they degrade and dishonor labor; that they never become citizens, and that an alien, degraded labor class, without desire of citizenship, without education and without interest in the country it inhabits, is an element both demoralizing and dangerous to the community within which it exists.[148]

Sparked by the agitation of labor leaders and politicians, the urban anti-Chinese movement entered a violent phase. Riots against the Chinese occurred in the major cities of the west. The first significant urban uprising took place in San Francisco in 1869,[149] and another far more serious riot occurred in the midst of a tong war in Los Angeles' Chinatown on October 24, 1871. After two policemen and a bystander had been killed, a white mob descended on the Chinese quarter and in but four hours killed at least nineteen Chinese, including women and children, burned several buildings and looted shops.[150] Six years later unemployed laborers burned and looted San Francisco's Chinese ghetto for several weeks without any significant interference by public agencies of law enforcement.[151] In 1880 an anti-Chinese riot occurred in Denver.[152] Five years later uprisings against the Chinese occurred in Rock Springs, Wyoming and in Tacoma and Seattle, Washington.[153] In 1907 labor-inspired agitation caused a mob of 15,000 white persons, led by some of the city's most prominent citizens, to descend on the Chinese and Japanese quarters of Vancouver, British Columbia; in response, the Orientals called a city-wide general strike which was only settled after intervention by the king of England and his representative William Lyon Mackenzie King.[154] Riots and assaults on the Chinese also occurred in smaller cities and towns of the West: at Gold Hill and Virginia City, Nevada in 1869; at Martinez, California in 1871; at Truckee, California, in 1878, during which 1000 Chinese were driven out; and in many other towns from Napa to Eureka in California and elsewhere.

Anti-Chinese legislation was of three kinds. The first consisted of state and ultimately federal laws to restrict or exclude the Chinese altogether from this country. California experimented for twenty-five years with immigration laws which were consistently declared unconstitutional. Only after the anti-Chinese movement had escalated from a sectional to a national issue did the federal government pass the first exclusion act. The second type of law sought to eliminate Chinese from those occupations in which they allegedly competed "unfairly" with white labor. Finally, a number of laws were passed which had either a punitive or harassing intent.

Among the laws passed in California perhaps the most infamous was Article XIX of the State Constitution, added in the Convention of 1879. This amendment forbade the employment of Chinese in any corporation formed in the state, on any state, municipal and county public works, and provided for legislation whereby any city or town might expel its Chinese inhabitants. Much of this amendment was rendered inoperative by judicial decisions.[156]

Additional city and state ordinances adversely affected Chinese laundrymen, fishermen and farmers. San Francisco sought to limit the activities of Chinese washmen by laws which limited the hours, arbitrarily licensed the laundry buildings, and taxed persons who used poles to deliver goods or traveled from house to house without a vehicle or horse. Some of these laws survived judicial scrutiny, but most of them fell before the unusually sharp eye of the justices of the Supreme Court.[157] In other states, including Nevada and Montana[158] laws or collective action sought the elimination of the peaceful Chinese laundrymen. Chinese fishermen were excluded from fishing by a law excluding aliens ineligible from citizenship from obtaining a license. After this ordinance ran afoul of the courts, a tax law made fishing expensive. California's second law denying fishing licenses to aliens ineligible to citizenship was passed after Chinese became eligible for naturalization and was directed against the Japanese. It too was declared unconstitutional.[159] Under the guise of protecting land and resources from aliens, California forbade nonnaturalizable citizens from obtaining land in 1913 and only after four decades of fruitless legal challenges was this anti-Oriental legislation declared void.[160] Even though much of California's anti-Chinese legislation was declared unconstitutional, its intent was realized by successful labor agitation which resulted in the firing of Chinese workers in nearly every urban industry in which they had thrived and their retreat into Chinatown.[161]

The most outrageous of the punitive and harassing legislation were the "lodging house" and "queue-cutting" ordinances passed in San Francisco and subsequently enacted as state laws. A law requiring 500 cubic feet of air space for each person inhabiting any public hostelry was enforced solely against the Chinese after 1873. When the Chinese combined to resist the law by refusing to pay the fines and crowding the jails so that there was less than five hundred cubic feet of air space per person in them, the Board of Supervisors retaliated with a vengeance. A vehicle tax on Chinese laundrymen, a prohibition on returning the dead to China, and a public health ordinance ordering the cutting of queues were proposed and sent on to the mayor for signature. Mayor Alvord vetoed the ordinances, but in 1876 they were enacted over the signature of Mayor Bryant. A court case against these laws was started and on July 7, 1879 the Circuit Court of the United States invalidated the law that had forced Chinese to be deprived of their badge of citizenship in the Chinese Empire. The prohibition on the removal of the dead from county burial plots, unless a physician's certificate was obtained, was upheld by the Supreme Court in the same year.[162]

In addition to their abuse by outraged mobs, their victimization and deprivations by legislative enactments and the discriminatory attacks on them by organized labor, the Chinese were also denied the right to testify in California courts and were segregated in several of the states' public schools. According to a ruling by California's twenty-nine year old Chief Justice, Chinese were declared to be Indians and as such were ineligible to testify in any case involving a white man. This ruling, making Chinese vulnerable to any kind of otherwise illegal treatment by whites so long as only Chinese witnessed the evil, remained in force from 1854 to 1875.[163]

California's Superintendent of Education complained bitterly of the presence of Chinese and other minorities in the public schools in 1859: "Had it been intended by the framers of the education law that the children of the inferior races should be educated side by side with the whites, it is manifest the census would have included children of all colors. If this attempt to force Africans, Chinese, and Diggers into one school is persisted in it must result in the ruin of the schools. The great mass of our citizens will not associate on terms of equality with these inferior races; nor will they consent that their children should do so."[164] The state legislature acquiesced to Superintendent Moulder's request and in 1860 delegated to him the power to withhold public funds from any school which admitted the proscribed minorities. Provision for separate schools was made, and a Chinese school operated irregularly in San Francisco after 1860. In later years, modifications of the law permitted admission of non-whites if whites did not object, but this law of 1866 had little effect in subsequent years. Chinese brought suit to desegregate the state's public schools in 1902 but were unsuccessful.[165] Twenty-five years later Chinese in Mississippi failed in another attempt to desegregate schools and subsequently refused to send their children to the schools established for "colored" pupils.[166] Since 1954 school segregation had been illegal, but de facto segregation still persists in the Chinese as well as other non-white ghettos.

Conclusion

The Chinese were truly strangers in a strange land. They had come suddenly to a frontier area, bringing with them cherished values and deeply engrained customs which, together with their physical distinctiveness, caused them to stand out and apart from the general population. It would not be unfair to point out that the Chinese had very few friends or sympathizers in the American West. Neither radicals nor reactionaires, liberals nor conservatives were interested in defending--much less understanding-- them. The radical intellectuals and labor leaders were with rare exception notorious for their fulminations against the hapless Chinese.[167]

Reactionaries, racists, demagogues, nativists and know-nothings seized upon "the Chinese question" to ride to power in California. Occasionally a Protestant missionary, men such as A.W. Loomis and Otis Gibson, took a sympathetic interest in and assumed a protective posture toward the Chinese. But when conversions proved to be few in number, these brave souls deserted the field and in some instances turned against their former charges. The Catholics remained almost universally opposed to the Chinese, preferring to serve their Irish flock and even to minister to its Sinophobia.[168]

A few officials and attorneys, possessed of a sense of noblesse oblige or moved to defend civil rights,--Hall McAllister, Colonel Frederick A. Bee and Benjamin S. Brooks--accepted the challenge of the Chinese presence and strove manfully to maintain their liberties and defend their lives and property. But these men were effective in the courts; they could not stop the violence of aroused mobs nor could they counter the invective and organization of the anti-Chinese unions. In the end the Chinese were forced to retreat behind the "walls" which prejudice and discrimination had erected; they returned to the ghetto and inside attempted to build a secure if not prosperous life.

By the turn of the century the Chinese were isolated, neglected and demoralized. Located inside the Chinatowns of American cities they achieved some sense of cultural freedom, a relaxation of tensions and a precarious independence. Some found a new sense of freedom in giving support to Sun Yat-sen's liberation movement for China; a few prospered as merchants and gained political and social power in the ghetto, but most remained homeless and trapped, too poor to return to China and too oppressed to enter fully into American society. Sojourners without wives, they could not procreate a second generation which, had it been born, might have succeeded like the second generation of other immigrant groups. Only after 1930 were there enough Chinese women present in America to guarantee that a new generation of significant proportions would develop in the next two decades. The much-vaunted Chinese family remained but an idea in Chinatown for eight remorseless decades.

Today, America and its Chinese are beginning to sense the legacy of the nineteenth century. The children of the immigrants, born in America, growing up in a period of relative tolerance and burgeoning civil rights, educated in public schools and emancipated from Chinese tradition, have left Chinatown for the professions, the suburbs and the rest of the American dream. To be sure, they still encounter discrimination in housing and in certain occupations, and they still must silently wince at the gauche pretensions of toleration which often accompany white "acceptance." Meanwhile, inside Chinatown, the old elite, composed of executives of the clans, hui kuans and secret societies, continues to hold sway at the expense of their subjects over whom they exercise a benevolent but despotic authority.

The mass of Chinatowners may be divided into four groups for whom life holds varying degrees of promise and poverty. The aged bachelors live in tiny, cold, unkempt, rooms, suffer from tuberculosis and other diseases not prevalent in the metropolis and contribute to Chinatown's alarming suicide rate. The shopkeepers and restauranteurs thrive on a tourist trade but privately worry about the effects of America's foreign policy on their fortunes. The new immigrants find themselves doubly estranged and alienated--they cannot bow to the authority of the Chinatown elites, but they lack the language and skill with which they might enter the American mainstream. Some work in the garment sweatshops, ekeing out a meager living from a production system that was once the horror of every humane Occidental but has not all but disappeared except in Chinatown. The youthful immigrants are angry and militant, and in their outcry against a seemingly pitiless system, sound a call like that of the Negro and other minority groups seeking independence and identity. The American-born school dropouts, those who for one reason or another have not made it into white America, are estranged from their immigrant peers by culture and language, but enjoined from white or Chinese-American middle-class life by their academic and occupational failures. Imbued with a new spirit born of desperation and vague radicalism, they too have assumed the posture of late of an independent group seeking not assimilation but liberty. Chinatown's future lies with its people. As some sociologists are realizing, it is as problematic and unpredictable as America is as a whole. One step in understanding its present is a knowledge of its past.

---

[1] Georg Simmel, "The Stranger," in THE SOCIOLOGY OF GEORG SIMMEL, Glencoe: The Free Press, 1950, p. 402 (Translated and edited by Kurt Wolff).

[2] See Paul C.P. Siu, "The Sojourner," AMERICAN JOURNAL OF SOCIOLOGY, VIII, (July, 1952), pp. 32-44.

[3] Cf. Harold Isaacs, IMAGES OF ASIA: AMERICAN VIEWS OF CHINA AND INDIA, New York: Capricorn, 1962, pp. 63-238.

[4] See Arthur O. Lovejoy, "The Chinese Origin of a Romanticism," ESSAYS IN THE HISTORY OF IDEAS, New York: Capricorn, 1960, pp. 99-135.

[5] Foster Rhea Dulles, CHINA AND AMERICA: THE STORY OF THEIR RELATIONS SINCE 1784, Princeton: Princeton University Press, 1946, pp. 6-7.

[6] George H. Danton, THE CULTURE CONTACTS OF THE UNITED STATES AND CHINA: THE EARLIEST SINO-AMERICAN CULTURE CONTACTS, 1784-1844, New York: Columbia University Press, 1931, pp. 29, 33.

[7] See Clay Lancaster, THE JAPANESE INFLUENCE IN AMERICA, New York: Walton H. Rawls, 1963, pp. 1-41.

[8] Kenneth Scott Latourette, THE HISTORY OF THE EARLY RELATIONS BETWEEN THE UNITED STATES AND CHINA, 1784-1844, Transactions of the Connecticut Academy of Arts and Sciences, 22 (August, 1917) pp. 16-17. New York: Kraus Reprint Corp., 1964. See also Robert Glass Cleland, "Asiatic Trade and American Occupation of the Pacific Coast," ANNUAL REPORT OF THE AMERICAN HISTORICAL ASSOCIATION FOR THE YEAR 1914, I (Washington, 1916), pp. 283-289. For Shaw's own account of his days in China see Joseph Quincy, THE JOURNALS OF MAJOR SAMUEL SHAW, THE FIRST AMERICAN CONSUL AT CANTON, WITH A LIFE OF THE AUTHOR, Taipei: Cheng-wen Publishing Co., 1968. (Originally published in 1848).

[9] See CHINA IN THE 16TH CENTURY: THE JOURNALS OF MATTHEW RICCI, 1583-1610, New York: Random House, 1952, pp. 41-58. (Translated by Louis J. Gallagher, S.J.). The "American farmer," J. Hector St. John de Crevecoeur, wrote in 1782 that "The American father thus ploughing with his child, and to feed his family, is inferior only to the emperor of China ploughing as an example to his kingdom." LETTERS FROM AN AMERICAN FARMER, New York: E.P. Dutton, 1957, p. 21. The 1765 catalogue of the private Union Library of Philadelphia contained among its titles CHINESE TALES, a book so popular the librarian had had to advertise for its return in 1764. Carl and Jessica Bridenbaugh, REBELS AND GENTLEMEN: PHILADELPHIA IN THE AGE OF FRANKLIN, New York: Oxford Hesperides, 1962, p. 87.

[10] See NILES REGISTER, Feb. 23, 1822; June 18, 1835. Quoted in Danton, op. cit., p. 11n. There also was a considerable respect for China's developments in agriculture and conveniences. Thus, the first volume of the AMERICAN PHILOSOPHICAL SOCIETY wished that America "could be so fortunate as to introduce the industry of the Chinese, their arts of living, and improvements in husbandry...(so that) America might become in time as populous as China." And as late as 1840 HUNT'S MERCHANTS' MAGAZINE wrote, "The industry and ingenuity of the Chinese in all that relates to the conveniences of life are remarkable: the origin among them of several arts of comparatively recent date in Europe, is lost in the night of time." Quoted in Latourette, op. cit., p. 124.

Respect for the Chinese government, originating in the 16th century Jesuit praises of the Peking administration, died down after Lord Macartney vividly contrasted the old Chinese order with that imposed after 1644 by the Manchus. He wrote, "The government as it now stands is properly the tyranny of a handful of Tartars over more than three hundred millions of Chinese...A series of two hundred years in the succession of eight Ch'ien-lung a Chinese. He remains at this hour, in all his maxims of policy, as true a Tartar as any of his ancestors." AN EMBASSY TO CHINA: BEING THE JOURNAL KEPT BY LORD MACARTNEY DURING HIS EMBASSY TO THE EMPEROR CH'IEN LUNG, 1793-1794, Hamden, Conn.: Archon, 1963 (Edited by J.C. Crammer-Byng), pp. 236-237. By the mid-nineteenth century the Chinese emperor's ability to keep Anglo-American ministers from the capital and to bottle them up with local officialdom was a matter of keen consternation. See, e.g., Laurence Oliphant, NARRATIVE OF THE EARL OF ELGIN'S MISSION TO CHINA AND JAPAN IN THE YEARS 1857, '58, '59, New York: Harper and Brothers, 1888, pp. 276-281.

[11] George I. Quimby, "Culture Contact on the Northwest Coast, 1785-1795," AMERICAN ANTHROPOLOGIST, 50 (April-June, 1948), pp. 247-255. See also Margaret Ormsby, BRITISH COLUMBIA: A HISTORY, Vancouver: Macmillans in Canada, 1958, pp. 16-19.

[12] Homer H. Dubs and Robert S. Smith, "Chinese in Mexico City in 1635," FAR EASTERN QUARTERLY, I (August, 1942), pp. 387-389. See also William Lytle Schurz, THE MANILA GALLEON, New York: E.P. Dutton, 1959, pp. 63-98.

[13] For the Chinese in Pennsylvania see R.L. Brunhouse, "Lascars in Pennsylvania: A Sidelight on the China Trade," PENNSYLVANIA HISTORY, January, 1940, pp. 20-30. For the role of the Chinese in early New England see Samuel Eliot Morison, THE MARITIME HISTORY OF MASSACHUSETTS, 1783-1860, Boston: Houghton Mifflin, 1961, p. 354 et passim.

[14] Dulles, op. cit., p. 39.

[15] Morison, op. cit., p. 203.

[16] Dulles, loc. cit.; Morison, op. cit., p. 240, 273.

[17] Latourette, op. cit., p. 123.

[18] Danton, op. cit., p. 102.

[19] Charles Gold to George Danton. Reported in Danton, op. cit., pp. 102-103.

[20] For the life of Yung Wing see Yung Wing, MY LIFE IN CHINA AND AMERICA, New York: Henry Holt & Co., 1909; Lo Hsiang-lin, HONG KONG AND WESTERN CULTURES, Honolulu: East West Center Press, 1964, pp. 86-156; Edmund H. Worthy, Jr., "Yung Wing in America," PACIFIC HISTORICAL REVIEW, XXXIV (August, 1965), pp. 265-288.

[21] See Tyler Dennet, AMERICANS IN EASTERN ASIA, New York: Barnes and Noble, 1963, p. 545n. for a personal report to this effect.

[22] Y.C. Wang, CHINESE INTELLECTUALS AND THE WEST, 1872-1949, Chapel Hill: University of North Carolina Press, 1966, pp. 42-45. For the fate of the Chinese returnees, many of whom led distinguished lives in China, see Lo Hsiang-lin, op. cit., pp. 125-144.

[23] Richard H. Dillon, THE HATCHET MEN: THE STORY OF THE TONG WARS IN SAN FRANCISCO'S CHINATOWN, New York: Coward-McCann, 1962, p. 30.

[24] Howard M. Chapin, "The Chinese Junk Ke Ying at Providence," RHODE ISLAND HISTORICAL SOCIETY COLLECTIONS, 27 (January, 1934), pp. 5-12.

[25] For a popular account which, despite the author's lack of social criticism, reveals the hostility directed against Chinese and the cruel pranks played upon them see Lucius Beebe and Charles Clegg, "The Heathen Chinese," THE AMERICAN WEST, New York: E.P. Dutton, 1955, pp. 318-335. Mark Twain documented the numerous attacks on Chinese, attacks which took place nearly every day. See, e.g., "Those Blasted Children," NEW YORK SUNDAY MER-

CURY, March 27, 1865. Reprinted in Bernard Taper, (Editor), MARK TWAIN'S SAN FRANCISCO, New York: McGraw Hill, 1963, pp. 27-33. Many of the songs of Gold Rush California derided the Chinese for his queue. See Richard A. Dwyer and Richard E. Lingenfelter THE SONGS OF THE GOLD RUSH, Berkeley: University of California Press, 1964, pp. 112-113, 119, 121 et passim. The Chinese queue was also a stereotypical feature of humorous drama about the Chinese in the nineteenth century. See Stewart W. Hyde, "The Chinese Stereotype in American Melodrama," CALIFORNIA HISTORICAL SOCIETY QUARTERLY, December, 1955, pp. 357-367.

[26]B.S. Brooks, "History of the Legislation of the Supervisors of the City of San Francisco Against the Chinese, Culminating in the Passage of the Present Ordinance Generally known as the 'Queue Cutting Ordinance'..." APPENDIX. THE INVALIDITY OF THE QUEUE ORDINANCE OF THE CITY AND COUNTY OF SAN FRANCISCO, San Francisco: J.L. Rice and Co., 1879, pp. 15-43.

[27]Latourette, op. cit., p. 123; Dillon, op. cit., p. 30. The definitive work on the subject is Howard S. Levy, CHINESE FOOTBINDING: THE HISTORY OF A CURIOUS AND EROTIC CUSTOM, New York: Walton Rawls, 1966.

[28]Levy, op. cit., pp. 95-99, 276-281.

[29]Thomas Taylor Meadows, THE CHINESE AND THEIR REBELLIONS, Stanford: Academic Reprints, n. d. [originally published in 1856], pp. 34-50, 112-122; J. Thomson, THE STRAITS OF MALACCA, INDO-CHINA, AND CHINA; OR TEN YEARS' TRAVELS, ADVERTURES, AND RESIDENCE ABROAD, New York: Harper and Brothers, 1875, pp. 46-48.

[30]Ping-ti Ho, STUDIES ON THE POPULATION OF CHINA, 1368-1953, Cambridge: Harvard University Press, 1959, pp. 101-280.

[31]Hosea Ballou Morse, THE TRADE AND ADMINISTRATION OF THE CHINESE EMPIRE, Shanghai: Kelly and Walsh, 1908, pp. 175-351; John King Fairbank, TRADE AND DIPLOMACY ON THE CHINA COAST: THE OPENING OF THE TREATY PORTS, 1842-1854, Cambridge: Harvard University Press, 1964. (One volume edition); W.C. Hunter, THE 'FAN KWAE' AT CANTON BEFORE TREATY DAYS, 1825-1844, Taipei: Ch'eng-wen Publishing Co., 1965; Victor Purcell, CHINA, London: Ernest Bann, 1962, pp. 52-61; Edgar Holt, THE OPIUM WARS IN CHINA, London: Putnam, 1964.

[32]"The Celestials at Home and Abroad," LITTELL'S LIVING AGE, 430 (August 14, 1852), p. 294.

[33]loc. cit.

[34]For a careful analysis of casualties during the Taiping Rebellion see Ping-ti Ho, op. cit., pp. 236-247, 275. The Taiping insurrection has been a continuous source of Sinological study. For some representative works see Meadows, op. cit.; Vincent C.Y. Shih, THE TAIPING IDEOLOGY: ITS SOURCES, INTERPRETATIONS AND INFLUENCES, Seattle: University of Washington Press, 1967; Franz Michael in collaboration with Chung-li Chang, THE TAIPING REBELLION: HISTORY AND DOCUMENTS; Vol. 1: History, Seattle: University of Washington Press, 1966; Eugene Powers Boardman, CHRISTIAN INFLUENCE UPON THE IDEOLOGY OF THE TAIPING REBELLION, 1851-1865, Madison: University of Wisconsin Press, 1952; J.C. Cheng, CHINESE SOURCES FOR THE TAIPING REBELLION, 1850-1864, Hong Kong: Hong Kong University Press, 1963; Lady Flavia Anderson, THE REBEL EMPEROR, London: Victor Gollancz, 1958.

[35]Oliphant, op. cit., pp. 75-300; Meadows, op. cit., pp. 74-492; Robert Fortune, A RESIDENCE AMONG THE CHINESE: INLAND, ON THE COAST, AND AT SEA. BEING A NARRATIVE OF SCENES AND ADVENTURES DURING A THIRD VISIT TO CHINA FROM 1853 TO 1856... WITH SUGGESTIONS ON THE PRESENT WAR, London: John Murray, 1857, pp. 1-22, 423-440; S. Wells Williams, THE MIDDLE KINGDOM: A SURVEY OF THE GEOGRAPHY, GOVERNMENT, EDUCATION, SOCIAL LIFE, ARTS, RELIGION, ETC., OF THE CHINESE EMPIRE AND ITS INHABITANTS... New York: John Wiley, 1853. Third Edition, Vol. II, pp. 417-604. For the Hakka-Punti War see Leon Comber, CHINESE SECRET SOCIETIES IN MALAYA: A SURVEY OF THE TRIAD SOCIETY FROM 1800 to 1900, Locust Valley: J.J. Augustin, 1959, pp. 28-29. For the American participation in the Taiping hostilities see Robert S. Rantoul, FREDERICK TOWNSEND WARD: ORGANIZER AND FIRST COMMANDER OF THE 'EVER VICTORIOUS ARMY' IN THE TAI PING REBELLION, Salem: Essex Institute, 1908. Historical Collections of the Essex Institute, Vol. XLIV.

[36]Arthur Waley, THE OPIUM WAR THROUGH CHINESE EYES, Stanford: Stanford University Press, 1968; Siang-Tseh Chiang, THE NIEN REBELLION, Seattle: University of Washington Press, 1954; THE BOXER UPRISING: A HISTORY OF THE BOXER TROUBLE IN CHINA, New York: Paragon, 1967; Victor Purcell, THE BOXER UPRISING: A BACKGROUND STUDY, Cambridge University Press, 1963.

[37]"The Discovery of Gold in California," HUTCHINGS' CALIFORNIA MAGAZINE, II (November, 1857), pp. 194-202. Articles by John A. Sutter and James W. Marshall. Reprinted in John A. Hawgood, AMERICA'S WESTERN FRONTIERS: THE EXPLORATION AND SETTLEMENT OF THE TRANS-MISSISSIPPI WEST, New York: Alfred A. Knopf, 1967, pp. 189-198.

[38]"Quite a large number of the Celestials have arrived among us of late, enticed

hither by the golden romance which has filled the world. Scarcely a ship arrives here that does not bring a increase to this worthy integer of our population; and we hear, by China papers, and private advices from that empire, that the feeling is spreading all through the sea-board, and, as a consequence, nearly all the vessels that are up for this country are so for the prospect of passengers. A few Chinamen have returned, taking home with them some thousands of dollars in California gold, and have thus given an impetus to the spirit of emigration from their fatherland which is not likely to abate for some years to come." DAILY ALTA CALIFORNIA, May 12, 1851.

[39] For circulars used in 1862, 1868, and 1870 see Hubert Howe Bancroft, THE NEW PACIFIC, New York: The Bancroft Co., 1915, pp. 413-414. Third Edition.

[40] A full discussion of all the ramifications of Chinese immigration is beyond the scope of this paper. For good accounts see Pyau Ling, "Causes of Chinese Emigration," ANNALS OF THE AMERICAN ACADEMY OF POLITICAL AND SOCIAL SCIENCE, XXXIX (January, 1912), pp. 74-82; Ta Chen, "Chinese Migrations, with Special Reference to Labor Conditions," BULLETIN OF THE UNITED STATES BUREAU OF LABOR STATISTICS, No. 340, Washington, D.C.: Government Printing Office, 1923; Wu Ching-ch'ao, "Chinese Immigration in the Pacific Area," CHINESE SOCIAL AND POLITICAL SCIENCE REVIEW, XII-XIII (October, 1928, January, 1929, April, 1929), pp. 543-560, 50-76, 161-182; Tin-Yuke Char, "Legal Restrictions on Chinese in English-Speaking Countries of the Pacific," CHINESE SOCIAL AND POLITICAL SCIENCE REVIEW, XVI (January 4, 1933), pp. 472-513.

[41] See Warren B. Smith, WHITE SERVITUDE IN COLONIAL SOUTH CAROLINA, Columbia: University of South Carolina Press, 1961; Carl Bridenbaugh, VEXED AND TROUBLED ENGLISHMEN, 1590-1642, New York: Oxford University Press, 1968, pp. 210, 421-424; Oscar Handlin, THE AMERICANS: A NEW HISTORY OF THE PEOPLE OF THE UNITED STATES, Boston: Atlantic-Little, Brown, 1963, pp. 20-22.

[42] See Theodore Saloutos, THEY REMEMBER AMERICA: THE STORY OF THE REPATRIATED GREEK-AMERICANS, Berkeley: University of California Press, 1956, pp. 16-17; Oscar Handlin, BOSTON'S IMMIGRANTS, 1790-1880: A STUDY IN ACCULTURATION, New York: Atheneum, 1968, pp. 70-71.

[43] Persia Crawford Campbell, CHINESE COOLIE EMIGRATION TO COUNTRIES WITHIN THE BRITISH EMPIRE, London: King and Sons, 1923, pp. XVII-XIX, 28-39, 150-151.

[44] For a complete discussion see Stanford M. Lyman, THE STRUCTURE OF CHINESE SOCIETY IN NINETEENTH CENTURY AMERICA, unpublished Ph.D. dissertation, University of California, Berkeley, 1961.

That the Chinese migrant to California was often the loser in an unprofitable venture is illustrated in this incident related by the distinguished historian Hosea Ballou Morse:

"An incident which occurred to the author in 1893 throws some light on the usual result to a returned Chinese emigrant. At a railway station in Formosa he was addressed in fluent and correct English by the proprietor-cook of the station restaurant; and in answer to an expression of astonishment, the Chinese explained why he was there. He had returned from California with a fortune of $2000. He had first to disburse heavily to remain unmolested by the magistrate and his underlings; then he had to relieve the necessities of his aged father; then an uncle, who had fallen into business difficulties, must be rescued from impending bankruptcy; and then he found he had only enough left to procure himself a wife, with a few dollars margin wherewith to establish himself in his present business, which at most would require $100 capital." THE INTERNATIONAL RELATIONS OF THE CHINESE EMPIRE, VOLUME II: THE PERIOD OF SUBMISSION, 1861-1893, Taipei: Book World Co., n.d. (Originally published in 1910), p. 166n.

[45] For the early maltreatment of Chinese by American sea captains see the account of the infamous "ROBERT BROWN incident" in Earl B. Swisher, CHINA'S MANAGEMENT OF THE AMERICAN BARBARIANS: A STUDY OF SINO-AMERICAN RELATIONS, 1841-1861, New Haven: Far Eastern, 1951, pp. 179-205. For the corruption of American officials at Canton see the Testimony of Thomas H. King in REPORT OF THE JOINT SPECIAL COMMITTEE TO INVESTIGATE CHINESE IMMIGRATION. U.S. Congress. Senate. 44th Congress. 2nd Session. Report No. 689. February, 1877, p. 93; Testimony of Governor F. F. Low and Testimony of Charles Wolcott Brooks in "Chinese Immigration: Its Social, Moral, and Political Effects." REPORT TO THE CALIFORNIA STATE SENATE OF ITS SPECIAL COMMITTEE ON CHINESE EMIGRATION, Sacramento: 1878, pp. 70, 101-102. See also Charles Wolcott Brooks, "THE Chinese Labor Problem," OVERLAND MONTHLY, November, 1869, pp. 407-419.

[46] The entire incident may be pieced together from documents and articles which appeared at the time. For the Memphis convention see the report of its Committee on Chinese Labor in John R. Commons et al., A DOCUMENTARY HISTORY OF AMERICAN INDUSTRIAL SOCIETY, Cleveland: A.H. Clark, 1910-1911, Vol. IX, pp. 80-84. The whole scheme was debated in the South's most prominent journal. See William M. Burwell, 'Science and the Mechanic

Arts Against Coolies," DE BOW'S REVIEW, (July, 1869), pp. 557-571; A.P. Merrill, "Southern Labor," Ibid, pp. 586-592; William M. Burwell, "The Cooley-ite Controversy," Ibid., (August, 1869), pp. 709-724; "Our Chamber of Commerce - The Chinese Labor Question," Ibid., pp. 669-701. For the character of Tye Kim Orr see Edward Jenkins, THE COOLIE - HIS RIGHTS AND WRONGS, New York: Routledge and Sons, 1871, pp. 114-116. For the Chinese reaction see the Testimony of T.H. King in REPORT OF THE JOINT-SPECIAL COMMITTEE...op. cit., p. 93. For Koopmanschap see Gunther Barth, BITTER STRENGTH: A HISTORY OF THE CHINESE IN THE UNITED STATES, 1850-1870, Cambridge: Harvard University Press, 1964, pp. 60, 117, 190-196. For a contemporary favorable account of Koopmanschap's Southern plan see "The Chinese Again," HUNTS MERCHANTS' MAGAZINE, LXI (September, 1869), pp. 214-217.

[47] Chinese had appeared in Kansas in 1859. During the Reconstruction Period gangs of Chinese were employed in various kinds of work in several southern states. See Barth, op. cit., pp. 187-198. For the Chinese in Mississippi see Robert W. O'Brien, "Status of Chinese in the Mississippi Delta," SOCIAL FORCES 19 (March, 1941), pp. 386-390, Barth.

[48] See, e.g., Barth, op. cit., p. 189.

[49] Patricia K. Ourada, "The Chinese in Colorado," THE COLORADO MAGAZINE XXIX (October, 1952), pp. 273-283.

[50] James J. O'Meara, "The Chinese in Early Days," OVERLAND MONTHLY, IV (May, 1884), p. 447.

[51] Mary R. Coolidge, CHINESE IMMIGRATION, New York: Henry Holt, 1909, pp. 22-25.

[52] Signs of racism and xenophobia had appeared earlier. The hostilities to Australians, Chileans, Mexicans, Peruvians and Pacific Islanders and the early attempts to bar Negroes from the State have been attributed, by one recent careful researcher, to the "respectable" American white middle class settlers' desire for "order." See Leonard Pitt, "The Beginnings of Nativism in California," PACIFIC HISTORICAL REVIEW 30 (February, 1961), pp. 23-38. For a recent analysis of the Negro question in the West, see Eugene H. Berwanger, THE FRONTIER AGAINST SLAVERY: WESTERN ANTI-NEGRO PREJUDICE AND THE SLAVERY EXTENSION CONTROVERSY, Urbana: University of Illinois Press, 1967. For an excellent example of California gubernatorial policy directed against the Negroes see "The First Annual Message of the Governor of California," December 21, 1849, CALIFORNIA STATE JOURNAL. FIRST SESSION. 1849-1850, pp. 30-41.

[53] For description of Chinese miners see "Mining Life in California," HARPER'S WEEKLY, October 3, 1857, pp. 632-634; J.D. Borthwick, THREE YEARS IN CALIFORNIA, Edinburgh and London: Blackwood, 1857, chapter 17.

[54] See "Report of the Committee on Mines and Mining Interests," ASSEMBLY JOURNAL. California State Legislature. 4th Session. 1853. APPENDIX, pp. 7-12; see also Coolidge, op. cit., pp. 26-40.

[55] See PEOPLE vs. DOWNER 7 Cal. 169 (1857); LIN SING vs. WASHBURN 20 Cal. 534 (1863); IN RE AH FONG, 3 Sawyer 144 (1874); CHY LUNG vs. FREEMAN 92 U.S. 275 (1876). See also Elmer C. Sandmeyer, "California Anti-Chinese Legislation and the Federal Courts: A Study in Federal Relations," PACIFIC HISTORICAL REVIEW, 5 (September, 1936), pp. 189-211.

[56] For the attack at Chinese Camp see Theodore Hittel, HISTORY OF CALIFORNIA, San Francisco: N.J. Stone, 1897, Vol. IV, p. 102. The resolution against Chinese miners at Marysville will be found in the Marysville HERALD, May 4, 1852.

[57] SACRAMENTO UNION, May 2, 1852.

[58] Charles Howard Shinn, MINING CAMPS: A STUDY IN AMERICAN FRONTIER GOVERNMENT, New York: Harper "Torchbooks," 1965. Originally published in 1884. (Edited by Rodman Wilson Paul), p. 246.

[59] Ibid., p. 248.

[60] Ibid., p. 213.

[61] SACRAMENTO UNION, December 29, 30, 1858; March 5-10; July 16, 25, 1859. Coolidge, op. cit., p. 255n.

[62] "By 1859 the white miners had abandoned a large part of the American River, the original home of river mining, to the Chinese, and by the close of 1863 the Asiatics had inherited the greater part of the river claims throughout the state. The fact that the whites no longer desired the claims for themselves is conclusive evidence of the declining profitableness of this once great type of mining." Rodman W. Paul, CALIFORNIA GOLD: THE BEGINNING OF MINING IN THE FAR WEST, Lincoln: University of Nebraska Press, 1947, p. 130. See also Rodman W. Paul, MINING FRONTIERS OF THE FAR WEST, 1848-1880, New York: Holt, Rinehart, and Winston, 1963, pp. 35-36.

[63] "How We Get Gold in California," HARPER'S NEW MONTHLY MAGAZINE, April, 1860. Reprinted in Milo Miltin Quaife, PICTURES OF GOLD RUSH CALIFORNIA, New York: Citadel, 1967, p. 197.

[64] Ibid., p. 199.

[65] UP AND DOWN CALIFORNIA IN 1860-1861: THE JOURNAL OF WILLIAM H. BREWER, Berkeley: University of California Press, 1966, pp. 329-330, 455, 481. (Edited by Francis P. Farquhar).

[66] Helen Rocca Goss, "The Celestials," LIFE AND DEATH OF A QUICKSILVER MINE, Los Angeles: Historical Society of Southern California, 1958, pp. 63-86.

[67] Rossiter W. Raymond, STATISTICS OF MINES AND MINING IN THE STATES AND TERRITORIES WEST OF THE ROCKY MOUNTAINS, Washington: Government Printing Office, 1872, p. 4. Quoted in Paul, CALIFORNIA GOLD, op. cit., p. 322.

[68] Paul, CALIFORNIA GOLD, op. cit., pp. 329-330.

[69] Lynwood Carranco, "Chinese Expulsion from Humboldt County," PACIFIC HISTORICAL REVIEW, 30 (November, 1961), pp. 329-340.

[70] Charlotte T. Miller, GRAPES, QUEUES, AND QUICKSILVER, unpublished manuscript in possession of the author.

[71] Larry D. Quinn," 'Chink Chink Chinamen': the Beginnings of Nativism in Montana," PACIFIC NORTHWEST QUARTERLY 58 (April, 1967), pp. 82-89.

[72] A circular recruiting labor in Hong Kong for Oregon in 1862 tells part of the story: To the countrymen of Au Chan! There are laborers wanted in the land of Oregon, in the United States, in America. There is much inducement to go to this new country, as they have many great works there which are not in our own country. They will supply good houses and plenty of food. They will pay you $28 a month after your arrival, and treat you considerately when you arrive. There is no fear of slavery. All is nice. The ship is now going and will take all who can pay their passage. The money required is $54. Persons having property can have it sold for them by correspondents, or borrow money of me upon security. I cannot take security on your children or your wife. Come to me in Hongkong and I will take care for you until you start. The ship is substantial and convenient.--(signed) Au Chan
Quoted in Rhoda Hoff, AMERICA'S IMMIGRANTS: ADVENTURES IN EYEWITNESS HISTORY, New York: Henry Z. Walck, 1967, pp. 74-75. For the rise and decline of Chinese miners in Oregon see Rodman W. Paul, MINING FRONTIER...op. cit., p. 149.

[73] Ibid., pp. 143-144.

[74] Rose Hum Lee, THE CHINESE IN THE UNITED STATES OF AMERICA, Hong Kong: Hong Kong University Press, 1960, pp. 189-190.

[75] James M. Hulse, THE NEVADA ADVENTURE: A HISTORY, Reno: University of Nevada Press, 1966, p. 79.

[76] Dan DeQuille (Pseudonym for William Wright), HISTORY OF THE BIG BONANZA: AN AUTHENTIC ACCOUNT OF THE DISCOVERY, HISTORY, AND WORKING OF THE WORLD RENOWNED COMSTOCK SILVER LODE OF NEVADA, San Francisco: Hartford Publishing Co., A.L. Bancroft & Co., 1876. The section on Chinatown is reprinted in Robert Kirsch and William S. Murphy, WEST OF THE WEST: WITNESSES TO THE CALIFORNIA EXPERIENCE, 1542-1906, New York: E.P. Dutton, 1967, pp. 409-411.

[77] THE CHINESE MASSACRE AT ROCK SPRINGS, WYOMING TERRITORY, SEPTEMBER 2, 1885, Boston: Franklin Press, Rand Avery and Co., 1886. For a debate over whether the Chinese "deserved" to be the victims of a riotous lynch mob see A.A. Sargent, "The Wyoming Anti-Chinese Riot'--Another View," OVERLAND MONTHLY, VI (December, 1885), pp. 573-576.

[78] Pierre Lamoureux, "Les Premieres Anees De L'immigration Chinoise au Canada," REVUE CANADIENNE DE GEOGRAPHIE, 9 (January-March, 1955), pp. 9-28.

[79] Ormsby, op. cit., pp. 167, 281.

[80] Ted C. Hinckley, "Prospectors, Profits, and Prejudice," THE AMERICAN WEST, II (Spring, 1965). pp. 58-65.

[81] TOMBSTONE EPITAPH, February 13, 1882. Quoted in Duane A. Smith, ROCKY MOUNTAIN MINING CAMPS: THE URBAN FRONTIER, Bloomington: Indiana University Press, 1967, p. 31.

[82] OWYHEE AVALANCHE, June 23, 1866. Quoted in Smith, op. cit., p. 32.

[83] MOUNTANIAN, March 27, 1873. Quoted in Larry Barsness, GOLD CAMP: ALDER GULCH AND VIRGINIA CITY, MONTANA, New York: Hastings House, 1962, p. 239.

[84] GOVERNOR'S MESSAGE, DELIVERED TO THE TWO HOUSES OF THE MONTANA LEGISLATURE ASSEMBLY AT VIRGINIA CITY, December 11, 1869. Helena, 1869, p. 8. Quoted in Quinn, op. cit., p. 83. Cf. "Special Message from the Governor of California to the Senate and Assembly of California in Relation to Asiatic Emigrations," CALIFORNIA SENATE JOURNAL, THIRD SESSION. April 23, 1852.

[85] Springfield REPUBLICAN, June 7, 1870; Boston TRANSCRIPT, June 13, 1870; Boston COMMONWEALTH, June 25, 1870; Boston INVESTIGATOR, July 6, 1870. See also Frederick Rudolph, "Chinamen in Yankeedom: Anti-Unionism in Massachusetts," AMERICAN HISTORICAL REVIEW, 53 (October, 1947), pp. 1-29.

[86] Albert Rhodes, "The Chinese at Beaver Falls," LIPPINCOTT'S MAGAZINE, 19 (June, 1877), pp. 708-714.

[87] Cincinnati ENQUIRER, January 8, April 11, June 24, 1870; Cleveland LEADER, June 6, 1870; OHIO STATE JOURNAL, November 3, 1873. Quoted in Carl Wittke, WE WHO BUILT AMERICA, New York: Prentice-Hall, 1948, pp. 460-461.

[88] Samuel Gompers, SEVENTY YEARS OF LIFE AND LABOR: AN AUTOBIOGRAPHY, New York: E.P. Dutton, 1925, Vol. I, pp. 216-217, 304-305; Vol. II, pp. 162-169. For Gompers' racism see Herbert Hill, "The Racial Practices of Organized Labor--the Age of Gompers and After," in Arthur Ross and Herbert Hill, (Editors), EMPLOYMENT, RACE, AND POVERTY: A CRITICAL STUDY OF THE DISADVANTAGED STATUS OF NEGRO WORKERS, FROM 1865-1965, New York: Harcourt, Brace, and World, 1967, pp. 365-402.

[89] Selig Perlman, THE HISTORY OF TRADE UNIONISM IN THE UNITED STATES, New York: Augustus Kelley, 1950, p. 52.

[90] See Stanford M. Lyman, "Contrasts in the Community Organization of Chinese and Japanese in North America," CANADIAN REVIEW OF SOCIOLOGY AND ANTHROPOLOGY. 5 (May, 1968), pp. 51-67.

[91] For the Chinese in agriculture see Carey McWilliams, FACTORIES IN THE FIELDS: THE STORY OF MIGRATORY FARM LABOR IN CALIFORNIA, Boston: Little, Brown, 1939, pp. 66-88; McWilliams, SOUTHERN CALIFORNIA COUNTRY: AN ISLAND ON THE LAND, New York: Duell, Sloan, and Pearce, 1946, pp. 84-95; Ping Chiu, CHINESE LABOR IN CALIFORNIA, 1850-1880, Madison: State Historical Society of Wisconsin, 1963, pp. 67-88.

[92] See Rose Hum Lee "The Decline of Chinatowns in the United States," AMERICAN JOURNAL OF SOCIOLOGY, (March, 1949), pp. 422-432.

[93] For the Chinese in railroad work see Alexander Saxton, "The Army of Canton in the High Sierra," PACIFIC HISTORICAL REVIEW XXXV (May, 1966) pp. 141-152. Chinese were also employed in digging the tunnels for California's vineyards; many were killed in tunnel collapses. They also worked as pickers of grapes, strawberries, cotton and other crops, and at a variety of other laboring and menial tasks. See A.W. Loomis, "How Our Chinamen Are Employed," OVERLAND MONTHLY, (March, 1869), pp. 231-240; H.C. Bennett, "The Chinese in California, Their Numbers and Significance," SACRAMENTO DAILY UNION, November 27, 1869, p. 8; Ping Chiu, op. cit., pp. 40-128.

[94] Testimony of the Hon. Frank M. Pixley, REPORT OF THE JOINT SPECIAL COMMITTEE... op. cit., p. 12.

[95] See the table in Coolidge, op. cit., p. 503.

[96] The diaspora of Chinese since the sixteenth century has made Chinatown an ubiquitous phenomenon in countries of Asia, Africa, Europe, and Latin America. For some representative descriptions see Shelland Bradley "Calcutta's Chinatown," CORNHILL MAGAZINE, LVII (September, 1924), pp. 277-285; Tsien Tsche-hao. "La vie sociale des Chinois a Madagascar," COMPARATIVE STUDIES IN SOCIETY AND HISTORY, III (January, 1961), pp. 170-181; A. Dupouy, "Un Camp de Chinois," REVEUE DE PARIS, 25 (November, 1919), pp. 146-162; P. LeMonnyer, "Les Chinois de Paris," L'ILLUSTRATION, 82 (November 1, 1924), pp. 406-407; Christopher Driver, "The Tiger Balm Community," THE GUARDIAN (January 2, 1962); Ng Kwee Choo, THE CHINESE IN LONDON, London: Oxford University Press, 1968; Leonard Broom, "The Social Differentiation of Jamaica," AMERICAN SOCIOLOGICAL REVIEW XIX (April, 1954), pp. 115-124.

[97] See Maurice Freedman, LINEAGE ORGANIZATION IN SOUTHEASTERN CHINA, London: The Athlone Press, 1958 and Freedman, CHINESE LINEAGE AND SOCIETY: FUKIEN AND KWANGTUNG, London: The Athlone Press, 1966.

[98] "Whenever any persons having the same family name intermarry, the parties and the contractor of the marriage shall each receive 60 blows, and the marriage being null and void, the man and woman shall be separated, and the marriage-presents forfeited to government." Sir George Thomas Staunton, TSA TSING LEU LEE: BEING THE FUNDAMENTAL LAWS AND A SELECTION FROM THE SUPPLEMENTARY STATUTES OF THE PENAL CODE OF CHINA... London, 1810, p. 114. Quoted in Freedman, LINEAGE ORGANIZATION...op. cit., p. 4n. Overseas this rule has been relaxed as more and more Chinese-Americans refuse to recognize an incest taboo that runs counter to that of the American kinship system. However, only a decade ago, one Chinese-American college student told me that his mother would be furious if she knew he was dating a girl with his own surname. Clan exogamy has been seen as one of the principal reasons for the decline of small, i.e., four clan, Chinatowns in the United States. Marriageable men migrate to the larger urban Chinese communities to have a greater choice in mate selection. See Rose Hum Lee, "The Decline of Chinatonw..." op. cit.

[99] San Francisco Chinese Chamber of Commerce, SAN FRANCISCO'S CHINATOWN, HISTORY, FUNCTION, AND IMPORTANCE OF SOCIAL ORGANIZATION, San Francisco, 1953, pp. 2-4. Space does not permit a complex discussion of overseas clans. See Stanford M. Lyman, THE STRUCTURE OF CHINESE SOCIETY... op. cit., 164-178 and William Willmott, "Chinese Clan Associations in Vancouver," MAN LXIV (March-April, 1964), pp. 33-37.

[100] See Chinese Chamber of Commerce, op. cit., p. 3. See also the discussion in Rose Hum Lee, THE CHINESE IN THE UNITED STATES OF AMERICA, op. cit., pp. 136-137, 164-165-264.

[101] See Calvin Lee, CHINATOWN, U.S.A.: A HISTORY AND GUIDE, Garden City: Doubleday, 1965, pp. 31-34. For the nature of intra-clan disputes and disharmony see Milton L. Barnett, "Kinship as a Factor Affecting Cantonese Economic Adjustment in the United States," HUMAN ORGANIZATION, 19 (Spring, 1960), pp. 40-46.

[102] The definitive work on the subject is Ping-ti Ho, CHUNG-KUO HUI-KUAN SHIH-LEUH. [An Historical Survey of LANDSMANNSCHAFTEN in China], Taipei: Student Publishing Co., 1966. For brief accounts see Ping-ti Ho, "Salient Aspects of China's Heritage," in Ping-ti Ho and Tang Tsou, (Editors), CHINA IN CRISIS: CHINA'S HERITAGE AND THE COMMUNIST POLITICAL SYSTEM, Chicago: University of Chicago Press, 1968, Vol. I, Book 1, pp. 34-35; and Francis L.K. Hsu, "Chinese Kinship and Chinese Behavior," Ibid., Vol. I, Book 2, pp. 588-589. See also D.J. Macgowan, "Chinese Guilds or Chambers of Commerce and Trades Unions," JOURNAL OF THE ROYAL ASIATIC SOCIETY, NORTH CHINA BRANCH, August 1886, pp. 133-192; and Hosea Ballou Morse, THE GILDS OF CHINA--WITH AN ACCOUNT OF THE GILD MERCHANT OR CO-HONG OF CANTON, Shangha: Kelly and Walsh, 1932.

[103] See A.W. Loomis, "The Six Chinese Companies," OVERLAND MONTHLY, New Series, 2 (September, 1868), pp. 221-227; William Speer, "Democracy of the Chinese,' HARPER'S MONTHLY, XXXVII (November, 1868), pp. 844-846; Richard Hay Drayton, "The Chinese Six Companies," THE CALIFORNIAN ILLUSTRATED MAGAZINE, IV (August, 1893), pp. 472-477; Fong Kum Ngon (Walter N. Fong), "The Chinese Six Companies," OVERLAND MONTHLY, (May 1894), pp. 519-526; Charles Frederick Holder, "The Dragon in America: Being an Account of the Workings of the Chinese Six Companies in America and its Population of the United States with Chinese," THE ARENA, XXXII (August, 1904), pp. 113-122; William Hoy, THE CHINESE SIX COMAPNIES, San Francisco: Chinese Consolidated Benevolent Association, 1942; Tin-Yuke Char, "Immigrant Chinese Societies in Hawaii," SIXTY-FIRST ANNUAL REPORT OF THE HAWAIIAN HISTORICAL SOCIETY, Honolulu: Advertiser Publishing Co., 1953, pp. 29-32; Chu Chai, "Administration of Law Among the Chinese in Chicago," JOURNAL OF CRIMINAL LAW, 22 (March, 1932), pp. 806-818.

[104] See Rose Hum Lee, THE CHINESE IN THE UNITED STATES OF AMERICA, op. cit., pp. 147-161; Calvin Lee, op. cit., pp. 34-35. In Canada a crackdown on illegal immigration from Hong Kong and China led to a highly misleading article attacking the Chinese in racist innuendoes and accusing the Chinese Benevolent Association of complicity on the crimes. See Alan Phillips, "The Criminal Society that Dominates the Chinese in Canada," MACLEAN'S: CANADA'S NATIONAL MAGAZINE, 75 (April 7, 1962), pp. 11, 42-44 and the letter from Stanford Lyman and William Willmott to the Editor in Ibid., 75 (May 19, 1962), p. 6. Recently in San Francisco disaffected immigrant Chinese youth and disenchanted American-born youth have formed separate associations and publicly rebuked the Chinese Six Companies for their insensitivity in Chinatown. See the San Francisco CHRONICLE, March 18, 19, 1968. News of this effort is regularly reported in EAST-WEST, a San Francisco Journal published in Chinatown. For the New York community's social problems, see Stuart H. Cattel, HEALTH, WELFARE, AND SOCIAL ORGANIZATION IN CHINATOWN New York: Community Service Society, 1962, pp. 20-90.

[105] The Six Companies aroused the ire of impoverished Chinese, a few missionaries, and an occasional sea captain for its ruthless and unstinting efforts to collect debts. See Otis Gibson, THE CHINESE IN AMERICA, Cincinnati: Hitchcock and Walden, 1877, pp. 339-344; A.W. Loomis, "The Six Chinese Companies," op. cit., p. 223; Testimony of Thomas H. King, REPORT OF THE JOINT SPECIAL COMMITTEE...op. cit., p. 95. It still collected debts from departing Chinese as late as 1942 and also required those returning to China to pay a departure fee. See Hoy. op. cit., pp. 23-24.

[106] In the following there is only a brief discussion of one of the most fascinating elements of overseas Chinese life. For a more complete discussion see Stanford M. Lyman, "Chinese Secret Societies in the Occident: Notes and Suggestions for Research on the Sociology of Secrecy," CANADIAN REVIEW OF SOCIOLOGY AND ANTHROPOLOGY, I (May, 1964), pp. 79-102.

[107] Thomas Taylor Meadows, op. cit., pp. 112-120. Sun Yat-sen's relations with secret societies is described in S.Y. Teng, "Dr. Sun Yat-sen and Chinese Secret Societies," in Robert Sakai, (Editor), STUDIES ON ASIA, 1963, Lincoln: University of Nebraska Press, 1963, pp. 81-99; Sun Yat Sen, MEMOIRS OF A CHINESE REVOLUTIONARY: A PROGRAMME OF NATIONAL RECONSTRUCTION FOR CHINA, London: Hutchinson & Co., n.d., pp. 184-224. See also James Cantlie and C. Sheridan Jones, SUN YAT SEN AND THE AWAKENING OF CHINA, New York: Fleming H. Revell, 1912, pp. 86-126; Stephen Chen and Robert Payne, SUN YAT-SEN: A PORTRAIT, New York: John Day, 1946, pp. 1-176; Marius B. Jansen, THE JAPANESE AND SUN YAT-SEN, Cambridge: Harvard University Press, 1954, pp. 59-130; Shao Chuan Leng and Norman D. Palmer, SUN YAT-SEN AND COMMUNISM, London: Thames and Hudson, 1962, pp. 1-34; Paul Linebarger, SUN YAT SEN AND THE CHINESE REPUBLIC, New York: Century, 1925, pp. 115-282; Mariano Ponce,

SUN YAT-SEN: THE FOUNDER OF THE REPUBLIC OF CHINA, Manila: Filipino-Chinese Cultural Foundation, 1965; Lyon Sharman, SUN YAT-SEN: HIS LIFE AND ITS MEETING--A CRITICAL BIOGRAPHY, Hamden, Conn.: Archon, 1965, pp. 29, 61-64, 84-86, 97, 109, 113-114; Henry Bond Restarick, SUN YAT SEN: LIBERATOR OF CHINA, New Haven: Yale University Press, 1931, pp. 11-108. Two post-1949 Chinese publications also speak of Dr. Sun's relations with secret societies: DR. SUN YAT-SEN: COMMEMORATIVE ARTICLES AND SPEECHES BY MAO TSE-TUNG, SOONG CHING LINN, CHOU EN-LAI, AND OTHERS, Peking: Foreign Languages Press, 1957, pp. 14-16, 70-72; Wu Yu-chang, THE REVOLUTION OF 1911: A GREAT DEMOCRATIC REVOLUTION OF CHINA, Peking: Foreign Languages Press, 1962, pp. 16-30. For the communist suppression of secret societies see A. Doak Barnett, CHINA ON THE EVE OF COMMUNIST TAKEOVER, New York: Proeger, 1963, pp. 83, 91-92, 126-129; Theodore H.E. Chen, THOUGHT REFORM OF THE CHINESE INTELLECTUALS, Hong Kong: Hong Kong University Press, 1960, pp. 108-111.

[108]In addition to Leon Comber, op. cit., see J.S.M. Ward and W.G. Stirling, THE HUNG SOCIETY OR THE SOCIETY OF HEAVEN AND EARTH, London: Baskerville Press, 1925-6, 3 vols.; Mervyn Llewelyn Wynne, TRIAD AND TABUT: A SURVEY OF THE ORIGIN AND DIFFUSION OF CHINESE AND MOHAMMEDAN SECRET SOCIETIES IN THE MALAY PENINSULA, A.D. 1800-1935, Singapore: Government Printing Office, 1941; J.M. Gullick, THE STORY OF EARLY KUALA LUMPUR, Singapore: Donald Moore, 1956; J.M. Gullick, A HISTORY OF SELANGOR, 1742-1957, Singapore: Eastern Universities Press, 1960, pp. 41-90; Maurice Feedman, "Immigrants and Associations: Chinese in Nineteenth-Century Singapore," COMPARATIVE STUDIES IN SOCIETY AND HISTORY, III (October, 1960), pp. 25-48; Song Ong Siang, ONE HUNDRED YEARS' HISTORY OF THE CHINESE IN SINGAPORE, Singapore: University of Malaya Press, 1967; Chen Mock Hock, THE EARLY CHINESE NEWSPAPERS OF SINGAPORE, 1881-1912, Singapore: University of Malaya Press, 1967, pp. 46-47, 59-60, 82, 95-97, 119, 138-139.

[109]Stanford M. Lyman, W.E. Willmott, and Berching Ho, "Rules of a Chinese Secret Society in British Columbia," BULLETIN OF THE SCHOOL OF ORIENTAL AND AFRICAN STUDIES, XXVII, 3 (1964) pp. 530-539.

[110]See the three essays by Stewart Culin, "Chinese Secret Societies in the United States," JOURNAL OF AMERICAN FOLK-LORE, III (January-March, 1890), pp. 39-43; "The I Hing or 'Patriotic Rising,' A Secret Society Among the Chinese in America," REPORT OF THE PROCEEDINGS OF THE NUMISMATIC AND ANTIQUARIAN SOCIETY OF PHILADELPHIA FOR THE YEARS 1887-1889, November 3, 1887, pp. 51-58; "The Gambling Games of the Chinese in America," PUBLICATIONS OF THE UNIVERSITY OF PENNSYLVANIA. SERIES IN PHILOLOGY, LITERATURE, AND ARCHAEOLOGY, 1:4 (1891), pp. 1-17. For Dr. Sun's skepticism about the Chinese secret societies in America see Sun Yat Sen, op. cit., pp. 190-191, 215; for his skepticism about those in Malaya see Chen Mock Hock, op. cit., pp. 95-97n.

[111]Alexander McLeod, PIGTAILS AND GOLD DUST: A PANORAMA OF CHINESE LIFE IN EARLY CALIFORNIA, Caldwell, Idaho: Caxton, 1947, pp. 149-150; Carl Glick, DOUBLE TEN: CAPTAIN O'BANION'S STORY OF THE CHINESE REVOLUTION, New York: Whittesley House, 1945; Henry Bond Restarick, op. cit., p. 103.

[112]Information on Seto May-tong is from AN APPEAL FOR THE CONTRIBUTION OF ESSAYS CELEBRATING THE EIGHTY-FIRST BIRTHDAY OF MR. SETO MAY-TONG AND FOR MONETARY GIFTS SERVING AS THE FOUNDATION FUND OF THE MAY-TONG MEMORIAL SCHOOL, (1948), a document in Chinese presented to the author by a former member of the CHIH-KUNG T'ANG.

[113]CHUNG-KUO HUNG-MUN MING-TSE TANG DECLARATION, POLITICAL OUTLINE, AND CONSTITUTION, Shanghai, September 1947; THE DECLARATION OF ALLIANCE OF MIDDLE PARTIES, Shanghai and Nanking, February 21, 1948. These documents are in possession of the author.

[114]See Stanford M. Lyman, "Chinese Secret Societies..." op. cit., pp. 99-100.

[115]Calvin Lee, op. cit., pp. 34-37.

[116]Sixteenth Census of the United States, "Characteristics of the Non-white Population by Race," p. 7; "Race by Nativity and Sex for the United States, 1850-1940," p. 19; Seventeenth Census of the United States, "Non-white Population by Race," p. 3B-19. See also Coolidge, op. cit., p. 502.

[117]United States Population Census, 1960, "Non-white Population by Race." FINAL REPORT, PC (2) - 1C. Washington, D.C., 1963, p. 4.

[118]Two settlements of Chinese -- one in Trinidad in 1806-1814, the other in Hawaii in 1852 -- foundered because of the failure of Chinese women to join the men in the overseas venture. See Eric Williams, HISTORY OF THE PEOPLE OF TRINIDAD AND TOBAGO, Port-of-Spain: PNM Publishing Co., 1962, p. 77 and Ralph S. Kuykendall. THE HAWAIIAN KINGDOM: FOUNDATION AND TRANSFORMATION, 1778-1854, Honolulu: University of Hawaii Press, 1957, p. 329.

[119]See Stanford M. Lyman, "Marriage and the Family Among Chinese Immigrants to America, 1850-1960," PHYLON QUARTERLY, 29 (Winter, 1968), pp. 321-330.

[120]Freedman, LINEAGE ORGANIZATION... op. cit., pp. 19-20, 32, 101-105. There was much variation in practice. See Freedman, CHINESE LINEAGE AND SOCIETY... op. cit., pp. 43-67. See also Wen Yen Tsao, "The Chinese Family from Customary Law to Positive Law," HASTINGS LAW JOURNAL, 17 (May, 1966), pp. 727-765.

[121] For a good fictional account see James A. Michener, HAWAII, New York: Random House, 1959, pp. 399-401.

[122] The remittances continued well into the twentieth century and were a principal element of the Republican economy. See Arthur N. Young, CHINA AND THE HELPING HAND, 1937-1945, Cambridge: Harvard University Press, 1963, pp. 79, 178, 262-263. From July, 1937 to December, 1941 the Chinese Overseas Affairs Commission reported receipt of $61,985 from the United States. Chinese Ministry of Information, (compiler), CHINA HANDBOOK, 1937-1943: A COMPREHENSIVE SURVEY OF MAJOR DEVELOPMENTS IN CHINA IN SIX YEARS OF WAR, New York: Macmillan, 1943, p. 37.

[123] See Paul C.P. Siu, op. cit., pp. 35-41. See also Paul C.P. Siu, "The Isolation of the Chinese Laundryman," in Ernest W. Burgess and Donald Bogue, CONTRIBUTIONS TO URBAN SOCIOLOGY, Chicago: University of Chicago Press, 1964, pp. 429-442.

[124] A good example is found in a United States Government report: "The Chinese coolie seldom or never removes his wife or family from his original domicile. They are left to represent his home interest with his ancestral divinities. The women are still less inclined to travel than the men. Without any education or mental development, Chinese females cherish exaggerated terrors of the fierce 'outside barbarians,' and of the tempestuous seas. A number of high class females have arrived in this country, the wives of intelligent merchants and business men, whose belief in the popular creed is not more profound than that which the ancient philosophers cherished for the classic mythology; but of the laboring classes it is believed that not a single instance of this character has yet been reported... It is evident, that with the Chinese female immigration already secured, no permanent family organization can be expected, and that consequently the Chinese race will not be propogated in this country. Their continuance as part of our population is then limited to the natural life of the immigrant." "Chinese Labor in Agriculture," U.S. DEPARTMENT OF AGRICULTURE REPORTS: 1870, pp. 573-574.

[125] CASE OF THE CHINESE WIFE, 21 Fed. 785 (1884); Huang Tsen-ming, op. cit. pp. 84-85.

[126] Timothy J. Molloy, "A Century of Chinese Immigration: A Brief Review," MONTHLY REVIEW OF THE UNITED STATES IMMIGRATION AND NATURALIZATION SERVICE, V (December, 1947), pp. 69-75.

[127] From a silver mining camp in Nevada in 1869 comes a terrible incident: "None were treated as beastly as the Chinese women from the brothels. One prostitute tried to run away from her owner and hide in the hills, but she was finally captured and held prisoner. Living in the open, exposed to the elements during her brief period of freedom, she had frozen both feet. The flesh feel away from the bones before her master asked admission to the hospital for her and then both feet had to be amputated. Although the wounds healed rapidly, the patient courted death, refusing to take medicine or food. She was eventually returned to the home of her owner to pass into oblivion without a protest from society." W. Turrentine Jackson, TREASURE HILL: PORTRAIT OF A SILVER MINING CAMP, Tucson: University of Arizona Press, 1963, p. 65.

[128] Horace Greeley, "California Mines and Mining," Sacramento, August 7, 1859, in Horace Greeley, AN OVERLAND JOURNEY: FROM NEW YORK TO SAN FRANCISCO IN THE SUMMER OF 1859, New York: Knopf, 1964, pp. 245-246 (Edited by Charles T. Duncan).

[129] Henryk Sienkiwicz, PORTRAIT OF AMERICA, New York: Columbia University Press, 1959, p. 255.

[130] A.W. Loomis, "Chinese Women in California," OVERLAND MONTHLY, 3 (April, 1869), pp. 344-351; Charles Frederick Holder, "Chinese Slavery in America," NORTH AMERICAN REVIEW, 165 (July, 1897), pp. 288-294; Louis J. Beck, NEW YORK'S CHINATOWN: AN HISTORICAL PRESENTATION OF ITS PEOPLE AND PLACES, New York: Bohemia Publishing Co., 1898, pp. 107-121; Carol Green Wilson, CHINATOWN QUEST: THE LIFE ADVENTURES OF DONALDINA CAMERON, Stanford: Stanford University Press, 1950.

[131] The situation might have been mitigated if Chinese had been able to intermarry into the white population. In other areas of Chinese settlement, such as Indonesia, Chinese did intermarry. (See Donald Earl Willmott, THE CHINESE OF SEMARANG: A CHANGING MINORITY COMMUNITY IN INDONESIA, Ithaca: Cornell University Press, 1960, pp. 103-116). However, in the United States, racial intermarriage has been illegal in thirty-nine states. In fourteen of these states the law specifically prohibited marriage between Chinese or "Mongolians" and whites. California's anti-miscegenation statute was originally enacted in 1872 to prohibit marriage between Negroes or mulattoes; in 1906 it was amended to prohibit marriages between whites and "Mongolians." See Huang Tsen-ming, op. cit., pp. 260-262; Fowler V. Harper and Jerome Skolnick, PROBLEMS OF THE FAMILY, Indianapolis: Bobbs Merrill, 1962, pp. 96-99; PEREZ VS. SHARP, 32 Cal. 711 (2nd Ser.), 1948; Andrew D. Weinberger, "A Reappraisal of the Constitutionality of 'Miscegenation" Statutes," in Ashley Montagu, MAN'S MOST DANGEROUS MYTH: THE FALLACY OF RACE, Cleveland: Meridian Books, World Publishing Co., 1964, pp. 402-424.

[132] Remigio B. Ronquillo, "The Administration of Law Among the Chinese in Chicago," JOURNAL OF CRIMINAL LAW, 25 (July, 1934), pp. 205-224.

[133] Jacob A. Riis, HOW THE OTHER HALF LIVES: STUDIES AMONG THE TENEMENTS OF NEW YORK, New York: Sagamore Press, 1957, p. 76.

[134] Frank Soule, John H. Gihon, and James Nisbet, THE ANNALS OF SAN FRANCISCO, Palo Alto: Lewis Osborne, 1966, pp. 411-412. (Originally published in 1855).

[135] Samuel Wells Williams, "The City of the Golden Gate," SCRIBNER'S MONTHLY, X (July, 1875), pp. 272-273.

[136] Frank Soule, John H. Gihon, and James Nisbet, op. cit., pp. 378-379.

[137] CALIFORNIA SENATE JOURNAL. THIRD SESSION. 1852. pp. 168, 192, 205, 217.

[138] "Minority Report of the Select Committee on Senate Bill No. 63..." CALIFORNIA SENATE JOURNAL. THIRD SESSION. APPENDIX March 20, 1852, p. 671.

[139] Ping Chiu, op. cit., pp. 89-128.

[140] See James Bryce, "Kearneyism in California," THE AMERICAN COMMONWEALTH, New York: The Macmillan Co., 1901, Vol. II, pp. 425-448, and "Appendix," pp. 878-880. See also Doyce B. Nunis, Jr., "The Demagogue and the Demographer: Correspondence of Denis Kearney and Lord Bryce," PACIFIC HISTORICAL REVIEW XXXVI (August, 1967), pp. 269-288.

[141] See Philip S. Foner, MARK TWAIN: SOCIAL CRITIC, New York: International Publishers, 1958, pp. 182-192.

[142] Morton Keller, THE ART AND POLITICS OF THOMAS NAST, New York: Oxford University Press, 1968, pp. 217-242.

[143] Philip S. Foner, THE LIFE AND WRITINGS OF FREDERICK DOUGLASS, Vol. IV: RECONSTRUCTION AND AFTER, New York: International Publishers, 1955, pp. 46, 222, 262-266, 282, 339, 349, 352, 385, 440.

[144] See Leon Litwack, NORTH OF SLAVERY: THE NEGRO IN THE FREE STATES, 1790-1860, Chicago: University of Chicago Press, 1965, pp. 167-168.

[145] See Forrest G. Wood, BLACK SCARE: THE RACIST RESPONSE TO EMANCIPATION AND RECONSTRUCTION, Berkeley: University of California Press, 1968, pp. 97-101.

[146] Bryce, op. cit., Vol. II, p. 880.

[147] THE WORKINGMEN'S PARTY OF CALIFORNIA, San Francisco: Bacon and Co., 1878. Quoted in N. Ray Gilmore and Gladys Gilmore, (Editors), READINGS IN CALIFORNIA HISTORY, New York: Thomas Y. Crowell, 1966, pp. 200-203.

[148] Testimony of Frank M. Pixley in REPORT OF THE JOINT SPECIAL COMMITTEE... op. cit., p. 22.

[149] Coolidge, op. cit., p. 259.

[150] C.P. Dorland, "Chinese Massacre at Los Angeles in 1871," ANNUAL PUBLICATION OF THE HISTORICAL SOCIETY OF SOUTHERN CALIFORNIA, Los Angeles, 1894, pp. 22-26.

[151] Coolidge, op. cit., p. 265-266; Oscar Lewis, SAN FRANCISCO: MISSION TO METROPOLIS, Berkeley: Howell-North, 1966, pp. 136-139.

[152] Patricia K. Ourada, op. cit.

[153] B.P. Wilcox, "Anti-Chinese Riots in Washington," WASHINGTON HISTORICAL QUARTERLY, 20 (July, 1929), pp. 204-212; Jules Alexander Karlin, "The Anti-Chinese Outbreaks in Seattle, 1885-1886", PACIFIC NORTHWEST QUARTERLY, XXXIX (April, 1948), pp. 103-130; Karlin, "The Anti-Chinese Outbreak in Tacoma, 1885," PACIFIC HISTORICAL REVIEW, 23 (August, 1954), pp. 271-283; Murray Morgan, SKID ROAD: AN INFORMAL PORTRAIT OF SEATTLE, New York: Viking, 1960, pp. 84-102.

[154] Alan Morley, VANCOUVER: FROM MILLTOWN TO METROPOLIS, Vancouver: Mitchell Press, 1961 pp. 121-126.

[155] Eliot Lord, COMSTOCK MINING AND MINERS, Berkeley: Howell-North, 1959, pp. 355-359 (Originally Published in 1883); Coolidge, op. cit., pp. 254-277; Lewis, op. cit., pp. 139-140; Vardis Fisher and Opal Laurel Holmes, GOLD RUSHES AND MINING CAMPS OF THE EARLY AMERICAN WEST, Caldwell, Idaho: Caxton Printers, 1968, pp. 262-265, 272-273.

[156] IN RE TIBURCIO PARROT, 6 Sawyer 349 (1879); IN RE AH CHONG, 6 Sawyer 451 IN RE LEE SING, 43 Fed. 359 (1890).

[157] See SOON HING VS. CROWLEY, 113 U.S. 713 (1880); PEOPLE VS. SOON KUNG, unreported (1874); PEOPLE VS. EX PARTE ASHBURY reported in DAILY ALTA CALIFORNIAN, February 5, 1871; YICK WO VS. HOPKINS 118 U. S. 356 (1885).

[158] Fisher and Holmes, op. cit., pp. 263-264; Rose Hum Lee, THE CHINESE IN THE UNITED STATES OF AMERICA, op. cit., p. 267.

[159] Coolidge, op. cit., pp. 72-73; TAKAHASHI VS. FISH AND GAME COMMISSION OF CALIFORNIA, 334 U.S. 410 (1947).

[160] TERRACE VS. THOMPSON, 263 U.S. 197 (1923); PORTERFIELD VS. WEBB, 263 U.S. 225 (1923); WEBB VS. O'BRIEN, 263 U.S. 313 (1923); FRICK VS. WEBB, 263 U.S. 326 (1923); MOTT VS. CLINE, 200 Cal. 434 (1927); MORRISON VS. CALIFORNIA, 291 U. S. 82 (1934); OYAMA VS. CALIFORNIA, 322 U.S. 633 (1927); SEI FUJI VS. STATE OF CALIFORNIA, 242 P2nd 617 (1952).

[161] See REPORT OF THE IMMIGRATION COMMISSION. IMMIGRANTS IN INDUSTRY. JAPANESE AND OTHER IMMIGRANT RACES IN THE PACIFIC COAST AND ROCKY MOUNTAIN STATES. United States Congress. Senate. 61st Congress, 2nd Session. Senate Document 633, Vol. III, Washington, D.C.: Government Printing Office 1911, pp. 411-413.

[162] THE INVALIDITY OF THE QUEUE ORDINANCE, op. cit., APPENDIX, pp. 15-43; HO AH KOW VS. MATTHEW NUNAN, 5 Sawyer 552 (1879); Sandmeyer, op. cit., pp. 54-55.

[163] PEOPLE VS. HALL, 4 California 399 (1854); SPEER VS. SEE YUP, 13 California 73 (1855); PEOPLE VS. ELYEA, 14 California 144 (1855).

[164] Quoted in William Warren Ferrier, NINETY YEARS OF EDUCATION IN CALIFORNIA, 1846-1936, Berkeley: Sather Gate Book Shop, 1937, p. 98.

[165] Ferrier, op. cit., pp. 98-104. WONG HIN VS. CALLAHAN 119 Fed. 381 (1902).

[166] GONG LUM VS. RICE 275 U.S. 78 (1927).

[167] See, e.g., Cameron H. King Jr., "Asiatic Exclusion," INTERNATIONAL SOCIALIST REVIEW, 8 (May, 1908), pp. 661-669. A few exceptions to the general anti-Chinese sentiment of organized labor were found among the "radicals" who organized the International Workers of the World, the United Mine Workers of British Columbia, and the American Labor Union. The division among labor unions on "The Chinese Question" is documented in Philip S. Foner, HISTORY OF THE LABOR MOVEMENT IN THE UNITED STATES, New York: International Publishers, 1957-1965, Vol. I: FROM COLONIAL TIMES TO THE FOUNDING OF THE AMERICAN REPUBLIC, pp. 425-428, 488-493; Vol. II: FROM THE FOUNDING OF THE AMERICAN FEDERATION OF LABOR TO THE EMERGENCE OF AMERICAN IMPERIALISM, pp. 58-60, 204-205; Vol. III: THE POLICIES AND PRACTICES OF THE AMERICAN FEDERATION OF LABOR, 1900-1909, pp. 274-279, 426-429; Vol. IV: THE INDUSTRIAL WORKERS OF THE WORLD, 1905-1917, pp. 81-82, 123-124.

[168] Robert Seagar II, "Some Denominational Reactions to Chinese Immigration to California," PACIFIC HISTORICAL REVIEW, February, 1959, pp. 49-66.

Filipino Immigration: the Creation of a New Social Problem

VIOLET RABAYA

ACQUISITION

From its inception, relations between the United States and the Philippine Islands have been marked by an aura of uncertainty, deception, and a general character of hypocrisy. This rather stunted relationship was typified most characteristically in the acquisition of the Philippines.

In 1898, the United States was the least known for imperialism and the Philippines was the most known for nationalism. However, at that time, the United States was the only major western power which did not have territorial landholdings in Asia. The Philippines, a possession of Spain, was viewed by many of the imperialists in political power (Roosevelt, Lodge) as a solution to this "problem." Advocates of a takeover of the Philippines pointed out that it would be advantageous to the Filipino people, themselves, to accept American guidance since the United States intended to liberalize them from Spanish rule and, besides, according to President McKinley, there was a moral duty to "educate the Filipinos, and uplift and civilize and Christianize them."[1] Both of these motives were ludicrous in light of the fact that Philippine nationalists were well on their way to fighting off Spanish dominance by themselves and had already been "educated and Christianized" by the Spaniards.

Alternative motives for acquisition were cited by other historians. Quite clearly, the Philippines, being very close to China, could be seen as a potential trading post or three-fourths house to China. "It is possible that the United States had reached its own territorial limits and had an 'energy' which still needed release in more territorial gain; it was possible that the United States was just beginning to realize its own strength (an industrial revolution was occurring in the U.S.); and, it was possible that the United States took over the "white man's burden" since Spain was no longer capable of ruling."[2]

The Spanish-American War was the stepping stone for American naval intrusion into the political affairs of the Philippines. The Filipinos, inspired by the martyrdom of Jose Rizal in 1895 and led by the dynamic nationalist Emilio Aguinaldo, had been engaged in a furious revolution against the Spaniards from 1896-1898. "The last part of the revolution was held under the very eyes and with the help of American officials. It extended throughout the entire Philippines, having rested from Spanish hands practically every foot of Philippine territory except Manila, which was in the hands of the Americans. It set up the first republic in the Far East based on a constitutional government."[3] But, the foothold the Americans had in Manila Bay, due to Admiral Dewey's victory over the Spanish fleet, was to precipitate a series of events which was to result in American annexation of the entire archipelago. The victory unleashed an "imperialistic enthusiasm generated within patriotic circles in America ...who saw in the situation the hand of God beckoning America to glorious 'manifest destiny'."[4]

Before the treaty between the United States and Spain was signed, ceding the Philippines to America, a "coup" by the Americans took place. Aguinaldo, who had always been suspicious of the Americans,

---

Reprinted by permission of the author. Miss Rabaya is a recent graduate of UCLA in history and intends to enter law school.

had agreed to join forces with Dewey to capture the Manila fortress. The victory in Manila came a few hours before Washington had signed the peace protocol with Spain. "Aguinaldo said that Dewey promised him independence, but the Admiral denied this allegation."[5] At this point, Aguinaldo and his nationals resumed the revolution, but this time it was directed against the Americans. The end of the republic so heartily fought for by the Filipinos was thus brought about by American intervention. "It was, naturally, a one-sided struggle which showed the firmness and desire of the Filipino people for an independent existence."[6] To say that America was responsible for finally liberating the Philippines, even politically, in 1946 was, indeed, a misconception.

THE "INTRUSION"

Filipino immigration to the United States did not begin until after the military occupation by the United States Government in the Philippines was ended in 1901. The peoples of the United States up until 1907 were not yet consciously aware of another oriental group which would, like the Japanese and Chinese before them, soon stir national concern. Before the end of the third decade of the century, much sentiment, predominantly begun by agitations on the West Coast, arose under the familiar face of "exclusion," a movement built around the irony that the Filipinos had never really wanted anything to do with America. Filipino immigration to the United States was to become a creation of still another "social problem" on the American soil.

The first Filipinos to come to the United States came virtually unnoticed. When Hawaii was annexed to the United States in 1898, the same year the Philippines came under U.S. sovereignty, the orientals in the territory numbered nearly 31,000[7] with 25,654 Japanese and 5,969 Chinese, mostly employed in the famed Hawaiian sugar plantations. The Chinese Exclusion Law, which took effect in 1900, had very little effect on the labor situation there due to their small numbers; but the Gentleman's Agreement in 1907, excluding Japanese, caused a drastic upheaval in the labor forces. The Hawaiian sugar planters were forced to find another source of cheap labor. Since the Gentleman's Agreement with Japan, the only two large potential reservoirs of labor were Puerto Rico and the Philippines. Due to occupation and control by America, these two countries seemed naturally free from the danger of being abruptly closed by restrictive immigration legislation. The Puerto Ricans were first introduced in 1901, but did not reach major proportions until 1922. The Filipinos, given a try in 1907, then became the most available of all potential labor supplies. Filipino immigration, thus may be said to have begun by the insertion of about 160 laborers into the Hawaiian labor syndrome in 1906-7 by the sugar planters. In view of the recruitment practices of Hawaiian labor, the subsequent so-called "Filipino invasion" clearly was not precipitated by the Filipinos, but instead by the labor entrepreneurs in Hawaii, a largely white bureaucracy.

Between the years of 1907-1919, the loss of Filipinos from Hawaii to the continental United States was negligible--only 2,000 of the 25,000 Filipinos in Hawaii went over to the mainland. And, according to the 1920 census, only 5,603 Filipinos were residing in the United States coming from anywhere (that is, Hawaii, the Philippines, and other oriental ports, principally Hong Kong and Shanghai in China and Kobe and Yokohama in Japan). Therefore, the problems of mass immigration were not yet alarming to the whites in the United States. Most of the Filipinos, of the little that there were, came as students hoping to complete a professional education and possibly return to the Philippines. Many of them had government fellowships, called pensionados, and had expectations of going into government service. Naturally, these initial immigrants were the products of the more wealthy sector of the Philippines and their status was looked upon favorably since they were seen in the educational echelons of this society. They were described as neat, amiable, well-dressed, articulate and well-mannered. This image, of course, was to change within the coming decade. It seems that as more Filipinos came, the less favorable their image became. The larger numbers, if they can be called that (there were twice as many Japanese on the continent), began to erase the initial impression of the Filipinos, and they were soon to be regarded as social derelicts, another "yellow peril."

Beginning around 1920, stimulated by Japanese labor strikes and a labor shortage in California in 1924, the Hawaiian labor force was heavily drawn upon. Also, a large plantation strike in 1924 drew Filipinos to Hawaii, and in turn, to the continental United States. Then, too, by 1927, Filipino labor organizations stimulated the move to the mainland. And, although the Filipino population in Hawaii by 1930 was still larger than the estimated 56,000 in the United States at that time, Americans began to panic.

Outside Hawaii there were other causes of the Filipino influx to America. At the end of World War I Filipino recruits in the United States navy who had enlisted in Manila secured discharges in continental ports. These men took occupations in the mercantile marine, so that by 1930, an estimated 25,000[8] of the nearly 60,000 Filipinos in the United States were Navy enlistees. By request, these Filipinos largely concentrated on the West Coast, prompted by American propaganda claiming San Francisco's Golden Gate as "the gateway to liberty and opportunity in America." This new Filipino man-type, the hard-working laborer, was to occasion a "threat" to the working classes in the United States. With Filipinos landing in harbors on the West Coast, it was quite natural that anti-Filipino stirrings and proposals for exclusion were heard there, first, especially in the State of California.

A PECULIAR PROBLEM

The Filipino immigration problem was a peculiar one. There was a major difference in the immigration of the Filipino to the United States when compared to Chinese and Japanese immigration. While the Immigration Act of 1924 definitely and specifically excluded the Chinese and Japanese, because of their ineligibility of citizenship, Filipinos were neither considered aliens nor citizens. They were "subjects" of the United States Government and could therefore permeate the American frontier unchecked. Furthermore, by a Legislative Act of 1925, Filipinos were deemed ineligible for citizenship unless they served three years in the American Navy.

Meanwhile, there was a massive revival movement in the Philippines, a highly regarded possession of the United States, for national independence. The Americans had taught their lessons of "equality and freedom" too well, and nationalists were violently urging independence. All men, according to the American lifestyle, were "endowed by their Creator with certain <u>inalienable</u> rights..." --- the idea of exclusion was a virtual bonfire. Already, the United States had damaged its relations with the Orient with the exclusion of the Japanese and Chinese. The exclusion of the Filipino could be seen as a final breaking point with the Far East, the catalyst which could ignite an explosion for complete severance with the Orient. Thus, the United States was faced with a multiple situation: diplomatic relations with the Far East, a re-ferment of nationalism in the Philippines itself, and a major U. S. economic loss in the Philippines, if it were, indeed, lost. These warnings for American composure, however, did not stop agitating forces demanding exclusion in California and the West Coast. The West's loud cry for exclusion was to be heard nationwide.

In 1923, 2,426 Filipinos were admitted to California and the "Filipino invasion" was said to have begun. Over half or 56% of these immigrants came from Hawaii; and 35% from the Philippines.[9] By 1929, the proportion of Filipinos from Hawaii evened with those from the Philippines at about 45%. These new arrivals were no longer predominantly of the student class, but were instead ambitious laborers seeking the "American dream." They became, according to a California report, an "unjust and unfair competition to American labor, nullifying the beneficial results to be expected from a national policy of restrictive immigration."[10]

This same report revealed that the Filipinos were largely a male immigrant group (14 to 1 ratio); preponderantly young (under the age of thirty); and largely unmarried (77.3%). Due to their mobility they were labelled a threat to the California and West Coast working class. Their maleness, youth and singularity were named as causes for concern. However, as has been mentioned before, it was a Supreme Court decision that specified that only those serving three years in the navy were eligible for citizenship. Women, quite naturally, could not serve in the Navy and were not inticed to come. Also, it was the desire and recruiting practices of the Americans which naturally demanded young, single males to do their plantation and agricultural labor. Bearing this in mind, it could hardly be faulted to the Filipino that he immigrated to the United States as such.

As has been mentioned, the Filipinos, like the Japanese, were largely used in agriculture employed as "stoop" laborers, especially in asparagus and lettuce. Because of their small stature they were highly adaptable to picking berries, tomatoes, grapes, lettuce, etc. They were also seen employed as houseboys, cooks, dishwashers, waiters, busboys, janitors, bell boys, and in other general domestic occupations. But it was their role in the agricultural climate of California and the West that was cited as reason for immediate concern.

Many employers preferred Filipino workers to whites because they were more dependable and more "tractable." That is, "they were willing to put up with longer hours, poorer board, and worse lodging conditions; white workers may feel restive and disgruntled because of bad working conditions. The Filipino newcomer is satisfied with staying on the job without kicking."[11] The reliability of this description of the Filipino immigrant is, however, highly debatable, since it was apparent that the Filipinos, like many other minority groups, were offered nothing more than those conditions. It was not by choice that the Filipinos lived in nearly sub-human accommodations. That they were satisfied with such treatment is untrue. Filipinos protested these conditions many a time with organized strikes. "The Filipino is a real fighter and his strikes have been dangerous. In August 1934, about 3,000 Filipinos went on strike in the valuable lettuce fields near Salinas, California. On September 3 a union of white workers employed in the packing sheds returned to work under an agreement to arbitrate. In fact, they were told to return to work by Joseph Casey, AFL official. But the Filipino field workers refused to call off the strike."[12]

The Filipinos implicated that only by insisting on traditional wages could they escape the violent opposition to their presence on the part of the white workers. Possibly, because they had very little control as a truly intimidating labor force against the white plantation overlords and farm owners, they made the impression of being satisfied in their roles as "cheap labor." However, this was hardly the case.

It was true that in 1930 America was in the midst of an overwhelming economic depression. Therefore, it would seem natural that the sentiment for immigration restriction was sincerely activated because of a fear of economic instability among the Americans themselves. Jobs could be taken by invading foreigners which would normally be allotted to the predominantly Caucasian citizens of the United States. The fear of hordes of foreigners taking over potential job holdings was, on the surface, a real threat. Yet, it must be noted that the depression this country was experiencing was largely an industrial one. Surely, it would be naive to suggest that agriculture is not affected by industry, but it would be equally naive to suggest that the Filipinos actually replaced the white workers in agriculture. Most agricultural jobs in California have been, and still are, performed by minority labor, whether it be Mexican, Japanese, Chinese, Black or Filipino. White agricultural laborers are not the heart of agricultural production--white owners, not laborers, are the rule. This may be the reason why agricultural laborers today are experiencing difficulty in unionizing--organized labor may be reluctant to create a cohesive coalition of non-white workers.

In 1930, the daily wage of the Filipino laborers in agriculture was about $2.50 per day or $1.00 per 100 pounds of asparagus cut.[13] These wages, understandably, were lower than the normal wages expected by the whites employed in the fields. Quite logically, it was beneficial to the farmer to employ those accepting lower wages. So, even in the eyes of the depression, it can be argued that the inclusion of Filipinos in agriculture actually aided those Americans who were citizens.

There were numerous groups on the West Coast yearning to keep the area white, and especially so because of the social unrest caused by the Depression. One of the loudest spokesmen for exclusion during this time was the American Federation of Labor, who along with the California Federation of Labor, distributed the bulk of the literature for exclusion. Labor sought to warn the people of the disadvantage of the Filipino presence and tried to do so with a multitude of irrational proposals. After suggesting that the Filipino was incapable of organization into a union group (already shown to be untrue in this paper), they made claims that the Filipino perpetuated an outdated system, the latifundia system, in California agriculture.[14] Yet, according to Harold Fisher, California labor was a system which had always relied on contract labor for survival since it is an "unstructured market."[15] Filipino labor contractors who acted as go-betweens between the farmer and the laborer did not create any such system of agriculture, they merely fit into an already established agricultural market. And even if they are accused of fostering this so-called "feudal system," it can also be asserted that the Filipino represented, possibly, the only skilled labor force in all of agriculture (as they were used exclusively in asparagus and lettuce) and therefore could be accredited as a stabilizing force in the agricultural structure.

Still, the Filipino was treated as an unwanted element in agriculture. With his lower wages the Filipino facilitated higher profits for the growers and subsequently, these profits would become reflected in the sale price of products to the American public. Thus, the argument that the Filipino threatened the American labor force, especially during such a time as the depression, is largely without merit. The "cheap labor" argument was a flimsy one. Whites had always been unwilling, even before minority labor, to do menial tasks, whether it be in the fields or in domestic labor. If there had not been non-white labor to perform these tasks, they possibly would not have been done at all.

And, while it is still feasible to claim that under such an economic strain as was being experienced under the depression, lower class white workers were put out of jobs, it lies not within the character of the Filipino but within the character of the white owners that such "injustices" occurred. Surely, the Filipino would rather have worked side by side with the whites and received the same wages. Blame, then, if anyone is pointing a finger, should not be leveled at the Filipino. The "unfair and unjust" labor practices were the practices of the white owner, not the Filipino laborer.

RACIAL CONFLICT

A more plausible reason for agitation against the Filipino, as in the case of the Chinese and Japanese, was a racial one. "The Filipinos have attracted considerable attention because of their social adjustments---the principle objection to the Filipino arises from the fact that they cross the race line in their relations with white women. They are found to be frequenters of Chinese gambling establishments and police officials regard them as potential criminals."[16] It was also said that they differed from most immigrant groups in the United States in matters of isolation and social aggressiveness. The Filipinos came to the United States with a feeling of belonging, due to their long occupation by U.S. forces and expected to be treated as equals. "Associations, however, in many cases are possible only with other strangers in the United States and with Americans who are also unadjusted."[17] Clearly, it was the Filipino color, like the Japanese and Chinese, which prevented assimilation into white society, not their threat as a labor force replacing whites. Yet, even while the racial case against the Filipino was evident, white Americans found ways of blaming the Filipino---they were "problems to themselves in a cultural organization where they do not have complete acceptance."[18]

According to Bruno Lasker who was assigned to look into Filipino immigration during the turmoil caused by the West Coast, the demand for exclusion of the Filipino was a part of a larger movement to restrict immigration to prevent the further infiltration of non-Caucasian races into the mainstream of the population of the United States. In fact, it was made very plain that organizers for exclusion were acting on a racist basis with the statement by the secretary of the California Joint Immigration Committee, V. S. McClatchy, who pushed a program aiming at "restriction of immigration into the United States whereby racial and political solidarity may be accomplished with the least delay."[19] The statements claiming that Filipinos were culturally unassimilable was made as vehemently concerning the Filipino as it was made concerning the Japanese and Chinese. To quote Mr. McClatchy once more,[20]

"There is a basic racial or biological difference which does not permit assimilation or absorption of one race by the other, and therefore the presence in either country of large groups of the other race must create friction and possible international difficulty. The fault in such cases lies with neither race. The usual dislike of one race for another, frequently assumed to be purely a matter of prejudice, is perhaps really a wise provision of nature, acting as a safeguard against miscegenation.

The coalition for exclusion apparently needed to rationalize its racist views.

Notably, then, outbreaks against the Filipino were prompted by racial conflict. In Exeter, California, in October of 1929, itinerant white American workers started a riot. Three hundred of them bandied together and went to a small Filipino ranch demanding their dismissal. Failing to do this, they smashed automobiles and damaged property. Of course, officers of the State Industrial Commission investigated and reported that it was only the Filipino's presence in taking away potential white jobs that produced the riot, not the presence of any racial undertones. However, a conflicting report states that, at a carnival, whites were throwing missiles at the Filipinos, especially those in company with white women. One Filipino, after being harrassed for that reason, stabbed a white man with a bolo knife. The riot then ensued.

In Watsonville, California, anti-Filipino riots reached even larger proportions.[21] In January, 1930, three months following the Exeter riot, a Filipino lettuce picker was found dead in his bunk with a bullet through his heart. Other Filipinos were badly beaten and attacked by white mobs. The fracas lasted for days. And, the immediate cause of the riot was not Filipino employment in the fields, but the employment by Filipinos of white female entertainment at the Palm Beach Club in Watsonville. Before the riot, a proclamation issued by the Chamber of Commerce of Northern Monterey County, at Pajaro, California, passed the following resolution:[22]

Whereas any foreign peoples coming to the U.S.A. who, by their customs, habits and standards of living prohibit them from assimilating with and adopting our standard of living are detrimental and dangerous to our social conditions; and

Whereas the unrestricted immigration into the State of California of natives of the Philippine Islands is viewed with alarm from both a moral and sanitary standpoint while constituting a menace to white labor: Therefore be it

Resolved, That we, the Chamber of Commerce of Northern Monterey County in regular session, do petition the county, State, and National Governments to adopt such methods and means to prevent further immigration.

The Filipinos, however, did not sit back and take the insult. They responded three days later with a resolution of their own, passed at the Monterey Bay Filipino Club:[23]

Whereas the Northern Monterey Chamber of Commerce adopted a resolution designating Filipinos in this district as undesirables and possessing unhealthy habits and destructive to the living wage scale of other nationalities in agriculture and industrial pursuits; and

Whereas that, in the opinion of the honorable Judge D. W. Rohrback after his comprehensive study as he claims it, denounces the presence of Filipinos in the State of California as a detriment to the attainment of a higher standard of man and womanhood; and

Whereas in this interview he baptizes in his own way the Filipinos coming to this country as little brown men attired like Solomon in all his glory; strutting like peacocks and endeavoring to attract the eyes of young American and Mexican girls, but 10 years removed from the bolo and breachcloth; and

Whereas that in the language of the honorable Judge Rohrback the Filipinos are unsanitary in their living habits and disease carriers of meningitis spreading germs, and that 15 of them will live in one or two rooms and contenting themselves with squatting on the floors and eating rice and fish; and

Whereas that the judge's malicious and very sweeping statements made to the press have deeply wounded the high sense of Filipino self-respect; such criticisms phrased in a gross and insulting language being false, unjust and personal in nature; without the least sense of propriety and consideration to those born of the same flesh and blood as he is; and the judge has even gone beyond his limit by taking the chance of utilizing the present state of affairs as a solution to the Philippine Independence question, which notion could never be thought by an American statesman: Now, therefore, be it

Resolved, That the Filipinos in this section of California present a solid front for a most vigorous protest against the resolution adopted by the above-mentioned chamber and be demonstrated in a form of this kind so as to show the Northern Monterey Chamber of Commerce and the honorable judge, author of the said resolution, that the Filipinos have self-respect and also are endowed with the same human attributes enjoyed by other people; and be it

Resolved, That our home government, through the Philippine Legislature, including the Resident Commissioners at Washington, D. C., they be, and are hereby, urged and requested to use all just and honorable means by appropriate legislative measures for the preservation of mutual trust and confidence of the peoples concerned; and be it further

Resolved, That duly authenticated copies of this resolution be transmitted to the Philippine Legislature and Resident Commissioners, respectively, for a just and equitable remedy.

The Filipinos were completely aware that they were victims of prejudice. Reaching back into the heart of America's foothold in the Philippines, an irate Filipino asked, "Is it because the Filipinos have no Japanese Emperor, Chinese President, Mexican President, or a Mussolini behind them?" that they are so abused. The message being quite clear, then, legislation for exclusion introduced in 1929 and 1930 did not pass. Filipinos were not to be officially excluded as an immigrant group. Government officials were wary of the consequences of exclusion, knowing that the claims by Californians and other West Coast peoples were not really based on labor competition. The U.S. Government chose to leave Filipino Immigration alone. Ironically, so as to keep their slates clean, labor groups and racist organizations sought passage of the Filipino Independence Act claiming that Filipino leaders advocated passage of the bill, which indeed they did. The bill for independence was recognized by Congress in 1935. "Under the Philippine Independence Act, an immigration quota of 50 a year was fixed for the Filipino, which, of course, was tantamount to exclusion."[24]

With exclusion virtually accomplished by the Independence Act, leaders of anti-Filipino agitation sought further extraction of Filipinos from the American soil. "On July 11, 1935, President Roosevelt signed a measure which they had sponsored, known as The Repatriation Act. Under this act the government undertook to pay the transportation expenses of Filipinos who desired to return to the Philippines, but the act contained the provision that those who returned could not later re-enter the United States."[25] Exclusionists wanted to bolt the door on Filipino immigration. However, only about 2,000 Filipinos took the option. Emory Bogardus explained that the sense of pride of the Filipino coupled with resentment (since they felt it was a final scheme to get rid of them) prevented him from accepting "free exile." In the meantime, while exclusionists groups were busy celebrating their victory, the Filipinos already here contemplated their exclusion as a resident group in a hostile and predominantly white society.

A WAVERING SOCIAL POSITION

With no official proclamation against them by the United States Government, Filipinos were left in an unstable situation within the American society. It could be suggested that since no official exclusion bill was passed against Filipino Immigration, the Filipino experienced an even greater problem of assimilation than other oriental groups. In the first place, the Filipino inherited already organized attitudes against the oriental when he arrived on the American soil. The Pacific Coast was the major area which instigated racial discrimination against the oriental, and accordingly, the Filipino went face down in dirt as soon as he arrived. To add to his woes, the Filipino was not even allowed the solidarity that racial identity can bring in such a situation. The Filipino was not easily recognized. He was classified unwittingly as merely a Mongoloid or "type of oriental." The national pride he brought with him was obliterated by this lack of social identity. "The racial affiliation of the Filipinos has been a debatable question ever since their first entrance to the U.S."[26] This question actually became a Superior Court issue at Los Angeles in February, 1930. At that time, Dr. Fay-Cooper Cole, a noted anthropologist, described the Filipinos in the following manner:[27]

> The Filipinos are Malays, who in turn are Southern Mongoloids and may be spoken of as Orientals. To be specific, it appears that the Malay is an ancient mixture made up of a small fraction of aboriginal pygmy blacks, and a rather strong sprinkling of early Caucasoid, but all predominantly Southern Mongoloid. Racially they are close to the Southern Chinese and the bulk of the Japanese population.

In an atmosphere hostile to orientals in general, the Filipinos, being young and male and largely without a family unit, found themselves as social outcasts. They wanted to be Americans, but could not be; they knew themselves as a race of Filipinos, but could not retain such an identity. Turning to the Japanese and Chinese for strength, there, too, they were oftentimes met with hostility. Because the Japanese and Chinese were more economically settled and socially established on the West Coast, they tended to frown upon the Filipino since he occupied the least desirable occupations and living quarters in the community. Certainly, this snubbing by other orientals was not always the case, but cases of non-acceptance were not merely examples of a few isolated cases. It is still occurring today. In relation to this problem, it is apparent that competition for jobs among orientals resulted in such hostility among them. Where the status of the resident oriental was established, the disposition toward the newcomer Filipino was good. But a sense of antagonism was displayed "where they (the orientals) are more directly in competition, and also at times where their own prestige, as Orientals, seems to be impaired by the incoming numbers of other 'Orientals' with lower social status."[28]

The Filipino was a man "without a country." He was severely discriminated against by the whites; he was forced to live in the "oriental ghetto" and, yet, he was not always accepted by the other orientals who were there with him. Surely much of this ambivalence in social identity was prompted by the ignorance of the Americans, themselves, for not being able to classify and recognize the Filipino. And, even while it would have been more desirable that he not be classified by his race and simply accepted into the mainstream of society, this did not occur. "If I were alone in such an experience it wouldn't be important. But I am one of many thousands of young men, born under the American flag, raised as loyal idealistic Americans under your promises of equality for all, and enticed by glowing tales of educational opportunity. Once here we are met by exploiters, shunted into slums, greeted by only gamblers and prostitutes, taught only the worst of your civilization.. and here I am lost in a jungle of dish-washing jobs and racial dislikes and economic discrimination. America came to us with bright-winged promises of liberty, equality, fraternity. What has become of them?"[29]

The only refuge for the Filipino was to cling to his oriental identity. Here, too, he was met unwillingly. "As an Oriental people, geographically and racially close to the great cultures of the East, yet Westernized to a large degree through familiarity with Western language, law, custom, religion, the Filipinos were the hybrid orphans of the Far East."[30] Therefore, it is understandable, though lamentable, that many Filipinos rejected their identity, much like the Blacks had done before them, in order to find a place within the society. Battered back and forth with diplomatic, then racial, discourse during the period between their first arrival in the United States and final independence of the Philippines in 1946, the scars left by such a long period of misjudgment and maladjustment were too deep to be erased. George Taylor described the situation in this manner:[31]

> That it is difficult for the small number of Americans who cannot get rid of the "little brown brother" attitude, or for the few Filipinos who continue to behave as colonials, is not important. The main fact is that in order to formulate an effective policy for the Philippines we shall certainly have to understand the charac-

ter and ideological content of Filipino nationalism. For fifty years the United States imposed upon the Filipino people its own concept of what a nation should be, and large elements in this concept have been accepted. But today the Filipinos themselves are deciding who they are and where they are going, and it is with this issue that they are more engaged. It is the theme of much of their art and literature, of their religious life, and of all discussions of educational policy, domestic politics, and foreign relations. It nags at the Filipino in his endless conflicts over the national language, and it confronts him at every national election; it haunts him, especially in Asia, when he travels abroad. The search for national identity is the basic problem of the Filipino.

This description of the problems which the newly liberated Islands experienced in 1946 is the same problem the immigrant faced in the United States.
In recent interviews with Filipinos, the problem of unity and identity among Filipino-Americans is evident. T. A. Mendoza, the current national president of the Filipino American Political Association which has been instrumental in politically influencing legislation to aid Filipinos, discussed this situation:[32]
Though the general consensus shows good feelings toward Americans, many people are disappointed, especially those in higher professional levels, since discrimination still exists. Doctors, dentists, lawyers, optometrists, find it hard to procure jobs even when they are highly qualified. They are told to return to college. But two and a half years ago, FAPA pushed a bill in the California State Assembly which required that dentists only pass a dental examination to be eligible to practice. Before that they had to go through college courses again, which was merely a duplication of work already completed in the Philippines. Pending is a bill, also pushed by FAPA, to give Filipino optometrists the same option.
You should notice that all features in American government which have promoted a more liberal attitude toward the Filipino have been prompted by Filipino action before the Americans reacted. Yet, even with this demonstration of unity, there is still a feeling among the young of 1) shame attached to Filipino heritage, 2) a desire to completely break away from any "old-timer" Filipino identity, and 3) a yearning to be totally assimilated as Americans. While many youths sooner or later return to their rich heritage and cultural traditions, due to what I consider an inborn trait to get back "home," I feel that much needs to be done to erase the feelings of embarrassment associated with being a Filipino, so that a positive image of Filipino-Americans can be created. FAPA hopes to create some solutions to Filipino problems of this sort.

Fernando Agbulas, 38, who arrived in the United States just last year, believes that young Filipinos are no longer brainwashed by American superiority. However, he feels that this new outlook has not changed or helped Filipinos in America to a very large degree. "Discrimination is still present. I worked in show business for 8 years in Manila as a television technician, but I couldn't get a job here because of my color. I wouldn't be working for a travel agency (which is operated by Filipinos) now if things were right. I had much higher hopes and my reaction to America is anger."[33]

Tony Jaramillo, now 28, came to America at the age of 15, and is a prime example of both Philippine and American background. He described his experiences in this way:[34]
When I went to high school here I was left out because I couldn't speak English well. I found out that because of my being Filipino I was unwanted. Everybody hated Filipinos, even the Filipinos, sometimes. Half-breeds usually went toward their other half and denied any Filipino heritage.
Today the old and new Filipinos in America are forced to accept lower jobs. When some of the professionals do manage to get employment in their fields they are paid a lower wage than the white professionals. Most of them don't really get visibly upset because they really don't know their rights and they feel they have to act like good boys or it's back to the Philippines. The most common way Filipinos are kept out of jobs is made possible by employers asking them if they have any local experience. Of course, they don't so they are turned away and have to seek employment elsewhere. I think there is a lack of unity among Filipino-Amer-

icans partly because of jealousy when somebody makes it, but mostly because Filipinos were never really given their independence. They don't know which way to turn. Half of them are pro-American and half of them dislike America, but it would be no consolation to go home because the Americans still economically rule the Islands. American presence and a feeling of inferiority haunt them wherever they choose to turn.

The opinions of these three Filipinos who represent nearly every type of Filipino who has come to America certainly illustrates the problem Filipinos have encountered on this soil. However, the most revealing interview concerning Filipino identity and the Filipino's place in American society came from Linda Escalona, 21 a Filipino-American born in the United States. Miss Escalona revealed:[35]

> Most of the Filipinos we knew were farm workers or busboys who didn't have much of a future. No Filipino teachers taught me and when they did come around it was a big thing. This is partly the reason I grew up looking down on the Filipino. On forms where it asked for my father's occupation I was hesitant. My father ran a bar in Chinatown, which is Delano's oriental ghetto, and this is where the Filipinos congregated. Mostly oldtimers went to this bar. I never wanted to identify with this image of my father. Education was another reason I belittled my own people. I was brainwashed into thinking Filipinos were lower. I actually used to wish I was white. I would never go outside in the sun because I was paranoid about getting any browner than I already was. Besides that, all the boys, at least the popular ones at school, were white, and they would never date you if you acted Filipino. It was simple. If you didn't at least pretend you were a white American, you were totally outcast. So, you just tried to forget that you were Filipino.
> I first felt real discrimination when I went to meet my boyfriend's white middle-class parents. He made me wait in the car, and his parents told him they didn't want me to set foot in their house. This was the first time I was really hurt because of race.
> All of these things have caused an identity crisis for me. I'm sort of getting over it, but I still have things in the back of my mind which tell me "wouldn't it be better if I were white?"

With the years of discrimination behind him and still in front of him by whites and other orientals alike, the Filipino today is left as a double social outcast. His immigration to the United States was not as beneficial as he had hoped. Sometimes he was highly educated, but he worked as a busboy. Sometimes he chose to procure an American education, but he was forced to work in the fields. And always, he was regarded as an "undesirable." While fighting for acceptance on two levels, the oriental one and the American one, he has lost his grip with his own land, the Philippines. According to an American writer, Erich H. Jacoby,[36]

> For the spiritual development of the Filipinos, however, American influence and education became of decisive importance. The American creed of equality and liberty, and the confidence in progress and in a high standard of living for everybody, have changed the Filipino. He feels different from his ancestors and has accepted Western ideology and ways of thinking, not as an additional attribute, but almost an inherited right. This process of mental assimilation cannot be emphasized too strongly. It explains the vigorous resistance of the Filipino peasants against the Japanese invaders and their "Asia for the Asiatics" program.

The Filipino has revolted against his own kind.

The Filipino's fight for a stable social position has thus taken on various forms. The notable lack of unity among the Filipino-Americans as evidenced in the interviews, has resulted in many different types of Filipino-Americans. He may appear as an American to the core; he may appear as an Oriental for Asia; or, simply as a Philippine nationalist. Then, too, he may a appear as one who is searching for a social position which can link all of these identities in the American society.

In summary, Filipino immigration, as peculiar a problem as it was in the beginning, has created an even more peculiar problem today. The problems American immigration officials had to contend with during the immigration melee of 1930 have taken its toll on the Filipino-American. It is the Filipino who has severed his contacts with the Far East; it is the Filipino who has lost his independence; and, it is the Filipino who has remained a "subject" of the United States. Perhaps, then, official exclusion of the Filipino would have been a lesser evil than the total "social exclusion" he is experiencing in America today.

---

[1] G. Kirk, PHILIPPINE INDEPENDENCE, p. 17.

[2] Dr. SarDesai, University of California, Los Angeles, lecture notes (History of Southeast Asia).

[3] FILIPINO APPEAL FOR FREEDOM, p. 11.

[4] J. Cady, SOUTHEAST ASIA: ITS HISTORICAL DEVELOPMENT, p. 466.

[5] L. Mills, NEW WORLD OF SOUTHEAST ASIA, p. 89.

[6] APPEAL FOR FREEDOM, p. 12.

[7] FILIPINO IMMIGRATION, p. 29.

[8] Statement of Brigadier General F. Le J. Parker, Chief of the Bureau of Insular Affairs, before the House Committee on Immigration and Naturalization, Hearings on H.R. 8708, April 11, 1930, p. 88.

[9] FACTS ABOUT FILIPINO IMMIGRATION TO CALIFORNIA, p. 1.

[10] FILIPINO IMMIGRATION, p. 34.

[11] FACTS, p. 2.

[12] C. McWilliams, "Exit the Filipino," NATION. September, 1935, p. 265.

[13] FACTS, p. 4.

[14] D.J. Pivar, "American Federation of Labor and Filipino Exclusion, 1927-1935." INSTITUTE OF ASIAN STUDIES OCCASIONAL PAPERS, p. 35.

[15] H. Fisher, HARVEST LABOR MARKET IN CALIFORNIA, p. 7.

[16] Guy Brown. IMMIGRATION, p. 169.

[17] Ibid., p. 170.

[18] FILIPINO IMMIGRATION, p. 10.

[19] Ibid., p. 34.

[20] Ibid., p. 36.

[21] "Anti-Filipino Race Riots", a special report made to the Ingram Institute of Social Science of San Diego, by E.S. Bogardus, U.S.C., May, 1930.

[22] FACTS, p. 48.

[23] Ibid., p. 51.

[24] C. McWilliams, BROTHERS UNDER THE SKIN, p. 244.

[25] Ibid., p. 244.

[26] G. Brown. IMMIGRATION, p. 167.

[27] A. Palmer, ORIENTALS IN AMERICAN LIFE, p. 89.

[28] FILIPINO IMMIGRATION, p. 11.

[29] M.J. Buaken, "Where is the Heart of America?", NEW REPUBLIC, September, 1940, p. 103.

[30] BROTHERS UNDER THE SKIN, p. 233.

[31] G. Taylor, THE PHILIPPINES AND THE UNITED STATES: PROBLEMS OF PARTNERSHIP, p. 15.

[32] Personal interview, May, 1971.

[33] Personal interview, June, 1971.

[34] Personal interview, June, 1971.

[35] Personal interview, June, 1971.

[36] Editorials on Filipino Immigration, PHILIPPINE NEWS, March and February issues, 1971.

BIBLIOGRAPHY

BOOKS:

Block, Louis. FACTS ABOUT FILIPINO IMMIGRATION INTO CALIFORNIA. Washington: U.S. Government Printing Office, 1930.

Bogardus, E.S. IMMIGRATION AND RACE ATTITUDES. Boston, New York, Chicago and others: D.C. Heath and Co., 1928.

Brown, Guy Lawrence. IMMIGRATION. New York: Longmans, Green and Company, 1933.

Buaken, Manuel. I HAVE LIVED WITH THE AMERICAN PEOPLE. Idaho: Caxton Printers, Ltd., 1948.

Cady, John F. SOUTHEAST ASIA: ITS HISTORICAL DEVELOPMENT. New York: McGraw-Hill Book Company, 1964.

Fisher, Lloyd H. THE HARVEST LABOR MARKET IN CALIFORNIA, Cambridge: Harvard University Press, 1953.

Fuller, Varden. LABOR RELATIONS IN AGRICULTURE. Berkeley: University of California, 1957.

Kirk, Grayson, PHILIPPINE INDEPENDENCE. New York: Farrar and Rhinehart, Inc., 1936.

Lasker, Bruno. FILIPINO IMMIGRATION TO THE CONTINENTAL UNITED STATES AND HAWAII. Chicago: University of Chicago Press, 1931.

McWilliams, Carey. BROTHERS UNDER THE SKIN. Boston: Little, Brown and Company, 1964.

McWilliams, Carey. ILL FARES THE LAND. Boston: Little, Brown and Company, 1942.

Palmer, Albert W. ORIENTALS IN AMERICAN LIFE. New York: Friendship Press, 1934.

Philippine Parliamentary Mission. FILIPINO APPEAL FOR FREEDOM. Washington: U.S. Government Printing Office, 1923.

Quezon, Philippines, University of the Philippines, Institute of Asian Studies. THE FILIPINO EXCLUSION MOVEMENT, 1927-1935. Quezon City, Philippines: University of the Philippines, 1967.

Shotwell, Louisa R. THE HARVESTERS. New York: Doubleday and Company, 1961.

Taylor, George E. THE PHILIPPINES AND THE UNITED STATES: PROBLEMS OF PARTNERSHIP. New York: Frederick A. Praeger, 1964.

Vinacke, Harold M. A HISTORY OF THE FAR EAST IN MODERN TIMES. New York: Appleton-Century-Crofts, Inc., 1950, 1959.

Walovits, Sonia Emily. THE FILIPINOS IN CALIFORNIA. Los Angeles: University of Southern California, 1966.

PERIODICALS:

Anthony, Donald E. "Filipino Labor in Central California." SOCIOLOGY AND SOCIAL RESEARCH, 16:149-156, September-October, 1931.

Barrows, David P. "The Desirability of the Filipino." COMMONWEALTH CLUB OF CALIFORNIA TRANSACTIONS. 24:321-326, November, 1929.

Bogardus, E.S. "American Attitudes toward Filipinos." SOCIOLOGY AND SOCIAL RESEARCH, 14:469-479, May-June, 1930.

Bogardus, E.S. "Citizenship for Filipinos." SOCIOLOGY AND SOCIAL RESEARCH, September, 1944, p. 53.

Bogardus, E.S. "Filipino Repatriation." SOCIOLOGY AND SOCIAL RESEARCH, 21:67-71, September-August, 1936-1937.

Bogardus, E.S. "The Filipino Immigrant Problem." SOCIOLOGY AND SOCIAL RESEARCH, 13:472-479, May-June, 1929.

Buaken, M.J. "Where is the Heart of America?" NEW REPUBLIC, 103:410. September, 1940.

Catapusan, Benicio T. "Filipino Immigrants and Relief in the United States." SOCIOLOGY AND SOCIAL RESEARCH, 23:546-554. July-August, 1939.

Catapusan, B.T. "Leisure Time Problems of Filipino Immigrants." SOCIOLOGY AND SOCIAL RESEARCH, 24:541-549. July, 1940.

DeMotte, Marshall. "California, White or Yellow?" A.A. OF P. AND S.S. ANNALS, 93:18, 1921.

Ebright, George E. "Is the Filipino a Health Menace?" COMMONWEALTH CLUB OF CALIFORNIA TRANSACTIONS, 24:356-360, November, 1929.

Goethe, C.M. "Filipino Immigration Viewed as a Peril." CURRENT HISTORY, 34:354-355, June, 1931.

Kirk, Grayson. "Filipinos." A.A. OF P. AND S.S. ANNALS, 223:45-48, September, 1942.

McWilliams, Carey. "Exit the Filipino." NATION, 141-265, September 4, 1935.

"Migration of Filipino Labor to and from Hawaii." MONTHLY LABOR REVIEW. 28:404-405, February, 1929.

"Migration of Filipino Labor to and from Hawaii, 1929-33." MONTHLY LABOR REVIEW. 40:14-16, May, 1935.

Perry, J.C. "The Filipino in Relation to Public Health." COMMONWEALTH CLUB OF CALIFORNIA TRANSACTIONS. 24:361-364, November, 1929.

Seward, G.F. "Mongolian Immigration." NORTH AMERICAN REVIEW, 134:562-578.

Williams, Judge D.F. "Filipino Immigration Cannot be Restricted." COMMONWEALTH CLUB OF CALIFORNIA TRANSACTIONS. 24:331-338, November, 1929.

Wilson, J.F. "The Filipino as I Knew Him." COMMONWEALTH CLUB OF CALIFORNIA TRANSACTIONS. 24:361-364, November, 1929.

KOREANS IN AMERICA

LINDA SHIN

Until 1945, Koreans in America constituted a small and largely isolated minority, with about 6,500 in Hawaii and about 3,000 scattered about on the North American mainland. While their color and ethnic heritage set them apart from white society, their distinctive social organization and outlook set them apart from other racial and ethnic minorities in America. Also, the Japanese annexation of Korea after 1910 cut many Koreans off from their homeland and increased their sense of isolation. Small numbers and intense isolation are central to understanding Korean society in America before 1945.

Korean emigration to the Americas began in 1902, when representatives from Hawaiian sugar plantations came to the port of Inchŏn seeking agricultural workers. Christian missionaries in Korea encouraged their converts to emigrate, while the Korean Government also became interested in emigration as a possible solution to the distress caused by a drought in Pyŏngan Province, in northwest Korea. The first group of 93 contract laborers arrived in Honolulu early in 1903, coached by their employers to pass through immigration inspection as free laborers. Their numbers were quickly augmented by further shiploads of Korean laborers. By the end of 1904, 6,647 Koreans had been admitted to Hawaii. When the Korean Government put an end to emigration late in 1905, about 11,000 had already come to Honolulu.[1]

Although some of the migrants came from southern provinces, the bulk of them came from Pyŏngan and Hwanghae provinces in northwest Korea. Even before the drought had brought widespread economic difficulties, northwest Korea seethed with many discontents. Under the regional factionalism of the Yi Dynasty (1392-1910), northerners were consistently denied access to official positions or power within the Court. Living in the North was viewed as a kind of exile by many disaffected yangban, or members of the nobility. In contrast to the (traditional and) more conservative South, northern Korea was relatively lacking in clan and other traditional forms of social

Reprinted by permission of the author. Mrs. Shin has done graduate study in history at the University of California and Cambridge University.

1903–1945

alism prevalent within it.[4]

Although the advertisements of the Hawaiian plantation contractors made the Islands sound like a paradise, life in fact was difficult for the Korean laborers. Typical wages were about seventy cents for a ten-hour day in the fields.[5] It was hard, if not impossible, for the contract laborers to accumulate enough money to return to Korea, much less to get a new economic start in life. Hence, many Korean laborers in Hawaii were attracted by the prospects of work on the West Coast of the mainland. In 1904 American railway companies sent representatives to Honolulu to recruit Korean and Japanese workers, and a steamship company began operations between Honolulu and San Francisco, charging $28 per person as steerage fare.[6] When emigration from Hawaii to the mainland was halted in 1907, about 2,000 Koreans had already arrived in San Francisco. Another 1,000 Koreans went as contract laborers to sugar plantations in Yucatan, Mexico, and Cuba.[7]

Wages on the mainland were somewhat better than in Hawaii--wages for railway work were from $1.20 to $1.50 per day, depending upon the contract--but competition for jobs seems to have been intense. The earliest Korean organization on the mainland, in addition to providing lodging and companionship, were also employment bureaus with which Korean workers registered in order to find jobs. A typical mode of employment was for a Korean boss to deal directly with the employer and contract to do a job for a certain sum. He would then recruit the workers and pay them himself from the sum he received from the employer. Under this system, the Korean boss had all the responsibility for his men and exercised considerable power over them.[8]

By 1910 there were small groups of Korean farm laborers scattered up and down the West Coast. Towns like Dinuba and Reedley in the San Joaquin Valley became centers of small but flourishing Korean communities that survive to this day. By 1910, however, the center of Korean activity on the mainland had shifted from San Francisco to Los Angeles, since the expansion of agriculture in Southern California created more jobs for Korean farm workers there.[9] Towns and cities throughout the West, such as Denver, Seattle, Salt Lake City and Butte, Montana, each had numbers of migratory Korean miners and railway workers, some of whom settled where they were to form

organization, and comparatively receptive to millenarian religious movements that swept through the area with chiliastic fervor.[2] Christianity, of the American fundamentalist and revivalist sort, also met its greatest successes in this area.

Hence, most of the emigrants who came to Hawaii before 1906 were relatively unorganized in traditional social groups. In contrast to the Chinese communities abroad and to some extent the Japanese as well, Korean society in the United States was largely lacking in clan associations, merchant guilds, district or regional associations and lodges, and gentry-type benevolent associations. In their absence, many of their social functions and services were performed by Korean Christian churches. Missionaries and, later, Korean Christian pastors established chapels on plantations employing large numbers of Koreans in Hawaii, where they soon became the centers of organizational life. In Korean communities in the mainland, Christian churches formed the core of the organizational structure of Korean society and reflected all of the schismatic faction-

small, isolated farming communities. In the decade to come, they were joined by almost 1,000 "picture brides."[10]

One incident involving Korean farm laborers was widely reported in American newspapers in 1913. Eleven Korean workers were recruited to pick apricots in Hemet Valley, in Southern California, by Korean contractors whose contracts with the growers were said to stipulate a rate two or three cents per box lower than that asked by white laborers. Upon their arrival in Hemet, the Koreans were met by an angry crowd of several hundred white farm workers who attacked them and demanded that they return to Los Angeles immediately. As they left, their baggage was thrown on the train after them.[11]

This incident, which was not isolated,[12] was widely reported, ironically enough, only because the crowd of white workers had mistaken the Koreans for Japanese. Diplomatic relations between Japan and the United States were severely strained at that time due to the passage of the Alien Land Act in California, and the Hemet incident was newsworthy because the American State Department feared a further worsening of relations with Japan. The Mayor of Hemet issued an apology and the American Government hinted that an investigation would be forthcoming. When it was discovered that the "Japanese" were in fact Koreans, Washington hinted that it was willing to regard them as under the protection of the Japanese Government, something the Koreans abhorred. Representatives from the Japanese Consulate in Los Angeles visited the Korean contractors in Riverside in preparation for launching a diplomatic protest, but the Koreans told them that they didn't want the protection of the Japanese Government. The head of the Southern California Korean National Association wired the Secretary of State asking that the matter be dropped. Since the growers had paid the train fare for the Korean workers, they were willing to forget the matter rather than allow Japan to assert authority over overseas Koreans in America. The Japanese also dropped the issue. Japanese officials in San Francisco described the incident as a "prank of overgrown boys," but not to be outdone, the "school boys" replied that the Koreans "were as objectionable as Japanese, and ... the people of Hemet wanted neither race among them." The ranchers subsequently agreed to keep Hemet a "white man's valley."[13]

The diplomatic repercussions of this incident illustrate the ambiguity of the legal status of Koreans in America. After the Russo-Japanese War, 1904-1905, Korea became a protectorate of Japan's. Control over foreign relations, finances and many domestic matters passed out of the Court's hands and into those of the Japanese Resident-General. Overseas Korean communities in America strenuously protested the Japanese encroachments. Soon they were joined by small numbers of students and intellectuals, who, disaffected by the Japanese, came to America as exiles and provided leadership for what proved to be the nucleus of the Korean independence movement. The importance of overseas Koreans was recognized by the Japanese-dominated government, for one of its first acts was to prohibit emigration. In part this decision was motivated by reports of ill-treatment of Korean laborers in Hawaii and the United States, but also because the Japanese feared the potentially seditious activities of Koreans abroad.

Indeed, in 1905, 8,000 Koreans in Hawaii held a mass meeting and drafted a petition to send to President Theodore Roosevelt asking him to use his influence to protect Korean independence during the forthcoming Portsmouth Conference between the Japanese and the Russians. The Reverend P.K. Yoon of Honolulu and Syngman Rhee, later to be first president of the Republic of Korea, were deputed to present the petition, but their mission was unsuccessful largely because Roosevelt had already privately agreed to the Japanese request that Korea be considered within its sphere of influence.[14]

In 1907 the Korean King smuggled two emissaries out of Korea with an appeal to the Hague Peace Conference. When the appeal was ignored, the emissaries committed suicide publicly and the Japanese responded by forcing the King to abdicate. Insurgent forces numbering several thousands, poorly armed and disorganized, were annihilated by the Japanese military. Koreans in America organized themselves to plan and finance resistance activities. Organizations and churches that had hitherto performed social and religious functions only now took on a distinctly political cast. Several existing associations were amalgamated into the new Korean National Association (<u>Kungmin Hoe</u>), which henceforth met regularly in areas with significant Korean populations, and which attempted to unify the many diverse groups into a force capable of supporting resistance to Japan.[15]

With the failure of the appeal to world public opinion and losses by the insurgents in Korea, Koreans in America and elsewhere turned to terrorism to combat the Japanese. In 1907 an unsuccessful attempt to assassinate several pro-Japanese Korean officials was planned by

Koreans in San Francisco. Then, in 1908, Koreans in San Francisco assassinated Durham W. Stevens, an American who had served in the Japanese Foreign Ministry for several years and who had been appointed by the Japanese to serve as foreign affairs advisor to the Korean Court under the Japanese Resident-General, where he had assumed de facto control over foreign policy. On leave from his post in 1908, he stated in an interview in San Francisco that Japanese rule in Korea was benevolent and in the best interest of the Koreans, who were unable to govern themselves. Korean organizations and church representatives in San Francisco decided to send a group to visit him at his hotel and ask him to rescind his statement. When he refused, they decided to kill him. Chŏn Myŏng-hun was deputed to shoot him, but when he missed his chance, Chang In-hwan stepped from behind him and succeeded. Stevens died three days later from his wounds and Chang was convicted of second-degree murder. Funds for his defense were raised by Koreans in America and Hawaii. He was sentenced to serve twenty-five years in jail and released in 1919.[16]

The Japanese response to this and other acts of terrorism was to further tighten their control over Korea. In 1909 a Korean patriot assassinated Ito Hirobumi, Resident-General of Korea, and in the following year Korea was annexed to the Japanese Empire and all pretense of sovereignty lost. In the years following annexation and leading up to the March 1, 1919 independence demonstrations, about 300 Koreans entered the United States as students. In fact, they were exiled intellectuals and political figures, many with Christian backgrounds, who were singled out by the Japanese for close surveillance in Korea. Those who could afford the steerage fare (about $80) came to the United States from Shanghai or Manchuria, often with letters of introduction from American missionaries. Since they carried no passports, they were allowed to enter by special order of President Wilson, but at the same time their status as students was carefully scrutinized and several were rejected at San Francisco and other ports of entry.[17]

Small communities of Korean students developed in New York, Chicago, Washington, D.C., and college towns throughout the East and Midwest, where the students formed a Korean Students' Association and provided manpower and leadership for the Korean independence movement. Many of them, however, found the economic struggle for survival an all-consuming process. Whatever their socioeconomic status in Korea had been, they nevertheless found themselves at the bottom of the economic barrel in America. Most students had to work part- or even full-time as farm laborers, factory workers, cooks, chauffeurs, houseboys, dishwashers or at other poorly paying jobs, while Korean women mostly worked as seamstresses. Others peddled farm produce and other commodities. When they could scrape up enough capital, some tried small businesses, such as Chinese restaurants, import-export firms, and small manufacturing companies, but there were few economic success stories among them. Although their educational level was unusually high, the prevailing white racism generally prevented them from moving into professional occupations.

Cities on the mainland with substantial numbers of Koreans, such as Los Angeles, with about 800 Koreans by 1945, New York, with about 300, and Chicago, also with about 300, had small ghetto-like Korean residential and business areas that generally existed within a larger Asian ghetto or else on its periphery. Since the Koreans constituted so small a group, their specialized needs, such as for groceries, were generally met by the facilities of the Chinese or Japanese ghetto areas.[18]

Considering their small numbers and isolation, one might expect a trend towards disintegration through intermarriage and assimilation. Indeed, in Hawaii after 1930, the outmarriage rate for Koreans was among the largest of the various ethnic groups.[19] Yet many factors worked against the disintegratory trend. Except for Hawaii, where Koreans could be assimilated into a larger Asian-Hawaiian culture, racist attitudes and social conditions on the mainland generally prevented Koreans from intermarrying and assimilating into white culture. At the same time, Korean community leaders assiduously resisted the trend towards assimilation by cultivating national pride and emphasizing the distinctiveness of Koreans from Chinese and especially Japanese. As early as 1915, Syngman Rhee broke with the Methodist Church in Hawaii, with which he had been closely linked, over the issue of cultural amalgamation. Henceforth, Rhee and other nationalists in Hawaii and the mainland established Korean language schools, often affiliated with Korean Christian churches, where youngsters were taught Korean history and culture in strongly nationalist and separatist terms in addition to language.[20] Hence the ideology and activities of the Korean independence movement among Koreans in America was highly important in maintaining the separateness of the

Korean community.

Independence activities among Koreans in America after 1910 were principally oriented, first, towards the March 1, 1919 movement, then towards Korean participation in the war effort to defeat the Japanese after 1937. In the March 1 movement, independence leaders in Korea and abroad secretly planned a series of popular, peaceful demonstrations to demonstrate to the representatives of the Big Four nations meeting at the Versailles Conference the desire of the Korean people for independence. The demonstrations caught the Japanese military rulers of Korea by complete surprise and they reacted with ruthlessness in suppressing them. Although the movement failed to obtain its objectives and many thousands were killed or imprisoned, the movement was nevertheless an extraordinary achievement of the Korean people and remains the most glorious moment in the history of the independence movement.[21]

Koreans in America played an important role in the March 1 movement and in the establishment of the Korean Provisional Government in Shanghai that followed it. In 1918 officers and members of the Korean National Association sponsored two delegates to observe the proceedings at the Versailles Conference, Syngman Rhee and Henry Chung, but they were unable to leave the United States because they had no passports and the United States Government would not grant them documents necessary to depart. Their appeal to President Wilson was ignored, in spite of Wilson's professed sympathy for the Koreans and his friendship with Rhee.[22] Following the March 1 movement Koreans in America planned a Korean Congress to meet in Philadelphia in April 1919. About 70 delegates from the United States, Mexico and Hawaii attended, along with numerous American religious and political figures.[23] A Korean Commission was established under Rhee in Washington, D.C. and an active publishing campaign designed to attract sympathy and support for Korea was begun, and with considerable success.[24] Through the Korean Commission in Washington, funds were collected from Koreans in the United States and Hawaii to establish and support the Korean Provisional Government in Shanghai. These funds were vital to the Provisional Government, and Rhee's decision in 1924 to withhold funds greatly contributed to its demise.[25]

Rhee's decision reflected the factionalism within the Korean independence movement and within the Korean community in the United States as well. In part the factionalism was due to ideological differences, but also to personality differences and regionalism. Pak Yong-man and other Koreans in America and Hawaii split with Rhee at an early stage over the question of strategies in the independence movement. Pak and others wanted to provide military training for the eventual military reconquest of Korea by Koreans. In 1912 a military training school was established for Koreans in Hastings, Nebraska, by Pak, which was attended by about 150 persons and from which thirteen were graduated.[26] Similar schools were established in Hawaii. In general, Rhee eschewed military preparedness in favor of appeals to enlightened world public opinion, especially that of the United States, in forcing the Japanese to leave Korea.

As a result of this and other differences, Rhee broke with the Korean National Association and established his own organization, the *Tongji hoe*, or Comrades' Association, and in Los Angeles, his own church group, the Los Angeles Free Church. His support was principally from persons who came from southern Korea, which, while substantial in Hawaii, was negligible on the mainland. Rhee's principal rival among Koreans on the mainland was Ahn Chang-ho, a Christian intellectual from North Korea who had organized the first societies for Koreans in the United States in 1903 and who had spent many years in California before returning to Korea, ultimately to die in a Japanese prison in 1938. In addition to receiving support from the Korean National Association, Ahn formed his own organization, *Hungsa dan*, or Corps to Promote Leadership, which was loosely allied with the Korean Presbyterian Church in Los Angeles and elsewhere. Relations between these two and other factions were so bitter that many of those who had opposed Rhee in the United States found themselves unable to visit Korea after he became President in 1948, for fear of being labelled communist.[27]

Although largely quiescent during the 1920's, the independence movement was revitalized with the Japanese seizure of Manchuria in 1931 and especially after the outbreak of the Sino-Japanese War in 1937. As during the earlier periods of activity, Koreans in America emphasized military preparedness and appeals to American public opinion, with the emphasis generally upon the latter. Throughout the 1930's the Korean National Association urged the United States to implement an embargo against Japan and staged demonstrations each March 1 against the Japanese Consulate in Los Angeles and elsewhere.[28]

With the American entry into the war, Koreans began to actively plan for the day of Korea's imminent liberation. A major concern of Rhee and other Koreans in America was that they would not be taken into consideration by the United States in its postwar decisions respecting Korea. Hence, many activities of the Koreans in America were designed to convince the American Government and public that Koreans should not be given the same treatment as Japanese and that Koreans should be allowed to govern their own nation. In the case of Rhee, he was also especially concerned with proving to the American Government that he was the legitimate representative of the Korean people in America and Korea, but he was largely unsuccessful at that time.[29]

In part to accomplish these aims, Koreans in America organized and financed a volunteer force that was trained in guerilla tactics to be used against the Japanese in Korea. Although about 300 Koreans were trained in this unit, it apparently never did link up with the large numbers of Korean guerilla units that had been active in Manchuria and along the Korean border throughout the 1930's. Another 100 Koreans in Southern California were organized into a special unit in the California National Guard and trained for warfare.[30] In addition to military training and financial support for it through contributions and purchase of defense bonds, Koreans also joined in anti-Japanese war propaganda with great fervor. Declaring themselves to be "the champion Jap-haters of the world,"[31] Koreans unanimously supported the move to intern Japanese-Americans during the war and in other ways declared their allegiance to the Allied cause.[32]

In spite of their aspirations, Koreans in the United States found themselves largely frustrated by the postwar solutions worked out by the great powers. At the Potsdam Conference, it was decided to divide Korea at the thirty-eighth parallel, with the American Military Government ruling the southern sector only. As Syngman Rhee began to rise in power within the American sector, those who were not part of his organization in the United States found themselves alienated. A fifteen-man delegation of Koreans from America to Korea in the postwar period was forced to leave when it found itself frozen out by Rhee and the American military authorities.[33] Hence the division of Korea and Rhee's assumption of power in the South, together with the cultural dislocation felt by some Koreans after their long years in America, worked to alienate Koreans from America in Korea and provide for their continued residence in the United States. Thus, many Koreans found themselves doubly exiled.

The character of the Korean community in the United States has changed considerably in the past twenty years, largely due to the influx of students and other immigrants. Including Hawaii, the Korean population in America may number as many as 50,000. Their social conditions, outlook and goals may differ considerably from the pre-1945 Koreans, but the experiences of the latter, including their problems and their many achievements, remain an important part of the heritage of Koreans and other Asians in America.

---

[1] No Chae-yon, CHAE MI HANIN SARYAK. (A Short History of Koreans in America.) Los Angeles, 1951, v. 1, pp. 1-4, 30.

[2] The great Tonghak movement of the nineteenth century originated in northern Korea in the 1860's before erupting in major rebellion in the 1890's. See Benjamin Weems, REFORM, REBELLION AND THE HEAVENLY WAY. Tucson, 1964.

[3] L. G. Paik, THE HISTORY OF PROTESTANT MISSIONS IN KOREA. (Pyongyang, 1929; repr. Seoul, 1969).

[4] No, pp. 17, 19, 35 and passim. for churches on Hawaiian plantations; see Kyung Lee, SETTLEMENT PATTERNS OF LOS ANGELES KOREANS. (M. A. Thesis, UCLA, 1969) pp. 32-37 on churches in Los Angeles.

[5] No, p. 8.

[6] No, p. 15.

[7] Although the contracts in Mexico were for four years, the Koreans found themselves stranded without any money when their contracts expired. Their living conditions were said to be the most terrible of all the overseas Koreans. Ahn Chang-ho and other Korean leaders visited them repeatedly. In 1921, after a large drought in northwest Mexico, many of the Koreans there moved to Cuba. There is still a substantial scattering of Koreans in Mexico, Central America and the Caribbean.

[8] No, p. 15.

[9] As early as 1904 Ahn Chang-ho came to Riverside to survey prospects for employment for Koreans in the orchards in the vicinity. In 1905 he established a section of his organization, Chin-mok hoe, in Redlands, which became the basis of the Korean National Association in Southern California. See No, pp. 13, 26.

[10] A 1910 survey by the Los Angeles newspaper, Shin Han Min Po, showed the distribution of Koreans throughout the West and the size of their respective contributions to the independence movement. See No, pp. 55-57. On the Korean community in Butte, Montana, see also Dale White, "Koreans in Montana," ASIA, 45 (1945): 156. The 200-odd Koreans there came in 1914 as section hands on the Milwaukee and Northern Pacific railway. On the picture brides, see No, p. 58.

[11] No, pp.65-66. The Los Angeles TIMES reported that 25-30 Koreans were involved. TIMES, June 27, 1913, p. 1, p. 5; June 28, 1913, p. 1.

[12] In an interview given to Miss Aija Paik and myself in Fall, 1969, Mr. Kwak Im-tae recalled similar incidents in Southern California orange groves during the 1910's. After one especially serious incident, he organized support from white church groups.

[13] Los Angeles TIMES, June 28, 1913, p. 1.

[14] The petition is reprinted in F. A. McKenzie, THE TRAGEDY OF KOREA. (London, 1928) pp. 311-312. See also Robert T. Oliver, SYNGMAN RHEE; THE MAN BEHIND THE MYTH. (New York, 1960) pp. 82-92: No, p. 18.

[15] On the development of early organizations, see Warren Y. Kim CHAE MI HANIN OSHIMNYON SA. (Fifty Year History of Koreans in America). (Reedley, Calif., 1959), pp. 83ff.

[16] Kim, pp. 327-331; No, pp. 44-46: San Francisco CHRONICLE, Mar. 24, 1908, p. 1, 2, 3; Mar. 25, p. 1, 2; Mar. 26, p. 1; Mar. 27, p. 1, 2.

[17] One of the results of the Hemet incident was that the Korean National Association henceforth agreed to guarantee all entering Koreans. No, op. cit. Interview with Mr. Park Lee Kuen, Fall, 1969.

[18] Kyung Lee, op. cit., passim.

[19] Cheng Ch'eng'k'un and Douglas S. Yamamura, "Interracial Marriage and Divorce in Hawaii," SOCIAL FORCES, 36 (Oct. 1957) pp. 80, 82, 83.

[20] Oliver, pp. 122-124.

[21] The March 1 or Samil Movement is treated fully in Chong-sik Lee, THE POLITICS OF KOREAN NATIONALISM. (Berkeley, 1963) pp. 101-126.

[22] Chong-sik Lee, pp. 102-103.

[23] See the record of the conference, FIRST KOREAN CONGRESS,...(Philadelphia, 1919).

[24] McKenzie's work, cited above, and THE CASE OF KOREA, by Henry Chung (New York, 1921) were two of the more notable works sponsored by the Korean Commission, which also published the KOREA REVIEW.

[25] Chong-sik Lee, pp. 166-168.

[26] No, p. 62.

[27] See, e.g., interviews with Mrs. Ahn Chang-ho (posthumous) and Reverend Kim Sung-nak, Fall, 1969.

[28] See, e.g., New York TIMES, February 18, 1932, p. 16. On the demonstrations before the Japanese Consulate in Los Angeles, see LOS ANGELES TIMES, March 2, 1941, II, p. 1.

[29] In characteristic fashion, Rhee blamed his lack of influence in Washington on communist infiltration of the American Government. See Oliver, pp. 182-183; 192 ff.

[30] Oliver, pp. 184-185. A Liberty Conference held in 1942 gave rise to the formation of the United Korean Committee in America, dedicated to support of the war effort and of Korean forces in China. See Chong-sik Lee, pp. 228-229.

[31] New York TIMES, January 25, 1942, p. 33.

[32] E.g., New York TIMES, April 28, 1943, p. 6.

[33] Interview with Reverend Kim Sung-nak, Fall, 1969.

the failure of democracy in a time of crisis
the war-time internment of the japanese americans and its relevance today

ISAO FUJIMOTO

Every generation is held accountable for its abstentions or stands on moral issues. The spectre of Eichmann prompts Germans to be asked, "You were alive and free when Hitler began his genocide campaign, so what did you do?" Subsequent generations can ask of us, "What were you doing when the police and dogs lunged at Negro school children at Birmingham?; What were you doing when people were napalmed in Vietnam?; What were you doing when we had the opportunity to prevent millions of mental defectives by sharing your daily bread with starving Biafrans in Africa and Navajos, Blacks, Mexican-Americans, and poor whites in America in 1968?" Many of us were alive and aware at a time in American history when democracy faced another crucial moral test. I refer to the war-time concentration of 110,000 American residents whose sole crime was their Japanese parentage.

But at that time few people bothered to even ask the basic questions or even noticed that democracy was on trial and found lacking. It may be argued that viewed against a background of total war the numbers affected by the war-time relocation of Japanese-Americans do not loom large. But what does loom large is the legacy that accompanies this generation and all generations which must evaluate the merits of democracy and consider the consequences when democracy fails to live up to its meaning during the time of crisis.

I was a part of the statistics bearing witness to this misguided experience in the practice of American democratic government. I was then eight years old--too young to know my rights but old enough to realize that something was wrong. Also, as a product of an ethnic ghetto, I've internalized the subtle ways in which the larger society reminds one to stay in his place. Like many other Japanese Americans, I've been infused with a philosophy that stresses: "Let's make the most of a bad situation and push ahead." This diverted me from critically appraising the past, the understanding of which is directly relevant to many of the issues that all of us--not just minority Americans--face today.

Reprinted from GIDRA, September, 1969. A modified version of this article appeared in THE BLACK POLITICIAN, October, 1969, under the title, "Who Can We Count On?"

The years I spent in camp have become a part of my identity. Whenever I meet another Japanese American I almost invariably ask, "What camp were you in?" I still find myself doing this. I am reminded of this bond when I try to relate the situation in the camps to those who do not share this experience. Many Americans on the West Coast knew of the evacuations but I found Americans elsewhere in the country with little knowledge of what went on, let alone comprehending the unresolved issues concerning the camps, particularly as they threaten the freedoms of all Americans. It is even a rarer opportunity to meet people who tried to do something about it when it occurred.

A few years ago, I met Dorothy Day, anarchist, communist, humanitarian and founder of the Catholic Worker. She told me many things about her life, her work on behalf of women, labor, and for men on the Bowery of New York City. Our conversation got around to peace and war and her concerns for the Japanese evacuated during the Second World War. She told me she had protested the move and picketed one of the centers. I had never met anyone who had done this. I asked where. When she replied, "Outside the Portland Livestock Pavilion," I looked at her and felt a strange bond of comradeship for my family and I had been inside the Portland Center. That moment gave me an insight of the empathy peasants feel towards communist cadres who come to help in the villages despite what our own propaganda claims to the contrary. I cared little that our political views differed for what struck me as significant was the feeling that here was a person who knew and cared about the issues involved; who backed me up with action, not rhetoric, when the chips were down; who was on my side when it counted most.

My early years were spent on the Yakima Indian reservation in the state of Washington. I lived among Indians and immigrant farmers from Japan. I didn't realize this was a rural ghetto until I started going to school--when I saw so many people who looked different, with round eyes and big noses, people who looked so pale--which I thought was due to their not eating enough rice.

But even our small, closed society was affected when World War II began. About a week after Pearl Harbor, two FBI agents arrived one night and took my father away. Our family did not see him for another year and a half. My father was in a detention camp in Missoula, Montana which he described to us in letters written to my mother. I remember these letters more for their form than their content. They had holes in them scissored out by censors. Because everything seemed so uncertain, my mother went ahead, had the fields prepared and planted crops for the coming year. Eventually, orders replaced the rumors and notices appeared for our evacuation. For reasons of general public safety and fear of possible subversive activities, the U.S. Army ordered the removal of all Japanese-American citizens and aliens living within 200 miles of the Pacific Ocean. So we let the field go and moved into the Buddhist Church in town. Our family was sent to the Portland, Oregon Assembly Center, one of the 15 make-shift centers converted mainly from West Coast racetracks and fairgrounds.

The Portland Assembly Center was like a giant honeycomb. Livestock stalls were converted into family quarters. I recall visiting friends who were sitting on suitcases outside of stalls still containing fresh hay and manure. Guard towers with armed soldiers and barbed wire surrounded us. Right after internment started, our Buddhist minister took pains to impress upon us the need to respect the laws inside the camps. We were warned that children had been shot for wandering too close to the barbed wire. Unfortunately, there were incidents which substantiated these fears.

All told, some 110,000 men, women, and children, 70,000 of them citizens of the United States, were uprooted from their homes into inland relocation centers.

There was no recourse to the courts; guilt was assumed, the charge being, "They look like the enemy." Voluntary migration inland was permitted, but Lt. General Dewitt, Commander of the Western Defense Command, made no attempts to prepare the way for the execution of this alternative. Although some 9,000 responded, most were turned back by armed posses at state lines, refused gas and food, and in general, intimidated. Public Law 503 closed all movements and Executive Order 9066 authorized the evacuation. So rife was clamour and support for this action in the name of law and order, that Milton Eisenhower, initial director of the War Relocation Authority, expressed discouragement at the low concern for human rights and constitutional guarantees by Congressmen advocating this uncompromising program of federal internment.

While the evacuees temporarily filled the 15 Assembly Centers, the U. S. Government had examined some 200 possible sites to permanently concentrate the Japanese evacuees. Ten of these were finally selected for best meeting the following criteria--safe distance from military zones, location in areas which could support a large scale work program, location on federal land which would not influence private land values. These camps were located in such places as Poston and Gila, Arizona; Rowher and Jerome, Arkansas; Heart Mountain, Wyoming; Minidoka, Idaho; Amache, Colorado; Manzanar and Tule Lake, California; and Topaz, Utah. The evacuation orders divided the West Coast into a military jigsaw puzzle. They scattered the Japanese-American population--first into different assembly centers then again into the ten camps. Some, like our family, were moved for the third time.

Our family, now identified mainly by a number--37205, was relocated to Heart Mountain, Wyoming. A three-day trip over the Rockies in a special train heavily guarded by armed soldiers brought us to a dusty treeless plateau in northwestern Wyoming. One of the first things I remember doing at Heart Mountain was to look for my mother and eight-month-old sister. We had been separated because my sister contracted measles and was quarantined. I found the two of them in a barren barracks in an empty block devoid of people. They had no provisions whatsoever. As soon as she saw me, my mother asked me to look around for water.

Heart Mountain held about 10,000 people distributed into thirty blocks each with 40 to 50 families. Each block had its community mess halls, boiler rooms, laundry, and toilets between the two rows of barracks, each holding from three to four families. Both space and possessions were very limited, not only for the families, but for the public facilities provided by camp authorities. For the first half year in Heart Mountain, the school I attended consisted only of benches, period. The playing field was marked off by two coal piles which serviced boiler rooms at opposite ends of the block.

In the process of being uprooted, many were victimized by those capitalizing on the knowledge that the victims had no alternatives but to leave things behind or get what little they could. Speculators offered a few dollars for household belongings which took many a life-time to accumulate. Unscrupulous operators took over the land without paying rent and confiscated equipment or waited until harvest to collect the spoils. Encouraging rumors that the government would seize all property, speculators would then make ridiculously low bids. When the Japanese refused such offers, the speculators threatened to report the would-be victims to the FBI. The public remained indifferent or gave in to this hysteria of the time. They used the very act of evacuation as reason against the victims. They reasoned: "There's something wrong about those people or the Army wouldn't have taken them under wraps. That's all I need to know." As for the Government, it offered none of the constitutional liberties which are the basis of its very existence and to which all of its citizens are entitled. The stipulation of the Fifth Amendment--that no person can be deprived of life, liberty or property without due process of law--were far from fulfilled.

About the time my father was reunited with the family, the War Relocation Authority inaugurated a program of mass registration for the purposes of processing the adults for resettlement and leave clearance. In essence, this is ironic in that they were asking for the loyalty of the very persons to whom they originally granted constitutional guarantees. Question 27 of the War Relocation Authority Leave Clearance Form concerned willingness to serve in the Armed Forces of the United States. Question 28 asked: "Will you support unqualified allegiance or obedience to the Japanese Emperor or any other foreign government, power, or organization?" To those already confused, troubled and resentful, the ambiguity of this question added further difficulty. To the Isseis, first generation Japanese born in Japan, the question was unfair and impossible to answer in the affirmative. Even had he been a veteran of the Spanish-American War, an Issei could not become a citizen of the United States. In fact, it was not until the McCarran Act of 1950, that the right of naturalization was granted to immigrants from the Orient. The question thus called the Issei to remove the only nationality he had. If he answered yes, he became a man without a country. My father chose to answer no and the family was evacuated to Tule Lake, California.

Like the others, Tule Lake was a maximum security camp but even more so-- with its double roll of barbed wire and cyclone fencing and armed guards in towers spaced every 100 yards around the camp. Located in Modoc County, near the town of Newell, it was also the largest of the camps holding 22,000 people. It was once invaded by troops reinforced by tanks, machine guns, and tear gas bombs. Such was the situation between November 1943 and January 1944, a few months prior to my transfer there. Just four days after our family got there, an army sentry killed a truck driver after ordering him from the truck following an argument concerning a pass.

As seen in retrospect, life at Tule Lake was tense, faction-ridden and chaotic--to say nothing of the complications wrought by people--many of them driven to extreme positions--by their resentment of unjust acts by a government claiming to be just. With more than its share of recalcitrants, Tule Lake became the official "segregation center." It is not surprising that of the 5,700 internees who protested the evacuation by filing applications to renounce their U.S. citizenship, the majority of them came from the Tule Lake Center.

What characterized Tule Lake from all the other camps was that life was very much oriented towards Japan. Youth were organized into squads which got up at five o'clock, took cold showers, ran and sang for two miles. Some blocks outlawed the use of English. Also, there were many homemade shortwave radios which were tuned in to propaganda programs from Japan. In the morning in Japanese school, the day started with all of the children assembled in the school yard and bowing towards the East. In the afternoon, I went to American school which began with all of the children standing up to pledge allegiance to the flag of the United States.

Although not apparent to me at that time, an incident occurred that illustrates how seriously the internees were recognized as Americans. On the way home from American school--which was voluntary, in contrast to Japanese school which was compulsory--I spotted some non-Orientals, with the letters "POW" on their shirts, cleaning out an irrigation ditch that ran through the camp. On the bank of the ditch was an armed American soldier guarding them as they worked. I later learned that they were Italian prisoners of war captured in North Africa. But these prisoners lived outside the confines of the barbed wires that enclosed us. Not only were we not different from the POW's but we were even more confined. We were no longer temporary refugees--we were enemies--enemies of our own country against whom we had committed no crime nor even had the opportunity to exercise the rights which we undoubtedly no longer had.

In December, 1945, four years after the FBI took away my father, our family was released from camp. Just as a prisoner leaves a jail with a suit and pocket money, our family was given $50.00 and a job assignment. But just as a prisoner carries with him a certain stigma, resettlement reintroduced to the public the very emotional outbursts that brought on the evacuation. In fact, the War Relocation Authority sent out teams of anthropologists to evaluate various towns as to their degree of hostility or tolerance towards the resettlement of Japanese Americans. Some of the super-patriots had publicly hoped that the Nisei landowners would be killed in combat. In this way, they could easily lay claim to a land they had been farming for nothing all during the war. The organization which took hypocritical stands in the guise of Americanism do not make a very proud list, for they include many of the organizations that still exist in our communities today.

Forewarned of such groups--by letters sent back to camp by early resettlers' interpretations of advice from anthropologists and the ever-present rumors concerning the actions of racists--our re-entry into American society was accompanied by a mixture of fear, insecurity, hope and confusion.

Our family resettled in the town of Pleasanton, California, where my father got a job as a laborer with the Southern Pacific Railroad. I remember my first day back in school: I was about to go into the class when I heard the class getting up to salute the flag. I had mixed feelings, and I chose to wait it out. Sensing my hesitation, my teacher, perhaps in an effort to reassure me, told me that this town was all right. He told me there were other towns which posted signs warning, "Tar and feathers for Japs." Not too many days later an adult brushed me aside with the warning, "All you Japs better get out of town." There are certain experiences, fleeting though they may be, that one never shakes off. The tortured look of hate expressed by that man remains indelible.

It is easy to believe in democracy in a time of ease and just as easy to accept the benefits of democracy without participation. It is also easy to dismiss what we don't want to believe, especially if it appears so novel that we rarely hear of it or consider it deviant. When we compare the overground with the underground information sources regarding concentration camps, we find a relative vacuum in the world most of us are tuned to. This involves the world brought to us and described by the San Francisco Chronicle, The Sacramento Bee, The Davis Enterprise, Channel 3, 4, or 9, or even KPFA--to mention a few of the information channels available to those of us in the San Francisco - Sacramento areas of California. But in the same area, if one were to tune in to the world reported by Flatlands, The Berkeley Barb, The Black Panther, El Malcriado, and other ethnic, ghetto and hip media circulating among the minorities and invisibles --be they non-white, the youth, the disaffected--one would discover the rather consistent concerns over the actions of such groups as HUAC, the 1967 up-dating of the McCarren Act, the efforts of Senator Eastland and his 19 Senate colleagues to introduce the 1968 Internal Security Act, and recommendations for additional powers for the Subversives Control Board.

However, such information which has been the concern of the underground has recently surfaced in such regional and national outlets as the San Francisco Examiner, and Look magazine, and even in the local papers. A word can be said for the legitimacy of the issue when such an "all-American" publication as Playboy elaborates commentary on the concentration camps which was part of an article on dissent in its September issue.

To check the validity of the variety of stories on the McCarren Act camps, I wrote to several Congressmen, Senators, and representatives of the Justice Department. The replies all dismissed the rumors about the camps, assured me that no appropriations were allocated for the maintenance of such facilities and that adequate precautions would be exercised before provisions of the 1950 McCarren Internal Security Act would be implemented. Title II of the McCarren Act also authorizes the Attorney General to issue a warrant "For the apprehension of each person as to whom there is a reasonable ground to believe that such persons <u>probably will</u> engage in or probably will conspire with others to engage in acts of espionage and sabotage." This kind of evidence can be turned in by a neighbor who dislikes you. Since the government is under no final obligation to produce a source of evidence, the burden of proving innocence rests on the suspected person. According to the Internal Security Act provisions, six detention facilities including Tule Lake were reconstituted. All letters received to date state that they were maintained only through 1957 and none exist today even on a stand-by basis.

However, the precedent of the Japanese experience makes all these arguments irrelevant. First of all, the war-time experience showed that the lack of camps is no deterrent to mass detention. That experience has taught us that any place for horses and cows can hold people. The Japanese-Americans were evacuated into fifteen assembly centers which included such famous racetracks as Tanforan and Santa Anita. Other assembly centers were the fairgrounds at places such as Fresno Turlock, Stockton, Sacramento, and Marysville. These were in operation--anywhere from a month to half a year--until the more permanent relocation centers could be built inland. Furthermore, all it took to bring about the evacuation was an executive order. The fact that a law exists today legitimizes what many insist couldn't happen again.

The fact that the Act is on the books is significant in terms of the stress Americans place on law and order. Americans pride themselves on being law-abiding citizens but when laws such as Title II of the McCarran Act remain on the books they cannot be dismissed as some anachronism out of the McCarthy period. Added to this dilemma is that the constitutionality of the war-time evacuation was upheld by the Supreme Court; Title II of the McCarran Act has yet to be tested. We are living with a predicament. If the law was enacted, it would be our awkward duty as citizens to abide by the law. The choice is to obey a bad law for the sake of law and order or to disobey a bad law out of concern for law and justice.

The Japanese were interned because they looked like the enemy. The threat of expansion of the Vietnam War involving China has sent rumors through Chinatowns concerning detention. "It happened before --will we be next?" is a question not easily shrugged off as a rumor. In the non-white ethnic ghettos which have witnessed repression, more than rhetorical assurance will be needed to offset the anxiety that circulates in the ghetto communication network.

The arbitrary basis of detention is an added concern. I referred, earlier, to my father being separated from us. We were told that the FBI wanted the leaders. My father was a farmer and also an experienced carpenter. Because of his skills, people in the community relied on him to direct the building of a Buddhist temple in the little town in which I grew up. In the eyes of the FBI, he was a leader and thus taken away. The suspect in such a situation is no different from the prisoner described in Kafka's THE TRIAL, where the suspect never knows the crime for which he is charged or why he is arrested; or he can be like Camus' THE STRANGER, who is never addressed by name, not even by his lawyer who does not regard him as human. But we need not rely on the imagination of novelists to supply us with examples. Poet Leroi Jones did not know till the day of his recent sentencing in New York that he was on trial for having written a poem.

The Japanese-American experience has relevance to numerous issues today. One issue is the matter of distinguishing between the victim and the social context in which the victim is found. The focus on the victim results in asking questions such as "Did you enjoy the camp?"; "How were you treated there?", etc., which takes away from the major issue--Why does a free society have to have camps at all? Why do people in a free society not only obey but support repressive laws? The victim approach misleads us from seeing the issues. This perspective would have us attempt to understand anti-semitism by studying Jews, to seek solutions to the ghetto problems by studying the migrant workers. This approach also assumes that it is the victim who needs correction and that programs be constructed that will help him adjust to society. It does not question that society itself might be at fault. This insistence that society is all right lengthens the gap between rhetoric and reality--resulting in a society of many paradoxes.

We have a society wherein the rich enjoy the fruits of socialism and the poor get tossed the rhetoric of free enterprise. We have a society wherein law and order get more attention than law and justice. We have a society where, in many fields, in order to "make it," you already have to "have it made." We have a situation where education, rather than being considered a process of opening up a person to new possibilities, is seen as a system to beat while one collects credits and units in the same way we gather Blue Chip stamps. We have a system whereby our commitments are limited, where we approach our challenges with our eyes downward and our palms upward. The current mood of our society sees government as good when it protects property but bad when it tries to help people--a far cry from what Lincoln said about government doing for people what the people couldn't do for themselves. We have a democracy by deal, sometimes by dole, but too seldom by decency.

The Japanese-American internment shows that people of good will are forced to limit their response to emergencies. Gestures of coffee and doughnuts were appreciated by the people being sent away to camps, as were the packages that arrived at Christmas. But while these efforts eased the stress of the experience, they were too little and too late--the feeble gestures of a people rendered helpless by the very system which was supposed to respond to their demands. But perhaps that was the problem--there were too few demands for justice, too few voices of protest. What was needed were people to put their bodies on the line--on the railroad lines--to keep the trains from moving to the camps. What was needed were leaders such as the King of Denmark who had all Danes wear Stars of David when the Nazis came to round up the Jews.

Thirdly, the Japanese-American experience warns us of the price we pay when we abstain from our moral duty to work against forces of repression in our daily lives. This means taking action against acts of injustice--be they involvement or complicity with discrimination in our local country clubs; research or service that aids entrepreneurs who violate laws of health, sanitation and decency for workers; arbitrary stands taken by the local school board on issues of public relevance; or subtle racism. As an example of supporting subtle racism, how many times have we ourselves said or heard Blacks and Mexican-Americans told to emulate the Oriental-American as an example of minorities who have made it. The subtlety of this logic also says "Be like them-- they know their place--they don't complain." This focuses attention on the minorities, pits them against each other, while absolving the larger society from looking at itself. In reaction to being used in this way, there's been an emergence of Yellow Power Groups. The latter, by the way, are not a front pushing bananas for the United Fruit Company. A recent local incident illustrates an expression of this concern. This spring, minority students--Blacks, Browns, and Orientals, walked out of Sacramento High School. When the Orientals were asked why they were walking out they answered, "We're joining because we're sick and tired of being used as examples of minorities who have made it, because we haven't!"

Fourthly, the Japanese-American experience warns us to discard the idea that "it won't happen to me." It is not just non-white Americans or citizens of the underground that are concerned about the concentration camps. The very fact that the government--by pressure from a few--is free to make its own arbitrary definition of subversives, should make us realize that this is a matter of concern for all Americans.

Furthermore, we should not fool ourselves into nitpicking by attacking the narrator because we didn't like the narration. If a fellow American--be he Black, Brown, Yellow, Red, or White--has endured unjust experiences brought about by such basic denials of due process, we should be able to listen to that experience and place it in its proper context rather than dismiss the relator of that experience as being bitter, biased, or disenchanted. Also, it is not enough to identify with the victim, by eating soul food, using him as a token guest, or insisting that all has been done to demonstrate fairness. Instead, we need a better grasp of what we mean by democracy and how it must function in a time of crisis. To maintain this health of a democracy so that it remains a channel through which all kinds of groups can move towards constructive goals, justice must be accomplished by benevolence and sympathy, zeal by patience and forebearance. These qualities were indeed limited during the war-time experience.

The sobering lessons of the Japanese-American relocation also force us to ask, "Can civil liberties, rights of individuals, and of the minority be tolerated, let alone protected, in a time of crises?" We acted on the basis of stereotype and we still too often operate by looking at him. When police teach only white housewives how to use firearms, this is racism in its most blatant form. If anything, the war-time evacuation has set the dangerous precedent of over-emphasizing racial and national strains in our population and using this as a criteria for discrimination and abrogation of human rights--something we see repeated now.

Democracy is in theory nothing more than the determination to live peacefully, and in practice nothing more than continuous experiment for doing so. The spirit of democracy involves integration of private convictions and public tolerance and involves the recognition of the will to live one's life consistent with good will to others. This was totally disregarded in the case of the internment of Japanese-Americans. It would do well to ask how much disregard for the rights of others applies to the situation we are living through today--whether the minority is the Black Panthers, the Latins for Justice, boys with long hair, girls with short skirts, or soldiers who do not want to kill.

Discussion and the pooling of ideas are instrumental to the maintenance of democracy. Yet what is also at issue is the vast gap between the rhetoric and action, between what is promised and what is actualized, what we say can't happen and what did happen. As Lord Clement Atlee of England said, "Democracy means government by discussion but it is only effective if you can stop people talking." The words of Pastor Martin Niemoller remind us of the price we pay when we renege on our responsibilities as participants in a democratic society:

"In Germany they came for the Communists and I didn't speak up because I wasn't a Communist. Then they came for the Jews, and I didn't speak up because I wasn't a Jew. Then they came for the trade unionists, and I didn't speak up because I wasn't a trade unionist. Then they came for the Catholics and I didn't speak up because I was a Protestant. Then they came for me--and by that time there was no one left to speak up."

It is hard enough to act constructively, let alone dissent creatively in our everyday lives. Crises situations challenge us to harness our rhetoric and respond to reality. We are in a time of crises where neither democracy, nor we, can afford to fail.

the Cherishing of Liberty: the american nisei

BILL HOSOKAWA

Shortly after his arrival in the United States, Manjiro Nakahama, the first Japanese "immigrant," found himself embroiled in a controversy that was not of his choosing. Manjiro was a shipwrecked fisherman who was rescued from a desert island in the Pacific by an American whaling captain, William H. Whitfield, and taken to Fairhaven, Massachusetts, in 1843.

The controversy arose when some members of the captain's church objected to Manjiro sitting in the Whitfield family pew. They contended the Japanese boy should sit in the segregated section with the Negroes.

History does not record Captain Whitfield's position on the slavery issue, but he felt discrimination against Manjiro was uncalled for. He resigned from the church to protest and affiliated himself with another congregation that was willing to accept Manjiro as an equal in the sight of God. In those times, however, it was widely believed that only those of European origins were entitled to enjoy without abridgement the rights and privileges of a nation whose independence was declared in a document that, ironically, opened its second paragraph with these noble words:

> "We hold these truths to be self-evident, that all men are created equal, that they are endowed by their Creator with certain unalienable rights, that among these are Life, Liberty and the pursuit of Happiness."

Manjiro's experience was only the first of a long series of rebuffs, many of them given a measure of sanctity by legal steps, that marks the history of persons of Japanese origins in the United States. Most of these persons, like Manjiro, were caught up in controversy without seeking it. The controversy came to them for the simple reason that they were of a race different from that of the Anglo-Saxon majority. These acts of racially-based discrimination were climaxed by the mass evacuation of all persons of Japanese blood to interior concentration camps during the hysteria engendered by World War II. Perhaps it is a tribute to the forebearance of both nations that their relations are as warm as they are today. Certainly it is a credit to the United States that, one step at a time, it has repealed discriminatory laws and abolished discriminatory practices so that Japanese, and other Asians who were similarly discriminated against, have relatively little to complain about today.

II

To understand the reason for this discrimination, it is necessary to go back into history, to the time when the first Asians arrived in the United States. The first to enter America in significant numbers were the Chinese. As early as 1848, the year gold was discovered in California, there were 54 Chinese known to be in that state. By 1850 the number had jumped to 3,227. The Chinese were imported to undertake the menial, unpleasant kind of work that frontiersmen shunned. Most of these Chinese were uneducated coolies from impoverished areas of south China, capable of prodigious amounts of work and enduring enormous hardships without complaint. Keeping to themselves and cherishing their own customs, it was inevitable that they should be looked down upon as different and therefore somewhat less than human. In some areas of the West, killing a Chinese was considered no more of a crime than killing a dog, for the testimony of a Chinese carried no weight in court.

So long as there was plenty of work—building the railroads that linked the West Coast with the East—the Chinese were tolerated. But when the railroads were com-

Reprinted from PACIFIC COMMUNITY, January, 1971, by permission of the Pacific News Community, the Jiji Press, Ltd., Tokyo, Japan.

pleted the Chinese began to compete for white men's jobs, and this was a different matter. Pressured by complaints against "cheap Asiatic labor," Congress was persuaded in 1882 to pass the Exclusion Act that barred further Chinese immigration for 10 years. The Act was extended another 10 years in 1892, and in 1902 it was extended for an indefinite period.

There is little doubt that Japanese government officials were aware of the treatment the Chinese were receiving in the United States. Even though numbers of bright young Japanese were being sent to the U.S. for their education during this period, immigration was prohibited. The Japanese reasoned that immigrants would come from the most humble classes, and the officials proudly declared they did not want their nation to be judged by the character of those going abroad. Emigration finally was legalized in 1886, in no small part at the urging of the United States which was looking for workmen to fill the void created by the embargo against Chinese labor.

In inheriting the jobs the Chinese once had filled, it was predictable that the Japanese also should fall heir to the prejudices and discriminatory legislation their predecessors knew. After all, were not the Japanese and Chinese of mutual racial stock? By 1924, a brief time as history is calculated, the Japanese also were barred from entry into the United States on the basis of race. Many observers believe the seeds for war between the two nations, which sprouted violently on December 7, 1941, were sown at that time. As Professor Yamato Ichihashi has noted: "No self-respecting nation can afford to be discriminated against on account of race."

Basic to the legalized discrimination the Japanese faced were statutes that restricted the privilege of naturalization to "free white persons" and those of African descent. Since there was no provision for persons who were neither black nor white, the Japanese found themselves "aliens ineligible for citizenship." A number of Japanese were permitted to become naturalized despite this law, apparently through the ignorance of local officials. One source estimates that as many as 460 Japanese immigrants received citizenship. The vast majority, however, did not even bother to apply, and the phrase "aliens ineligible for citizenship" was utilized to deny Japanese immigrants ownership of land in many states and prevent them from entering certain professions. The logic was that if under federal laws these persons were not worthy of being accepted as citizens, they certainly should not be permitted to own real property.

III

Ultimately a landmark United States Supreme Court decision upheld the validity of the discriminatory naturalization statutes. Takao Ozawa, born in Japan but a graduate of high school in Berkeley, California, and for some time a student at the University of California, brought suit to gain citizenship. One objective of his suit was to test California's Alien Land Act. The high court found the statute constitutional. Ozawa, being neither white nor African, remained an alien and therefore unable to enjoy the benefits of land ownership.

This decision was further reinforced in 1925 when the Supreme Court denied citizenship to Japanese who had served in the armed forces of the United States in World War I. Congress had passed a law offering citizenship to "any person of foreign birth who served" in the war, hoping thereby to stimulate enlistments. Japanese aliens had been among those who responded. The court ruled that inasmuch as Japanese aliens without military service could not become naturalized, the same rule would hold regardless of service in the armed forces.

Along with these setbacks, however, there were minor triumphs in the cause of justice. Take, for example, the San Francisco Board of Education's attempt to send all "Chinese, Japanese and Korean children" to a segregated Oriental school. On May 6, 1905, the school board announced such a segregation policy to protect white children from being "affected by association with pupils of the Mongolian race," but did not attempt to put it into force. Less than a year later the city was rocked by an earthquake followed by fire. On the pretext that the surviving schools were overcrowded, the school board implemented the segregation order.

Washington and Tokyo quickly took note of San Francisco's action. The embarrassed President Theodore Roosevelt sent a member of his cabinet to San Francisco to investigate. He found that the issue involved a grand total of 93 pupils, 25 of whom were American-born, distributed among 23 schools. Ultimately, San Francisco authorities were invited to Washington to work out a solution, the upshot of which was that immigrant children who had been in classes with much younger children because of language inadequacies were transferred to a separate school where they could be given special help with English. All other Japanese children were permitted to return to their neighborhood schools. The significance of this incident is that a relatively small local issue had become an international matter and forced the President of the United States to take action.

During much of this period some Americans, notably in California, for their own reasons spread the impression that it was official Japanese policy to flood the United States with immigrants. We have seen that Japan had refused to permit migration to the United States until 1886. Even after this law was changed many restrictions impeded the flow. Until 1907, the largest number of Japanese to enter the United States in a single year was 20,041 in 1903. During this same period tens of thousands of immigrants were entering the U.S. from Europe to meet the demand for labor in Eastern cities and populate the vast prairies of the West. Still, the fact that the Japanese were easily distinguishable physically and tended to concentrate in the West Coast states made them easy targets for "Yellow Peril" fears. In 1907, Secretary of State Elihu Root and Japanese Minister Kogoro Takahira negotiated a "Gentlemen's Agreement" whereby Japan pledged not to issue passports to laborers desiring to enter the United States, certainly a placatory action on Japan's part. The agreement was scheduled to become effective in 1908; seeking to beat the deadline, 30,824 Japanese entered the United States in 1907. But that was the high water mark. By 1909 the number of Japanese immigration exceeded 10,000 in only two years, and every year without exception women outnumbered male immigrants as the Japanese already in the U.S. took wives. Then, in 1921, the Japanese government stopped female emigration because of continued American hostility, thus effectively depriving many Japanese men in the U.S. of the opportunity to marry; Oriental-white unions were legally prohibited in a number of states, including California.

Despite these conciliatory efforts the United States finally slammed the door in Japan's face--in fact, the face of all Asia--by revising immigration statutes to prohibit the entry of any alien ineligible for citizenship. Some Senators favored an immigration quota for Japan, putting her on the same general basis as other nations. Such a quota, permitting the entry of 146 immigrants a year, would have lifted the stigma of undesirability and permitted Japan to save face. But even this token quota was rejected by Congress. The new, stringent immigration law was passed 308 to 62 in the House of Representatives, 69 to 9 in the Senate. President Calvin Coolidge said he disapproved of the Japanese exclusion provision, but signed the bill because he considered other portions of the measure vital to U.S. policy. A wave of resentment at the racial slight swept Japan. The U.S. Ambassador in Tokyo, C. E. Woods, resigned in protest, declaring: "Japan does not want to force emigrants upon the United States if we do not wish to receive them. The Japanese government, I believe, would be willing to agree to almost any form of restrictive treaty, but the exclusion provision of the immigration bill has struck a blow to their natural pride."

Among approximately 125,000 persons of Japanese blood in the United States at that time, about 100,000 of whom were aliens, the Congressional action spread consternation. It seemed to be confirmation of their fears of discriminatory treatment in perpetuity--denial of citizenship, the right to buy land, and now of their hopes of being treated on an equal basis with people of other national origins. Yet the vast majority did not want to return to Japan; the United States with all its repressions was the more desirable place to live--and to bring up families of American-born children who were citizens by birth.

These American-born, the Nisei, were educated in the public schools and quickly adopted the American heritage as their own, just as the sons and daughters of immigrants from Europe did. But there was one undeniable difference. The offspring of European immigrants could be assimilated quickly into the American melting pot. This was not true for the Nisei, who were of a different race. On the telephone a Nisei sounded as American as the next fellow, but in person his appearance set him aside. And so the

Nisei were subjected to subtle and often not so subtle social and economic discrimination. As more and more of their numbers completed their education and reached maturity, they found invisible barriers that kept all but the most aggressive and able individuals inside their own communities. Thus did the "Little Tokyo" settlements become established in centers like Los Angeles, San Francisco, Portland and Seattle.

This was the situation when the tragedy of World War II exploded over the Pacific.

IV

At first calm voices pointed out the need to distinguish between the enemy that had attacked Pearl Harbor and the peaceful, law-abiding "Japanese" in America, two-thirds of whom by now were Nisei citizens. Yet the government itself failed to make the distinction. At the same time federal agents were arresting Little Tokyo community leaders--an understandable precaution-- other officials ordered a blanket freeze on the funds of all persons with Japanese names. The family whose breadwinner had been seized by the Federal Bureau of Investigation suddenly found its bank accounts tied up. When the cash on hand ran out, it was impossible to buy food, pay bills, give employees their salaries. No distinction was made in this order between citizens and aliens, and even though the freeze was soon lifted, it was a warning of more stringent restrictions to come.

The campaign to "do something" about "the Japanese in our midst" did not pick up momentum until some five weeks after the outbreak of war. It is the charitable point of view to assume that a genuine though unjustified fear of possible fifth column activity motivated many of those who demanded restrictive action against the Japanese Americans. But there is ample evidence that many of the most militant were motivated by economic reasons or an opportunity to make political capital. At any rate, the demand that Japanese Americans be placed in concentration camps as a security measure began to be heard about five weeks after the beginning of the war, and the cries soon quickened and grew more strident.

The gist of most of the arguments was that the Japanese Americans were an unknown quantity, and that while many undoubtedly were loyal to the United States, it was impossible to separate the good from the bad. Shades of the inscrutible Oriental! Therefore, it was necessary to incarcerate the entire racial group. The racist implications were clear; Italian and German aliens are of the white race and therefore less suspect that Japanese aliens and their American-born offspring. Earl Warren, then attorney general of California and later to become the liberal Chief Justice of the United States Supreme Court, added another dimension to the argument for restrictions when he contended that the fact there had been no sabotage and no fifth column activities was "the most ominous sign in our whole situation." Warren contended that the Japanese Americans in California were only waiting for a signal from Tokyo to launch an uprising, probably to coincide with a Japanese attack on the West Coast. This point of view was embraced by, among others, the eminent commentator Walter Lippmann who wrote in his syndicated column that the fact there had been no sabotage is "a sign that the blow is well organized and that it is held back until it can be struck with maximum effect." In other words, Warren and Lippmann held that the absence of sabotage was a sign of Japanese American disloyalty, a remarkably illogical line of reasoning.

The federal government did little to quiet fears of a fifth column. The first garbled reports of the attack on Pearl Harbor had included charges of sabotage by Japanese Americans in Hawaii. In truth, they had distinguished themselves in many ways, and key officials later testified to their complete loyalty. But this testimony was not made public until much later, long after the evacuation decision had been made. Meanwhile, members of Congress repeated rumors of disloyalty and no one in authority attempted to clear the record. Secretary of the Navy Frank Knox, in his official report after a quick inspection of Pearl Harbor, made no mention of fifth column activity and he praised Hawaiian Nisei who had rushed to man guns against the attackers. But in a press conference coinciding with release of his report, he was quoted as saying: "I think the most effective fifth column work of the entire war was done in Hawaii, with the possible exception of Norway." No one bothered to refute that charge, either.

Inevitably, all persons of Japanese blood were removed from California, the western half of Oregon and Washington, and the southernmost portions of Arizona, to inland concentration camps which were euphemistically called War Relocation Centers. Approximately 110,000 men, women and children, two-thirds of whom were American citizens, were involved. No charges of disloyalty were filed against them, and in the absence of charges, no hearings were held. The evacuation was a racially-based measure in a war being fought, ironically, to defend the democratic way of life.

The economic loss to the evacuees has been estimated by the Federal Reserve Bank at $400,000,000. The loss in terms of human dignity, democratic ideals, pride and other intangible values, is incalculable.

Even as the Army executed the evacuation at gunpoint, another arm of the U.S. government was being organized to ease the shock and bitterness. This was the War Relocation Authority, a civilian agency charged with operation of the camps and, more important, for returning the evacuees as rapidly as possible to normal life outside the camps.

The camps were elementary barracks towns, no worse than camps being occupied by thousands of Army recruits. The basic difference, however, was that recruits are vigorous young men; the evacuees included women and children as well as men of all ages. Moreover, the evacuees had been segregated by race. Even so, they enjoyed a small measure of self-government and contributed largely to the operation and maintenance of the camps. The War Relocation Authority's main thrust, however, was on returning its charges back into the American lifestream. By the end of the war, half the 110,000 evacuees had left the camps for freedom in the Mountain states, the Midwest and the East.

V

Shortly before war's end the United States Supreme Court finally got around to ruling on several cases having to do with the evacuation. The first involved Fred T. Korematsu, a California Nisei shipyard welder who had been convicted of remaining in a military area from which persons of Japanese ancestry had been excluded. The Supreme Court upheld the conviction, recognizing the right of the Army to order the exclusion of any persons from specified military areas.

The second case involved Mitsuye Endo, a Nisei woman who had sued the government for release from War Relocation Authority custody. The Supreme Court ruled that since it had not been shown that Miss Endo was disloyal, under the Constitution she should be free to come and go as she pleased, even to California where she had lived.

In effect, the Supreme Court had ruled that the Army was justified in evacuating Japanese Americans from a prohibited zone, but once evacuated, loyal Japanese Americans could not continue to be excluded from their former homes. The practical effect was to enable the evacuees to go back to the West Coast if they wished. The Supreme Court agreed unanimously in the Endo decision. Three justices dissented in the Korematsu case. One of them, Robert H. Jackson, made a point that has broad ramifications beyond the rights of Japanese Americans, and which continues to be of concern to many observers.

Mr. Justice Jackson contended that the Supreme Court, in finding that the Constitution sanctions a military order against a specific minority, "for all time has validated the principle of racial discrimination in criminal procedure and of transplanting American citizens." He contined: "The principle then lies about like a loaded weapon ready for the hand of any authority that can bring forward a plausible claim of an urgent need." In these times of militant civil unrest the precedent indeed lies like a loaded weapon threatening dissident minorities.

At this point it may be pertinent to note that of some 120,000 Japanese Americans, only 4,724 left the United States as repatriates or expatriates as a result of the war experience. This amounted to less than four per cent of the total, and many of them were minors who had little choice but to accompany their parents. The breakdown goes like this:
 1,659 aliens repatriated to Japan.
 1,949 American citizens, virtually all minors, accompanying their parents.
 1,116 adults who renounced their American citizenship. Most of these were Kibei-- persons who had received an important part of their education in Japan and had experienced considerable difficulty adjusting to life in the United States.

Meanwhile, the Japanese American Citizens League, the only national organization of Americans of Japanese ancestry, set out to right the wrongs perpetrated during the war and before, and to eliminate the legal bases for discrimination. Three primary goals were set up:
 --To gain the right of naturalization

for Japanese aliens.
- --To remove racial discrimination from immigration laws.
- --To collect idemnity for economic losses suffered as a result of the evacuation.

The League's Washington representative, Mike Masaru Masaoka, a decorated veteran of service with the all-Nisei 442nd Regimental Combat Team, was given the responsibility of lobbying remedial legislation through Congress. Even though the objectives seemed impossible in view of lingering animosities, Masaoka achieved the objectives one by one. Several factors, in addition to Masaoka's persistence and skills, worked in his favor. One was a growing realization that the evacuation had been a ghastly error and amends were overdue. Another was the Nisei war record, a demonstration of loyalty that could not be ignored in weighing the cause of justice.

Characteristically, Congress agreed on compensation for the evacuees before it did anything about human rights. On July 2, 1949, President Harry Truman signed the Japanese American Evacuation Claims Act. The evacuees filed 23,689 claims totaling $131,949,176. About 60 per cent of these claims were for less than $2,500--"pots and pans" claims for loss of household items. In all, some $38,000,000 was paid by the federal government--less than 10 cents for every dollar lost.

Masaoka was moved to observe: "This was not a generous program. But it represents a major triumph in that Congress recognized the error of the evacuation and the justice of the claims."

Next, after a series of court cases, the California alien land law, after which land laws in many other states were patterned, was ruled discriminatory and unconstitutional by the U.S. Supreme Court.

The greatest triumph was yet to come. In 1950 Masaoka succeeded in having introduced a simple measure that would authorize the naturalization of any qualified alien without respect fo race or national origin. Congress approved the measure, but because other issues objectionable to President Truman were attached to it, he vetoed the entire bill. Two years later the Walter-McCarran Immigration and Naturalization Act provided for repeal of the Oriental Exclusion Act of 1924 and extended to Japan and other Asian nations a token immigration quota. It also eliminated race as a barrier to naturalization. Once again President Truman vetoed the measure for reasons not linked to the Japanese. This time Congress overrode the veto, and two ancient injustices that had been the source of ill-feeling between Japan and the United States were eliminated.

Finally, in 1965, shortcomings that had continued to discriminate subtly against Asians were eliminated in another immigration bill signed by President Lyndon B. Johnson. The law now specifies that the 350,000 immigrants permitted to enter the U.S. annually will be admitted on a basis of their skills and relationship to those already here, and not on the basis of race, creed or nationality.

Today, what Manjiro Nakahama encountered first has run full circle. The meaning of all this was explained not long ago by Representative Patsy Takemoto Mink, first and so far only woman to serve the State of Hawaii in Congress. In a speech she observed:

"Exclusion acts, Yellow Peril laws, miscegenation laws, World War II relocation camps, hate campaigns, arbitrary firings from jobs, housing and employment discrimination; all these were suffered by the Japanese, alien or citizen, during our recent memory. Yet the astounding truth is that despite all this, this persecuted minority--classified as 'enemy' during the war--refused to believe that America did not offer them the best opportunities to be free, to be secure, to be prosperous, and to be happy. And so with deliberateness they sought to regain the confidence and trust of a suspicious nation.

"I believe this struggle for acceptance as Americans has been won; and this victory is not ours but belongs to white America for having found that those of the 'yellow' race have the same capacity as they to love their country, to honor and revere its heroes, to fight and die for its honor, and to cherish the blessings of liberty. May all of us who have flourished in this land become an emissary of brotherhood and love so that all who still suffer the indignities of the unequal shall have the chance that was ours."

BOOK REVIEW
Nisei: The Quiet Americans

YUJI ICHIOKA

"God Bless America"--so the refrain rings in William K. Hosokawa's new book: NISEI: THE QUIET AMERICANS. Much has been written and said about the title before its publication--many people objected to the word "quiet." Now we have an opportunity to examine its content and theme, and the refrain, sad to say but not too surprisingly, rings hollow and discordant.

Mr. Hosokawa's book is popular history. It fits the classic genre of histories written by other ethnic groups which might be labeled "We Too Made A Contribution." Professional historians call this type of history filiopietistic--filio because it insists upon remaining faithful to an ethnic group; pietistic because it relates that group's contributions to America with platitudes while extolling the virtues of America. Reading such histories, ethnic readers can be self-congratulatory and the larger society can continue to uphold its doctrine of "Americanism." In judging the merits and demerits of his book, this point should be kept foremost in mind.

It is clear that its origin predetermined its content and theme. NISEI is part of the larger Japanese American Research Project, begun in 1962 and still in operation at UCLA, under the initiative of the JACL. Aside from the "academic" volumes which are scheduled for later publication, Mr. Hosokawa was commissioned to write a popular history of the Nisei. Hence it is not unexpected to discover that his work is essentially about Nisei JACLers and the JACL itself. Two-thirds of it deals with the establishment of the JACL, its subsequent trials and accomplishments, and its leading luminaries. The book jacket which contains the further sub-title, "A Story of a People", is therefore very misleading. The book is not about all Nisei--it is about Nisei JACLers, unless of course one equates the JACL with all Nisei. And its platitudes specifically concern that organization.

Reprinted from GIDRA, January, 1970.

The theme is simple: it says, "We've Made It!" in so many words. Edwin O. Reischauer, in his foreword, gives us more than an indication:

"No immigrant group encountered higher walls of prejudice and discrimination than did the Japanese...None experienced a more dramatic crisis than they did when...one hundred thousand of them...were herded from the West Coast into what amounted to concentration camps. None retained greater faith in the basic ideals of America or showed stronger determination to establish their rights to full equality and justice, even when their fellow Americans seemed determined to deny them both. None showed greater loyalty to the United States or greater willingness to make sacrifices on the battlefield or at home for their country. The outcome, of course, has been the great American success story writ large-- a Horatio Alger tale on an ethnic scale."

Mr. Hosokawa simply relates this Horatio Alger story in terms of the JACL. The book is divided into three parts: "The Early Years," covering the pre-war period in a superficial fashion; "The Years of Travail," focusing upon the World War II ordeal; and "The Years of Fulfillment," treating the post-war era through the early 1950's. The first part relates the origins of immigration and the early immigrant experience. It ends with the emergence of the Nisei population and the birth of the JACL. Thus the stage is set for the drama. Already faced with seemingly insurmountable obstacles, the Japanese must contend with even more. The attack on Pearl Harbor occurs, and the travail begins, opening the second part of the book. The "dedicated" JACL leaders then enter, and the JACL acts out its "monumental role in the history of the Japanese in America." The leaders are all depicted as flawless characters, single-minded in their devotion and commitment to American ideals. And many interesting episodes and anecdotes are related in the course of the narrative--Mike Masaoka's idea, for example, proposing a volunteer Nisei "suicide battalion" to fight in the Pacific to prove Nisei loyalty to America; the "sinister" implications ascribed by intelligence agencies to the fact that Nisei students at UCLA were studying German. The third part finally orchestrates the theme to its logical crescendo: because of the inspired leadership of the JACL, the doors of opportunity at last open to the Nisei.

At no time does Mr. Hosokawa allude to possible psychological damages which Nisei may have incurred because of their minority experience and the trauma of World War II. He does go into a short discourse on Nisei passivity, inability to articulate, and lack of general aggressiveness (which even Mike Masaoka is said to have observed upon his initial contacts with Nisei). But he does no more than gloss over this observation. Many people have attempted to explain Nisei conservatism by stressing, in one way or another, the importance of transmitted cultural value--the "shikata ga nai" or family structure or related explanation. A much better one might be sought in the Nisei experience in an overtly hostile, racist America. Given his success ideology, however, Mr. Hosokawa has his blinders on. He fails to recognize, let alone analize, the price Nisei have had to pay for their loyalty obsession. An obsession is abnormal, especially in proportion to its persistence. Mr. Hosokawa writes about past JACL obsessions which persist down to today--which explains why he avoids this discomforting issue. For to do so, he would have to reevaluate his Horatio Alger story.

The Sansei should be particularly disturbed by this book. The clear implication for them is that they should be grateful. The rich harvest of America is now available to be reaped because of JACL's commitment to American ideals. It appears, ironically, at the very moment when Sansei activists are asking: what have we been integrating into? Into a nation conducting a politically and morally bankrupt war against Vietnamese people in the name of freedom and democracy? A nation bent upon exterminating militant Black leaders? A nation which is moving to extreme right in the name of law and order? A nation in which the so-called "American Dream" has turned out to be a violent nightmare? His theme is totally out of touch with the hard realities of the time. In 1969, "Americanism" still basically means racism, superpatriotism, and rightwing politics.

NISEI in sum is an idealized monument to the old guard JACL leaders, justifying their existence and lifetime work. No one can deny the important role and work JACL performed in the past. But today we need to question old assumptions; the last thing we need is filiopietistic, popular history. In this time of political, social, and moral crisis in America, old and new problems demand radical approaches, not tired orations. And so having had their testament for posterity written, we bid the old guard to retire as "quiet Americans."

the u.s. in asia
and asians in america

FRANKLIN ODO WITH MARY UYEMATSU, KEN HANADA, PEGGY LI, AND MARIE CHUNG

All ethnic groups in the United States work with the assumption, explicit at some times, implicit at others, that the nature of the relations between the U.S. and the nations from which they or their ancestors came have much to do with their own fates.[1] This is why Black Americans confront the issue of American policies toward African nations--and particularly the problem of U.S. investment in the most blatantly racist ones like South Africa or Rhodesia. Their responses vary, to be sure, but Blacks understand that the racism manifested in movies set in Africa (e.g., "Tarzan" types) are of critical importance to them.

The same reasons apply when Chicanos attack the "Frito Bandito" commercials or movies set in Latin America like "Butch Cassidy and the Sundance Kid." One important factor is the image of these groups portrayed to and internalized by White and other Americans. More crucial, now, is the understanding that those portrayals have real and deleterious effects on the attitude of members of that ethnic group-- particularly the children. Many American Jews were quick to understand that Israel meant more to them than a symbol. Few Jews have, after all, emigrated here from Israel but the survival and image of the Israeli State are problems of immediacy because they can do much to affect the lives of all Jews in the United States. Asian Americans are no exception--as this volume's selections on the media ought to make clear.

In times of crisis, however, the issues become more dramatic and more clearly delineated. The most glaring example is the World War II relocation of Japanese Americans on the West Coast to concentration camps farther inland. Whatever their sympathies (and many issei, in particular, were understandably ambivalent about the United States-Japan was for Pacific hegemony) they had had no way of influencing the policies of either belligerent but were assumed dangerous on racist grounds.

Legislation affecting Asians in America at all levels of government has both influenced and been influenced by the historical conditions of U.S.-Asian relations. Immigration laws were good examples--the weakness of the Ch'ing court prevented China from mustering any real international voice to stop or allay U.S. efforts at ending Chinese immigration in 1882. It took World War II when China became an ally against Japan before even token immigration was finally allowed in 1943 (annual quota of 100).

Anti-Chinese attitudes exhibited against Chinese Americans intensified with the emergence of a stronger (and communist) China in 1949, and J. Edgar Hoover's notorious statement to the House Un-American Activities Committee in April 1969 was hardly calculated to reassure Chinese in America. Recent "ping pong diplomacy" notwithstanding, there is little reason to believe that he (and thus the F.B.I.) does not continue to believe that the 300,000 Chinese in the U.S. pose a potential source of mainland agents for espionage/sabotage. It would be foolish, therefore, for any leader in the Chinese American community to assume that he or she is not under some form of surveillance by one or more security agencies. The same holds true for virtually all ethnic minority communities.

Most recently, the war in Southeast Asia has brought home to many Asian Americans the fact of racism in the United States. We look like the enemy and often pressures of the war encourage non-Asian G.I.'s to give vent to their frustrations by attacking yellow comrades in arms or, later, civilian Asians in the U.S. After all, no effort is made to "debrief" G.I.'s who are trained to hate and despise the "gooks." National efforts to counteract heroin addiction among returning veterans is belatedly being recognized but few people bother to even consider the extent of anti-Asian racism being generated or boosted by the war.

At this most immediate level it is relatively easy to understand the concern Asian Americans must have in the face of a continuing U.S. presence in Asia. More important because more fundamental, however, is a second level of analysis which suggests that there are useful analogies between the U.S. treatment of Asians in Asia and the position of Asians in America. Here, the working concept of internal colonialism attempts to relate the position of countries of the Third World to the colored communities of America.

The assumption of eventual Asian assimilation into mainstream America has implied the disintegration of "ghettos" since ethnicity was to become increasingly irrelevant. In fact, however, the 1970 census will probably show large pockets of Asian peoples--with the poor in the larger cities and the middle classes in certain specific suburban neighborhoods. It would be difficult to argue a point by point analogy between neo-colonialism (economic control) abroad and the position of Asian Americans but certain elements are worth noting.

In both cases (neo-colonies and Asian Americans) the two distinctive patterns are their relative powerlessness and the systematic exploitative relationships that exist between us and our government. This is not to deny the existence of the Inouye's, Mink's, Fong's and Hayakawa's. They perform useful functions--but primarily (and they would no doubt agree) in the service of the "larger" community rather than as representatives of any ethnic groups. Who, then, represents the interests of Asians in the U.S.? We are still a largely powerless group.

Asian Americans have been systematically exploited--few would question that assertion in the face of the history of labor in Hawaii and on the West Coast over the past century.[2] More would deny the present existence of such a relationship today in spite of the exposure of ghetto conditions in Chinatown with sweatshop labor conditions; or references to the struggles of Filipino farm workers who have survived decades of abuse.[3] Working class Asian Americans face the dual problem of racism and class conflict. Other, more "successful", types work with systematic discrimination in higher civil service positions and the "middle-management ceiling" which appears to exist for Asian Americans in business. A recent survey of top-level businessmen in the San Francisco and Los Angeles-San Diego metropolitan areas revealed continuing patterns of prejudice against the promotion of Asian Americans into executive positions.[4] Two basic factors were prominent: first, the executives themselves admitted to anti-Asian prejudices (reinforced by combat participation in World War II, Korea or Vietnam); and, second, the assumption that customers shared these prejudices.

With few exceptions, then, Asians face relatively powerless and circumscribed lives. We contribute in taxes or labor to the disproportionate gain of others and accept as inevitable or unchallengeable (as do most colonized peoples) our own limited horizons. But conditions change and so do the people involved.

A third level of analysis which links Asian Americans to Asians in Asia is the ideological posture assumed by proponents of a Third World concept. But the Third World is a slippery entity--both in conceptual terms and in practice. As originally conceived, the Third World denoted an independent, capitalist Europe competing with the post-World War II super power empires, the Soviet Union and the United States. For various reasons, including the fact that capitalism has assumed an increasingly multi-national character, the economic interests of the U.S. and Europe (and Japan) are becoming more monolithic.

In their struggles against foreign exploitation, the nations of Africa, Asia, Latin America and the Middle East are urged to unite in a common struggle against the imperialism of the "two worlds." Peoples of color in the U.S. have responded to the analytical and emotional attractiveness of the Third World concept and growing numbers insist on a world view which places them in positions related to their brothers overseas. Racism and capitalism work together to perpetuate some of the major ills borne by Third World countries abroad and Third World communities at home. In both cases the logic calls for resistance and revolution but the unification struggles and effective coalitions are hampered by the unbalanced power relationship (counterinsurgency, foreign and domestic) and the immediate needs of each nation or ethnic group. Complicating the picture is the growth of relatively privileged groups who help perpetuate the relationship because it appears to be in their interest. Client regimes or puppet governments abroad are matched by ethnic counterparts here--the leadership dominated by "toms," "apples," "coconuts," and "bananas,"--all colors on the outside but white on the inside. Under these conditions some people will form liberation struggles along ethnic lines as well as ideological ones and considerable energy is expended in the attempt to integrate the two.

It is possible for concerned Asian Americans to respond variously to the three levels of analysis but the most interesting ones include the following: a) on a personal level we recognize the direct effects on ourselves of this exploitative and racist war and we participate in or support protests; or b) we understand the critical nature of the "neo-colonial" situation within the U.S. and seek to reorient our priorities so that working within our ethnic communities (i.e., restructuring of power within the U.S.) is seen as a necessary prerequisite to the reformulation of foreign policy; or c) we attempt a comprehensive analysis which ties in the problems of Third World countries with the lives of all workers and peoples of color in the U.S. The common link is the corporate structure which is used to dominate both in the unceasing grasp for economic expansion. "Evil" motivations are unnecessary--the capitalist who refuses to pursue economic growth in all ways and all areas is, after all, being totally irresponsible.

There are not a great number of ways in which Asian Americans can begin to explore the ideas presented above. One of them should be the formal institutions of education--like the college or university. Unfortunately, the problems are great. Courses normally offered are given with a rather different frame of reference. An unusual seminar presented the opportunity for research into the general problem of Asian American perspectives on the U.S. in Asia and the analysis that follows reflects part of our efforts. First, however, it will be useful to provide a brief description of the seminar itself, its members, goals, methodology, limitations and advantages.[5]

Designed and structured to explore the relationship between Asian Americans and U.S. policies in Asia, the fourteen students (from all four undergraduate classes) and instructor spent the first three weeks reading and discussing major works dealing with revisionist or radical interpretations. All entered the seminar with some background in a) U.S. history; b) history of Asians in America; or c) U.S. foreign policy; a general background of conventional interpretations was thus assumed. Works by William A. Williams, Gabriel Kolko, Thomas McCormick, Pierre Jalee, Franz Schurmann, Harry Magdoff, and Paul Sweezy contributed much to the focus the group was to develop.

One essential decision was to do whatever possible to make the results of our efforts available to a wider audience. We all agreed very quickly that the problem area was important, sometimes critical, to the lives of Asian Americans. World War II alone was enough of a "lesson." It was more difficult, however, to agree on any single perspective.

The geographical target area was limited to S.E. Asia because of its immediate concern as well as to demonstrate the historical and longer range considerations of U.S. interests there. Members selected more precisely defined subjects to research in smaller groups which met separately and reported back to the entire seminar. Individual assignments were coordinated at both levels.

After considerable discussion and debate the seminar agreed to pursue the question of U.S. economic interests in the area and their implications for policy. In spite of the prevailing contemporary anti-war sentiment in the U.S. the fundamental nature of our involvement is too often clouded by references to "mistakes" and bad judgment or to the megalomania of individual men in high places rather than to self-interest.[6] We sought to examine the degree of economic motivation and the mechanisms through which it is implemented. Once that was done the research areas became more obvious. The following, with the students involved, are the principal ones selected and suggest the outlines of the collective undertaking:

1. Historical Background (Rob Murakami, Merilynne Hamano).
2. Natural Resources in S.E. Asia--Oil (Ken Hanada, Russel Kubota, Dyan Nakaji).
3. U.S. Aid and Financial Network in Asia (Mary Uyematsu, Betty Hom).
4. Cultural Imperialism (Peggy Li).
5. Research and Development--Counterinsurgency (Marie Chung).
6. Politics and the Military (Jack Ng, Jerry Wong).
7. Vietnam (Tony Inzana).
8. Ecocide (Mike Miyamoto).

Our conclusions were far more detailed than the following account could include but the outline above indicates the major points. The U.S. has had a long tradition of economic interest in Asia--at least from the eighteenth century. It has also been an expansionist country from its inception and been an integral part of a larger movement of European colonialism and imperialism. Few were disposed to accept a simplistic notion of economic determinism as explanation of historical causation but the group argued for its inclusion as central to any understanding of the U.S. in Asia.

The search for markets has been a part of American business concern since the second half of the nineteenth century when Asia became crucial as a vast area with teeming multitudes whose purchases could keep domestic industries expanding. Markets are still important but raw materials are more concrete and recent evidence suggested the critical nature of new oil discoveries in Asia. So the question of U.S. oil interests and their activities became an important part of our research. Assuming, then, that Asia is being regarded as crucial to our corporations, the next step was determining the mechanisms for gaining or securing these markets and resources for our business leaders. Here we discovered one of the keys to American "success" to be a rich and varied approach with many levels of strategy and tactics. Prominent among these is the use of economic aid to "developing countries" or, more precisely, for their ruling elites. The growth of a financial network (banks; other lending institutions) throughout S.E. Asia has been impressive--and bankers themselves have stressed the importance of investment in the area.

Other important means of maintaining governments friendly to U.S. business interests are covered under the rubric "cultural imperialism"--social and educational methods of increasing Asian dependence on the U.S. Its importance lies in the need for business to operate under secure and predictable conditions. Thus the selective extension of scholarships enabling Asian students to study American institutions and business practice (the virtues of capitalism and democracy) is regarded as "overhead" in business terms.

But aid, trade, banks and education are not always enough. The U.S. is deeply involved in research and development aimed at improving our counterinsurgency policies. Everything from the use of bedbugs to help in early warning systems for combat troops in guerrilla warfare situations to total social redistribution (strategic hamlet, free fire zones, etc.) is the grist for the "R plus D equals CI" mill. Power, of course, is the name of the game and politics is the expression of power. The uses of political institutions and politicians was also explored. But when all else fails, the military must be called in to protect our interests. Some of us find it misleading to call the U.S. a "warmongering" or "militaristic" society bent on destroying the world. The military is better understood as the last resort and it has been (and will continue to be) used in Asia when other means seem to fail.

All this may be seen in the case of Vietnam and the rest of S.E. Asia. What remains is the brutal fact of ecocide for non-cooperating Asian nations and powerlessness (vulnerability) in the lives of Asians in America--unless more fundamental changes occur--and the reexamination of our present situation is a critical first step. There is no reason, after all, to believe that conflict in Asia will cease in the near future. The following sections exerpted from the more useful papers, may be of some help in assessing the fundamental posture of the U.S. in Asia. The first, by Mary Uyematsu presents an important alternative to the views of those who now see Vietnam as a series of "mistakes" and "miscalculations."

....

INTERNATIONAL DEVELOPMENT OF THE U.S.

It is the assumption of many Americans that United States foreign aid is a function of the theory of "the White Man's Burden." This theory claims that "the dirty work of sustaining Western Civilization for the benefit of the underdeveloped world and for the civilized West now lies heavily on the conscience of the U.S."[7] Thus, the United States is supporting the rest of the world by helping underdeveloped countries get on their feet and by keeping the "civilized West" stable in its economy through aid.

When Americans hear about different countries of the world protesting against United States policies through revolutionary guerrilla movements, student protests and other anti-U.S. movements, they feel great indignation that these countries should dare be so arrogant as to bear any grudge against the American government, when America is financially supporting their livelihood. But the contradiction does not lie so much in those rebellious countries which are receiving aid as in the disparity between what Americans believe to be the purposes of foreign aid and the essential functions of foreign aid.

"The White Man's Burden" has been used as a rationale for the U.S. government and businessmen to show their "fellow" Americans what a great and generous country America is. Capitalism and racism work hand in hand to keep this belief alive. The capitalist outlook sees the rest of the world as something meant to be used--whatever we do for the rest of the world could only make it better than what is already is. Therefore, whether we build factories, develop other economies "like" ours, or "change" a government so that it is more "receptive" to ours, we are doing it for their own good. America is the principal benefactor to the rest of the world for it is giving everyone else the "privilege" to be a part of the "civilized West."

President John F. Kennedy explained foreign aid: "Foreign aid is a method by which the U.S. maintains a position of influence and control around the world and sustains a good many countries which would definitely collapse, OR PASS INTO THE COMMUNIST BLOC."[8] The House Committee on Foreign Affairs was as explicit: "The most important reason (for "pure" economic assistance) is that nations are DETERMINED to develop. Only by participation in that process will we have an opportunity to DIRECT their development along lines that will BEST SERVE OUR INTERESTS."[9]

Our policy makers are not necessarily cynical in thinking that we are helping underdeveloped countries by providing them with a capitalist economy. They base their thinking on "sound economics" which is itself based on a balance of profits and deficits. But the most important assumption here is that the U.S. economy is "the" economy to be concerned with, a natural pattern of thought since it is U.S. policy makers and economists who are involved. If anything, then, other countries are helping America. They are supporting the American economy; subservient to and dependent on the American economy.

HOW IS THIS SO?

In providing foreign aid to a country, the U.S. has a number of devices through which it secures support for its own economy. As underdeveloped countries feel the need for financial assistance to become a working industrial nation, they become subject to "strings" which are attached to that aid. Through negotiations for foreign aid to recipient countries, the U.S. has been able to:
1. Implement world-wide military and political policies of the U.S.
2. Enforce the open-door policy: for freedom of access to raw materials, trade, and investment opportunities.
3. Ensure that such economic development as does take place in underdeveloped countries is firmly rooted in capitalist ways and practices.
4. To obtain immediate economic gains for U.S. businessmen seeking trade and investment opportunities.
5. To make the receivers of aid increasingly dependent on the U.S. and other capital markets. (debts created by loans extended perpetuate bondage of aid receivers to the capital markets of the metropolitan centers.)[10]

In order to illustrate some of the advances of American capitalists have been able to make through foreign negotiations, the recent examples of aid to Southeast Asia will be most useful. In Vietnam, the first important trade with the United States took place with the introduction of American aid in that country in 1965. U.S. aid allowed for the increase of economic expansion which in turn led to a rise in foreign exchange for import markets. The Commercial Import Program provided Vietnam with $150.7 million to pay for U.S. import goods for civilians during the fiscal year of 1965. This excluded military assistance which went toward supplies and construction. Thus, what the U.S. has done is provide more markets for U.S. goods in the guise of foreign aid. Public Law 480, which allows for almost all of Vietnam's imports of flour, dairy products and leaf tobacco, is an act through which the U.S. government finances these agricultural products. The goods, however, are sold through the usual trade channels and the income becomes further U.S. financial power in the local currency of that country (often used for further loans to the government of that country).[11] Hence, there is no real giving away of money through foreign aid. America is simply furthering her bargaining power and foreign exchange with these "economic assistance" programs.

The use of foreign aid to provide more markets for U.S. goods not only functions to open these trade markets, but the American people's taxes are fronting this money, that is lending these countries their foreign exchange power. Thus, for those who directly profit from these foreign market sales--namely "big business"--their tax money is merely being returned to them through sales profits. But for the rest of us who are in no way connected with foreign market sales "profits", we are indirectly supporting the further wealth of "American Business."

Indonesia provides an example of how the U.S. has "created" a government through which it can attain profits from a country--via foreign aid. It was long understood that Indonesia held vast potential for profit with its wealth of raw resources. Logically, the United States has involved itself directly and indirectly in making that country accessible to American private investors. In 1953, Eisenhower defended American aid to France in their war with the Vietnamese, rationalizing that if the "free world"--of which France is an integral part--should lose Vietnam and Malaysia, then there was no way that it could "hold the rich empire of Indonesia." Thus, $400 million was given to aid the French war.[12] In April of 1966, the New York Times reported:

In southeast Asia over the last decade, the CIA has been so active that the agency in some countries has become the principle are of American policy. It is said, for instance, to have been so successful in infiltrating the top of the Indonesian government and Army that the U.S. was reluctant to disrupt CIA covering operations by withdrawing aid and informative programs in 1964 and 1965.[13]

Thus, the overthrow of Sukarno by General Suharto in 1965 was determined not just by CIA infiltration but also through American aid to Suharto's forces through various third world countries. As Suharto's forces were at times in meagre supply of food and munitions, "aid" must certainly have helped their overthrow.[14]

Sukarno needed to be ousted--through American policy eyes--to turn back the socialistic changes he was making in the Indonesian economy to the U.S. benefit. General Suharto's coup resulted in the return of U.S. private ownership to Goodyear, Uniroyal, Unilever, Caltex, and Stanvac--enterprises which Sukarno had nationalized.[15]

Indonesia then turned to the International Monetary Fund (IMF) and the World Bank (International Bank for Reconstruction and Development--IBRD) for "stabilization loans" to restabilize the economy Sukarno has set up (and upset) with his attempts at reform. FORTUNE MAGAZINE noted that when the rescheduled debts are due in the mid-1970's, repayments will result in inflation again. Thus, in addition to "stabilization loans" Indonesia has launched an "austerity" program aimed at restabilizing as "needed to halt inflation, but it also means a low level of economic activity and reduced revenue for development spending."[16] Thus, Indonesia is caught in a bind of trying to stabilize her economy through measures which are keeping her from developing those necessary projects which will get her back on her feet. As a result, Indonesia plans to "increase their foreign debt from $3 billion to $6 billion by 1974" in order to finance the needed "development projects."[17]

Indonesia now has little choice but to keep borrowing from "lending institutions" for her chances of regaining a balanced economy look slim in terms of the debt she has already acquired. They will look even slimmer for as Harry Magdoff describes this "economic-financial dependency trap", it becomes "more pronounced when the country tries to advance via the established capitalist path."[18] This becomes more than true if we look at the situation that has developed within the last three decades. In the period between 1938 and 1963, the trend in the world trade market for exports from underdeveloped countries (composed mainly of raw materials) increased by two-thirds, while the markets for manufactured goods (produced by the industrialized nations) jumped up 250 per cent.[19] (This is where the opening of markets through foreign aid is ironic). Prices for these raw exports fell as compared to those of manufactured goods. Additionally, since the most "fruitful spheres of manufacturing activity are usually taken over by foreign investors"[20] via open door policies attained through "aid negotiations" in these underdeveloped countries, plus the "high degree of monopolization in the manufacturing centers"[21] thereby industrialized nations or foreign investors can keep their prices at a "profit" level, then underdeveloped countries stand no chance of getting their economies "together". In the example of Indonesia, one of the richest resources of the world, she may as well sink back in the ocean until American capitalists and capitalists alike are forced to play another game. To further confound the relationship between developed and underdeveloped countries, capitalist countries like the U.S. have tariff systems that cut off U.S. markets from "direct competition that might arise from underdeveloped countries." Thus, for underdeveloped countries to develop processing industries for their raw exports, they are met with "protective devices" for the processing industries in industrialist countries.[22] Underdeveloped countries are left with limitations as to what they can sell to the United States, cutting their rate of exports--which further lessens their power to catch up in the capitalistic game that the industrialist nations are now controlling.

There is an additional structure which further enhances underdeveloped countries' dependencies on to the capitalist "machine." This is the "world banking system." Such institutions as the World Bank, International Monetary Fund, International Finance Corporation, and Development Assistance Committee have been created for the basic purpose of being "loan agencies" to those countries needing extra capital to develop their economy. Just as foreign aid has found meaningful ways of supporting the existing structure of the donor, such is also the case with these establishments. IMF, IBRD, and DAC work "in cooperation" with U.S. foreign aid programs.[23] The working relationship between foreign aid and these lending agencies comes in the form of both working to accomplish the same end. Lending agencies have the same amount of "strings" as do foreign aid grants and loans. They are controlled by the U.S. and other leading industrial nations,[24] and they are therefore managed in such a way as to "bind" underdeveloped countries into certain specific "relationships" with capitalist economies.

IBRD, better known as the World Bank, was created in 1944 at the time of the Breton Woods Economic Conference, and it started business in 1946. It granted loans to the governments of member nations, official bodies, and "private enterprises"--(it is interesting that private enterprises be afforded similar status as governments and official bodies of peoples. Perhaps this reflects the attitude that their member governments and official bodies are much the same as private enterprises). Of the 103 member nations of June 30, 1966, 50 per cent of the voting power was "controlled" by the United States, Britain, France, West Germany, and Nationalist China.[25] This means that either "strong influence" or direct control is vested in these five countries "interests." World Bank's activities include withholding capital from needy countries unless they follow the "desirable practices,":

> In the face of demand from the underdeveloped for the maximum amount of capital on the easiest possible terms in the shortest period of time, the IBRD was replying, in effect, that they really did not need as much capital as they imagined; the capital they did need was private, not public; and the reason they were short of private capital was that their governments were following undesirable policies.[26]

What then results is either the compliance of the underdeveloped to increased private investment--or no loans.

Agency for International Development has been mentioned in connection with working closely with IBRD.[27] AID is the primary aid agency of the U.S. for economic assistance.[28] Its varied activities give one insight into the true role of American foreign aid in the world:

> ...if the United States, or any other aid dispensing country is to exert influence on the domestic policies of an aid-receiving country, either directly or via an international agency, its representatives must have a clear idea, based on careful analysis, of what it wants this country to do. Frequently, such ideas have been lacking. Recently AID has given increased attention to this problem and has attempted to formulate for some of the principal aid-receiving countries a so-called Long-Range-Assistance Strategy which spells out U.S. economic, political, and security interests in the countries in question, the conditions necessary to their attainment, and the relevant instruments of foreign policy.[29]

The various ingredients that go into the real making of U.S. foreign policy via AID cover a wide spectrum of activities--from the relocating of Vietnamese civilians to foreign exchange activities. In 1961, 90 per cent of South Vietnam's 15,000,000 people were to be put into 11,000 "strategic hamlets" or "fortified villages." Many were forced into these "concentration camps" against their will. By 1964, three-fourths of the people were in hamlets. This program was run by a former CIA man for AID.[30]

AID serves as an information source for the CIA's Intelligence Division.[31] In addition, it is an information source in itself for American businessmen. In "Businessmen's Information Center: Investment in Southeast Asia," AID has produced a complete and detailed manuscript on the current economic situations of the Southeast Asian countries, giving guidelines as to where profits and "insured investments" (those countries having Investment Guaranty Programs insure U.S. citizens and corporations against losses due to nationalization and the incovertibility of local currency of U.S. dollars)[32] lie.

In 1967, AID conducted studies in Thailand on "peasant reactions to U.S. plans for 'radical' changes in traditional agriculture methods and consequent disruption of rural life."[33] Results of these studies give a better analysis of the situation whereby changes the U.S. is planning for Thailand can be given better control over the existing population there.

In the Department State Bulletin of December 1970, it was reported that government programs involving "exchange activities" were in the range of $400 million. These "exchange activities" are run by two agencies: Bureau of Education and Cultural Affairs and AID. Seven thousand persons a year are brought to the U.S., of whom about half are under the age of thirty. Recent budget cuts in this program were reversed by Assistant Secretary John Richardson and increased by an additional $5 million.[34] These "exchange activities" can be utilized by foreign policy makers in "cultivating the generals and admirals in power" and others who may serve as future governing agents, well-educated in American policy and "ideals."[35] Ngo Dinh Diem of South Vietnam, who chose exile rather than "actively oppose" the French, spent the early 1950's in the U.S. In June 1954, the French, at the "American urging" took Diem as premier of South Vietnam.[36]

India provides a concrete example where U.S. aid does not just go to any underdeveloped country for the simple reason of "development." In the 1960's, India turned to the U.S. for aid to build a steel mill at Bokaro. Not only would this mean that India would be receiving aid for the largest aid project ever undertaken, nor that India had recently gotten the "biggest piece of the pie" in aid, but that this aid money would be going towards a "government owned, socialized industry." Although Kennedy was in word saying "yes, you can have aid for your project," in action he commissioned two studies which eventually paved the way to block aid for the project.[37]

Of the studies that were commissioned,

one was a "feasibility study" of the project--U.S. Steel Corporation was given the contract by AID, costing the government (which means tax money of the American people) $686,344. U.S. Steel's analysis found the project to be unfavorable, judging that no exports were expected until 1976. On the other hand, it raised the question in Congress of the "likelihood" of India becoming self-sufficient in steel production meaning a reduction in U.S. steel exports to India under the aid program.[38]

In the other commissioned study, the Clay Report, the following was concluded:

If countries with a free will are to become or remain so, and if their governments are to prove to their peoples that the democratic non-communist route to political and economical well-being is far the better one some form of extensive assistance to their internal efforts is necessary.
We believe the U.S. should not aid a foreign government in projects establishing government owned industry and communist enterprises which compete with existing private endeavors. While we realize that in aiding foreign countries we cannot insist upon the establishment of our own economic system despite its remarkable success and progress, we should not extend aid which is inconsistent with our beliefs, democratic tradition and knowledge of economic organization and consequences.[39]

The government of India withdrew the request for the project and the Foreign Assistance Act of 1963 placed general restrictions on assistance for projects "establishing or otherwise assisting government-owned manufacturing, utility, merchandising, or processing enterprises in any country or area, except where it clearly appears that goods or services of the same general class are not or cannot be adequately provided by private business located within such country or area."[40]

Recent issues of foreign aid and policy surrounding the war in Vietnam have had interesting projections into the future--and interesting trends in foreign aid to various Southeast Asian countries. In Secretary of State Rogers' appropriation requests for the coming fiscal year, he has requested aid for the smooth withdrawing of U.S. troops.[41] This means more military and economic assistance to insure the "free" governments economic stabilities and military efforts against the revolutionary fronts. Thus, direct U.S. involvement via American troops is being reduced, while increasing indirect involvement via foreign aid to maintain U.S. policies.[42] Though the title of Rogers' statement in the Department of State Bulletin was "Self-Help and Search for Peace"--the new foreign aid appropriations in no way imply "peace." There is a direct contradiction between a "search for peace" and military assistance aid. If anything, Rogers is talking about a "search for piece". The continuance of U.S. policy in its more "subtle" form through the governments of Thailand, South Vietnam, South Korea, Cambodia, and Indonesia will still be in conflict with the revolutionary struggles of those same countries.

For now the U.S. has to continue to expand foreign aid appropriations in order to keep her influence in Southeast Asia. Nixon now realizes that "poverty that was accepted for centuries is accepted no longer. Military security has to rest, ultimately, on economic and political stability... The people, in the broadest sense have become an entity to be served rather than used."[43] Thus, his basic policy now is no longer ignoring this segment in foreign policy aims--but at least acknowledging them just enough to keep operative U.S. influence over Asia. Nixon has thus suggested a "minimal level of economic growth fostered by an influx of foreign aid to 'buy off' social unrest without significantly altering the capitalist social structure and power relations that created the poverty and oppression in the first place."[44] As a result, economic aid for Southeast Asia has risen by 41 per cent between 1968 and 1969.[45]

The role of foreign aid, as has been exemplified by Southeast Asia, is a vital and determining factor in United States foreign policy "goals" for the world. Through foreign aid, underdeveloped countries are caught up in the conflict between socialist and capitalist doctrines. The U.S. and the other big industrialist nations have created a vast and complex system of dependencies and safeguards for the capitalist system in which underdeveloped countries are "exploited" for the resources they have for the continuance of the capitalist structure. They become immediately enmeshed in various traps and games which have been created by the big capitalists. In the specific instance of Southeast Asia, it is a contradiction for Asian Americans to be supporting the U.S. government through taxes which are being used to "abuse" the economies of fellow Asians on the other side of the world. Especially since we are not a part of the "corporate structure" which is profiting off of the foreign aid measures, it is merely supporting and reinforcing the existing structures present by being unaware

of the true situation at hand. Asian Americans and all Americans alike must come to grips with the U.S. political and business enterprise in order to determine a reality without contradictions in our lives and in the lives of others.
Mary Uyematsu

The most critical business enterprise may well be petroleum--oil points to some of the problems linking Asians in America and U.S. policies in Asia. Oil and water do not mix but oil and war seem to be inseparable. Oil and related industries account for perhaps one half of our one trillion dollar GNP and 71 per cent of U.S. investment in Third World countries involves petroleum. "Oil companies control the capital, resources, and order of American society and of dozens of other nations--just as oil and its by-products control the ecology of the atmosphere and the waters."[46] Ken Hanada turns our attention to oil in Asia.

CHEVRON ISLAND: THE OIL STAMPEDE TO SOUTHEAST ASIA

The current plundering by U.S. Multinational Oil "parasites" that have permeated Southeast Asia is not merely an "explorative gamble" for oil, but a necessity for capitalism to survive, and retain global economic influence and control of economies throughout the Third World. For imperialism, according to the Leninist thesis, constitutes the last phase of capitalism--that being the stagnation, decay, and dying period. In that light, one can conceive of U.S. oil interests and exploitation as the last gasp of economic permeation before death.

From President Nixon's inauguration to the present, there has been a disparity between winning the war and economic incentives that have caused Nixon and the "Multi-Capitalists" to be ambivalent and skeptical towards policies directing Southeast Asia and more precisely, the Vietnam War. It is an ambivalence that reflects the economic incentives of whether Nixon should withdraw or escalate the war. Now, however, there is emerging the possibility of a new economic bloc (oil) that could dangerously shift a vital portion of a hitherto neutral or hostile sector of big business and banking into the strongly pro-war camp.

In 1967 some U.S. oil companies did initial research into the possible existence of rich oil deposits in Southeast Asia; the project was followed up in 1969-70 by ten oil companies and the government of South Vietnam--seismic surveys, geological probings, and other forms of research were conducted in offshore areas. As a result, it has been determined that there is great potential for massive oil deposits on the continental shelf off South Vietnam. Specifically, the area is off the Southeastern part of the country between the Mekong River and Camau Point.[47]

The American oil giants' stampede to Southeast Asia began after the 1965 coup in Indonesia by pro-American generals which left a half million Indonesians dead but opened the door wide to foreign investment. Southeast Asian oil's importance was heightened by the Six Day War in 1967, which cut off the Suez Canal to important Middle Eastern oil shipments. "Major companies are eager to diversify their sources of petroleum because of political uncertainty in the Middle East, the World's major source of crude (oil) today."[48]

On December 1, 1970, the Thieu-Ky government issued Public Law No. 011/70 regarding the "exploration and exploitation of petroleum and related taxation, fees and exchange regulations." This law gives the official go-ahead for negotiating offshore leasing arrangements between South Vietnam and twenty-one contending petroleum companies, mostly American. Extensive American petroleum exploration in Indochina and South Vietnam has been conducted for more than two years under the auspices of the United Nations Economic Commission for Asia and the Far East (ECAFE).[49] This is nothing but an act to legalize the Nixon Administration's policy of plundering oil resources in South Vietnam and to step up the efforts of U.S. neo-colonialism.

Potentials of Southeast Asian Oil:

The potential of the South Vietnamese oil fields is apparently immense. The May 22 issue of the German magazine WELTWOCHE quotes "a top oil company official" as saying that "compared to the Southeast Asian offshore deposits, those of Louisiana are like a postage stamp on the back of an elephant." WELTWOCHE paraphrases a U.S. oil expert with fifteen years experience in Southeast Asia as saying that in five years, "the offshore oil fields of Thailand, Cambodia, Malaysia, South Vietnam, and Indonesia will be ready to produce...more than is now produced in the whole Western World."[50] In addition, along the rich alluvial plains of the Mekong Delta, potential petroleum deposits have been detected along a continental shelf that connects Japan, Indochina, Indonesia, and Australia. With more than 1 million square miles of Southeast Asian jungles and shallow seas, this continental shelf is the largest in the world. Also, it appears to hold the largest deposit of petroleum.[51] WORLD OIL MAGAZINE (August 15) predicts "a daily average crude production of 400 million barrels by 1975 from this area." In essence, whoever controls this area will control three-fourths of the world petroleum production.

Indonesia:

Foreign firms are eager to get into the Indonesian oil business. Caltex and Stanvac both plan to increase the output of their operations on Sumatra. Caltex is by far the bigger of the two, owning 70% of Sumatran Oil. Caltex earns roughly $80 million per year in foreign exchange, about 1/5 of Indonesia's total. Stanvac (Standard) owns 10% of the Sumatran oil, and the state-owned company, Pertamina, owns the rest. The biggest oil reserves, however, lie in the offshore fields, thought to be nearly as rich as the Persian Gulf.[52]

At present, offshore oil concessions dot a map of Southeast Asian waters, and by the end of 1971 Indonesian petroleum production is expected to reach 1 million barrels a day, with American interests dominating 80 percent of production. U.S. investment in Indonesian oil has sprinted from $100 million in 1969 to $130 million in 1970 and is expected to climb to $160 million in 1971.[53]

Oil Firms in Indonesia: Caltex Oil Co., Stanvac Oil Co., Petican Oil Co., Union Oil Co., Sinclair Oil Co., Continental Oil Co., Cities Service Oil Co., Gulf Oil Co., Phillips & Superior Oil, American Petroleum, Indotex Oil Co. (Texaco), Virginia International & Roy M. Huffington Inc., Frontier Oil Co.,--all of which are U.S. Other oil firms are: Japex, Asamera, Nosopex, which are Japanese firms.

Responses by the Folks at Home:

The testing off South Vietnam is what recently got the oil companies into hot water with the peace movement. One West Coast group, called Another Mother for Peace, is asking for an investigation of possible administration guarantees of oil company investments in Southeast Asia.

The most important and most outrageous aspect of these developments is the extent to which American military activities in Southeast Asia are in fact presently determined by the will to stabilize the political regimes of the region in order to allow for maximum profit-taking by the largest U.S. petroleum interest.[54]

"Do we continue to sustain the highly unpopular Thieu-Ky regime in order to aid U.S. oil interests?"

"Do we remain in South Vietnam in order to allow U.S. oil companies to obtain offshore oil leases?"

"Did the U.S. promote the Cambodian coup of General Lon Nol in the same manner as that of General Suharto in Indonesia, to pave the way for U.S. oil interests?"

"Does Petroleum wag the tail of the U.S. State Department (and Pentagon) in Indochina?"

"Are people dying in Indochina for noble ideas or the black profits of oil?"

These are good questions, especially as the PETROLEUM ENGINEER, in its June, 1970 issue, commented:

"If and when the U.S. wins its objectives there, oil exploration conceivably could be successful enough to turn that part of the world into another South-Louisiana-Texas-type producing area. It all depends on the Vietnam war, how long it takes to get the job and how well the job is done."[55]

In reference to South Vietnam, Jacques Decornoy, Southeast Asian editor for LE MONDE, asked on January 8, "Have the oil companies perhaps received some solid assurances from Washington concerning the willingness of the U.S. to hold Indochina, and South Vietnam in particular? One is tempted to think so, for the companies have already begun to invest."

Gabriel Kolko expounds on this subject by saying that "The Thieu-Ky regime has grasped the significance of these possibilities and in recent months has adroitly attempted to deepen the American stake in its future as well as solve the potentially fatal economic illness it now confronts. During the summer of last year, Saigon divided its offshore waters into 18 immense blocks and then rewrote its investment laws to facilitate foreign entry on terms that will tempt even the most cautious investors. Last December 1 it issued a new oil law containing tax rates far lower than prevailing world standards, and it embarked on a public relations campaign to make what was admittedly a very promising situation look like, to quote Saigon sources, one of the most spectacular oil deposits in the world. Explicitly releasing it in the context of an attack on a coalition-government solution to the war, Saigon has also just published DOING BUSINESS IN VIETNAM and is distributing it free in the U.S. As Thieu's men never tire of pointing out, whether American business will reap the harvest depends on a regime ready to co-operate with the United States on most generous terms. Such a government precludes both a political settlement to the war and American withdrawal."[56]

The Oil Giant-Standard:

The government of the U.S. extends innumerable special privileges to the private petroleum industry--among them the oil depletion allowance which alone has cost the American tax-payer over $140 billion since its inception.[57] To quote BUSINESS WEEK: "In industry after industry, U.S. companies found that their overseas earnings were soaring, and that their return on investment abroad frequently was much higher than in the U.S.... As earnings abroad began to rise, profit margins from domestic operations started to shrink... This is the combination that forced development of the multi-national company." The most explicit example is Standard Oil.

Standard Oil of California is part of the entire Standard Oil Empire and the vast holdings of the Rockefeller family. The Rockefellers own a controlling interest of 11.9% in Standard of California, which operates in 35 countries with over 100 subsidiaries.[58] The Standard Oil Companies are intimately involved in exploration and development throughout Indochina. At present, as already noted, the government of South Vietnam is about to offer offshore concessions mostly to American oil companies for a potential oil field of 400 million barrels a year. U.S. oil companies today control 50% of the oil production in the Mid-East. Standard Oil of California in 1969 was the 42nd largest war contractor in the U.S. with $148.5 million in contracts.[59] This example of a multi-national corporation exemplifies a small "isolated" example of the oil stampede or parasitic permeation into Southeast Asia.

Military Escalation:

Many American statesmen and businessmen have long thought of Southeast Asia as a treasure chest of raw materials "one of the world's richest areas is open to the winner in Indochina." wrote U.S. NEWS AND WORLD REPORT just before Dien Bien Phu fell in April, 1954. "Tin, rubber, rice, key strategic raw materials are what the war is really about. The U.S. sees it as a place to hold--at any cost."[60]

Speaking in Boston in 1965, LBJ's ambassador to Vietnam, Henry Cabot Lodge, extended that analysis--"He who holds or has influence in Vietnam can affect the future of the Philippines and Formosa to the east, Thailand and Burma with their huge rice surpluses to the west, rubber, oil, and tin to the south. Vietnam thus does not exist in a geographical vacuum--from it large storehouses of wealth and population can be influenced and undermined."[61] Thus, the U.S. must hold these areas at "any cost."

It appears that recent military escalations in Cambodia and Laos coincided with the actual determination of petroleum deposits in Indochina. A story sent out by the wire service Agence France-Presse on February 7, 1971, states: "The very recent discovery of important oil deposits in Thailand and South Vietnam explains in great part the resurgence of military activities in Indochina, particularly the recent events in Laos."[62]

The controversy over the sovereignty of the Tiao-yu Islands, off of Taiwan, arose from the discovery of rich deposits of oil around these islands in 1968. The attempts to control these deposits are only part of a large-scale oil rush in the whole South China Sea area.[63] This latest scramble for the Tiao-yu Tai oil deposits reflects the U.S.-Japanese corporations' move to control, directly or indirectly, all areas in Third World countries with the aim of exploiting raw materials for their benefit.

The ultimate reason for the American companies' passionate interest in the Vietnamese and other Southeast Asian oil fields is not simple profit, but control of vital oil reserves. As has been the case since World War II, American economic hegemony in Asia rests partly on the American ability to control Japan's supply of raw materials and its available markets. An independent, socialist, resurgent Southeast Asia would pull Japan into expanded trade both with itself and China and end its reliance on the U.S.[64] Nixon's current strategy of fighting a protracted air and mechanized war does assure, however, an important reduction of U.S. manpower and costs (Vietnamization). Oil investments would partially compensate for this new economic drain and it would gain the Administration what it hitherto lacked: a politically and economically powerful constituency--the international oil firms--with a tangible vested interest in Indochina puppet regimes and a protracted war to consolidate U.S. hegemony in the region.[65]

What frightens the major international oil companies is the prospect of an independent Southeast Asia, developing its own resources for the needs of its own people. As Southeast Asia's important natural resources include not only oil, but also tin, tungsten, iron, bauxite, copper, nickel, and rubber, Southeast Asian development is not only possible, but likely, if current independence movements achieve victory.

Should Congress, the press, and the people eventually consider the implications of massive oil investments to the future of the war, the first effect will be to expose, further, Nixon's claims to favor U.S. withdrawal; for economic penetration, given the predictable Southeast Asian people's commitment to national liberation struggles, will require what is tantamount to a U.S. colony and a war that can only shift in tactics. If major oil firms decide the war is still worth the gains, and actively back Nixon's undertaking, then the balance of political forces within the U.S. will be very different than in March, 1968 when, according to Townsend Hoopes' account, major financial and industrial interests prevailed on President Johnson not to further escalate manpower in Vietnam for fear of aggravating the already sagging health of the economy and society.[66]

But America's great oil families, who stand to lose most if Southeast Asian oil comes under Southeast Asian control, already have a strong ally in the White House. The Mellons (Gulf), the Rockefellers and other oil families contributed some $600,000 to Nixon's 1968 presidential campaign. They need only remind him that his political fortunes rest upon the continued expansion of American corporate capitalism--an expansion fueled by <u>Asian oil</u> and <u>Asian oil revenues</u>.[67]

Ken Hanada

···

Economic "aid" then, has always been explicitly regarded by business and government leaders as one means of extending and maintaining U.S. domination over Asian markets and resources. One need not advocate a simplistic "devil" theory to see that our benevolence has been effected by realistic people whose self-interest was always a factor. It is in this context that the following paragraphs, excerpted from Peggy Li's study, should be read. "Cultural imperialism," broadly and simply defined, is the use of social functions (particularly education) by one country to extend its power over another. In economic terms it is clear that the existence of a ruling elite schooled in and pledged to the ways of American business practices is a most desirable and, at times, essential prerequisite to the "normal" functioning of international capitalism.

···

CULTURAL IMPERIALISM

That grants and loans are intended to help change these nations culturally is revealed by the August, 1968 issue of BUSINESS WEEK, concerning awards to foreign students: "the program to train foreign students in U.S. business ways has dual aims: to spread respect for American methods and to supply manpower for international corporations."[68] One of these "investments" is the International Enterprise Fellowship program. Its purpose is to "train executives under the theory that students can improve their understanding of the private enterprise system through first-hand exposure to American business. When the year-round training is up, the IEF and participating companies work to place fellows in managerial jobs in their country."[69]

The number of foreign students encouraged to study abroad is impressive. In 1966 alone, there were 111,000 foreign citizens from 172 countries and territories studying, teaching, or doing research in our colleges and universities. Of these, 70% of them came from developing nations.[70] It is evident, then, that economic assistance helps to maintain these countries' dependence upon our economic aid on the one hand, while our aid "spreads the system" on the other.

But economic assistance is not a reliable means to maintain a <u>long-term</u> political ally for the United States. That is the reason why we have to "make the world safe for Democracy." What this amounts to is further penetration into the social structure. This is accomplished by means of technical assistance--the distribution of knowledge rather than money, since it is "obvious that there is not enough (money) in the world to relieve the suffering of the peoples of the underdeveloped areas, but ... there is, for the first time in history, enough knowledge to do the job."[71]

This concept is especially appealing to the idealistic partisans who are, no doubt, convinced of its morality as well as its material superiority. Thus in 1963, we had an outpouring of 6,500 technicians and 5,000 Peace Corpsmen while 10,700 students and trainees were financed for foreign study or training courses. Furthermore, the Development Association Committee, consisting of the "developed" areas such as Taiwan, European Allies,

South Korea, and the Indochina successor states, supplied 82,000 technicians and 42,000 scholarships for foreign studies and research, thus setting an organized network for cultural reform for which the United States is at the command post.[72]

Under technical assistance, there is importation of raw materials, machinery, and surplus food for "economic development" because "more rapid economic growth tends to result in more rapid subsequent improvement in levels of social development, and vice versa."[73] But while the development of human skills or technical assistance is on a temporary exchange basis, the equipment, the raw materials and even the buildings these newly-trained teachers used had to be financed by the recipient countries. In cases where countries are unable to pay for these goods they then seek financial aid (from the U.S.) in a reimbursable plan, thus setting an economic trap for these nations.[74]

Of the four areas in which technical assistance is emphasized: health, agriculture, public administration and education, only programs for education have expanded consistently. The other three aid programs have not received as much attention because they are only "leverage" aids; for the reduction of discontent and grievances to help prevent the growth of "communist" influence. Education, on the other hand, can:
1) maintain the status quo for perpetuating an elite class, thus
2) producing potential leadership, which will
3) give legitimacy to our political and ideological expansion.

The maintenance of the status quo in these nations was recently revealed in a book review in NATION (January 20, 1969) stating that, "the schools of the Third-World are often less concerned with development than with perpetuation of an elite class, 'the stronghold of the elites... a class of over-privileged rulers more concerned with cars and other material goodies than with progress, holding the masses in profound contempt.' Supporting such schools, the Peace Corps has laid itself open to the charge that it is implicitly encouraging the ruling school system while starving the nation's other needs."[75]

Peggy Li

In the meantime the continuous development of national liberation struggles in Asian countries presents the most effective danger to the strategy outlined in the papers above. The NLF in Vietnam is only the most visible of these; Northeast Thailand has long been alienated from the Bangkok government and a sanctuary for mass organization and armed struggles. "Insurgents" all, the people in these movements threaten the security of the relationships established between the U.S. and client regimes in Asia and have forced us to spend considerable effort and enormous amounts of money to devise counter-insurgency tactics. Marie Chung has explored the particular equation which has recently turned university campuses into battlegrounds.

RESEARCH AND DEVELOPMENT: WEAPONS OF INTERVENTION AND COUNTERINSURGENCY (R AND D=CI)

Buttressed by industrial cooperation, the military is the tool of the capitalist state, whose theory of freedom and equality falls apart in the avalanche of violence perpetrated against the self-determination of the peoples of the Third World. Moreover, not only are the "colonies" exploited, but in using the same military process that America has used in foreign countries, she has turned her own people into a colony as well. Within the context of the nation-state, national leaders and institutionalized propaganda of the military sought to infect the population with their false consciousness of reality. The liberal ad hoc reforms momentarily coddled the lower classes so that contracts could be negotiated with private business, universities, and the research corporations. So when Juan Bosch refers to "pentagonism"[76] as the enslavement of the people of the mother country, he apparently sees little distinction between the status of the contract laborer and that of the worker under the contract mechanism in this national security state.

Those who engage in military contracts are locked into a symbiotic arrangement with the Department of Defense. Melman's notion of pentagonism capitalism analyzes the military-industrial complex with respect to a state-management structure in which the government takes the role of private entrepreneur. The management, the Dept. of Defense, gauges the accumulation of capital, decides what to produce, how much to produce, and controls the use of assets. The convergence of the

DoD with its major contractors has greatly reduced the differences between the public and private sectors of the American economy. Hence, government is a business based on the political economy of war.

According to the grand design implemented by Robert McNamara in 1960, decision-making authority became centralized in the hands of the Secretary of Defense with a budget planned for five years in advance. The senior officers of the state-management which controlled the multi-divisions of industrial firms also became the prominent political officers of the U.S. government. The covert feature of this totalization no less diminishes its resemblance to the modern Soviet state which is a military-industrial complex, true to Stalin's design in the first Five Year Plan.[77] The New Class (Milovan Djilas) of the political bureaucracy controls special privileges and economic preferences resulting from this administrative monopoly. After military expenditures have been allocated, the Soviets probe into the amount left over for consumption and for raising the standard of living. Not dissimilar has been this nation's priorities--cloaked in the guise of national security, the American people pay the taxes which enrich the manufacturers of arms, warships, fighter planes, who feed on the politics of intervention under the "Vietnam Wars Program." One crucial element in the entire R and D establishment is the university and related institutions.

The Institute for Defense Analysis (IDA) is a non-profit research advisory corporation established at the request of the Secretary of Defense to "provide an independent and objective source of analyses, evaluations, and advice on problems of national security,"[78] to the Weapons Systems Evaluation Group of the Joint Chiefs of Staff. The consortium of universities included MIT, CalTech, Stanford, Michigan, California, Princeton, and Penn State. The board of trustees consists of large stock holders of defense industry corporations, as well as former industrial employees. The issue of conflict of interest is not put to question.

> "In some cases, the man who designs a weapon, the think tank employee who evaluates it, and the defense department official who awards the contracts may be associated with the same corporation, if they are not one and the same individual."[79]

A special program called the Jason Division sets up a defense "summer camp" in which 40 scientists and graduate students work on technical problems related to the national interest: missile re-entry, anti-submarine warfare, nuclear test detection, weapons effects and personnel detection. During 1969 Professor Luis W. Alvarez of the University of California, a 1968 Nobel Prize winner in physics was appointed Jason Advisor.[80] Many a scientist finds it increasingly difficult to avoid participating in the government's exploitation of the universities. Sometimes defense projects are the only means to gain access to information needed for research in a given area.

The IDA was among the first to recognize the importance of limited war and counterinsurgency, emphasizing the importance of a counterforce capability. Southeast Asia was frequently the target for these research topics:

Chemical Control of Vegetation in Relation to Military Needs
Night Vision for Counterinsurgents
A Rational Approach to the Development of Non-Lethal Chemical Warfare Agents[81]

As the major research institution of the DoD, IDA has influenced the posture of foreign policy in the development of electronic "village protection systems," sophisticated radio communications, and hand-held radar devices.

The structure of the university differs little from that of a corporation, both owing their existence to an outside party--the Pentagon. The University of California has an "interlocking directorate" relationship with the Pentagon and the defense industry. President Hitch was the Assistant Secretary of Defense to McNamara. The last three Defense Research and Engineering directors have come from the UC Radiation Lab: Herbert York, Harold Brown, and John S. Foster, Jr. Chancellor Franklin D. Murphy was on the board of Ford.[82] In much the same fashion that 25 defense contractors dominate nearly half of the contracts, the top 50 university-affiliated institutions obtain about 75% of the federal funds for scientific research.

The linkage of the universities to counterinsurgency missions created considerable sensationalism in the first disclosures at Michigan State in 1965. A contract between MSU and the Diem regime was designed to assist the government to strengthen the economy, the civil service, and the police.[83] Professors from Yale, University of Pittsburgh, UCLA, as well as representatives from the FBI and CIA were instrumental in arming and training the internal security forces of the Saigon regime.

> "The University Group was for all practical purposes the sole supplier of weapons, ammunition, vehicles, and equipment to the entire South Vietnamese secret police, mu-

nicipal police, Civil Guard, and palace guard."[84]

The Willow Run Lab at the University of Michigan became involved in a counterinsurgency project between the Advanced Research Projects Agency (ARPA) and the Royal Thai military. Thai military officers attended a course in engineering, physics, and reconnaissance technology and infrared imagery. Various scientists were sent to develop an operational lab in Bangkok.[85]

There are three sophisticated private research groups associated with universities that illustrate the extent of the interlocking defense complex at the corporate and decision-making levels. The Hoover Institution on War, Revolution, and Peace (affiliated with Stanford) was designed by director Wesley Glenn Campbell (also member of UC Regents) to "demonstrate the evils of the doctrines of Karl Marx . . .and to reaffirm the validity of the American system."[86] He believes that "an important first step toward assuring the primacy of national security is to stop the further expansion of federal expenditures for domestic benefits."[87] Included on the board of directors are top executives from Standard Oil of New York, Gulf, Mobil, Union Carbide, American Cyanamid, US Steel, Republic Steel, and Lockheed. Of the 56 member advisory board, only two are educators. The Hoover Institute is inclined to advocate an agressive foreign policy. A study made for the US Arms Control and Disarmament Agency suggested a reduction of arms in the Far East would not be prudent.

The think-tank at Georgetown University, the Center for Strategic and International Studies, is primarily financed by companies concerned with US military protection for their investments. Industrial ties to the advisory board include GE, Westinghouse, Chrysler, Jones and Laughlin Steel, Goodyear, North American, and Pan American. The publications support a greater military presence abroad and a more aggressive defense build-up at home. Chairman Arleigh Burke, who was on Nixon's task force on national security stated that "our government should take initiative in confronting communism, using everything from specially trained guerilla forces to nuclear weapons."[88] Some of their recent reports have dealt with the conduct of the Vietnam war, the challenges of Soviet technology, and arms control.

The third of these university-affiliated research centers is the Foreign Policy Research Institute of Pennsylvania, known as one of the most influential sources of cold war strategy. The Institute has prepared course material and lectures for seminars at the National War College. An Air Force contract "Counterforce and Alternative US Strategies," analyzed the feasibility of maintaining a second strike counterforce strategy, with aid from consultants from GE, Stanford Research Institute, Hudson Institute, and Rand. In the past the institute has done research for foundations with foreign investments like the Rockefeller Foundation study on the political and strategic value of Central America to American security.[89] Influencing public policy is a major goal of these institutes. More closely related to government, military and industry than to the world of education, the speculations of their private investment interests in relation to foreign policy, show up in the heavy corporate subsidizing.

Research and development projects are given an experimental outlet in the Southeast Asian war, and subtly become part of the network of counterinsurgency tactics which has begun to envelope areas such as Thailand. An associate of the Academic Advisory Council on Thailand at UCLA stated that "the thrust of current US policy in Thailand is counter-insurgency."[90] The AACT is funded by AID to support the Royal Thai government in its effort to contain, control and eliminate the communist insurgency in rural areas.[91] In a 1962 report done for Rand by David Wilson, executive secretary of AACT at UCLA, "Certain Effects of Culture and Social Organization on Internal Security in Thailand," a recommendation for the recruitment of a village defense corps became implemented later as the Village Security Force.[92] The Village Security Force comprises 9400 men who participate in an 11-week training session in anti-communism and civic action. With concentration in the three northeastern provinces, each five to ten villages would be patrolled by an eight to twenty man police post.

The project also organizes and conducts investigations and seminars dealing with counterinsurgency problems and in fact serves as consultant for US policy makers. On July 24-27, 1970 such a conference was held at UCLA to inquire about the capacity of development of local authority in rural Thailand,[93] and resulted in the publication "Local Authority and Administration in Thailand." David Wilson has traveled to Thailand on various occasions to consult with Royal Thai officers and members of the Border Patrol Police.

Research and development has been manipulated to exploit Asian resources not only in the extraction of oil, tin, and rubber and in laying the groundworks for investments by corporations, but also in training and educating an elite city-state of 50,000 bourgeoisie in Bangkok. Following the theme of Vietnamization, the US relies on the puppet Thai forces to maintain law and order and control over other Asians by proxy.

R and D in chemical and biological warfare includes a more complicated dimension since most projects are kept secret and classified and are, furthermore, disguised as scientific or medical inquiries, replete with esoteric terminologies attached to them. The Pentagon has a tendency to distribute different aspects of a CBW project to several agencies. As an example, in a survey of plant life in Vietnam by the Agricultural Research Service,[94] research on chemical defoliants was done by the University of California, leaf studies were done at UC Davis and the Purdue Research Foundation.

Chemical and bacteriological weapons can be produced at a relatively low cost compared to the development of even a crude atomic weapons system, since most of the basic research is readily available. The major problem rests in determining the type of delivery systems, and in the protection of one's forces. Bacteriological weapons seem to fit in military planning under the flexible response strategy:

"They are noteworthy for their ability to accomplish their effects...with little or no physical destruction. They kill people, do not destroy property and are self-multiplying."[95]

The "limited war" mentality is aimed at debilitating a small population which upsets the balance of power with the large.

"We must hurt them badly enough to deter them from interfering with us or our allies, but not as badly as they know we would hurt them if they retaliated with actual warfare. The damage on them would be of the type for which we could provide relief and restoration--once the country concerned changed its attitude."[96]

Just enough to make the people dependent on the present regime. In a leaflet dropped over target areas where a herbicide mission was conducted, pressure was put on the people to do no less than to be permanently relocated.

"The Government of the Republic of Vietnam has adopted the use of defoliants which will ruin your rice crop and other crop plants in the field. This has been necessary as your rice fields are located in areas supplying food to the Vietcong. However, you should not be disappointed as the Government will compensate for all the damage done to your rice crop; meanwhile the Government will at all times help evacuate you to other places with food, lodging and clothing provided until the next harvesting season, if you so desire."[97]

The implications of the R and D directed to squelch revolutionary movements do not terminate merely upon confrontation of the guerrilla with foreign intervention. An equally disastrous manifestation is the imminent colonization of the American people. Juan Bosch calls this mode of exploitation "pentagonism", an extension of imperialism, in which the terms "law and order" on the homefront are practically tantamount to crushing "exported" revolution abroad. Be it known that the form of government most frequently supported by the US is not a democracy of egalitarian liberty, but a military dictatorship such as the ones receiving US aid in the Congo, Iran, Ethiopia, South Africa, Port Territories, Thailand, South Vietnam, Brazil, and Greece.

A nation that exports repression has most assuredly the potential to turn that force inward to perpetuate its image of reality. The Pentagon has more money than the federal government does, and in fact is the biggest "business" in the entire world. Although not originally conceived in a conspiratorial ring, the Pentagon has virtually become a state within a state with limbs extending into industrial and academic institutions, and having the power and resources to influence national and international policy. Elaborate security measures are taken to police those industries related to defense. The objectives of the Defense Industrial Security Program was to detect hostile espionage involving US industry.[98]

When the relationship between external affairs and domestic repression becomes clearer, we are that much nearer to the consciousness of our struggle. When even the triteness of rhetoric begins to dissolve, so too does the distinction between foreign and domestic policy. It is not an accident that mace and CS gas came into use for riot-control "coincidentally" with the widespread CB tactics in Southeast Asia. Nor should it surprise us to note the introduction of electronic devices in the context of urban surveillance of the American people. Following the crude "divide and conquer" routine, the imposition of a natural state of alienation on the American people may be seen in our telephones being bugged, our shopping places being equipped with television detectors, our actions recorded in intelligence dossiers, and our neighborhoods being surveyed from the air. Law and order on the homefront is analogous to counterinsurgency in the foreign context.

The research institutes are applying the same logic and techniques to design programs for internal stability. The urban renewal programs which give rise to the "strategic hamlets" of the ghettoes are insufficient solutions for political and social alienation, but instrumental in controlling the actions of the Third World communities. We have our "village security forces" operating among us disguised as our peers by the CIA and the FBI.

The "Oriental middle-man" has learned his lesson well--conditioned in the historic mission of the national bourgeoisie to transmit the bourgeois ethics to his community. Proposed like the Thieu-Ky puppets, he leaves the Chinatown's and Little Tokyo's to be prostituted like a center of "rest and recreation" under the guise of tourism for the pleasure of the ruling-class bourgeoisie.

Armed with the knowledge of the consequences of one's actions, passive inaction is the most severe indictment:

"The fact that one participates passively in bourgeois economy, that one does not oneself wield the bludgeon or fire the cannon, so far from being a defense really makes one's position more disgusting, just as a fence is more unpleasant than a burglar, and a pimp than a prostitute... The bourgeois pacifist occupies perhaps the most ignoble place of a man in any civilization... He sits on the head of the worker and, while the big bourgeois kicks him, advises him to lie quiet... The pacifist is obsessed with the lazy lust of the absolute."[99]

There is nothing without its effects on others--nothing rests in absolutes--acts involve consequences and our responsibility is to discover the laws of social relationships which link which causes to which effects. Self-awareness through self-criticism is the nature of our protracted struggle to purge our bourgeois inclinations. Even after 20 years, the Chinese felt the need for the introspection of the Proletarian Cultural Revolution to eradicate the individualism of bourgeois conditioning. By knowing ourselves and our weaknesses we will be able to carry on the struggle. The knowledge gained through research efforts that is used in counter-revolutionary strategy must be seized and co-opted into our revolutionary principles to liberate the oppressed peoples of the world. Research is only one part of the duality--the theory. Knowledge and information must be extracted from the marketplace and united with a practice which is consistent with our assumptions of reality. Part of the strategy and tactics necessary for the people's victory must come first by using the enemy's weapons--"opposing counter-revolutionary war with revolutionary war."

Marie Chung

．．．

But military means must be at hand when economic aid and penetration, cultural exchange and development of research used for the protection of U.S. interests in Asia all fail to create and preserve conditions suitable for American business expansion.[100] Unfortunately for the U.S. war planners, the American public is beginning to resent the loss of life and treasure involved in the Southeast Asian venture. Strategists have devised a three-pronged strategy to try to resolve this contradiction by minimizing direct U.S. battlefield involvement while maintaining control of future guerrilla areas.

The first of these prongs is directed at the creation and support of client regimes which function as providers of indigenous troops for counterinsurgency purposes. At the same time, a second thrust goes directly to those nations controlled by whites--the former colonies of Great Britain--in order to maintain an inner circle, an "Anglo-Saxon Alliance". Third is the formation of an elite counterinsurgency force backed by the best in modern technology. This "fire brigade," comprised of servicemen trained in guerrilla warfare, can be flown in division strength almost at moment's notice from U.S. bases to crisis spots in Asia.

Previous sections of this paper have dealt with the means by which U.S. leaders hope to maintain client regimes. South Vietnam is the most blatant example but the presence of troops from South Korea, Thailand and the Philippines is a good indication of our control over the regimes controlling those Asian nations as well. The use of Asian troops in Asian contexts (Nixon's "Vietnamization") reduces the level of U.S. troops overseas and, thus, domestic discontent; it also lowers the visibility of American control over the client regimes; provides counterinsurgency battlefield training for troops from the other Asian nations whose regimes will probably need to employ them in their own defense against national liberation struggles--the Thais rotate their approximately 10,000 man force as often as possible; allows for combat testing of new weapons and techniques devised and constantly revised to help defeat a people's war; and, of course, it serves its overt purpose of appearing to "internationalize" and thus "legitimize" the U.S. intervention.

Sometimes, as the recent "Pentagon Papers" have revealed, the U.S. destroys its own creations--as in the case of the South Vietnamese coup which removed and killed Diem. An interesting sidelight is Madame Nhu's recent allegation that the U.S. was actively involved in the 1963 Buddhist uprisings in Saigon, thus setting the stage for the actual removal of the Diem regime which had been operating far too independently for our taste. Madame Nhu alluded to contact with Hanoi and efforts at a South Vietnamese form of socialism--neither of which could pass muster under the Kennedy regimes. Since, then, the client regimes themselves are not always trustworthy, the U.S. military and CIA have bypassed the regular armed forces to train, arm, pay and directly command bands of mercenaries, often recruited from ethnic minorities of that country (Montagnards in Vietnam and Meo in Laos). We do that here as well with Third World communities offering up their sons who volunteer because their own conditions make higher combat pay and status attractive to them.

With only precarious footholds in many Asian countries and undependable client regimes, the U.S. assiduously cultivates an inner circle rimming the Pacific. These happen to be former colonies of Great Britain, ruled by whites and even more racist in their immigration and social policies than is the U.S. Friendship and commitment to the Vietnam's, Korea's, and Thailand's are of a different order from the stronger bonds with New Zealand, Australia and Canada with whom the U.S. shares far more of its military secrets. This fact may be seen in the existence of the ANZUS Pact (Security treaty among Australia, New Zealand and United States) in spite of the fact that SEATO (Southeast Asia Treaty Organization) already serves as an area defense pact including Thailand and the Philippines. Here is one area where racism and capitalism may be seen clearly complementing each other in the preservation of their respective and overlapping spheres of control.

The third prong of this sophisticated approach to our goals in Asia is the fire brigade, vital prerequisite to the U.S. ability to withdraw large numbers of troops now stationed in Asia. The capability of airlifting troops from the U.S. rather than stationing them overseas eases diplomatic and economic pressures while preserving a flexible tactical force. Development of the CX-HLS Heavy Logistics Transport (C-5A) has made this approach practicable. This super-transport-jet can carry 600 fully-equipped troops or their equivalent. The first groups of 58 C-5A's can airlift, within hours, an entire combat division, with supplies, over 6,000 miles without refueling. High floatation landing gear enables the C-5A to land on relatively short and primitive airfields constructed rapidly by combat engineers. All of this is not to imply that the U.S. is leaving, or is about to leave, the approximately 200 military bases in Asia with well over half a million men stationed there. The end of the Vietnam phase of the war in Southeast Asia may signal the withdrawal of some troops and the closing of some bases. It will not, unfortunately, mean that the U.S. is embarked on a more reasonable approach to Asia—less exploitative, less racist, les dangerous or less threatening to the fortunes of Asians in Asia and Asian Americans as well.

A final caveat for those Asian Americans, the Japanese, who feel most secure as a result of post-World War II U.S. policies in Asia--they would be ill advised to neglect the role Japan has been developing in the Pacific economy. Usually considered a source of pride for those Japanese Americans who had suffered the consequences of the Pacific War, the "modern" Japanese miracle is problematic enough to ensure increased vulnerability in the future. It should be noted, first of all, that the economic miracle was encouraged and supported by the U.S. in order to produce a capitalist bastion in the Pacific--Japan was to stand as the Western "enclave" in the face of the growing power of the People's Republic of China. For the Japanese the move meant the end of the occupation reforms which had promised to level the military, bureaucratic and business oligarchies and produce a genuine democracy. The need for economic growth took precedence over those goals and the trend toward a reinvigorated business-bureaucratic complex was firmly established.[101]

Increasing cooperation between U.S. and Japanese corporations has prompted some observers to examine the "Pacific Rim Strategy," which envisions an expansion of U.S. economic penetration in those countries on the rim of the Pacific Ocean with Japan as a junior partner. The search for markets and raw materials (e.g., Southeast Asian oil) would be marked by a coordinated effort supported by both governments. Where Japanese technology/products are superior to American, the U.S. effort would be concentrated on direct investments in those Japanese firms--hence, the quid pro quo of lowered restrictive barriers to U.S. capital investment in return for the restoration of Japanese rule over Okinawa.

Japanese Americans may feel some ambivalence about this course which is propelling Japan into the forefront of the world's economies. There is pride in the accomplishment but concern for the exploited. For other Asian Americans who remember the Japanese drive for a "Greater East Asia Co-prosperity Sphere," the present direction is frighteningly reminiscent of the 1930's. Japanese Americans, who should remember their own history of struggle in the U.S., could be expected to "identify" with the exploited both within Japan and in the rest of Asia. But perhaps that is one of the central problems with the present "identity crisis"-- too many Japanese Americans try to identify with the exploiters rather than the working class, the poor and the Third World communities with whom they share such strong traditions.

The preceding line of reasoning may strike "realists" (who like to be on the victorious side) as irrelevant. They too, however, should consider the nature and future of the U.S.-Japan-Pacific Rim nexus. A number of Japanese critics have questioned the recent move toward further militarization and the growing emphasis on protecting a Japanese sphere of economic influence. It is quite possible, after all, that Japan may again "adapt herself too well to the power play of new imperialism as an efficient subcontractor of the worldwide socio-economic and political engineering initiated and managed by the West."[103] Whether as "subcontractor" or competitor, the new Japan is likely to assert itself more forcefully and thus challenge the U.S. position-- with predictably unfortunate implications for Japanese in America. The current spate of articles condemning the Japanese "economic animal" will surely increase and the intensity of the still largely latent racism will grow. We can already see political cartoons, editorials and business articles using the stereotypical linguistic devices that inflame anti-Japanese sentiments.[104]

A repeat of the concentration camp experience may be unlikely for a variety of reasons but the failure of the intensive drive to repeal Title II of the McCarran Act which legalizes "protective detention" should give all Americans some cause for reflection. This failure is particularly noteworthy because all concerned are fully aware that legislation is hardly necessary to legitimize such actions during times of proclaimed national "emergency." Title II is unnecessary; the legislative refusal to repeal it must be interpreted as a warning to all indentifiable groups, ethnic in particular, who might engage in acts unfriendly to the ruling class. Because Asian Americans are especially vulnerable to the effects of U.S. policies in Asia, and since those policies are based on a structure which demands corporate expansion in Asia in the face of growing national liberation struggles, the future is grim. Unless, of course, those policies can be changed--and the only way for such fundamental changes to be effected is for a revolutionary redistribution of power to take place--power to the people of the Asian countries with which the U.S. deals and power to the people in the United States.

----

[1] Native Americans constitute an important exception. This factor has done much to further submerge their experiences since international exposure has been one element considered in government policies toward ethnic groups in the United States.

[2] See Karl Yoneda's article in this volume.

[3] See paper in this Reader by Violet Rabaya on "Filipino Immigration."

[4] Unpublished student paper submitted to class on the "Asian American Experience," Occidental College, Fall, 1970. See introduction for methodology and details.

[5] Offered Spring, 1971, as CED 144, "Asian Americans and U.S. Policies in Asia" at UCLA. Previously offered in Winter, 1970, that course resulted in a film on the subject.

[6] A recent attempt to interpret the war in terms of power followed closely on the heels of the N.Y. TIMES "Project X" revealing secret papers regarding the origins of the war in Vietnam. In William Pfaff's view we went to war "out of an impulse to power--out of power's notorious tendency to intoxicate and corrupt...These men, and we as a nation, went to war for no more complicated or subtle reason than to force these Vietnamese who defied us to submit to our will." L.A. TIMES, Opinion Section, p. 2 (June 20, 1971). But Pfaff ignores the vital question of the nature of that "will". We may well have become a super-arrogant, power-hungry nation, as he says, but we have not indiscriminately preyed upon smaller countries. Areas rich in resources or people or which have strategic importance have always assumed priority. Southeast Asia qualifies on all three counts. It stands to reason we will not leave willingly.

[7] Harry Magdoff, THE AGE OF IMPERIALISM (New York, 1969), p. 137.

[8] Ibid., p. 117. Emphasis mine.

[9] Ibid., p. 125. Emphasis mine.

[10] Ibid., p. 117.
[11] Agency for International Development, Businessmen's Information Center: INVESTMENT IN SOUTHEAST ASIA, July, 1966, Washington D.C.
[12] Pacific Research and World Empire Telegram, "Indonesia: The Making of a Neo-Colony," August 3, 1969, Volume 1, Number 1, pp. 6-15.
[13] Ibid.
[14] Ibid.
[15] Ibid.
[16] Ibid.
[17] Ibid.
[18] Harry Magdoff, op. cit., p. 149.
[19] Ibid., pp. 156-157.
[20] Ibid., p. 159.
[21] Ibid., p. 157.
[22] Ibid., p. 164.
[23] Ibid., p. 142.
[24] Ibid.
[25] Pierre Jalee, THE PILLAGE OF THE THIRD WORLD.
[26] Harry Magdoff, op. cit., p. 143-144.
[27] Harry Magdoff, op. cit., p. 142.
[28] B. Maheshwari, INTERNATIONAL STUDIES: ISSUES IN U.S. FOREIGN POLICY, "Bokaro: The Politics of American Aid," (New Delhi, 1968) July-October 1968, Volume 10, Numbers 1-2, pp. 163-190.
[29] Harry Magdoff, op. cit., p. 143.
[30] David Wise and Thomas B. Ross, THE INVISIBLE GOVERNMENT.
[31] Ibid.
[32] Harry Magdoff, op. cit., p. 127.
[33] Banning Garrett, op. cit.
[34] DEPARTMENT STATE BULLETIN, "Youth, Change and Foreign Policy," December 14, 1970, Volume 63, pp. 718-722.
[35] Harry Magdoff, op. cit., p. 121
[36] David Wise and Thomas B. Ross, op. cit.
[37] B. Maheshwari, op. cit.
[38] Ibid.
[39] Ibid.
[40] Ibid.
[41] DEPARTMENT STATE BULLETIN, "Self-Help and Search for Peace," December 14, 1970, Volume 63, pp. 713-717.
[42] Ibid.
[43] Ibid.
[44] Ibid.
[45] Ibid.
[46] Bay Area Institute, "Pamphlet on Oil" (S.F., n.d.).
[47] BOSTON GLOBE, February 22, 1971.
[48] Adam Bennion, "Southeast Asian Oil," PACIFIC RESEARCH & WORLD EMPIRE TELEGRAM, March-April, 1971, p. 7.
[49] Barry Weisberg, "Oil and Southeast Asia," CURRENT AFFAIRS, May, 1971, p. 47.
[50] Bennion, p. 7.
[51] Barry Weisberg, p. 47.
[52] Ibid., p. 12.
[53] Ibid.
[54] BAY INSTITUTE WEEKLY, January, 1971.
[55] PETROLEUM ENGINEER (June, 1970).
[56] Gabriel Kolko, "Oiling the Escalator," NEW REPUBLIC, March 13, 1971, p. 20.
[57] BAY INSTITUTE WEEKLY, "What is the Record of Standard of California."
[58] Ibid.
[59] Ibid.
[60] PACIFIC RESEARCH & WET, Vol. II, No. 3, March-April, 1971, p. 7.
[61] Ibid.
[62] Weisberg, p. 48.
[63] TIAO-YU TAI SPECIAL, March, 1971, p. 1.
[64] PACIFIC RESEARCH & WET, March-April, 1971, p. 7.
[65] Weisberg, op. cit.
[66] Kolko, p. 20.
[67] PACIFIC RESEARCH, p. 8.
[68] BUSINESS WEEK, August 17, 1968, p. 84.

[69] Ibid.

[70] "Corporation and Education," DUNS REVIEW, February, 1968, Vol. 91, p. 20.

[71] Eric Goldman, THE CRUCIAL DECADE--AND AFTER 1945-1960, p. 94, speech by Johnathan Bingham on the Point Four Program.

[72] Jacob Kaplan, CHALLENGE OF FOREIGN AID, p. 296.

[73] "Social Development: Key Growth Sector," INTERNATIONAL DEVELOPMENT REVIEW, March, 1965, speech by H.W. Singer.

[74] Kaplan, p. 294.

[75] "Agents of Change," NATION, January 20, 1969, p. 86-87, book review of Hargood and Bennett's book.

[76] Bosch, Juan, PENTAGONISM.

[77] Armstrong, "Military-Industrial Complex--Russian Style", FORTUNE, August 1, 1969.

[78] Institute for Defense Analysis, ANNUAL REPORT, 1969.

[79] VIET REPORT, January, 1968, p. 12.

[80] Institute for Defense Analysis, op. cit., p. 32.

[81] VIET REPORT, January, 1968, p. 10.

[82] Sidney Lens, THE MILITARY-INDUSTRIAL COMPLEX, p. 136.

[83] VIET REPORT, January, 1968, p. 12.

[84] VIET REPORT, February, 1966, p. 18.

[85] VIET REPORT, January, 1968, p. 23.

[86] Berkeley Rice, "The Cold-War College Think-Tanks," WASHINGTON MONTHLY, June, 1969, p. 24.

[87] Ibid., p. 27. Emphasis added.

[88] Ibid., p. 29.

[89] Ibid.

[90] G. Wetherhill, "The Nature of War-Related Activities at UCLA," p. 14.

[91] "The Three Wars," Issues of UCLA Strike: 1970.

[92] Banning Garrett, "The Dominoization of Thailand," RAMPARTS, p. 11, November, 1970.

[93] "The Three Wars," loc. cit.

[94] VIET REPORT, June, 1966, p. 26.

[95] Melman, PENTAGON CAPITALISM, p. 13.

[96] VIET REPORT, June, 1966, p. 38.

[97] Ibid., p. 39.

[98] Colonel George Zacharias, "Industrial Security Program," DEFENSE INDUSTRY BULLETIN, November, 1970, p. 25.

[99] Christopher Caudwell, STUDIES IN A DYING CULTURE, London: 1938.

[100] The following remarks are largely based on research done for the seminar by Jack Yen Ng.

[101] For documentation see the impressive work by Kozo Yamamura, ECONOMIC POLICY IN POST-WAR JAPAN; GROWTH VERSUS ECONOMIC DEMOCRACY.

[102] The tendency of Japanese Americans to follow this with approval is criticized to good effect in Yuji Ichioka, "JACL and the U.S.-Japan Security Pact," GIDRA, (June/July, 1970), pp. 10, 16-17. Mr. Ichioka notes with alarm the failure to critically examine "the fearful collaboration between Japan and America designed to maintain and expand American power in Asia at the expense of popular, indigenous nationalist movements."

[103] Koji Taira, "Japan's Economic Relations with Asia," CURRENT HISTORY (April, 1971), p. 230.

[104] A recent newspaper article outlining the ominous shift in the balance of trade at the expense of the United States was headlined, "U.S., Japan Trade: Ah, So Different," (L.A. TIMES, July 11, 1971), Section F, page 1.

3
COMMUNITY

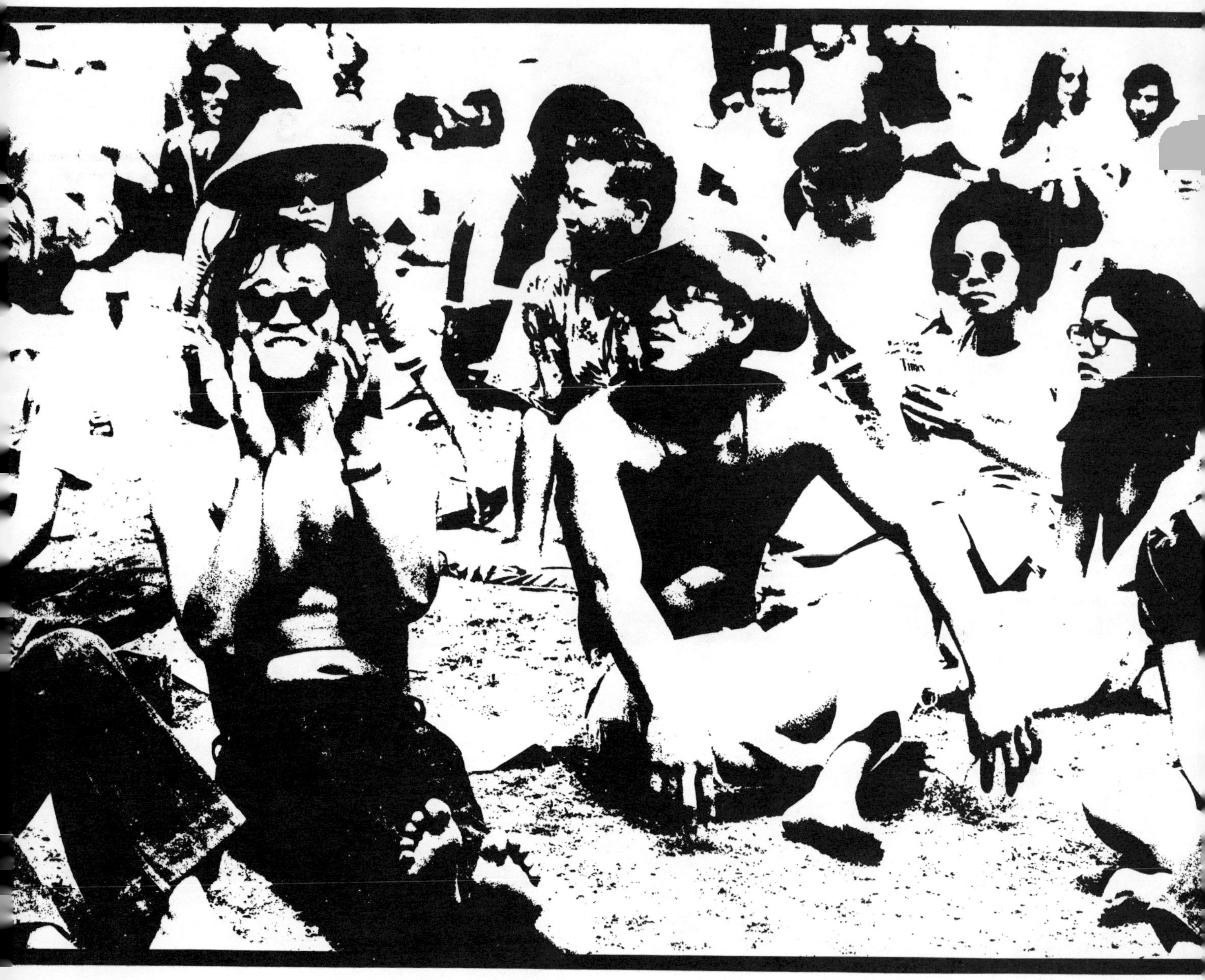

INTRODUCTION

Community analysis has been a relatively new phenomenon for Asian American communities. Though sociological studies have been conducted on Asian American communities in the past, it has only been within recent years that the community itself has undergone a process of self-evaluation. Casting aside the stereotype of community cohesion and passive assimilation, the community has been impelled by the twin forces of internal dissension and external conflict to redefine its image and relationship to the general society. Propelled by the awakened racial/social/political consciousness brought forth by the civil rights and Black power movements in the Sixties and by the anti-Asian racism spawned by the U.S.-Indo-China War, Asian Americans have begun re-examining the stable, inoffensive facade of the model minority community against the very real forces of social change and racial conflict. As Asian Americans are recovering their identity and rediscovering their history in America, there is a greater identification with their communities and its problems and people. What is emerging perhaps is a true community, entailing a recognition of responsibility among Asian people toward one another that supercedes the geographical boundaries of the community. For what is truly being considered is the collective fate of Asian people in a society racked by a racist war in Asia and by racial and economic inequities at home.

The community section of the reader will present three interrelated aspects of the Asian American communities: perspectives on community concept and community organization, analysis of community problems, and documentation of the Asian American movement. Thus, we hope to combine traditional sociological research with personal evaluations by community leaders and activists. In addition, we have included short articles from movement journals and newspapers to offer a cursory examination of the principles and goals of the now loosely-defined Asian American movement.

In any discussion of the Asian American movement, it is important to acknowledge historical roots as well as contemporary practice. Throughout the Asian experience in America, there has been a long tradition of struggle against economic exploitation and racism. Resistance took many forms: law suits against discriminatory laws by community groups (e.g., Chinese-American Citizens Alliance), labor organizing, and cultural resistance through preservation of Asian language and history. There are numerous examples.

In "An Interview with Pat Sumi" and "Activism, 1946 Style" (GIDRA, February, 1971), an important legacy of radical political activity among Nisei is brought to the surface. Such groups as the Japanese American Committee for Democracy (JACD) and Nisei Democrats represent the outspoken, politically progressive segments of the community buried under the "quiet American" stereotype. With their dreams of a better world destroyed, in the brutal repression of the McCarthy era that brought loss of jobs and blacklisting, many retreated to the quiet obscurity of suburban life. "...what they're afraid of is that they lost once," syas Pat Sumi. "The camps...the end of the radical movement in the late forties and early fifties...were real defeats. Whenever people are defensive...Nisei come up with 'we tried too...we resisted'. The question is to awaken that feeling in people again and get them to fight back in one direction....They really are courageous only they need something to fight for." As Pat Sumi points out, we must make the connection with this other generation of Asians who fought long ago for ideals now held by the younger generation.

In the Sixties, a new generation of Asian Americans were entering high schools and colleges. During this decade, violent confrontations over the contradictions of racism and poverty in an "equal" and prosperous society brought many students out of their comfortable isolation on campus. In "An Interview with Pat Sumi," we see one person's struggle to seek an understanding of herself and the society around her. Like many students, she became involved in the civil rights movement. From that initial step, Pat describes her gradual evolution towards a more radical point-of-view. Also included is her assessment of the Asian American movement and community.

Because of the numerous Asian Americans

at colleges and universities, it is no coincidence that a major part of the Asian American movement occurred on campuses. As part of the growing demand by Third World people to have their true history and contemporary situation reflected in educational curriculum, Asians participated in the struggles to implement ethnic studies. From the San Francisco State strike and the U. C. Berkeley Third World strike, Asian American student groups emerged bringing forth an articulation of both a Third World perspective, expressing solidarity with black, brown, and native American people, and an Asian American awareness expressing a unity of all Asians, Chinese, Japanese, Filipino, Korean, Samoan, and Hawaiian, while recognizing each group's unique communities.

Two articles from the Asian American Political Alliance (AAPA) illustrate the ideals and rhetoric expressed in student organizing efforts. "AAPA Perspectives" and "Understanding AAPA" are examples of the movement's approach toward a humanistic idealism with a critical social/political analysis. The existence of an Asian American Political Alliance, along with its radical politics, have angered many segments of the community. By presenting the unpopular aspects of the success story myth, including the dangers of being quiet Americans, AAPA performs a valuable service in polarizing issues to bring into sharp focus the different values and interpretations of reality. For without an alternative to the Olympian pronouncements of the Hayakawa's of this world, a one-sided picture of the community is perpetuated upon an already ignorant white society.

As a natural extension of student organizing, AAPA members became involved in organizing ethnic studies. Studies offered an institutional means to reach more Asian students. Judging from the large class enrollment in Asian American studies courses at numerous colleges, studies is fulfilling an expressed need. Yet, operating within the university presents everything from the dangers of co-optation to bureaucratic myopia and eventual isolation. "Concepts of Asian Studies" presents a clearly articulated political awareness of their responsibility to Asian people from within the educational establishment.

As a logical extension of Asian American studies, students began to study Asian American communities in order to ascertain means of identifying and resolving problems in each of the ethnic communities. While realizing that all Asians are Third World people, being Asians also means concretely different sources of oppression. In "An Interview with Warren Furutani," Community Involvement Director, JACL, he expresses the dilemma of the nonsingular Asian American community. He states, "...whether you use nationalism or...Third World to organize people depends upon your realistic analysis of that particular community." As Warren points out, different issues apply to various communities. While many Chinese still live in geographically-defined urban ghettos, many Japanese live in suburbs. Thus, Chinatown is a situation "where you can use the contradiction of racism... identity...and economics...in terms of self-determination and community control. The Japanese community...we've been defining as a psychological thing....Japanese people relate to Japanese institutions."

Much of the early student-community work started in the inner-city ghettos typified by San Francisco or New York Chinatown and Los Angeles' Little Tokyo. It was in these communities where wealth and poverty existed side by side with prosperous restaurants flanked by crumbling, overcrowded hotels for elderly Chinese, Filipinos, and Issei (first-generation Japanese), that students initiated and participated in self-help programs for the elderly, English tutorial programs for adults and children, and youth service centers. A variety of groups began to emerge ranging from tutorial projects to politically-oriented community service groups like I Wor Kuen in New York City.

"Asian Community Center" illustrates the type of multi-service organization that has emerged to meet the pressing social needs. The community center concept has been implemented in numerous Asian American communities. As each community has unique problems and a different social composition, the centers must offer special services. In Los Angeles' Little Tokyo, the Pioneer Center run by the Pioneer Project, an Issei-Sansei self-help group for the Issei in the Downtown area, provides multiple services from social security and welfare information referrals and flu vaccinations to a yearly recreational and social program. The JCYC Drop-In Center (Japanese Community Youth Council, San Francisco) provides a place for young people to gather and participate in art and photography workshops. The growing problem of drug abuse among young people is also confronted through the community centers; Asian American Hot Line, a drug counseling phone-in for crisis situations, operating from the Japanese American Community Services; Asian Involvement (JACS/AI) office, a Los Angeles umbrella organization of various self-help groups, including Asian Sisters, Asian American Hardcore, and Yellow Brotherhood.

An historical overview of Asian American communities is equally as valuable as contemporary analyses. Many of the contemporary problems have their seeds rooted in the historical development of the community. Buck Wong traces the development of San Francisco Chinatown from the early settlement of Chinese in California and renders a brief sketch of changes within Chinatown from the turn of the century to the present. In Part III of his essay, "A Social and Economic Look at Chinatown," the development of a Chinese slum is documented from the growth of an insular, segregated community born of anti-Chinese agitation through the institutionalization of a ghetto mentality characterized by low expectations and resigned acceptance of subservient status to the exacerbated social and economic problems attendant to the new immigration.

"An Interview with L. Ling-Chi Wang," the former director of San Francisco Youth Services Center, provides a short history of juvenile delinquency problems in Chinatown from the 1940's to the present. In discussing the failures to resolve critical youth problems raised by the activist movements of '68 and '69, Mr. Wang postulates possible future directions in community organizing and provides a model of community power structures. He reaffirms the importance of student work in the community and offers a challenging and useful critique of past and present efforts.

Jim Matsuoka's article, "Little Tokyo, Searching the Past and Analyzing the Future," reconstructs a view of the thriving, pre-war community of Little Tokyo. Drawing upon interviews with longtime community residents, Matsuoka successfully renders a personal look of that community from the early settlement to the present redevelopment project. A basic theme of Japanese influence upon the Japanese American community in Little Tokyo through the Japanese government ties past, present, and future together in a critical analysis of community interests versus covert economic control.

New York Chinatown displays many similarities to San Francisco Chinatown. However, as Rocky Chin points out in "New York Chinatown Today: Community in Crisis," "New York City is not San Francisco. It is older, larger and louder. Also denser, dirtier, richer and poorer." 90 percent of the housing is pre-1901; 76.5 percent of the housing is roach-infested. For Chinatown, this means that housing, education, youth problems, and community power alignments are main features of Chin's extensive essay. In addition, a fairly detailed account of the Chinatown radical group I Wor Kuen is given. As evident from "I Wor Kuen 12-Point Platform and Program," their revolutionary politics represent a threat to the reactionary Chinatown establishment and a radical answer to poverty and ghetto conditions. I Wor Kuen is now a national political organization based in San Francisco and New York City.

Chinatown and Asian American ghettos are not confined to urban settings. Ken Suyama's article, "The Asian American Experience in the Sacramento River Delta," gives a history of Asian migration to the farming areas and river towns of the Delta. After working the fields as labor hands, successive migrations of Chinese, Japanese, Filipino, Korean, and Hindu people settled in tiny segregated ghettos in Locke, Courtland, and Walnut Grove, California.

In this rural labor experience, racism also reaps its toll. Suyama presents the formation of a ghetto mentality of fear toward strangers and powerless acquiescence to the dominant white land owners. Poverty, poor housing, youth problems, and inadequate care for the elderly stand as visible manifestations of that ghetto situation.

The contemporary chapter of the Asian rural experience is the Filipino farmworker. With the major contradiction of large land owners profiting at the expense of 'cheap' labor still in practice, Filipinos today bear the burden of economic exploitation. In "Sour Grapes: Symbol of Oppression," Philip Vera Cruz recounts his personal experiences as a grape picker in Delano, California, from 1943 to the Delano Grape Strike of 1965. Mr. Vera Cruz desribes the life styles of Filipinos in Delano, giving vivid illustrations of racist attacks upon the community, the exploitation of Filipino labor and the ghetto environment.

Today, Philip Vera Cruz is a Vice President of United Farm Workers Organizing Committee (UFWOC). In "An Interview with Philip Vera Cruz," he presents a brief history of the Filipino involvement in initiating the Delano strike as well as his analysis of future directions for the union. Drawing upon his experience as an organizer, he analyzes the Asian American movement and stresses its need to strongly ally with other Third World movements and radical white groups. Furthermore, he sees a growing unity between Filipinos in the city and in rural areas from their common struggle for human rights.

Two articles illustrate the Filipino situation in cities: "International Hotel" and "Filipinos: A Fast Growing U.S. Minority -- Philippines: Revolution." The community control struggle over the preservation of the Hotel against the expansionist schemes of the land-hungry Financial District has gone on for three years. The issue centers around the need for low-cost housing for elderly Filipinos and Chinese or the further expropriation of land from the community by big business. The other article is a KALAYAAN (Philippine International News Service, San Francisco) editorial which rebuts many false impressions presented in a recent NEW YORK TIMES article on Filipinos.

A common, unifying issue among Asian American communities is land alienation. From the struggles over the densely populated, highly valuable properties in Chinatown and Little Tokyo to the restricted purchase and subsequent theft of farm lands from Japanese during World War II relocation, land has played and continues to play a significant role in our communities. Perhaps, the clearest example of land alienation rests in the expropriation of native Hawaiian land by white missionaries and adventurers. In "This Land Is Mine," the author states, "Many of our most dynamic political and economic problems can be directly attributed to the unequal and shortage (sic) of land. In exploring our economy, one discovers the connection between the land problem and every aspect of economic life -- especially in agriculture, tourism and defense." Ownership of land insures at least a means toward economic independence.

"Save Kalama Valley" and "Hawaii Homestead Struggle" drive home the relationship between land and the self-sustaining community. Without community control of land and its resources, there is no guarantee that people's basic needs for shelter, food, clothing, education, and medical aid will be met. Within the Hawaiian experience, this contradiction has been translated into white dominance over the native Hawaiians and poorer Asians. Like their Chinatown counterparts, Hawaiians "...accept passively being at the bottom of social and economic life." ("Hawaiian War Chant," ROLLING STONE MAGAZINE, #87, July 22, 1971). Native Hawaiians, or kanakas, according to author Paul Jacobs, hold a contemptuous, self-hating image, playing the happy-go-lucky, stupid, worthless "boy" haoles (whites) expect.

But changes are evident today. A growing movement for racial pride exemplified by the Hawaiians and Kokua Kalama are not only reassessing their identity and demanding return of their lands but are re-evaluating the "benefits" of tourism. "Tourism -- Decline of Aloha" reveals the negative aspects of tourism: inflation, pollution and deteriorating Asian-haole relations. The growing militancy of the Hawaiian movement is reflected in their Third World perspective as declared in "Raising the Fist."

Another area of community involvement concerns the middle-class Asian American professional. Teachers, social workers, and professionals have organized within their occupational fields to form Asian educational task forces, medical service committees and social workers organizations. One striking example of their involvement occurred in the dismissal of L.A. County Coroner Thomas Noguchi. In a reprint of JUST's (Japanese United in the Search for Truth, organized for fundraising and political pressure on Noguchi's behalf) L.A. TIMES advertisement, one can note a break from the usual quiet acceptance of injustice so often associated with the Asian community.

Other middle-class based groups have been formed. With strong student-Nisei alliances, Asian Americans for Action (AAA) in New York City and Asian Americans for Peace in Los Angeles, have organized demonstrations in protest of U.S. involvement in Southeast Asia. Other more established groups such as the Japanese American Citizens League (JACL) have vigorously urged the repeal of Title II of the Internal Security Act which provides for internment camps in times of "national emergency."

A final article on the movement shows the development of an Asian women's movement. "Asian Women as Leaders" explores both the racial inequities and stereotypes enforced upon all Asians and Third World people as well as the particular roles assigned to women in society and within the movement.

As a concluding note, we hope that these articles are of use to the Asian American communities not only in analyzing past and present problem areas but in charting future directions. In moving towards a political community, much more needs to be done in defining a viable politics within each community, organizing people around those issues and uniting our communities with other Third World communities. We must remember that Asian people have historically struggled bravely against their oppressors; today, we must redefine the sources of oppression within each community and righteously continue that struggle towards self-determination and liberation.

All Power to the People
Lokahi A Kuppa -- Unite and Stand Fast

EDDIE WONG

EDITORS NOTE
We regret that we could not complete an interview with the San Francisco Asian Legal Services in time for this printing of the reader. We thank the Asian Legal Services for their cooperation.

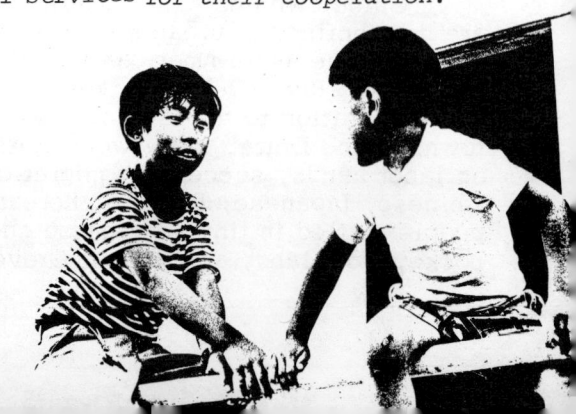

aapa perspectives

The Asian American Political Alliance is people. It is a people's alliance to effect social and political changes. We believe that the American society is historically racist and one which has systematically employed social discrimination and economic imperialism, both domestically and internationally, exploiting all non-white people in the process of building up their affluent society.

They did so at the expense of all of us. Uncontrolled capitalism has pushed all of the non-white people into a social position so that only manual jobs with subhuman pay are open to them. Consequently, we have been psychologically so conditioned by the blue-eye-blond-hair standard that many of us have lost our perspective. We can only survive if "we know our place"--shut up and accept what we are given. We resent this kind of domination and we are determined to change it.

The goal of AAPA is political education and advancement of the movement among Asian people, so that they may make all decisions that affect their own lives, in a society that never asks people to do so. AAPA is not an isolated group, and should never profess to be such. Its only legitimacy and value is in the effects it has on many people, not just a small group of people. In the same vein, AAPA is not meant to isolate Asians from other people; it is unhealthy as well as unwise to do such a thing. AAPA must constantly expand and grow, and reach out to other people and groups. At the same time, AAPA must meet the needs of its own members and deal with its own problems.

In the past political organizations have tended to subject themselves to rigid, traditional levels of structure in which a few make the decisions, present them to the body, and the body can vote either "yes" or "no."

This hierarchistic organization, however, is only a manifestation of the elite control, primidal structure mentality in which you are not capable of making your own decisions, an idea drilled into you from the foundations of this society.

AAPA is only what the people make it. We have adopted a structure which better fits the needs and goals of our alliance, not a structure to which we have to adjust ourselves. Furthermore, there is no membership in AAPA in the strict sense of the word. There are workers who for common interests join together with one or more people to intensify the effectiveness of an action.

Since May, 1968, AAPA has grown from a small group of students and community workers to a powerhouse for Asian thought and action. AAPA is now a member of the Third World Liberation Front, Asian Association, and Asian Coalition. Some past activities of Berkeley AAPA include: Free Huey Rallies at the Oakland Courthouse, Chinatown Forums, McCarran Act lobbies, MASC Boycott, Third World Liberation Front Strike, development of Asian Studies, and liaison with and development of other AAPA's throughout the state.

AAPA is only a transition for developing our own social identity, a multiplication of efforts. In fact, AAPA itself is not the important link but the ideas generated into action from it--that we Asian Americans are no longer going to kowtow to white America in order to gain an ounce of respect; that we must begin to build our own society alongside our black, brown and red brothers as well as those whites willing to effect fundamental social, economic, political changes; that we have the right for determining our own lives and asserting our yellow identity as a positive force in a new life based on human relationships and cooperation.

Reprinted from ASIAN AMERICAN POLITICAL ALLIANCE, Vol. I, No. 6, October, 1969. Berkeley, page 3.

understanding aapa

We Asian Americans believe that we must develop an American Society which is just, humane, equal, and gives the people the right to control their own lives before we can begin to end the oppression and inequality that exists in this nation.

We Asian Americans realize that America was always and still is a White Racist Society. Asian Americans have been continuously exploited and oppressed by the racist majority and have survived only through hard work and resourcefulness, but their souls have not survived.

We Asian Americans refuse to cooperate with the White Racism in this society which exploits us as well as other Third World people, and affirm the right of Self-Determination.

We Asian Americans support all oppressed peoples and their struggles for Liberation and believe that Third World People must have complete control over the political, economic, and educational institutions within their communities.

We Asian Americans oppose the imperialistic policies being pursued by the American Government.

Reprinted from the ASIAN AMERICAN POLITICAL ALLIANCE NEWSPAPER, Summer Issue, Volume I, Number 5, Berkeley, California.

EDITORIAL BOARD
JULY, 1971

AN INTERVIEW WITH

PAT SUMI

QUESTION: Could you elaborate a little bit on your personal background, and how you evolved into becoming a radical?

SUMI: It seems to me that becoming a radical is only a logical conclusion to the resolution of contradictions not only in your own life but between you and society; if you keep pushing yourself to find answers to problems you see, you wind up having a radical perspective.
In high school, I was the model Asian. I got good grades and ran for student body offices and had good citizenship marks. I couldn't understand the "rowdies", you know, the Pachucos and the Chicanos and the low-riders and all. I was kind of intimidated by them and I didn't have any idea what they were about. I grew up in a mostly white, upper middle class neighborhood. There were some Chinese families around but it wasn't like the Westside or the most nitty-grit of J-flats.
Mao has a story about a frog sitting at the bottom of the well and he thinks the sky's no bigger than the well, while, in fact, the sky is much bigger than that. Coming from the background that I came from, I was the perfect frog in the well. I knew exactly what the well defined for me and nothing more.
I had a very narrow conception of life; I was into getting good grades at school. I didn't know exactly what I was going to do with it afterwards. But then I went to Occidental College, a predominantly Christian, Caucasian college, and most of the people came from South Pasadena. And just because it was that kind of thing, it raised those contradictions in my life.
I had to ask myself, was I white? Was I middle class? Was I Japanese, was I not Japanese? What was I? For the four years I was in college, I went through a series of experiences that really sharpened those questions.
I went to Japan between my freshman and sophomore years and visited and traveled around not only to see the sights, but also to see relatives--farmers-- the kind of middle peasant types in Japan. It was kind of a mind-blower because I felt as if I had gone home. I was surprised. I hadn't any idea that I was really Japanese in that sense. I'm more so, I think, than most Sansei, because I lived with my grandparents all my life. But still, it was a very surprising experience. I came back and re-entered this white world and I began to resent things like people saying, "Wow, do Japanese really eat raw fish?" But at the same time I was going through these contradictory changes about my mother

An excellent interview with Pat Sumi appears in ASIAN WOMEN, Dwinelle Hall, U.C. Berkeley, Copyright 1971, in the section on the "Politics of Womanhood."
*Editor's note: An extensive interview with Pat Sumi on the Anti-Imperialist Peoples delegation to Asia appears in RODAN, November, 1970.

being old-fashioned--why didn't my grandparents ever become citizens--not ever understanding about the history of what they had been through; but more of just thinking, "Wow, if we're in America, and by God, the majority is white and middle class, well, why don't we assimilate? Why do we have to stand out so much? Why do we have to be so obviously Japanese?"--at the same time resenting white people asking racist questions and that "How quaint to eat with chopsticks" type of attitude.

Another thing about racism towards Black people. At that time, I considered it a separate thing from racism toward Asian people. I didn't even know if it was racism toward Asian people, because certainly what was happening to Black people seemed to be different.

That crystalized when I went to Africa in 1965; I went with a kind of missionary attitude toward primitive Black people, but I discovered that they had many things in common with my relatives in Japan. They were not very wealthy farmers. They had a rich, traditional family structure--a lot of traditional folk material. They came from what I consider a very rich cultural heritage. Immediately, that meant that you could not explain the conditions of Black people in America by saying that they came from a more primitive type of society than Japanese. That's one of the arguments used about how we're assimilated and supposedly Black people aren't--because we come from such a rich tradition and a high civilization and Black people don't. I discovered that it just wasn't true.

So I came back and the next summer, after I graduated from college--I got a B.A. in history, which doesn't really mean much--I went to the South. I decided that if Black people were separate, it must be because of segregation. Of course, the "answer" was to integrate. And I found for the first time in my life that someone wanted to kill me because of my beliefs. We walked around in this demonstration with almost two hundred crazy rednecks; a lot of them very young people in their twenties who literally wouldn't mind--as they were throwing bricks and things at us--if they accidently bashed your head in. It's kind of a scary thing, to say the least. It was my first experience of the police being on the other side, not protecting the interest of poor people, but interested in protecting the privileged people.

I couldn't understand it. Those white people weren't privileged either; they were privileged because they were white, but they certainly weren't privileged economically--they lived in shacks just like Black people. The plantation owners didn't even bother to come to those demonstrations; they just sat up in their air-conditioned plantation houses. It was very confusing.

I worked there at that time in an O.E.O. (Office of Economic Opportunity) program called Child Development Group of Mississippi in the Health Department. We came up with some pretty astonishing figures--80 percent of one county's Head Start Children were anemic; anywhere from 10-40 percent so anemic, that if they were white middle class children, they would be hospitalized. We also had the experience of having a two and one-half year old child in the program die from complications from malnutrition. He died from diarrhea and just didn't have strength to deal with it.

There was at that time, a great reform movement about food for starving people in the United States--one of those publicity campaigns that the pigs are so good at, making people think things are changing. So me, two older Black people from Humphrey County and two little kids from Belzoni, Mississippi went to Washington to lobby for the passage of an emergency food bill. We met with various politicians and press people and were uniformly turned back by all of them.

I was just amazed at the so-called democratic system that could not respond to the needs of starving people. Now I know that there are other people in the Northern cities who starve, including our own Asian people. To be told that it wasn't politically expedient to raise the issue of starvation really blew my mind.

It didn't seem to me that democracy had anything left to offer. I now know that this is bourgeois democracy, where the rich people really have the control. I just said, "Later for the congressional system." Whether it's the people in it or the system that turns the people into those kinds of monsters, I have no interest anymore in appealing to them to help people, because it's obvious they don't care. They're more interested in the internal machination of Congress and the power plays. The real needs of people outside have no meaning to them. After this I went back to graduate school. That was my second year of graduate school (Cornell), and I was determined to find some answers. It was fruitless to pursue it. The other students and professors weren't even interested in that field. They were interested in their degrees and dissertations, classes, and full-time teaching status. It was a drag. I just packed up my books, my two cats, and all my belongings and came West. I just said, "Later, I just can't deal with this at all."

I wound up in a hippie commune--now that I look back on it, a comical commune-- of people in Palo Alto, which had been one of the founding forces of the draft resistance movement in early '67. It had all the problems of a hippie commune: it was male chauvinist, elitist, racist...but again, in that context, it was a step forward for me. By then I had decided that the war in Vietnam was wrong. Again, I didn't know exactly why. Sometimes adults will put down young people by saying "Well, you don't really understand what you're getting into, so what are you doing it for? You're just a bunch of wild-eyed half-baked, unclear radicals." That's partly true; that's a criticism on all of us who have something more clear in mind on what we're doing and don't make sure that newer people have that perspective. But still, there's something very great to be said about courage that the young have today. We may not know exactly where this is going to lead us. It may lead us to six feet under the ground or to jail, but insofar as we have a life that has to be dedicated to something, we will and should dedicate that life to making this wrong right, however we can do it.

It seemed to me at that time that the best way to stop the war was to keep people from joining the army. I did not realize at the time that white middle class people could afford to go to jail, could afford the psychological burden of resisting the draft in an individualistic moral stand--whereas lower class and third world people could not afford that, and that a lot of minorities had been to jail and didn't want to go again.

I thought everyone was just like me--educated and middle class.

I lived in that commune a little more than a year. In that time, significant things happened to me. I worked in a minority education program at a junior college, the College of San Mateo--that's where I met Warren Furutani.

Warren wanted to front me off as an Asian counselor because I had a college degree and a Japanese name. I didn't want to ask him then, but I couldn't understand "why an Asian counselor?" Asians don't need counselors, I thought-- we've all got it made. The cat was so earnest and enthusiastic about an Asian counselor and minority program--so I kind of just said "Yeah, sure", not at all realizing what I got myself into.

Also, at the same time, I got into my first attempt to organize G.I.'s. My job was to organize the leafleting team to go out and leaflet all the bases and bus stations and airports about a G.I. peace march in San Francisco. We found that G.I.'s were very willing and receptive--well, not all of them; some were very hostile, mostly career and officer types. You cannot go on government reservations; it's not for people. You cannot hand out literature unless it's been approved by the commanding officer. I was detained on two bases; Hamilton Air Force Base and finally arrested at Treasure Island Naval Base, San Francisco Bay.

Also, at that point, I suddenly found myself being one of the eleven demands being put forth by the minority students at San Mateo and being hired as a counselor. So I went to work there for little less than two months, and was finally ushered out the door by the administration.

I found out that it doesn't really matter if you're quiet and non-violent, and petitioned peacefully and discussed things in a reasonable way with people, because as long as they had the power, you could be as reasonable as you wanted to, but they weren't going to give you control over anything that really affected your life--especially not minority students.

By then, I began to realize why Asians had to be included--because there were a whole lot of poor Asians I had never known about who were trying to struggle through this crazy program and who were getting arrested and so on. I found out what institutional racism looked like, just glaring us in the face. Unless you have the power to control that institution, you just have no way to change that institution.

I just decided that I was tired of the hippie commune. I just couldn't relate to that racism, the bullshit, anymore. So we decided to start a G.I. coffeehouse at Camp Pendleton in Oceanside, California. That's where I consider I really began to become a radical organizer, as opposed to a sympathizer or "misguided youth,"--because at that point, I came into direct conflict with the powers that control this country.

When you organize in the military, you organize directly counter to American foreign policy because American troops are the rifle point of that policy. When you start messing with the troops, you're messing with the power that the man has to control most of the so-called "free world."

Again, I think that if I really knew what I was getting into, I don't think I would have had the nerve to do it. But it's precisely because you felt not only you had to do it, but that--like the American Indians have a saying, "It's a good day to die"--you just think that this is something that's worth dying for, whether you fully understand all the political reasoning or not. You go with that faith, that the world can be made better by human effort and it has to be...even if it means human sacrifice.

It was a phenomenal response from the G.I.'s. We sort of forced the military to go through everything from liberalism to absolute fascism in about six months! The brass were just terrified...about the organization, Movement for Democratic Military.

We just began out of the faith that the G.I.'s should be self-determined people too--that they were oppressed, that they could educate themselves, politically educate others, write newspapers, and organize themselves to deal with their oppression. The problem was the issues weren't clearly defined at all. Often, we just confused the issues and a lot of people's minds down there. But we did a whole lot of things right. We succeeded in having a couple of really great demonstrations--one in which a thousand G.I.'s turned out.

QUESTION: What happened to them?

SUMI: Well, M.D.M. still exists in the minds of people--but that's not an organization, we discovered. We discovered what the Black Panthers have since discovered-- that mass sympathy does not at all mean mass organization. Mass sympathy does not give you the power to change anything. We didn't understand what an organization was.

We really messed up some G.I.'s. A lot of them went to jail. Some had to go A.W.O.L. A few went to Canada. We had no way really to organize power to protect G.I.'s when they were arrested or harassed. Finally, the thing that really broke us was in April of 1970, last year. Someone fired 12 rounds into the M.D.M. house and nearly killed a G.I. That was when we discovered we had no organizational way to respond. That was it. That was the crisis. That was when the pigs decided to confront us. That was when we discovered we had no real power. After that, it was downhill for the organization.

I didn't understand all this. Last summer, I was running around in Asia telling everyone about M.D.M. when, in fact, it was really falling to pieces. I came home and there was no M.D.M. left. But it was for the really impressive G.I.

work that we did do that I was chosen to go as a representative of the G.I. movement in the delegation to Asia. And again, naively, I went trotting off to see Asia, not knowing what I was getting into.

QUESTION: You talked about the people's delegation before.* Do you have any further thoughts on it?

SUMI: I discovered that in relating to international revolutionary movements, you have to represent something. For most of us, except for the Panthers--and even now for the Panthers, it is a question of who do they really represent--you shouldn't get a bunch of individuals to go. It's not useful. I suppose what it did do was to heighten my consciousness of the real critical need in the American movement for a party; some kind of guiding force that can take leadership in struggle. We don't have it yet. Everyone is floundering around, trying to find direction on their own. I suspect this period of pre-party struggle will last a great deal longer; in fact, too long. I think we're going to find that we'll have to have a party, because a whole lot of us are going to wind up in jail. There's a good possibility in the next two, three, four years that there's going to be a massive repression. I don't think it'll kill a whole lot of us--but it will put a whole lot of us away. People are going to understand what we understood when the pigs decide to confront us, that if you don't have the organizational power to meet that crisis, then comes the question--"Can you make it, can you make an organization? Will you have that power?"

QUESTION: Is that when you started getting involved in the Asian Movement? A lot of people see you in different roles--as an organizer, as a movement, as a P.R. person. How do you see yourself?

SUMI: At this point, right now, it's not clear to me what I have to do. I think the political development in Los Angeles has come to a certain point which is an important construction point. The question is of my role in that. I don't know if I have a role here or elsewhere, geographically speaking, in the Asian movement.

QUESTION: In terms of the need for organization, how do you see that happening in the Asian community? Is that organization to be on an ethnic basis?

SUMI: Leadership is the critical question in a revolution. Leadership that the masses of people can relate to and trust. If you don't have that leadership then the masses of people are just not going to automatically rise up. There is a kind of belief among one whole line in the Asian movement, which I call the Social Services line--that if you merely present the people with contradictions, e.g., welfare not being given to aliens, that people will rise up and become very radical. In fact, practice has shown that's not necessarily true. In the same sense that I thought draft resistance was the answer to the war, social services is not the answer to the critical needs to the community. Ultimately, what can make it (the Asian community) a healthy positive environment for people to grow up and live in, is a question of the larger environment of this society--the interplay between the two.
What we need is Asian leadership--political leadership. Not the old style community leaders, but political leaders. A whole new breed of people who are dedicated to the notion that it's only a revolution, and at that, a Marxist, Leninist, Maoist type of revolution that's going to free our people. This is really a hard point. I don't know how to explain it very clearly right now except that people will become leaders when they fully understand the context in which we operate. I think that a lot of Asian young people now operate on the assumption that capitalism, racism, imperialism are all part of the same package of oppressors, and that socialism is the way out. But as to how to fight one to get the other is the question. That's where you need leadership.

Leadership comes from several things. It comes from study, practice, and self-conscious practice...going out and seeing if your theories work. If you develop a political line--let's say that Japanese people need to organize a strong Japanese leadership movement, which can ally itself with other strong groups in other communities--well, what you need are people who not only see that as a necessity but are also willing to take the risks, to expend the energy to go out and try to build that organization.

One of the things I'm trying to understand is that revolution is really a science... of how people interreact, how society moves and changes. And if it's a science, then we have to apply a revolutionary scientific method. What we need are people with the wisdom to be able to abstract revolutionary hypotheses and then the courage to test them.

We have a lot of leaders in the old style sense...like me, who are looked up to because we've been big talkers and have a certain knowledge. But that's not leadership in the sense I mean leadership.

I think there have been two things accomplished in the Asian movement that are important. One is that there are thousands of young people all over the United States who believe in socialism as an answer to capitalism, imperialism, and racism. That's one whole huge accomplishment. We've broken the brain-washing by immigrant parents from China and the anti-communism from Nisei parents. The other thing we've learned is serving people's needs--the little that has been done--is not the most direct route to the revolution. The question is now what is the most direct route? Who are the most important people in our community to be organizing--the most advanced people? We don't even know who are going to be our bravest people.

There are very good examples, though. I just found out yesterday that Doug Yamamoto (U.C. Santa Cruz student, charged with fire bombing the Santa Cruz Armed Services Recruiting Center, following the February '71 invasion of Laos) was sentenced for three years. The judge told him that we can't have people like you running around loose and "I was lenient in letting you plead guilty to the lesser charge"--that kind of attitude. They didn't even have the courage to tell Doug's people where they were taking him. As soon as the gavel came down they handcuffed him and took him out of the court and that was it. Apparently as he left, he said "Keep the spirit up," which we should take as an admonition from a very courageous brother who decided that things had come to a certain point in his own life. He may not have known the exact reasons, but he decided that he had to do something besides being peaceful, calm about things. That's a very courageous thing for him to have done. In my own view of Doug's trial, he didn't deserve to be in jail.

QUESTION: What does being a people mean? What does being a community mean?

SUMI: First of all, we have to understand that we're all Third World people inside the United States--and it's not really clear at this point, what that actually means in terms of organizing for the revolution. What it does mean is that we have a certain common basis of oppression; our enemy is the same. We have to get together as Third World people to fight the same enemy.

Ultimately, our goal in organizing is to be able to build that Third World solidarity within the United States. But in terms of what it means to be an Asian people. I think there are two things to that. One is how are we oppressed? The second is how have we fought in the past, how shall we fight in the present and into the future? That then means that we're not just Asians. We are Filipinos, Koreans, Samoans, Chinese, Japanese, and so on. It means that the ways we are oppressed concretely are different. It means that most Filipinos are rural proletariats who are farm workers while most Japanese are urban worker-types: gardeners, seamstresses...While there are Chinese who live in ghettoes, there are not many Japanese ghettoes left.

On the other hand, the largest slogans, the ones that try and move people forward quickly, are the ones that do bind us together--that we are all oppressed as Asian people, that racism toward Asian people looks a certain way at this point in history, as opposed to the way it looks towards Blacks. I suspect the more militant we get, the more it'll look like the stuff that comes down on Black people. When you organize--when you talk to your mother, you talk to her about specific things that have happened to her because she's Chinese. And you also try and mention the things that are similar to Chinese people as to Japanese people as to Filipino people. Ultimately, you'll have to mention why it's similar to Black, Brown, Red, Vietnamese, South African, Palestinian, everybody else. That's what it means to me to be an Asian people, for myself. Organizing on a mass level, it means being Japanese; on the revolutionary level, it means being Third World. They're all one and the same. We are oppressed people. Third World people have always been oppressed people in this country. To fight means we must fight together. One million Asians combined with thirty million Blacks, combined with fifteen million Browns is a whole lot of people.

QUESTION: You mentioned that there's some common issues like the anti-war movement that can unite all segments of the Asian community because they all have an interest in this anti-Asian racism that's being disseminated. How has the organization gone on that one issue?

SUMI: I think that if you take a more militant stand it seems to go better than a liberal stand. I marched in the April 24 demonstration in San Francisco with the Asian contingent. That was everybody: Filipinos, Chinese, Koreans, Japanese. We marched together, waving red books and carried the People's Chinese flag, a Pathet Lao flag, some North Korean flags, Vietnamese flags, a Chinese flag--and it was good! There was more unity under that kind of militant feeling of politics than I felt at Peace Sunday (Anti-War Teach-in, Los Angeles, May, 1971) even though Peace Sunday was an important event.

QUESTION: You've always stressed the fact that Asian people have expressed a solidarity with the American people. They also stress how important the American movement is, and many times, it seems that the movement fails the Indo-Chinese, because of all the internal bickering. What kinds of concrete expression can Asian Americans give to the Indo-Chinese?

SUMI: First of all, they should be concrete ones. We have to confront anti-Asian racism coming home and over in Asia. Steps are being taken to recognize that racism against Asians comes in special forms as against black or brown people. The People's Coalition for Peace and Justice just held its national convention and decided to call national actions on Hiroshima-Nagasaki weekend to protest Asian genocide. And that's a great step forward for the white movement to be thinking on those terms. I think Asian people need to take a greater leadership position in opposing the war. We are in fact the visible reminder in this country of what is going on over there. And that has to be brought up to the American people over and over again.
Our own brothers continue to go into the military, willingly, without questions asked. Draft counseling has to be stepped up. Parents have to be educated to keep their sons out of the military by any means necessary. There already are surprising numbers of Japanese and Chinese draft resisters and A.W.O.L.'s in Canada. And that's a big step.
Another simple thing we can do is letter writing campaigns to Washington instead of Hanoi saying that if you want the P.O.W.'s released, set a date to withdraw. The Indo-Chinese that I've met do have a special feeling for us as blood relatives and it's a shame we don't have the same feeling for them.
I want to say a couple of things about what S.I. Hayakawa said. One, about the bomb and Hiroshima. And the other is about the radicals copying the Panthers.

I think they're tied together. We can't look at the history of Asians like a series of slides, a series of incidents. The history of our people in this country is tied together with a couple of threads. One is that we've been oppressed by racism and economic oppression. And the second thing is that we've had to fight back to survive. Those two things run from the first time the Chinese came over in a large group in the 1840's all the way to the present.

It's true to an extent that suddenly the Sanseis have discovered who they are. But that's really because we've been forced to. You can't integrate into white society. A few individuals can and they always allow those few to do it and then hold those individuals up as examples. But the mass of Japanese people cannot become white. Anyways, who wants to become white? Who wants to become part of the society that started the Indo-Chinese War and Korean War and invented the bomb and pollution?

The question is how do we solve our problem of white racism and economic oppression amongst our people? If Hayakawa thinks that we're just aping the Panthers just to imitate the Panthers, he's really mistaken because he really doesn't understand the objective conditions in the community--those things that make people upset: dope; people dying in the street; people going to jail, and not having money for lawyers; old people falling apart in the streets because they don't have enough money for medical care; and just having to live forty, fifty years of humiliation. Those are real problems but he may not see them because he's living with his white friends up in Mill Valley, thinking that he's white. That's the whole point of being accepted in that kind of society in the first place so you don't see the problems of your own people because you don't even recognize that you're part of your own people. Once you do make that connection that you are in fact Japanese, and you look around, you find all kinds of problems. If you really try to confront the contradiction: why is there dope; why are there people starving; why is there people dying in the street; why is there no medical care? Then you ultimately get yourself to the understanding that it's the system that we live in. We can't even blame it on Nixon; you can't just blame a few individuals. How do all the military men come back calling people "gook"? They didn't learn that individually; they learned that because of a racist institution, the military.

How are we going to fight this? First of all, we have to understand we're not by ourselves. Our people have fought back as long as we've been here. That's one of the whole things about institutional racism in the first place. They never tell you that we ever fought back. You just begin to read the history of some of the things our people have done and it blows your mind. A Japanese helped found the American Communist Party; Japanese were deported for being members of the Communist Party in the U.S.; Japanese were almost deported in the 50's because of the McCarthy thing. People organized and became parts of unions and other radical organizations. They tried to organize Japanese into Gardeners' Federations, housemaid-houseboy organizations. That unity once existed amongst our people. Right now, we're trying to give our people their courage just for them to tell us what their life was like.

I consider people like Hayakawa traitors--that they sold out to becoming white racists themselves. The stand he took at San Francisco State was obviously the same stand any white racist would have taken; it's not even with an understanding that he himself is oppressed to the point where he hates himself and his own people.

Hiroshima was a racist experiment on Third World people to see what the bomb would do. There's no other possible justification for it. The Emperor already sued for peace but was ignored because the bomb wasn't quite ready for use. Then immediately after the bombing, he again sued for peace; and of course, isn't that a real military victory? Six hundred thousand Asians to save a few thousand whites...that's exactly the logic behind Vietnamization--as long as Asian people are dying, that's O.K., but not white people.

QUESTION: Hayakawa has the habit of always looking for the positive aspects of the most negative things and saying that as the main point. He said the relocation camps were the best thing for the Japanese--evacuation moved the Japanese to Chicago and gave them mobility.

SUMI: Well, you have to do that. The camps were so awful that you had to fight it or try to look at the good side of things. That's one of the things human beings do to survive. People had to say, "Well, at least we're not getting beat up by white people anymore because we're in the camps." If you really looked at the reality of the camps, you either would have had mass revolts and massacres, or people would have gone crazy. In a situation like that, perversely, you get grateful for people not massacring you.

I suppose that's why identity is such an important question for Asians. Who are we as an Asian people? If you identify with your people, then you become part of their suffering and also part of their fighting power. But if you don't, you become like Hayakawa--very isolated and cynical, or you become very insular like the frog at the bottom of the well--because that's a measure of self-protection. I know a lot of Japanese kids, especially middle class kids from all Asian communities that are much into looking at things from the bottom of the well. They want to be assimilated and accepted. They don't want to fight. Well, after all, no one wants to fight. You only do it after you come to the conclusion that you have to.

For the time being, at least now for the Japanese, there seem to be other choices: Dodge Dusters, Toyotas, a bike, a good-looking girl friend or a boyfriend, or some alternative which seems to be meaningful. Everybody seems to know what they want. As long as you can bury your head in Montebello and you don't have to confront the rest of the sky, everybody thinks that's cool. The problem is that you never get to or are allowed to because racism reaches you wherever you try and hide. You either recognize that racism and struggle against it or let it destroy your life and the life of your children--watch them go into dope because they have no strength, no identity. Or let them run in gangs, because they have no strength on their own. Then people will finally understand that material comforts are not going to make it. It's a frightening thing for a lot of Niseis--that's why they so much oppose radical young people. They know that Sanseis are saying that it didn't work, that you may be making money but then you're making less money than a white man at the same job. You may be comfortable with your wall-to-wall carpeting, but your kids are on dope. You may think things are O.K., but they aren't. Racism didn't end in 1945. You can't run away from it. That's what's making a lot of parents upset. They see us as raising questions, challenging them about their entire life for the last twenty years. We're asking them, do you find it that meaningful? Because we find our life as young radicals more meaningful than having wall-to-wall carpeting. That really puts people uptight.

QUESTION: But how does the movement respond to that alienation? For one thing, the Nisei are alienated. They get ulcers all the time. Sansei are very alienated too, to the extent that the young generations identify less with Asians. How can a movement deal with that?

SUMI: First of all, I think we have to understand the power of the people. Power to the people means figuring out who the people are. The people are not abstract. They are human beings--all of them, each one of them. That means our parents, our friends who are bikers, low riders, friends who are into having two kids and living out in Monterey Park. Those are the people. Of course, some are going to be more willing to fight on their own behalf. Poor people and oppressed people are going to be more willing to fight than people in Monterey Park. But at the same time, when you talk about struggle against racism, racism has affected all of us. Economic exploitation has affected all of us in some degree

or other. It means that we have to approach those people with respect instead of "You bourgeois reactionary so-and-so's. I come to tell you the word." You just can't approach people with that attitude. The revolution is a mission in the sense of making things better. But not in the sense that you have to proselytize people because they're in the dark. People are not "saved by the revolutionary word"--because people are wise. Not wise in the sense that you just point out a contradiction and they'll say give me the gun. But they're wise in the sense that they know the implications of a society-wide revolution and that it includes them. They are wise because they've lived in this country. One of the things they're afraid of is that it's only them.
The Nisei, the middle-aged ones, and the Chinese who live in Chinatown are really isolated from each other. They lived through a terrible period of history and they became very afraid; afraid of informers; afraid of each other because twenty Asians together was a mob. Carmen Chow (from I Wor Kuen) tells a story of a man who came from Chinatown to a meeting called by people to hear the Young Lords and the Panther Party to talk about their programs. The old man turned to comment afterwards--"Well, I'm so glad. I knew the Chinese wouldn't be able to do something by themselves, but I'm so glad that the Blacks and Browns are with us. Then maybe we'll have a chance to win."
Basically, I think if we investigate where our parents and grandparents are at, what they're afraid of is that they lost once. The camps were a real defeat for our people. Further, the end of the radical movement in the late 40's and early 50's in which many of our parents and grandparents participated was a real defeat. You just don't get over a defeat like that. You learn a lot of distrust because, most of all, people didn't know why they were defeated. They learned to distrust organized Communists and radicals. They learned to distrust ideology. They felt betrayed and they were. They didn't know just exactly what had gone wrong. For us to approach people who have battle scars from many previous battles with condescension instead of respect isn't in any sense building a movement. It alienates people. We should give them a sense that they had interesting lives, that they have lived battles, that they are good and brave people, and that we have a lot of respect for them.
I know whenever people are defensive, Nisei in particular, they always come up with "We tried too. We tried to make a better world when we were young." They'll even bring up examples of "We resisted." Everyone has examples of that. You just don't live in this country for so many years without somewhere in their memory having some event where they fought back. The question is to awaken that feeling in people again and get them all to fight back in one direction; then there's real power. If you begin to really listen to your parents and grandparents and all their friends, you begin to understand what the power of people really means, because they really do have power. They really are courageous, only they need something to fight for. They need a sense of strength in our organization and leadership and some reason to fight.

QUESTION: The Filipinos in Delano have always asked for Asian support, but there has never been any organized effort to help them.

SUMI: I think the Filipinos are very much organized behind the strike. The Japanese thing I don't understand because many are ex-farm workers. I don't know as we've really tried. There have been a lot of real issues we've let go--Vietnam is one, Delano is another. They're real issues raised for Asian people in this country and we've kind of let them slide.

QUESTION: What other issues do you see coming up?

SUMI: The rise of Japanese militarism is something that we've got to confront. And Japanese have to do that. Otherwise, it's going to be purely a nationalist thing with Chinese and Filipinos. Japanese have to begin to educate their people about what is really happening in Japan. I think Korea is just going to explode soon. There's going to be war in Korea with the U.S. involved and the guerrilla movement in the South. And we've got to be prepared for that.

We've never been really able to deal with the issue of drugs. One thing we haven't really done for people who have gotten off drugs is to provide a movement alternative for them that meets them from where they're at. They are street people, and they want confrontation. They want something much more militant, and we've failed to provide that. Many have come into the J.A.C.S. office or a similar project for two months and they go right back out and back on dope. Movement people bad mouth them, call them failures. But people don't fail themselves. They fail because there is a failure of leadership to explain and make viable something to do.

I've been rereading Edgar Snow's RED STAR OVER CHINA. It's very interesting how Chairman Mao became a radical. He went through more changes than I've been through--more kinds of liberalism and political philosophies. At every critical point, there was some leadership to guide him to something more correct and because he was a student and from the middle class background, it was alright for him to go through changes like that. But street people are not like that, especially poor street people. They're not willing to skate around and live an interesting life. They really want action to confront the pigs. They know that the pigs have been oppressing them. It may be for a while that we'll continue to lose them. A lot of those people did not become part of the movement until there was a viable Red Army in China. Then they came in droves. Whole gangs of bandits and city lumpen joined the Red Army. But even then, some drifted back into banditry and were eventually killed by the people who had then been armed.

I'm trying to absorb what this means. I have a sense that things are a lot more urgent than we think they are in Los Angeles. I think Nixon's got something planned after '72 or even before in order to win the election. Millions die each year in this country and around the world because of this country's economic system and government. We have to stand up sometime. And I think that time is now. If the Chinese get sent to the camps, it's too late to start talking about them then. We have to fight racism and our racist government right now.

QUESTION: What future plans do you have?

SUMI: I feel that it's very necessary to find out what leadership means in a revolutionary sense, not only for myself but community wise--finding and developing new forms of leadership. It's necessary to find other parts of our community, the working people, the poorer people--and get them to understanding that self-determination means that they must become organized and powerful. I really want to write some more.

QUESTION: What about working with Asian women's groups?

SUMI: I think I'd be interested in working with war brides, but I don't know where to begin...I don't think it's useful politically to mobilize women except to help them become stronger themselves, at this point, until a leadership organization and the most militant segments of our community are mobilized. I could see having women's groups among the most militant...then you have something to talk about and organize around. You'll have some really committed and dedicated people.

For a lot of people still--for most people in L.A.--I get the feeling that it's still a game. I'm bothered by that because I can remember what it was like when you had to live with the day-to-day fear of getting killed. I remember what it's like to be an Indo-Chinese wondering when the bombs are coming next. That sense of real purpose, of real dedication to confronting the enemy still is lacking. As long as it's lacking, the most militant people will not be mobilized.

All of this is a lot of words just to say what I summed up in the beginning--that as Asian people, if we seek to explain the problems of ourselves, our community and all poor and oppressed peoples in the United States, we come to the conclusion that revolution is the only answer. We must cease being Japanese frogs at the bottom of the white American well seeing only what that defines for us. We must make our own definitions by seeing the totality of who we are and where that puts us.

All Power to the People!

ASIAN STUDIES: THE CONCEPT OF ASIAN STUDIES

EDITORIAL STAFF OF ASIAN AMERICAN POLITICAL ALLIANCE

Introduction

The creation of the Asian Studies Division stemmed directly from the political action of the Third World Strike, in the Winter Quarter, 1969. The original demand of a Third World College was partially met with an interim Ethnic Studies Department, to be implemented in the Fall of 1969. The Strike met with very little understanding or flexibility from the Berkeley Administration, which used police terror and bureaucratic hang-ups to discourage creative thinking, and threatened ideas. It is the goal of the Asian students in the Third World Liberation Front Berkeley to continue and strenthen the goals of the Strike: self-determination for Third World (and all) people, and an end to the current system dominant in the United States and the world--based on property individualism and professional bureaucracy. The hope of the Asian students is that these goals will be embodied both in the goals, as well as the running of, the Asian Studies Division and the future Department.

We hope that Asian students at other campuses and institutions will cooperate with us in this venture, and share their ideas and feelings with us. It is only with brotherhood and trust in one another that we will build a society where we can be ourselves.

For the Asian students who have developed the Asian Studies aspect of Third World Studies, self-determination includes meeting our own needs in education. Under the traditional mechanisms of the University, the Regents and the Administration decide what the students' educational needs are and direct those decisions downward, through the bureaucracy, for the students to respond to. The Regents and the Administration are clearly neither Third World nor students. They do not know what our needs are. They know their own needs--what is best for big business, and what is best for remaining secure in an administrative position. Their common need to maintain the status quo is obviously not in the interests of Third World people. Yet, the Regents and the Administration continue to make decisions which affect our lives. The students of the Asian Studies Committee believe that the educational hierarchy must be inverted. We are best suited to assess and deal with our own needs; the Regents and the Administration must respond to us.

The University establishment has told us that we lack background and training, yet Asian Studies has existed since the Winter quarter of the past academic year. Asian Studies began with one course under the Board of Educational Development. Since then, six classes have been offered, with a total enrollment of at least six hundred students. Each class has been designed, run, and taught by students. In addition, the Asian Studies Division, unlike the other Third World divisions, does not have a coordinator. A committee of six graduate and six undergraduate students make policy and decisions. This is innovative--the Administration has been pressured into recognizing students rather than a coordinator whose only qualification may be a Ph.D..

Innovation is not accomplished without

Reprinted from ASIAN AMERICAN POLITICAL ALLIANCE, Volume I, Number 6 (October, 1969), Berkeley.

struggle. But struggle has produced four Asian Studies courses and a Third World Colloquium for the Fall quarter.

Direction of Asian Studies

Asian Studies at this stage will emphasize Asians in America. The program in Asian Studies is a strongly community-oriented program of study. The system of high education in America today is effectively siphoning much needed talent from the Third World communities, and specifically the Asian-American communities have and are continuing to evolve into economic, political, cultural, and psychological ghettos. Talented individuals who could otherwise function effectively as integral and constructive elements in the community are now being channeled out of this environment, thus leaving detrimental evolution to continue.

The study program is designed with the intention of reversing this trend. In order to accomplish this goal, community-oriented subjects and actual community work is stressed in order to facilitate a more comprehensive understanding of the community and its network of internal and external relations. Community work is also essential in establishing the necessary dialogue between ourselves and the community in order that the department itself has the necessary understanding to relate the subject to the students. To prevent the Asian-American community from being a cultural and psychological ghetto, the program concentrates on two aspects of scholarship: Asia and Asian culture, the roots of Asian-Americans; and racism, the primary cause of oppression and exploitation of Third World people in the United States.

Too often, the plight of the Asian-American is one of forced rejection of his own culture in favor of the dominant one in order to survive. This process of accommodation, which often appears under the guise of acculturation, has produced considerable psychological damage. An awareness of this predicament is essential, not only in understanding the self, but also in evolving a new value system so that the Asian-American can carve out a cultural existence as well as an economic existence in this country.

Therefore, the study program of Asian Studies is to include the following areas of scholarship: community commitment, awareness of the Asian-American identity, Asian and Asian-American culture, and the dynamics of racism.

NEED FOR AWARENESS:
an essay on chinatown, san francisco

BUCK WONG

Introduction

Writing for Holiday in August of 1954, Sidney Small said of San Francisco's Chinatown, "An authority takes you behind the paper lanterns and shows you a wondrous city as tourists rarely see it--its traditions, its festivals, its intimate family life."[1] In reality, behind the neon signs and paper lanterns lies not Small's wondrous city, but a swarming, sweatshop world of long hours, low pay, hard work, and fear. It is rather unjust that one of America's most wretched slums should have its deplorable social condition masked by an image as a tourist haven. Chinatown is a sector which in the mid-1960's had forty thousand people crowded into the forty-two blocks between the streets of Bush, Broadway, Kearney and Powell.[2] In addition, thirty thousand Chinese spilled into the North and the West as well as ten thousand others throughout the Bay Area. Upon viewing Chinatown, there is no mistaking the fact that it is a ghetto.

To understand the situation of Chinatown comprehensively, it becomes necessary to understand the major aspects of Chinese life in America. In so many ways, Chinatown is a microcosm of the larger context--acquiring the detrimental characteristics of a segregated urban slum as the Chinese, in general, found themselves relegated to a second class status. In recent years, the slum conditions of Chinatown have intensified, but it is crucial to realize that its economic and social ills have a

Reprinted by permission of the author. Buck Wong is a graduate student in history at the University of California, Los Angeles.

long historical background.

History of a Chinese Slum

There is a shakey account that the first Chinese in California was a seaman in 1793. A cook named Ah Nam is said to have come in 1815, a Chinese cabin boy in 1838, and two men and a woman in 1848[4], but only with the advent of the Gold Rush did the immigration of the Chinese really start. Since San Francisco was a port city, it naturally became a place of congregation for these new foreigners. Though many of the Chinese were in California to look for gold or were merchants, menial white labor was scarce so they often took any necessary work that was offered. Many Chinese began to stay in San Francisco, and Chinatown began when they took over the old buildings around Portsmouth Square, upon which the city had originally started. By the mid-1850's, a definite community had developed. Among other distinctive features, it had thirty-three general stores, five restaurants, five butchers, three tailors, and two bakers.[5]

The Chinese population in San Francisco was soon to become the major concentration of Chinese in America. In the 1850's and 60's however, a large majority of the Chinese immigrants were in the mining areas. After the mining activity subsided, the Central Pacific Railroad employed between ten and twelve thousand Chinese for cheap labor until its completion in 1869.[6] Railroad and mining work grew scarce by the 1870's, leading to an increase in the Chinese population--both in overall size and as a percentage of the total population. The Chinese came to San Francisco to find work in the factories or in the domestic field, and while a substantial number resorted to argricultural work, many of them might have resided in San Francisco in the off-season. Another factor was that as the anti-Chinese agitation mounted, many Chinese felt compelled to draw into a more segregated environment. (To be discussed further in Section III) As a result, from a population of 2719, the third largest Chinese settlement in the state in 1860, it grew to 12,022 in 1870, thus becoming the largest in the state and the country.[7]

As Chinatown was increasing in size, the pattern of Chinese occupational status in the city began to emerge. The Chinese found numerous types of domestic work in San Francisco; they became servants, vegetable men, broom sellers, and flower vendors. In these domestic fields, the Chinese earned more than the white person because they attained a reputation for efficiency, but on the other hand, they found work in the factories because they would underbid the whites. As a result, in 1870, 191 out of 211 workers in the slipper industry of the city were Chinese. Also, nineteen per cent of the workers in shoe factories in 1870 were Chinese.[8] The state wool industry started in San Francisco about this time, and Chinese labor monopolized it. Workers in cigar factories were almost exclusively Chinese. In 1876, 907 out of 3479 people in the sewing trade--many of these in San Francisco--were Chinese.[9] In addition, the Chinese owned a vast percentage of the factories. Eleven out of twelve slipper factories in 1870 belonged to Chinese, and they owned fifty per cent of the city's cigar factories in 1866.[10] Also, by the 1870's the trend of the Chinese laundries and restaurants was beginning to be set. Chinese restaurants and teahouses were in existence in the city as early as July, 1849, and by 1870, most of the laundries in California were Chinese-owned.

The Chinatown population continued to increase until the national policy of Chinese exclusion took effect. From 1870 to 1890, its population increased from 12,022 to 25,833 as immigrants streamed into the country,[11] and even after the Exclusion Act of 1882 excluded laborers, over sixty thousand came over after changing their status to that of merchants and students. The Geary Act of 1892 extended the exclusion of the 1882 act and served to terrify and drive out many Chinese.[12] The prohibition of Chinese immigration was extended indefinitely in 1902, and the 1924 Alien Act tightened the loopholes for immigration by such acts as defining students as only those aspiring for graduate degrees. The consequences of those acts were substantial. From 1890 to 1940, Chinese immigration generally averaged about twenty thousand per decade, and the overall Chinese population in America stabilized itself at between sixty and eighty thousand.[13] Chinatown's population dropped to 13,954 in 1900 and remained about the same for forty years. In 1930, it was 16,303 and only increased to 17,782 in 1940.[14]

Meanwhile, Chinatown had acquired the characteristics of a closely-knit community--a city within a city. As the concentration intensified, the Chinese constructed a society of their own which was symbolic of the Far East in which the pattern of behavior was predominately that of a village culture rather than that of an urban sector. The shops were Chinese-owned; there were Chinese newspapers; oriental attire was common; and soon Chinatown existed outside the mainstream of society. Also, by the end of the nineteenth century, the laundry and restaurant occupations began to dominate the economic framework of the Chinese in America. In 1870, there were only 3653 laundry workers and sixty-six restaurant workers in America, but by 1900, laundry workers numbered 25,483. In 1920, out of 45,614 Chinese workers, 12,559 were laundry workers and 11,438 were restaurant workers.[15] Naturally, San Francisco reflected such a restrictive occupational development, and it served to accentuate the close-knit characteristics of the Chinese sector.

The large role of the Six companies was another trenchant illustration of the detachment of Chinatown from the larger society. As the major clan and district associations joined together into the Chinese Six Companies in the 1850's it quickly established itself as the major organization of the California Chinese. It assumed a vital role for the Chinese community in San Francisco by providing educational, recreational, medical and even legal services. Some, however, have said that the Chinese "institutions (Six Companies) contributed in various degrees to the maintenance of an invisible Chinese world which controlled the indentured emigrants."[16] Nonetheless, as the Six Companies became the principal spokesman for the Chinese to white America, the distinctiveness of the Chinatown section became more and more apparent until most of its social and economic functions were of an esoteric nature.

The situation of Chinatown remained basically static until World War II. The war brought some changes to Chinatown, as it did to Chinese Americans in general, by creating a personnel shortage, and thus, allowing Chinese college men and women to secure proper employment. The Chinese had always placed a premium upon education, but they had previously had to be content with inferior jobs. Now, professional employment jumped from 2.8 per cent in 1940 to 7.1 per cent in 1950.[17] Overall, the changes that affected Chinatown were anything but substantial as the ghetto problems of housing and health still existed.

After the war, immigration restriction eased up, beginning with the repeal of the 1924 Alien Act. Though only a quota of 105 a year was set up, non-quota immigration through acts like the War Brides Act of 1947 and the Immigration Act of 1952 (allowing students) pushed immigration from a low point of about five thousand in the 1930's to 16,709 in the 1940's and to 9,657 in the 1950's. There was one change concurrent with the immigration that was to have vast consequences for Chinatown. In 1949, the Communists took control of China, and the United States imposed a quarantine on China. Now the Chinese had to become citizens or permanent residents of this country, and a new generation began to emerge in Chinatown as well as in all Chinese communities which was oriented toward assimilation.

With the 1960's came the most significant loosening up of the immigration regulations for the Chinese, and San Francisco reflected those changes as it continued to be a docking point for so many of the new immigrants. In 1963, President Kennedy issued a directive to ease the refugee situation in Hong Kong. Then, President Johnson signed into law a new immigrant act in 1965, to become fully effective in July, 1968, which repealed the quota system based on national origins and substituted in its place an entry procedures based on skills and a means for the reuniting of families.[18] In 1966, 8482 immigrants came to America, and the number increased to 14,045 in 1967.[19] The result was to place a greater burden upon the Chinatown situation, as many of those immigrants moved into San Francisco. District Immigration Director C. W. Fullilove estimated that since 1968, approximately 1200 per year enter San Francisco with the intention of remaining.[20] While the economic situation of many Chinese has improved and a professional and white collar class has emerged, the poverty in Chinatown remains today as the middle class leave the ghetto and make it a place inhabited by immigrants, the poor, and the elderly.

A Social and Economic Look at Chinatown

Like all immigrant groups in America, the Chinese attempted to retain a strong hold on their culture by sustaining ethnic enclaves, promoting immigrant associations, and preserving native customs. However, the idea that Chinatown grew as a self-imposed ghetto is far from correct. There was a definite tone of subtle coercion and often a policy of blatant discrimination throughout the history of the Chinese in America which forced them to accept the status of living in a blighted urban sector.[21]

It was very possible that people in early San Francisco regarded the Chinese with interest and curiosity rather than hostility, but it was not long before racial and social prejudice, arising out of a disdain for anything different, took its toll on the Chinese. On February 16, 1854, the Alta California stated, "If the city continues to fill up with these people, it will ere long become necessary to make them the subjects of special legislation."[22] Only two years before, this same newspaper had spoken of the Chinese as "excellent citizens." The increasing antipathy reflected the general tone of anti-Chinese agitation embodied in political actions like the Foreign Miner's Tax and the Exclusion Acts beginning in 1882 which gave official sanction to the prevalent hostility toward the Chinese. California' second constitution in 1879 also prohibited employment of Chinese in state, county, and municipal government work. The violence directed at the Chinese surfaced on various occasions throughout the nineteenth century. In the Los Angeles Riot of 1871, a white mob killed at least nineteen Chinese; in the Rock Springs massacre of 1885 in Wyoming, twenty-eight Chinese were killed; at Truckee, California, in 1878, 1000 Chinese were driven out of town.[23]

The general prejudice was also to be found on a local scale in San Francisco. The first significant urban uprising occurred in the city in 1869.[24] In 1870, an ordinance directed at the Chinese to forbid the firing of rooms with less than five hundred cubic feet of air per person met defeat in the county court, but in the same year, an ordinance preventing the use of poles to carry objects was upheld. Another city ordinance provided that every Chinese in jail must have his hair cut to one inch from his scalp, thus imposing queue cutting. San Francisco was also the center of the Workingmen's Patry, led by the demogogic Denis Kearney, which adopted the slogan "the Chinese must go" and was instrumental in arousing public sentiment for Chinese exclusion. In July of 1877, Kearney incited the Sand Lot Riots, lasting for several days, in which white gangs terrorized the Chinatown section. When faced by that kind of treatment, the Chinese acquired a tendency to look for security and satisfaction within a segregated community.

In addition, Chinatown attracted many Chinese because it fulfilled important social functions as well as providing for economic needs and offering insulation from anti-Chinese agitation. The Chinatown community filled the void caused by the lack of an adequate family structure in America. "Ideally, Chinese custom held that a wife should remain in the household of her husband's parents, even in the event that her husband went abroad."[25] So as late as 1890, though there were 26,720 married Chinese men in America, there were only 1,951 married Chinese women.[26] The situation worsened in 1884 when a U.S. Federal Court ruled that the Exclusion Act of 1882 excluded not only a Chinese laborer, but his wife as well. Under such conditions, the male-female ratio for the Chinese has remained abnormally high; it was 18.58 in 1860, 12.84 in 1870, 21.06 in 1880, 26.79 in 1890, and even in 1960 was still 1.33.[27] As a result, the Chinese men who remained abroad were left to form a homeless men's community and sought the friendlier and more secure confines of a larger Chinese community.

With the advent of the exclusion policy, Chinatown entered a static period in which contact and association with the greater society became minimal as an impenetrable social, political, and economic wall divided the Chinese and the larger culture. The withdrawal into a tight social structure had gigantic consequences because, while the United States went through some truly profound changes from 1880 to 1940, San Francisco's Chinese ghetto remained essentially the same. It could not really become independent economically, but its closed social system prevented it from joining the mainstream of social change. It was a period when the Chinese found themselves limited to occupations in domestic work, laundries, restaurants, sewing, and grocery stores. In the twentieth century, the Chinese gained a reputation for being very well educated, but they usually found that society refused to employ their talents. As one author stated, except for a few professional workers "within the limits of Chinatown..." and some in civil service work, the educated Chinese found no adequate future.[28]

The Chinese in the Chinatown community also remained politically indifferent during the period from 1880 to 1940; the cause for such an attitude can be expressed as a combination of a ghetto and sojourner mentality. Especially in the early years of immigration, many of the Chinese in this country were sojourners, wishing only to work for a few years until they could save enough money to go home.[29] Many Chinese were consequently reluctant to assimilate with the greater society and to protest the injustices done to them. Nonetheless, more and more Chinese began to make America their permanent home,--in fact if not in declaration--but still the Chinese in San Francisco acquiesced in the inequalities of the society. A ghetto mentality among the Chinese had developed, resulting in the prevalence of low expectations and the willingness to accept a subservient status in American society.

By the twentieth century, Chinatown had acquired all the characteristics that today make it a slum section. Perhaps the major consequence of the creation of the Chinese slum was the physical handicaps incurred through the existence of inferior living conditions. If not for the 1906 earthquake, it is conceivable that buildings constructed before 1900 could still be around. As it was, the Chinese took over one of the older parts of the city, and they only acquired more old buildings when they moved out into the blocks surrounding Portsmouth Square. In 1941, fifteen thousand Chinese lived in a twenty block area where 3000 out of 3830 dwelling units were without heat.[30] The deplorable situation becomes more apparent when one considers that the twenty block area had been primarily dedicated to the operation of shops and restaurants. Though the male-female ratio evened up with the passage of time, the lack of women in early Chinatown led to an indulgence in prostitution, gambling, and opium smoking during the late 1800's which resulted in the association of Chinatown with an atmosphere of vice. Even more dominant, however was the growing image of Chinatown as a tourist center. Its appearance was a result of the economic depravity that affected the sector, but tourists saw it as a quaint and amusing example of Far Eastern culture. Of course, the shop-keepers and merchants found it economically expedient to capitalize upon this aspect of Chinatown, so the image of tourist town became further enhanced.

Chinese Americans benefited from some social and economic changes in the years since World War II, but there has really been no fundamental change in Chinatown. As mentioned, the professional and white collar employment of Chinese has increased since the 1940's. There are many Chinese engineers and professors now; some are even city councilmen or judges. While the social integration is welcomed, it creates a dilemma for Chinatown as the more well-to-do Chinese move out of the ghetto and leave the less fortunate to remain. In addition, the quarantine on Red China stung the Chinese with the realization that they could no longer return to their homeland.

In fact, as more people populated Chinatown through natural birthrates and immigration of the 1960's, the conditions only got worse. In 1960, education in Chinatown averaged 1.7 years while it was twelve years for the rest of the city. Unemployment was 12.8 per cent compared to the overall rate of 6.7 per cent, density of population was 885.1 per acre while it was 81.9 per acre in the rest of the city, and substandard housing in Chinatown was sixty-seven per cent compared to a city-wide rate of nineteen per cent.[31] Most of the architecture in Chinatown was inferior. The tourist retail business was poor with many shops selling only about thirty dollars worth of goods a day while having to pay monthly rents of three to five hundred dollars. Tuberculosis rates, which serve as indicators of the detrimental effects of ghettos, ranged from 2.9 to 4.7 cases per one thousand persons in Chinatown while the city average was .8 per one thousand persons.[32] Still common were cases where fifty to one hundred people used one kitchen and where separate bathrooms were lacking. So one wonders if Chinatown has changed much in recent years.

The conditions in Chinatown have become increasingly critical due to the influx caused by the recent immigration. Chinatown now has a density in population second only to Harlem. In addition, the younger element of San Francisco Chinatown has increased greatly in the last few years, due to the offspring from more Chinese marriages and the large number of young Chinese in the recent immigration. The youth and young adults of Chinatown have been the ones who are leading the protest against deplorable slum conditions that become worse instead of better. However, the crucial factor to remember is that the recent immigration and population influx into Chinatown accentuates already critical ghetto problems that have persisted throughout the existence of this Chinese slum. The Chinatown crisis is not a new phenomenon!

IV. The Struggle for Awareness

Even the broad picture of Chinatown clearly reveals that the urgency to correct the social situation of this sector should be as great as in any urban area in the nation. Concern for these problems, however, will never develop if the mainstream of American society persists in a trend of thinking which promulgates the idea of Grant Avenue as having become "an asset to the commercial life of the city as one of its main tourist attractions."[33] Chinatown still suffers from this image and the stereo-typing which says that the Chinese like to live with their own, that they can take care of their own, and that they are law-abiding.

This pattern of projecting the Chinese as a successful minority is extremely dangerous because it hides the problems of the Chinatown community and facilitates deterioration. Efforts are being made to overcome the ignorance of the outside society and also to combat the social ills from within. However, the problems are immense and require aggressive and tenacious action.

All Americans should realize that no one really _wants_ to live in a ghetto. There is evidence that if not for the anti-Chinese agitation of the early years after the start of immigration, there would certainly be more social integration today. People should not mistake the resignation and apathy derived from a ghetto mentality for a personal desire to remain in Chinatown. It seems to be easy for whites to look at people who were scholars in China and are now waiters and to praise them for a willingness to do something. Outsiders of Chinatown can also easily absolve themselves of any concern for constructive change when they operate from the misguided idea that the Chinese can take care of themselves. Well, the days of the association like the Six Companies, of the Far Eastern social structure, and of the unique patriarchal family system are gone; such a system can not adequately cope with the present problems--and they never really could. If the Chinese could subsist adequately as a separate entity, they would not suffer from the living conditions that they do. I submit that the mainstream of America has willingly grabbed these ideas and perpetuated the image of the happy-go-lucky, law-abiding, and self-sustaining Chinese, thus, maintaining a _social distance_ between greater San Francisco and Chinatown which is immensely farther than the actual walk across a street.

What is being done though? If the people outside of Chinatown remain callous, has Chinatown itself taken any action? For a number of reasons, Chinatown has responded very little until recently to its adverse conditions. In a broad sense, one might say that it suffers from a ghetto mentality, but the problem can not be confined within such a narrow boundary. Much of the answer is to be found in the history of Chinatown because as the Chinese withdrew into the safety of a homogeneous group, survival and endurance became a virtue. The survival philosophy led to an inclination toward non-involvement and distrust of government.[34] As the ratio of American born to foreign born went from twenty-one to seventy-nine in 1910 to a ratio of fifty-three to forty-seven in 1950, involvement in American society increased, but apolitical feelings still persisted.[35] Another factor that contributed to the lack of drive in the Chinese community, of course, was the establishment of poverty as a way of life. Many of the residents of Chinatown have lived there most of their lives, and there is also a large number of immigrants from China who have known a way of life that has been just as harsh as an American ghetto.

However, the dissatisfaction is there, and it is beginning to show itself as various segments of the Chinatown community have responded indignantly and vociferously to the existing problems. The uproar has led to the initiation of major Chinatown studies by groups such as the City Planning Commission and the Bay Area Social Planning Council. The Chinatown-North Beach Economic Development Agency functions as the local federal target agency, but unfortunately, "it has failed to involve the community, and has failed to find leadership from the indigenous poor."[36] Prior to 1956, there was only one politically active organization, the Chinese American Citizens Alliance, but some felt that it had turned conservative and, thus, formed the Chinese American Democratic Club which takes a stand on almost every social issue and is the strongest political voice in Chinatown.

The newer element of the Chinatown community, the youth, has suffered greatly as a result of the intensification of the ghetto problems and has responded in a belligerent and sometimes spontaneous manner. Native born youths have found that the price of success is often abandonment of language, culture, and much of their ethnic identity. The immigrant youth find that the Americanization inherent in the school system compounds their cultural shock and causes many to drop out.

A hint that something was wrong appeared in early 1963 when a threatened inter-racial gang fight resulted in the arrest of four young Chinese Americans and the confiscation of several weapons. In 1964, the Bugs, a young Chinese burglary ring, was uncovered. Then, in the 1969 New Year parade, a confrontation between young people and the S.F. Police Tactical Squad led to a small scale riot in which cherry bombs dipped in glue and BBs were thrown. These incidents seem to reflect more than just trouble due to a small knot of delinquent young people.

The youth have also responded in an organized manner. In 1968, the Wah Ching formed and is credited as the first group to publicize Chinatown's youth problems. This loose group of 200-300 Hong Kong youth was unable to attain funds for activities such as building a recreation clubhouse, and by 1969, the Wah Ching had split into three camps. One group returned to the streets, gambling, and burglaries, while the other two groups have been hired by two Chinatown tongs as bodyguards.

In April, 1967, about seventeen native born Chinese youths created Le Way (Legitimate Ways) as a self-help group to eliminate loitering and street fighting. The group grew to about 400 and obtained enough funds to maintain a pool hall and soda fountain. In early 1969, a small group split from Le Way and formed the Red Guard Party. Meanwhile, Le Way found increasing difficulty in functioning as the police continually raided the pool hall in search of criminal suspects and as good jobs eluded the reach of the Le Way youths.

Another group, the Intercollegiate Chinese for Social Action is an organization of young people working out of San Francisco State whose activities have centered on creating a school of ethnic studies and providing tutoring and summer activities for Chinese youngsters. Now, the Chinatown-North Beach Area Youth Council, an offshoot of the Economic Development Agency, serves as an umbrella group for fifteen youth groups that range from church groups to Le Way and ICSA. It hopes to build good relations between the native and foreign born youth and bridge the gap between Chinatown and city hall.

The leadership of Chinatown is shifting to organizations like ICSA, the CCAC, and the CADC, but to the outside world, the Six Companies has kept its reputation as the official representative organization of the Chinese in America. People still listened when Dr. Dennis Wong of the Six Companies said that Chinatown should respond to its problems by resorting to the "old ways of love, understanding, compassion, perseverance, fidelity, instead of wanting everything now."[38] The following specious and fallacious response made by Dr. Kalfred Lum of the Six Companies to the SF EXAMINER's articles (during August of 1968) on Chinatown's social and economic ills indicates the water-treading philosophy of the older establishment.

On the whole, the fascinating and virtuous charm of San Francisco Chinatown must not be hurt by slanderous and erroneous statements. San Francisco Chinatown will continue to meet its problems which can be solved with proper understanding and guidance from public officials. This, in our opinion, is the proper solution.[39]

As a result, the Six Companies has become a major stumbling block to reform.

As efforts are made to rectify the Chinatown ills, tremendous obstacles exist. The garment-making sweat shops of Chinatown best reveal the dilemma in combating Chinatown's seemingly insurmountable problems. Many of the 3000 workers in the community's 150 garment factories were immigrant workers who worked ten to twelve hours a day for less than a dollar an hour.[40] In August, 1967, pickets from the International Ladies Garment Workers Union demonstrated to obtain legal minimum wages, but by May, 1968, the first strike in Chinatown history collapsed--it got little support from the workers. Any effort to alleviate the conditions of Chinatown runs into similar obstacles because many of the people living in the core of Chinatown are immigrants, most of whom are isolated individuals or families too busy surviving to worry about political maneuvers like group leadership and community representation. This is a crucial factor because most of the future leadership of Chinatown must eventually come from this group.

It is also important to remember that the crisis in San Francisco is part of a larger problem which has enveloped other Chinese communities in cities like New York, Los Angeles, and Oakland. Until very recently New York was the only other good sized Chinese community in America, and it went through many of the experiences of an isolated ethnic enclave that San Francisco did. Since it serves as the second major docking point for the recent immigration, it has also seen its Chinatown problems intensify in the last few years.[41] Communities such as Los Angeles and Oakland Chinatown have not had quite as intense historical problems as those existing in New York and San Francisco, but they are beginning to acquire more serious urban difficulties. Similar changes have occurred in Oakland due to the overflow of Chinese from San Francisco. While each of these communities have their distinct characteristics, their increasing problems accent the intensification of San Francisco Chinatown's ills.

What lies in the future? It is impossible to propose a schematic plan that would serve as a panacea for Chinatown's complex problems, but there is clearly a need to attain and maintain a sharp state of awareness within the Chinese community. In order to affect any strong community effort, a powerful sense of unity must prevail in Chinatown. The organizations that exist now must work diligently to create viable changes and ease tensions within Chinatown. Efforts should continue to be made to involve the poor, but these community workers (whether they be students or middle class adults) must work with the people in Chinatown instead of condescending toward them. A delicate balance between the hard sell and soft sell approach must be taken to stimulate an oppressed community, bent upon survival, into action.

At the same time, the outside community must realize that the changes to be made in Chinatown are long overdue. Unfortunately, due to the nature of the power structure in the society, Chinatown needs the funding and other material benefits available from a sympathetic public. So the question is, will the larger society react favorably to the increasing self-awareness of Chinatown? But on the other hand, will the changes within Chinatown kindle a deep-seated belief of the Chinese as both inferior and threatening, a belief perhaps made "benign by a minority group's tacit agreement to live behind the invisible wall of an urban ghetto?"[42] Yet, in many ways, the answers to these questions are peripheral to the whole issue of initiating change because any campaign to find cures for the Chinatown ills must begin first from within the community. Hopefully, the larger society will join in creating a solution with an equal sense of urgency, but it is crucial that those who are oppressed commence the fight for liberation and change.

---

[1] Sidney Small, "San Francisco's Chinatown," HOLIDAY, Vol. 16, (August, 1954), p. 98.
[2] "Chinaman's Chance," TIME, Vol. 90, (September 8, 1967), p. 18.
[4] Thomas W. Chinn, ed., A HISTORY OF THE CHINESE IN CALIFORNIA (San Francisco, 1969), p. 8.
[5] Ibid., p. 10.
[6] Charles Caldwell Dobie, SAN FRANCISCO'S CHINATOWN (New York: Appleton and Century Co., 1936), p. 72.
[7] Chinn, op. cit., p. 21.
[8] Ibid., p. 52.
[9] Ibid., p. 54.
[10] Ibid., p. 49.
[11] Ibid., p. 21.
[12] Carey McWilliams, BROTHERS UNDER THE SKIN (Boston: Little, Brown, and Co., 1964), p. 95.
[13] Shien-woo Kung, CHINESE IN AMERICAN LIFE (Seattle: University of Washington Press, 1962), p. 43.
[14] Stanford M. Lyman, THE ASIAN IN THE WEST (Reno and Las Vegas: Western Studies Center, 1970), p. 69.
[15] Kung, op. cit., p. 57.
[16] Gunther Barth, BITTER STRENGTH (Cambridge: Harvard University Press, 1964), p. 78.
[17] Kung, op. cit., p. 57.
[18] Lyman, op. cit., p. 102.
[19] Chinn, op. cit., p. 29.
[20] Lyman, op. cit., p. 102.
[21] Continual investigation needs to be done to ascertain better the forces that led to the crowded, segregated Chinese community, but up-to-date research indicates that the nature of racial prejudice played a major role in creating the detrimental conditions that have existed in Chinatown.
[22] Dobie, op. cit., p. 54.
[23] Lyman, op. cit., pps. 22-3; Alexander Saxton, THE INDISPENSABLE ENEMY (Berkeley: Univery of California Press, 1971), p. 202.
[24] Lyman, op. cit., p. 22.
[25] Lyman, op. cit., p. 18.--One must ask the question of how such a custom would have survived if the Chinese had been allowed to participate more in American society, and thereupon, create an incentive to bring over families and settle.
[26] Kung, op. cit., p. 35.
[27] Lyman, op. cit., pp. 79 and 101.
[28] Elizabeth Colman, CHINATOWN, USA (New York: John Day Co., 1946), p. 14.
[29] Paul Siu, "The Sojourner," AMERICAN JOURNAL OF SOCIOLOGY, Vol. 8, (July, 1952), pp. 32-44.
[30] McWilliams, op. cit., p. 109.
[31] L. Ling-chi Wang, "Chinatown in Transition," THE ASIAN EXPERIENCE IN AMERICA (University of California, Davis: 1969).
[32] Gerald J. Chan, "The Other Side of San Francisco's Chinatown," CHINATOWN-NORTH BEACH STUDY PACKET (San Francisco: 1965-66).
[33] Colman, op. cit., p. 20.

³⁴The tendency toward non-involvement may have been also reinforced by what Mary Coolidge, in her book, CHINESE IMMIGRATION, called the lack of a public spirit in China. She said that the development of a national feeling had been retarded by the large number of dialects and the difficulty in travel and communication.
³⁵Kung, op. cit., p. 40.
³⁶George Chu, "Chinatown," SAN FRANCISCO, (June, 1969).--The article provides a good brief overview of the current situation in Chinatown and a rundown of the major organizations that are attempting to affect change.
³⁷The youth scene is a turbulent, fluid situation which seems to defy understanding and analysis, but several fine articles on the Chinatown youth include: Ben Fong-Torres, "Chinatown Youth," SAN FRANCISCO, (June, 1969); Stanford Lyman, "Red Guard on Grant Avenue," THE ASIAN IN THE WEST (Reno and Las Vegas: Western Studies Center, 1970); Tom Wolfe, "The New Yellow Peril," ESQUIRE, Vol. 73, (December, 1969).
³⁸Tom Wolfe, "The New Yellow Peril," ESQUIRE, Vol. 73, (December, 1969), p. 197.
³⁹Dr. Kalfred Dip Lum, "The Misunderstanding in Chinatown," GIDRA, (July, 1969).
⁴⁰Chu, op. cit.
⁴¹Rocky Chin, "New York Chinatown Today: Community in Crisis," AMERASIA JOURNAL, Vol. 1 (March, 1971).--The article gives the reader an excellent picture of the contemporary situation in New York Chinatown.
⁴²Lyman, op. cit., p. 117.

ASIAN COMMUNITY CENTER

EDITORIAL STAFF OF RODAN

Asian people in America are living in a contradictory society. The present United States government and the racist society which perpetuates it claims this country stands for freedom, liberty, and happiness. From the injustices, Third World (non-white) people have experienced in this country, there are no such conceptions as freedom, liberty, or happiness. We don't even have any rights to protect us from exploitation and brutality. Third World people are suffering from hunger, disease, unemployment, poor housing, miseducation, and Racism and Death. Asian and other Third World communities are actually internal colonies which this racist society uses to exploit our manpower and labor for low wages. Our people are caught in these colonies and are forced to suffer. The big businessmen and the rich landlord drain us of our resources, the military drags our young men to fight in imperialist wars to kill other Third World people, the school system operates jails which brainwash our younger brothers and sisters to be ashamed of their cultural and racial heritage, and the universities rob us of the people we need to return to rebuild and to serve the community. To keep us weak and unable to resist effectively, the Man permits disease, corruption, narcotics, subhuman housing, and hunger to flourish throughout the Third World colonies. Every Asian community, whether it is Chinatown, Manilatown, or Japanesetown, are internal colonies of the United States--exploited to the hilt, insulted constantly, and brutalized by the forces of law and order.

In December of 1969, a group of young people from the Chinese community in San Francisco made a move into the old, dark and shoddy basement of the United States Filipino Association Hall. They maintained an informal office and showed movies to the people of Chinatown and Manilatown during the weekends. The basement was cleaned up and posters from China were put up. We leafletted the community to inform the people of the free movies at the basement. We set up reading tables with magazines from Asia, particularly from China. People began to come down and talk to us. Within a short period of two months, after analyzing the objective conditions in Chinatown, it was clear that the United Filipino Association Hall at 832 Kearny Street would have to become an Asian Community Center. Its purchase was to provide a base where the youth of the community could serve people of Chinatown to solve its problems and attempt to find cures to the ailments plaguing it; to encourage the people of the community to work collectively for their physical and mental well-being and to educate them to the real enemy who is shamelessly exploiting our community and our culture.

Reprinted from RODAN, Northern California Asian American Community News, Volume I, Number 5 (November 1970).

The Asian Community Center emerged not because we thought it would be a nice missionary trip to do, but that we realized that the Chinatown community was indeed an internal colony of the United States--kept down solely to be exploited. There are over 47,500 people living on the small area which Chinatown is situated upon. There are about 600 to 800 people per acreage in Chinatown, making it an area with the highest density next to Manhattan. The tuberculosis problem is the worst of any area within the United States and the suicide rate is no better. There used to be a TB clinic in Chinatown but due to lack of Federal funds needed for it to operate, it was terminated. Now there are no clinics in Chinatown to treat people with TB. Many parents find it hard to find good jobs because of their language difficulties and many times both parents are forced into accepting menial jobs in order to make enough to keep their family alive. Since there are no real recreational facilities, many young people are forced into the streets to spend their time. The community is extremely over-crowded and more new immigrants from Hong Kong are coming in every year and the housing situation in Chinatown is rapidly deteriorating--the Ping Yuen housing projects are already overcrowded and families of six are forced much of the time, to move into small apartments or flop houses, paying high rents, forced to find work. Many mothers are forced to work in the numerous garment factory sweatshops in Chinatown for the lowest of wages--as low as fifty cents an hour. The Chinese mothers have become a source of cheap labor.

The situation and the rotten conditions that the people of Chinatown were subjected to demanded that there be an organization such as the Asian Community Center to be established.

We knew that we had to inform the people of the community of our motives and objectives so they can understand and relate to what we were trying to do. We drew up a platfrom which reflected the needs of the people and relayed our ideas:

PLATFORM OF THE ASIAN COMMUNITY CENTER

What We See

> We see the breakdown of our community and families.
> We see our people suffering from malnutrition, tuberculosis, and high suicide rates.
> We see destruction of our cultural pride.
> We see our elderly forgotten and alone.
> We see our youth subjected to racism in the classroom and in the streets.
> We see our Mothers and Fathers forced into meaningless jobs to make a living.
> We see American Society preventing us from fulfilling our needs.

What We Want

> We want adequate housing, medical care, employemnt, and education.

What We Believe

> To solve our community problems, all Asian people must work together.
> Our people must be educated to move collectively for direct action.
> We will employ any effective means that our people see necessary.

The programs of the Asian Community Center include the Chinatown COOP Food Program, the Free Film Program, during the summer, the Youth Summer Workshop. The Food Program was created to provide the community with a proper diet so that its children grow up healthy. We were providing surplus government food to cover 300 families once every month. The food was U.S. surplus which the Community Center obtained by paying for it, unloading it off the trucks, and packing it in bags ourselves to distribute it to the families. Every weekend we show movies about China and Mao Tse Tung and other political films about the Liberation struggles all over the world and in the United States. The Film Program was very popular because Chinese people like to see movies about their motherland and how it has progressed after the Revolution. During the showings, we provided hot tea and cookies. During the summer, the Youth Summer Worksop took young people on field trips, taught them Asian American history, and introduced them to photography, carpentry, and kung-fu workshops.

The Asian Community Center has for the last nine months been serving the San Francisco Chinatown community. The Center has become a place where young and old can come together to discuss politics, play chess and ping pong, listen to music from China, and read about struggles in Southeast Asian and other Third World nations against the imperialist policies of the United States and its lackeys. As of November 15, 1970, the Asian Community Center will be moving from its location at 832 Kearny Street. The lease has been terminated. We are getting kicked out. Upon investigation, we have discovered that pressures by the reactionary Chinatown Establishment (the Chinese Six Companies and the Kuomintang--the Chinese Nationalist party) has led to much of our troubles. This only goes to show that the Chinatown Establishment is not necessarily interested in

their control in Chinatown. Power for its own sake, not for the people of Chinatown. But we, and the other progressive forces of Chinatown, will grow powerful because the people can distinguish between the lackeys of the United States and the other reactionaries and those who serve the people.

The Asian Community Center will continue to serve the people from our new location at 846 Kearny Street. The Center is more than helping the people of Chinatown. The Establishment is only interested in maintaining just a physical place, but an idea, an idea that will unite the people of Chinatown to change the poverty conditions of the Chinatown colony. It is an idea that will get people to help each other as in the rest of American Society. In the final analysis, regardless of what difficulties we have to face, we must keep the welfare of the people foremost in our minds and hearts.

ALL POWER TO THE PEOPLE!

AN INTERVIEW WITH

L. LING-CHI WANG

EDITORIAL BOARD
JUNE, 1971

WANG: In the Chinese community for many years there have been a lot of claims that the Chinese community is free from juvenile delinquency and that if there are a few, that the family and community together will take care of those juvenile problems. Because of this traditional attitude a lot of the juvenile delinquency problems are really not taken care of. In fact, I guess you can trace the problem all the way back to around the 1940's, and it was reaching the point where the delinquency problem was so bad that there was no choice except for the community to admit that it is a serious problem and that something must be done, and indeed we started this place (Youth Services Center) a year ago.
The rate of delinquency increase is tremendously high. Between 1964 and 1969 for Chinese juveniles, the rate of increase was around 600%. And I dare say that's probably the highest increase among any of the ethnic groups in San Francisco and maybe in the rest of the U.S. So what we try to do here is to try to bring the traditional Youth Services agencies and services, the probation department, California Youth Authority, San Francisco Board of Education, lawyers, and social workers, together and to work with the juvenile that gets into trouble.

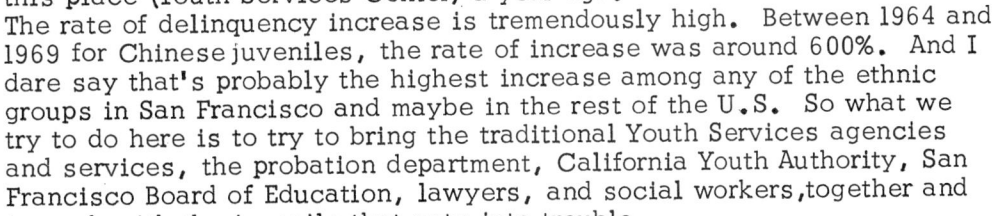

QUESTION: What kind of program do you carry on here?

WANG: We don't have any program. We only offer direct service to an individual and his family.

QUESTION: What are the usual charges... drug abuse, petty theft?

WANG: No, drug abuse is primarily limited to the American born-youth, who are more, in many ways, assimilated, into the American youth culture, whereas the foreign-born because of language barriers and cultural differences, they are not quite in with the drug scene. But there are other things common to both American-born and immigrant youth, especially at younger age brackets: truancy, staying away from home, petty theft, shoplifting. These are very common among both boys and girls at the younger age. But as they get older they go into heavier things such as burglary and auto theft, very common for both American and foreign-born. I guess there are two reasons. Partly because they are not tied to the family for all kinds of purposes: they just work; they need money to subsist so some of them go into burglary. But others, just for kicks because they get so bored. And there is really not much a young person in Chinatown would do because there are no recreational facilities and many of them are alienated from schools and families.

QUESTION: You said the rate of increase is 600% since 1964. What do you attribute that to? What major things caused it? Why wasn't there a high rate before that?

WANG: Well, there was delinquency as far back as 1940 that we know but in the past we have that reputation because there were no juveniles around. I think you know the history of Chinese in the U.S.--for that matter, also the Japanese. The people who came over there were unmarried male laborers. They came here to supply the cheap labor demand. The law prevented them from bringing their wives and children over. And so there was a scarcity of women and more so of children. So in the community there were very few juveniles just to begin with.
The ones that really appeared in the public's eye came at the time of the early fifties, right after the 2nd World War, Chinese-American GI's who fought during the 2nd World War in the Far East because there was a scarcity of women, took the advantage of being over there and married some Chinese girls over there. Just to show you how the law prevented the Chinese from bringing their wives over, these American GI's who fought for the U.S. could not bring their wives over because of the law. So the Congress had to enact a special legislation called the War Bride Act to allow 5,000 of these war brides to come here. And when they came over some of them brought their children over and then more children were born. So by the time of 1951 and 1952, juvenile delinquency was already quite a problem.

QUESTION: But it was a function not so much of upbringing or something of that sort but part of the density of youth in Chinatown.

WANG: That's part of it. However, the other part of it is that when you have a family brought over, there's an old concept of the Chinese family as a close knit type of family situation where there is strict control of children on the one hand, and on the other hand a tremendous respect for the elderly. And when you have that kind of structure, usually delinquency doesn't creep in quite so early.

QUESTION: It's taken care of within the family.

WANG: Right. That kind of family structure is workable primarily only in an agrarian society such as China. But when you transplant that family from China into the U.S. in a highly urbanized, technologically advanced society such as the U.S. and San Francisco in particular, what happened here was that the economic and social life was completely disrupted. The society around the family does not support, or sanction, the traditional Chinese structure. Furthermore, the economic life of the family has changed and you have both parents working, whereas in China that is not the case. You find that the man sometimes is not earning as much as the wife which again also upsets the traditional demand for the wife to respect the husband and the husband to be the head of the household. Then also childen going to school receiving white middle-class type of education and coming home and already taught to to be an individualist, to think on his own and to make decisions by himself. What this means with the traditional Chinese family structure is that you don't have to respect your parents whereas in the past you always listened to your parents and obeyed whatever they told you, but now you're taught to think on your own. You don't have to listen. In fact, you're taught to demand scientific proof on everything and of course the parents who have not received the same kind of education...

QUESTION: Don't know how to deal with it...

WANG: Yeah, and so there is tremendous conflict within the family to begin with.

And this is why the gap between Chinese and their children and their parents is considerably wider. In fact, very often the parents and children don't communicate because when the children get into school they were taught to suppress their Chinese language speaking ability. In fact, the teacher tends to frown upon their Chinese...laugh at them for their Chinese accent and to try to indoctrinate them that the English language is _the_ language. So children unconsciously suppress their language ability and then their parents on the other hand don't get the opportunity to learn English. So sometimes it reaches the point where we have to act as interpreters with the parents--between parents and their children because they just don't communicate.

We only act in a crisis situation because the kid gets busted. So we intervene in their behalf. At those times, there is very little we can do as far as bridging that gap. That gap has been built up in the last ten, fifteen to twenty years. We just cannot undo it. We spend a lot of time trying to educate the parents about why their children behave in a certain manner, what kind of education they're getting in school. And then we also, at the same time, try to tell the Board of Education the kind of things they must do. Certainly, teachers who have disrespect for the Chinese language and culture should have no business teaching in school. I think the problem is that the children are not taught anything about their own cultural background. And I guess this is why Asian studies is really very important. But unfortunately it hasn't really gone down to the elementary kindergarten level, which is where it really counts, because the suppression of Chinese language and culture occur as early as kindergarten, and unless the teachers are sensitive to these things and the schools take an initiative in trying to include that into their curriculum, there is nothing we can do. It's too late.

QUESTION: Since '68 and '69 when there was a strong activist movement among youth, the Wah Ching demands, the Red Guard Party and all the other groups, looking back on it now and the last couple of years, how do you evaluate the position of the youth; has it improved or worsened?

WANG: I think it's gotten worse, because there was really nothing for them. You can help a few individuals. You can get them a job, send them back to school or something like that. But then the new generation comes up, and there is nothing in the community to offer them. The schools remain fairly unresponsive to their needs. As all these kids are not going to school or are still alienated from school, they're going to be truant. When they're truant they get into trouble. You can predict a lot of times from the later elementary age how that one fellow is going to become. For many of them, they form these street gangs--in the papers two days ago you probably read about in San Francisco an extortion racket among the youth in Chinatown-- now that's been going on for two years, and in a way what do they have in Chinatown? Nothing. They can't find a job outside of Chinatown, they can't get into school and the only finite thing in Chinatown for them is being a busboy or kitchen help, jobs that are totally below their dignity. They have a little bit of education, a little bit of taste of the badder aspect of American life, so they're frustrated and resort to crime and violence. Young people are more demanding of immediate results, concrete results and rewards. In the past the Tongs also provided very tight control. See, the trouble in Chinatown is that the adults certainly don't set a good example for the youth; these adults are involved much in illegal activities. So the young people say if you can do it, why can't I do it.

QUESTION: In the matter of extortion, they're supposedly extorting businessmen but aren't they really extorting the illegal gambling that businessmen are running. That's the whole myth. The businessmen get together and say to the white community that our youth are extorting businessmen and that they are the real criminals, whereas the businessmen themselves running illegal gambling are as criminal as the people extorting them.

WANG: Yes, and then also the businessmen are the ones providing substandard wages to these people, and it's illegal to pay below minimum wages. And so it's really a question of it you can do it, why can't I.

QUESTION: How did you personally get involved in the Asian community and from your own personal background, being born in Asia, teaching at U.C. Berkeley?

WANG: Well, you know my background is mostly Eastern. Up to high school, I was in China. Then I came here for college, most of which was out in the Midwest and out East. But in 1966 I came out here to school at Berkeley. And that's when I began to get involved in the Chinese community here. My first involvement here was working with young people, youth groups. Then pretty soon I found out that solving the youth problem is really not the right approach to the community problems because the youth problems are really created by the community as a whole--and how that community is related to the White society. So then I eventually got deeper involved in it.

QUESTION: If you made a distinction between an organizer, a sort of welfare technician, or any number of roles you could categorize, what would you typify your role as?

WANG: I see myself as an advocate, not as an organizer. Though a lot of people think I am an organizer, if you examine the type of people I work with, there may be some organizational effort behind it, but organization to me meaning organizing the people at a grass roots level...that I have not done yet. What we have done so far really is raise the level of political and social consciousness of people who are somewhat in professional fields and business and not the working people yet. And this is why in many ways I feel that the work that we have done so far is not really that significant. Certainly not yet, because we have not reached the people down at the grass roots level. There is no grass roots organization.
I am very discouraged in many ways by the fact that...when we came into Chinatown, we criticized the Chinese establishment, the Chinese Chamber of Commerce, all the family associations and the Chinese American Citizens Alliance for being not able to do anything in the community, for suppressing the problems in Chinatown, for exploiting the people of Chinatown. All those things we have said already and I think that out of these a number of social service agencies have been established in Chinatown between 1966 and now. But what we have done in many ways is we brought in social service technicians into Chinatown who have some specialized skills in offering social services but are really not that interested in organizing the community and making sure that the community is aware of what is going on politically.
So what I see now is a new group of elites in Chinatown. This group of elites is made up of the professional people who are dispensing the services. They are by no means a spokesman for the community. Their number is no more than the number that used to be the so-called traditional Chinese establishment. At first there was the Chinese Six Companies and Chamber of Commerce. That has been challenged and their effectiveness and credentials have been totally destroyed. Also they don't have the competence and ability to deal politically with the outside white leaders. If they have, we wouldn't have been in such a miserable position. And now these new professionals who came in who have some technical ability. At least they demonstrated an ability to provide services and also bring in government services to Chinatown. But these people are by no means leaders and unfortunately because of the need for leadership, they're being looked upon as the new leaders of Chinatown even though their competence is often times limited to just services. And this is very bad. These leaders unless they become politically aware, they have no business to be political leaders or spokesmen for Chinatown. In fact, that's what I find now again after being involved here since 1966. We really have to re-examine the role of these professionals. And the community is far from being a political community which is essential for any minority group to deal with the predominant white society.

QUESTION: You have said that the situation of youth has worsened and that all the efforts of organizing the youth such as the Wah Ching have really brought no results outside the community, support from the white community, or from within the community. What future directions can you foresee outside of some sort of explosion of frustration, the whole prediction of the riot scene that was already laid down in '68; where can it go?

WANG: Well, the description in the newspaper is bordering on anarchy in Chinatown now. In many ways it is. They (Wah Ching) just walk into a theater, watch movies, and harass the audience. They walk into a restaurant and order a big banquet and walk out. If anybody who prints things, who records about these incidents, their newspaper windows get busted. If that's not anarchy I don't know what is. I don't know if there will be a riot or not. It is certainly a possibility. But the situation now is kind of anarchy.

QUESTION: What role do political groups like Red Guard and Leway, who polarize the scene--who bring out the issue in a political context within an anarchical situation, have? What can they do?

WANG: There is no relation between the American-born and the foreign-born youth. They have no contacts with each other. And the foreign-born do not see things in a political perspective maybe partly because--certainly because of the language barrier, but they're not politically as aware of what's going on. And the Chinese newspapers are equally politically unaware. Of course, a lot of political activities in the community are generated from the college students. You really have to be a middle class to afford the political luxury. For people who are struggling on a day to day basis, it's hard. But I'm not ruling out the possibility. I think people can be poor, fighting for survival and at the same time being able to articulate their needs in political terms. This is what I think that all the professional people who have been working here have failed to do. When I say the professional people who have failed I include myself. And I am probably one of the prime offenders of this type of situation. In fact, my commitment to this place is to set it up and get it established, then I'm leaving. I mean this is important--a direct services on a piece-meal approach is important because it does serve some immediate needs. But I think we have to do something broader, a community-based type of activity, to change some of the situation.

What do you plan to go on to next?

WANG: No plans yet. I hope to be a full-time volunteer for a while. I'd like to at least do some community education type of program.

QUESTION: What top three priorities do you see in the community before it becomes organized and emerges from anarchy? What really needs to be done?

WANG: Well, I think for one thing the schools have to do something about the teaching methods and in such a way that it becomes relevant to the kids. The kids now don't see what they're getting in school as having anything to do with what they will be in the future. Secondly, the restaurant and garment shop workers must be organized. But that's a tremendous job. I think, of course, the third thing which I spent a lot of time doing and will continue to do is to fight against white racism outside of Chinatown. But on the whole I'd like to say that the number one priority is to turn the Chinese community into a political community.

QUESTION: What sort of direction or politics should it be oriented toward?

WANG: What do you mean?

QUESTION: There are already various political levels in the community from conservative reactionary, moderate liberals, to radicals. One idea of a political community for liberals might be to help Chinatown assimilate further into American society whereas a revolutionary might say that the solution to problems in Chinatown lie in restructuring all of society, which means the destruction of capitalism and racism. So when you say political community, do you mean just a general awareness of politics or do you mean a certain direction it has to go, say along radical lines?

WANG: No, I think by political community, I mean a community that will have differences of opinion but at the same time a consciousness that we are a Chinese community and that whenever we move, we move somehow as a unit in a certain direction and that direction is really up to the people. Right now we don't have that. I think we must try to achieve that. I think we have a number of really good issues that are current. I consider the U.S.-China relation as a new critical issue for the Chinatown community. There's a lot of interest for one thing. Just for sheer survival, I think that a good relationship is definitely good for the survival of the Chinese community here. Certainly, we don't want the U.S. to go to the war with China and then have all of us end up in concentration camps. That's quite inevitable if it should happen. All this hostile propaganda that the government dished out to the public against China has a tremendous psychological effect on the public as a whole which will definitely limit us in the area of jobs, housing, and education. You can't help reading J. Edgar Hoover saying that these Chinese might be spies. The other thing is that I really think that the Chinese community here could play a very leading role in promoting better relationships between China and the U.S.. Partly because I think we are Chinese and do know something about China.

QUESTION: Where do you see Chinatown being five years from now given the direction it has now?

WANG: Not much really. I think it's going to take a while to get Chinatown together.

QUESTION: Can you separate certain roles that have to be taken? Do you see a need that certain segments of the community can do certain things; for example, the liberal section may accomplish a certain amount of reforms and young radical youth can do other functions? Do you see that separation of tasks or is that separation a necessity for moving the community?

WANG: That's the means of moving towards a political community. But at this moment, of course, there is so much intolerance. And a lot of it is motivated by these young people on ego trips. They will only really slow down the evolution of the community into a really political community.

QUESTION: Could you give us an example of that kind of intolerance?

WANG: I think that the radicals have a tendency to ask for instant results and overlook the immediate needs. For instance, and I'm really not criticizing the radical people, on the issue related to the Chinese Cultural Center in the Holiday Inn, the structure is going to be there and Holiday Inn is going to occupy it whether we like it or not. On one hand, the liberals would say, "Let's try to salvage what we can out of this thing." The radicals would say, "No, we're going to take over that building for low-cost senior citizen housing," which is fine. It's a good idea. The two groups somehow just can't get together on it. For one thing, I'd like to see the radicals actually carry out their objectives in a more complete fashion rather than just shouting rhetoric. I think they want to occupy it--go and occupy it. It may do some good.

QUESTION: Do you see a procedure by which community organization might be carried out? In Los Angeles, problemwise and sizewise, it is may be five to ten years behind San Francisco--these are really arbitrary figures. What sort of procedure would you recommend judging from San Francisco's mistakes?

WANG: There are certain things that you can learn. The attack against the establishment, the establishment of a new professional elite, and hopefully that there will be some people to attack the new professional elite and then really you have the mass movement going--I think that kind of procedure will probably follow. But I'd hate to generalize it. The Los Angeles community is a little different in the sense that it is more business oriented, less of a residential nature. But New York City is more like here. And I think New York can probably benefit more in this respect and the same thing is true in Boston where the business and residents are one and the same.

The other thing that especially for the younger people should really learn from here...the college students, which is a very important factor for community change, must learn more about the Chinese community. A lot of college students are still not aware of what is going on in this community even though they're physically down here in the Asian Community Center. But they really don't know what's across the street from Kearny on the other side of Chinatown. Mao has a short phrase--"Serve the people, learn from the people." And really I think college students have a lot to learn from the people in Chinatown. They may not be able to use all the academic jargon just to describe the assimilation process, underemployment rates and statistical analysis, but these people really know what's going on and that's something that the college students don't know. The only way to learn it is by identifying with the people, to work with them.

There are two things college students must overcome. When they come to the community that they do not feel themselves to be outsiders. That's a tremendous psychological barrier that I noticed a lot of students could not overcome. They still have this outsider's mentality. I really can't blame them because a lot of them are brought up in the suburbs and white middle class areas. And when they come here, they feel a gap. First, they must feel they are part of the community. Secondly, they must try to learn from the people rather than coming in with their preconceived idea of what the Chinese community needs and that would be just exactly the same as the liberals that have come in. They have all these preconceived ideas of "This is good for Chinatown." And we're no different in many ways from the white missionaries who went to China or the white missionaries who come to Chinatown. The white missionary in providing food and medicine for the suffering people then stick a little bible on the people. And of course, the radicals are doing the same thing. They make them go through their food stamp and surplus food issues and try to stick a little red book to the people. They're the same. No respect for the people at all.

QUESTION: How can the student from the outside in his desire to learn from the people and talk with the people, how can he do that on a day-to-day basis? What would he do outside of working in community centers and starting these projects? Or are those the things they should do?

WANG: I think there are certain projects that you can do. And I think we should be more selective on the type of projects the college students want to do. Certainly projects where you come into dealings with the people constantly. For instance, if you go to work with the self help for the elderly, you will be taking people to the hospitals, to collect their welfare check, to see a doctor, to visit relatives, or to their home. As simple as these things, these are the opportunities for the college student to learn from the people. I'm not saying that everybody can do it. I think there are some people who just can't do this kind of thing, and I think those people ought to spend time doing community research. Not research just for the sake of research, but research that will have some impact on the community, for the people doing the planning to try to bring in new programs into the community.

QUESTION: Do you see any optimistic signs for change in Chinatown?

WANG: Yes, I think so. Chinatown really has changed a lot, and things are changing each day. You're going to find some liberal people who got disillusioned with working in the community, and I think this year people are tired. They're beginning to feel increasingly the hostility from the masses. Because after a while, if what you're doing is not really relevant to people's needs, people are going to criticize you and then, of course you will feel hurt. I can never forget the movie, THE SEVEN SAMURAI. I can't help but draw the analogy there when the villagers hire the Samurai to get rid of these bandits and finally also get rid of the Samurai. And that just may happen. Because as long as you don't have a stake in the community, your attitude will set you aside from the rest of the people. Unless you'll be part of the community, eventually the hostility will be turned against you because you are not part of this community.

NEW YORK CHINATOWN TODAY:
COMMUNITY IN CRISIS

ROCKY CHIN

Remember 1970. First year of a new decade and for Chinatown, New York, a new era. The profound events of 1970 were not unpredictable fluke happenings, but in many ways had their genesis in past history, the Communist takeover of the Mainland in 1949, the United States involvement in Southeast Asia, the new massive Chinese immigration to this country after 1965, and the Black Movement in America. This article is about Chinatown today and the profound events of 1970. But it is also about what they portend for Chinatown tomorrow.

Setting: The Lower East Side

New York City is not San Francisco. It is older, larger and louder. Also denser, dirtier, richer and poorer. Chinatown is located on the "Lower East Side" of Manhattan Island. The highest concentration of Chinese establishments--restaurants, food, drug, and hardware stores, gift and candy shops, offices and factories, association and club headquarters--are crowded onto nine irregularly-shaped blocks which comprise "central Chinatown", bounded on the north by Canal Street and "Little Italy", on the east by the Bowery, and on the south and west by Government Center and "The Tombs (Manhattan Men's House of Detention)."

Massive new immigration in recent years and an already overcrowded central Chinatown is forcing many of these new arrivals to settle outside the nine-block area, some as far north as 14th Street, others as far east as the public housing projects flanking the East River.

The neighborhoods surrounding Chinatown have seen many immigrant groups come and go--usually after having been through several generations and having saved up enough money for the move out to the suburbs. Thus today's Lower East Side Puerto Ricans and Blacks have replaced yesterday's Jews, Irish, Rumanians, Italians, Poles, Ukrainians and Turks. Chinatown has seen only a nominal amount of out-migration itself, notably to parts of Queens and Long Island.

But Chinatown remains. The concrete consequence of almost a century of discrimination and oppression.

History and Development of Chinatown

Chinatown is a unique ghetto colony. Most of the early settlers arrived between 1870 and 1882, the latter date being that of the Chinese Exclusion Act. Many were seeking new opportunities on the East Coast, having been victims of an intense campaign of racism and repression on the West Coast. Some of these early overseas Chinese or "huaqiao"

> regarded themselves as 'sojourners', others decided to become permanent settlers. The unbreakable bond between the Chinese and his homeland and his culture was a decisive factor in the development of the sojourner attitude.[2]

Alien and adverse conditions on the East Coast also contributed towards the colonization of Chinatown.

> External and internal influences, therefore, led to the creation and maintenance of a duplicated Chinese society or ghetto on foreign soil--a society, of sojourners and permanent settlers, that was strongly oriented toward China and that looked to China, vainly and helplessly, for leadership and protection in times of persecution.[3]

The early proliferation of family name, district and merchant associations all had their counterpart in Imperial China.

> The family name association has its counterpart in the "feudalistic concept of _zu_ which was the heart of the Chinese patrilineal kinship system."[4]

This clan or kinship system was particularly strong and prevalent in southeastern China, the region from which most of Chinatown's inhabitants emigrated.[5] These associations, numbering around 40 today, once served as quasi-judicial, service and social organizations, handling such important matters as business affairs, family disputes and immigration problems. Today they have become primarily social organizations and face the future with uncertainty.

That the family name associations would decline in power and influence might be attributable to the following explanations:
1. Many of the wealthy supporters of the associations had invested substantial

sums ("patriotically") in Nationalist Chinese stocks and bonds, only to lose fortunes in 1949. The associations must now raise money from Chinatown residents who are not wealthy.

2. Several government-funded social service organizations have begun to take over many of the services once offered by the family name groups. For example, the Gold Age Club has a very large membership of elderly Chinatown residents, but it is administratively operated out of the N.Y.C. Department of Social Services and Welfare.

3. New immigrants find aspects of the associations anachronistic. Though in theory new immigrants are automatically members of their family name group, some 80 percent of Chinatown residents surveyed by the Chinatown Study in 1969 do not participate in any family name organization.

4. Financial services offered by the associations are less in demand today as an increasing number of Chinatown residents are accepting banks, stock brokers, credit unions and other once-suspect institutions and practices. The Lee family nevertheless maintains a revolving credit fund of one million dollars, loaned at an attractive 5 percent interest rate to members.

While the family name associations are declining in influence and power, the merchant associations have maintained theirs from a still formidable economic and financial base in the community. These organizations, or "tongs", are controlled by powerful business interests in and around Chinatown. The On Leong Merchants Association building on the corner of Canal and Mott, and the Hip Sing Headquarters on Pell Street, are unquestionably the only structures which can compare to the Chinatown palaces of San Francisco, Los Angeles or Chicago.

As the two most powerful tongs in New York, On Leong "controls" Mott and Hip Sing "controls" Pell and Doyers. Fees going to the controlling tong are exacted from commercial establishments on these streets. It is said that non-cooperation can result in severe economic and physical sanctions. Because the merchants associations have engaged in illegal "mafioso-like" activities in the past, many Chinatown residents assume that even today these tongs delve in police pay-offs, organized gambling, contracts, prostitution and the like. Residents speak of the tongs in whispers, never quite knowing themselves how widespread or insidious is their power today. But they do know the tongs are wealthy; that gambling is in Chinatown; that debts must be collected; and that in the past, the tongs have used youth groups for their own purposes. There is thus some apprehension that the new Hong Kong youth groups might be similarly used. It is out of this atmosphere of fear, ignorance and intimidation that the tongs command much of their power and false "respect".

As in other Chinatowns, the New York Chinese Consolidated Benevolent Association (or "CBA") claims to be the "official spokesman" and de facto "government" of the Chinatown Community. Ties between the CBA and the Chinese Government have always been strong. The CBA was registered with the Peking Imperial Government in 1883[6] before being incorporated under the laws of New York. Some seventy different organizations are represented in the CBA, though some, such as the two powerful tongs, exert effectively more power and control. The presidency (somewhat of a figurehead position) is alternated between Toisanese and Cantonese members.

During the past two decades, a number of other groups have gained popularity in Chinatown, such as the Lions Club, the Chamber and Junior Chamber of Commerce, the American Legion, and the Democratic and Republican Clubs. With the proliferation and popularity of such organizations, the power base in Chinatown is indeed shifting.

Serving The People

During the 1950's and 1960's, several social service organizations were created in Chinatown in response to the growing and neglected needs of the community. The CBA had their Chinese school (which charges tuition) and the family name associations had their traditional services. But these were woefully inadequate to meet the needs of the thousands of new arrivals.

One of the earliest of these new service organizations was the "experimental" branch office of the New York Community Services Society (CSS). Today, CSS staff offer primarily health and counseling services to families and the elderly.

The Chinatown Planning Council (CPC) offers more comprehensive services, but it is also under-financed and under-staffed. Some of their services include a day care program in P.S.23 (about 100 children), English classes, academic subject tutorials, youth programs, health and welfare counseling. CPC has a fulltime staff of 12 and is financed through private and public funds.

A third organization, the Chinatown Youth Council (CYC), had its origins in CPC. Established as a separate agency with OEO funds, CYC's staff of 8 (including recently 3 Vista Volunteers), sponsor English classes, youth programs and job placement.

All of these organizations have found it difficult to make significant inroads in the community. Some found themselves unwitting parties to internal political and personal feuds. Because there has been a considerable amount of in-fighting and disunity in Chinatown, recent efforts have been directed toward unification of the community.

Chinatown and China

The social, political and cultural climate of Chinatown was significantly affected by the 1949 Communist takeover of the Mainland and the subsequent United States policy of non-recognition. Sojourners felt the immediate consequences. America would be their home at least for the foreseeable future. Some could make the necessary adjustment. Others, denied of that all-important cultural link, became "marginal men"--strangers to both cultures.

Chinese professionals and workers alike were quick to adopt apolitical positions concerning Communist China, though some felt it necessary to lend their support to the Kuomintang out of genuine loyalty or out of a fear that anything less might be interpreted otherwise by United States authorities. Few residents wished to be deported.

During the McCarthy Era, Chinatown residents who might have been sympathetic to Mao kept mum. The CCBA felt it had to reassure American Society Chinese were indeed loyal and good citizens. Chinatown became thus not only "tourist attraction" but "model minority community". A number of "success story" articles were written during this period, perpetuating the existing stereotypes.

"Red-baiting" slackened somewhat during the early 1960's, but a number of television programs and some films, ever searching for a new villain, found him in the Chinese.

The intense anti-U.S. propaganda and isolationist stance of Communist China made it impossible to know what was going on except by reading unreliable secondary sources. For the most part, letter writing between relatives had to cease for mutual benefit. What little news there was in the Chinatown newspapers about Red China was always critical. Bookstores and newspaper stands refused to stock Communist Chinese literature.

Today, the situation is not much better. Only two Chinatown newspaper stands will carry the pro-Communist Chinese publication "China Daily News", which incidently survived the McCarthy Era. Despite the "news black-out", new immigrants coming from Kwangtung Province in China via Hong Kong inevitably bring with them their memories and experiences.

That the Establishment of Chinatown take a pro-Nationalist and anti-Communist stance is expected by United States authorities. Nevertheless, some officials persist in attacking the vulnerability of Chinese Americans. On April 17, 1969, F.B.I. Director J. Edgar Hoover heightened tensions and fears in Chinatown when he made the following statement to the House Appropriations Subcommittee:

> We are being confronted with a growing amount of work in being alert for Chinese Americans and others in this country who would assist Red China in supplying needed material or promoting Red Chinese propaganda. For one thing, Red China has been flooding the country with its propaganda and there are over 300,000 Chinese in the United States, some of whom could be susceptible to ties of hostage situations because of relatives in Communist China.[7]

Hoover's statement is irresponsible and slanderous. In Chinatown, it further intimidated the populace who had heard about it, many who justly wondered why they had been singled out. Some Asians recalled the incredibly unjust internment of the Japanese Americans during World War II.

During 1970, the topic of political discussions in Chinatown was the question of China's admission to and Taiwan's ouster from the United Nations. This issue came up every year and it was not surprising to see a full-page advertisement in the NEW YORK TIMES on November 10, 1970. The advertisement read as "An Open Letter from 17,500,000 Overseas Chinese to the United Nations General Assembly", submitted by 385 Chinese overseas organizations such as Benevolent and Merchant groups:

> We the undersigned, representing more than 17,500,000 overseas Chinese in various parts of the world wish to express once again our firm opposition to the admission of the Chinese Communist regime to this world organization.
> We are loyal citizens or residents of the countries in which we live. We are convinced that any attempt to put the seal of international approval upon the Peking Regime will strengthen the bondage of the people there and will impair their efforts to regain freedom...
> We entreat all the Delegates to reject forthright any resolution or proposal designed to admit the regime of Mao Tse-tung which is the enemy of the Chinese people and a threat to world peace.

Canada's decision to support Red

China's admission to the U.N. (along with Chile, Italy, etc.) drove the Nationalists deeper into Chinatowns in the United States. According to some sources,

> the Kuomintang...dominates the leadership of the (New York) Chinese Consolidated Benevolent Association more than the leadership of any other Chinatown on the continent.[8]

Because of this close relationship, it was also not surprising that the CBA hired buses for Chinatown residents to welcome the Vice-President of Taiwan who came on October 30, 1970 to address the United Nations. Kuomintang flags were freely distributed to children. Two anti-KMT groups showed up as well, the Taiwan Independence Movement and the Maoist-Third World New York group, I Wor Kuen.

Today's attitudes towards Chinese and residents of Chinatown are based on past pre-conceptions and stereotypes, but also on this country's foreign policy in Asia during this century. World War II, Korea and now Southeast Asia, have all had some adverse affects on Asians in America insofar as they have aroused sentiment against yellow people or seeded misunderstandings.

Chinatown and Southeast Asia

Being against the war in Southeast Asia in Chinatown was once, not long ago, rather like being for Red China. The mass of people in Chinatown, however, are not informed about international affairs and politics. They are much too busy working and surviving. Thus when draft counseling came to Chinatown in 1970, many immigrant families ignored it.

It was thus left to the so-called Asian American Movement which originated on the West Coast, to formulate this country's policies in Southeast Asia in terms of genocide. The movement saw a direct correlation between United States government policies abroad and domestic policies towards Chinatown at home. Vietnam, they further argued, was a "racist war" (witness Mylai, etc.) which could only portend hard times for people of yellow skin and almond eyes if it continued.

Chinatown Meets the Asian American Movement

No minority group can discount or dismiss the impact of the Civil Rights and later Human Rights Movement in America during the early 1960's. De jure discrimination wherever and however it may have been practiced was attacked vehemently and vigorously. Civil disobedience and marches came into the arsenal of the liberals once again. But it was the more recent "Black Power" Movement which caught on among the young of all colors, but particularly the poor and oppressed. Young Asian Americans (most often American-born) began to adopt "Black power" rhetoric and ideology. "Yellow Power" and an "Asian American Movement" was inevitable.

The Asian American Movement had its genesis on the West Coast. Young Asian students like their non-Asian peers were affected by "Black Power" (racial pride) and "New Left" politics. It wasn't long before Asians who had been in the various non-Asian political groups such as SDS, PLP, Women's Liberation, Third World Liberation saw the logic and need to create their own political alliances. On a number of California campuses, Asian American Political Alliances were formed. There organizations were markedly different from the traditional Chinese Students Associations on most campuses. Whereas the CSA's were socio-culturally oriented (though this is changing), AAPA's were quick to adopt the tactics, rhetoric and strategy of the various political movements from which their members had come.

In 1969, Asian American Student Associations were organized on a number of East Coast campuses, almost always through the initiative of some West Coast student. In New York, a liberal organization calling itself "Asian Americans for Action" or "Triple A" was already well-established. "Action" meant demonstrations, picketing, leafletting and holding forums on the problems of Asians in America, American Society and U.S. government foreign and domestic policies. During 1968 and 1969, Triple A's informal membership grew substantially as an increasing number of young Asians took an interest in the group and its activities. At Columbia, an AAPA was organized, many of its members having come to it through white radical politics. In New Haven, students at Yale put together a course on "Asians in America". Another effort was Dr. C.T. Wu's call for a "Congress for Chinese United " (CCU) which was organized in October of 1969 but never gained much support for a number of unrelated reasons. Some of the early members of the CCU later organized themselves into a group calling themselves "The Basement Workshop" located in Chinatown, with a similar purpose of serving the people.

To risk oversimplification, all these groups were fundamentally concerned about fighting injustice, racism and repression which particularly oppresses the poor, non-white minorities in America. It was inevitable that many of these students would turn towards Chinatown. The stage was thus set for the events of 1970.

Chinatown in 1970: turmoil and change

A. Immigration and Demography

On October 3, 1965, "national-origin" quotas were abolished with the passage of a more equitable immigration law. Thus ended some 83 years of one unjust immigration law after another--almost a century of blatant de jure discrimination against Chinatown and the Chinese people. We had the dubious distinction of being the only people "specifically named in legislation to be excluded from the United States."[11]

Chinatown is currently receiving a phenomenal 6-10,000 new arrivals per year.[12] Indeed, more Chinese immigrants have come to the United States during the past five years than during the previous fifty. Roughly 20 to 25 per cent of those entering report New York City as their intended permanent residence,[13] and about 80 to 90 per cent of these take up residence in Chinatown. There is no way, unfortunately, to determine the secondary migration from California and other parts of the country to New York, and vice versa. Some 15,000 Hong Kong Chinese (mostly refugees) were admitted to the United States between 1962-1966 under the "Hong Kong Refugee Parole Program."[14] If we account for these various flows, including natural increase, deserting Chinese crewmen and internal secondary migration, Chinatown's estimated population will be 62,000.[15]

Chinatown today is largely made up of new immigrants, most of whom have come from Kwangtung Province via Hong Kong. Almost one fourth (1/4) of Chinatown's population arrived in 1967-68, and more than one-half (1/2) of those now living in Chinatown came and settled between 1961 and 1969.[16] Chinatown has, in other words, undergone a complete population conversion within the last decade.

Place of Origin by birth:[17]
Kwangtung   50.9 per cent
U.S.   25.6 per cent
H.K.   15.9 per cent
Mainland   4.0 per cent (excluding Kwangtung
Other   2.2 per cent

The New Immigrants

Unlike Chinatown's early settlers and sojourners, recent immigrants are younger, female and more oriented to considering America as a permanent home. According to a special U.S. Census in 1957, the median age in Chinatown was 37.1. In 1969, however, the median age according to the Chinatown Study Report was 27.6. The age distribution has also changed radically. In 1957, some 25.2 per cent of the total Chinatown population (est. 13,285) were under 20 years of age. In 1969, more than 40 per cent were under 20.[18] The average number of persons per household today is 3.7, some 12 per cent of all households live alone, 7 per cent live with one to four roommates, and 14 per cent are couples. The remaining we assume, are families.[19] The most hopeful aspect of this new immigration is that in time it will balance out a most abnormal sex ratio in Chinatown. Earlier immigrants were predominantly male, not having been able to bring their wives over from China. They were also prevented from marrying non-Asians. In fact, it was only in the 1960's that the U.S. Supreme Court struck down anti-miscegenation laws which still existed in some states.

B. Getting together with I Wor Kuen

In February 1970, Chinatown residents were probably surprised to see young Chinese selling a newspaper on the corners of Mott and Bayard Streets in downtown Chinatown. The bi-lingual paper, "Getting Together", was put out by a new group in Chinatown calling themselves I Wor Kuen (IWK) after the Boxers (of the "Boxer Rebellion" in China, 1900). I Wor Kuen's original membership was composed of Asian college and high school students. Some had come from Triple A, others from Columbia AAPA and still others from "new left" political groups. They had decided to form a "collective" in 1969, setting it up originally on 30 Market Street in The Two Bridges Neighborhood. The first issue of "Getting Together" discussed "Chinatown and its problems", "Serving the People", "Yellow Power", "Free Health Clinic", "Concentration Camps in the USA", the "Black Panther Party Program" and other "Politically-charged" and controversial Chinatown subjects.

Of their own orientation they write: We are not a bunch of 'do-gooders' out to save somebody else; we only know that our own freedom and happiness are tied-in with the freedom and happiness of every Chinese and every Asian person. We are not going to turn ourselves into a bureaucratic agency to hand out charity; our programs will be the beginning blocks of the movement for Chinese,

YELLOW POWER. We are not out to demand this phoney reform or that, but to fight for the total self-determination of the Asian people in Chinatown. Our programs are a step on the road of thousand-li that leads to the freedom and power for all non-white (YELLOW,

BROWN, BLACK) peoples of this community. POWER TO THE COURAGEOUS, HARDWORKING, PROUD, ASIAN-AMERICAN PEOPLE![20]

The CBA Establishment may have initially passed IWK off as a group of "radical college kids", but IWK no doubt (did) upset (many) elders. Not only did it have its own media, but it offered services which were in fact needed in the community, thus gaining a clientele and a foothold in Chinatown. Nevertheless, rumors began to spread that they were communist-inspired and possibly communist-supported.

Though one might have criticized the group for not finely tailoring its politics and tactics to Chinatown (though there is by no means a consensus as to what that entails), no one could deny that Chinatown was going through some serious changes, which did demand attention, that the community was indeed impoverished and ignored by the City of New York, and that the existing community institutions were either irrelevant, antiquated or impotent in responding to these urgent community needs.

The older generation in Chinatown, having experienced more blatant forms of discrimination than their children, were afraid that their children would place themselves in serious jeopardy by associating with IWK, participating in demonstrations or in any way challenging the existing order. The increasing anti-U.S. propaganda and international status of Communist China and the con-commitant liberalism and radicalism on college campuses and in the high schools only nurtured these fears.

Much of the initial support of IWK thus came from those who were not residents of Chinatown. In time, that would change somewhat. These Chinese-Americans who did not grow up in Chinatown were less vulnerable to intimidation. Through free films and other programs and services, IWK did begin to build up support among those who did not fear being "red-baited".

One of the early demonstrations by Asian Americans in New York City was on the afternoon of November 21, 1969. Some 40-50 Asian-Americans protested J. Edgar Hoover's statement in front of the FBI headquarters, thus demonstrating their new "militancy".

In April, Chinatown was reminded that I Wor Kuen was still alive and well. The second issue of "Getting Together" came out, much more strongly pro-Mao and pro-Red China. By this time the turmoil and changes in Chinatown were beginning to be picked up in nationally circulated periodicals. ESQUIRE and NEWSWEEK both ran feature articles on San Francisco Chinatown.[21] TRANSACTION MAGAZINE included a somewhat more in-depth article on Chinatown by Stanford Lyman.[22] Several New York City colleges were investigating the possibility of a course on Asians in America. It was thus in March and April of 1970 that many of the various activities going on among Asians on the East Coast suddenly got together, first in a conference at Princeton University, then in a March Against the Vietnam War in Washington, D.C. (April 12), a week later in an anti-Tourist Bus demonstration in Chinatown (sponsored by IWK), and finally in a conference on "Asians in America" at Yale (April 25, sponsored by Yale's AASA).

Few Chinatown residents participated in any of these events, however. Young people from Hong Kong did not relate to their America-born peers, and that was mutual. Life-styles, language and cultural experiences were too divergent. What these events during March and April did do was to start people thinking, about themselves, American Society and about their Asian communities such as Chinatown.

The Economy

The Tourist Bus Demonstration in April was adversely and indignantly received by Chinatown's merchants. Though the demonstration had been against "whistle-stop" tour groups which shoved people onto the streets and patronized only one restaurant (by prior agreement) on Pell Street, it was misunderstood as being against Chinatown's most important business, tourism. The following day, a large sign saying "Chinatown Welcomes all Tourists" was draped across Mott Street in front of the CBA building.

There are over 200 restaurants in Chinatown and a larger number scattered throughout New York City. There are grocery stores, seafood markets, pastry and gift shops, laundries, barber and beauty shops, movie theaters, banks, travel agencies, drug stores, churches, funeral homes, factories, printing presses, liquor stores and homes. Chinatown is indeed an economically self-contained and self-sufficient community. Thus it is possible that a resident never ventures outside of Chinatown's boundaries during his entire life.

Employment
Status of Chinatown Residents between 18 & 64

Full-time	56.7
Part-time	7.9
Student	10.4
Housewife	14.4
Retired	2.0
Welfare	1.0
Unemployed	3.0
Refused to Respond	4.5

The Chinatown garment industry, now consisting of about 140 factories (most of which are Chinese owned), employs 75 per cent[26] of all working women in Chinatown, which make up about 80 to 90 per cent of the total employees in the Chinatown industry. The recession and the available supply of workers is having deleterious affects on on the industry. There is even some talk that the entire uptown Department is therefore currently undertaking a study of the entire question, but they are finding data on Chinatown's factories not readily accessible. Needless to say, whatever happens to the garment industry will have profound repercussions on Chinatown's economy. The other major employers in Chinatown are the food and noodle factories.[27]

About 54 per cent of Chinatown is between the ages of 18 and 64.[28] Of the 10.5 per cent over 65 years,[29] some 66.7 per cent are retired but some 17.9 per cent are still working either part-time or full-time.

It is difficult to get precise figures about people's wages. What one earns has always been somewhat of a private matter. What data we do have indicates a median annual income of Chinatown residents between $4,000 and $5,000.[30]

For many years, the Chinatown Garment Industry exploited its employees. Today, there are still several factories which persist. Because the industry is vulnerable to the whims of fashion designers and the increasingly independent wills of women, the contractor must be skillful in pricing a pattern right. After a price is reached between the contractor and the manufacturer, the cheaper the contractor can make the garment, the greater his profit.

The number of factories in and around Chinatown has grown as a result of cheap labor in good supply as well as the desire to cash in on the high profits one can make if one is a "good pricer." The new immigrant women are not familiar with their rights as employees and do not speak much English. They are, however, very anxious to get a job, often in order to help raise plane fare for another family member still in Hong Kong. It is not surprising that unethical contractors do exploit these women. Hence, almost two-thirds of all garment industry violations in New York City are found in the Chinese shops![31]

There are theoretically two wages offered a worker: a minimum wage and a piece-work wage.[32] The minimum wages vary from one garment job to another and are supposedly standardized by the international Ladies Garment Workers Union. The price a worker is paid per piece, however, is negotiated between employer and employee. There is still much truth to the "sweat shop" image of the industry today, though there are some changes worth noting. The union offers English classes and most shops publish union notes and other circulars in Chinese and English. Each shop is supposed to have a Chinese-speaking shop steward.

But wages remain low. One source estimated that some 2,000 to 3,000 workers earn less than the minimum wage. Most of the women still work often 10 to 12 hours a day, six days a week. Oftentimes their children will join them after school and even help out. The factory has inevitably become part of the workers social life. Many older women could retire but stay for the company. If minimum wage laws were strictly enforced, some of these women would be either laid-off or placed on part-time roles. To eliminate wage gouging and exploitation some people have talked of creating a cooperative garment shop.

Commercial Space

Commercial space in Chinatown is limited and expensive. Land in 1967 was about $30-$35 per square foot in the Chinatown area and the area immediately adjacent.[33] Land values in reality are much higher because of Chinatown's proximity to Government Center and Wall Street commercial area. Garment factories are located in old and deteriorating lofts in and around Chinatown. Many have begun to locate elsewhere around "Greater Chinatown" because of the lack of space and the changing settlement patterns of new arrivals. Retail stores are following their Chinese clientele north of Canal Street and east of the Bowery.

D. Housing

Spring had passed and summer came with most college and high school students still recovering from Cambodia, Kent State and the nationwide student strike. Chinatown was quiet. I Wor Kuen was showing films and still pushing their politics. They had moved to a new storefront at 24 Market. It had plate-glass windows but they were soon broken--by reactionaries, they claim, in the neighborhood.

In July, I Wor Kuen decided to show the pro-communist film, "The East is Red," in an open vacant-lot playground on the corner of Market and Henry Streets. Several hundred families and single men and women came out to see the Peking-opera style depiction of the Communist Revolution. The film was shown on three consecutive nights, and only on one was there an incident. Some water and garbage was dumped on the crowd from an adjacent tenement roof top, but IWK managed to keep the situation under control and assure protection of the families, a majority of which had stayed. The incident was evidence that political climate in Chinatown was still obviously charged, but there were some signs of growing tolerance.

Around the block from that playground, a sign was put up across the street during the summer saying "We Won't Move!". This was the slogan of a tenants' movement on one block of Madison Street in the Two Bridges Neighborhood. The New York Telephone Company, having made a gross underestimate of demand in Lower Manhattan, was seeking a site on which to construct a switching station. The Two Bridges Neighborhood Council, made up of Blacks, Puerto Ricans, Italians and Chinese, got word that this block was being bought up and immediately began organizing the community to fight. After months of block organizing, parties, marches and demonstrations, their case is now in court. "Squatting" (moving into locked, sealed and abandoned buildings which have been slated for demolition) is prevalent throughout the block. The "We Won't Move" situation epitomizes the frustrating housing situation in New York City and the Lower East Side.

New York's Chinatown has one of the oldest housing stocks in the country. More than 90 per cent[34] of the residential dwelling units in Central Chinatown were built before 1901. There are only three middle-income elevator apartments in "Greater Chinatown": Chatham Green, a snakelike brick structure just south of the core area, Chatham Towers, two towers of cast-concrete fronting Columbus Park, and 50 Bayard, an older cooperative on the corner of Elizabeth and Bayard Streets in the heart of Chinatown. Rents in these so-called "middle-income" buildings range from $40 to $60 per room per month.

Many Chinese live in the high rise public housing projects along the East River. One project, Rutgers Houses, has some 40 per cent of its dwelling units occupied by Chinese families.[37] Many single elderly men live in dormitories in converted old factory lofts in Chinatown. Windows of their cubbyholes can be seen from the streets, papered-over and curtained. These elderly are among the most poorly housed and neglected in Chinatown.

Housing Conditions[38]

Pest control is a major problem in the Chinatown tenements. About 35.2 percent of the dwellings have rats, 76.5 percent have roaches. The crumbling tenements only provide more places for such pests to hide, more openings through which to invade apartments.

Some 27.8 percent of the apartments have rooms which require individual heating. 6.7 percent have no refrigerators, 4.8 percent share their kitchen with another family, 6.2 percent share their bathroom, and 62.7 percent have not been painted during the past three years as required under code regulation.

Many families do not even know where their landlord lives (46.1 percent). Nevertheless, further information indicates that most landlords do live in and around Chinatown. Nevertheless, there is little the landlord can do to substantially improve his building except "cosmetic" or "veneer" rehabilitation. Nothing short of complete "gut rehabilitation" or "new construction" will stop the steady deterioration over time and usage.

Rents

Rents are controlled in the majority of buildings in Chinatown, but "key money" is used to circumvent the law. About one-fourth[39] of those families living in rent controlled apartments have paid this fee which is most always in cash and non-refundable. "Key money", which can amount to a few thousand dollars, amounts to being a payment for information of a housing vacancy. Without this payment, rents are among the lowest in the City. Some 56.4 percent[40] reported a total rent in 1969 (before the recent rent increases) of less than $50 per month per apartment.

E. Crime

Fortunately for the tourist trade, most outsiders still consider Chinatown a safe neighborhood. Many residents do not. In the past, the CBA did have control over "asocial behavior"--either by preventing it or by withholding news of it from the American press. New immigration has meant more young residents, youths who find recreational activities and facilities woefully inadequate. As Chinatown grows in population, it has inevitably begun to push into other ethnic communities in the Lower East Side, some of which have severe drug addiction and crime problems.

When asked in the Chinatown Study survey what they least liked about Chinatown, 28.1 per cent of the total number of respondents and 71 per cent of those who lived in public housing projects felt the area was unsafe. In central Chinatown, 20 per cent of the respondents had experienced robberies. Those who lived in public housing projects were the most vulnerable, with 31 per cent having experienced muggings and/or robberies.[41] In another question, 51.1 per cent of those surveyed indicated that protection of the public was the major deficiency in Chinatown (sanitation services, 39.4 per cent and recreational facilities, 22.1 per cent were the other major "deficiencies"). These are of course, only one indication of public dissatisfaction with their neighborhood.

Some years ago, the Fifth Police Precinct, which is located in the heart of Chinatown on Elizabeth Street, informed residents of its plans to move out of Chinatown. The community's response was a remarkable demonstration of some 4,000 residents protesting the decision. The Fifth Precinct stayed.[42]

Of the current situation, police captain James McDonald analyzed the situation as follows in a WCBS-radio special on Chinatown:[43]

In 1964, we had one Chinese youth under 21 years of age arrested for a serious crime. In 1969 we had 30 youths under 21 years of age arrested for a serious crime. We've had a tremendous influx of foreign-born young Chinese into the community the last couple of years. They bring with them the tremendous problem of the language barrier. In addition to this, when they get into our schools, they find themselves with American-born Chinese and with American youth that are much younger than they are. This coupled with the language barrier causes a tremendous dropout in the school system. The result is that we find them hanging on the street with nothing to do and the youth goes completely unsupervised.

In 1970, the "arrest statistics" were running even with 1969.

Police-community relations have never been intimate, primarily because of language and cultural differences. An auxiliary Chinese force of men and women have been hired part-time to the Fifth Precinct. Relations between police and many youth groups remain strained.

Chinatown leaders are quick to blame the current rise in crime on the new arrivals from Hong Kong, yet the CBA has no active youth program and its gymnasium, the only one of its kind in central Chinatown, is closed to the community.

On August 3, 1970, 14-year-old William Wong was fatally stabbed in the face, head and chest on a busy Chinatown Street. When officers of the Fifth Precinct arrived, they did not have a first aid kit and thus, many youths felt, were in some part responsible for Wong's bleeding to death. William Wong's family had come from Hong Kong five years ago. Like many of his friends, he had joined a street gang which had its own turf and its own hangouts. If Wong was the victim of a gang feud, he would neither be the first nor unfortunately, many residents feel, the last.

When this news broke, it was immediately picked up by all the New York City newspapers before being reported in the Chinatown publications. Few people in Chinatown wished to discuss the issue with reporters.

At the office of the CHINESE TRIBUNE, a Chinese-language daily newspaper, for example, no one would conceed...that such things as teen-age gangs existed in the community. The same reluctance to speak of such things came from shopkeepers and men and women and teenagers on the streets...at 62 Mott Street, in the (Consolidated Benevolent) Association's offices, a man who declined to identify himself said: "Gangs. What gangs? You'll have to go to the Fifth Precinct." (N.Y. TIMES, August 6, 24:6, 1970)

Drugs and drug addiction is another potentially serious problem in Chinatown, particularly among the youth. Hard drugs are available and quite pervasive in parts of the Lower East Side. The City is just beginning to acknowledge the potential widespread use of drugs in the Chinatown area. The City's Addiction Services Agency has hired recently a Chinese youth, Peter Chan, to work with some of Chinatown's youth groups. He is one of the few individuals who are actively doing so at the present time.

The rise in crime rate and the increasing concern about community safety among residents is but one indication of severe turmoil and change in the Chinatown community. The recent activities and demands of Chinatown youth is another.

F. Youth & Recreation

Some 35.5 per cent of Chinatown's total population is under 17 years of age.[44] Chinatown's youth however, are not a homogenous group. There are, to begin with, those who were born in America ("jooksing") and those who were born abroad ("jook-kok").[45] American-born youth may speak Chinese fluently or not at all. Few know how to read and write Chinese, though many have gone to the CBA Chinese School when they were young. Youths from abroad may have been born in Hong Kong or in China (most likely, Kwangtung Province). Many have difficulty speaking English. In school, on the streets and in sports, the youth sift themselves out into these various groups.

Another group of Chinese youth should be mentioned here because several are becoming involved in Chinatown, not as outside "missionary" do-gooders, but as actual community-based residents. I Wor Kuen has been mentioned previously, However, there are many others who are active in Chinatown but for one reason or another have not joined IWK. "Corky" Lee, for example, is a recent graduate of Queens College who is now Chinese Community Organizer for the Two Bridges Neighborhood

Council. Lee grew up in Queens, speaks some Toisanese, and now lives in and works in Chinatown. Though he has been working in the community for less than a year, he has made himself quite "visible" through a "Two Bridges Newsletter" (tri-lingual in English, Chinese and Spanish) and through his assumed role as an advocate for the youth. Each of the social service agencies has their "youth worker".[46]

For all Chinatown youths, recreational facilities and activities are very important. However, there is only one full-sized gymnasium in central Chinatown and it is closed. There is only one park in this area and it is intensely used during all hours of the day, as a sitting place for the elderly, a playground for a nearby elementary school, and a recreational area for teen-agers (basketball, etc.). But even this beloved grassless park, in the shadow of the monolithic "Tombs" prison on Mulberry Bend, is threatened to be narrowed by the highway department in order to improve access to Government Center. Because of the incredible lack of recreational facilities in Chinatown and the wide popularity of basketball, it soon became obvious to a group of community youths during the spring of 1970 that the CBA gym must be opened. Their efforts to "Free the Gym!" ultimately brought them into direct confrontation with the Chinese Consolidated Benevolent Association itself. It is this event which occurred in September of 1970 which best epitomizes the changes in Chinatown.

Free the Gym: A Confrontation

Sunday is Chinatown's busiest. As a regional center for Chinese groceries and food products, it draws Chinese from as far away as New Haven and distant parts of Long Island. Sunday is also often the only day off during the week for Chinatown residents. In addition, tourists pour into the area seeking good food and activity. It was thus on Sunday, September 13, 1970 that a group of 100 young Chinatown residents chose to confront the CBA at their doorstep on 62 Mott.

This significant confrontation began as an issue some four years earlier. At that time, the CBA had just closed its gym to the community after having experienced some vandalism. When the CBA building was built, it was intended to be the Chinatown Community Center. Funds for the gym were raised from the community and from the Police Athletic League. The building houses the gymnasium, showers, lockers, offices, classrooms and an auditorium.

After the closing of the gym, several attempts were made to re-open it. These failed. The argument given was that proper supervision was needed and operating costs had to be funded. Thus, for four years the facility lay most of the year idle, only occasionally rented out for a dance or meeting.

The youths who got together in May of 1970 had each been actively involved in community sports programs. Negotiations were begun between one member of the "Sports Committee" and N.B. Lee of the CBA. All through the summer while these negotiations were going on, various "strategy" meetings were called. The Sports resisted turning their efforts into "radical student politics" and at no time were they ever controlled by non-Chinatown groups. In fact when I Wor Kuen's newspaper carried a story about the gym, many of the committee members were openly resentful and very much afraid their issue would be marked as "communist inspired". As the summer wore on, efforts by the "Sports Committee" to elicit support from various community groups, agencies, and churches were met with sympathy which did not extend to support. Support of the "Sports Committee" most groups felt would be seen as being against the CBA, a position some Chinatown agencies had once put themselves in and did not wish to repeat; two longtime youth workers, Mike Gill of the Young Life organization and Harold Lui of Hamilton-Madison House did lend their support. The decision to demonstrate thus came after frustrated efforts to negotiate in good faith and the lack of public support from the various Chinatown groups.

On September 13th, the CBA was presented with several non-negotiable demands. "Demands" were decided upon as a way to get the CBA to negotiate seriously and in good faith. In fact, of course, the demands had forced the Association into a corner without leaving it a dignified route to escape. Thus though the demonstration itself drew many people from the press and radio stations, it did not succeed in forcing the CBA's hand. There were some stall tactics (promises to open the gym couched in certain vague terms) and the issue eventually died. Word was released later in the fall that the gym would be converted into a classroom, though that idea was dropped. To date it remains closed.

Several things were gleaned from this affair. The power of the CBA is apparently still formidable. At the height of the gym controversy, some members of the "Sports Committee" actually were fearful that "contracts" had been sent out to discourage them. But the affair also indicated that Chinatown residents could and would stand up. No longer could the CBA claim representation of all the Chinatown people, and the prospects of future such confrontation between the CBA and other groups are probable.

G. Health

Health facilities and services are also inadequate in Chinatown. There is no public health clinic in the Chinatown area, and the nearest hospitals are inconvenient walking distances away. Residents work long hours in poor conditions, live in crowded and deteriorating tenements, infested by rats and roaches. Diseases such as asthma, tuberculosis and psychological disorders have been common in the Chinatown area, which is not surprising to find in a ghetto neighborhood.

In 1946, tuberculosis was a major health problem in Chinatown. Officials in the Health Department had "discovered that the relapse rate among Chinese discharged from tuberculosis sanitoria was particularly high."[47] T.B. tests are given by IWK, CSS and a clinic supported by the CBA on Madison Street. IWK and CSS both have Chinese doctors.

New immigrants particularly prefer Chinese doctors, of which there are about twenty, not including 9 herbalists and 5 dentists.[48] Only one third of Chinatown residents surveyed in the Health Project have been to a clinic or hospital for medical treatment. Some do not like the long lines, others the inconvenient hours and the non-Chinese staff (about 20).[49] The hospital is also working on translating medical terms into Chinese and vice versa--no small task!

Two thirds of all residents are covered by health insurance, but only a little more than 11 per cent have medicaid, a surprising figure compared to the number of residents eligible.[50]

The plight of the elderly in Chinatown matches that of the young. Many are without families and relatives. Housing is poor and the tenement stairs often restrict the elderly to their rooms. Many also need the services of a translator, or perhaps a person to go and buy some medicine if they are sick. But these services are not provided free by the associations. Translating a letter may cost $5 to $10.[51]

The most serious health problem today and possibly in the future may be the mental health of Chinatown residents. As there are few psychiatrists and even fewer bi-lingual Chinese psychiatrists, para-professional counseling services are desperately needed. Mental illness, suicide, asocial behavior and withdrawal from society are all commonly found in various ghetto environments. Many of the new immigrants face cultural shock, and many of the old sojourners, knowing they can never go back to China, fall into severe states of depression and psychosis. It was not surprising that 1970 had its suicides. On the morning of September 4, a 78 year-old man jumped down from the fifth floor of 11 Bowery Street. He was killed instantly. He was an old overseas Chinese, Lo Wen Shen, who had been in the U.S. for 50 years.[52]

H. Education

There are some half dozen primary schools in Greater Chinatown, and most are crowded, old and in poor condition.[53] Bi-lingual staff and teachers are necessary but the City has not made the appropriations. Unlike the "massive aid to the Hungarian, Cuban and Czechoslovakian" immigrant,[54] the Chinese immigrants have received no assistance from the United States government to ease their adjustment. Worse yet, it is illegal for the city to hire non-citizens for any Federal jobs. Federal funding for a bi-lingual center is being sought by the Chinatown Advisory Council's Education Committee, chaired by lawyer Irving Chin. If they are successful, this should be a major contribution to the Chinatown community.

The average number of years of education of those residents between 18 and 64 years of age is 7.4 years, with the breakdown as follows:

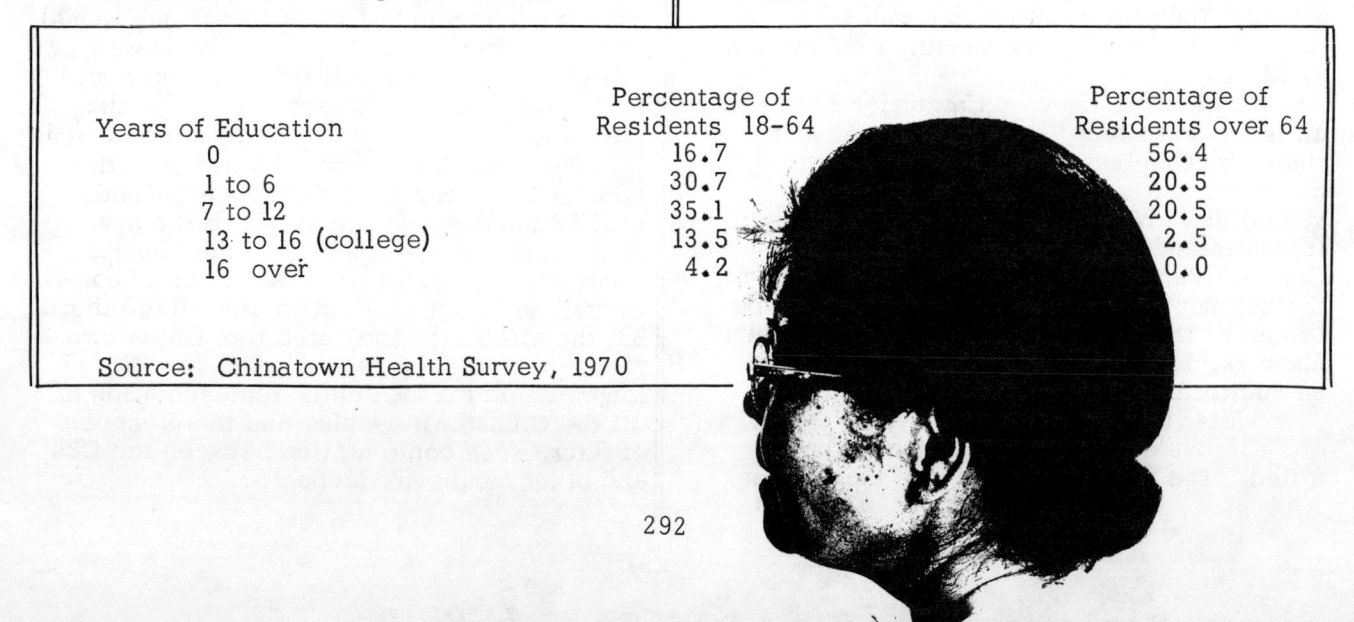

Years of Education	Percentage of Residents 18-64	Percentage of Residents over 64
0	16.7	56.4
1 to 6	30.7	20.5
7 to 12	35.1	20.5
13 to 16 (college)	13.5	2.5
16 over	4.2	0.0

Source: Chinatown Health Survey, 1970

Almost 90 per cent[55] of all those Chinatown residents who have received a total of 6 to 11 years of education, received that education in Hong Kong or China. In Hong Kong, public education is not free, which accounts for the high illiteracy rate among new immigrants. In this country, the immigrant youth must also adjust to the different school system which still nurtures many stereotypes of the Chinese and which also attempts to inculcate middle class American values. Because of the totally inadequate histories for all grades, many of our school children are left with warped versions—often humiliating—of the early Chinese immigrant history to the present. Chinatown students are also subject to the personal racial misconceptions of their teachers and, importantly, the radio, television, show and news media. Within this context as well as the context of the Black and Asian American Movement, many college-aged Asian Americans, particularly the American-born second and third generations, are undergoing an "identity crisis".

On the East Coast as on the West Coast, numerous colleges and universities are beginning to realize not all Chinese have "made it" and have equal opportunity of education. Some have begun to recruit from Chinatown high schools. But to date, there is no major foundation which has recognized the unique situation and problems of the Asian American by designating scholarship funds or grants accordingly. There is some indication that in time this will change.

Prospects for the Future

The gym demonstration was covered by the New York media. WCBS radio ran a special week-long report on Chinatown under its "Minority Report." On November 1st, a march was held in Chinatown by IWK and its college student sympathizers. It was a "Third World March" supporting all "wars of national liberation." After the Chinatown March, participants went uptown to join the main march (consisting of Blacks, Puerto Ricans and other Third World Peoples) up through Harlem.[56]

By the Fall of 1970, the "radical underground" and "liberal establishment" were well informed about IWK's activities in Chinatown[57] as well as some of the changes going on in the community. Indeed, many people were of the impression that the only young people working actively in Chinatown were members of I Wor Kuen. This, of course, was not true, but IWK was indeed one of the most colorful and controversial youth groups to come into Chinatown for a long time. By the end of 1970 Chinatown residents had begun to accept IWK's existence and even began to show some greater tolerance for their tactics.

December opened with a conference in New York on "Asian American Reality" and closed with a demonstration by the "Oriental Actors" of New York against the broadway musical, "Lovely Ladies and Kind Gentlemen." The conference, the first in New York City, was held on two consecutive days and drew almost 500 students from the metropolitan area and more distant campuses along the East Coast. Speakers included members of I Wor Kuen, Alex Hing of the San Francisco "Red Guard", author William Hinton (FANSHEN),[58] writer Grace Lee Boggs and Mary Kochiyama (Japanese-American Third World Activist). Workshops ranged from the "Asian American Movement" to "Women's Liberation" to "Chinatown."

The conference had attempted to attract high school students from Chinatown. Not many showed up. Again, like many other such conferences, there was a general sentiment of "where do we go from here?"

I Wor Kuen offers one approach to the community and the movement. The Chinatown Planning Council, for example, offers another. There are still many other alternatives. Time and circumstance will test each of these various approaches, though not always fairly. Student visions of the "revolution" may be just visions. But Chinatown's needs and problems are urgent and real. We cannot continue to ignore and neglect them.

For Chinatown, future continued massive immigration, without the substantial resources necessary to improve all aspects of community services, will lead to further social, cultural and political disorientation and turmoil. This country's foreign policies in Asia will likewise have significant impact of easing or increasing tensions in the community. Physical changes will also affect Chinatown's future growth and development. The possibility of a 2nd Avenue subway stop at Chatham Square would dramatically change circulation flows and access patterns in and around and to Chinatown. A turn-off connecting the Manhattan Bridge and the East River Drive could ease truck traffic on Canal but it would require housing demolition and hence, family relocation. Any widening of Baxter Street which fronts the western length of Columbus Park would result in the loss of precious park and recreational space. Finally, anything affecting the Garment Industry will have its impact felt in Chinatown.

To John V. Lindsay (and possibly 8 million other New Yorkers), Chinatown is a tourist smorgasbord of neon lights, crowded crooked streets, late evening atmosphere and basement cuisine—all garnished somewhat tawdrily in "oriental motif" (after San Francisco). But Chinatown should mean much more than that to us as Asians and Chinese in America.

Today, the majority of Chinese in America live in Chinatowns across the country, and theirs is not a "small immigrant success story" as Fox Butterfield's uninformed and misleading article in the NEW YORK TIMES might have led one to believe.[59]

Current social, cultural and political upheaval in Chinatown is reflected in the seriously urgent problems which we have already explored. These are problems which demand attention now. No one individual or group of individuals can or will have all the answers and proper approaches. What is clear, however, is that massive resources are going to be required, resources which we can only expect to obtain through united creative efforts on the part of all Asians and Chinese in America. In the years ahead, the people in Chinatown must also be able to participate fully and meaningfully in the decisions which will affect their lives.

As a minority in America (between .5 per cent and .9 per cent), we cannot allow ourselves the luxury of thinking we have "made it" when our brothers have not. We cannot afford to fight among ourselves or exploit each other for the sake of personal advancement and self-aggrandizement. Insteady, we must discover how we can, through whatever skills or resources we have been given, work towards bettering the condition of all Asians in America. Because we know of no "right" approach or strategy, we must also become more tolerant of individual ideological differences and the wide range of means now and in the future which will be used towards obtaining the goals we have in common--freedom from racism, poverty and oppression, the right to determine our own destinies, and the establishment of ethnic pride and consciousness as Asian Americans.

---

[1] See L. Ling-chi Wang's "Chinatown in Transition," TING MAGAZINE, August 30, 1969. Wang's article is one of the best and most concise pieces around on what San Francisco's Chinatown is really like today.

[2] Ibid.

[3] Ibid.

[4] Stuart H. Cattel, HEALTH, WELFARE AND SOCIAL ORGANIZATIONS IN CHINATOWN NEW YORK CITY (New York: Community Services Society, 1962). This study is drawn from a small sample taken from the CSS Clientele and cannot be said to represent the total population. Cattel, an anthropologist, develops an academic analysis of the social structure of the community which lacks the nuances of one who really understands the political tugs and pulls of the community. Good beginning bibliography. General concentration is on health.

[5] Wang.

[6] Y.K. Chu.

[7] THE NEW YORK TIMES, November 22, 1969.

[8] THE VILLAGE VOICE, September 10, 1970.

[9] CHINATOWN STUDY REPORT, 1969. The project director of this study was Danny Yung, an urban planning and design student at Columbia who had previously studied architecture at Berkeley. Yung, a foreign-born student, also worked with Dr. Roy Eng on the Chinatown Health Project, 1970. He is now active in the Basement Workshop, Inc. in Chinatown. With a large sample size of 565 residents carefully selected, this survey probably comes closest to representing the population.

[10] CHINATOWN HEALTH PROJECT, 1970. Under the direction of Dr. Roy Eng, this project had a federal grant to investigate health facilities, etc. Sample size is representative.

[11] Betty Lee Sung, MOUNTAIN OF GOLD, (New York, MacMillan, 1967).

[12] New York City Planning Department, PLAN FOR NEW YORK CITY; MANHATTAN, vol. 4, 1970.

[13] U.S. Immigration and Naturalization Service, ANNUAL REPORT, 1966, Table 12B, 1960-1969.

[14] Ibid., p. 7.

[15] CHINATOWN HEALTH PROJECT, 1970.

[16] CHINATOWN STUDY REPORT, 1969.

[17] CHINATOWN HEALTH PROJECT, 1970

[18] Ibid.

[19] Ibid.

[20] GETTING TOGETHER, February, 1970.

[21] Tom Wolfe, "The New Yellow Peril," ESQUIRE MAGAZINE, December, 1969. Note: satirical and facetious treatment of a serious situation which has developed in S.F. Chinatown. Min Yee, "Chinatown in Crisis," NEWSWEEK MAGAZINE, February 23, 1970.

[22] Stanford Lyman, "Red Guard on Grant Avenue," TRANSACTION, April, 1970.

[23] CHINATOWN STUDY PROJECT, 1969.

[24] Hart, Krivatsky and Stubee, consultants to the New York Department of City Planning, CHINATOWN NEW YORK: a report on the conditions and needs of a unique community, July, 1968. This merely rehashes existing material and is not meant to be an in-depth study of the community. It explores but does not develop several important planning questions.

[25] Ibid.

[26] CHINATOWN STUDY PROJECT, 1969.
[27] Hart, Krivatsky and Stubee.
[28] CHINATOWN HEALTH PROJECT, 1970.
[29] Ibid.
[30] CHINATOWN STUDY PROJECT, 1969.
[31] Norman L. Kee, New York Chinatown attorney.
[32] CHINATOWN STUDY PROJECT, 1969.
[33] Hart, Krivatsky and Stubee.
[34] Department of Buildings, Housing and Development Administration, building print-outs, 1969.
[35] Roy Lubove, THE PROGRESSIVES AND THE SLUMS; THE TENEMENT HOUSE REFORM IN NEW YORK CITY, 1890-1917 (Pittsburgh: University of Pittsburg Press, 1963) pp. 29, 31. See also Lawrence M. Friedman, GOVERNMENT AND SLUM HOUSING (Chicago: Rand McNally, 1968).
[36] Jacob Riis, HOW THE OTHER HALF LIVES (New York: Hill and Wang, 1957). The colorful, shocking and influential account of the tenements on the Lower East Side, with an interesting chapter on Chinatown as seen by Riis in 1890 when this book was first published.
[37] CHINATOWN HEALTH PROJECT, 1970.
[38] Ibid.
[39] Ibid.
[40] Ibid.
[41] Ibid.
[42] Rumors were that the Establishment didn't want to pay another group of policemen off. These are unsubstantiated.
[43] WCBS Radio, "Minority Report," September 21-25, 1970.
[44] CHINATOWN HEALTH PROJECT, 1970.
[45] ..."Jook sing," refers to the hollow portion of the bamboo stick; "Jook kok" refers to the stiff outer portion. (Generally derogatory of American-born but now somewhat widely accepted, depending, of course, on the context in which it is used.)
[46] Chinatown Planning Council, Jimmy Lo; Chinatown Youth Council, David Ho and Wing Wong.
[47] Cattel.
[48] CHINATOWN HEALTH PROJECT, 1970.
[49] Hart, Krivatsky, and Stubee.
[50] CHINATOWN HEALTH PROJECT, 1970.
[51] Hart, Krivatsky and Stubee.
[52] GETTING TOGETHER, September-October, 1970.
[53] Hart, Krivatsky and Stubee.
[54] L. Ling-chi Wang.
[55] CHINATOWN HEALTH PROJECT, 1970
[56] Many of these participants had marched in the "Asian Coalition" on August 8, 1970, to protest the bombing of Hiroshima and Nagasaki and current atrocities.
[57] THE VILLAGE VOICE, September 3 and 10, 1970.
[58] William Hinton, FANSHEN: A DOCUMENTARY OF REVOLUTION IN A CHINESE VILLAGE, (New York: Random House, 1966).
[59] Fox Butterfield, "Orientals Find Bias Is Down Sharply In U.S.," NEW YORK TIMES, December 13, 1970.

I WOR KUEN
12 Point Platform and Program

Asian people in Amerika have been continually oppressed by the greedy, traitorous gangsters of our own communities and by the wider racist exploitative Amerikan society. We have been bombarded by the media (newspapers, T.V., radio and schools) with false ideas about how we should accept our position in this society. They have tried to brainwash us and have even coerced us into going overseas and fighting against our own people in S.E. Asia.

But, Asian Amerikans have been fighting back against the oppression of this country ever since we first tasted the bitterness of Amerika's racism and exploitation. The long and heroic history of the Asian Amerikan struggle inspired and strengthened us in our purpose. No longer can we endure these oppressive conditions. We cannot let our ancestors' struggles go down in vain. We know who are our real enemies and friends and we have found new strength for we are joining our sisters and brothers within this country and around the world to fight for freedom and justice against the rulers of this country.

We have tried the peaceful means of petition, courts, voting and even demonstrations. But our situation remained the same. We are not free.

We want to improve the living conditions of our people and are preparing to defend our communities against repression and for revolutionary armed war against the gangsters, businessmen, politicians and police. When a government oppresses the people and no longer serves the needs of the people, we have the right to abolish it and create a new one.

We are working for a world of peace, where the needs of the people come first, which is without class distinctions and is based upon the love and unity of all peoples.

The following 12 points are what we are fighting for:

1. WE WANT SELF-DETERMINATION FOR ASIAN AMERICANS.

The masses of Asian people in Amerika live in ghettoes which are like small colonies. The Amerikan capitalists continually attempt to make profit off us by trying to alter our entire way of life for their own benefit. We want liberation from this enslavement so we can determine our own destinies.

2. WE WANT SELF-DETERMINATION FOR ALL ASIANS.

Western imperialists have been invading and colonizing countries in Asia for the past 500 years. Amerikan imperialism, concentrating in Asia is now engaged in the most sadistic and genocidal war of aggression the world has ever seen. We want an immediate end to Amerikan imperialism.

3. WE WANT LIBERATION OF ALL THIRD WORLD PEOPLES AND OTHER OPPRESSED PEOPLES.

People of color, Asian, Black, Brown, Red are all fighting for liberation from Amerika's racist oppression. Millions and millions of white people are also rising up to fight our common oppressor. We recognize that only when the oppression of all people is ended can we all really be free.

4. WE WANT AN END TO MALE CHAUVINISM AND SEXUAL EXPLOITATION.

The thousands of years of oppression under feudalism and capitalism have created institutions and myths of male supremacy over women. Man must fight along with sisters in the struggle for economic and social equality and must recognize that sisters make up over half of the revolutionary army. Sisters and brothers are equals fighting for our people.

5. WE WANT COMMUNITY CONTROL OF OUR INSTITUTIONS AND LAND.

Those institutions in our communities such as the police, schools, health, housing, transportation, sanitation, anti-pollution, and welfare must be controlled by and serve the needs of our people and not be geared to the making of money. We want an end to our community being used to make profit for outsiders, such as slumlords and tourist agencies.

6. WE WANT AN EDUCATION WHICH EXPOSES THE TRUE HISTORY OF WESTERN IMPERIALISM IN ASIA AND AROUND THE WORLD: WHICH TEACHES US THE HARDSHIPS AND STRUGGLES OF OUR ANCESTORS IN THIS LAND AND WHICH REVEALS THE TRULY DECADENT EXPLOITATIVE NATURE OF AMERIKAN SOCIETY.

The Amerikan imperialists have tried to justify their world empire by covering up the inhuman deeds they perpetrated in Asia and to the rest of the Third World. They also try to brainwash us in school with racist history which does not tell of the degradation, oppression and humiliation Asians and other Third World People have been forced to suffer in Amerika. We want to learn of the heroic and inspiring struggles Asian people have conducted throughout the world as well as in Amerika.

7. WE WANT DECENT HOUSING AND HEALTH AND CHILD CARE.

The institutions of housing, health and child care are set up only to make money for landlords, doctors, hospitals and drug companies. We want housing, health and child care that gives us life and not slow death.

8. WE WANT FREEDOM FOR ALL POLITICAL PRISONERS AND ALL ASIANS.

Our Asian brothers and sisters in Amerika's racist jails should be set free for they were not tried by their peers (other Asian brothers and sisters). Political prisoners are jailed because they fought for their freedom and basic rights as human beings. They all must be set free.

9. WE WANT AN END TO THE AMERIKAN MILITARY.

The Amerikan military machine is butchering people throughout the world, especially in Asia. The end of the Amerikan military will be one of the greatest events in the history of the liberation of mankind. We want all Asian Amerikans exempt from military servitude.

10. WE WANT AN END TO RACISM.

White racism has been oppressing Third World People for the past 500 years. Although we recognize and firmly support the progressive white people in the anti-imperialist struggle, we should continue to struggle against white racism on all levels. The racism among Third World People toward each other is being broken down and a new unity is being created in our struggle against our common enemy.

11. WE WANT AN END TO THE GEOGRAPHIC BOUNDARIES OF AMERIKA.

From its beginning, Amerika has been a robber country. It stole land by the use of armed force from native Americans, Chicanos and Latinos, and other peoples. Amerika can now only maintain its present boundaries both internally and externally by the threat and use of violence. We want free passage of all people to and from Amerika. The people of the world have built Amerika, and they must now determine its destiny. Amerika has also tried to blind those who live here as to the realities of socialism by restricting information from and travel to the People's Republic of China, Cuba, Albania, North Korea, and North Vietnam. We want open boundaries and an end to immigration and emmigration harrassment.

12. WE WANT A SOCIALIST SOCIETY.

What exists in Amerika today is a society where one man in order to survive must exploit his fellow man. We want a society that works for the fulfillment of human needs. We want decent housing, health, child care, employment, sanitation and old age care. We want a society where no man or woman will die due to lack of food, medical care or housing, where each gives according to his ability and takes according to his need.

ASIAN WOMEN AS LEADERS
EDITORIAL STAFF of RODAN

American society is broken up into different levels based on economic income, education, politics, color and sex. Each level has a prescribed set of rules for action and interplay--roles that are enforced by the levels above. At the bottom of these varying gradations are women of color. Third World women face domination by both racism and sexism (discrimination based on sex). Both racism and sexism are means by which American society controls and oppresses everyone. Everyone is forced to conform to the values and roles established by the dominant group in order to "succeed." For the Asian movement to progress, it must have a clear understanding of sexism, racism, and imperialism; and deal with them simultaneously.

For Asian women in general, the stereotypes or roles have been of two major kinds: either docile, submissive Oriental dolls who will cater to the whims of any man; or the Suzie Wong, sex-pot, exotic bitch-body. Between these two are the efficient secretary, sexy stewardess, the good housekeeper and domestic, the girl any guy would like to marry.

Women in the Asian movement find that these stereotypes are still hovering over their heads. Not only these but new stereotypes, too: i.e., Asian men have tried to define for "their women" what it means to be "heavy." Men in the Asian movement also find themselves tied down to stereotypes. Perhaps they may feel that to be a MAN one must have authority and responsibility. In the same light, they will frown on women who take on a lot of responsibility (and the authority that goes along with it), labelling them as "unfeminine." Women then tend to fear this loss of "femininity" and so they do the clerical work and the cleaning up, activities for which intellect is not essential or expected. Women may also fulfill these jobs because they do them best: And why do they do them the best? Because women are never encouraged to do anything else; women's potential abilities as a leader are left untapped and undeveloped. She loses her confidence in being able to handle such responsibility.

The sisters who have achieved a position of authority in the movement are a minority and are still trapped by the stereotypes that society has created. It is a struggle for women to attain the top leadership positions. Women who "make it" into such positions have had to reject the stereotypes already imposed upon them. But because the new definition of "the Asian woman" has not yet evolved, women find themselves in a "limbo." Some find themselves being labelled as Bitches-- women who speak out loudly and strongly; who are authoritarian, who boss people around, and command some form of respect. Some must resort to being overly diligent and efficient to prove themselves as worthy of the same leadership positions as the men. Others gain respect by appearing to accomplish work in a multitude of projects but actually only completing a few tasks. And still others attain their leadership positions as token gestures. Some women can gain respect only by putting up with put-downs on other women, i.e., "you're not one of those bird-brained little girls," or "You're as strong as a man!"

Once women do get into leadership posi-

Reprinted from RODAN, Northern California Asian American Community News, Vol. I, No. 9 (April, 1971).

tions, they find that their ideas are usurped by the men, who then take credit for the idea as being their own. Women are often heard but not listened to. Many times, the woman must play her old role in order to get things done: "Oh, please, can you help me carry this. It's much too heavy for little old me..."

How can these problems be solved? People must recognize that women are half of the working force in the movement against oppression, exploitation, and imperialism. They are half of the working force in creating the new revolutionary lifestyle. Men and women in the movement must therefore begin to live the ideals and goals they are working for. To do this, they must not let chauvinist acts slide by. People cannot work together effectively if there are hidden tensions or if people let little annoyances build up inside themselves. They must deal with racism or imperialism. They must be able to develop as human beings, not subject to categorizations and stereotypes. Developing as people confident in themselves, in their ideas, they will not be afraid of criticism; they will see the need for criticism, self-criticism in order to move forward. The struggle is not men against women nor women against men, but it is a united front striving for a new society, a new way of life.

If I go forward,
Follow me.
Push me if I fall behind.
If I betray you,
If they take me,
Avenge me then in kind.

THE ASIAN AMERICAN EXPERIENCE IN THE SACRAMENTO RIVER DELTA

KEN SUYAMA

About thirty miles south of Sacramento lies a unique region--the Delta. Much like the better known Mississippi Delta, it consists of numerous waterways, rich farmlands, assorted wildlife, and sleepy river towns. The similarities between the two regions are surprisingly numerous also with respect to a more relevant issue: racism. In Mississippi, the Blacks are persecuted-- while in the Sacramento Delta Asians and Chicanos are the objects of racial prejudice.

I have lived in the Delta region for all of my nineteen years in a small river town named Courtland. When I was small, we lived in a house owned by the rancher for whom my father worked. I was too young then to even think about my racial background. Of course I realized that I was Oriental, but my friends were of all races and at the age of seven, no one can care less about the color of his skin. When I was twelve, the people my parents worked for were divorced and we had to move out. Unable to find housing, I remember my mother telling my father when he was considering one house that the people who owned it probably would not sell to a Japanese family. Later, when my father got a job as a school gardener, he expressed surprise that the state school system would hire him. These incidents did not make an impression on me at the time, but as I got older, I began to wonder why comments like that were necessary here in America.

The following are reports on three small towns in the Delta, each with an Asian population. The data gathered are mostly first-hand from interviews and personal experiences. The dates are from the "River News-Herald", a newspaper published in Rio Vista, California.

Courtland

Courtland is a small town of about 600 which was founded in 1870. It quickly became a booming rivertown due to the rich surrounding farmlands. Chinese farm labor was introduced and a Chinatown was born. One Chinatown which stood along the riverbank burned down completely in 1885 and a Chinatown was built in town. Today the same buildings stand along a gutted, narrow road and old men pass the time away while chickens and dogs scamper about. Although some Mexicans and one Chinese family live outside of "old Chinatown" today, it was originally planned to keep the minorities in Chinatown. (During World War II, anti-Japanese sentiment was extremely intense and no Japanese at all were tolerated. Even today, only one Japanese family actually

Reprinted by permission of the author. This article was a student paper submitted to the "Asian Experience in America" course at U.C. Davis, Spring, 1969.

lives within the limits of Courtland. The rest, like my family, live on farms a few miles outside of town.)

Courtland High School (which unified with Clarksburg High School to become Delta High three years ago) was comprised of about 40% Chinese, Japanese, Mexican, and Black students. However, all the teachers and school board members were white. Money was lacking and facilities were poor. It was finally condemned during my senior year and we had to move to another school. Even today, at Delta High, money, facilities and qualified teachers are scarce.

Since Courtland is predominantly white and the people are conservative, getting information was extremely difficult. The minority members of Courtland are perhaps aware of the racial forces working on them but they do not want to "make waves" for fear of censureship (which is quite real in a town of 600). Sadly enough, my parents belong in this category for they felt that it is wisest to remain quiet and stay out of trouble. The same general feeling prevails among the rest of the older generation Courtland minorities.

The youth of Courtland are of two categories: (1) Those who get an education and leave town and (2) Those who drop out of school and become farm laborers. The future of Courtland is not very bright--for without any industries besides farming to attract the young, there is no population growth. It is safe to assume that Courtland's booming era ended when the last steamboat stopped running on the river.

Locke

Locke, an all Chinese rural ghetto, was established in 1915 by "Charley" Lee Bing (the grandfather of a friend of mine) after a fire in the Chinatown of Walnut Grove left the Chinese there homeless. Locke was built practically overnight and today the same buildings still stand. Like Courtland, Locke's heyday is long gone. Once a busy town filled with wine, women, and song, today it is little more than a quaint, sleepy town that is slowly dying. Old men sit in their chairs and stare blankly out into narrow, gravel streets. Locke has had publicity brought to it in the form of newspaper and magazine write-ups that capitalized on its "quaintness". The papers did not show the living conditions of those who inhabit Locke. Houses that were cheaply built fifty years ago and which are ready to collapse are still being occupied by families. Rusting, wrecked autos and stagnant ponds lie within the backyards of many of these houses. Two of my friends whose families have played prominent roles in Locke's history live in quite comfortable homes. The housing is, however, inadequate and outdated.

I know many of the kids that live there and most of them plan on leaving as soon as they can. Of course they will come to visit, but not to live. Those who do stay, are destined to become laborers or welfare recipients, like the old men who live there now.

It is interesting to compare Locke, a rural ghetto, to Chinatown, San Francisco, an urban ghetto. In both communities, housing is poor and the youth are faced with many problems. Like Chinatown, Locke has had trouble with juvenile delinquency. Parents prefer to iron out their own problems rather than call in outside officials. Both are in a sense removed and in a world of their own, for once inside Locke, you are in an all Chinese community, a smaller version of Chinatown. Both towns capitalize on the tourist trade. Although Locke does not have the numerous shops that Chinatown has, the main businesses in Locke are restaurants and stores.

The main difference between the two

communities is their location--one is in the heart of a great city while the other is hidden along a river. Both share common problems: youth, housing, etc. but since Chinatown's location makes it hard to ignore, its problems are gradually being brought out and examined while Locke has been easy to forget.

The future of Locke is uncertain, for the youth are drawn away to the cities and all who remain are the uneducated, the old, and the people tied to Locke by property which range from a restaurant or store to a shanty behind a rusting junkpile. It is difficult for me to project into Locke's future, but I can say with reasonable certainty that it will exist on the roadmap as long as a handful of its citizens remain and operate the small businesses there. However, its significance and relevance to the rest of the world is handicapped by its location and its existence will be a limited and perhaps a digressive one.

Walnut Grove

Less than half a mile south from Locke lies Walnut Grove, a larger town of about 1,000 Caucasians, Chinese, Japanese, and Mexicans. It was founded in 1850 and like the other rivertowns, the steamboats and farming kept it alive during its early years. The Chinese, Japanese, and the Mexicans moved into the area as farm laborers during the early 1900's. The Chinese remained as laborers or opened small businesses, stores, restaurants, etc. The Japanese, who also started out as laborers gradually acquired land and became farmers. My grandfather, who was one of these men, owned a farm a few miles outside of town. Most of the Japanese, in fact, before World War II lived on nearby farms rather than in the town itself. The Chinese lived in a section of the main town until a fire forced them to move and establish Locke. The Mexicans arrived later and remained as farm laborers.

Like many rivertowns along the Sacramento and the Mississippi Rivers, Walnut Grove was and still is segregated. It lies on two sides of the river and the story of how the minorities came to live on one side is interesting. During its early days, the town was centered on the east side. At the time, Walnut Grove, except for a Chinatown, was predominately white. Gradually, as more Chinese, Japanese, Filipinos, and Mexicans came and settled on the east side, the whites moved out to the west side. Thus the whites came to live on the west side (called Clampett Tract by the local residents) while the poor whites and the minorities lived on the east side and it has remained this way.

The story of how the Japanese came to live in one section of east side is one which reflects the forces which were at work after the war. Many of the Japanese farmers (including my grandfather) lost their land during internment, and after returning from camp, they settled to one side of the railroad track that ran behind the east side. Anti-Japanese sentiment was strong and thus they had to lease instead of buy the land upon which they built their homes. These homes were built from war surplus materials and as housing, were poor. Asphalt shingles, used lumber, and corrugated steel were the common building materials. Jobs for the Japanese were scarce, many of them (like my uncles) turned to farmwork.

As the years went by, the Japanese once more became assimilated into the community and better jobs were found. Today, many of them live in quite comfortable homes but they still do not own the land. This peculiar situation of owning the house but not the land it stands on became very awkward to say the least. The land owners who live in the bay area refused to sell the land for anything less than a ridiculously high sum. The owners did nothing to improve the land and yet they continued to charge rent at an increasing rate. This state of affairs led to the recent rent strike by the Japanese, the results of which are still to be evaluated. The problem of land ownership hindered many attempts at home improvement. For example, only recently did this section of town acquire an efficient sewer system due to the problems of land ownership. (Editor's note: The East side of Walnut Grove involves three different areas owned by three different landowners. Only families of one area--the area Ken Suyama refers to in the preceding paragraph-- participated in the rent strike. The strike was finally settled in February, 1970 after two years of negotiations. The forty households--some households consist of one *Issei* man or lady--formed the Delta Estates Cooperative Society and purchased the land for $57,500.)

I must also point out that while many of the Japanese live in comfortable homes, many others live in the shoddy, old houses built after the war. My aunt and uncle, for example, still live in a house built practically overnight. These homes, for the most part, are overcrowded and unsafe. My aunt, for instance, has a television set but not hot water. The housing is inadequate and outdated but the residents seem to make the most of what they have.

The schools of Walnut Grove hold a history of their own with regard to racism. Up until the second World War, the schools were segregated: the white kids went to one school while the minority students went to another school, poorer in facilities and faculty. Both of these schoolhouses stand today and by looking and comparing the two, one can tell which housed the white kids. The idea of segregated schools seems to suggest the deep south and how strange it seems to find it so close to home.

The conditions of the present day east and west side reflects the racism involved in their development. Today, the west side boasts paved, lighted streets, nice homes, a new telephone building (completed just last year), a recent housing tract development and many other attributes common to white upper and middle class areas. The atmosphere that one gets when visiting the west side is one of exclusiveness with regard to race. In fact when my father was considering renting a house on the west side, (buying was out of the question) the owner had to first check with the rest of the community to see if they would accept a Japanese neighbor. They all approved, but having to ask in the first place reflects the racist attitudes of the community.

The east side in contrast has narrow, gravel streets, crowded old houses, no drainage system, and relatively few street lights. In the winter the streets become mud holes and during the summer are an endless source of dust. There are several small stores owned mostly by Chinese or Japanese, a run-down pool hall, and a few eating places. The entire east side looks old and tired.

The people of Walnut Grove, like the people of Courtland and Locke, are very conservative and uptight. At this point, I must give credit to those who participated in the rent strike but on the whole, many of them feel that they are comfortable, that things are all right and want to avoid trouble. When talking to them, I could not help getting the feeling that deep inside, some of them realize that certain things are not right but they feel unable to effect any changes. Tradition and fear of censureship also contribute to their feelings of helplessness.

Most of the Japanese men have jobs connected with agriculture while women who work are employed as housemaids or in canneries. My aunt works in a cannery and picks grapes while the mother of a friend of mine works as a housemaid. The Chinese either own small businesses or work in agriculture. Almost all the Filipinos and the Mexicans work as farm laborers. The Caucasians own farms or businesses and control most of the land.

Most of the youth of Walnut Grove finish at least high school and many graduate from college. The white kids usually finish college and return to take over their father's property which in most cases is a business or a farm. Some of them, of course, do not return, but the fact that family property is located in town assures the return of someone. In contrast, the minority kids whose parents own little besides their house, have little incentive to return and build up the community. Those who drop out of high school or college get drafted and usually return to some job in farming. The Orientals who finish school rarely return to Walnut Grove except for visits. Several of the Chinese kids whose parents own a business have returned to take over, but since business in Walnut Grove is slow, the number returning is diminishing. For the youth in general, there is no future in Walnut Grove, only a past. Most of them leave for Sacramento or the Bay area.

The future of Walnut Grove, though not as bleak as Locke's, is not very bright. The rich white class living there will assure its survival, however, and perhaps even hold hope for its eventual improvement.

The three towns described above are similar and yet different, but the environment is generally uniform and the people think in much the same way. The old generation remembers the heyday of these rivertowns as they slowly pass the time away. For them, these towns hold cherished memories and most of them choose to live in the Delta because of friends, home, and relatives. The generation to which my parents belong are for the most part, destined to stay in the Delta. They realize the shortcomings of living in small towns, but they have learned to live with it and are relatively content for they have more or less found what they wanted out of life in the Delta. The feeling I got from talking with most parents is that although they are content to remain in the Delta, they want something better for their children. They feel that there is not much of a future in the Delta besides farming and accordingly, their children would be better off in Sacramento or somewhere else. Even some of the parents who owned businesses or farms expressed feelings that perhaps a brighter future for their children can be found elsewhere. When asked to comment on the racism found in the Delta, most of them acknowledged its existence but hardly anybody had any solutions or even strong opinions on the matter.

The youth of the Delta in general are not very race conscious, for growing up with friends of all races makes color of skin irrelevant. However, much like youth everywhere, the kids in the Delta are awakening to contemporary racial and social problems. As more and more kids go to college and get an education, they begin to realize the problems of our society in terms of their own environment. The youth of the Delta face many frustrations and problems parallel to the ones faced by youth everywhere and yet unique due to the environmental factors involved. Nevertheless, the insulating isolation of the Delta is gradually eroding.

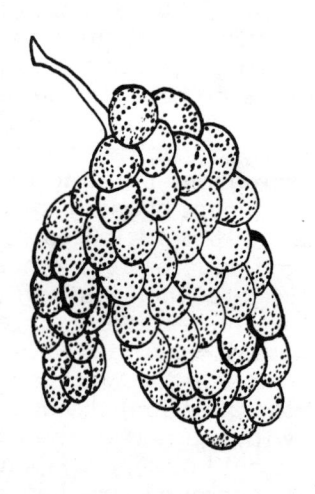

PHILIP VERA CRUZ

SOUR GRAPES: SYMBOL OF OPPRESSION

From the slum district in the near Northside across the river in Chicago, I came and lived in the shantytowns in California. Being used to city life, I thought I would go back and be with my friends again. Instead I started working in the grape vineyards in the early Spring of 1943 and stayed on until the Delano Grape Strike in September 1965.

For the first few years in California, I considered Delano as my hometown. Though I went to work in the Arvin-Lamont area for thinning plums, picking and packing grapes for different growers, cut raising grapes in Selma, cut asparagus in Byron and worked in the salmon cannery in Alaska, I always returned to Delano. There was nothing especially interesting for me about the old town. But, as I was a stranger in the state, it was the only place where I met most of my new friends.

While in town on Saturdays, I would walk across the railroad tracks to the business district comprising about two and a half blocks between the 9th and 12th avenues in Main Street. Country people coming to town once a week lined up the sidewalks and flocked into those few stores. Parents brought their children with them for new experiences in life.

There was a bank, a post office and a theater. All were small but quaint. Employees like those in the stores were lily-white, arrogant and sarcastic. You could always feel their sense of racial superiority.

Reprinted from GIDRA, November, 1970.

The Delano Theater practiced racial segregation. Seats in the northside and in the center were reserved for whites only. A small part of the theater in the southside was for the minority grape-pickers--Orientals, Mexicans, Blacks, Puerto Ricans, Arabs, etc. People didn't like or care for each other but themselves.

Even the attitude of Filipinos towards their own people was cold with indifference. An unpleasant thrill runs through my spine by just looking at acquaintances as they pass me by without the slightest sign of a friendly greeting. I had talked to them before and even ate with them at the same tables, but they moved around me as if we never met. This prevalent attitude has been hurting people. Communication among them was very slight because of strained personal relations. But, this damaging attitude is just a faint reflection of a racist community.

Filipinos in Delano have worked in the grape vineyards for a long time. Some of them told me the common practice of hiring during the depression years. They said that "in the pruning season, a grower required new employees to get to the labor camp two of three days, or more, for training without pay. In the training and practice period, those new helps were charged 75 cents for board a day. At least the black slaves in the South had their meals free. But, those Filipino trainees paid theirs while working in an agribusiness ranch for gratis. Then, after those recruits learned the job, they were paid ten to fifteen cents an hour.

In those depression years, Filipinos were blamed for taking the Anglos' jobs. Racist growers and politicians picked on the Filipino minority as an easy target for discrimination and attack. Filipinos were harassed and driven from their camps. But, the sad thing was they didn't have anywhere else to go. They were pushed to the wall and the whole town was against them. The police made false arrests and threw them in jail. In certain cases the courts imposed excessive fines. Those poor unwanted people risked their lives even just to go and buy their groceries. In those race riots staged in their camps, some were hurt and one was shot dead in bed.

While working in different labor camps in the Delano area, I observed that on Saturdays and Sundays during the harvest grape seasons, Filipinos concentrated in Chinatown west of the railroad tracks. (The habit still continued to the present.) They were not welcome in other places in town, so they didn't have any other place to go. Though their job was strenuous, it was also monotonous. After the day's work was done, a quick shower and hurried dinner, the would walk slowly by a small restaurant, or bar, and go close to those windows, screen their eyes and peep through to see who was there. They seemed to be always looking for someone, or some acquaintances or friends, but really there were no particular people in their minds.

There were many standing in groups talking about grapes--names of growers, location of ranches, acreage, wages and bonuses, hours of work, cooks, board per day, etc. Most important was how the growers were. Were they reasonable to work for? To go through that noisy crowd, one had to take a detour or get off from the sidewalk to the middle of Glenwood Street.

The whole sidewalk in Chinatown was the busiest Employment Service in all Delano. It was an open HIRING HALL for the Filipino grape pickers. A foreman or anyone ordered to get an additional worker by a grower was a dispatcher. One could be hired in Chinatown but rejected when reporting on the job, or one could be accepted and later fired without reasons. That was why even a small owner acted like a dictator. Right or wrong, or wise or foolish, his word was law. He was the supreme court whose decision was absolute.

Other Filipino brothers were quite shy. Some of them were just standing and watching the passers-by, or looking at the north end of that buzzing sidewalk then turning to the south to see what was happening. There were some squatting or sitting on copies of the DELANO RECORD on the edge of the sidewalk. Like brown owls, they turned their head from one side to the other to check if the entire flock along the block was still in peace.

Moving into the restaurants, bars, cardrooms and pool halls, I sometimes found them packed with Filipino grapepickers. For a change of environment on weekends, they didn't mind paying the high prices on the menu or for beer at the bar. Some were hungry and eating, others were just lingering around and flirting with the waitresses or girls behind the bar. Cardrooms and pool halls were usually together. Women were all over the place participating in all those activities. The whole business looked like a mixed-up affair.

One might prefer to go to the pool hall. To feel and look important, he would walk erectly, seemingly with dignity, stop at the counter and survey those Havana cigars, and would fill his shirt pocket with those long fat cigars. Lighting and smoking a big cigar in the corner of his mouth gave him the feeling and semblance of a prosperous grower, or maybe a banker. But, he could be easing his nervousness or could just be addicted to that habit-forming stimulant.

In that pool hall, sputum of tobacco juice spotted the floor along the walls, especially in the corners. Reflected against the bright light, the gamblers in the adjoining room played cards or dominos in the cloud of smoke. After inhaling that foul air for several years, each made his saddest and loneliest first, and maybe his last trip--to the tuberculosis sanitarium. Loss of precious health and lives were the unnecessary but inevitably cruel effects of forced racial segregation.

Sometimes a squabble would start in a cardroom. A guy got caught cheating in a "paralasi game" and another stood up and pulled a knife on him. The others grabbed the former to calm him down, while the latter ran quickly out through the door knocking down a few men sitting and talking on the sidewalk.

Another fight ensued, worse than the first one. At this time, more men were involved. Thinking that those fights and the confusion were giving the business a bad reputation, the proprietor called the Delano Police Department. He believed that the good relations he had with the city police would always help him with his headaches with those roughnecks.

Within a few minutes, the police arrived and mixed with the crowd. Not knowing who were fighting, they arrested people on the sidewalk at random. But, before the police left, the chief gave a stern, curt statement, "You are supposed to be in the labor camps to pick grapes when the growers need you. If you don't do that, then go back where you belong, or I'll throw you all in jail. I don't want to see you here in town again."

An elderly man, reflecting on what had happened that evening remarked, "All these people have been moving from one place to the other. Wherever I went, there was a place for Filipinos to gather together and just be among themselves. Like any other rendezvous of our people (a slum district), Chinatown in Delano is a hobos' paradise. Unfortunately, most Filipino community leaders have taken advantage of this situation. They choose to live on the rackets--bars for the disgusted and despondent, gambling for the unjust and greedy, and dance halls for the lonely and unhappy. These businesses are the sources of easy but questionable money. But, since they are at the mercy of the city council, police and sheriff department, the proprietors align themselves with them and exploit the minorities. They must make money to stay in the rackets. They would sell a guy for a few dollars because they themselves have no guiding principles." As the growers control the town, so do these leaders take the employers' side in a labor dispute with management.

The next morning, the people in Chinatown went to work for the first picking of the seedless Thompson grapes. With many years of experience, they know grapes. They complained that the bunches were too green. But the growers gave the orders, through their ranch managers and foremen, to pick and pack more for the "high prices in the market." The workers were bothered with their conscience but could not use their own judgment. So, they worked as ordered.

In the afternoon, an inspector went to a packing house and tested the packed grapes. He found the content deficient and told the owners to stop the picking.

The whole crew was ordered to repack the green grapes, without pay. While all the workers were busy repacking, the inspector was closely watching them. But when he went away, the big grower himself was there and told them to load those sour grapes, first into the boxcar with the repacked boxes on top. This is one of the magic tricks of the growers in the table-grape industry.

With brands from other ranches, the Delano Sour Grapes were sent as delicacies to the metropolis of the United States. The uniform bunches and solid berries, packed beautifully, could have been the choice grapes of the world if the growers had waited just a few more days for Nature to sweeten the fruit.

Premature harvest in the grape industry has been the common practice of the family farm and agri-business. It is caused by cutthroat competition tainted with deceit and unsatisfied personal greed. Customers spend their money for sour grapes not fit to eat. The orders from the growers overpower the conscience and decency of workers to do what is right in their work.

Those accumulated profits of agribusiness are generating economic power for the oppression and enslavement of farm workers. They are used to influence legislation to enhance agri-business interests in an ever expanding growth. They perpetuate poverty and shantytowns located in the richest states of the nation. For the children, living in those filthy shacks is a disaster to their welfare and future. Conscience and justice are foreign to the ruthless nature of agri-business. Equipped with the right to property, agri-business is turning the United States into a fascist state. Excessive expansion and oppressive power of agri-business must be checked as a protection for the people's rights.

AN INTERVIEW WITH
Philip Vera Cruz

EDITORIAL BOARD
DELANO, JUNE, 1971

BOARD OF DIRECTORS AND VICE-PRESIDENT, UNITED FARM WORKERS ORGANIZING COMMITTEE, A.F.L.-C.I.O.

VERA CRUZ: The farm workers today: I think the way the publicity runs, it looks that people who are now in the Movement have started and accomplished everything. But I don't think that's the truth. It started from the beginning and every little principle has been fought. It was really the Filipinos and the Mexicans who started to build it in Coachella Valley. But the fact was that most of the foremen were Filipinos, and then the crews were mixed workers, Filipinos and Mexicans. Then they staged a strike there, because Secretary of Labor Willard Wirtz put up the criteria of $1.04 an hour to be met by the growers who applied for braceros in Mexico. And so the local workers, including the Filipinos themselves, thought that it was unfair for them to receive $1.20 an hour while the new guys from across the border would be paid $1.04 an hour. That triggered the strike. Well, in Coachella they paid $1.04 an hour because the location was such that there was no, even now there is no, stable work force. But when that one was finished, and they moved to the Arvin-Lamont area and came to the Delano area, where you have a stable force of workers, because they live here. And so the advantage is to get the first price in the market which is high. So they paid the 10¢ more in wages, but the union didn't get the contract. So when they came over here the growers refused to give them 10¢ more because they thought that the people would work anyway-- because it had been done during the past. On September 8, the Filipinos met in the Filipino hall and they wanted $1.04 an hour. The growers rejected it so they went on strike. Officially it was the Filipinos who declared the strike. After 8 days Cesar Chavez and his union joined the strike, but while we were striking together, we were still in separate organizations. The National Farm Workers Organization--that was Cesar's organization.

The Agricultural Workers of the National Committee, A.F.L.-C.I.O. (A.W.O.C.), was the one that really declared the strike and to which the Filipinos belonged. Some unforeseen events came in; the Teamsters Union came into A.W.O.C. and they said that they would like to help the farm workers organize their own union. But when the farm workers became organized, they were in competition with us. That happened during the Di Gorgio campaign. But the Teamsters Union was trying to sign contracts that were really not getting much benefit. And that's why the growers liked the Teamsters Union because they spend less. But then we did not want to give it up. We claimed that it was our right to organize the farm workers, and we claimed that it was out of their jurisdiction. And so the fight went on and we beat them here. Now it reoccurred in the Salinas Valley. Because while we were still trying to boycott and sign the grape growers, they already had been organizing in the Salinas and Santa Maria Valley. So because of the threat of the Teamsters Union, we merged into one--and that's the United Farm Workers Organizing Committee. That's why we are in one union now.

Now I would like to give you the differences that I see between the A.W.O.C. and the N.F.W.O.A., Cesar's organization. Now in the A.W.O.C., it is a straight labor organization. But in the N.F.W.O.A., it's a mixture of many things--like the students and the churches are involved; C.O.R.E.; the people who are going to the South and participated there in civil rights; the Peace Corps; and all those things. So we have all kinds of people. To tell you frankly, I believe that the other side has even more motivation, has given even more inspiration. There were certain other goals beyond money. They were fighting really for the rights of people and the dignity of human beings. And so that's why those eight years that they had are being expanded as we get more contacts because a lot of people are talking to us. So education is a two-way street. While we try to give information about our struggle and how we live on farms to others, why they come over here also, and educated us in their own way. So now the union has gone beyond the dollars and cents, prices as the standards of progress. I think the dollars and cents are only incidents that have come into a struggle for livelihood. Because of the involvement of many people, the goals of the union have also expanded--the union is trying to build one big co-operative. Then under the big co-operative, it will have multiple services, like cleaning, and then there could be a bank. We have to get a plan for health and welfare and even the legal services, and many others that could be done.

QUESTION: How long have you had the idea of a co-op...since the beginning of the union?

VERA CRUZ: I think they (N.F.W.A.) even had it before the merger, and after the merger we adopted the project of the union. Really that one there (the union headquarters known as 40 acres) is not really a co-op. It's only used by the gasoline station. We have not sold any shares yet.

QUESTION: Are you going to sell only to the workers?

VERA CRUZ: Yeah, the workers. 'Course we have our credit union. And the workers are encouraged to save their money, like putting in $5 a share. Then we charge them 25¢ more in the beginning for stamps and office things. When he puts his money there, it grows at 1% interest, and then when he borrows, it also charges 1%. So the idea is to get the people's money and loan it to people who need the money.

QUESTION: What areas in the state are you going to have these services available?

VERA CRUZ: Well, we've got to start in Delano. And then, we've got to build them around, where other farm workers are, because it would be impossible for them to come in. Those are the hopes of the plan that the union is trying to achieve. The most important thing is that the farm workers will be organized. That's the only way where you could make changes. Again, Cesar had been mentioning that the union should have land. If the union would acquire land, and then the workers would work on it, the ownership will be collective. So when you put up a co-op, it is not limited to retirement villages alone. The retirement village is housing, but it will have some assets, but the difference is that the ownership will be collective. I think that the seed of socialism is being planted--and that's why I'm interested.

QUESTION: Do you expect any sort of repression against implementing your socialist model of the co-op? Do you expect the government and the growers to really come down on you?

VERA CRUZ: Oh yes, they will fight us. But in the beginning we have to fight them. Everything that you gain, you've got to fight for it. That was one big mistake that we made in the beginning. These are different categories of conflict. Of course the capitalists are your enemies. Capitalism cannot exist without exploitation, and you know exploitation is not fair; it's unjust. So if you are an honest man, then you don't like it. The conflicts are inside...are personal things. In an organization, you have honest people and opportunists. Right here in my experience in organizing you've got to fight within and without. There are conflicts of personalities, and ambitions, and ideas that you've got to start fighting in the beginning. Of course there are a lot of considerations that you've got to make. For instance if you fight within the organization in the beginning and try to start this other (the boycott), then you don't have a union. I mentioned this because we will be attempting to organize the young people, and we got to keep it in the right direction.

QUESTION: How is the union organized--the relationship of the leadership to the followers? Who initiates the programs? Do the programs start from the people, or do they start from the leadership?

VERA CRUZ: We are kind of fishing. Good leadership listens. And that's why Cesar is smart, because he listens. Then there is the tendency that when you become too popular and you think you are somebody, you are still the same shit, you know. But you feel kind of bigger and bigger. That happens to some guys, and then they lose contact of the people. And then they cannot communicate with them anymore.

QUESTION: How do you decide on what tactics to use?

VERA CRUZ: You've got to vote for it. You've got to tell them that they should not be so offended in being criticized, because if you don't criticize others' ideas, then how could you improve? Now I say what I think is right, but then, I'm not the judge. So if we try to hear from each others' viewpoints, we will arrive to a better conclusion. But you've got to be sure that they understand that within the system you've got no way out. They find out that the strike is going on, and the boycott is effective; now they are trying to legislate the state and federal laws. This government is supposed to be a democratic form of government--a representative form of government, but in fact it's not. Whether you are going to elect a Democrat or a Republican, there is no difference, because he will do the same bullshit.

  For example, in the state of Idaho, now they require that the workers are working for 6 days before they are able to be a striker. Then nobody would help us. It would be illegal. Not only that but during the harvest season, to be able to do that, it doesn't take very long to harvest the crops, for grapes, two weeks. Another example is that Cory Bill, State of California, which is trying to restrict boycotting.* They had a hearing in Sacramento and they have some powerful people. It's not far-fetched at all. The reason why they could do that is because the people in the state legislature and in Congress are elected because of the money big companies and corporations give them. Everybody is trying to get his share of the loot that they robbed from the people. So they don't give a shit. They can make a bill and pass it overnight because

---

*Editor's note: The Cory Bill was defeated, largely because a major campaign and publicity drew widespread support for the U.F.W.O.C. cause.

they are not protecting the people, but they are protecting business. Automation will accelerate the changes. Automation is here right now and there is a sociologist that I have read, Daniel Moynihan, offering a guaranteed wage. It's not a matter of charity, but a matter of right. He offered $3200 a year for four. Of course that's not enough. Even if the government will appropriate some money as a guaranteed wage, it will always be too little. In the problem of automation--I believe in automation--and then let the people be employed for social services, and further their studies, get educated, so they will know better how to live together. Then the ownership has to be changed. All the system's got to be changed--and it's got to be socialism because if you stick to private enterprise, private enterprise will always claim all the production. And he won't let it go until he gets the profits. Now that way, the production will always be here on the profits instead of what the people need. So there is always misappropriation--others will be wealthy, and too many people will be without. And they will be hungry, and those are the causes of problems.

QUESTION: You talked about youth organizing before. What sort of plans do you have for that area?

VERA CRUZ: I feel that the Asians don't have the number for the pressure like the blacks and the Mexicans. So we got to put the Asians together. It would be easier for us because we are pretty close together. You look like one another, you cannot tell really which one is which. To start with that's a good thing. But we cannot win alone, and so we got to ally ourselves and the other minorities and also with the Anglos who are really in sympathy with our ideas.

I feel that the young people are very revolutionary. The people who are coming are mostly coming from the middle class and these young people I think are disappointed because what they learn in school really does not fit what is around outside. They think that they're not getting the real information about what is going on. It disturbs them. It has a lot to do with their accumulation of property; the middle class... they got their good homes, conveniences, they got money invested, their folks are professionals, and so on. And so they are not worried about the next day. They always got something to eat. They have their pride to sustain them.

QUESTION: What about with Asian people?

VERA CRUZ: Asians...they're just as bad as the others. Take for instance the business people (Asian business people). They're just as conservative as the Anglos. And I guess there is some reason for that. They are in the minority and it scares them to death. If they involve themselves with this kind of struggle, then they might lose all they got. So they will be reduced to working people. And they don't want to lose that advantage.

QUESTION: You said that some of the Anglo young children have rebelled against their parents, against all the materials goods they have. Do you see the same things happening for Asians?

VERA CRUZ: I think so too. They're also rebelling, but you see Mama is not so rich. Maybe in the middle class, but she's not too rich. Some have really got wealth; very few. They (the kids) don't fight them (their parents) but they do what they want. I find that among the Chinese and the Japanese and also some Filipinos. However, the parents of young Filipinos today are not like the Japanese and Chinese. The Japanese and Chinese got some kind of security. They have gone into business and they become professionals. So the young people are not very worried much about being kicked out. But for the Filipino it's going to have bad effects. The parents are poor. And they got a helluva time to get him through college. And so if he joins the demonstration and is jailed, he will get hell at home. But the Japanese and Chinese young people are more free because if Mama gives hell, they (kids) say, well, they don't want me, I'll go out, and then Mama will call him back anyway. And Mama is not so hard up. That is the difference.

Asians are like any other people. What makes them rebel is that they feel repressed, and they're not getting the rights they hope to have. Another thing is they also have their own ideas--their eyes are open wide, and they understand the idea of this parent/child conflict today, and the fact that China is the real, unquestionable power in Asia. I think they feel stronger also. There's a great difference between belonging to a little country and a big one, because Asia someday, one by one or in groups, the others will follow in line. And it's just a matter of time...

QUESTION: Before all the Asian countries are strong.

VERA CRUZ: Yeah, I mean when they will be on the same system. Even today I think the Filipinos are rebelling because of that knowledge they got. I think that other countries will not really risk a dangerous war when China is ready because they will know better then. The Asiatics have been insulted, since they were here. They also try to place the Asians as dumb-bells, and imitating and cannot figure out anything. But the atomic bomb was created by China. They did not steal any goddamn secrets from the U.S. like Russia. They have their own intellectuals. As long as there are problems, there is somebody to solve them.

QUESTION: How are relations between the Chicanos and Filipinos?

VERA CRUZ: I think the more sensible ones will put the union together; the others are irresponsible; they're not disciplined. The Filipinos and the Mexicans...you got to get the other groups, too! We will not have any power, not enough to effect some kind of changes. That's why I would like to have the Asians work together to begin with.

QUESTION: How do the Filipinos here get along with the Filipinos in the city?

VERA CRUZ: It looks like they know each other exactly. They have been a long time and they have been also moving from the city to the farm, from the farm to the city; so they're pretty well acquainted now. It's not like in the beginning.

QUESTION: Do you think the problems are the same?

VERA CRUZ: They're identical. That's why you can connect the city people and the farm people, because the principles are the same. For instance, in the farms you get injunctions, and that is to prohibit you from picketing. Now you're fighting for your freedom of speech and information (in the cities). In both cases they are fighting for their own rights, which are fundamentally the same. And so the poor...you can connect the two. You isolate one side, then the other one will be powerless. When you put them together, it's a great power, and you apply that pressure to change things. You're working in an alliance with the other groups, like the middle class. You see, there are two revolutions today in the U.S. One is coming from the bottom, the other one is coming from the middle class. The middle class really is the greatest resistance to progress because it has votes that determine the officials in the state to the federal level. You can look back in history that the significant leaders who have made changes in the world have been middle class. There are reasons for that--they are educated and are well-equipped for leadership. They are not afraid of economic

QUESTION: shortcoming, because they've got money. When these guys are educated, they don't care how many billions the other guys got, but they think that their programs are superior to those people; so when they stand up, they are backed up by the people. That's where leadership comes in.

QUESTION: What would you include as part of the middle class revolution--what sort of movements are there?

VERA CRUZ: They're coming to the students and the unions and some political organizations. You've got the socialists, communists, and students. Then you have also some changes in the churches. The movement tends to be split, and the progressive side seems to be gaining more everyday. I think the changes will be faster, because once you start a movement, the momentum, the inertia is always operating, and it's pretty hard to stop it. You cannot even stop it. One individual cannot stop it. You stop now, and somebody picks it up, and it keeps going.

INTERNATIONAL HOTEL

Chinatown and Manilatown occupy seventy square bocks in North San Francisco. To the north are the gaudy nightclubs of North Beach, to the south and east stand the buildings of San Francisco's financial district, and to the west are the plush hotels of Nob Hill. The crowded, shabby streets of Chinatown and Manilatown stand in sharp contrast to the affluent surroundings.

The Chinatown-Manilatown area has the highest population density of elderly persons in the nation. The overcrowding and poverty result in the highest tuberculosis and suicide rate in the nation. Every year 6,000 newly arrived immigrants take up residence in the Chinatown ghetto adding to the problems.

Evicted

In December 1968 residents of the International Hotel, one of the few low-income housing facilities in the area, were told to vacate the hotel immiediately so that a parking lot could be built on the site. Protests and demonstrations were mounted in the community in an effort to save the hoetl. Findally the owner of the hotel, Milton Meyer, Inc., agreed to lease the hotel to the United Filipino Association (UFA).

The lease, however, was never signed. The night before the signing of the lease was to take place, a mysterious fire broke out in the hotel. Three tenants were killed in the blaze that completely destroyed the north wing of the building. Lease negotiations were broken off. Evidence pointed to arson as the cause. However, both Milton Meyer, Inc., and city officials claimed the fire was an accident.

Immediately after the fire, the city moved to condemn the building. They offered to tear the building down for Milton Meyer, Inc., at no cost. Hotel tenants and the United Filipino Association decided to fight the condemnation. Picket lines appeared in front of city hall and the offices of Milton Meyer, Inc.. UFA lawyers filed a suit against Milton Meyer, Inc., charging that the company was negligent in its operation of the hotel.

Reprinted from PAUNAWA, October, 1970.

Hassled

Meanwhile, hotel residents were harassed and intimidated. Kitchen facilities were locked up. Tenants often found themselves without electricity. Sanitary facilities were not maintained. The city relocation agency began to displace tenants out of the hotel. Mr. Wing Lew, a resident of the hotel for twenty years, was forcibly moved to another hotel three blocks away. He struggled back despite the fact that he could barely walk. Unfortunately strained from the constant harassment, some tenants sought other housing.

The picketing and the campaign to mount public opinion against Milton Meyer, Inc., began to have its effect. In the face of declining business and mounting public support for the UFA campaign to save the hotel, Milton Meyer, Inc., agreed in July, 1969, to lease the hotel to UFA for two years, with a third year optional.

However, the signing of the lease was not a total victory for the UFA. Under the new lease the United Filipino Association agreed to pay rent of $40,000 per year. In addition, the UFA would pay property taxes on the building which amount to around $25,000 per year.

The UFA found itself in possession of a dilapidated, unsanitary, unsafe building. In the course of time, tenants of the hotel and Asian students began to rebuild. The volunteers came from as far away as Los Angeles and New York to make the hotel a decent, low-cost dwelling. The first step was to repair the fire ravaged North wing at a cost of $80,000. The cost would have been considerably higher if much of the work had not been done by student and community volunteers.

Donations of furniture, paint, and building materials together with an abundance of manpower brought about the change. What was once a run-down hotel is now a real home for the elderly Filipino and Chinese residents. Cracks and holes were patched, walls were repainted, and old furniture was repaired or replaced. Often on Saturdays, the hotel was jammed with volunteer workers. As rooms were renovated, people moved into the storefronts on the ground floor. Most of the spaces were sub-leased to service-oriented programs. They sought to serve the needs of the community. The Asian Community Center provides a supplemental food program for expectant mothers with small children. In addition, they have a free film every weekend for the elderly in the community. Also housed in the building is the Chinatown Youth Council, an organization that attempts to serve the needs of street kids.

The services offered at the International Hotel and the entire block have achieved recognition in the community to help overcome the tremendous problems which plague it.

Recreation programs were created in the hotel. Excursions outside the community, monthly dinners, weekly brunches, and a few other successful programs were instituted by the workers to reach out to the tenants. The tenants themselves have taken the responsibility of running many of the programs.

Unity

The generation gap between young workers and the elderly has been bridged through their interaction at these recreation events. Also, tenant participation in the rebuilding of the hotel has given strength and spirit to the whole hotel community.

All in all, the underlying bond between the tenant and the worker is their common goal: to build a new way of life, and a new home.

The strength behind the hotel is the people who are served. They come not only from the Chinatown-Manilatown community, but from as far away as New York and Hong Kong. In the coming struggle, they along with the tenants of the International Hotel will deal decisively with the owner. Then, hopefully, he will understand that human rights are more important than property rights.

FILIPINOS: A FAST GROWING U.S. MINORITY
-- PHILIPPINES REVOLUTION

On March 5th of this year the NEW YORK TIMES carried a fairly long article on Filipinos written by Earl Caldwell. The story concerned the increase in Filipino immigration in recent years and some descriptions of the growing Filipino "minority" community. The title is FILIPINOS: A FAST GROWING MINORITY and the basic contents run as follows:

The Filipinos since the new immigration law of 1965, have jumped to second rank in total number of entries into the U.S., only slightly behind the Mexican people. In 1965, Filipino immigration was 2,545, whereas in 1970, 25,417 Filipinos entered this country. In San Francisco, Filipinos make up the fastest growing minority. The number of Filipinos has doubled in the last five years bringing the total number to over 20,000; in Portland, Oregon the number has gone from 1,000 in 1965 to over 3,000 in 1970. In New York, as well as San Francisco, clusters of Filipino restaurants and grocery stores are becoming a more and more common sight. In addition, movie houses featuring films in Tagalog can be found in the Mission District of San Francisco.

In the Philippines, the economic and political situation is becoming more unstable. Professionally-trained people have very few opportunities for employment at home. The visa costs for immigration to the U.S. is about $1,000 and professionals are given first preference.

Consequently, today the majority of Filipino immigrants are doctors, lawyers, engineers, teachers, nurses, and other professionals. They are "well educated" and speak English. This is in sharp contrast to the Filipino immigrants of former times who were illiterate, unaccustomed to American ways and worked as servants and farm laborers.

However, the most recent newcomers, despite their professional education in the Philippines, are finding difficulty in getting jobs that suit their occupational and educational levels. But the Filipinos 'adapt very well' and commonly accept jobs outside their profession. So Filipino lawyers work as clerks; teachers as secretaries; dentists as aides; engineers as mechanics; and many professionals work also as laborers and janitors. But Filipinos interviewed agree that accepting such jobs here in America is still financially better than working within their professions back home in the Philippines. Despite the financial benefits in the U.S., some Filipinos for social reasons would prefer to live and work in the Philippines, but they will not return home for economic reasons.

Filipinos interviewed had divided opinions as to whether or not they were discriminated against. But the article concludes by suggesting that the inability of Filipinos to find jobs can be accounted for by a combination of racial prejudice and the worsening economic situation in the U.S.

Caldwell's article does not describe accurately the situation of Filipinos. It contains many half-truths, many things are stated out of context and many questions that should have been asked were never asked or answered. Consequently, the article is generally misleading and inaccurate.

Romantic Descriptions

To begin with, the Mission District of San Francisco is described in "romantic" terms. Like some "ideal community" complete with Filipino movies! Filipinos and Chicanos who live in the Mission District do not own their homes; they all rent from landlords they have never seen. A five-room flat rents for about $140 to $150 a month; anything cheaper is not fit to live in. Unemployment of the men is common; many mothers hold down jobs for the family's survival. Filipino mothers commonly work as salesgirls in Woolworth, Emporium and other Market St. stores, many also work in the American Can Factory and as nurses' aides, etc. Mission district schools have some of the highest truancy rates in the city, mainly because the schools are con-

Reprinted from KALAYAAN INTERNATIONAL, Vol. 1, No. 1 (June, 1971).

Miss Asuncion Guevara, Candidate for 1930 Rizal Day Contest, San Francisco Calif. Under the Auspices of Associated Filipino Organisations. Billones photo.

trolled by racist and incompetent people. Outside of this, there are few activities available for kids other than pool halls and "hard drugs." So the fact that some films in Tagalog are shown in the community doesn't tell very much of the story.

Caldwell also fails to describe accurately the situation under which the Filipinos come to this country. Many have to sell their homes and land and borrow from relatives in order to get the money for visa and transportation expenses. Young men often come on "visitors" visas, hoping to get them transferred to immigrant visas once they get here, which is almost impossible. Meanwhile the parents have mortgaged what little they have to provide money for the trip. The travel agents in the Philippines, as well as the government and educational system, is directly responsible for creating a false image of America as the land of "endless opportunity and harmony". Filipinos, when they arrive, find that along with the higher wages is a high cost of living they have never fully imagined. Ideas of easily saving money and someday returning home rich quickly vanish and are replaced by just trying to make ends meet and scrimping to send even small amounts of money back home.

Caldwell's article doesn't even begin to describe the dilemma which faces most Filipinos who have recently come to America. The anxiety of feeling lonely here and wanting very much to return home yet feeling there are even less opportunities back home for a decent livelihood. Feeling inadequate to fully understand the social forces shaking America and yet every year they remain here, they become less capable of understanding the social forces changing their homeland. For many, the question of returning home has become simply a financial impossibility. But for most, it is a combination of financial costs and feeling anxiety at not being able to fulfill the "expectations" of the people back home.

Racist Stereotypes

The facts that Caldwell states in comparing former Filipino immigrants to the more recent immigrants contain some truth. However, by stating these facts without any further explanations, he only fosters the racist stereotypes that exist about the first groups of Filipinos that were brought to America and Hawaii. The fact that Filipinos were even allowed to enter the U.S. and Hawaii was only because they were a convenient source of cheap labor for American capitalists, most especially the Sugar Trust barons of Hawaii and California. After American colonization, the expansion of tobacco plantations in the Ilocos region of Luzon began to cause serious dislocation of small farm settlements and the rural population. The fact that there were few educational facilities built either by the Spanish or the American colonials accounts for why many were illiterate. For most of these young peasants, the first film they ever saw was American propaganda inviting them to work in the fields of Hawaii and California and see America (in that order). Of course, they had to become "indentured laborers" and sign contracts for a number of years before being allowed to embark for the "land of the free, home of the brave." Once here, they were cruelly exploited, making their strong desires for a decent life seem day by day more impossible. Their dreams of self-advancement and education faded after years of blatant racial oppression and discrimination. These men were the victims of American colonialism and once they were here, they became victims of capitalist exploitation and white racism--in such a hostile environment they fought and survived. Survival is an act of heroism in certain social systems (like America).

The names and deeds of most of these "first Filipinos" are forgotten, but we should never let ourselves forget the harsh conditions they faced or the struggles they waged for survival. There is much to learn from their experiences and example the fundamental nature of American society HAS NOT CHANGED since the 1930's and 40's. The system is still essentially exploitative and oppressive in nature, especially to non-whites. Therefore, to simply state that Filipino immigrants in the past were poor, illiterate, unaccustomed to American ways and worked as farm laborers and household servants says nothing about "why" or "how" such a situation developed. Consequently, it implies something negative about Filipinos rather than something negative about American society. For this reason, it is racist.

In the article, Earl Caldwell quotes many people. As the author, he chooses what quotes to include and in what order, so as to create the tone of the article. We have disagreements not only with the overall tone of the article but also with some of the people who were quoted in it.

"Green Pastures"

Mrs. Nicanor, from the New York area says, "Here in America, we've found a greener pasture." If this Filipina has found a "greener pasture" in the New York state, she should write and tell us exactly where it is because many Filipinos haven't come across it yet, to say nothing of the millions of blacks and Puerto Rican people who are trying to live in that area.

A Catholic priest from San Francisco says, "They (Filipinos) adapt very well. If they have to work as janitors, they can do it--and they will do it very well." Obviously this priest has never questioned himself at any length on why engineers, teachers, dentists, etc. should be asked to work as janitors. What do Filipinos adapt very well to? To the American ethic of "survival of the fittest"--with advantages given to the white people? Is it a sign of high moral character that Filipinos who have spent many years and much money in educating themselves should humbly accept the obstacles placed in the way of their practicing their professions here in America? Or is it that America has reached such a high degree of "civilization" that teachers, engineers and nurses are in excess because all the basic needs of the people have been met? (Bullshit).

It is clear that those who encourage acceptance and meekness in the face of injustice are only serving to perpetuate the injustice. The only appropriate response to injustice is organized resistance. To say that the Filipino people "adapt very well" to the injustice is not only deceptive but irresponsible, especially coming from a person who is in a position to influence many people.

Furthermore, there are many young priests and ministers who, through their words and actions, are saying that not to encourage the people to fight against injustice is unchristian. It seems strange that Earl Caldwell could not find one of these men to interview.

Mr. Caldwell also quotes Jose Arcega as saying there is a "surplus of professionals" in the Philippines. If Mr. Arcega's statement was said in a different way, it would be more correct, that is, the Philippines is an underdeveloped country which does not have the industrial or technological base to support a large number of highly trained people. Consequently many "professionals" lack the opportunities to work in their own country and seek employment in the highly developed countries. Stated in this way we begin to get to the root of the problem which Caldwell's article does not even begin to hint at.

Root of the Problem

Why the influx of highly trained Filipinos to the U.S. when there is such a greater need for them at home? Why are the people with the knowledge and education capable of assisting the transformation of Philippine society encouraged to leave the country? Basically, what accounts for the inability of the Philippines to develop and fully utilize its resources and highly trained people?

Underdevelopment of a country is a condition which is created and perpetuated by the control of foreign investment from the advanced industrial countries over the direction and development of the economies of the underdeveloped countries. It means that the Philippines for over 50 years and up till today has served mainly as a source of raw materials and cheap labor. The profits from this has not in the past and does not today go into developing national industry or manufacture, but rather, most of it leaves the country and is reflected in Wall Street dividends and Swiss bank accounts. Most of the industries that do exist are controlled by foreign capitalists and are in extract material production for export. Meanwhile the Philippines imports even the most basic items for domestic consumption. These are items that could be easily produced by Filipinos given a restructuring of power relations within the society and a rational utilization of the resources and talents of the Philippines and the Filipino people.

Only a country whose government does not have as its first priority the educational development and physical well-being of its people cannot utilize all the teachers, doctors and nurses. A country whose "leaders" have been consistently trained to be subservient to the interests of foreign capitalists never truly assists the development of a strong independent national economy. And it is only when a country is too bankrupt and corrupt to build irrigation systems and hydro-electric power plants and housing that it sends away its chemists and engineers to other countries.

The question is never asked: Why are there no job opportunities in the Philippines? Why is the economy so bankrupt? Why is the political situation so volatile? The answer is never forthcoming...imperialism. Imperialism is not simply a word, it is a real force in the world today. A force that systematically creates poverty and perpetuates underdevelopment in the majority of nations within the world. It is a force that tries to convince people of these countries that their poverty is natural and inherent in their "cultural backwardness." However, imperialism is being challenged all over the world by another force stronger than itself-- national democratic revolutions. The Philippines is no exception. In the Philippines, the major imperialist power has always been the United States. The amount of wealth extracted from the Philippines by the U.S. monopoly capitalist business interests is so massive it has never been fully calculated. We can never understand our experience as Filipinos in America apart from understanding the nature of imperialism. The first wave of Filipinos came here because America colonized the Philippines and needed cheap labor in the farm valleys of California and in the sugar cane fields of Hawaii. The second major wave were Filipinos serving in the U.S. Navy and Army, mostly as cooks and servants to officers. The third major wave are professionals displaced by a corrupt and underdeveloped national economy at home. It is clear that the U.S. colonial and imperialist relationship with the Philippines is closely connected to the existence of a Filipino minority in this country, the conditions by which they live once they arrive here.

Finally, the fact that so many Filipinos are coming to this country in the last few years is not simply because of a new U.S. immigration law. It is misleading for Caldwell to look at the arrival of large numbers of Filipinos and ask nothing about the conditions they are leaving behind them at home. To ask nothing about the forces in the Philippines that are calling for fundamental changes in the society. To ask nothing about the future of the Philippines or how basic changes there would affect the Filipino minority here. How many will return? Under what conditions? If there is a successful revolution and the long hard struggle begins to develop an independent, truly democratic Philippines, without corruption and exploitation, how many doctors, teachers, engineers, chemists, laborers will ask to be repatriated to their homeland? Or what will the effect of a growing revolution in the Philippines have on how Filipinos identify themselves here in this country? The article creates a mistaken impression that Filipinos once they arrive here consider themselves as an "American minority." It underestimates the relation between Filipinos who have emigrated and their lifelong relationship to the Philippines. Mr. Caldwell fails to realize that even after 20 years of living here and even having children here, most Filipinos still see themselves as being Filipinos. The notion of being an "American minority" is always a secondary aspect of their identity. Therefore, to look at thousands and thousands of newly arrived Filipinos and not examine Philippine society is a serious mistake.

We feel Earl Caldwell is friendly to the Filipino people and he was well meaning in his article. However, his perspective on the subject of Filipinos is inaccurate and limited. We criticize some of his basic assumptions and his basic hypothesis. The total effect of his article is to reinforce the idea of America as a refuge for "displaced" people--the Statue of Liberty image. This seriously clouds the fact that the American Dream is now and always has been a myth.

SAVE KALAMA VALLEY—HAWAII

On October 31, 1968, a hearing was held by the City and County Planning Commission on rezoning Kalama Valley and Queen's Beach, referred to as Maunalua. Bishop Estate holds title to the land and has leased it to the Kaiser Hawaii-Kai Development Company. Kaiser Hawaii-Kai asked for the restricted Residential area to Class A, A-1, and AA Residential. Over 800 acres of land were involved. Residents of Kalama Valley had no knowledge of this hearing and none of them attended. The land was zoned according to Kaiser Hawaii-Kai's request.

As late as March 1970, 67 families lived in the Valley, among them were Hawaiians, part-Hawaiians, Portuguese, and Japanese. There was strong sentiment against the rezoning and planned eviction of residents from the Valley, but little hope or organizational effort to fight the Bishop Estate. The deadline for clearing residents out of the Valley was set for June 30, 1970, by the Estate. Those who could afford to, moved out. Others, who could not afford to move, were forced into substandard and overcrowded homes. Some of those who moved were forced to liquidate their pig farms for want of suitable land. Several families stayed.

On July 1st, Hawaii-Kai bulldozers appeared in the Valley and started to knock down homes on order of Bishop Estate Officials. An attempt was made by Kokua Kalama to save these homes from destruction. The people were arrested and charged with trespassing by the Estate. The same thing was repeated on July 10th, and seven persons were arrested. The bulldozing came to a halt. Fires broke out in the Valley for several nights after this. The psychological effect of the bulldozing and fires caused some residents to flee the Valley.

Kokua Kalama (community organization) organized a tour of the Valley to get more of the community aware of what was happening there and to build a base of support for the residents' struggle. Two thousand people made the tour on September 7th, along with representatives from the media. Concern over the issue mounted. A rally was held at the State Capital on October 28. Almost a thousand people unanimously adopted the following statement:

We demand that the development planned for Kalama Valley by the Hawaii-Kai Corporation with the cooperation of the Bishop Estate be brought to a complete and permanent halt. We want that land returned to the local residents and rezoned to agricultural use. We want the residents in the Valley given the right to remain.

We want those families already evicted to have the right to return. Any improvements made on the Valley should be done in cooperation with these families and for their benefit. We know the Bishop Estate can afford these improvements. We also believe that in so doing, the Bishop Estate will fulfill its pledge to help the Hawaiians and at the same time, help itself. We believe our demand is reasonable and just.

The Kalama Valley-Queen's Beach complex is planned for 30,000 people--half tourist and the other half high income people. Ten hotels, a golf course, high rise apartments, low rise apartments, shopping facilities, and homes are planned for Kalama.

There is a lot at stake in Kalama Valley for the farmers, Hawaiians, local people, and the environment. What is happening to Kalama is a symptom of the disease which is ravaging the islands and its local inhabitants. The Kalama project must be stopped right now as a start toward the total re-evaluation of Hawaii's priorities.

DEMANDS OF THE PEOPLE

1. *We must stop the rezoning of agricultural land for urban use and halt tourist and urban development.*
2. *We must control immigration. Our local people must come first.*
3. *We must guard the ecology of our islands.*
4. *We must free our people from the land monopolies.*
5. *We must work towards economic self-sufficiency for our islands.*
6. *We demand that the development planned for Kalama Valley by the Hawaii-Kai Development Corporation with the cooperation of the Bishop Estate be brought to a complete and permanent halt.*

Reprinted from THE BLACK PANTHER, Vol. VI, No. 15 (May 8, 1971), p. 1.

this land is mine

Unlike many mainland areas, Hawaii has an extremely limited supply of land and natural resources. Many of our most dynamic political and economic problems can be directly attributed to the unequal distribution and shortage of land. In exploring our economy one discovers the connections between the land problem and every aspect of economic life--especially in agriculture, tourism, and defense. One must fully understand that land is the basic factor in the production and control of any economy.

Land, Hawaii's most valuable "commodity," is highly concentrated among a few wealthy families, descendants of Hawaii's missionaries, large private corporations, and the state and Federal governments. The monopoly is historic. A century or more ago, the land was controlled by the King and his various chiefs. This is still partly true today--it's just that the King and the chiefs are now the State, large private landholders, and the Federal government.

Out of 4,050,176 acres in the entire state, the armed forces control close to 252,000 acres; or almost 10 percent of all land in the state's territory. This ranks the military with the large private corporations like Castle & Cooke and Bishop Estate (B.E.: 369,699 acres; C. & C.: 154,759 acres. The military and Castle & Cooke both have something in common, they both own islands). The military also leases from the state 43,167 acres and some 21,866 acres of precious Hawaiian Homes Land. This does not account for the sizable portions it rents from private landholders like Campbell Estate in the Kahuku area, and the McCandless Estate in the Waikane area, for jungle warfare practice. These land owners are thus silent accomplices in America's genocidal policies upon the people of Southeast Asia. In contrast, less than 6 percent of Hawaii's general populace of small land owners own no more than 134,981 acres collectively.

The Department of Defense maintains property around the world, including 29.5 million acres of land, buildings, utility systems, streets and parking areas. Specifically in Hawaii, much of the 252,000 acres of land, and the 150 bases and minor installations the military operates, was acquired by absolute order of the War Department.

Under the direction of the Joint Chiefs of Staff, the forces of the Army, Navy, and Air Force stationed here in the Pacific are grouped together into a single command, known as the Pacific Command (covering more than one-third of the earth's surface, it is the largest geographical command in the world). The military depends on land, and the strategic Hawaii "property" area must be maintained if the United States intends to perpetuate and expand its economic, political and military domination in the world.

While many of Hawaii's people are landless, pay exhorbitant land taxes and high rents, and without property to farm or make a subsistence living from, the Armed Forces have obtained a disproportionate amount of property for the storage of gas, fuel and weapons, for the placement of tracking and radar stations and missile sites, for bombing and strafing purposes, and for the training in jungle warfare and counter-insurgency, which is then put into practice in the countries of Southeast Asia. Hawaii's situation is no different from Okinawa and Puerto Rico, for much of our best, cultivatable and livable land is either controlled or leased to the U.S. military.

While we have over 600,000 permanent residents living on Oahu with more people coming in each day, and a population density in Honolulu that now exceeds 3880 inhabitants per square mile (the density of Hong Kong is 3578 persons per square mile), close to 140,000 acres of land is within the hands of the Federal government. While military personnel have much land, shelter, room and space, many of us are crowded into dense complexes within the city, or like Hawaii's original inhabitants, within the enclaves of Kuhio Park Terrace, Kam IV Housing and Kalihi-Palama.

The contradictions of the military's use of land can be clearly seen. As time goes on, the people, especially the young of our islands, will comprehend the fact that while much of our land can be used for crop production and creative purposes, the military uses it for war, death, and destruction of our cultural heritage.

The U.S. military bases in Hawaii are essential to America's war effort in Southeast Asia and the establishment of its dominance in the Pacific Rim Basin. Out of all the property and territory that the military controls throughout the world, why is Hawaii so important? Hawaii is vitally important to America

---

Reprinted from GIDRA, February, 1971. This article was part of a pamphlet distributed at the Interim Session Ethnic Studies Conference sponsored by the University of Hawaii, held in January, 1971.

because of its (1) strategic position in the Pacific, (2) superb ports and harbors, (3) verdant jungle and forest areas for the training of combat troops used in the suppression of revolutionary movements in Asia, (4) passive, easily manipulated 442nd mentality type of citizenry. In other words, America needs Hawaii. Hawaii is essential in establishing a base of operations for the planning, research and conducting of America's military exploits. Hawaii is being used. And, with the help of the Federal and State governments, the military will fight to keep Hawaii under its thumb.

Hawaii has a limited amount of land available for her own people for housing since one-half of the state is owned and controlled by either the military, or major corporations like Alexander and Baldwin. Eighty percent of military housing shortage is acute for they have yet to provide for almost 11,000 of their dependents.

This is one unfortunate aspect of Hawaii's housing shortage: that the military itself cannot provide enough housing for its dependents. Because of this, the low ranking military personnel who receive no base housing and no housing allowance are thrust into direct competition with Hawaii's own low income residents. These low men on the military totem pole are applying for state aid which they are successful in obtaining, and they now constitute fourteen percent of the Hawaiian Housing Authority (HHA) clientele.

The contradictions that are evidenced in the scramble for living space in Hawaii reveal that the people who can least afford housing are paying more while those that are capable of paying more are, in fact, paying less. The pressures that are exerted on Hawaii's housing market come from the outside, and its effects are most sorely felt by Hawaii's low income residents. These people are forced into competition against the military which leased hundreds of homes and apartments on the open market, and they also contend with the subsidies given to military dependents by their own state government which, in essence, may be seen as working indirectly through the HHA as a subsidizer.

The military population in Hawaii will continue to increase in the future. What will happen to Hawaii's low income population which are, even now, being inadequately cared for?

raisin' the fist ..

Many people have asked what the fist symbolizes. It is a symbol of struggle. A symbol of struggle by the people, for the people. The fist stands for all the people sticking together — together tight like a fist. It means all power to the people. All power to the people. Black power to the black people, brown power to the brown people red power to red people, yellow power to yellow people, and white power to white people. There can't be one of these without all the rest. White people are not free if black people are not free and black people are not free if white people are not free. So it's ALL POWER TO THE PEOPLE.

TOURISM: DECLINE OF ALOHA
ROY TSUMOTO

Two Faces

No one can argue that tourism has played a major role in the increased prosperity of Hawaii over the years. Tourism is the largest "industry" in Hawaii, and is second only to the military as a source of income to the residents. In 1969 tourist expenditures totaled $577 million as compared to defense spending of $654.6 million that same year.

Why then has the sentiment against tourism been mounting among the Hawaiian people in such an accelerated manner during the past few years? The answer is an ironic one. The lamentable fact is that the manifestations of the industry itself are destroying the very "magic" that lures the tourist to the Islands. Crowded roads, sidewalks, and beaches, destruction of the Islands' natural beauty (for people who may spend ten to twelve days of their lives there), inadequate housing for the Islanders, a soaring cost of living, and an increased intensity of materialistic competition have all contributed to the diminution of that magic called Aloha.

The increased bitterness among the kamaainas ("old-timers") is noticeable. Our daily attitudes are taking on the taints of suspicion, defensiveness, and cynicism--not unlike that attitude I have found to be so prevalent on the mainland. It is bad enough when this bitterness is released upon scapegoats such as the haole tourists, hippies, and servicemen, but this bitterness becomes so ingested and internalized that the Islanders begin to vent this aggression upon each other.

Growth

Approximately 1.6 million tourists descend upon the Islands each year. The number has quadrupled in the last decade and about doubled in the last four years. With an average of over 25,000 tourists in the Islands at any given moment, it is no wonder that their presence is so much more felt that it was before statehood.

It is estimated that 24,000 jobs are directly related to tourism, about half of that being hotel employees. In 1966 hotel workers accounted for four percent of the labor force and only 1.4 percent of the total income--in jobs, mind you, directly related to the state's

HAWAIIAN HOMESTEAD STRUGGLE

It came like a cool westerly breeze, sharp with the smell of the sea. And in the camps of the Hawaiians, the people began to awake from a long sleep of uninvolvement. Thus begins the Great Awakening.

The Hawaiians, at one time, before the coming of the White Man, were a strong people in numbers and in strength. In stature, they were like giants. In legend it is said that Kamehameha crossed over to the other islands by foot!

The Hawaiians were a proud and humble people. Their life was simple. They lived off the land and off the sea. And the land was theirs from the mountains to the sea.

Then, Captain Cook and the eventual settling of the missionaries. And the Hawaiians being full of aloha, welcomed these fair skinned people who came from across the ocean. And the land began to change hands, from the Hawaiians to the White Man. The rest is History. Perhaps history will be made again.

"The Hawaiians" is an organization of Hawaiian people all concerned with the Hawaiian Homestead Act. The first organizing community was Waimanalo, but the movement has spread rapidly as the issue is one of deep concern for all persons of Hawaiian ancestry, persons with half or more Hawaiian blood.

The Hawaiians have a registered membership of over 180 and with hundreds are aiming for a statewide organization. The present chairman, Pae Galdeira, and his staff, are working hard to establish clear ideas and strategies to help the Homestead problem.

Research is a vital part of the group as this whole movement is concerned with the Federal Hawaiian Homestead Act, 1920.

An immediate problem is the fact that

largest and most prosperous industry. In 1968 the average weekly earnings of hotel workers was $76.16. The weekly expenditures necessary in Honolulu in 1967 to maintain a "moderate" standard of living (according to the U.S. Bureau of Labor Statistics) was $209.65; for a "lower" standard of living, $139.34! It must be kept in mind that next to Anchorage, Alaska, Honolulu has the highest cost of living in any major city in the U.S. In 1967 the cost of a city worker's family budget in Hawaii was at least twenty percent above the national average.

Hawaii Visitors Bureau

The HVB spends over $1 million every year on advertising, publicity, and promotion in order to attract tourists, conventions, and military personnel from the East and West. The bulk of these military personnel come to the Islands on R&R from active duty stations in Asia. The Bureau takes pride in its role of overseer for the whole tourist industry. It enters into cooperative advertisement programs with major air and sea carriers. It runs ads in business magazines to attract investors and developers in building or expanding hotel and resort facilities. It has given "top priority" to the long-range planning and development of the necessary plant and manpower needs, to ensure the orderly growth of tourism for the state, and to ensure maximum year-round occupancy.

Sources of HVB Funds

In fiscal 1967-68 about seventy-five percent of the HVB's funds came from the State Government and the rest from private contributors (i.e., the business community,) but the Bureau planned to shift more of the burden of its costs onto the private sector by the following fiscal year.

The HVB and the State Department of Planning and Economic Development must negotiate the allocation of the State funds yearly. The remainder of funds comes from the HVB's 1800 or so "members", half of whom are so-called "first line beneficiaries" (hotels, air and sea carriers, tour and travel agencies, etc.) The other half of the private sector is composed of individuals and businesses that profit indirectly from tourism, and this is the sector from which the HVB intends to secure more "dues" in the future. Thus we can clearly see that the HVB's very existence is dependent upon the community's encouragement and the financial support (including State Government funds.)

Reprinted from HAWAIIAN ETHOS, Volume I, Number I (January-February, 1971).

.... LAURA ALANCASTRE and GLORIA BURBAGE

there is not enough land being opened up for house lots. The numbered waiting list is 1,600 people (each person representing one family) with an approximate 500 unnumbered. Many on the waiting list have applied as far back as 30 years ago and still no land.

Much of the Homestead land is being leased out to various corporations with the intent of bringing funds into the Hawaiian Homestead Loan Fund.

Of an approximate 190,000 acres, only about 40,000 is being used by Hawaiians for 1) house lots, 2) agriculture lots, and 3) grazing lots. The different parties leasing Hawaiian Homestead Land include sugar companies, pineapple companies, Sea Life Park, and the Military establishments. Rent of the leases to such parties is not high enough. Why?

Funds needed to build homes, start subsistence farming to increase cattle heads are not available for said Hawaiian People.

The H.H.C. priority system is outdated. If you are priority three (one-half of the children are not eligible), one should forget about the possibility of receiving land before your first 40 years on the waiting list! Connections within the H.H.C. always makes distinctly dishonest difference!

To establish your Hawaiian blood line requires birth certificates as far back as your great-grandparents! In those days many people were not registered at birth.

Presently there is a study being done on H.H.C. funded ($90,000) by the legislature and the head man is a haole with no Hawaiians working with him. This report will take a total of 15 months, and according to such persons, the report will propose "drastic changes" within the H.H.C. This is doubtful, for as long as haoles keep on writing, and analyzing, deciding "for us" Hawaiians, nothing will change.

Reprinted from HAWAII FREE PEOPLE'S PRESS, Vol. II, Issue V (November, 1970).

The history of Los Angeles' Little Tokyo reaches back almost a hundred years to the economic boom period of the late 1880's when Los Angeles was transformed into a boisterous city of some 50,000 inhabitants. Among the newcomers were a few handful of Japanese who had followed the "trail of opportunity" to the Southland from San Francisco. These very early Issei settled in what is now the downtown area of Los Angeles, choosing to eventually develop their community in the First and San Pedro Street area which has since become synonamous with Little Tokyo. Although the East First Street district had existed for many years before it evolved into a Japanese district, the presence of many buildings in this area with shop space on the street floor and living quarters for workers above, proved an agreeable quality which was sure to draw many of these workers from abroad. The proximity also of Chinatown, which was just North of the East First Street district, near the present day site of the Union Station, was inviting.

The early Japanese of Little Tokyo geared much of their economic activities around the laborers for many of their own came from this category. Excellent business opportunities were present in providing services for the working man, thus we find that many of the first Japanese restaurants, barber shops etc., often catered to non-Japanese groups, although they still tended to hire one another when help was needed. Many activities, however, started through purely servicing the needs of Japanese laborers. These workers needed boarding houses, employment agencies and recreational places where they could spend some of their off-work time (often pool halls and bars). Much to the discomfort of the more conservative individuals within the community, the drinking bars (nomiyas) and the large vice quarters (Los Angeles had an extensive and infamous red light district during the 1900 period) which proved to be a powerful attraction of many of these young men, especially after a hard day's work on farm fields and orchards or with the railroad. Gambling, too, proved to be a major source of diversion among the Issei and indications are that it played a large role in the "development" of Little Tokyo.

By the early part of the 1900's, Little Tokyo was beginning to grow into a more stable community with the steady influx of more Japanese from the North, especially some with families. The movement south was greatly accelerated in 1906 by the earthquake which smashed San Francisco and also swept the city with fire. Many women during this period came to America under the "picture bride" category which in most instances were marriages arranged between two parties by photo. Many of these marriages were however between parties that had known each other since childhood, or were brides that were acceptable to the suitor's family in Japan. More likely than not, these marriages were arranged between persons from the same village or at least from the same prefecture in Japan.

Little Tokyo grew larger as people with families moved into the simple white frame houses that dotted the area around the First Street section, as well as homes which lay across

Reprinted by permission of the author. Jim Matsuoka has been a Hi-Potential instructor at UCLA and an Asian American studies instructor at Cal State Los Angeles.

LITTLE TOKYO, SEARCHING THE PAST AND ANALYZING THE FUTURE

JIM H. MATSUOKA

the Los Angeles River in the Boyle Heights district. Single men, of course, continued to live in the boarding houses and to this day, many of the recent arrivals from Japan are scattered throughout the Los Angeles region, still living in such bachelor quarters. The Japanese also found that they were moving into an area soon to be active with small industrial firms, stores, food processing shops and wholesale vegetable markets (pre-dating the huge Japanese dominated wholesale markets to come at 10th and San Pedro Streets). The Little Tokyo residents of this period often found themselves living next door to foundaries and warehouses, but they resolutely put together temples, newspapers, shops and homes, next to the noise of the metal shops and the rumble of the freight trains as they made their way slowly through the East First district.

Little Tokyo's Heyday

The "heyday" of Little Tokyo occurred during the decades of the 1920's and the 1930's. By this time, Little Tokyo had clearly become the center of Japanese activity within Southern California and a new generation of Japanese Americans, eligible for citizenship now by birth, were growing up. The majority of the Nisei (the second generation) were born during this period (1920-1930) and tend to remember Little Tokyo fondly. Going to "Nihonjinmachi" might mean being treated to some form of Japanese "kashi" or sweets as they knew that their parents would not miss this opportunity to buy some favorite Japanese treat especially if they were traveling some distance to reach downtown. It might also mean that they were going to learn some sort of cultural art or that the family was at least headed for some event (meaning a wedding or funeral or hopefully--a Samurai movie popularly termed "chambara"). Japanese merchants were quick to appreciate the Nisei fascination for East First Street, especially so during the rough days of the 1932 Depression. Recognizing the attraction "Nihonmachi" had for the Nisei, the hard pressed businessmen helped to organize the Nisei Week Festival as an inducement to keep the young people's interest focused on Little Tokyo, rather than have it drift away toward downtown White Los Angeles. Nisei Week proved to be so successful that it was then launched as an annual event.

By this time, East First Street had become a solid Japanese business district with a large population of Japanese families occupying the area between East First and the wholesale produce markets on 10th and San Pedro Streets. Many basic significant economic changes had taken place within the Japanese community in Southern California as a whole, and many

Japanese were now small farm operators instead of providing only the labor as had characterized the very earliest Japanese of the Los Angeles area. In those periods (1900-1910) a wagonload of Japanese laborers were often available for work within the hour, if one called upon a Japanese operated employment agency.

"The Temper of the Times"

In attempting to reconstruct the "temper of the times" more clearly, Mr. Roy Tazawa, an Issei who is now in his 60's was interviewed. Mr. Tazawa came to Los Angeles in 1930 after his business had failed in San Francisco. He subsequently worked for the Japanese newspapers, first with the RAFU SHIMPO and then as Editor of the SANGYO NIPPO, a paper which reflected the interests of the Japanese small farmer. Mr. Tazawa spent the war years in the Poston Relocation Camp and while there, helped the Issei organize the canteen in order to keep it out of the hands of officials who Mr. Tazawa charges supplied the people with poor quality items at high prices. After the war, Mr. Tazawa worked briefly as a translator in the East, however giving that up to return to the Los Angeles area. Joining the interview are Franklin Odo and Eddie Wong from UCLA.

QUESTION: We would sort of like to get the feel of what Little Tokyo was like; in other words, what sort of social and economic conditions existed there during the 1930's, the feelings of the people, the scope of the community itself?

TAZAWA: The basis of the community was farming...that and farm laboring. Japanese farmers and laborers came to Little Tokyo for lots of reasons...especially to get things from Japan. They would even use many of the large dry goods and grocery firms as banks because they did not understand the language at American banks. People would come to shop and then leave what was left over deposited with such large dry goods stores such as Asia Company, Hori Company, Kimura Company and Tomio Company.

QUESTION: Little Tokyo then grew because they carried goods that no one else had and provided services to them?

TAZAWA: That's right. Nowadays, even big chain stores carry Japanese foods but in the old days you can't even get rice outside of Little Tokyo...but not only food, but things like clothes. Japanese were small and skinny, and it was hard to find suits for them outside of Little Tokyo.

QUESTION: How big was Little Tokyo?

TAZAWA: Los Angeles Street to Alameda...East Second Street to North San Pedro was the business section. The residential section was mostly in Boyle Heights...some on the Westside around Normandie and 36th...there were lots of Japanese around there...but I think more people lived in Boyle Heights as it was more convenient. Of course, there were a lot of cheap hotels around there and lots of farmers and farm laborers stayed there when they had to stay overnight...especially around Alameda Street where they would only charge one dollar to a dollar and a half a night.

QUESTION: When the farmers came in to Little Tokyo, what did they do? Were they there for recreation...to buy goods?

TAZAWA: Mostly recreation--some show or movie. They had to buy everything in Little Tokyo...dress, groceries, etc.

QUESTION: How many movie theaters did they have in Little Tokyo?

TAZAWA: Only one movie theater. The Nishi Hongwanji (temple) and the Koyasan (temple) had halls where they had theater shows. The theater shows come in connection with the Tokyo Club, which was a gambling joint, you know. They (the Tokyo Club) had to draw in everybody...just gambling couldn't draw in all the people, so they sent to Japan to have singers, actors and actresses perform here. These singers, actors and actresses would perform two or three nights in Little Tokyo and then tour all over California...like Santa Ana, Garden Grove, San Diego, Watsonville, Salinas...all over California.

QUESTION: Perhaps you could elaborate on the Tokyo Club. I take it that it was an illegal gambling hall and that they had connections in Little Tokyo. How influential was the Tokyo Club? I want to put it in its proper perspective.

TAZAWA: The Tokyo Club and Japanese town were very close. Many important businessmen were connected with the Tokyo Club. The people from the country spent their money in Little Tokyo, that's why. They ate, stayed in the hotels and bought things. The Tokyo Club and Japanese town were very close. The Tokyo club had watchmen all over...across the street from the Club they had a little grocery and candy store with a signal in it connected to the gambling hall upstairs. When the alarm was pushed, the gambling tools could be taken all out. Just like Capone in Chicago, if a small Japanese store started gambling in the back, the Tokyo Club would find out and go beat them up.

FRANKLIN ODO: Did anyone go to Chinatown for recreation?

TAZAWA: Some of them. I think about half went to the Tokyo Club and the other half went to Chinatown. Many people were afraid to go to the Tokyo Club as they would be recognized, but Chinatown was far from Japanese town.

QUESTION: Gambling was a pretty important recreation then?

TAZAWA: Not only here but all over. If you go to Watsonville, Monterey, lots of farming communities have gambling...Fresno, Stockton.

QUESTION: Why was there such an emphasis on gambling?

TAZAWA: I don't know. They like to be rich quick, I guess.

MATSUOKA: It could be because of the economics of America at that time. They were just coming out of a depression...you know, whenever you have an economic condition that is very depressed, people have a tendency to move towards get rich quick schemes. A lot of countries which have economic problems are really attracted to the lottery and things of that nature because you have a dream of becoming wealthy in one shot. But let's go on to some of the more legitimate institutions of the Japanese community. Can you give us a rundown on some of the leading institutions in Little Tokyo?

TAZAWA: The Central Japanese Association not only controlled Los Angeles but all of Southern California; Garden Grove had a Japanese Association; Anaheim, another one; but the Central Japanese Association was on top.
(Note: Almost all Japanese communities were organized under its own Japanese Associations. These local associations included most of the leadership of the Japanese community and were affiliated with other small local groups into "districts." Southern California's Central Japanese Association had some 20 local associations affiliated with it, while the San Francisco based association had some 38 local branches throughout Central and Northern California. Other major groupings of associations include the Northwest American Japanese Association based in Seattle with some 14 local chapters and the Japanese Association of Oregon with links to the 5 associations of Idaho. Other smaller organizations existed in such states as Colorado, Arizona, Utah, Texas, Illinois and New York.)

TAZAWA: The Central Japanese Association was active in Sacramento where they had a lobbyist by the name of Walter Tsukamoto. He was a graduate of the University of California Law School.

QUESTION: In other words the Central Japanese Association was the most powerful overall community organization...something like an umbrella organization, and they retained a lobbyist in Sacramento.

TAZAWA: And they were also connected to the Japanese Consulate, because half of the money came from the Japanese community and half from the Japanese government.

EDDIE WONG: What did they do with the money?

TAZAWA: In 1914, American communities in California started an anti-Japanese movement and the Japanese can't own or even lease land. All the farmers had a hard time...they were supposed to deal with things like that. My wife was the owner of a farm, although she was only 12 years old at the time, because she was the only Nisei.

(Note: The California Alien Land Laws forbade the ownership or the leasing of land to "aliens ineligible for citizenship"...which was a polite terminology to exclude Japanese, Chinese, and all Asians as they were not eligible to become citizens. The Japanese got around this by registering the land in the name of their offspring who became American citizens by birthright.)

QUESTION: The Japanese Associations were composed of all aliens then, and they had ties with the Japanese Consulate?

TAZAWA: That's right. The Nisei were too young and they couldn't do anything.

QUESTION: How did the Central Japanese Association exert its power within the community? Was it through consensus? Did everyone voluntarily follow its leadership?

TAZAWA: They had several meetings every year in Los Angeles...sometimes at the Kawafuku using a whole floor...sometimes at the Nishihongwanji. Every local association sent a representative there; then they would elect a president, vice-president, treasurer, etc.

QUESTION: Did they just appoint themselves as the leaders, or did they have a lot of ties into all parts of the community?

TAZAWA: They're elected.

QUESTION: No, I mean did everybody more or less follow the leadership of the Central Association?

TAZAWA: At that time, the Japanese didn't have much political experience or knowledge because they didn't have political rights as Japanese (either in America or Japan). But they paid attention. People who were asked to put in so much money, paid, because they were glad to fight discrimination. They had to rely on the Central Association.

FRANKLIN ODO: It's interesting to me that the Japanese Consul was providing half the money. Can you tell us a little bit more about the ties between the Japanese and the Japanese Government?

TAZAWA: The Japanese Government was interested in the Japanese people here. They had to protect them, that's their main business here. The Consulate had connections to the Federal Government through the Japanese Ambassador...that's why the Consulate is connected with the Japanese Associations. It's much easier to fight anti-Japanese movements that way.

QUESTION: How much influence did the Consulate have on the Central Association? According to the United States Attorney General's Office, they claim that the Consulate controlled the Central Association. In other words, could the Consulate tell the Central Association to move in a direction and would they do so obediently?

TAZAWA: Well, of course they would discuss it...this is not Japan and they're not yes-men. Sometimes they discuss it and always they take in account the interest of the Japanese here.

QUESTION: Were most of their alliances in terms of fighting discrimination?

TAZAWA: That's right.

QUESTION: The charges that the Attorney General made were that they were completely controlled. In other words, the Central Association was nothing but a front. How would you react to something like that?

TAZAWA: I don't think so. I think half the expenses were paid by the Japanese Government because this community cannot afford to spend so much money for Sacramento. The Japanese community is a small community, comparatively speaking. The Consulate and the Japanese community's interest were the same.

QUESTION: Let's move on to the political feelings of the times. What were the political attitudes? I hate to use labels, but did they have a strong rightest element in the community that was pro-Japan?

TAZAWA: Japanese are always very conservative. You know that the Japanese are mostly farmers. They work hard...sometimes 13-14 hours everyday to make money, to save money. That's why they were conservative.

QUESTION: What about the very nationalistic types?

TAZAWA: That's most of the Japanese...very nationalistic. They were educated in Japan during the Meiji Era. They were raised there so they strongly supported Japan's stance in Asia. They even raised money to send an airplane to fight the Chinese when the war started with China.

EDDIE WONG: What about the other side, the leftist side?

TAZAWA; Many were people from Okinawa. Here about 40 or 50 people belonged to the Communist Party and many of them were from Okinawa. Even after the war, they are very strong in Hawaii. In Honolulu, they even had a newspaper there and they distributed it all over the United States and Canada.

EDDIE WONG: This political climate of conservatism...how did that show up when they had conflicts with the outside, White community?

TAZAWA: The Japanese had no conncection with the White people at that time. After the Nisei grew up, we had connections with the White community, but before the war we didn't have any connections. They didn't have any advantage in talking with the Hakujin. The Japanese are in the country farming; they spend their money in Little Tokyo. The White community didn't have anything that they wanted.

QUESTION: You're saying that the reason they didn't have anything to do with the White community was that they really had nothing to offer them...or is it perhaps because of discrimination they may have encountered? Could it be a combination of both?

TAZAWA: Of course, there's discrimination. The Japanese had an awful time finding a house even if they pay high rents. Look at the way they lived in San Francisco. The Japanese community lived in basements. They can't live on the ground floor or the upstairs-- they lived in the basements. Another thing was that the Japanese community didn't get any relief before the war from the county or the state. When people had trouble, the Japanese community stepped in and helped each other.

QUESTION: How did the community fare during the Depression?

TAZAWA: I heard some people slept under the East First Street bridge. If they can't live in a hotel, they go to a friend; they're glad to let them stay a few days. Friends tried to help each other.

EDDIE WONG: How were conflicts handled within your community? Let's say two people had an argument about a business matter. How would that be solved?

TAZAWA: The Japanese Chamber of Commerce handled those things and they would usually compromise someway.

EDDIE WONG: Let's say someone was wrong. How would he be punished?

TAZAWA: I don't think they have any punishment. When they're wrong, nobody would speak to them.

EDDIE WONG: Would that essentially kill off that person's business?

TAZAWA: That's right.

QUESTION: Generally speaking, of the people that came here from Japan, which class would you say they were from?

TAZAWA: Usually poor, but they're not all poor. Some people I know in Texas were rich in Japan. In Texas they're big rice farmers and they came here because they didn't like it in Japan.

QUESTION: How much money did it take to leave Japan? Did it take a certain amount of capital to get you out of there to come here?

TAZAWA: They have to have the fare and at least $50 in cash when they come in to port. Immigration would ask you how much you got, and usually you have to have $50 because on that you could live about one month.

EDDIE WONG: It seems times were very hard and the Japanese people worked very hard. What were their feelings about being in America even though life was so hard working on the farms?

TAZAWA: Comparing it to Japan, things were much better because here they could eat rice three times a day. In Japan, sometimes they can't eat rice and have to eat potatoes.

EDDIE WONG: Did they intend to stay?

TAZAWA: Yes, many wanted to stay, but most of the people who stayed in the cities might have wanted to go back. Most of the people in the city wanted to stay about 3 years and save enough money to go back to Japan, but some can't save that much money...some stayed over 50 years.

QUESTION: What was the influence of the J.A.C.L. before the war?

TAZAWA: Not very much.
(Note: Prior to the war, the J.A.C.L. was a small organization composed primarily of young Nisei throughout the West Coast. In the Issei dominated Japanese communities, they carried relatively little influence until the war brought them into prominence as "spokesmen" for the Japanese...a title and responsibility which they may not have wanted and carried heavily.)

The War Years

World War II and the evacuation of the Japanese from the West Coast stripped Little Tokyo clean. What was once a vigorous center of activity became a lifeless community as the Japanese left for the relocation camps by train and bus. This state of inactivity did not last long in the First Street area as the tremendous demand for labor in the war industries on the West Coast attracted a new group of immigrants, those from the rural South. Little Tokyo during the war years became a temporary Black community and it was to be many years before the shattered remnants of the pre-war Japanese community would try to re-establish their historic claim to First and San Pedro Streets.

Little Tokyo 1970-1980

Having survived the war years, the Japanese community and Little Tokyo now faces its most important series of changes since the community got together before the turn of the century. Little Tokyo is part of a massive effort to renew the heart of Los Angeles and a staggering $80 million plus will be spent through the Redevelopment Project in an effort to maintain and rebuild the district. To discuss what the Redevelopment of Little Tokyo means to the Japanese community of Southern California, an interview and discussion is presented with George Umezawa, Information Specialist for the Little Tokyo Redevelopment Project, along with members of the U.C.L.A. Asian American Studies Center, Franklin Odo, Eddie Wong, Amy Tachiki and Peter Lin.

MATSUOKA: I'd like to ask George, in your capacity as an Information Specialist with the Little Tokyo Redevelopment Project, in which direction do you think Little Tokyo is heading for? You can define that (direction) as loosely as you want.

UMEZAWA: I can only really speak in terms of the Redevelopment Project. The important idea is the fact that it has to be in existence if the community is to continue. Little Tokyo has been here since 1885, and it's always been the core of the community...in terms of commercial activity and cultural activity. Most of the community organizations have headquarters in the Little Tokyo area now. The direction that Little Tokyo is taking through the Redevelopment Project is for many more years of use, especially for the Japanese people in Southern California. Just briefly, to go over some of the things that are happening in the Redevelopment Project, you have developments that will ensure the commercial continuity of the community; there is also a project in the works which will preserve and expand the cultural and community service aspects for the community; and also a project which will bring back to Little Tokyo some of the residential aspects that it had in its earlier history. That's the senior citizens housing program that is right on the threshold of being realized. The name of the project is the Little Tokyo Towers and it's being sponsored by four of the larger Japanese community organizations in Southern California: the Southern California Christian Church Federation, the Buddhist Church Federation, the J.A.C.L. and the Southern California Gardeners Federation.

QUESTION: When is this going to be done?

UMEZAWA: The way things are going now, construction can begin next year as land acquisition will start taking place within the next few months. The significance of it is that the residential section will be brought back into the community. The whole reason for the Redevelopment Project is that the people saw that because of the age of the buildings and the deterioration of them, Little Tokyo would be gone in about 20 years if nothing was to be done. In 1950, there was a whole section of Little Tokyo on First Street where the Police Administration Building is, that was leveled because of the expansion of the Civic Center...the fact that it was considered a deteriorated area made it very easy for the Police Administration Building to be moved in. In addition, there are buildings in the area that have already been demolished and condemned for safety factors, and this has been going on little by little.

There was an effort to build up Little Tokyo by the community itself, but it was such a monumental task that they could not handle it by themselves. The costs were prohibitive to the community so they eventually got Federal funding.

MATSUOKA: I might add that a Community Redevelopment Agency survey conducted on the buildings show that 75% of the structures in the area were substandard.

UMEZAWA: The last earthquake proved out the survey that Jim was talking about very graphically. There were about 20 buildings that suffered extensive damages. Two hotels in the area had to be evacuated because of the damage done to those buildings and 3 more buildings have since been condemned by the City Building and Safety Commission because they were inspected and found to be unsuitable for human occupancy. You can visualize the problem because most of the buildings are like 50-60 years old...most of them are merely brick frames...unreinforced brick buildings that were built before restrictive standards were put up.

MATSUOKA: George, most people think that Little Tokyo is a collection of little restaurants and curio shops. What are examples of some of the services you can find there?

UMEZAWA: We have something like 25 doctors, 5 financial institutions, 18 gift shops, 20 cultural schools, groups and instructors, 1 Buddhist temple, 1 Christian church, 28 restaurants, 2 bookstores, 16 hotels and apartments, 10 social service organizations, 1 employment agency, 14 dentists, 4 ethnic newspapers, 10 investment counseling services, 12 law offices, etc.

MATSUOKA: And that probably is just a partial listing. What it brings out is that Little Tokyo provides a variety of services to people which makes it more than just a small curiosity type of place.

UMEZAWA: There is another survey I read which the Agency took, which showed that of the 100,000 Japanese living in Southern California, approximately half of these people, some 50,000, make a trip to Little Tokyo from wherever they are, the San Fernando Valley, Long Beach, Orange County, wherever, to Little Tokyo at least twice a month. That's a lot of people coming in to this little area. It's because of a lot of these services, and sometimes, it's just to come back to the community.

MATSUOKA: What are some of the serious problems that urban redevelopment projects have? In some instances it has meant minority dislocation in many ways. How is Little Tokyo trying to deal with this situation?

UMEZAWA: To start off, the whole Redevelopment Program was the idea of the community itself. The Little Tokyo leaders saw what was happening to Little Tokyo because of the deterioration. And I think they also saw that this was a bad thing to happen for every Japanese person in Los Angeles. And so they got together and it was the community's idea to establish a redevelopment program with the purpose of preserving the area. In other programs you'll find that it's somebody outside of the community that decides to have the redevelopment program for you, because they don't like an area because it's blighted and it looks ugly. Bunker Hill was a perfect example of this where you did have many low income minority people living in an area...a blight area, next to the Civic Center. Through political machinations, a redevelopment program was started there by outside interests. It's an arbitrary removal of a lot of people with no real sensitivity to the problems that the people would encounter once they've left. Anyway, this is like a picture of urban renewal at its worst. In Little Tokyo's case, because it is to preserve the community, its plan is to go step by step, to improve and rebuild the area and at the same time not trying to force anybody outside the area. In other words, when it's complete, the people that are in the community now, will still be there.

*Editor's note: The United Way which receives substantial contributions from the Los Angeles Japanese community refused to fund drug abuse, care for the elderly and other projects sponsored by Japanese American Community Services, Asian Involvement (JACS/AI).

QUESTION: In concrete terms, is there any way of being able to say that the senior citizens living there now would be able to afford to move into the Little Tokyo Towers?

UMEZAWA: This gets into the problems with the project. It's not going to solve everything. You will have problems with not only the senior citizens but also businessmen who will be forced to pay higher rents because of the new buildings and everything else. Right now because of the Federal funding programs for senior citizens housing, we're hoping that the rent rates will be low enough to accommodate all the people in the area. The senior citizens in the area have first priority to get those housing units. According to our figures, they can get a rental unit at about $108 a month (estimate), and that's quite a lot for many people. But there's also a special rent supplement program. Under this program, it allows those eligible senior citizens to pay not more than one quarter of their income toward the rent so if he's only making $100 a month, he will be able to get the rental unit for $25. But only 10% of the total renters will be allowed this supplement and the number of people that can't afford that may run over the 10% of the renters, so it is a definite problem. That's something that we'll have to deal with.

QUESTION: This is by no means a closed subject yet?

UMEZAWA: They're in the process of applying for the funds right now, and when we receive the funds and we know we can build the thing, then we'll be getting into that area.

"We Have Seen the Enemy and He Looks Like Us"

An entirely new phase of the discussion began when the topic of the influx of Japanese corporate power coming into Little Tokyo was brought up. Some of the conclusions that were arrived at offer an insight into the new uncharted world that Little Tokyo may be entering into.

MATSUOKA: Now redevelopment brings in mind the San Francisco experience with its Trade Center. A lot of criticism has been directed at it because there's been sort of a takeover of the Trade Center by Japanese business groups. What do you think of the influx of Japanese imports in terms of money, businessmen and what have you, into Little Tokyo itself?

UMEZAWA: I don't know if I can really answer that. My background on this is not that great. The only place where I see the Japanese businesses becoming a factor in the Redevelopment Project is within the cultural-community center project. And this was done almost purposefully in a way to draw in money to help build the structure which is going to be a $3 million project...and at the same time guards are being put against them "bogarding" the whole show, by having them in only as part of a larger corporation (non-profit) which will allow a lot of other people to have a say in what the cultural-community center does and how its facilities are used.

FRANKLIN ODO: There is a danger of the "Japanese-Japanese" moving in with a great deal more capital.

MATSUOKA: I see this as a very interesting facet of what's going on in Little Tokyo today... that they're developing almost a Little Tokyo of segments, where you have this group from Japan with I won't say unlimited, but with huge expense accounts at their disposal. You can see it in the restaurants down there. You can tell, the "natives" eat on one side of the street and they eat on the other. There is no question of their influence in terms of money, in terms of confidence, in terms of their expertise in many areas. They're setting up a sort of social system where the Japanese Consul is becoming the social leader again, and he's reasserting his leadership. People are beginning to look toward him now.

FRANKLIN ODO: This is like pre-war days then.

MATSUOKA: In a way, because all we're seeing now is a resurgence of Japan in general, and as Mr. Tazawa stated, you know how much influence Japan had before. Of course, we're beginning to get a resurgence of this again.

PETER LIN: Before it seemed that the interests of the Consulate and the interests of the people were the same, but if the San Francisco Tokyo and the Little Tokyo experience is any kind of indication, it seems that the foreign involvement in the U.S. now is not so much concerned with people who live here. They're now concerned rather with their own businesses.

MATSUOKA: You've hit the crucial difference right there. I think that's really a most crucial thing that we have to watch and look at...just where are the interests of the Japanese "interests." Are they with and for the people of the community or are they with and for whoever rules Japan--and that would be the business corporations. The biggest source of money around right now and that's available in vast amounts is probably from Japan.
    One of the things in the Redevelopment Project that they've done in order to retain local ownership as much as possible is to create property owner local development corporations.

UMEZAWA: This is where property owners whose property is acquired by the Agency are getting the first priority to form a corporation to build up whatever development is being planned for that area. They will be responsible for the financing of the project, for developing it and management once it's completed. In this way the same people that have control of that land now will also retain control of it in the future.

FRANKLIN ODO: What about the residents themselves? You talk about the people within the community--but of people within the community with particular rights. What about the residents?

UMEZAWA: This is a weakness I see also. The Redevelopment Project has what is called the Little Tokyo Community Development Advisory Committee and supposedly, this is the advisory group to the Redevelopment Project. They're supposed to be in on all the planning and setting up of priorities for the project...I see a lot of businessmen in there, a lot of professional people, but few residents. This is a problem that I see, and I don't know how it can be alleviated.

MATSUOKA: I think one of the problems with the residents is that a large number are transients. They're here one day and gone the next and you can't keep track of them. The remaining group are the elderly and their economic positions are very poor in many ways. It's difficult to get people like this to participate in some sort of advisory body, you know, but granted they will participate if you make strong efforts to get them...I doubt very much if anybody has made that kind of an effort to get people like this.
    One of the things we might want to talk about are some of the segments within the community today. The most significant one to watch I believe are the Japanese from Japan... how much power they'll eventually have and how much influence they'll exert. Another segment of course is the commercial element that have been there for years that is taking an integral part in the redevelopment of the community. Another, a third force that is making a lot of changes within the community, is of course the young people. This is a thing to watch too as I think there might be a time of increasing conflict because the younger people are beginning to make significant inroads into the community. Before the older people had a tendency to dismiss the young people as "here today, gone tomorrow" type of thing, but they're beginning to realize the seriousness of the thrust and are sort of moving against it. I think Chinatown had a similar experience when the Six Companies really moved against any group that threatens to upset things.
    The Little Tokyo community has taken a little longer to respond, but many of the people are beginning to realize the seriousness of the younger people's intentions of working within Little Tokyo, and working with Little Tokyo as a means of recreating a community and moving towards some changes in this society. They definitely see it as a threat.

AMY TACHIKI: Does the Redevelopment Project have the support of the younger faction?

MATSUOKA: I think right now there is no opposition to it from the younger people. The Little Tokyo Redevelopment Agency group in J-town has gone to great lengths to align themselves in many ways with many of the social programs that the young people have developed. They've helped with programs like Community Information Service Day, and they've taken strong stands as individuals on the United Way conflict*...they're very sensitive to what the young people are asking for in Little Tokyo. The key issue, this is why I keep harping on it, still goes back to the role of the Japanese from Japan...the key issues will come from there.

UMEZAWA: You notice that the most impressive structure is maybe the Kajima (Sumitomo Bank) Building.

MATSUOKA: The money power behind things like that is awesome; it's overwhelming.

AMY TACHIKI: Is there any merging between powerful Nisei business figures with some of the Japan-based businesses? I'm talking about those Nisei businessmen who are developing profitable business relationships with Japanese firms.

MATSUOKA: I don't know exactly how much influence is being moved around there, but I think it's beginning to grow. Did you ever see a list of Japanese corporation representatives in Southern California? It's fantastic.

EDDIE WONG: We were talking before about the political nature of the community, and as Mr. Tazawa said before, it was a basically conservative community. What direction is it moving in politically given that now there is an international push for the Pacific-Rim strategy and using key cities on the West Coast as sort of major trade centers, and using Little Tokyo as a center? How is that going to affect the politics of the community?

MATSUOKA: I think politics are strange here in Little Tokyo...an almost schizophrenic condition. People always have a tendency to vote where their interests lie. You'll find the funny situation of having a lot of Republicans there, because they see their business interests tied in. Many of these same people are also cognizant of the fact of what they've suffered under discrimination so you have a situation where they are sympathetic at times toward certain radical changes because of the knowledge that they're Japanese. It's a really funny situation. You really don't know where they line up sometimes.

UMEZAWA: The impression that I get is really weird. When you refer to Little Tokyo in terms of politics, I don't think you can use that word sometimes. Only a certain element is actively involved in that sort of thing. The politics again is internal. It's like dealing with things that are happening within Little Tokyo and not looking outside of that.

FRANKLIN ODO: I've seen references to a strange kind of neo-colonial situation developing with Japanese control of certain areas of America by using Nisei capital, and being able to establish branch factories or plants or services in the U.S., building on the money that's being deposited in the banks by Japanese Americans...and then extending that kind of control to who gets credit and who doesn't, so that a good deal of the community development, say in Little Tokyo, might be controlled not so much by Japanese-Americans, but by the bank executives who are native Japanese.

EDDIE WONG: That puts the position of the Japanese-American in a very perilous state. It's like a cycle going back to the 30's and the pre-war days again, where the Japanese community is conservative and imperialist because the very structure in the community such as banking and all the businesses are being run and controlled by the Japanese in Japan.

MATSUOKA: Our control may well be gone. There will be faces down there that look Oriental, but we'll be pushed out to the hinterlands of Crenshaw. We may be on the outlying areas looking in and we'll see a whole bunch of people and it won't be us, and when I say "us", I include businessmen. It won't even be us in that respect.

FRANKLIN ODO: Is there any chance that Crenshaw might develop really divorced from the Little Tokyo area? To what extent will even Monterey Park develop as an autonomous Asian American, Japanese-American unity?

MATSUOKA: Personally, I feel that Little Tokyo should always be a center of Japanese-American activity if we aren't pushed out. I don't think outlying areas like Crenshaw and Monterey Park can offer the same sort of things that Little Tokyo can. They are more Americanized and they really are not the type of thing that Little Tokyo is...its strong association with the culture of Japan and its background of history for the Japanese in America. Those other places are sort of like a Japanese community—it's got the beauty shops, etc., but these are just services that you can get anywhere else...it just happens to be that they're owned by Japanese Americans. The center for the cultural arts...the schools...most of them are located around the Little Tokyo area if not inside it or somewhere close by. Your established social organizations like the J.A.C.L., the Japanese Chamber of Commerce, J.A.C.S. these sort of things will always be in Little Tokyo. Little Tokyo will stay important to the entire Japanese community.

PROPERTY

UREAU   REAL ESTATE

AN INTERVIEW with WARREN FURUTANI

EDITORIAL BOARD
JULY, 1971

NATIONAL COMMUNITY INVOLVEMENT COORDINATOR, JAPANESE AMERICAN CITIZENS LEAGUE

QUESTION: You spoke about the movement as setting an example for other people to follow and from that, the movement now needs a lot more structure and discipline. Has any of that progressed?

FURUTANI: In terms of progressing to structure, I think that people are at least coming to the conclusion that they need it. Up to this point, it's been a situation where a lot of the movement's philosophy has been "do your thing," which is a very middle class philosophy but nonetheless was our philosophy. And Los Angeles, in particular, our emphasis has always been doing. We were turned off very much to rhetoric; action was the direction we wanted to go. So the last two, three years, we've been so action-oriented and so busy doing, we, on one level, have developed a pretty good credibility in the community because we have so many programs. But on another level, a much more important level, we developed a misunderstanding as to what we're doing. Because we're so busy doing now, our programs are short-range oriented. For example, working with people on the level of survival community services, it's a very subjective thing. In other words, you get very involved in it emotionally and personally. You work with these people, see their problems, want to solve their problem immediately, and in doing that, you become very short-range oriented. Well, this is all well and good today, but what happens tomorrow? What happens with the next generation? In other words, our long-range goal really suffers because we really get hung up on short range. You come to the conclusion that the only way you can do it is by having some sort of organization where you have discipline and with

Warren Furutani is a well known community worker and speaker in the Asian community. He attended Gardena High School in Gardena, California, and was active in the College Readiness Program at the College of San Mateo.

principles. The reason you need these two things is because principles, for example, give you an overall guideline of what you're going to do. It's a situation where we lack principles to give us a base, a level of debate. The way arguments go these days are once again very subjective, very emotional. They talk about how "I feel the need for change" or "I see the Issei and it just turns my stomach inside" or "I see Chinatown and I get uptight." That's all well and good because it motivates you. But you have to know how to explain that motivation to someone, for example, who lives in Gardena, who lives in another part of town; to someone who doesn't have the same experiences. You have to be able to explain that to him, not just emotionally but be able to logically break it down, because they're liable to say, "Well, I didn't live there so I don't know. I never felt racism. I never felt economic oppression." So in order to explain these things you have to explain it to him with logic and with reason and to have continuity in terms of our whole philosophy. It's a situation where we have to be at meetings on time, we have to cut out dope, and so on and so forth. That's all good except that a lot of people didn't know why they had to do it. This is the level we've come to. As far as really developing that structure, it's got a little bit more to come.

QUESTION: When you talk about ideology of a movement, in the case of an Asian American movement, there seem to be two forces moving at once: one is a very strong psychological undercurrent of finding one's identity again; but most other political movements have had as their objective, political power. In other words, seizing means of controlling one's life. How does that apply to the Asian American movement? Is it both or what is it?

FURUTANI: There's really a dilemma in the movement right now. The Asian American, in particular, because one level of involvement in the movement is that of having and showing contradictions like racism and identity, which are very important things; on another level of the movement is where it deals on an economic level. It's a situation where everything is so inter-related that it's really hard to divide it. But I think the most important thing we have to look at is when we talk about Asian American movement or the Asian American community--we have to define that; we have to look at out communities. For example, we have something like Chinatown, San Francisco, New York, Los Angeles, it's a situation where you can use the contradiction of racism and you can use the contradictions of identity, of Chinese Americans especially. But also there you can use the contradiction of economics. There you can talk in terms of self-determination, community control. You can talk in terms of community merchants in that area of being responsive to the people who buy in that area because that is a real geographic community. A situation with Little Tokyo is pretty much the same thing. But if you talk about other Asian communities, like the Crenshaw area and Gardena, or Sawtelle, or different areas in San Francisco, New York, you come to the conclusion that the Japanese community, the Chinese community, the Asian community, is not a geographic one. So to me, the most important thing when you define a community is that you have to look at it in real terms. For example, the Japanese community--we've been defining it as a mental thing, a psychological thing. Many of the Japanese people relate to Japanese institutions. For example, they come to Little Tokyo and shop here; they relate to Japanese churches, Japanese schools. But what's happening, for especially the younger Asian Americans--Chinese, Japanese, Korean, Filipino, that the most dominant thing in their life, in terms of identity, is the fact that they're a minority in America. It's a situation where they've felt limited racism, where identity is so assimilated or so acculturated into the American mainstream of life that it's hard for them to relate to things like identity and racism. So, another means of organizing in geographic areas is that you take a geographic area of Third World people and the basis which you organize Third World people is on issues which affect them in that area. If you live in the same area, that means you relate to the same institutions; you relate to the same schools; you shop at the same stores. So this is the common bond you have. In terms of organizing people, the first thing you have to do is to create bonds--create some sort of common ground to show that we are in this thing together, so whatever we deal with, we'll solve our problems. There's a situation where nationalism is an organizing tool,

FURUTANI: We've been able to point out contradictions showing people problems on many levels; if L.A. County Hospital is all messed up, we have to have an alternative. We have to say come to this clinic or come to the Free Clinic. And we haven't been able to develop that alternative. The reason is obviously because we don't have the professional people; we're trying to eventually get into the area of student mobilization again--talking to medical students, law students, professional people, because we need the revolutionary technologists to deal with alternative institutions. In terms of life style, this has been a problem of the movement from the beginning. We've tried to create alternative life styles but the people have seen the hypocrisies in ourselves so much that it's hard for them to relate to the Amerasian movement. For example, in the beginning of the movement and even now to a certain extent, there was a high degree of arrogance. We flaunted it with rhetoric by dressing differently, "being different," and trying to show the differences rather than showing unity. Our life style has been on the surface. Our whole thing has been external changes: changing the way we look, changing the institutions, changing the churches...and so forth. In terms of internal changes where people will relate to our movement and our identity is living differently-- sharing collectively and cooperatively in terms of dealing with male chauvinism, our relationships to material things, our relationship to pleasure, how much time we have for pleasure, and how important it is to us.

QUESTION: Many people are concerned about the upcoming generations and how it's impossible not to become assimilated anymore because of the mass media's influence and how society is structured. Just what kinds of things do you foresee in future generations?

FURUTANI: This question of culture and identity, for example, has a lot to do with generations coming up. We have stronger ties with our nationalism within the country in terms of being an Asian in this country--rather than relating to Japan and China, relating to our ethnicity in this country. When you go rap at high schools and talk to younger people about racism and identity, they really question racism. They don't know what it is; they have very seldom felt it; if they did, it was very subtle and you have to explain it; then they see it. But still they don't relate that strongly to it. The area where they can perhaps start relating to is identity, when they start talking about new life styles, new ways of looking at things. But that isn't necessarily "Asian"--that's like only toward themselves, their youth culture, and the way they look at things.

QUESTION: Do you see that the Third World concept is still a very viable concept to organize minority people?

FURUTANI: Well, the Third World concept, once again like nationalism, is obviously a means to an end. And whether you use nationalism or you use Third World to organize people, depends upon your realistic analysis of that particular community. If you don't have a real community or real issues in terms of Third World people in that community, then trying to apply that to the situation will not work. Examples of that are the Third World strikes on campuses. Now those were really noble, righteous struggles and very important for our development. But the fact is after the struggle was over, every Third World situation just totally broke down; and the reason it broke down was that it wasn't really a situation. They abstracted principles; Third World was placed upon these people but the campus community was not a living, real community. So the situation was an abstract theory. But if you take a community like Crenshaw or like the communities in many areas on Eastside, which are definitely Third World, and you organize along Third World lines, then that will be a reality because that's the way they live--in terms of Third World.
But the thing that's affecting the generations to come that didn't really affect us that profoundly is one important contradiction--drugs. The fact that it is an increasing problem with younger people and generations. I think the problems we had, the problems the Nisei had, the problems of racism in terms of that being a tool of capitalism will provide different problems for each generation. So what I'm saying is that for each generation

where you use nationalism as a common bond. In terms of younger Asian Americans, in particular, the generations coming up and in areas where they're so assimilated or so spread out, it's a situation where the common bond cannot be nationalism. The common bond has to be geographic, in terms of where they live in the same area, where they relate to the same institutions. So this is like the two types of things that are being set up: Nationalism as a means, obviously; and organizing along the lines of geographic area and class. Both of them are important; both of them work. But it's a situation where you have to apply each one in its proper situation. For example, using nationalism in Crenshaw Square is very incorrect because nationalism is not the common bond. But just going along the lines, not talking about racism or identity is still not the way either.

QUESTION: Do you set any priorities, like which areas can be organized better, for greater power or for anything like that?

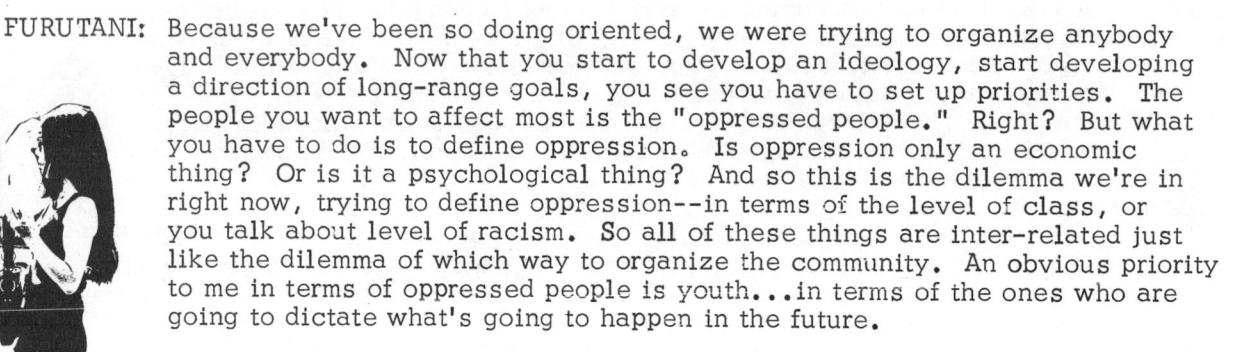

FURUTANI: Because we've been so doing oriented, we were trying to organize anybody and everybody. Now that you start to develop an ideology, start developing a direction of long-range goals, you see you have to set up priorities. The people you want to affect most is the "oppressed people." Right? But what you have to do is to define oppression. Is oppression only an economic thing? Or is it a psychological thing? And so this is the dilemma we're in right now, trying to define oppression--in terms of the level of class, or you talk about level of racism. So all of these things are inter-related just like the dilemma of which way to organize the community. An obvious priority to me in terms of oppressed people is youth...in terms of the ones who are going to dictate what's going to happen in the future.

I think our organizing up to this point has been aimed at a different segment of the community. It's been aimed at the Issei or the older members and more "established" members of the community. Although we've been working with the Issei and with the youth, still our whole orientation has been to older people. For example, a stereotype has been created in the Asian movement already, and it's our fault in Los Angeles, in that when people talk about community organization, they say that if you're going to organize in the community, that means you can't be political. In other words, we have created a difference between political organizing and community organizing when in actuality they shouldn't be different at all. The reason we did it was we weren't afraid we'd turn off the old people or the young people; it was that we're afraid we'd turn off the middle-age people because they're the ones with power in the institutions, with the money in the communities, who seem to have the informal or formal power in our communities. So what we're going to have to do right now is take a good look at what type of potential the middle-age people have in our communities. They have a great amount of power in terms of resources. But they have the tendency of just becoming liberals. Their help is all the way to a certain extent--as long as we're working with Issei and drug problems. But as soon as we point our finger to the real problems in this country, then we're digging at the roots of their whole life, where we start talking domestically about the major contradictions in this country--there's competition; there's capitalism, where everybody is so busy fighting each other, so busy trying to compete, so busy trying to make it that the pressures are so great for young people that one alternative they turn to is drugs. Now once we really start pointing our finger at the problems and admitting (because we're going to have to start admitting to the community) that we're never going to stop the drug problem until we change this whole country. The drug problem is so imbedded into the whole nature of this society in terms of the competition and the pressure and the need to escape from that. Big business makes a big bundle of dough on it, and big business is a very important part of the government.

QUESTION: In trying to reach just any class--middle-class, young, or old, a lot of movements had to present real alternatives to them. We can point out all the contradictions but without really providing an alternative model or providing some other direction for people to go to, they're hesitant. Do you see your concept of Amerasia as a viable alternative?

coming up, they will not be a normal generation. They will all be abnormal generations because of the initial problem way back when and it'll be a different thing for each generation.

QUESTION: Right. It seems like a major theme throughout the Asian American experience is alienation. And it manifests itself in different generations: for the Nisei, it may be overaccumulation of material goods; for the Sansei, it's just a sort of being lost, or it'll be drugs. Do you see any way a political movement may deal with that kind of alienation? How would it do it--in terms of getting power or teaching?

FURUTANI: Getting power and having the cultural change as well at the same time is the ultimate thing. But in terms of getting to that point is like education is the most important thing right now. Education on the level like with words and media, but also educating them by example. I mean example in the sense that they'll see an alternative and come to that alternative and help create an alternative organization for young people; this organization will give them, in a sense, self-determination and self-respect. Right now in terms of a vehicle, what we need to develop is an organization that younger people can relate to, be a part of, and help steer. So this, in terms of short-range goals, seems the most important thing in the immediate future--an organization that's going to provide this.

QUESTION: If your analysis of the Asian American community is that each one is different, do you see any issues which can unite them on a thematic basis, like the war? Do you see any common issues that each one of the communities would have regardless of their unique problems or unique composition?

FURUTANI: The war is one of the main contradictions. The biggest contradiction in this country is, obviously, the war--is imperialism. I think that's a mass organizing tool for all people--especially the Asian community. If we can get to the fact that they are Asians and that those people over there, getting fucked over are Asians, and the reasons they're getting fucked over is economic, and the way they're doing it is with racism, by calling them "gook." Then draw the parallels, draw the similarities in terms of the camps, in terms of our experiences here, in terms of "Yellow Peril," I think these can be very important issues in terms of education. With Third World internationalism and the world getting smaller, internationalism is a very good educational tool to draw similarities, to draw parallels; but when it comes down to really getting out in the street and really wanting to move and organize, it's not going to be a very intellectual thing, a far away thing. It's going to be something at home. It's going to be thirty-eight students at Dorsey High School getting arrested for no reason whatsoever except that they were in the vicinity of drugs.

QUESTION: Do you see that as a necessity getting out in the streets in terms of seizing power? How is that process going to be taken?

FURUTANI: What I mean by getting out on the streets is not getting out and breaking windows. I'm talking about organizations like ours--informal organizations, where we start walking the streets, talking to the people on the streets, moving with the people and the institutions on the streets; I think the way we've been organizing has shown our insecurities. We've developed hierarchies and bureaucracies because we're really insecure--we're afraid to get out to talk to people on the streets, canvass and things of this nature.

QUESTION: A lot of people are sort of complaining that the Sansei movement or any radical movement brings out the paranoia in the American society where everyone is afraid just about everywhere. S.I. Hayakawa especially has this charge that the Sanseis are following the paranoia cut out by the Black Panthers--like the "war is racism." All these images which are bad, negative influences on America reinforce all the negative images they already have of us and so they would say "be quiet and be cool." How would you answer that?

FURUTANI: I think that once again relates to looking at things in terms of reality. Like if Hayakawa really wants to know how people think about him and if he's quiet, he's never going to find out. Like he got up in San Francisco State and did his thing and was very boastful, did his trip, and now he knows how people feel about him. Some people hate his guts, some people like him. It's a situation where the Asians and our movement; "Outwhiting the whites" (NEWSWEEK article) and stuff like that: as long as we're quiet and industrious and do our work and do our trip; it's a situation where there's no problems, no racism. I've talked to a lot of Niseis who will say there's no racism. But soon as you get out picketing some play or something like that--all those things will come back: "Go back to China; go back to Japan; China, this; Jap, that." It's just a matter of whether you want to see it or not, and I think in terms of people raising paranoia, or bringing up the negativeness toward Asian people, or that whole trip: it's there-- it's just a matter of what's happening. If the United States goes to war with China, and if they want to see racism toward Asians, it'll come all back just the way it was before; it's historical: racism towards Chinese people and Japanese people, in terms of "Yellow Peril" in the late 1800's, early 1900's. During the mid part of the 1900's, the 20's and 30's, everybody was disappearing--all that heavy racism towards Asians was slowly but surely disappearing. And then 1940, probably if you talk to a lot of Niseis, they would say racism was not around, very little racism. Boom! 1942-- CAMP. Right? Racism as big as life. The same things that were printed in the 20's Yellow Peril, they printed during World War II. Almost the same headlines! And this'll happen again. J. Edgar Hoover already made one headline. It's a situation where racism, all these negative things, are there. It's just a matter if you want to look at the real situation or you want to live in Disneyland, and Hayakawa just happens to live in Disneyland. He really does.

One more thing I'd like to say is that all the things I say...are not our own ideas--everybody thinks what everybody says are their own thoughts and that they had a revelation...Bullshit! A lot of other brothers and sisters have already done the thinking--so no use of us having to do it. It's just a conglomeration of all the people we've met and all our experiences, and so it's like anything that we say is like something anybody else would say.

A PLEA FOR JUSTICE
IF THIS CAN HAPPEN TO ONE OF US, IT CAN HAPPEN TO ONE OF YOU

WHAT HAPPENED?
A nationally known doctor and scientist was humiliated, disgraced and fired from a civil service post without a hearing, amid charges so bizarre yet so degrading and odious that a victim's reputation could be forever stained by their very publication.

WHO WAS FIRED?
THOMAS T. NOGUCHI, M.D., CITIZEN, JAPANESE-AMERICAN, with a record of 7 years of dedicated service to the County of Los Angeles, was summarily SUSPENDED on Mar. 4, 1969 from his position as CHIEF MEDICAL EXAMINER-CORONER, by the County Board of Supervisors, composed of Supervisors Frank G. Bonelli, Burton W. Chace, Ernest E. Debs, Warren M. Dorn and Kenneth Hahn.
Two weeks later, Dr. Noguchi was DISCHARGED on the word of one man, still without having been given a chance to answer the charges.

THE CHARGES
Dr. Noguchi was accused of being mentally ill, In need of psychiatric care, and of excessive use of drugs, among others.

WHO MADE THE CHARGES?
The man on whose word the Supervisors fired Dr. Noguchi was LINDON S. HOLLINGER, the County's CHIEF ADMINISTRATIVE OFFICER, who testified at a subsequent Civil Service Commission hearing:

1. That he could not remember or did not know of any of the details of the charges because the Investigation was conducted by members of his staff. (Not one of whom took the witness stand.)
2. That he "thought (Dr. Noguchi) was a sick man," further stating, "I MAY REACH ANY CONCLUSION I CHOOSE."
3. That as to his qualification to determine whether Dr. Noguchi was sick Mr. Hollinger further testified, "I'M QUALIFIED TO REACH ANY IMPRESSION I CHOOSE TO REACH."
4. That he talked to only 6 employees of the Coroner's office and did not even make notes of his Interviews.
5. That he saw no reason to question the remaining 125 employees in the Coroner's office.
6. That when he signed the letter recommending Dr. Noguchi's discharge he did not personally examine any supporting data because
"I sign hundreds of letters each week, and I don't look at detailed material on any . . . It is SIMPLY ANOTHER ADMINISTRATIVE MATTER." Yet he admitted he had never before signed a letter recommending discharge of a department head.

WHAT DID THE SUPERVISORS SAY?
SUPERVISOR BONELLI, voting for Dr. Noguchi's immediate SUSPENSION, "All these ACCUSATIONS are going to have to be documented BEYOND a SHADOW OF DOUBT. I support the (suspension) motion with a qualification that proof must be provided."

SUPERVISOR CHACE, voting for his DISCHARGE without a prior hearing, stated: "We cannot take the charges leveled against Noguchi too lightly. They are serious and HAVE SHAKEN PUBLIC CONFIDENCE in the office of the county medical examiner-coroner . . ."
(During the hearing the charge that Dr. Noguchi had "shaken public confidence" was dismissed by the Commission for complete lack of proof.)

SUPERVISOR HAHN, joining the discharge action called the charges "the most serious ever placed against any county employee, let alone a department head." On the day before the discharge, Supervisor Hahn had said at a Board Meeting: "No other coroner in the history of the United States . . . had had the heavy work load in one year's time. On June 5 was the shooting of Sen. Robert Kennedy. Dr. Noguchi had to supervise that autopsy, which medical experts say was the most thorough ever made in the United States . . . 2 helicopter crashes . . . 2 airline crashes . . . Now the pressure on this man has been terrific and we all admit he had difficult surroundings and equipment."

SUPERVISOR DORN had said: "Certainly this gentleman has been TRIED ALREADY, the way I see it, IN THE PRESS. I feel that It is perhaps the worst handling of anything I have seen since I have been in the County."

PUBLICATION OF CHARGES
The degrading and inflammatory charges were published on Mar. 19, 1969. It was not until 7 weeks later that Dr. Noguchi had a chance to answer the charges, by which time his reputation had been seriously undermined and his dignity degraded.

ADDITIONAL CHARGE
Not content with the original charges, the County on April 30, 1969 (10 months after the Kennedy autopsy, 43 days after Dr. Noguchi was discharged) ADDED the following charge:
"During the KENNEDY AUTOPSY, your eyes went glazed, your behavior was erratic and your dictation of the events surrounding the autopsy was so disassociated that it was all but unintelligible."

J.U.S.T. FORMED
At this juncture, concerned Japanese Americans, formed a Committee called Japanese-Americans United In Their Search For Truth (J.U.S.T.), to offer Dr. Noguchi moral and financial assistance in his lonely and expensive uphill fight to regain his position, professional reputation, personal honor, and human dignity, in the face of determined opposition by the County, with its almost unlimited resources in manpower and political influence.

HEARING BEGINS
The hearing began on May 12, 1969 before the County Civil Service Commission, composed of COMMISSIONERS: Mr. O. RICHARD CAPEN, President; MR. HARRY ALBERT, and MRS. THELMA MAHONEY.

DR. NOGUCHI'S WITNESSES
Many people willingly testified at the Commission hearing on his behalf, including a Chief of Police, homicide officers, doctors, newsmen, prominent citizens, colleagues, experts, and numerous employees of the Coroner's office, whose only interest was in seeing justice done.

Medical Experts — Among the medical experts who testified as to his HIGH PROFESSIONAL STANDING AND CHARACTER were:

Dr. William G. Eckert, Chairman of the Pathology and Biology Section of the American Academy of Forensic Sciences.
Dr. John Burton, Chief Medical Examiner, Detroit, Michigan.
Dr. Bernard Knight, Forensic Pathologist with a British university In Wales.
Dr. Cyril Wecht, Chief Forensic Pathologist for Alleghany County, Penna.
Dr. Victor J. Rosen, Deputy Medical Examiner and Pathologist at Cedars-Sinai Hospital.
Dr. William Sturner, Deputy Medical Examiner—Cook County, Ill.
Dr. George Schwartz, Legal medicine specialist and cardiologist.
Dr. Isaac Sanders, radiologist at White Memorial Medical Center who testified, "Most of us are ordinary men who try to do our job a little bit better each day, but in every era, there are special people, they have special talent — men who make a definite contribution, who open doors. And Thomas Noguchi is such a man. And this individual before you now feels that THIS IS NOT AN ORDINARY MAN, BUT A SPECIAL MAN."

Thanks to the testimony of the witnesses, and the crusading zeal of ATTY. GODFREY ISAAC, a turning point was reached in Dr. Noguchi's uphill fight—at long last.

COUNTY WITHDRAWS KENNEDY AUTOPSY CHARGE
On May 26, the very first day that Dr. Noguchi began to call his witnesses, the County withdrew its odious Kennedy autopsy charge, and STIPULATED that Dr. NOGUCHI HAD PERFORMED THE AUTOPSY IN A "SUPERIOR" MANNER.

5 MORE CHARGES DISMISSED
The following week, 5 of the remaining charges were DISMISSED by the Commission for COMPLETE LACK OF PROOF.

JUST DECISION AWAITED
The commission is the first line of defense against arbitrary action by the County against its some 60,000 employees. Its independence must be preserved. Despite the fact that the Commission obtains legal advice from the Office of County Counsel and despite the fact that the Commissioners are appointed by the Supervisors, WE AWAIT THE COMMISSION'S JUST AND UNBIASED DECISION.

UNANSWERED QUESTIONS
Supervisor Chace had stated at the time the Board discharged Dr. Noguchi that he will receive "a full and fair public hearing" before the Commission, and emphasized, "THE MATTER MUST BE RESOLVED TO THE FULL SATISFACTION OF THE PUBLIC."

Before we are SATISFIED, we would like to know:

1. Prior to discharging Dr. Noguchi, WHY DID THE SUPERVISORS INSTRUCT HOLLINGER, of all persons, to "investigate" his own charges?
2. WHY DID THE COUNTY ADD THE KENNEDY AUTOPSY CHARGE, 43 days after discharging Dr. Noguchi, only to WITHDRAW IT on the day he called his first witness, THEREBY DEPRIVING HIM OF THE OPPORTUNITY TO EXPOSE THE SPURIOUS CHARGE?
3. WHY DID THE COUNTY, WITHOUT HAVING ANY SUPPORTING EVIDENCE, MAKE THE FOLLOWING UNFOUNDED CHARGES:
   a). That Dr. Noguchi "prayed that Mayor Yorty's helicopter would crash"?
   b). That Dr. Noguchi spoke to employees "with unwarranted profanity"?
   c). That Dr. Noguchi made fun of a pathologist who had one leg shorter than the other, driving him to quit the coroner's office.
   d). That Dr. Noguchi "suddenly changed the topic and started discussing totally unrelated subjects" during a conference last February?
   e). That he had "shaken public confidence" in the Coroner's office?
4. If Dr. Noguchi was too ill to handle autopsies, why did Hollinger and the Supervisors offer him, at the same salary, the post of Chief Pathologist at Rancho Los Amigos?

AROUSED JAPANESE-AMERICAN COMMUNITY
NEVER HAS THE JAPANESE AMERICAN COMMUNITY BEEN — *More Aroused* than by the CALLOUS and INHUMAN TREATMENT meted out to this sensitive and intelligent human being — *More Certain* of his COMPLETE INNOCENCE — *MORE SOLIDLY UNITED* as in their determination to seek vindication of his reputation, honor and human dignity.

J.U.S.T. (Japanese United In Search For Truth)
Takito Yamaguma, Co-Chairman
Ken Nakaoka, Co-Chairman

Frank Omatsu
Yoshio Yamaguchi　Henry N. Yamada　Katsuma Mukaeda　Masuo Mitamura　Saichi Fukui　Kenji Ito　Jim Kanno　Sam Shimoguchi　Alfred Hatate　Dr. Steve Yokoyama　Jeffrey Matsul　Don Karimoto　Wallace Ban　Ernest Fukumoto　Rev. Howard Toriumi　Arthur Katayama　George Takei　Ko Hoshizaki　Kats Kunitsugu　Isao Haga　Victor Ikeda

"A" Battery — 442nd Veterans Association of Los Angeles　American Federation of State County and Municipal Employees, Local 119 Los Angeles　Nanka Meiji Club　Shizuoka Kenjin Club　Taisho Club of Los Angeles　Venice Judo Boys Club　Shodo-kai Kokufuryu Shigin　Pomona Shinwa Kai　Los Angeles Buddhist Church Federation　Crown City Gardeners Association Inc.　Aichikenjin-Yushi Associates　San Fernando Valley Chapter-Japanese American Citizens League　Baido-kai　Jodo-Shu Y.A.B.C.　Backlashers Club　Santa Monica Nikkei Jin Kai　Nanka Fukuoka Kenjinkai　Rafu Seinan Kyogikai　Nanka Kanagawa Kenjinkai　Nanka Shiga Club Nanka Yamanashi Club　Nanka Yamaguchi-ken Club　Nanka Miyagi Kenjin Kai　Los Angeles Free Methodist Church　Japanese American Citizens League, National Headquarters　Japanese American Citizens League, Pacific Southwest District Council　Japanese Chamber of Commerce, So. Calif.　Japanese Amer-

Optimist Club　Crescent Bay Optimist Club　East Los Angeles Gardeners Association, Inc.　Nanka Fukushima Kenjinkai　Japanese American Citizens League, Pacific Northwest District Council　Japanese American Citizens League, San Jose Chapter　Japanese American Citizens League, North San Diego County　Japanese American Citizens League, East Los Angeles　Japanese American Citizens League, Santa Barbara Chapter　Rafu Sekokai　Issei Fujinkai　Nanka Fukui Kenjin Kai　Plaisted Episcopal Church　Japanese American Citizens League, Hollywood　Pioneer Club-Southern California Flower Market　Okinawa Club　Nisei Voters League of San Francisco　East Los Angeles Japanese Student Association　Ikenobo Ikebana Society of Los Angeles　Payallup Valley Japanese American Citizens League　Nanka Kenjin Kyogi Kai　Southern California Gardener's Fed., Inc.　M Ladies Club　Commodore Perry Post #525　Los Angeles Retail Fish Association　Riverside

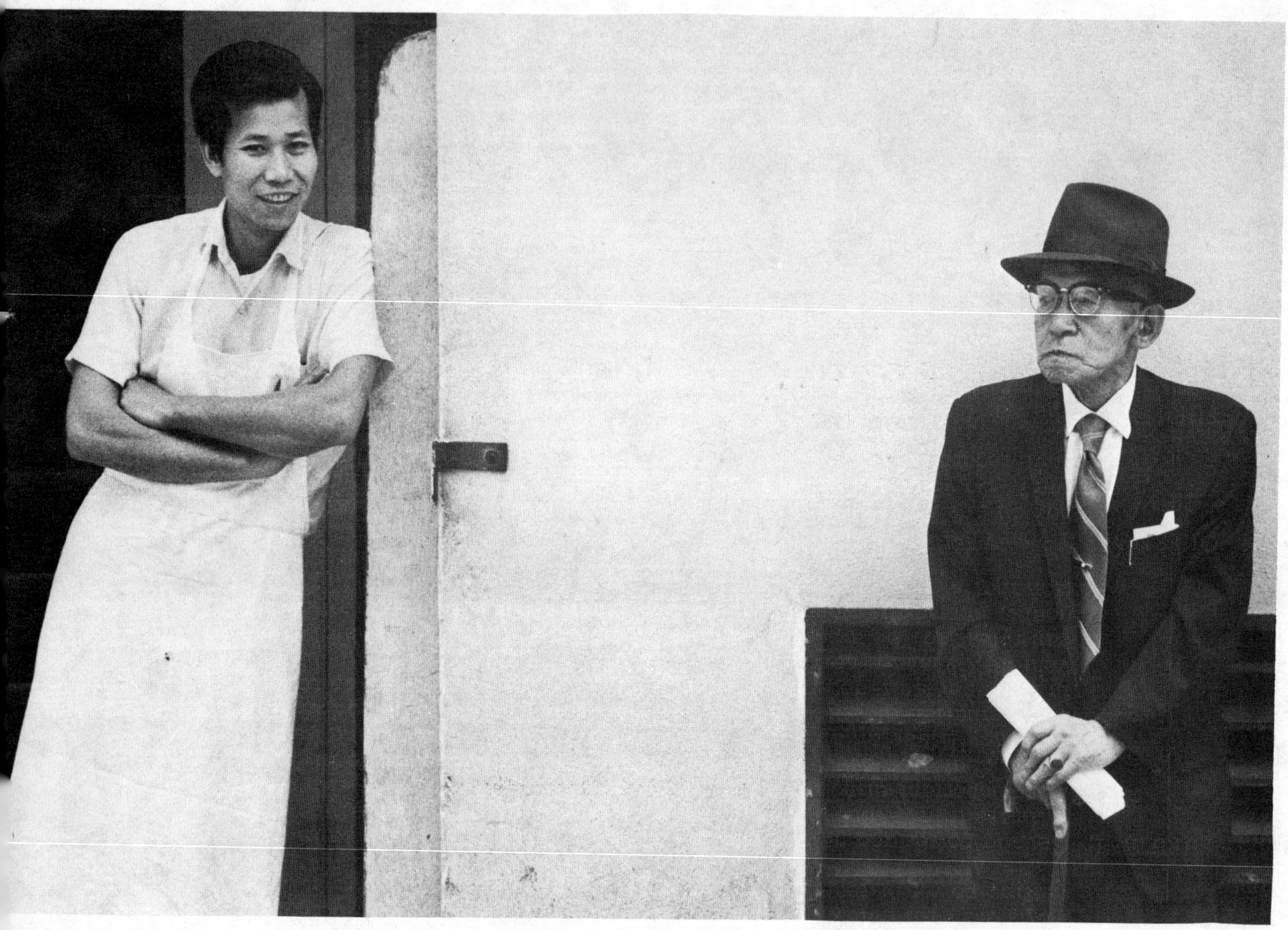

movement journals

AION (a quarterly publication)   675 Thirty-Fifth Avenue   San Francisco, Calif. 94121

AMERASIA JOURNAL (a quarterly publication)   c/o UCLA Asian American Studies Center,
             ($4.00 a year)   3235 Campbell Hall
             ($5.00 overseas rate)   Los Angeles, California 90024

ASIAN WOMEN'S JOURNAL   c/o Asian Women   3405 Dwinelle Hall   UC Berkeley, Calif. 94720
             ($2.50 a copy; $2.00 a copy for five or more)

GETTING TOGETHER   30 Market Street   New York City, New York 10002

GIDRA (monthly newspaper of the Asian American Community)   P. O. Box 18046
             ($2.50 a year)   Los Angeles, Calif. 90018

HAWAIIAN ETHOS   P. O. Box 10591   Honolulu, Hawaii 96816   ($2.50 for 12 issues)
                                                                     ($4.50 for 24 issues)

HAWAII FREE PEOPLE'S PRESS (a quarterly publication)   P. O. Box 352   Haleiwa, Hawaii

HAWAII PONO JOURNAL (a quarterly publication)   1776 University Avenue
                                                    Wist Hall 208, University of Hawaii
                                                    Honolulu, Hawaii 96822

KALAYAAN INTERNATIONAL   P. O. Box 2919   San Francisco, California 94124   ($3.00 a year)

RODAN (monthly newspaper of the Northern California Asian American Community)
             ($2.00 a year)   1808A Sutter Street
             ($5.00 for institutions)   San Francisco, California 94115

ACKNOWLEDGEMENTS

Laura Alancastre

AMERASIA JOURNAL

American Academy of Political
and Social Sciences

Asian American Studies Center,
UCLA

Asian American Studies Division,
UC Davis

Asian Legal Services, San Francisco

Bancroft Library Collection,
UC Berkeley

Gloria Burbage

Betty Chen

Rocky Chin

Morgan Chu

Marie Chung

Lowell Chun-Hoon

Roger Daniels

Isao Fujimoto

Nancy Fujimura

Warren Furutani

GIDRA

Kathy Fukami Glascock

Ken Hanada

HAWAII FREE PEOPLES PRESS

HAWAIIAN ETHOS

S. I. Hayakawa

Bill Hosokawa

Yuji Ichioka

Lawson Inada

Bruce Iwasaki

JACL National Visual Communications
Committee

Japanese American Research Project,
UCLA

KALAYAAN INTERNATIONAL

Harry Kitano

Peggy Li

Peter Lin

Pyau Ling

Ron Low

Stanford Lyman

Judy Maruyama

Magoroh Maruyama

Jim Matsuoka

Toyo Miyatake

Mike Murase

Bob Nakamura

Gail Nakamura

Norm Nakamura

National Council of Family Relations

Alan Nishio

Tom Okabe

Daniel Okimoto

Shin'ya Ono

Raymond Orbach

Pacific News Commentary,
 Jiji Press, Ltd.

Irvin Paik

PAUNAWA

Violet Rabaya

Andrea Rich

Al Robles

RODAN

Janet Kikuko Sanders

Linda Shin

Esther Soriano

All students enrolled in Asian
 American studies classes

Derald Sue

Stanley Sue

Pat Sumi

Ken Suyama

Ron Tanaka

Tomi Tanaka

Roy Tazawa

THE BLACK PANTHER

Tinnon-Brown, Inc.

Roy Tsumoto

UCLA Council on Educational
 Development

George Umezawa

University of California Press

Elsie Uyematsu

Mary Uyematsu

U. S. NEWS AND WORLD REPORT

Sherry Valparaiso

Philip Vera Cruz

L. Ling-Chi Wang

John Weatherhill, Inc.

Melford Weiss

Western Studies Center,
 Desert Research Institute

Donna Wong

Risa Yamamoto

Teri Yamamura

Karl Yoneda

Evelyn Yoshimura